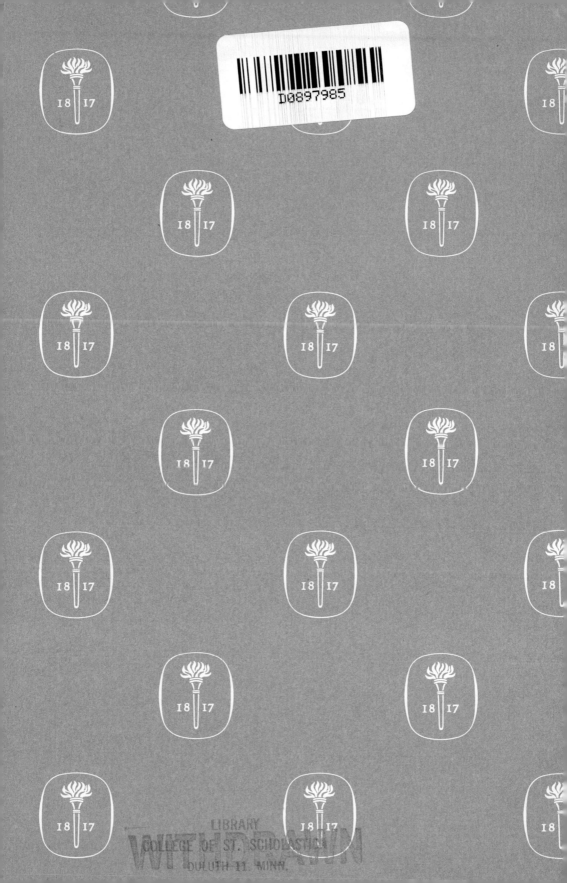

APPRAISING

VOCATIONAL

FITNESS

APPRAISING

VOCATIONAL

FITNESS

BY MEANS OF PSYCHOLOGICAL TESTS

REVISED EDITION

Donald E. Super M. A. (OXON) Ph.D.
Teachers College, Columbia University

John O. Crites, Ph.D.
University of Iowa

HARPER & ROW PUBLISHERS

New York and Evanston

APPRAISING VOCATIONAL FITNESS, REVISED EDITION
COPYRIGHT 1949 BY HARPER & ROW, PUBLISHERS, INCORPORATED
COPYRIGHT © 1962 BY DONALD SUPER AND JOHN O. CRITES
PRINTED IN THE UNITED STATES OF AMERICA

L-M

Library of Congress catalog card number: 61-7929

CONTENTS

v

CONTENTS

PREFACE TO THE SECOND EDITION

SINCE the appearance of the first edition of this text the use of tests in vocational guidance and personnel work has increased so greatly as to dwarf the "big business" figures cited in its preface. The number of tests on the market and the number of publishers distributing them and the volume of publication concerning tests in the psychological, educational and management journals have multiplied, making more information available but increasing the difficulty of finding the particular information needed to keep posted on existing tests and to learn about new instruments. Committees of the American Psychological Association, the American Educational Research Association, and the National Council on Measurements Used in Education, on two of which the senior author had the privilege of serving, have recognized the responsibility of the professional associations for setting standards for the development, publication, distribution, and use of tests. And Buros has continued the very useful work of compiling and publishing the *Mental Measurement Yearbook* to make comprehensive bibliographies and critical reviews of tests currently available to users.

This continuing activity has made a new edition of this text desirable to keep up to date a treatise to which many instructors, students, and practitioners refer as a guide to and synthesis of significant work with the most useful vocational tests. This second edition is, accordingly, a revision of the book which first appeared ten years ago. It is not a drastic revision, for the activity of the past decade has produced refinements, clarifications, and confirmations rather than radical changes. With few exceptions today, the most widely used tests and inventories, most esteemed by practicing psychologists, counselors, and personnel men, and best withstanding the revealing light of validation research, are the instruments dealt with in the first edition. We know more about them; we are surer of what we knew about them. A few new instruments have been studied with sufficient thoroughness to justify adding them to the armamentarium of the practitioner. This edition, therefore, brings a useful source book up to date.

A brief review of the changes made in this edition should be helpful to the user. Some tests and inventories discussed in the first edition which have practically been replaced by instruments constructed by more refined methods, or concerning which no significant new material has been published, have been dropped in order to save space: the Iowa Placement Examinations, the Bernreuter Personality Inventory, the Bell Adjustment Inventory, and the Minnesota Personality Scale. A few instruments which have been published since the first edition appeared have been added: the School and College Aptitude Tests, the Wechsler Adult Intelligence Scale, the Sequential Tests of Educational Placement, the Rotter Incomplete Sentences Test, and the Edwards Personal Preference Schedule. Certain other tests have been the subject of considerable significant research, making it possible to deal with them more thoroughly and more definitively than before: the Wechsler Intelligence Scales, the General Aptitude Test Battery, the Kuder Preference Record, Vocational, and the Minnesota Multiphasic Personality Inventory.

Changes in the content and depth of test manuals are beginning to permit changes in the type of treatment, thanks to the responsiveness of the professionally oriented test publishers and to scientific and professional opinion as formulated and expressed in the American Psychological Association's *Code of Ethics,* its *Technical Recommendations for Psychological Tests* and elsewhere. When the first edition of this text was written, virtually no test manual contained a comprehensive, detailed, unbiased digest and discussion of the research on a given test. Today, test manuals from some publishers and authors have begun to make available the kind of review which has been a distinctive characteristic of this treatise, but the manual for the Differential Aptitude Tests is still too rare an example. Perhaps by the time a third edition of this text is necessary the reader will have available in the manuals of the tests adequate summaries of the relevant research; it will then be possible to concentrate on conclusions concerning the use of the tests in counseling and selection. In the meantime, there is a real need for the encyclopedic treatment found in this text.

A change in the type of bibliographical work carried out in preparing this edition also needs comment. There has been so much publication that to mention *every* study bearing on a given test, as was the intent in the first edition, has become impossible. Instead, the customary search of the literature led to the selection of crucial and typical studies; these are included in the additions to the bibliography. Readers wanting complete lists of references on a given test are referred to the *Mental Measurement Yearbooks* and to other standard bibliographic aids.

Finally, focus in this edition is exclusively on the test user—the counselor in school, college, or community agency and the personnel worker in business, industry, or government—who uses standard tests for educational and vocational appraisal. Whereas in the first edition attention was given to promising new types of tests, with the psychologist who develops or experiments with tests as well as uses them in mind, this type of content has now been omitted. Advances in test development have made that a special subject, and the sharper focus which characterizes the second edition should make it more valuable as a text and handbook on tests used in vocational appraisal.

Courses in testing are, essentially, of three types. They deal with 1) basic principles, 2) use in practice, or 3) test construction. The field has become highly developed; many texts are now available for courses of the first type, with several in the second and third categories. This text belongs in the second category, and it may help to comment briefly on its role.

Treatises on the use of tests in appraisal for guidance or for personnel selection and evaluation can be of four types, essentially: 1) advanced basic texts which attempt to do more thoroughly what the introductory course in measurement attempts; 2) surveys of tests used particularly in guidance or personnel work and their applications; 3) detailed treatments of these same tests which concentrate on their development and validity to provide a basis for interpretation; or 4) studies of the use and interpretation of tests in appraisal, counseling, selection, and evaluation. This book has found its place in courses which seek to give the student a real knowledge and understanding of the instruments which he may use, and some skill in the methods of using them. The tests dealt with were selected because of their widespread use and the availability of relevant research. This book has also been found valuable by psychologists (clinical, counseling, educational, and personnel), counselors, and personnel workers desiring to deepen their knowledge of objective instruments of appraisal.

In preparing this revision I have had the collaboration of Dr. John O. Crites who appears on the title page as co-author; having begun as a graduate student compiling references and writing abstracts, he progressed to revising parts of the text and to writing some of the new sections, as well as to assuming a co-author's responsibility for other material. The collaboration has been pleasant and efficient; it is our common hope that the results will continue to serve our colleagues in the field.

Upper Montclair, N. J.   Donald E. Super
December, 1960.

FROM THE PREFACE TO THE FIRST EDITION

IT IS the aim of this book to bring together the results of the significant research which has been done with the most widely used and useful tests, to interpret these findings in the light of recent developments in testing theory and practice, and to view each test in the perspective gained by those who are currently using them in schools, colleges, consultation services, business, and industry.

But the objective of this book goes beyond that of providing a manual of currently usable tests. An attempt is made to familiarize the reader with the bibliographical sources and to take him through the processes of collection of data and synthesis of findings, so that he may develop work habits and thought processes which will enable him to evaluate instruments himself and to make new applications. Insofar as this goal is accomplished, the user of vocational tests will be enabled to keep abreast of progress in the field and to work on a high professional plane.

In this process, the student should develop an understanding of the basic procedures of the development of vocational tests. It is true, of course, that most vocational counselors, psychometrists, and personnel workers are and should be primarily users and interpreters rather than constructors of tests. It is rare that real skill as test technician and as counselor are combined in one person. But, to be an intelligent consumer, one must be familiar with the procedures and problems involved in the development or manufacture of the product which is to be used. This does not necessitate skill in manufacture, but it does require detailed knowledge of methods, materials and problems. As each test is studied, the methods used in constructing, standardizing, and validating it will therefore be described in some detail. The underlying assumptions will be pointed out, and the validity of the criteria used will be considered. Such knowledge is important in personnel selection, in which custom-built tests generally prove most effective, and in vocational counseling, in which generalizations are made on the basis of limited data.

As a result, the reader should become well acquainted with the demonstrated values and limitations of the most widely used vocational tests.

The word *demonstrated* should be emphasized, for during the past twenty or twenty-five years, and especially during the past decade, a great deal of research has been carried on and published on the validity of vocational tests. There is no longer any excuse for depending primarily on hunches as to the vocational significance of special aptitude tests, nor for going to the other extreme and concluding that, since "a test tests only what it tests," one can conclude nothing from psychological test results concerning vocational promise. Both of these attitudes and practices were widespread during the 1930's, when validity data were sketchy and often disappointing. Enough data have now been accumulated so that a more realistic and pragmatic approach is possible; the counselor can know, from experimental evidence, a good deal about the nature of the trait being measured and about its rôle in vocational adjustment. His interpretations of test results can therefore be based on objective evidence or, when the evidence does not go far enough, on logical analysis which uses fact rather than fancy as a starting point. For the test user the key question is, *"What does this test, and the score made on it by this person, tell me about his vocational promise?"*

It is around this question that the author has attempted to organize this book. Experience as counselor, personnel consultant, supervisor and instructor has shown that the user of vocational tests in diagnostic work starts with data about the *client,* which he then synthesizes and interprets in terms of *vocations.* It is true that he needs to make a decision as to what vocational goals are likely to be considered in order to select appropriate tests, and that this requires thinking in terms of occupations and constellations of abilities. However, test batteries for occupational families are not yet developed to a sufficient degree to make this the best approach in actually interpreting test results and counseling. Instead, the psychologist or counselor must tease what meaning, suggestions, and contra-indications he can from the test and other personal data on hand. In some of the most effective vocational counseling and personnel evaluation services vocational tests are used, not only for the occupational norms which permit comparison with successful workers, but also for the analysis of the psychological strengths and weaknesses of the client, which are then interpreted in terms of possible vocational opportunities. This latter type of analysis requires thorough knowledge of the tests used, supplemented by detailed knowledge of occupations from first-hand experience and from psychological research. Another unique feature in a text such as this is the material on the use of test results in counseling, that is, on putting test results to work.

The acknowledgments due to others in connection with the preparation of this book are numerous, varied, and a source of such pleasure that I have looked forward to the writing of these paragraphs. (In the interest of saving space in the revision their names are omitted from these excerpts. They are more numerous now than ever).

Upper Montclair, N.J.   DONALD E. SUPER
February, 1949

I
TESTING AND APPRAISAL IN VOCATIONAL COUNSELING

The Nature and Purposes of Vocational Guidance and Counseling

VOCATIONAL counseling has two fundamental purposes; to help people make good vocational adjustments, and to facilitate smooth functioning of the economy through the effective use of manpower.

These purposes imply that each individual has certain abilities, interests, personality traits, and other characteristics which, if he knows them and their potential value, will make him a happier man, a more effective worker, and a more useful citizen. Part of his education, therefore, consists of helping him to get a better understanding of his aptitudes for various skills, his adaptability to differing types of situations, and his interest in the numerous activities in which he might engage. Although less generally recognized as such, this self-understanding is just as much an objective of education as is the understanding of the world in which he lives. A well-educated man is one who has achieved both types of understanding; a well-adjusted man is one who has put these two types of knowledge to good use and has found a place for himself in society.

Some educational programs have assumed that the processes of mental discipline, intellectual development, and general education result in the desired self-understanding. However legitimate this assumption might be in an effective educational program, the result is not achieved in practice; the Regents Inquiry into the Character and Cost of Public Education in New York State, as reported in the monographs by Eckert and Marshall (1938) and by Spaulding (1938), made it clear that a large proportion of the products of our more or less traditional school systems have neither the self-understanding nor the understanding of the world around them that is necessary for good vocational adjustment or citizenship. This lack of insight and of social understanding has been revealed by numerous other studies of the relationship of the vocational aspirations of youth to both abilities and available opportunities (Super, 1957, Ch. 8).

What are the psychological processes necessary to bring about the understanding which experience alone so often fails to produce? They are, of course, those of vocational counseling, the process of helping the individual to ascertain, accept, understand, and apply the relevant facts about himself to the pertinent facts about the occupational world which are ascertained through incidental and planned exploratory activities. The techniques of vocational counseling vary from case to case and from counselor to counselor, depending partly upon the counselee's state of readiness and partly upon the time available to the counselor, the degree of skill he has attained, and his philosophy of counseling. In many cases these techniques fall naturally into two categories: those of appraisal, and those of treatment or counseling in the more limited sense. There is, however, one important school of thought which is sometimes described as opposed to the use of diagnostic or appraisal activities, at least of the traditional varieties and in the traditional ways. This point of view has been most ably and widely propounded by Carl Rogers and his students (1942, 1946, 1951; Rogers and Wallen, 1945) and is known as nondirective or client-centered counseling. Before embarking upon a discussion of the techniques of appraisal prefatory to the intensive study of appraisal through tests, some consideration should be given to this question of the role of appraisal in vocational and educational counseling.

To Appraise or Not to Appraise?

The topic of appraisal is a somewhat controversial one.* At one extreme, the nondirectivists question the use of appraisal techniques, and particularly the appraising attitude on the part of the counselor, on the ground that they may interfere with the release of growth forces within the client. More favorable to appraisal, but assigning it a limited role in counseling, are writers such as Bordin (1955) and Tyler (1953), who recognize that obtaining information by appraisal methods has a place in counseling, but question or limit the appraising role of the counselor. Further along the continuum are those who, like Meehl (1954) and Kelly (1954), recognize the importance of appraisal methods and approaches, but take a dim view of the results of efforts at appraisal, both because of their demonstrated low validity and because of the greater validity of more strictly psychometric methods. And, finally, we have others who, like Williamson (1950) and Froelich and Hoyt (1959), put their faith in the informed appraiser rather than in the uninformed and personally involved client.

* The passages which follow are adapted from material which first appeared in a paper by the senior author entitled "The Preliminary Appraisal in Vocational Counseling," *Personnel and Guidance Journal*, 1957, 36, 154-161.

The Place of Appraisal

The synonymous terms of appraisal and diagnosis are used with three different meanings, all of them relevant, all of them included in Williamson's definition, which is that "a diagnosis is a structured summary of significant case data" (1950, p. 199) . 1) *The problem* presented by the client must be identified and its seriousness appraised by the counselor, so that he may know what it is he is expected to work with, whether or not he should continue to work with it, and what kind of approach he might best use. 2) *The person* being counseled must be appraised, that is, the counselor must attempt to formulate an idea as to the manner of man with whom he is dealing and what the man's needs, capacities and resources are. 3) *The prognosis* stems directly from the appraisal of the person; it is, in other words, an appraisal of the person's prospects. These three meanings are commonly used but too rarely identified. Often they are confused, with resulting confusion in the literature on diagnosis and appraisal.

Problem Appraisal. The focus on appraisal of the client's problem is well illustrated by Shoben's discussion (1956) of a study reported by Bordin (1955a) . In this study Bordin ascertained the expectations of counseling manifested by clients at a counseling center; some of the clients came for help in making a particular decision while others came with a belief that they were themselves in need of help as the source of their own difficulties. Shoben writes: "The implications of this observation are manifold, but they place particular stress upon the importance of initial contacts, the process of structuring, and the appraisal of the client's adequacy. Seeking help in decision-making can be an act of strength as well as an admission of weakness . . ." and goes on to point up the different types of handling that may be called for with the different types of underlying problems.

Personal Appraisal. The focus on personal appraisal is illustrated by the typical clinical study of a person, as for example in the personal descriptions written on the basis of intelligence, aptitude, and personality tests. Bordin writes that description of the person is the primary appraisal objective of psychological counseling: ". . . psychological counseling is directly concerned with personality development. The implications of this reach farther than is at first evident. They mean, for one thing, that when a troubled person comes to the psychological counselor, as he often does, with concrete decisions to be made, specific problems to be solved, or particular situations to be clarified, the primary goal for the psychological counselor is not to contribute to the solution of these immediate situations.

That major goal lies further ahead. The primary goal requires understanding of the obstacles to further personality growth and development that are typified by this person's rather specific and, for the time being, limited difficulty (that is, it requires personality appraisal). The counselor tries to contribute to the removal of these deeper lying personal obstacles and to bring about reactivation of the psychological growth process in that person.

"Where before counselors had emphasized aiding the client to make a satisfactory decision, they began to see the process of helping him to make a decision as one that should also increase his capacity to make succeeding decisions . . . Today, to an increasing degree, counselors are examining their clients' efforts to solve vocational problems with a view toward understanding what there is about an individual's personality that makes these problems difficult for him to solve. . . For a mature and well-integrated client, the problem of vocational choice may arise only out of misinformation or ignorance, and the counselor will function as the most available informational source" (1955, pp. 9-13).

Bordin thus recognizes that some clients come with their personal problems solved or under control, needing only information about themselves and about occupations; to this we would add, help in using this information. This, then, is the domain of most vocational counselors.

Prognostic Appraisal. Appraisal for prognostic purposes is, as was pointed out above, generally an outcome of personal appraisal. That is, the study of personal data, school and work experiences, psychological tests, and job requirements leads to a prediction of the individual's prospects of success in one or more types of occupation. This is what many clients expect when they come for vocational counseling; it is what vocational counselors typically attempt to do, whether they aim to use the data to give the client a prediction or to help him understand himself and his situation so that he may reach a decision of his own. (Unfortunately, the emphasis on collecting data for appraisal purposes, especially the prognostic type, can and often does lead to the means becoming the end.)

Appraisal, then, can have quite different meanings. It can mean the initial appraisal of the type of problem presented. It can mean understanding a personality and its resources. It can mean obtaining a basis for a prediction. All three of these meanings are important. It may help if we make it clear that we are assuming the first type of appraisal has been made and that the problem is truly one of appraising vocational promise or fitness. We may then concentrate on the last two, intimately related, types of appraisal. While our interest is ultimately in the last type, that is in prognosis, in locating a sound vocational objective, the fact that prognosis is based on understanding means that we are interested in both.

Appraisal and Counseling

The role of the vocational appraiser has generally been described as that of an objective third person, who can assemble, evaluate, and synthesize facts in a detached manner (Froelich and Hoyt, 1959; Pepinsky and Pepinsky, 1954; Williamson, 1950). To nondirective counselors this has implied an attitude which makes accepting the client difficult if not impossible, and since acceptance and a permissive atmosphere are considered essential, diagnosis and appraisal are frowned upon (Rogers and Wallen, 1945, pp. 5-6). When during the 1940's, the conflict between these two points of view became clear, it left many vocational counselors in a confused state of mind. "To diagnose or not to diagnose" became the question.

But during the past few years synthesizing forces have been at work, as manifested in Tyler's work:

"In order to make searching diagnoses and evaluate prognoses in various directions, the counselor must adopt an objective third-person sort of attitude ... This is a quite different approach from the one he takes during an interview, when he attempts to get the 'feel' of the clients' experience. It would not seem that the conflict between the two attitudes would need to be irreconcilable, since a large part of the diagnostic thinking goes on *between,* rather than during, interviews ..." (1953, p. 86). Tyler continues:

"We have tried ... to avoid the difficulties that have grown up around the diagnosis issue by giving up the idea that the counselor's main business is prognosis, and shifting our attention to specific decisions which he does find it necessary to make. In disposing of diagnosis in this way, have we lost sight of anything important? The vocational guidance expert may feel that we have. If the counselor refuses to pass judgment on the facts and make the best prognosis that he can, is he not simply shifting the burden to the client's shoulders and thus demanding that predictions be made by someone much less qualified than himself to make them with accuracy? We would agree that a very essential part of the vocational counselor's task is the synthesizing of test results, background information, and expressed attitudes into a coherent, understandable whole. But this need not be regarded as diagnostic activity and it need not lead to definite predictions. If the counselor can convey his synthesis to the client and enable him to assimilate it, the decision that finally crystallizes out need not be the one occupation or educational plan carrying the best prognosis. It will be instead a course of action *for which the* client is completely willing to take the consequences" (1953, pp.101-103).

If we may add to Tyler's last sentence, her statement will express our own point of view very adequately: "It will be instead a course of action for which the client is completely willing to take the consequences, *leading to a goal which is based on a cooperative realistic appraisal of the factors involved."* By making this addition, the contribution of the appraisal process to the *quality* of the decision, as well as the *nature* of the decision making, is made clear. Society has an interest both in the nature of the decision making and in the quality of the decision.

Data Needed in Vocational Appraisal

In order to evaluate a person's vocational prospects, two types of information about him are needed: the *psychological* facts which describe his aptitudes, skills, interests, and personality traits, and the *social* facts which describe the environment in which he lives, the influences which are affecting him, and the resources which he has at his disposal. To depend upon one type of fact to the neglect of the other is unrealistic and disregards important elements in vocational adjustment, for the opportunities available to persons with similar aptitudes and interests may vary greatly, just as the abilities and traits of people in similar social situations differ from one person to the next. (It has, for instance, been demonstrated that many young men and women capable of benefitting from a college education do not attend college because of financial handicaps (Thomas, 1956, Ch. 14), just as many students who can afford to attend college drop out because of learning difficulties.)

The fact that many psychological characteristics are best judged by means of tests which require special study and have the appearance of objectivity and concreteness has often led to the relative neglect of social factors in counseling by those trained to use tests, and to the neglect of important psychological factors by those not trained to use tests. For these reasons it seems desirable, in considering the types of data needed in vocational diagnosis, to stress the need for both types of information and to use both testing and non-testing techniques. More will be said later about the methods of gathering data; first let us focus on the types of data needed.

Psychological data needed include information concerning the general intelligence of the individual, that is, his ability to comprehend and use symbols or to do abstract thinking. This academic aptitude is important not only in school situations, but also in everyday life situations in which ability to analyze a situation or a problem, to draw conclusions, to generalize, and to plan accordingly, is needed. Special aptitudes must also be explored. The work of recent years has shown that general intelligence manifests itself as special aptitudes such as verbal comprehension, arithmetic reasoning, and spatial reasoning (Staff, Div. of Occupational

Analysis, 1945). For this reason data concerning strength or weakness in any one of these special areas must be obtained. Other special aptitudes which play a part in clerical, technical, musical, artistic, and manual activities must be known. The subject's interests, attitudes, and personality traits need to be assessed, in terms of their vocational implications. And finally, data are needed as to his proficiency in using any of the skills which he has acquired.

Social data are needed in order to provide a framework in which to interpret the psychological data. The occupational level of the parents plays an important part, for example, in determining the vocational ambitions of a youth and in his drive to achieve them, as well as in fixing the financial resources upon which he can draw in furthering his ambitions. The vocational achievements of the subject's brothers and sisters may be indicative of his own probable level of achievement, but this prognosis is modified, in turn, by the age of the parents and their financial independence. It not infrequently happens that the youngest child fails to reach an occupational level as high as that of his siblings because of the need to contribute to his parents' support just at the time at which he might have been going to college. The industrial and cultural resources of the home and of the community, the educational experiences of the individual, his leisure-time activities, and his vocational experiences all need to be examined, in order that the resources open to him and the use he has made of them may be understood. To draw the line between psychological and social data is obviously impossible at times, for in finding out what influences have been at work on a person one also ascertains the ways in which he has reacted to them.

Techniques of Gathering Data

With the improvement of testing techniques it has become possible to measure an increasing number and variety of important psychological characteristics. In 1918 intelligence was the only psychological characteristic of vocational significance which could be effectively measured; in 1928 manual, mechanical, artistic, musical and spatial aptitudes, and vocational interest, could be added to the list, although the measures of these characteristics were then quite new and therefore relatively little understood. By 1938 a considerable amount of information had been gathered about and by means of these instruments, they had been refined and improved, and attitudes and clerical aptitude had been added to the list of measurable entities. By 1948, further improvements had been made in existing types of instruments. Now, more than a decade later, much more is known about their validity, and measures of personality have been developed to a point at which they appear to have clinical validity even though their vocational significance is not clear.

Despite the great progress in psychological testing since its beginnings, knowledge of the characteristics which can be measured still leaves a great deal to be desired. It will become clear in subsequent chapters that the measuring instruments we now use even for the most adequately measured traits such as intelligence and vocational interest are still not completely understood; those we use for measuring personality traits such as general adjustment, introversion and the need for recognition are still in embryonic stages; and there are no methods of testing creative imagination, persistence, and certain other traits and abilities which are often assumed to be important and which laboratory studies and other types of investigations have suggested may actually exist.

For these reasons the psychological study of a person's abilities and personality traits requires more than testing techniques. When a suitable test is available, its use will generally save time and obtain the information in a more objective, valid, and usable form than would otherwise be the case. This is especially true of intelligence, and it applies also to a variety of other traits. But some tests measure aspects of ability or interest which are so narrow as to make their use dangerously misleading unless the data obtained with them are thought of as being only one small part of the aptitude picture; for example, the existing tests of musical talent do not measure anything as broad as that term implies, but only certain minute aspects of musical aptitude. They need to be supplemented by observation of musical performance, ratings by musicians, history of interest in musical activities, etc. As the major part of this book is devoted to the uses of vocational tests, it is the purpose of this section to point out some things that tests cannot now do rather than to show ways in which they are useful. It aims to indicate briefly the nontesting techniques which must be used in order to obtain a well-rounded picture of a subject, rather than to discuss the useful testing techniques.

The *interview* is the most widely used subjective method of gathering personal data, as well as the principal treatment or counseling technique. In diagnosis as in counseling, there are traditionally two divergent points of view concerning interviewing. In one approach, the emphasis is on careful planning, in having a well-thought-out interview schedule or form which is to be completed during the interview. The interviewer asks direct questions, using the phraseology of his schedule and adhering to the order in which the questions appear on the schedule. In the other, the nondirective approach, the interviewer merely sets the topic ("structures the situation"), then accepts and reflects feeling in order to let the person being interviewed lead the discussion into the areas which are most important to him. Although the interviewer may not gather data on exactly the topics which he had considered important, he does obtain material on the problems which are of most importance to the client, and therefore most important for diagnosis. The Hawthorne Study well illustrates the development of this technique (Roethlisberger and Dickson, 1939, Ch. 13). A commonly used procedure is the patterned or semi-structured interview, in which the interviewer uses the schedule only as a guide. In this semi-directive type of diagnostic interviewing, the essence of the technique is to use key questions as a means of getting the client to talk freely on important topics, in the anticipation that desired facts will be brought up in a context which makes their interpretation more complete than it would be if the facts were given briefly and in response to a direct question. In either type of data-gathering interview, and especially in the less directive type, it is possible to obtain information not only on factual items such as those normally covered in the social history, but also on attitudes, ambitions, and other affective matters which constitute the psychological case history (see Fenlason, 1952; Kephart, 1952; Tyler, 1953, Ch. 23 for detailed discussions).

Questionnaires are frequently used in order to obtain data such as are commonly gathered in the interview. Super and Brophy (1941) demonstrated that with literate subjects who want to co-operate this is an effective time-saver in collecting factual material, but it is much less useful than the interview as a means of gaining insight into the attitudes and feelings of any but the most frank and insightful of individuals. Research by Landis and Katz (1934) and others has shown that factual items are generally reported with considerable accuracy when the subject has come for counseling, although there is evidence supplied by Green (1951) and Heron (1956) that others, whether subjected to diagnosis against their will or under scrutiny as applicants for positions, yield to the pressure to falsify facts and improve appearances as much as they consider possible. Useful material on attitudes can sometimes be gathered by questionnaire methods, often by transforming the questionnaire into an attitude scale, but Spencer (1938) has shown that the truthfulness of material obtained depends on the anonymity of the response and, by inference, on the confidence of the respondent in the person using the data. Symonds (1931, Ch. 4) has discussed the details of questionnaire construction at some length, pointing out steps which can be taken to improve the understanding of the questions by the various people filling out the form and thus to compensate as much as possible for the lack of flexibility inherent in the technique. If the questionnaire is well constructed and good rapport is established in its use, remarkably frank answers can be obtained concerning matters which the respondent is able to put into words, as shown in a study made under conditions of anonymity by Shaffer (1947).

Rating scales are a third widely used non-testing technique of gathering diagnostic data, although they resemble tests in that they attempt to quantify evidence and to be objective. A great deal of research, summarized by Symonds (1931, Ch. 3) and from the counselor's point of view by Strang (1949, Ch. 3), has demonstrated that despite its objective appearance the rating scale is a very subjective technique, being fundamentally the recording of opinion. Despite this defect, rating scales have been found useful in personnel selection and evaluation; but judging by the accumulated experience of those who have tried them, they have not proven very helpful to counselors interested in getting a picture of the characteristics of students or others with whom they are working.

Anecdotal records resemble some aspects of the better types of rating scales in that they call for descriptions of behavior as observed in concrete situations. The American Council on Education Personality Report, for instance, calls for a specific illustration of every characteristic rated on the graphic scale: if the student has shown evidence of leadership, the rater is asked to describe a situation in which this was demonstrated. An anecdotal record differs, in that it consists of a collection of such incidents described soon after the event and accumulated in the subject's file. If the incidents are well chosen and well described (neither of these desiderata can be taken for granted) it is then possible to analyze these records and construct a dynamic and characteristic picture of the individual in question and to make judgments concerning his probable behavior in other situations. This technique has been studied by Jarvie and Ellingson (1940), and is described by Strang (1949) and Froelich and Hoyt (1959).

Personnel records are another source of diagnostic data available to schools, colleges, and business enterprises. The data included therein are often so sketchy as to shed little or no light on the abilities, interests, personality traits, background, or family situation of the person in question; on the other hand, they frequently include a variety of important diagnostic data. In a school or college the student's courses and grades are at least likely to be available, while in an industrial concern his type and amount of education, previous employment history, marital status, earnings, and attendance are likely to be on record. The case histories of social agencies and credit ratings often provide other material. If the records go into more detail concerning the subject's special achievements and problems the counselor or personnel worker has as his disposal data on proficiency, interests, and personality traits which have the advantage of having been accumulated over a period of time and therefore of showing trends of development, and which generally reflect the judgment of a variety of people. The principal problem in using personnel records is to keep them sufficiently complete without making record keeping take time that is needed for appraisal and counseling. Strang (1949) and Tyler (1953) discuss the use of personnel records in schools and colleges; treatment of their business and industrial uses will be found in Scott and others (1954) and in Ghiselli and Brown (1955).

Essays and *autobiographies* provide another source of diagnostic data. Counselors and admissions officers in schools and colleges frequently ask students to write an autobiographical sketch, often focussing on their educational and vocational experiences and plans, in order to get an understanding of their interests and motivation. There has been much less systematic study of this technique than of most, despite its widespread use. It is used not only in educational institutions, but also by foundations granting fellowships, rarely by business enterprises. It is briefly discussed by Strang (1949) and by Froelich and Hoyt (1959) and at somewhat greater length by Fryer (1931, pp. 371-419).

The Contribution of Tests to Vocational Appraisal.   What has just been said should make it clear that psychological tests are only one way of obtaining information needed to understand a person whom one is counseling. To put it concretely, the intelligence of a young man two years out of high school can be judged by an intelligence test administered to him especially for that purpose, by his marks in high school, by his father's occupation, by his own occupational experience since leaving school, and by various other indices.

It is true that all of these methods have defects: the test may not truly represent his mental ability because of a reading handicap; his high school marks may not be a good index because of his poor motivation at that time; his father's occupation may be the result of social stratification rather than of his own enterprise and ability in a fluid society; and his own occupational experience may have been distorted by depression conditions. But they also have their own peculiar advantages: the young man's occupational history shows what he has actually done with his ability in a situation in which the economic factors are known; there is a demonstrated relationship between intelligence and occupational level, whether the occupation referred to is that of the father or of the person in question; high school marks correlate to a moderate extent with intelligence tests and with subsequent achievement in college; and good tests well given are relatively free from extraneous influences and do yield a prediction of performance or satisfaction in some types of activities which is as good as any other index available, sometimes much better.

The well-trained diagnostician therefore uses a variety of techniques for gathering data about a person he is going to counsel or concerning whose admission, employment, upgrading, or release he is to make a recommendation. He uses psychological tests to obtain information concerning aptitudes for analyzing new situations or for using fine instruments; he checks this evidence against interview material and personnel records which indicate what kinds of new situations the client has met in the past and how he has met them, or what courses he has taken and what hobbies he has engaged in which require manual dexterity and how successful he was in these. Ratings and reports from former teachers or employers provide evidence of proficiency in activities not covered by marks and for which no proficiency test data are available. They also supply data concerning the ability of the person concerned to get along with superiors, associates, and subordinates, something not assessable by means of the usual psychological tests. These illustrations could be extended indefinitely, but should be sufficient to illustrate the point that testing and non-testing techniques need to be used in combination for the effective gathering of psychological and social data.

The above discussion presupposes the validity of the psychological tests that are used, just as it presupposes the validity of the other methods of gathering data and of the data which they yield. Educators and business men who are not trained in statistics and in experimental methods, and some who are trained in experimentation in other fields but not in psychology, often fail to realize that in a blanket questioning of the validity of tests they assume the validity of some other criterion or predictor such as school marks, supervisors' ratings, production records, or their own judgment. They too often do not know how unreliable or invalid these other indices have been shown to be by objective investigations. Ample evidence on this subject will be presented later in this book, in connection with the problem of selecting a criterion and in discussing the validity of each test covered in detail. But it is pertinent at this point to introduce some evidence of the value of tests in vocational counseling.

The National Institute for Industrial Psychology conducted a number of studies in England and Scotland (Allen and Smith, 1940; Hunt, 1943; Hunt and Smith, 1945) in order to ascertain the value of vocational tests in counseling boys and girls in their early teens who were leaving school and taking employment. The results have been consistently favorable to counseling which utilizes test data along with other information rather than depending only upon traditional sources of data. Allen and Smith (1940), for example, followed up the children who had graduated from four elementary schools. A control group had been counseled without benefit of test data, whereas an experimental group had been tested with a variety of vocational tests and counseled in the light of all types of data. The vocational adjustment of the experimental group, as evidenced by job stability, satisfaction, earnings, and similar criteria of success, was significantly better than that of the control group.

Pitfalls in Diagnostic Testing

Four major types of error are frequently made by users of tests. These are: 1) the neglect of other methods of appraisal, 2) overemphasis on appraisal with the resulting tendency to neglect counseling, 3) failure to take into account the specific validity of the tests used, and, 4) the neglect of other methods of guidance which should normally accompany appraisal and counseling. The first two pitfalls have already been dealt with at some length in this chapter; the third is discussed in the next chapter; in concluding this chapter some remarks on the fourth type of error are in order.

Many of the earlier writers on vocational guidance, working at a time when psychological tests were first being developed and when interviewing was an unanalyzed art, were more impressed by the promise of exploratory activities in school and on the job than they were by diagnosis and counseling. Aware of the extremely limited usefulness of the tests of their day and of the subjectivity and inadequacy of the interview as then used, they had more faith in the ability of the individual to "find himself" as a result of exposure to a variety of experiences in his school work, leisure-time activities, summer jobs, and first few years of work than as a result of a counselor's work with him. This point of view is expressed as late as 1932 in Brewer's *Education as Guidance,* the title of which indicates its philosophy.

Not a few later writers on vocational guidance went to the other extreme, particularly those who have had a part in the development of vocational tests during the past thirty years. Impressed by the gains made in our ability to appraise and predict, they tended to emphasize the role of the counselor or employment manager and to minimize the importance of exploratory and induction activities. This emphasis is shown in the writings of some psychologists of the 1930's (Darley, 1943; Williamson, 1939), and again a score of years later when objective tests were shown to yield better predictions than other techniques (Kelly and Fiske, 1951; Meehl, 1954).

A third, also recent, group of writers has introduced still another emphasis, that on therapy or counseling at the expense of diagnosis and exploration, the first of which is considered positively harmful while the latter is not considered at all, because of the emphasis on personality adjustment (Rogers, 1946; Rogers and Wallen, 1945).

Rogers' and Williamson's points of view have already been discussed in another connection; the point which it is desired to bring out here is that both of these emphases have minimized the role of exploration by the individual and the use of exploratory activities by the counselor as a means of furthering vocational adjustment. In most contemporary thinking, appraisal and counseling are viewed as essential to a program of vocational guidance, and so is exploration. The effective vocational counselor is one who knows when and how to use appraisal techniques, when and how to rely primarily on counseling, and when and how to help the counselee engage in activities which will help him to obtain the insights and information needed. In industrial and business personnel work also, there are circumstances in which good selection is the crucial thing in securing well-adjusted employees, others in which helping them to understand themselves and their situations better is most important, and still others in which good induction into the new company and try-out in a variety of activities are the key to developing effective employees; the most competent personnel man relies on a combination of such procedures. To become so absorbed in the mechanics or dynamics of one aspect of vocational guidance or personnel work as to lose sight of the others, or to depend exclusively on one or two rather than using a combination of all three, is to impose an unnecessary limitation upon the effectiveness of one's work.

REFERENCES FOR CHAPTER I

Allen, E. P., and Smith, Patricia. *The Value of Vocational Tests as Aids to the Choice of Employment.* Birmingham, England: City of Birmingham Education Committee, 1940.

Bordin, E. S. *Psychological Counseling.* New York: Appleton-Century-Crofts, 1955.

———— "The implications of client expectations for the counseling process," *J. Counsel. Psychol.*, 2 (1955), 17-21.

————, and Bixler, R. H. "Test selection: a process of counseling," *Educ. Psychol. Measmt.*, 6 (1946), 361-374.

Bragdon, H. D. *Counseling the College Student.* Cambridge: Harvard University Press, 1929.

Brewer, J. M. *Education as Guidance.* New York: Macmillan, 1932.

Combs, A. W. "Nondirective techniques in vocational counseling," *Occupations,* 25 (1947), 262-267.

Covner, B. J. "Nondirective interviewing techniques in vocational counseling," *J. Consult. Psychol.*, 11 (1947), 70-73.

Darley, J. G. *Testing and Counseling in the High-School Guidance Program.* Chicago: Science Research Associates, 1943.

Dressel, P. L. "Counseling caprices," *Pers. Guid. J.*, 33 (1954), 4-7.

Eckert, Ruth, and Marshall, T. O. *When Youth Leave School.* New York: McGraw-Hill, 1938.

Fenlason, Anne F. *Essentials in Interviewing.* New York: Harper, 1952.

Fisher, V. E., and Hanna, J. V. *The Dissatisfied Worker.* New York: Macmillan, 1931.

Froelich, C. P., and Hoyt, K. B. *Guidance Testing and Other Student Appraisal Procedures for Teachers and Counselors*. Chicago: Science Research Associates, 1959.

Fryer, D. *The Measurement of Interests*. New York: Holt, 1931.

Ghiselli, E. E., and Brown, C. W. *Personnel and Industrial Psychology*. New York: McGraw-Hill, 1955.

Green, R. F. "Does a selection situation induce testees to bias their answers on interest and temperament tests?" *Educ. Psychol. Measmt.*, 11 (1951), 503-515.

Hahn, M. E., and Kendall, W. E. "Some comments in defense of non-nondirective counseling," *J. Consult. Psychol.*, 11 (1947), 74-81.

Heron, A. "The effects of real-life motivation on questionnaire response," *J. Appl. Psychol.*, 40 (1956), 65-68.

Hunt, Patricia. "The Birmingham experiments in vocational selection and guidance," *Occ. Psychol.*, 17 (1943), 53-63.

———, and Smith, P. "Vocational psychology and the choice of employment," *Occ. Psychol.*, 19 (1945), 109-116.

Jarvie, L. L., and Ellingson, M. *A Handbook of the Anecdotal Behavior Journal*. Chicago: University of Chicago Press, 1940.

Kelly, E. L. "Theory and techniques of assessment," *Annual Rev. Psychol.*, 5 (1954), 281-310.

———, and Fiske, D. W. *The Prediction of Performance in Clinical Psychology*. Ann Arbor: University of Michigan Press, 1951.

Kephart, N. C. *The Employment Interview in Industry*. New York: McGraw-Hill, 1952.

Landis, C., and Katz, S. E. "The validity of certain questions which purport to measure neurotic tendencies," *J. Appl. Psychol.*, 18 (1934), 343-356.

Meehl, P. E. *Clinical* vs. *Statistical Prediction*. Minneapolis: University of Minnesota Press, 1954.

Patterson, C. H. "Is psychotherapy dependent upon diagnosis?" *Amer. Psychol.*, 3 (1948), 155-159.

Pepinsky, H. B., and Pepinsky, Pauline N. *Counseling Theory and Practice*. New York: Ronald Press, 1954.

Roethlisberger, F. J., and Dickson, W. J. *Management and the Worker*. Cambridge: Harvard University Press, 1939.

Rogers, C. R. *Clinical Treatment of the Problem Child*. Boston: Houghton-Mifflin, 1939.

——— *Counseling and Psychotherapy*. Boston: Houghton-Mifflin, 1942.

——— "Psychometric tests and client-centered counseling," *Educ. Psychol. Measmt.* 6 (1946), 139-144.

——— *Client-centered Therapy*. Boston. Houghton-Mifflin, 1951.

———, and Wallen, J. L. *Counseling with Returned Servicemen*. Boston: Houghton-Mifflin, 1945.

Scott, W. D., Clothier, R. C., and Spriegel, W. R. *Personnel Management*. New York: McGraw-Hill, 1954.

Seeman, J. "A study of client self-selection of tests in vocational counseling," *Educ. Psychol. Measmt.*, 8 (1948), 327-346.

———. "A study of preliminary interview methods in vocational counseling," *J. Consult. Psychol.*, 12 (1948), 321-330.

Shaffer, L. F. "Fear and courage in aerial combat," *J. Consult. Psychol.*, 11 (1947), 137-143.

Shoben, E. J. "Counseling," *Annual Rev. Psychol.*, 7 (1956), 147-172.

Spaulding, F. T. *High School and Life*. New York: McGraw-Hill, 1938.

Spencer, D. *The Fulcra of Conflict*. Yonkers: World Book, 1938.

Staff, Div. of Occupational Analysis, WMC. "Factor analysis of occupational aptitude tests," *Educ. Psychol. Measmt.*, 5 (1945), 147-155.

Strang, Ruth. *Counseling Techniques in College and Secondary School.* New York: Harper, 1949.

Super, D. E. *The Psychology of Careers.* New York: Harper, 1957.

———, "The preliminary appraisal in vocational counseling," *Pers. Guid. J.,* 36 (1957), 154-161.

———, and Brophy, Dorothy A. "The role of the interview in vocational diagnosis," *Occupations,* 19 (1941), 323-327.

Symonds, P. M. *Diagnosing Personality and Conduct.* New York: Appleton-Century, 1931.

Thomas, L. G. *The Occupational Structure and Education.* Englewood Cliffs, N. J.: Prentice-Hall, 1956.

Tyler, Leona E. *The Work of the Counselor.* New York: Appleton-Century-Crofts, 1953.

Williamson, E. G. *How to Counsel Students.* New York: McGraw-Hill, 1939.

——— *Counseling Adolescents.* New York: McGraw-Hill, 1950.

II

TESTING AND PREDICTION IN VOCATIONAL SELECTION

The Peculiarities of Selection Testing

ALTHOUGH vocational counseling tests are often identical with those used in selection (i.e., placement and promotion), their uses generally differ considerably. In vocational counseling, the primary objective is the development of an understanding of an individual by himself and incidentally by the counselor, and the relating of personal to occupational data. This broad task, in our present state of knowledge, requires considerable dependence on non-testing techniques and subjectively obtained information concerning both counselee and occupations. Perhaps some day the dream of a comprehensive battery of tests and of test weights for all the major occupational fields, described by Hull (1928, Ch. 14), will be realized, but current opinion is in agreement that both people and occupations are too complex for this to be at all likely. In vocational selection, on the other hand, it has proved possible to rely more heavily on testing procedures. Familiarity with the reasons for this is essential to the effective use of tests in both counseling and selection.

Fundamental among the factors which make possible greater reliance on tests in vocational selection is the relative simplicity of validation, that is, of checking test results against behavior which one is attempting to predict. Whereas in counseling one is concerned with a great variety of occupations, in selection the focus is on suitability for one or at most several somewhat related jobs. The personnel man interested in improving the selection of employees for certain jobs in his company works with a relatively *uniform criterion group* (men in one job) and with a relatively *simple criterion*. He is therefore able to make a careful first-hand analysis of the activities involved in the job, to select or develop tests likely to prove valuable in predicting success in its activities, to check up on the actual value of the tests and of other indices such as the judgments of interviewers, and to utilize in his selection program the combination of techniques which has actually worked best for the job in

17

question. If, for example, the objective is to select effective operatives for a certain type of assembly work, an analysis can be made of the processes involved in the assembly and of the skills which seem to be required by them. Possible criteria of successful performance can then be examined, some of them designed to serve as overall indices of success, some perhaps selected to serve as measures of success in special aspects of the work in which specific aptitudes play an important part. In an assembly job the overall criterion may be the number of assemblies correctly completed per working day or other unit of time; specific criteria are not likely to be available in as simple a task as assembly work, although some such work can be broken down into processes requiring primarily gross and fine manual skills, spatial judgment, and perceptual speed. The frequently forced dependence on one overall criterion of an objective type has the advantage of reducing the amount of experimental work, but has the disadvantage of making it seem deceptively simple. Research has shown that production is affected by many factors, including payment methods, location of work, type of supervision, and union policies. Despite this fact, the use of vocational tests in selecting employees for one type of job in one company, in which most of these other factors are constant, is made relatively simple by the possibility of one fairly adequate criterion of success.

A third factor which operates to make the use of tests in vocational selection easier and more helpful than in counseling is the fact that the personnel man has some *control over the job situation.* As he is working for the company for which he is trying to improve employee selection the company has a stake in his success, and as he knows the situation in which he works, the people whose co-operation he must have, and the policies governing their work, he is likely to be able to obtain the co-operation which he needs and to be able to make changes in policies, schedules, and other aspects of operations in order to achieve his objectives. This improves both the chances of developing good tests and the prospects that the personnel whom he has selected will work under conditions which permit the success of qualified employees. It should be noted, however, that since the user of tests in personnel selection is part of an operating agency and must fit in with the operating needs of other officials he is subject to pressures which may handicap him in his work. Among these are the need for immediate results when preliminary work should be done before applications are made, the lack of sufficient numbers of employees in some jobs for adequate standardization and validation to be possible, the difficulty of obtaining adequate criteria (e.g., the impracticability in some situations of training supervisors to rate objectively), and the fact that certain operations cannot be interfered with in the way necessary to a particular project.

The fourth factor which generally operates to make possible greater dependence on tests in personnel selection than in counseling is the practicability and superiority of *custom-built tests*. Experience has repeatedly shown that, when a battery of tests is developed especially for use with one job or a group of jobs in the organization, specific local factors can be taken into account which make the tests more valid than tests which have been developed with more varied applicability in mind. This is a crucial point which should be borne in mind by every user or potential user of vocational tests for selection purposes; given the time and the highly-trained technical personnel necessary to such work, selection tests developed especially for use with certain jobs in a given organization are likely to prove much more valid than more widely applicable tests. A knowledge of the nature and validity of existing tests, such as it is the purpose of this book to provide, is essential to good testing of any kind, but the user of tests for selection purposes needs to master also the techniques of test construction and validation and to apply them to his work, or to obtain the services of a specialist who can, under his general supervision, carry on such work. The next chapter contains a discussion of the logic and methods of test construction and validation, but does not attempt to present the statistical procedures. As stated in the introduction, that should be the subject of another book.

An illustration of the superiority of custom-built tests will help make the point that selection-testing is more practicable than guidance testing. In selecting and classifying cadets for training as pilots, navigators, and bombardiers in World War II, some work was done with tests of spatial visualization such as Thurstone's Surface Development (Guilford, 1947, p. 273) with results which led to the conclusion that existing tests of this factor were not promising for aircrew selection (rbis=.16 with flying success). Work was begun along lines suggested by job analyses which involved tasks and materials resembling, at least superficially, the tasks in which success was to be predicted. One of these tests which factor analysis has shown to be a measure of spatial visualization in a way realistic for aviation (Guilford, 1947, pp. 479-486) was entitled the Instrument Comprehension Test. In it the examinee read airplane flight instruments such as the artificial horizon and decided which of the presented alternative pictures of an airplane in flight represented the attitude (position relative to the ground) of the plane indicated by the instruments. This test had validities of .39 and .48 (two different parts of the test) for the experimental group referred to above.

Most clearly a spatial visualization test for aviation, however, was the Visualization of Maneuvers Test (Guilford, 1947, pp. 277-284). The items consisted of a stem showing the attitude of an airplane and describing the turns, climbs, and dives it next makes, followed by five multiple-choice pictures of the same airplane in varying attitudes. The task was to indicate how the plane would be flying after completing the maneuvers described. This would seem logically to involve the ability to visualize the relationships of objects in space. Anecdotal evidence is available in the observation of experienced pilots taking the test and in their comments after taking it; they gesticulate with their hands and sway in their seats as they act out the maneuvers they are attempting to visualize, and say, afterwards, that they "just about twist your hand off trying to do those maneuvers." The correlation of this test with success in flying training has been shown to be .23 (Guilford, 1947, p. 283). These results demonstrate considerable validity for single tests, and more than that which characterized the more abstract type of spatial visualization tests.

With the advantages deriving from a relatively uniform situation over which he has some control, with a criterion of success which is simple enough to permit validation but broad enough to be related to a number of different tests, and with the greater similarity between test and criterion which results from the ability to use custom-built tests, the personnel man working on selection problems can well depend more on tests than can the counselor who is trying to help people with vocational choices.

The Importance of Other Techniques

Although the psychological factors which can be measured in selection are the same as those which can be measured for counseling purposes, there is less reason for thinking that non-measurable factors need to be measured in selection than in counseling, and more direct evidence to justify a greater dependence on the factors which can be measured.

Numerous studies of the employment interview, summarized by Bingham and Moore (1959) and by Wagner (1949), have shown that there is so little agreement among interviewers that employment interviews have little value. Since the bulk of these studies were made, improved techniques have been developed which make possible a reasonable degree of agreement between interviewers; these involve training interviewers, standardizing the interview situation, focussing on certain traits or aspects of behavior most readily observable in the interview, and providing standardized scales for the rating of traits or behavior and the notation of substantiating facts. Stone and Kendall (1956, Ch. 8) have a good discussion of methods and results. Despite such improvements experience continues to demonstrate that in many situations interviewing techniques do not contribute much to prediction for specific jobs. For example, an aviation psychologist met regularly with a flight surgeon as a member of a board which reviewed the cases of soldiers who made borderline scores on the aviation cadet classification tests. This board interviewed these cadets, reviewed relevant material, and decided whether they should be sent on to flying training or disqualified on the basis of low aptitude. The board's judgment was proved to be of little value. The procedure was soon dropped, and cadets were disqualified on the basis of test scores alone.

Another study was made somewhat earlier by the staff of the same Research Unit (Guilford, 1947, Ch. 24), in which a number of clinical techniques, as contrasted with objective tests, were studied in order to determine their validity in predicting success in flying training. These techniques included a standardized interview, observation of behavior in an informal "rest period" between tests, observation of behavior in two standardized situations in one of which the cadet took an apparatus test by himself and in the other of which he worked on a spatial assembly test as one of a group of three examinees, ratings of behavior in standard psychomotor tests, and others. The correlations between ratings based on these techniques and success in primary flying school were practically zero, except for coefficients of between .15 and .20 for the ratings based on observation in Heathers' Control Confusion Test and on Super's Interaction Test, the two experimental situations designed especially to bring out ratable behavior. The interview ratings had no validity, even though made by interviewers who had at least the equivalent of a master's degree in psychology with an emphasis on clinical work. The objective tests used in the standard selection and classification battery had validities which ranged from .29 to .51 in the experimental group of 1112 cadets (DuBois, 1947, p. 191). Dependence on tests rather than on interviewers' or observers' judgments is clearly justified by these two studies, although it is conceivable that a more valid interview or observation procedure might be devised and personnel trained to use it, as in the work of the Office of Strategic Services (Assessment Staff, 1948). Finding time for it would then be the problem when large numbers of candidates are involved. The AAF program tested cadets at a cost of five dollars per man, whereas the OSS procedure required three and one-half days, a hundred-acre farm, and fifteen professional staff members for a group of eighteen candidates.

One reason why tests have proved to be more valid than other techniques for gathering and evaluating personal data for the prediction of vocational success is that the tests themselves have been so constructed as to cover material which is often thought of as obtainable only by other methods. It is not meant to imply that the tests measured all relevant variables; a multiple correlation coefficient of .66 (DuBois, 1947, p. 191) makes it quite clear that other factors also were operating in the AAF studies, and the battery of tests avowedly was weak in measures of personality and temperament. But the factual material which is normally obtained by means of interviews and questionnaires and then interpreted subjectively was obtained in a Biographical Data Blank (Guilford, 1947, Ch. 27) devised by Laurance F. Shaffer, weighted according to the experimentally ascertained importance of each possible response to each question, and scored to yield a measure of background factors and experiences which play a part in flying success. It had a validity of .33 (DuBois, 1947, p. 191). The technique was not entirely new: it was used in the Civil Aeronautics Administration testing program by E. Lowell Kelly (Fiske, 1947) and prior to that had become a standard method in the selection of salesmen by a number of life insurance companies. In the latter, for example, a positive weight was given to affirmative answers to questions as to whether the examinee was married, had children, or carried insurance, since these were found to characterize men who made good salesmen.

Work done by German military psychologists (Farago, 1941), by Murray and his colleagues at Harvard, by the same investigator and the staff of the Office of Strategic Services (Assessment Staff, 1948), and by Bass (1954) and by Flanagan and others (1954) in more recent years, has demonstrated that there are possibilities in the development of the standardized situation test which should not be neglected in selection programs, nor, for that matter, in counseling programs. The ultimate form of such tests may perhaps not be comparable to the paper and pencil or apparatus tests that we now consider objective; instead, it may combine some of the standardized features of the objective test with some of the subjective features of the interview. But, in improving their validity by standardizing the situation and the method of evaluation, psychologists take them out of the category of non-testing techniques and into that of testing techniques. At present they are experimental and of limited validity, and so are briefly considered only as a promising technique for the evaluation of personality.

The Validity of Selection Tests

The problems and methods of validating tests for selection and counseling purposes are taken up in the next chapter. It is pertinent here, however, to examine the evidence concerning the value of tests in the selection of employees, for what has been said on that score while considering the limitation of other techniques has been piecemeal and incomplete.

Working with applicants for employment with a utilities company, Wadsworth (1935) gave two intelligence tests to an experimental group and no tests to a control group, the former numbering 108 and the latter

594 men and women. After employment, by the usual methods in the case of the non-tested applicants, data were gathered concerning their success on the job. Employees were classified as outstanding, satisfactory, or problem employees. The results, given in Table 1, show the superiority of test-selected personnel in this one enterprise, as only 5.5 percent of the latter were considered problem employees as contrasted with 29 percent of the non-test selected group.

TABLE I

TEST-SELECTED EMPLOYEES IN A UTILITY COMPANY PROVED
SATISFACTORY MORE OFTEN THAN OTHERS

Type Employee	Test-Selected	Non-Test-Selected
Outstanding	33%	22%
Satisfactory	61.5%	49%
Problem	5.5%	29%
Total Number	108	594

Strong used a different type of test with a different type of employment, obtaining his data in the somewhat less satisfactory manner of testing employees already on the job (1943, pp. 487-498). Despite this his data are impressive, and there is no reason to think that they would have been different if testing had preceded employment. Relevant to this topic is his finding that 56 percent of the life insurance salesmen who scored A on his life insurance salesman's scale sold $150,000 worth of insurance per year (enough to yield a living in commissions at that time), whereas only 6 percent of those who made scores of C sold that much insurance.

Finally, data from the army aviation testing program of World War II might be cited, because of the unusually large numbers tested, the extensive batteries of tests involved, and the nature of the criteria used. Figure 1 shows the percentage of cadets at each ability level (determined by tests) who were eliminated from primary flying training, the first nine weeks of actual flying as a student pilot. The trend is obvious at once: the short bar at the top shows that only four percent of the 21,474 cadets who entered training between October 1942 and December 1944 with pilot stanines of nine (standard scores expressed on a nine-point scale) were eliminated from primary flying school because of flying deficiency, fear, or their own request, whereas the long bar at the bottom of the graph shows that 77 percent of the 904 cadets who entered training during that same period with pilot stanines of one were eliminated. These low-scoring cadets were less numerous than the high-scoring, because of the raising of requirements as the use of tests became more completely accepted and as the progress of the war made smaller quotas of new pilots possible. By the end of the war it was possible to accept for pilot training only cadets with pilot stanines of seven. This meant that, instead of an elimination rate of 24 percent as in this group of 185,367 in the middle two years of the war, only 10 percent would be eliminated if other factors remained constant.

Even more conclusive evidence is available from the experimental group described in Report No. 2 of the Aviation Psychology series (DuBois, 1947) and by Flanagan (1947). As has been previously stated, this group was selected without reference to test scores, the only official requirement being the passing of the physical examination. Actually, the group was also somewhat selected according to traditional methods, as they were accepted at a time when the normally enforced standards were well known and the men presumably applied with the thought that they could meet them. This is shown by the fact that only 23 percent were not at least high

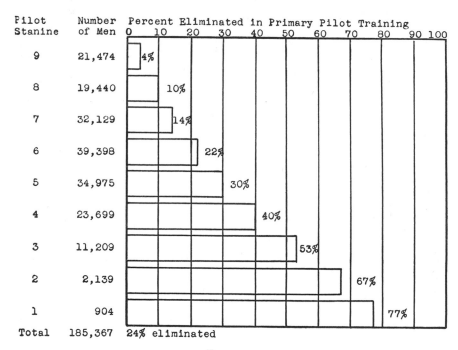

FIGURE 1

TEST SCORES AND SUCCESS IN AAA PRIMARY PILOT TRAINING
The bars indicate the percentage eliminated, at each pilot stanine (combined test score), for inability to fly, fear, and at own request. Credit for flying experience is included in the stanine. Data are for classes trained during 1943 (when some low stanine men were admitted), 1944, and 1945. After Flanagan (1947, p. 76).

school graduates, as contrasted with 37 percent of men-in-general at that age (Bell, 1938). Whereas the selection and classification tests normally admitted to training only one failure to every three or four successes, the non-test selected experimental group included one failure for every success. If, as there is reason to believe, other things such as the strictness of instructors, check riders, and elimination boards remained relatively constant, the use of tests was clearly an improvement over selecting merely on the basis of physical examination and, to a lesser extent, education.

Programs of Testing for Selection, Placement, and Upgrading

Despite the evidence which shows that subjective methods of evaluating applicants for employment add little or nothing to the predictive value of well-constructed and validated objective tests, personnel men and vocational psychologists continue to utilize interviews, application blanks, rating scales and letters of recommendation in selecting employees. This is partly because of an unreasoning distrust of purely objective methods, partly because of the knowledge that even the best of test batteries do not cover everything and the hope that other methods will supplement them, and also because, in practice, tests are often used without the thoroughgoing standardization and validation procedure necessary to know just how valid they are and whether or not selection is in fact improved by supplementing tests with other techniques.

When job analyses have been made the emphasis in testing is likely to be on *placement* on the right type of job; when differential ability data are lacking, it is likely to be on *selection* of generally promising employees.

One large corporation, to cite a concrete instance, uses psychological tests in three of its divisions. In one division of this corporation a new plant had been built and the personnel director was told that the management wanted to make it a model plant. He was accordingly directed to devise a battery of tests which would be appropriate to the jobs to be filled, and to select employees on the basis of tests and other data from the beginning. The need for selecting employees on *some* basis and the belief that even tests which had not been validated in that plant would help in the selection of better employees than would be selected without test results, caused the use of tests without the benefit of scientific preliminaries. The personnel director therefore put into use a battery of tests which, judging by results in other plants, seemed likely to prove valuable. They were used in an attempt to exclude from any type of job the most awkward, most maladjusted, and least intelligent, that is, for *selection*. At the same time provisions were made for the gathering of data concerning the success of the new employees on their jobs. Although the use of the tests in making decisions concerning selection could be expected to reduce the range of abilities in any one job, it was felt that the shortage of labor would result in a spread of abilities sufficient to reveal whether or not a relationship existed between test scores and job success. In such a situation it was only natural that previous experience, schooling, and similar background factors were weighted quite heavily by the employment manager in going over the results of tests, interviews, application blanks, and letters of recommendation.

In another division the psychologist in charge of testing began by making a systematic analysis of the jobs in question, using standard job psychographic techniques. He then selected and devised tests which he thought would be effective measures of the characteristics which appeared to differentiate the major types of jobs. The experimental battery of tests was administered to all applicants for factory employment and, as data accumulated, the test results were correlated with supervisors' ratings in order to determine their actual value in selection. One test was found to add nothing to the predictive value of the battery, but, as it took little testing time and appealed to applicants and foremen, it was retained; other tests which had some value were weighted accordingly and used in selection and in *placement* in appropriate jobs. The validities of the battery average about .50. No personal history or biographical data form of the type discussed earlier in this chapter is used, the battery being limited to aptitude tests. For these reasons the employment interview is depended upon rather heavily, and decisions are made after the background and manner of the applicant have been mentally (rather than statistically) weighted in combination with the test results by the employment manager, with the emphasis on placement in a suitable job.

The third division of this corporation operated in a part of the country in which labor shortages were serious. In practice, employee selection became more a matter of employee *placement*. The personnel manager, however, selected a battery of tests without regard to special aptitudes and abilities such as might be important in selecting for or in placing people in different types of jobs; believing that even selective placement was generally out of the question in that plant, the emphasis was placed on tests of certain basic general factors the understanding of which would help foremen and supervisors to induct and handle the new employee more effectively. The employment battery therefore consisted of a test of general intelligence, a measure of personality adjustment, and a measure of vocational interests. The nature of the tests was explained to supervisors, the scores of each new employee were discussed with them, and they were helped to understand the types of adjustment problems which the new employee might encounter. It was believed that the supervisors' interest in and intelligent use of this information was an important factor in the development of satisfactory employees, although no objective evidence was gathered on this subject.

Psychological tests are frequently put to use in business and industrial personnel work for the *upgrading* of personnel, that is, the evaluation of employees for possible promotion to more responsible positions. In this type of work two approaches are possible, one of them comparable to selection testing, the other to placement testing. In the former, tests and other techniques are used which will throw light on the general promise of the persons in question: their general intelligence, personality adjustment, leadership, and similar general characteristics are assessed by means of tests, inventories, ratings by superiors, and interviews. In the latter, data are gathered by similar methods, but they are data about special abilities, interests and personality traits that are known or thought to be important to success in specific jobs at higher levels.

For example, a number of aviation psychologists worked under the leadership of John C. Flanagan in the American Institute for Research, on the evaluation of airline first officers for possible promotion to captaincies. An analysis was made of the abilities and characteristics needed by the captain of a commercial airliner. Tests were selected which previous work with pilots had demonstrated to be correlated with success in flying twin and four engine planes; others were constructed to measure characteristics not covered by existing tests; and interview procedures were developed for tapping other factors which could most effectively be assessed in face-to-face contacts. Techniques for quantifying the results of interviews were developed, and the results obtained by any one interviewer were so treated as to make them comparable to the results obtained by others, thereby minimizing the subjective elements. At the same time, the flight records and ratings of first officers by captains and check pilots were utilized as objective measures of proficiency and achievement, after they had been subjected to a statistical study which demonstrated their reliability and validity. The resulting data were weighted to provide an overall score indicative of the pilot's promise as a captain; this, and a three hundred word sketch verbally summarizing the first officer's assets and liabilities and pointing out how they might be respectively utilized and corrected in this and other possible jobs, were turned over to company personnel officers for use in making decisions.

In such a program tests play an important part in assessing characteristics which are not called for in the job currently held, or the exercise of which cannot be well observed on the job. They help to isolate factors which, even though observable in the employee at work, are so intertwined with other factors that the observer has difficulty in determining the relative importance of a given strength or weakness. And, finally, they are free from the taint of possible bias.

REFERENCES FOR CHAPTER II

Assessment Staff. *The Assessment of Men*. New York: Rinehart, 1948.
Bass, B. M. "The leaderless group discussion," *Psychol. Bull.*, 51 (1954), 465-492.
Bell, H. M. *Youth Tell Their Story*. Washington, D. C.: American Council on Education, 1938.
Bingham, W. V., and Moore, B. V. *How to Interview*. New York: Harper, 1959.
DuBois, P. H. (ed.). *The Classification Program*. ("AAF Aviation Psychology Report," No. 2) Washington, D. C.: Government Printing Office, 1947.
Farago, L. (ed.). *German Psychological Warfare*. New York: Committee for National Morale, 1941.
Fiske, D. W. "Validation of Naval Aviation Cadet selection tests against training criteria," *J. Appl. Psychol.*, 31 (1947), 601-614.
Flanagan, J. C. *The Aviation Psychology Program in the AAF*. ("AAF Aviation Psychology Report," No. 1.) Washington, D. C.: Government Printing Office, 1947.
Guilford, J. P. (ed.). *Printed Classification Tests*. ("AAF Aviation Psychology Report," No. 5.) Washington, D. C.: Government Printing Office, 1947.
Hull, C. L. *Aptitude Testing*. Yonkers, N. Y.: World Book, 1928.
Stone, C. H., and Kendall, W. E. *Effective Personnel Selection Procedures*. Englewood Cliffs, N. J.: Prentice-Hall, 1956.
Wadsworth, G. W. "Tests prove their worth to a utility," *Pers. J.*, 14 (1935), 183-187.
Wagner, R. "The employment interview: a critical summary," *Pers. Psychol.*, 2 (1949), 17-46.

III

METHODS OF TEST CONSTRUCTION, STANDARDIZATION, AND VALIDATION

TO BE fully competent in the use of vocational tests one needs to know all stages and types of work with tests. This does not mean that the vocational counselor or personnel director must be an expert in test construction, nor that the developer of tests must also be expert in using them in counseling or selection. But it does mean that the vocational counselor must be familiar with the procedures and problems of test construction, and that the technician whose function it is to develop tests must understand their use in counseling and selection. It is therefore the purpose of this chapter to provide an orientation to test construction enabling the user of tests in counseling and personnel evaluation to read the published test research with a critical appreciation of the problems involved and thus to understand more completely the meaning of test results.

The development of a vocational test can be broken down into seven major steps. These are: job analysis, selection of traits to test, selection of criteria of success, item construction, standardization, validation, and cross-validation. In any given test construction project one or more of these steps may conceivably be slighted or omitted altogether; when this is the case, however, it should be because sufficient work has already been done along those lines to provide a basis for the next step, or because the pressure of time and circumstances makes the taking of short cuts necessary and dependence on hunches seems wise. The critical reader must judge for himself whether or not the omission of the steps was justifiable and whether or not the data are usable.

Job Analysis

Before tests can be selected or constructed for the measurement of aptitude or personality traits which affect success or satisfaction, it is necessary to have an understanding of the characteristics and abilities which play a part in the work in question. The process of collecting and analyz-

29

ing information which provides this understanding is called job analysis. It may be an armchair analysis, in which the test constructor draws on his familiarity with the job or occupation in order to set up hypotheses as to the characteristics which make for success in that work. It may involve bibliographical research, to ascertain what others have thought or found to be important in that occupation. It may be an analysis of manuals used in training in order to judge the abilities needed in mastering the fundamental skills. It may involve discussing it with supervisors, observing and interviewing workers doing the work, trying the operations oneself, or even learning the job and working at it for a period.

In analyzing the work of military pilots a combination of these methods was used as time and circumstances permitted. First, Flanagan analyzed the proceedings of boards which eliminated failing aviation cadets from primary flying training, in order to ascertain the reasons given for their failure by the boards. This resulted in a list of characteristics ranging from lack of co-ordination to poor motivation, and a table showing the incidence of each of these reasons in a large sample of eliminees. Then Hemphill, drawing on his own experience as a civilian flyer, and Super, depending on observations of military pilots at work and demonstrations of flying in which he performed some of the operations, made an analysis of training manuals in order to describe the pilot's tasks as a basis for setting up hypotheses concerning characteristics which would make for success in learning to fly. After this, Miller, Wallen, and Super went to a military flying school in which Miller and Super worked as participant observers, living in barracks with the cadets, attending ground school and physical training, handling planes on the flight line, learning to fly, and being graded for their flying on the same basis as cadets. Wallen worked in the station hospital, administering clinical tests to the cadets being studied, interviewing them concerning their background and development, and collecting other types of information from hospital, training, disciplinary, and other records. All three job analysts kept notes concerning the observed behavior of the twenty cadets of whom intensive case studies were being made, whether on the flight line, in the barracks, or on "open post" in the nearby town. The two investigators who were flying kept detailed records of their own experiences in learning to fly. These materials provided a basis for detailed study of the task of learning to fly, of emotional aspects of the experience of learning to fly, and of factors which made learning to fly easier or more difficult for a random sample of cadets. Fitts interviewed the returned members of a bombardment squadron to get their account of the nature and requirements of combat flying, analyzed the material, and made it available to aviation psychologists working on test construction. Flanagan spent some time in a combat theater studying records, interviewing flyers, and flying a number of missions in order to analyze combat flying at first hand. Later, research detachments conducted similar investigations on a larger scale in most theaters of the war (Lepley, 1947).

The above description of job analysis activities in one practical situation illustrates the variety of approaches used. In practice there is not necessarily one method of job analysis; it is more likely that there are several which will yield valuable information, and that more than one must be used if adequate data are to be made available as a basis for selecting or devising tests.

The most recent form of job analysis, adapted especially to vocational guidance because it deals with broadly rather than with narrowly defined jobs, is that widely applied by the Occupational Analysis Division of the United States Employment Service under Carrol L. Shartle (1959). Items which have a bearing on test construction include a description of the work performed, the amount and type of supervision received, the responsibility, knowledge, initiative, alertness, judgment, dexterity, and accuracy involved, the tools used, production standards, working conditions, physical demands, and other characteristics required for performance of the work. The use of this procedure yields a list of abilities and traits which are considered important in the occupation or job being studied.

Selection of Traits to Be Tested

The analysis of the job provides the test constructor with a list of aptitudes and traits which are deemed important in that job. But this list is subject to two serious limitations. These are the subjectivity of the evidence and the uncertainty that a particular factor, even if it proves to be important, will differentiate this job from others. The fact that ability to get along with others is thought important in a given job is, for example, ascertained only by the analyst's observations or by opinions transmitted to him by persons who know the work. The data are no more reliable than the judgment of the people gathering or supplying them. Furthermore, if the presence of the trait is subjectively ascertained in the first place, there may be no objective method of assessing it, for it may be a characteristic which has so far eluded the attempts at measurement. Granting that ability to get along with others is a prerequisite of the job being studied, there is still a question as to whether or not it differentiates this job from others. There are many jobs which require ability to get along with others; even if this trait could be measured, its measurement might contribute little that is of value to differential diagnosis and prediction.

Once the job analysis is complete and the list of presumably important characteristics is available, the first task of the test constructor is to decide on: 1) The relative importance of each trait or aptitude; 2) the availability of a suitable criterion against which to validate a test of this trait; 3) the chances that a given trait is important in this job and unimportant in others with which he is also concerned; 4) the unavailability of some reliable and economical non-testing technique for judging this characteristic; and 5) the prospects of being able to locate or devise a test which provides an objective measure of the characteristic in question. The job analysis should provide evidence of a subjective type concerning the first point. The next section deals with the important problems which arise in connection with the choice of criteria. A comparison of the job analysis data for the job in question with available evidence from other jobs should provide a basis for judgment of the third point. In connection with the fourth point, the use of school grades and supervisors' ratings should be considered. For the fifth, the psychologist must be well acquainted with the various types of tests which are already in existence and with the extensive literature on test construction in which abortive as well as successful efforts at test construction have been described. In the light of these considerations, the psychologist is able to draw up a list of aptitudes, skills, and personality traits ranked in the order of the likelihood with which they may be successfully studied.

Selection of the Criteria of Success

Jenkins (1946) has pointed out that the events of World War I taught American psychologists the *necessity* of validation, the next two decades taught them much about the *technique* of validation, and that World War II drove home the necessity of devoting much time and thought to the *basis* of validation. In most of the test validity research of the 1920's and 1930's much space is given to descriptions of the technique of test construction, the methods of securing data, the description of the criterion used, and the results of the relating of test scores to criterion data. Not infrequently one of these topics is somewhat neglected—that in which the criterion is described. But, even when the criterion is adequately *described,* too little attention is paid to its adequacy as an index of success.

This lack of emphasis on the criterion can be illustrated by a study (Sartain, 1945) in which the group of aircraft factory inspectors on which the battery of tests was validated were not defined as to type of material inspected, sex, or age, and were described as "probably representative" with no supporting statistical analysis; the raters who made the criterion judgments knew the subjects as students in a refresher course, but knew their job performance only in "most" cases; the ratings of two instructors had an intercorrelation of .77, and their correlation with subsequent ratings by supervisors was .42. The intercorrelations of ratings are relatively high; and yet with no more attention devoted to the criterion, it is difficult to interpret the results. For example: Specifically what type of performance was rated, that it correlated highly with intelligence (.64) and only moderately (.32) with mechanical comprehension? Data for engine and fuselage inspection might differ. Was the immediate criterion (instructors' ratings) only moderately related to the ultimate criterion (supervisors' ratings) because of low reliability of the latter, lack of common factors in the instructional and work situations, or some other uninvestigated factor? Admittedly the judgment of the instructors is one type of evidence that is available early in the new employees' job experience, but how valid a *criterion* is it, that is, how good a measure is it of what the tests are trying to predict? If a test has a correlation of .64 with the immediate criterion, and the immediate criterion has a relationship of only .42 with the ultimate criterion, the relationship between the first predictor and the ultimate criterion is not very high. A more thorough study of the nature and meaning of the criterion serves to clarify issues and suggest better predictive devices. At the same time, whether or not it is desirable to devote time to such a study depends on other factors; e.g., the savings that would be effected by improved procedures.

The typical but unwise procedure in test construction is, too often, to leave the detailed consideration of a criterion until somewhat later in the process than has been done in this discussion. Usually, having decided what factors he should try to test, the psychologist has proceeded to develop suitable tests, administer them to appropriate subjects, and then for the first time seriously consider the problem of criteria. The vague ideas that he has so far had are now crystallized, the most readily available index of success is used with little or no investigation beyond a cursory check on its reliability, and the relationship is computed.

The experience of Naval aviation psychologists summarized by Jenkins (1946), and the experience of Army aviation psychologists summarized by R. L. Thorndike (1947), suggest that the order of the steps taken in test construction needs to be changed, and that considerable emphasis needs to be put on the problem of selecting and evaluating a criterion early in the process. Once the traits to be measured have been determined, attention should be turned to the selection of a criterion and to the refinement of methods of collecting evidence against which the tests to be developed can be validated.

Thorndike (1947, 1949) and others have distinguished between *immediate, intermediate,* and *ultimate* criteria. In military aviation these are respectively illustrated by such evidence as ability to complete training as a bombardier, accuracy of bombing (indicated by average circular error) on the practice range in operational training, and accuracy of bombing in combat. Immediate criteria are generally partial, that is, they tend to emphasize limited aspects of performance. If grades in medical school, for example, are used as an index of success, some men with good academic ability but poor social adjustment will be rated as more successful than certain other students with somewhat less academic ability but superior social adjustment, whereas if an ultimate criterion of success in the practice of medicine can be utilized the latter may prove to be more successful than the former. Conversely, ultimate criteria are more complex than immediate or intermediate indices of success; for this reason, as well as because of the pressure of time, they are rarely used in test validation.

In the case of military pilots, for example, it was necessary to put a classification program into operation on a large scale shortly after the bombing of Pearl Harbor. This meant that there was no time in which to gather data on the subsequent combat success of cadets before establishing weights for the experimental tests. Collecting such data actually took more than two years. Instead it was necessary to use an immediate criterion, in this case evidence of the cadet's ability to graduate from primary flying school, which became available in about five months. This is by no means a simple criterion, as it is affected by a variety of factors such as the cadet's various abilities and personality traits, the attitudes of the instructors under whom he works, and the extent to which the school he attends adheres to or deviates from established practices and standards. But it is not an ultimate criterion, as ability to complete the first stage of flying training is not necessarily identical with ability to outfly enemy pilots or to withstand the greater and more enduring stresses of battle. Since pilots who cannot complete training never get to combat the criterion is, however, suitable in a negative way. The same argument applies to the selection or guidance of physicians, teachers, and any other group which must surmount a training hurdle before they can compete in practice.

It is noteworthy, however, that despite the fact that Ghiselli (1955) has demonstrated that tests tend to predict immediate (training) and not ultimate (job success) criteria, Distefano and Bass (1959) found that highly rated practicing lawyers had scored significantly higher than low-rated lawyers on the Law School Admission Test.

The first characteristic to be sought in selecting a criterion is *relevance*. If the immediate criterion is to be valid, it must adequately represent important aspects of the ultimate criterion. If success in completing training is to be a suitable immediate criterion, the activities and requirements of the training program must resemble those of the job. Fortunately, the job analysis should provide a fairly good basis for a subjective judgment of this matter. Jenkins (1946) cites the case of aerial gunnery, in which intelligence test scores were found to correlate highly with grades in training, and might therefore have been assumed to predict success in actual combat; but when the curriculum was revised to make it less abstract and more practical the correlation between intelligence and grades fell to zero.

A second characteristic of a good criterion is *reliability*. Thorndike (1947, p. 34) has pointed out that although high reliability is not essential in a criterion, provided it is stable enough to reveal the existence of a relationship, the more reliable the criterion is the more clearly the degree of the relationship is demonstrated. Low reliability is caused by intrinsic factors such as the inconsistency of the performance which is being studied, and by extrinsic factors such as variability in the conditions of work, the lack of agreement between raters either in the use of terms or in the interpretation of behavior, and bias in the situation. An illustration of *inconsistent performance* is provided by an analysis of errors in determining the position of an airplane at key points in the mission (Thorndike, 1947: 44), which showed that the number of such errors made in one mission has no relationship to the number of errors made in the next mission. As the reliability of performance on a single mission was considerably higher, it is probable that both the inconsistency of the performance of such a complex task and variations in external conditions played a part in the unreliability of performance from one mission to the next. *Variability in the conditions of work,* in these same aviation studies, consisted of such factors as temperature, visibility of targets, and turbulence of the air and consequent instability of the navigator's and bombardier's working platform. In business and industrial studies such variations are illustrated by differences between selling on an open floor on which the customer can approach the merchandise and the clerk can use his skill in approaching the customer, and selling behind a counter where the clerk can merely await the customer in a more passive way, or by differences in supervision which affect the attitudes and output of the workers. Meltzer (1944) has for example reported a study in which the Minnesota Rate of Manipulation Test (Placing) had a correlation of —.27 with output under one management, and of more than .20 in the same department under a different type of management and with the different attitudes which it engendered. The *lack of agreement between raters* is so well known a factor that it hardly needs elaboration; Jenkins (1946) mentions a study in which Naval aviation cadets were given successive check flights by two experienced instructors, with a correlation coefficient of approximately zero for the two sets of grades. *Bias in the situation* is well illustrated by differing standards in the judgment of performance in different training institutions from which graduation is the index of success, for example in traditional academic colleges on the one hand and in progressive colleges which emphasize more than intellectual accomplishment on the other.

Criteria may be classified as *proficiency measures, output records, ratings, self-ratings, administrative acts,* and *internal consistency measures.* As Thorndike (1947) points out, some of these are enduring records which can be scored with perfect agreement by different workers at different times (the first two categories), such as answers to a multiple-choice test or hits on a target; some leave no enduring record but can be recorded objectively by an observer (administrative acts, ratings and anecdotes), such as number of bounces in landing a plane or number of customers approached; and some are subjective evaluations for which no objective evidence of any type is available save the overall impression in the observer's mind (ratings).

The first five are types of *concurrent* or *predictive* validity criteria, the last has to do with *content* and *construct* validity (American Psychological Association, 1954). It has been well pointed out by Brayfield and Crockett (1955) that these different criteria often do not agree with each other, and indeed some should not be expected to agree.

Proficiency as measured by tests of information and skill in the performance of a task is sometimes used as an index of success. In some occupations, the work of which closely resembles the work of the proficiency test, this type of criterion may be quite appropriate. The work of a navigator in flight resembles that of the student of navigation in the classroom in many important respects, even though it may differ insofar as working conditions are concerned. The computations and instruments, and even the sequence in which they are used, can be made the same in the classroom or group test as in the airplane. This logical analysis is borne out by a correlation of .49 between final examinations in ground school and final average grade for missions (Flanagan, 1947, p. 122), although the coefficient is low enough to make it clear that there are factors operating in flight which do not operate in the classroom, probably factors of an emotional and perceptual nature. In many other occupations the proficiency test situation is too unlike that in which the actual work is performed for it to seem a satisfactory criterion. Knowledge of the operation of a .50 caliber machine gun, for example, would not appear to involve the same aptitudes and skills as ability to hit a moving target with it while standing on an unstable moving platform. Before an achievement test can be considered a good criterion of success, an analysis of the job and of the factors covered by the test is necessary.

Output can be gauged in a number of ways, varying with the nature of the task. In a production job it may be the number of units produced per hours, whether the units are identical parts turned on a lathe or pounds of butter wrapped, or it may be the average earnings over a given period when wages are based at least in part on volume produced. In a sales job it may be the number of units sold or the dollar value of the total sales, or a ratio of sales income to sales expense. In military aviation it may be the number of hits on a target in gunnery or the number of planes shot down by fighter pilots or gunners. Criteria such as these seem delightfully concrete and objective at first glance, but one of the bitter lessons learned by applied psychologists engaged in test construction work is that the appearance of objectivity is frequently deceptive.

Investigations of incentive systems have shown (Mathewson, 1931; Roethlisberger and Dickson, 1939), for example, that the output of indus trial workers is often governed by factors other than individual differences in abilities or motivation and that artificial limits are often set upon the amount produced per worker per hour. A detailed study by Rothe (1946, 1946a) showed that individual daily work curves of butter-wrappers vary greatly, but that nevertheless group trend lines were a stable and usable criterion. He found no evidence of restriction of output in his subjects. In sales work differences in territories, type of clientele, and the aspirations and circumstances of the salesmen often attenuate the relationship between volume of sales and abilities. Strong (1934) investigated the case of a life insurance salesman whose annual sales were not as great as would have been anticipated of one with a test score as high as his. It developed that he had a private income and therefore aspired to sell only enough insurance to supplement his income. In executive jobs company policies greatly affect the amount earned; E. L. Thorndike (1940:86) reported the cases of two presidents of equally important and well-known corporations, one of whom received a salary of $420,000 per annum, the other $125,000. A study of the reliability of bombing scores cited by Thorndike (1947) reports a median reliability of .08. As Kemp and others have shown (Kemp and Johnson, 1947:42-52), so many factors enter into the accuracy with which bombs are dropped that one cannot predict the performance of a given bombardier from one mission to the next unless he flies with the same crew and the personnel factors are thereby kept constant; even then, weather provides a vitally important but extraneous variable.

Output may also be judged somewhat more subjectively, by having experts evaluate the product as to quality. This is done by developing a score sheet on which specific aspects of the work are rated and the total score obtained by combining these ratings, a method commonly used in evaluating school systems and in phase checks or performance tests for aerial gunners, but it has not often been applied to civilian jobs. The work to be evaluated need not be tangible, but may instead be simply an observed performance. In the standard flight checks developed for pilots the cadet performs certain highly standardized maneuvers, while the check pilot or examiner records such objectively determined items as the angle of bank in a steep turn, the time taken to complete it, and changes in altitude. One group of 16 selected items had a reliability of .39 for cadets with 15 hours of training and .50 for men with 55 hours of flying (Thorndike, 1947, p. 47). Reviewing later work, McFarland (1953, p. 78) reports progress in improving these on-the-job tests.

Ratings of performance are a widely used criterion, probably the most common because of the relative ease of obtaining them. The history of ratings has, however, been extremely disappointing, and when they are relied upon today it should be only because of inability to find or devise a better criterion and after systematic steps have been taken to make them as reliable as possible. The literature on rating as a technique is too well known to need review here; it is well treated in several sources (Ghiselli and Brown, 1955; Thorndike and Hagen, 1955). From the point of view of the reader of the literature on the validity of tests, the questions to be kept in mind have to do with the extent to which the ratings of one judge agree with those of another, the possible influence of halo effect (the tendency to rate specific traits on the basis of an overall evaluation), and the relevance of the traits or behavior measured to the work in question. In one study (Thorndike, 1947, pp. 50-51) in which airplane commanders were rated while going through operational (combat) training, the rating for "likeableness" had the highest correlation of any of the ten traits rated with the overall rating of suitability for combat flying. There would seem to be little relevance in this case, and considerable halo effect.

In studies of the use of tests in vocational counseling conducted in England under the auspices of the National Institute for Industrial Psychology (Hunt, 1943; Hunt and Smith, 1945), and in a few American investigations (Cole, 1939; Seipp, 1935) ratings of vocational adjustment have been a criterion. The investigator usually makes a case study of the individual in his work and gives him a rating for vocational adjustment according to the extent to which he seems to be properly placed, satisfied with his work, and satisfactory to his employer. Little attention has as yet been paid to the adequacy of the judgments made by such investigators, presumably because of the labor involved in having more than one judge go over the necessary case material. In many respects, however, this would appear to be an ultimate criterion of so desirable a type as to justify giving time to devising more economical ways of using it and more thorough study of its reliability.

Most users of ratings have obtained ratings of the traits or behavior of individuals. In a few investigations the focus has been not on a person, but on some tangible product of that person's work. When this has been the case the results are somewhat more encouraging. One of the best examples is the Minnesota Mechanical Abilities Project (Paterson et al., 1930, p. 201), in which industrial arts teachers rated the shop products of junior high school boys for quality of workmanship. The identity of the worker can be disguised to avoid halo effect, thereby focussing attention on the specific aspects of craftsmanship to be judged. The reliability of the ratings in this study was .76 in the woodshop and .72 in the sheet-metal shop. The principal weakness in such criteria, as in the case of more objective output criteria, is the neglect of important human factors not directly revealed in the product of the worker.

Self-ratings have occasionally been used as a criterion of success in attempts to get at the less tangible and more personal aspects of vocational adjustment (Hoppock, 1935; Super, 1939; Brayfield and Crockett, 1955; Brayfield and Wells, 1957; Thorndike and Hagen, 1959). The focus in these investigations has generally been on the nature and extent of job satisfaction rather than on the predictive value of tests, although Sarbin and Anderson (1942) did study the relationship between Strong's Vocational Interest Blank and satisfaction in work, and Thorndike and Hagen (1959) correlated aptitude test results of 1943 with self-rated satisfaction in 1955. In studying the value of tests in vocational selection, the emphasis is appropriately on the effectiveness of the worker in performing his task as indicated by ratings of supervisors or by output, but as the use and study of vocational tests in counseling is improved it is probable that more attention will be paid to ratings based on case studies and to self-ratings, the former as an index of overall vocational adjustment, and the latter as a criterion of the worker's feelings of success and satisfaction in his work. As self-ratings of job satisfaction are further refined, to distinguish between *job* and *occupational satisfaction* and between the various components of each of these global concepts, as in studies by Brophy (1959), Friesen (1952) and in the SRA Employee Inventory (Burns et al., 1951), they will probably find increasing use in the validation of tests and inventories for vocational guidance.

Administrative acts which provide criteria of vocational success include the obtaining of employment in a given field, promotion, increase in pay, discharge or failure, and other tangible evidence that people employed in the field consider the individual in question a success or failure. These administrative acts have many of the drawbacks of ratings, and are in fact administrative outcomes of ratings; but they are generally made after more serious deliberation than a rating is, because of the obviousness and immediacy of their effects on employer as well as on employee. Ability to complete flying training was thus the best immediate criterion of success in the Aviation Psychology Program of the Army Air Forces; promotions, decorations, assignment to first or co-pilot duties, assignment to lead crews, removal from flying status for flying errors, and removal from combat because of operational fatigue (neurotic reactions to combat stress), were also used as intermediate and ultimate criteria (Thorndike, 1947, p. 55). The National Institute for Industrial Psychology has frequently used ability to keep a job as a criterion (Hunt, 1943; Hunt and Smith, 1945): in a period of depression, when jobs are scarce and promotions come slowly, this is presumably a sound criterion, but in more prosperous times, when transfers to better jobs are more easily obtained, and when the scarcity of labor makes employers retain marginal and submarginal employees, the criterion is obviously less adequate. This illustrates the defect inherent in all administrative criteria, that is, the degree to which they are affected by external factors. Ability to complete a training sequence may depend in part upon changes in standards from one time to another or from school to school; at one time, for example, one primary flying school consistently eliminated 50 percent of its students and another only 10 percent, despite control of the quality of the cadets sent to them for experimental purposes without their knowledge (Guilford, 1947, p. 116). In the last analysis, administrative acts make a good criterion because it is in terms of them that success and failure are judged in daily life; at the same time, it is important for the user of tests based on such indices to know just what factors were operating in the administrative situation at the time in question, and the effect of their presence on the criterion and on the test validities.

Internal consistency is frequently used as an index of the validity of a test, although it has no necessary significance for vocational prediction. In the case of general intelligence, the vocational significance of which has been demonstrated in numerous studies with a variety of tests and for the measurement of which certain types of items have amply been demonstrated to be effective, it may be sufficient to check the internal consistency of a new test and to standardize it on a good sample population for its results to be useful in vocational guidance. Ascertaining its validity for specific occupations would be helpful to counselors, but might be dispensed with if it interfered with better validation of other tests. On the other hand, measures of special aptitudes, of interest, and of personality are still so little understood, and the nature and operation of these characteristics in determining vocational success and satisfaction is so uncertain, that merely knowing that the items in a test measure the same thing is insufficient. People who score high on one half of the test should score high on the other half, in order that one may be sure the test is measuring something and measuring it well; but the vocational counselor, psychologist, and personnel man need to know that what is being measured is related to success in the activity or activities in question. This requires an external criterion of validity such as those discussed in the earlier paragraphs of this section.

Knowing the various types of criteria, and their advantages and limitations, the test constructor canvasses the situation in which he is working to ascertain what kind of criteria are already available to him, and which could be made available if proper steps were taken. Existing criterion data are analyzed in order to ascertain their reliability. Supervisors who already rate their employees may be given a refresher course in rating in order to make their results more reliable, or statistical corrections may be made for constant biases which the data have revealed in certain raters. Production records may be usable in their present form, or it may be found that there is too little variation among workers for them to serve as success criteria. If no suitable criterion already exists, the psychologist must decide which possible criterion lends itself most effectively to use in that situation and how data might be collected. The negligible interrelationships of different kinds of criteria received by Brayfield and Crockett (1955) and reported by Thorndike and Hagen (1959) point up the need to select an appropriate criterion; relevance should not be sacrificed to convenience or to objectivity. Establishing the *content, construct,* or even the *concurrent* validity of a test is only a useful first step; the most important criterion is that which the test predicts.

Test Construction

Once the nature of the characteristic to be tested and of the criterion to be used in validating the test have been decided upon, the *choice of type of test* and of test item is relatively easy. If the characteristic to be tested has been isolated by job analysis procedures it may be a relatively complex bit of behavior requiring a miniature situation test and therefore, as a rule, apparatus. Or the characteristic may have been broken down into relatively abstract components which lend themselves to paper and pencil testing; thus in aviation cadet testing a large fraction of the validity of certain apparatus tests lay in their measurement of spatial visualization, a factor which was well tested by paper and pencil tests used in the same battery (Guilford, 1947; Guilford and Zimmerman, 1947). Knowledge of the literature of aptitude and personality testing is also a source of ideas as to how to attempt measuring a given trait.

The type of test having been decided upon, the next step is to *construct* the apparatus or to *draw* or *write* items. In the case of an apparatus test first a sketch and then a rough pilot model is made in order to devise suitable mechanical or electrical methods, to ascertain the most effective size or sizes for the various parts, and to have a model for use in experimental trials. In paper and pencil test construction the procedure is to draw up an outline of the proposed contents of the test or inventory, write, photograph, or draw items of those types, and refine them by checking and rechecking. Thus in constructing a three-dimensional test of spatial relations one would cut blocks of wood of various sizes with various degrees of complexity, in order to ascertain which yield the best results; in the case of a general information test one canvasses encyclopedias, current magazines and newspapers in order to choose topics for items, and makes up questions with suitable right and wrong answers.

The preliminary form or forms of the test having been prepared, the test is *tried out* on a small group of subjects, who may be a sophisticated group of co-workers or a sample of the type of subjects for whom the test is designed. Ideally, both are done in order to get subjective comments and criticisms from the points of view of both test constructors and persons like those to be tested. In one project, for example, Super directed the development of a biographical inventory for the selection of telephone operators. The traits to be measured were ascertained from an analysis of a variety of data on differences between operators who stayed on the job more than six months and those who quit or were discharged. The items written by one staff member were reviewed by another, to make sure that multiple-choice alternatives were suitable and that phrasing was clear. Revised items were reviewed by a committee made up of two of the consultants and four representatives of the parent and branch companies which proposed to use the inventory. After further revamping and editing, a first form was tried out on 25 subjects in each of four companies, most of the applicants being interviewed to ascertain their reactions to and criticisms of the inventory. These comments provided the basis for one more revision before the large-scale collection of data began.

Further revision of the test results from the above procedures, and the test is reproduced for the *collection of data* on a larger scale. The actual number varies with the facilities for trial testing, but is normally large enough to make possible the establishment of time limits, the checking of the clarity and completeness of directions, the locating of ambiguous or offensive items, and the analysis of the internal consistency of the test. The subjects at this stage should be a sample of those for whom the test is designed, not only because different types of groups may require different amounts of time or need directions which go into varying amounts of detail, but also because items that work well with one type of subject may not work well with another: for example, a question may be well-phrased and have a right answer for unsophisticated subjects, but may be unanswerable by more sophisticated examinees because of simplification of matters which they know to be complex.

An *analysis of the internal consistency* of some tests is not possible at this stage, either because some apparatus tests with time scores have no items or parts, or because the test may not be scorable until it has been item-validated. If, as is generally the case with aptitude tests, there is an *a priori* method of scoring based on right and wrong answers, this scoring key needs to be analyzed to make sure that answers keyed as "right" are in fact generally chosen by those who make high total scores, and that the wrong answers are more frequently chosen by those whose total scores are low. The test is then *revised again,* in order to eliminate poor items and sharpen those that are ambiguous, after which it should be ready for large scale administration.

Standardization

The principal problem in administering vocational tests for standardization and validation is *whom* to test, and at what stage of their careers. The question of *how many* is more easily answered, at least in theory. Whether the test is to be used in guidance or in selection and promotion, it is obvious that it should be standardized on persons for whom the chosen criterion will be available. But this raises a problem which has plagued psychologists since the beginnings of aptitude testing, for if the test is standardized on a group who are already employed in the occupation, and for whom criterion data are presumably readily procurable, there will be a real question as to the value of the test when used with persons who have not yet entered the field. Specifically, will a low score made by a high school or college student indicate a relative lack of the aptitude measured, or will it reflect primarily what is already known, namely, his lack of training and experience? If, on the other hand, the test is administered to students or others who have not yet entered the field in question, how is one to validate it? The lag between testing time and that at which criteria of success become available may be considerable, and the loss of cases through entry into other fields not being investigated and through change of address is certain to be almost prohibitive.

Predictive validation studies of the type just mentioned are rare. Strong's studies of his Vocational Interest Blank have generally employed the *ex post facto* validation of differentiation between people employed in various occupations (1943, Ch. 7) , but he has also administered his inventory to miscellaneous college students and followed them up about twenty years later (1955) in order to ascertain the relationships between their test scores on the one hand and entry into and stability in various occupations on the other. Longitudinal validation has been used more in selection programs, especially those involving training after preliminary selection. The Armed Forces frequently selected on the basis of tests which were first validated by giving them as though for use in selection and then checking their results against success in training; Thorndike and Hagen (1955) have analyzed a mass of such data to predict later civilian occupations. As users of tests in personnel work have become more test sophisticated, as users of tests in guidance have become more exacting in their requirements, and as constructors of tests have raised their standards through familiarity with good practices, longitudinal validity studies have found better support and have become more numerous.

In the meantime concurrent validation studies are still a very common type. Strong first validated his inventory by contrasting the answers of men in one field with those of men in other fields; Kuder is now doing the same with his, although the first validation was by internal consistency; the numerous sets of norms compiled by the Minnesota Employment Stabilization Research Institute compare workers in one field with those in others or with the general population (Paterson and Darley, 1936); the material comprising the bulk of this book deals with *group differences* and relationship to *success in training,* rather than with *success in an occupation,* because of this emphasis in the research. It may be well to point out, however, that the result may not be as disastrous for vocational counseling as one might suppose, for work by Strong and by Carter (1944), the most complete along these lines, shows that the results of some *ex post facto* validated tests can legitimately be applied to untrained and inexperienced persons if one knows what corrections to make for maturation. This finding for Strong's Blank has been confirmed in other ways with other tests, for example, by determining the effects of training and of age on the Minnesota Clerical Test (see Ch. VIII).

The number of cases to be obtained, it has been stated, is more readily decided upon than whom to test and when to test, but is inextricably involved in both of these. The determining factors are the number needed in order to compute certain statistics and the number that can, in a given practical situation, be tested. If the test is being standardized for selection in a department which employs 200 workers in one job and hires fifty new people each year, and if results are to be available for use in a reasonable period of time, it is clear that pre-selection testing and validation cannot be based on more than 50 or 100 cases, and that validation upon persons already working is not likely to be feasible with more than 250 or 300 cases. As these numbers are large enough for computing correlation coefficients and critical ratios, test construction and validation may well be worth while in this situation. Certainly the sample would be adequate if the test is to be used only to select for that job in that concern providing labor market and job remain the same, as it includes the whole population in question rather than just a sample.

If the test is to be standardized for counseling in connection with the choice of an occupation the problems of numbers and sampling become much more acute. While it is relatively easy to make sure that a job in one factory is in fact *one* job rather than a number of *different* jobs, making sure that the persons who are nominally engaged in a given occupation are in reality doing the same type of work is difficult, for if they are to be a good sample they must be distributed throughout the country and analysis of their work is likely to be impossible. The test constructor has then to content himself with other devices which may help him select a well-defined and homogeneous group. He may, like Paterson and associates (1930) confine his study to a thoroughly studied and well-defined group of boys in one junior high school in one community; he may follow their lead in a series of other studies (Paterson and Darley, 1936), and select a cross section of the employed population of one city which is distributed among the major occupations in the same manner as the employed population of the United States as a whole. Both groups may then number only in the hundreds, being well selected. But in the former case, the counselor must assume that success in mechanical activities will be judged in the same way in his school or community as in Paterson's, and that the same psychological and social factors operate in his subjects in approximately the same way, or he must refuse to use the test without a local validation study of his own. In the latter case he must assume that stenographers and typists in Minneapolis do the same types of work, requiring the same *types* and *degrees* of aptitudes and skills, as stenographers in his own community, and similarly with retail salesmen, garage mechanics, policemen, etc.; or he must refrain from using the tests until he has gathered his own norms and his own validation data. The assumption may be quite sound in some instances and quite unsound in others; the writers suspect that it may be true for bank tellers, but false for retail sales-clerks. Observational evidence for the latter assumption lies in the differences between standards for clerks in dime stores and in more expensive establishments, which govern both the referral of girls to such stores by placement workers and their selection by employment managers.

The solutions to the sampling problem used by Strong, who faced it repeatedly and was primarily interested in the counseling values of his test, follow no uniform pattern and illustrate the opportunism which problems of time, money, and co-operation have forced upon test construction workers. The psychologists on whom Strong standardized his psychologist key constituted more than one third of the full members of the American Psychological Association at the time of standardization (some 200), and were scattered throughout the country, having been reached through the membership list of the Association. This would seem to be a good sample of academic psychologists, although changes in the field made necessary development of a new key twenty years later (Kriedt, 1949). On the other hand, the group upon whom the key for social science teacher was standardized consisted of more than 200 teachers employed in the state of Minnesota. They later proved to be a good sample, but there was no way of knowing whether they were also typical of social science teachers in other states such as Georgia with its different culture until Braasch (1954) so demonstrated. Obviously, the counselor using such a test needs to know the characteristics of the population on which it was validated, and the extent to which the latter resembles the population with which he is working, before he can draw any legitimate conclusions from its scores. It is, therefore, important for the test constructor to choose his validation group well and to describe it in detail.

Validation

The terms standardization and validation have been used synonymously in the preceding section, because the standardization of a vocational test involves collecting data on meaningful norm groups, and this makes possible drawing conclusions about concurrent validity or, in other instances where follow ups are made, predictive validity. In the sense in which the term is used in the sequence of steps outlined here, validation is therefore the statistical procedure of analyzing test results in relation to criterion data. In work with some types of tests this process consists of just one step, the determination of the relationship of test scores to the criterion; in work with other types of tests, however, it involves another step before scores can be validated, specifically, the validation of each item in the test.

Item validation, the determination of the extent to which a given question is answered one way by the "success" and other ways by the "failure" group, impresses the novice as a laborious procedure. It is this, but it frequently proves its worth and is often indispensable to test construction. For example, the senior author and co-workers developed a personality inventory, referred to previously, for use in aviation cadet selection and classification. When criterion data in the form of graduation-elimination reports arrived from primary flying schools, two *a priori keys* were found to have validities of approximately zero (Super, 1947). The next step was to validate each item against pass-fail in flying training; when this was done, a number of items were found to be answered predominantly in one way by the successes and in other ways by the failures. A new, empirical key was therefore made and cross-validated on another part of the sample not used in the item validation: it proved to have a validity of about .20 (significant at the 1 percent level). While this was not high, the test was unique enough for its contribution to the cadet classification battery to raise the latter's validity from about .66 to about .69, an improvement worth twenty minutes of testing time and a moment of scoring (Guilford, 1947, pp. 736-746).

This example brings out clearly the importance of item validation in tests and inventories which have no inherently right or wrong answers, for even the best logic often fails in constructing vocational tests. Even when a test has right and wrong answers, however, the right answer is not necessarily the best for persons in a given occupation. If, for example, knowing about stamps and stamp collecting were characteristic of men who *fail* in pilot training, the correct definition of the term would be a "wrong" answer for pilots. If the latter were the case a test of philatelic knowledge might be validated as a test, without item validation; but one would need to be certain that it was philatelic knowledge as such that was prognostic of failure, and not just knowledge of certain aspects of stamp collecting such as the technicalities of paper-making, colors, and perforations, as contrasted with the historical and geographic knowledge which a careful stamp collector also acquires. Hence the usefulness of item validation. This problem does not arise when the test is of a clearly homogeneous type, for example, a spatial visualization test utilizing two-dimensional forms in each item, for in their case both logical analysis and internal consistency indices demonstrate the fact that what is measured by one item is also measured by other items.

The *validation of scores* is generally done by correlating the score made on the test with the criterion data. Thus the validation of a test of employment stability in telephone operators involved computing biserial correlation coefficients for test scores and stay-quit reports of women applicants who had been hired after taking the test, and the validation of Strong's life insurance salesman's key for success in selling life insurance involved the correlation of dollar volume of sales with test scores (1934). In many cases other methods are used, the principal reliance in Strong's insurance study, for example, being placed on the analysis of the percentages of men with a given letter grade on the interest inventory selling enough insurance to make a living as a salesman. This method is known as the percent of overlapping technique using a cut-off score, and differs only superficially from a third, in which group differences are expressed by means of a critical ratio.

The choice of method is dictated by the form in which the data are expressed; pass-fail reports cannot be used in computing Pearsonian correlation coefficients, but do lend themselves to the use of biserial r's. Data like Strong's lent themselves to either correlation or percent-of-overlap analysis; although he used both procedures, more emphasis is placed on the latter technique, because the fact of earning or not earning enough money to live on seems more important in judging success as a salesman than differences above or below that amount.

Cross-Validation

Scoring keys based on item validation should be cross-validated, that is, another comparable group should be scored in the same way, to ascertain whether the validity for the second group is as high as for the first. This was brought out by the fact that validities in subsequent studies were often lower than those in the original study of a test, as a result of special factors present in the criterion group which are not present in the later validation groups. These factors operate especially in small samples in which, for example, a disproportionate number of members may, as a result of pure chance or of administrative bias, come from one part of the country, be younger than the occupational universe from which they are drawn, or have some other things in common which are not so common in other samples of the same occupational group.

Strong (1943, pp 637 ff.) studied this problem, and found that, although groups could sometimes be differentiated with as few as 50 or 100 cases in the criterion group, better differentiation was obtained, with minimal shrinkage in cross-validation, when criterion groups of from 250 to 500 are involved.

Although the need for cross-validation has been recognized in the literature it has in fact too often been honored in its breach because of practical reasons such as time, money, and the difficulty of obtaining co-operation from sufficiently large groups. Some dramatic instances of reversed relationships in cross-validation are reproduced from Stead and Shartle (1940) in Figures 4 and 5 (pp. 166 and 167).

The experiences of psychologists in World War II led to a consensus that cross-validation of item-validated scoring keys is essential, despite Strong's conclusion (1943, p. 650) that, when a large criterion group is used (and additional cases are difficult to obtain), cross-validation may be dispensed with. Experience repeatedly showed that a test validated on several hundred aviation cadets might appear valid until evidence was obtained on another sample, at which time it would lose all semblance of validity. In one study the Rorschach Psychodiagnostic was administered to cadets, and ratings of their probability of success in training were made by trained examiners who were also somewhat familiar with the requirements of flying training (Guilford, 1947, p. 625-637). In the validation or criterion group consisting of every other tested cadet ($N=283$) the biserial r with pass-fail was .23, the standard error being .09. When the cross-validation was completed on the other half of the tested group the correlation fell to approximately zero. The original figure was not very high, it is true, but with a battery of tests which occupied one and one-half days of the cadet's time and had a validity of .66, each research test which had a validity of .20 and a low correlation with the tests actually in use was carefully scrutinized as a potential contributor to the battery, and a number of such were found which repeatedly yielded validity coefficients of about the same size and added .03 or .04 to the validity of the battery.

The techniques of cross-validation are the same as those of validation with the original group. Sometimes they are applied after a second round of testing and the collection of new cases, but more commonly it is found more practical to gather enough data at first to carry out both procedures, doing the validation on even-numbered cases, for example, and the cross-validation on odd-numbered cases. This insures controlling the effect of the times at which data are obtained, and yet provides two groups for study.

Factor Analysis and Factor Validation

A further step in test construction and validation has been added by Guilford (1947, Ch. 28; 1948; Guilford and Zimmerman, 1947), through the application of factor analysis to test construction in personnel selection. It consists of analyzing tests in order to ascertain their factorial composition, and of analyzing the criterion in order to determine the nature and weight of the factors which enter into it. The former step makes possible the refinement of tests, cutting down the number of tests needed to predict success by eliminating overlapping and making each test do a maximum of work. Analysis of the criterion indicates what types of tests should be stressed in order to improve predictions.

Factorial Analysis of Tests. The use of factor analysis implies that tests can be statistically analyzed into a limited number of independent traits or aptitudes, or, conversely, that existing tests actually measure a number of traits which can be isolated by statistical analysis. To attempt to describe the procedures of factor analysis would be out-of-place in this text, but some understanding of the significance of factor analysis for test construction and validation is in order. The application of the Thurstone centroid method of factor analysis with rotation of axes (Thurstone, 1938) to a battery of tests results in the isolation of three types of variances or components: 1) several common factors, that is, components which appear in several tests; 2) possible specific factors, appearing in only one test; and 3) error variance, arising from the unreliability of the measures. These common factors, having been arrived at by a process which is largely mathematical, may or may not make psychological sense; it is by rotating the axes that meaningful factors are made to emerge. This is a somewhat subjective procedure, calling for judgments on the part of the statistician. Even more subjective is the naming of the factors that have been isolated; this is done by inspection of the kinds of tests which are saturated with a given factor, to ascertain what the common elements seem to involve.

Guilford (1948) provides an illustration of how factor analysis can help one better to understand what tests are measuring, graphically presented in Figure 2. This figure shows the proportions of factor variances in three

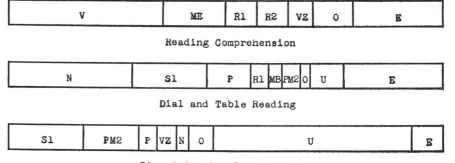

| V | | ME | R1 | R2 | VZ | O | E |

Reading Comprehension

| N | | S1 | P | R1 | MB | PM2 | O | U | E |

Dial and Table Reading

| S1 | PM2 | P | VZ | N | O | U | E |

Discrimination Reaction Time

V—verbal comprehension   N—numerical
ME—mechanical experience   MB—mathematical background
R1—reasoning I (general)   PM2—psychomotor II (precision)
R2—reasoning II (analogies)   O—other minor factors
VZ—visualization   U—unknown or specific
S1—space I (spatial relations)   E—error variances
P—perceptual speed

FIGURE 2

FACTORS MEASURED BY TWO PAPER AND PENCIL TESTS AND
ONE APPARATUS TEST, ADMINISTERED TO AVIATION CADETS
Illustrating the complexity of simple tests and the unknown quantities in miniature situation tests. After Guilford (1948).

of the tests used in the AAF Aviation Psychology Program. These tests were developed in the standard ways already described. That is, it was thought that reading comprehension might play some part in flying success, so a Reading Comprehension Test was developed with aviation types of materials. Pilots, navigators, and bombardiers make much use of books of tables and take many readings from dials. A Dial and Table Reading Test was therefore developed, using dials such as those in airplanes and tables such as are used in navigation. Reaction time is frequently mentioned by pilots as an important characteristic in flying, quick response to a variety of stimuli being obviously important in taking off, landing, and in emergencies; hence a Discrimination Reaction Time Test was constructed, along lines long used in laboratory studies in physiological psychology.

The job analysis procedures used in developing these tests were obviously those of observation and deduction. The tests were, in the cases of Reading Comprehension and Discrimination Reaction Time, attempts to measure more or less unitary traits, and, in the case of Dial and Table Reading, an attempt to duplicate the job situation in miniature.

As Figure 2 brings out, all three tests were complex in their factorial composition. This was true not only of the miniature situation test, which might have been expected to draw on a variety of abilities, but also of the two tests normally thought of as being simple in their composition. The reading test draws on the following abilities: verbal comprehension, mechanical experience (some of the content was mechanical), general reasoning, analogic reasoning, visualization, and several others. The discrimination reaction time test requires ability to judge spatial relations, psychomotor precision, perceptual speed, visualization, numerical ability, several minor factors, and a relatively large number of unknown factors, one of which might be reaction time. The dial and table test measures number, spatial relations, perceptual speed, general reasoning, mathematical experience, and psychomotor precision, a few minor factors, and some unknown factors. Such unknown factors, if not specific to the test, emerge because the test battery does not include enough other tests for them to be clearly recognizable.

These three tests were found to measure, not three traits, but a total of eleven. Of these, six are measured by more than one test. This is clearly not economical, as one good measure of a given factor would be less time-consuming than three tests. It is also inefficient from the point of view of prediction, as the validity of one test may be due to one of the factors it measures, whereas others that it also taps may actually tend to lower its validity, as when they correlate negatively with the criterion. In such a case positively and negatively significant factors tend to counteract and cancel each other in the same test.

The contribution of factor analysis to test construction is, therefore, to make possible the refinement and purification of tests, and to reveal what kinds of tests may actually be developed. The three tests just described yielded ideas for eleven different tests, some of which might be positively significant for pilot selection, some negatively, and some not at all. The construction of eleven separate tests makes possible the differential measurement of these eleven traits, and improves predictions based on the validities of these traits. Profiles showing the scores on independent traits are much more useful in counseling, provided the validity of the traits measured is known. Guilford's unique contribution lies in his having not only isolated the independent factors of this extensive battery of tests, but in having ascertained the significance of these factors for success in several occupations.

Factorial Analysis of the Criterion. When factor analysis is applied to the criterion of success, two major types of results are accomplished. First, the occupational significance of the factors is made clear, permitting the counseling of individuals on the basis of factor profiles or the weighting of factors rather than of tests in selection programs. As is pointed out in the discussion of multifactor test batteries (Ch. XV), the drawback of factorially pure tests has been the lack of evidence to guide the interpretation of their results. The second outcome is a better understanding of the nature of success in the occupation in question. Factor analysis of the criterion gives one an objective description of what is being predicted, to supplement the observational data of traditional job analysis and the deductions from test validities. But the very nature of factor analysis imposes some limitations of a very serious nature on the second type of use of the technique with the criterion. One can extract from a factor analysis only what was put into it. The only factors which can be isolated are those which are tapped by more than one test in a battery. If, therefore, the battery of tests used in the analysis is limited in scope and fails to include some traits which might be measured (and all batteries are more or less open to this criticism), the analysis of the criterion will leave undescribed some of the abilities which it requires. An indication of the extent of these unmeasured components is, of course, provided by the unknown-factor variances.

Figure 3, also taken from Guilford (1948), shows two criteria analyzed in the same way as the three tests already discussed. The pilot criterion was found to be composed of 27 common factors; about 52 percent of the variance of success or failure in pilot training could be accounted for by 23 of these factors. If other tests of appropriate but unknown types had been included in the battery, another 28 percent of the variance could perhaps have been predicted, leaving 20 percent of the variance in success or failure due to lack of reliability. Nine known factors accounted for about 56 percent of the navigator criterion; apparently success in navigation training was more easily predicted, and less complex in nature, than was success in flying training.

It is interesting to note that success in pilot and in navigator training have little in common, according to the data in Figure 3; only spatial relations and perceptual speed appear in both occupations. This contrasts with the three tests for which factorial data were presented and which overlapped more completely in their components.

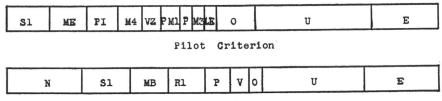

| S1 | ME | PI | M4 | VZ | PM1 | P | M3 | LE | O | U | E |

Pilot Criterion

| N | S1 | MB | R1 | P | V | O | U | E |

Navigator Criterion

V—verbal comprehension
ME—mechanical experience
R1—reasoning I (general)
VZ—visualization
N—numerical
S1—space I (spatial relations)
P—perceptual speed
MB—mathematical background

PI—pilot interest
M4—memory IV (content)
M3—memory III (picture-symbol)
PM1—psychomotor coordination
LE—length estimation
O—other minor factors
U—unknown or specific
E—error variance

FIGURE 3

FACTORS IN PILOT AND NAVIGATOR CRITERIA

As revealed by Army Air Forces factor analyses of success in training.
After Guilford (1948)

What these data make clear for vocational counseling is that number ability is not important in success in pilot training, and need not receive attention in profile interpretation; that mechanical experience, visualization, and psychomotor precision (among other abilities) differentiate pilots from navigators; and that navigators, on the other hand, are helped by the possession of number ability and mathematical background. These facts are brought out more clearly by factor analysis of the criterion than they could be, for example, by an analysis of the differential validities of impure tests such as that for reaction time or reading comprehension.

For improvement of predictions of success in pilot and navigator training these data make clear the facts that there is still considerable room for improvement in the test battery and for the development of tests measuring other factors. Approximately 28 percent of the variance in pilot success could still be predicted if suitable tests were available. The graph shows that there is probably less room for improvement in navigator selection. But just how this improvement is to be effected, or what types of traits should be tested, is not clear. In order to get clues as to what these traits are, one must depend on the traditional type of job analysis, whether for the selection of existing tests or for the devising of new instruments for inclusion in the battery and in the next factor analysis.

REFERENCES FOR CHAPTER III

American Psychological Association. *Technical Recommendations for Psychological Tests and Diagnostic Techniques.* Washington, D. C.: American Psychological Association, 1954.

Braasch, W. F. "Regional Differences in Occupational Interests." Unpublished Ph.D. dissertation, Teachers College, Columbia University, 1954.

Brayfield, A. H., and Crockett, W. H. "Employee attitudes and employee performance," *Psychol. Bull.,* 52 (1955), 396-424.

———, and Wells, R. V. "Interrelationships among measures of job satisfaction and general satisfaction," *J. Appl. Psychol.,* 41 (1957), 201-205.

Brophy, A. L. "Self, role, and satisfaction," *Genet. Psychol. Monog.,* 59, (1959).

Burns, R. K., Thurstone, L. L., Moore, D. G., and Baehr, Melany E. *The SRA Employee Inventory.* Chicago: Science Research Associates, 1951.

Carter, H. D. "Vocational interests and job orientation," *Appl. Psychol. Monog.,* 2 (1944).

Cohen, L., and Strauss, L. "Time study and the fundamental nature of manual skill," *J. Consult. Psychol.,* 10 (1946), 146-153.

Cole, R. C. "Evaluating a boys' club guidance program," *Occupations,* 17 (1939), 694-698.

Distefano, M. K., and Bass, B. M. "Prediction of an ultimate criterion of success as a lawyer," *J. Appl. Psychol.,* 43 (1959), 40-41.

Flanagan, J. C. *The Aviation Psychology Program in the AAF.* ("AAF Aviation Psychology Report," No. 1.) Washington, D. C.: Government Printing Office, 1947.

Friesen, E. P. "The incomplete sentences technique as a measure of employee attitudes," *Pers. Psychol.,* 5 (1952), 329-345.

Ghiselli, E. E., and Brown, C. W. *Personnel and Industrial Psychology.* New York: McGraw-Hill, 1955.

Gilbreth, F. B., and Gilbreth, L. M. *Applied Motion Study.* New York: Sturgis and Walton, 1917.

Guilford, J. P. (ed.). *Printed Classification Tests.* ("AAF Aviation Psychology Report," No. 5.) Washington, D. C.: Government Printing Office, 1947.

———. "Factor analysis in a test development program," *Psychol. Rev.,* 55 (1948), 79-94.

———, and Zimmerman, W. S. "Some AAF findings concerning aptitude factors," *Occupations,* 26 (1947), 154-159.

Hoppock, R. *Job Satisfaction.* New York: Harper, 1935.

Hunt, Patricia. "The Birmingham experiments in vocational selection and guidance," *Occ. Psychol.,* 17 (1943), 53-63.

———, and Smith, P. "Vocational psychology and the choice of employment," *Occ. Psychol.,* 19 (1945), 109-116.

Jenkins, J. G. "Validity for what?" *J. Consult. Psychol.,* 10 (1946), 93-98.

Kemp, E. H., and Johnson, A. P. *Psychological Research on Bombardier Training.* ("AAF Aviation Psychology Report," No. 9.) Washington, D. C.: Government Printing Office, 1947.

Kriedt, P. H. "Vocational interests of psychologists," *J. Appl. Psychol.,* 33 (1949), 482-488.

Lepley, W. M. (ed.). *Psychological Research in the Theatres of War.* ("AAF Aviation Psychology Report," No. 17.) Washington, D. C.: Government Printing Office, 1947.

Mathewson, S. B. *Restriction of Output among Unorganized Workers.* New York: Viking, 1931.

McFarland, R. A. *Human Factors in Air Transportation*. New York: McGraw-Hill, 1953.

Meltzer, H. "The approach of the clinical psychologist to management relationships," *J. Consult. Psychol.*, 8 (1944), 165-174.

Paterson, D. G., et al. *The Minnesota Mechanical Abilities Tests*. Minneapolis: University of Minnesota Press, 1930.

————., and Darley, J. G. *Men, Women, and Jobs*. Minneapolis: University of Minnesota Press, 1936.

Roethlisberger, F. J., and Dickson, W. J. *Management and the Worker*. Cambridge: Harvard University Press, 1939.

Rothe, H. F. "Output rates among butter wrappers: I. Work Curves and their stability," *J. Appl. Psychol.*, 30 (1946), 199-211.

————. "Output rates among butter wrappers: II. Frequency distributions and an hypothesis regarding the 'restriction of output'," *J. Appl. Psychol.*, 30 (1946), 320-327.

Sarbin, T. R., and Anderson, H.C. "Preliminary study of the relation of measured interest patterns and occupational dissatisfactions," *Educ. Psychol. Measmt*, 2 (1912), 23-36.

Sartain, A. Q. "The use of certain standardized tests in the selection of inspectors in an aircraft factory," *J. Consult. Psychol.*, 9 (1945), 234-235.

Seipp, E. *A Study of One Hundred Clients of the Adjustment Service*. New York: American Association for Adult Education, 1935.

Shartle, C. L. *Occupational Information*. Englewood Cliffs, N. J.: Prentice-Hall, 1959.

Stead, W. H., and Shartle, C. L. *Occupational Counseling Techniques*. New York: American Book Co., 1940.

Strong, E. K. "Interests and sales ability," *Pers. J.*, 13 (1934), 204-216.

————. *Vocational Interests of Men and Women*. Stanford: Stanford University Press, 1943.

————. *Vocational Interests 18 Years after College*. Minneapolis: University of Minnesota Press, 1955.

Super, D. E. "Occupational level and job satisfaction," *J. Appl. Psychol.*, 23 (1939), 547-564.

————. *Avocational Interest Patterns*. Stanford: Stanford University Press, 1940.

————. "The validity of standard and custom-built personality inventories in a pilot selection program," *Educ. Psychol. Measmt.*, 7 (1947), 735-744.

Taylor, F. W. *Principles of Scientific Management*. New York: Harper, 1915.

Thorndike, E. L. *Human Nature and the Social Order*. New York: Macmillan, 1940.

Thorndike, R. L. (ed.). *Research Problems and Techniques*. ("AAF Aviation Psychology Research Report," No. 3.) Washington, D. C.: Government Printing Office, 1947.

————. *Personnel Selection*. New York: Wiley, 1949.

————, and Hagen, Elizabeth. *Measurement and Evaluation in Psychology and Education*. New York: Wiley, 1955.

————, and Hagen, Elizabeth. *10,000 Careers*. New York: Wiley, 1959.

Thurstone, L. L. "Primary mental abilities," *Psychometrika Monog.*, 1 (1938).

Viteles, M. S. "Job specifications and diagnostic tests of job competency," *Psychol. Clinic*, 14 (1922), 83-105.

————. *Industrial Psychology*. New York: Norton, 1932.

IV

TEST ADMINISTRATION AND SCORING

A PSYCHOLOGICAL test is a measuring instrument. The reason for using measuring instruments rather than guesses or judgments based on unaided observation is that psychological tests, like rulers, micrometers, calipers, and scales, are more accurate than the naked eye. Since the fundamental reason for resorting to psychological tests is the accuracy of which they are capable, it should go without saying that the user of tests should take pains to give them according to the directions and to assure accurate results. And yet, in every-day practice, one observes countless careless errors in the use of tests, some of them probably not important, but others of vital importance.

The Minnesota Spatial Relations Test was originally designed and standardized as a black formboard, the small pieces which fit into the varied shaped holes also being painted black on top (see Ch. XI). Although none of the original publications dealing with it so state, it was administered in the validation studies with the subject standing (personal letter from Professor Donald G. Paterson, dated August 14, 1946). And yet the copies of the test, supplied by a well-known manufacturer and publisher of test materials, are painted black with *green* inserts which probably change the visual problem involved and perhaps make it easier, and the test is administered in some consultation services with the subject standing, in others with him sitting, and in still others either way, according to the client's preference! Super and Morris made a study of the effect of taking the tests in these two different ways, with the finding that the presumably improved perspective which is associated with standing above the formboard tends to result in better scores. The problem of color has not been investigated, but it seems likely that, contrary to widespread custom, the available norms can legitimately be used neither with the green inserts nor when the examinee is seated. Wilson and Carpenter (1948) have shown that the norms for the Crawford Spatial Relations Test, based on the original aluminum form, are not applicable to the marketed wooden form.

A psychometrist was giving the American Council on Education Psychological Examination to a client whose other test results seemed conflicting. There was some informal conversation first, after which the examiner rather casually read the directions and proceeded with the test. While working on the first timed part the client was puzzled and asked a question in the same informal way. The psychometrist answered the question in some detail, then, realizing that some time had been used in which the examinee should have been working on the test, allowed an extra minute for that part. As a result of both of these errors, the score could be considered only a crude measure of the client's intellectual status.

In scoring a test used in a large-scale testing program, a clerk failed to invert the scores in order to change the high *time* scores (score=number of seconds) to low *rank* scores. This error resulted in giving high standing to those who had the least aptitude, and low standing to those who had the most. Fortunately, the error was caught in a routine audit in time to prepare a new set of reports; had it not been, time and money, not to mention human energies, would have been wasted when many of the poorer risks failed to make good in an assignment to which they should never have been sent.

Perhaps the cause of errors such as the above lies in the very simplicity of the directions for giving and scoring most tests. The novice's reaction is that anyone can give most tests, if he knows how to read, and it is true that they are written out so that one should know exactly what to do. But their simplicity is deceptive, and errors are frequently made both in following the directions too slavishly when they are poorly written or inappropriate to the situation, and in departing from the directions when there is no need to do so, in ways not true to their intent. For this reason it is necessary to devote some space to the methods and problems of test administration, even when a background of knowledge of the field of measurement is taken for granted.

Arrangements for Test Administration

Freedom from distractions is one of the first considerations in providing space for test administration. If the examinees are to be free to concentrate on their work they must not be disturbed by people, incidents, noises, or views which draw attention away from the tests. This seems very simple, until one attempts to define distraction. Studies of the effects of noise on work have shown, for example, that typists are able to do as much work, with as high degree of accuracy, under noisy conditions as under quiet conditions, although more strain results in the former (Viteles, 1932, p. 506-511). Super, Braasch, and Shay (1947) found that "normal" distractions had no effect on test scores in an experiment with graduate students. Apparently a great deal depends upon how much the examinee wants to exclude the distracting factor from his attention; if he is well motivated, incidental noises will not bother him, whereas if he is not interested in doing well on the tests he will seize upon the slightest excuse for attending to other matters. As one cannot always take good motivation and good work habits for granted, the examiner must take what precautions he can to insure freedom from distractions. This means that he should have the use of a room through which there is no passage and to which no one needs to have access during testing, without disturbing views of passersby, not affected by noise in adjacent rooms, corridors, or play space, and in which the temperature is normal and constant.

Good working space for the individual examinee is a second consideration, whether testing is on an individual or group basis. In the former this means a table for the examinee, so placed that the examiner can sit opposite him, and a second table so placed that the examiner can reach and manipulate the test materials easily and inconspicuously. In group testing, good working space consists of a flat top large enough for the examinee to be able to rest his elbows without touching the persons next to him and to spread out his papers without exposing them to the eyes of his neighbors; this may be made somewhat smaller on especially constructed testing tables by building upright partitions about ten inches high to shut off the view of the neighbor's work. Tablet arm chairs such as are used in many college lecture rooms are not desirable for timed tests, especially if separate answer sheets are used, as Traxler and Hilkert (1942) have demonstrated. These two considerations of sufficiency of space and privacy of work are disregarded with surprising frequency. One can sometimes make the best of crowded conditions by alternating two forms of the same test.

Advance preparation of materials insures having everything needed during the testing (scratch paper for some parts of some tests is frequently forgotten in large-scale group testing), cuts down the time needed for test administration, and results in better morale among examinees. In group testing this involves preparing a list of items needed, from pencils to test blanks, and of the quantity to be provided; sorting the materials according to type and sequence in which they are to be used; and counting them out according to the number of subjects to be seated in each row and the number of rows in the room. This last step saves a great deal of time and confusion in handing out materials, and prevents the pocketing of excess copies of confidential test booklets. In individual testing the steps are essentially the same, but more attention is focused on placing the materials on the examiner's table for availability during testing.

Good proctoring is a prerequisite of good testing which results only from securing the assistance of enough proctors and seeing to it that they understand their work. Experience with large-scale testing programs with both students and military personnel has led to recognition of the fact that, when large numbers are being tested, there must be one proctor or testing assistant for every 20 or 25 examinees; if fewer proctors are provided, supervision is likely to be inadequate. The functions of the proctors are to distribute test materials, collect them after use, provide sharp pencils when needed, be alert for problems arising from inadequacy of materials (e.g., a blank page where there should be printing), from insufficient grasp of directions the understanding of which is assumed once directions have been given (e.g., marking answers on the booklet instead of on the separate answer sheet when provided), from "bugs" or defects in the test or test directions which should be recorded for the future improvement of the test, and from abnormal personality traits or poor motivation on the part of examinees. Proctors work most effectively when they have not only studied the tests and test directions, but also taken the tests and administered them. In large-scale testing operations which have considerable continuity the establishment of training programs to provide for these experiences is not uncommon; in other testing programs the administrator should make the best possible provisions for familiarizing the proctors with the tests and with problems which may be encountered in administering them. Testing assistants easily get the feeling that their function is a routine one with neither responsibility nor glory. Everything the administrator can do to make them aware of the responsibility they carry and thus insure their careful attention to their work is therefore worthy of consideration.

The duration of testing, assuming that more than one or two tests are to be given, depends on the maturity and motivation of those taking the tests. In testing for the vocational guidance of high school juniors and seniors and of college freshmen the writers have found two days of testing and filling out records, consisting of three hours each morning and two hours after lunch, quite acceptable to the students. The College Entrance Examination Board (1947) found that fatigue played no part in six hours of testing. When motivation is not so strong and co-operation not so good, periods of two hours may be all that are wise, and there may have to be fewer periods. For example, when testing returned combat fliers in a Redistribution Station it was found that two three-hour test sessions, both on the same day, were feasible, but the examiners and proctors needed special skill at times in the handling of recalcitrant officers and men who balked at the length of the testing period. Even in this military situation tact went further than authority, and one of the best examiners with poorly motivated returnees was a civilian woman psychologist who knew how both to jest with and to mother belligerent gunners and bombardiers. Making clear to examinees why they are taking the tests and how the results will affect them (discussed in a subsequent paragraph) and letting them know at the start just how long the test sessions will last are two essentials to the winning of co-operation in test administration. If the examinee wants to understand himself, wants to get a job, or wants to help others like himself (the desire to help other fliers who were *going* to combat motivated many *returnees* in the completing of research questionnaires), he can put in more than a full day of taking tests.

Provisions for the recording of the proceedings should also be made ahead of time. Decisions should be made as to the type of records to be kept, and appropriate forms provided. The times at which tests are begun and stopped should be recorded, as they are occasionally needed later when checks are being made on accuracy of timing. Problems arising during testing should be noted, for their value in interpreting the behavior of individuals or the significance of the test results. Examiner and proctors both have a part in this work.

Testing individuals in groups is frequently made necessary by lack of space and personnel even where schedules and needs vary from one person to the next. When there are a number of persons to be tested with different tests, and fewer examiners and rooms than there are batteries to be administered (a chronic condition in guidance centers and personnel offices), there is no alternative. The space must then be arranged so that individuals or small groups can be sufficiently isolated from others in the same room so that they can work undisturbed by directions not intended for them, stocks of materials must be kept in such a way as to make them readily available to all examiners as needed, and each examiner must develop skill in using several stop watches or chronometers and in shifting from individual to individual as timing requires. Space must, of course, permit easy circulation of examiners and of entering and departing examinees.

The Preliminaries to Testing

The checking of all arrangements discussed in the preceding section is naturally the first preliminary to the starting of testing, to be sure that everything necessary is ready for things to go as planned. Test administration seems so very simple to the average examinee that its smooth progress is important to rapport.

The introductory or motivating talk follows immediately after the arrival and seating of the examinees. In prior informal contacts examinees often ask questions of examiners or proctors, thereby demonstrating the widespread need for orientation to that which is to take place, even when testing is voluntary. The knowledge that he is about to put himself to a test makes the examinee somewhat insecure and self-conscious, so that he wants reassurance or feels the need to be somewhat aggressive and belligerent. The examiner or proctor, knowing this, can accept his remarks in a calm and friendly way, stating perhaps that something will be said about the nature of the tests before they are started. The motivating talk should be brief and to the point. Its objective is to set the stage for effective testing by giving the subject some idea of what he is going to do and how long it will take him, and to make him want to portray himself accurately on the tests by relating the taking of the tests to his goals. In vocational counseling the goal is self-understanding and better adjustment to the world of work; in vocational selection it is the obtaining of a job in which he will find success and satisfaction. These themes can be elaborated upon in ways appropriate to the age and occupational level of the examinee, but it is well to be sure that the goals are real to those being tested and that the language used in discussing them is appropriate both to the examiner and to the examinee.

The Sequence of Tests

In formal testing programs the nature of the tests which need to be given to a particular individual or group determines to some extent the sequence of tests. Within these limits, however, it is desirable to arrange the order in the way which is likely to interest the examinee most and to get the maximum co-operation from him. As a rule, the following principles have been found effective in arranging the sequence of tests.

The first test in the series should be something of a *buffer,* one on which the examinee can warm up, get some self-assurance, and develop some interest. For this reason it should not be too hard, should be relatively impersonal (i.e., neither an intelligence nor a personality test) and objective, and should have "face validity" or seem pertinent to the reason for taking tests (i.e., it should, in the case of pilot selection, look like a test that has something to do with flying an airplane).

Next should come a test or tests with long and difficult directions, *difficult content,* or other characteristics which make desirable an alert mind, ability to concentrate, and willingness to apply oneself. Tests of this type might come after one or two of the first type, depending on the number and length of those in each category, or they might alternate.

Tests which the examiner prefers not to have remembered in detail, if there are such, should come late in the sequence but not at the very end. Personality inventories which contain *touchy items* or which might be joked about afterwards are in this category. If taken after the difficult tests and before all the other tests have been given they provide some variety and relaxation when it is needed and are likely to be half-forgotten by the time testing is finished.

The last test should be relatively *short* and *pleasant,* to help the examinee leave with a good taste in his mouth. If a group is being tested together, it is often desirable to let the test be a speeded test so that all may stop and leave at the same time, as having some leave while others are working tends to make the latter finish hurriedly or carelessly, and keeping those who have finished for more than a few minutes is difficult because of restless eagerness to leave. When testing individuals in a group with different tests, untimed tests or inventories may be satisfactory to finish with; the individual can be left more or less to his own devices and others can be given attention.

Informal testing characterizes much counseling work carried on entirely by one counselor utilizing interviewing and other techniques (Bordin and Bixler, 1946; Super, 1950). Then nothing approaching a "test battery" is administered, but certain tests are used as questions come up on which it is believed they will throw light. In such testing the question of sequence is settled by the factors making testing seem desirable; the question to be answered provides the motivation for the test being used. The problem is then entirely one of selecting an appropriate test; bases for test selection are made clear in later chapters.

Following Directions in Testing

It has already been pointed out that the very ease with which tests are administered breeds errors. Group test administration is likely to be thought of as requiring less skill than other testing operations; group test proctors in aviation cadet classification testing referred to themselves as the "bunion brigade." Unless examiners and proctors are aware of the ease with which errors are made and are challenged by the need for care, they are likely soon to be guilty of unknowingly modifying the introduction to testing in such a way as to change the examinees' motivation for better or for worse, of changing directions in ways which give them either more or less help than they should have in taking the test, of answering questions which give an unfair advantage in comparison with the groups on whom norms were established, and even of allowing too much or too little time in which to take the tests.

The writers of *motivating talks* and of *test directions* intend to convey ideas to the examinees which will motivate them in certain ways and lead them to work according to certain methods. *If,* therefore, the examiner understood exactly what the test constructor intended to convey, and *if* he were able to express that idea just as clearly as the test author in words of his own, there would be no reason why he should not rephrase the directions to suit himself and vary his statements from time to time. Unfortunately, however, experience has demonstrated time and again that while the modifications made in test directions may be just as clear to the examiner as were the originals, they are rarely if ever as clear to the examinee. The reason for this is obvious enough: the directions supplied with a well-constructed test have been tried out a number of times on subjects like those for whom the test was developed before it was finally published, and each time they were rewritten somewhat and improved after criticism by examiners and examinees in order to make sure that the intended meaning and the understood meaning were identical. Obviously, the directions more or less casually phrased and even more casually tested by the user of a test are not likely to be as clearly and as uniformly understood as those that are printed with the test. Only a highly skilled examiner who knows both his test and his subjects well should allow himself the privilege of improvising or modifying directions. At the same time examiners need to scrutinize the printed directions carefully to be sure that they are well drafted. If they are not suitable for the group in question the suitability of the test itself may be open to question; if the test is suitable with different directions, the norms may no longer be applicable. These matters are subject to empirical check, and if judged important enough the answers may be found by experimental methods. It is good practice for examiners to have a manual or loose-leaf notebook of test directions, and to know these well in order to facilitate reading them while administrating tests.

Examinees' questions need to be viewed by the examiner as possible requests for changes in the test directions. If the information asked for was supposed to be conveyed by the directions, and if understanding of the directions was supposed to be achieved before beginning the test (rather than being a part of the test), the examiner should answer the questions promptly and concisely. If, on the other hand, answering the question would give the examinee an understanding of the test or information which the directions were not intended to convey, to do so would be to make his score meaningless, or at least impossible of comparison with those of others who took the test and on whom the norms were based. In such a case the best answer is "That's for you to decide" or some equivalent which makes it clear that the examinee must find the solution himself. It should be stressed that the number of questions asked, and their legitimacy, depends to a very considerable extent upon the manner of the examiner. If he gives directions in too businesslike and cold a manner questions which should be asked will not be voiced; if he is too informal and friendly too many unfair questions will come up; but if he gives directions clearly and pleasantly he will meet with an optimum number of questions concerning matters included in the directions (few but all necessary questions) and a minimum of questions of types which he should not answer.

This leads to the topic of the examiner's *voice and attitude,* both of which have considerable effect on the attitudes of examinees and therefore on the validity of the tests which they take. An examiner whose clear, confident, and friendly voice and interested, alert manner are noted by the examinees gives them the feeling that the tests are important, interesting, and worth taking seriously; one who is lackadaisical in manner, fearful in front of a group, or careless in his speech is not likely to create in his subjects attitudes which make for serious application and genuine co-operation. When proctors assist in test administration, the manner in which they walk the aisles and watch examinees or stand idly by with their minds obviously far away is equally important.

The need for *accuracy of timing* has already been mentioned. In administering tests by apparatus tests this necessitates a stop watch with its easily controlled second hand. Most paper and pencil tests, however, can be timed with sufficient accuracy by means of the second hand of an ordinary watch if the hand is long enough. A watch with a sweep-second hand is even better, although not as easily used as a stop watch because the examiner must watch the second hand enough to count the number of times it goes around. This is best done by tabulating on a pad. If a stop watch is available, the freedom to spend more time watching examinees and less time looking at the second hand is desirable. As stop watches are sometimes erratic, it is advisable to check their operation before testing, and to note the starting time on one's wrist watch or on a clock (or to have a proctor time with a second stop watch) in order to be sure that watch trouble does not prevent accurate timing of a test. Finally, when testing large groups it is good practice to instruct examinees to put their pencils down and lean back in their chairs at the word "Stop," thus making it easy for examiner and proctors to insure the respecting of time limits on strictly timed paper and pencil tests.

Observing the Behavior of Examinees

Careful observation of the manner and attitude of the examinees has long been standard practice in clinical testing, and has been carried over into vocational testing by those with clinical training. Baumgarten published a list of types of behavior which should be looked for by the user of vocational tests (1935) , and Bingham translated and converted this into an Examiner's Checklist (1937, pp. 229-235) . An abbreviated and somewhat modified form of this checklist is included here because of its value in suggesting types of behavior which may be worth noting and the possible

EXAMINER'S CHECKLIST

Examiner_____Subject_____

Date_____Test_____

BEHAVIOR	INTERPRETATION
I. *PRELIMINARIES* A. Attention to Examiner 1. Attentive_____ 2. Looks around_____	
B. Questions 1. Yes_____ 2. No_____	
C. Speed of Approach to Test 1. Rapid_____ 2. Slow_____ 3. Hesitating_____	
D. Seriousness of Attitude 1 Serious 2 Playful 3 Zealous	

E. Confidence in Approach
   1. Disparages task_____ 2. Enthusiastic_____
   3. Disparages Self_____	

F. Judgment of the Task 1. Vocal_____ 2. Gestures_____	

II. *EXECUTION*
A. Starting
   1. Deliberation
     a. Yes_____ b. No_____	

2. False Starts
     a. Yes_____ b. No_____
     a'. Perseverates_____ b'. Changes_____	

B. At Work
   1. Direction of Attention
     a. To task_____ b. Away_____	

2. Degree of Attention a. Concentrated_____ b. Distracted_____	
3. Expression of Feelings a. Yes_____ b. No_____	
4. Body Movements a. Co-ordinated_____ b. Not co-ordinated_____	

5. Hand Movements
          Yes_____   Yes_____   Yes_____
     a. Appropriate b. Sure c. Quick
          No _____ No _____ No _____	

6. Work Tempo a. Quick_____ b. Slow_____	
7. System a. Yes_____ b. No_____	

8. Regularity
              1 ⎱ Crescendo_____
     a. Yes_____ b. No___ 2 ⎰ Diminuendo_____
              3 ⎰ Alternately_____	

9. Care and Neatness a. Careful_____ b. Sloppy_____	

C. Frustration-Tolerance
   1. Asks no help_____
     a. Indifferent_____
     b. Gives up_____
     c. Solves problem_____	

2. Asks help_____ a. Once_____ b. Repeatedly_____	

3. Receives help_____
     a. Indifferently_____   d. Critically_____
     b. Happily_____   e. Trustfully_____
     c. Gratefully_____ f. With offense_____	

EXAMINER'S CHECKLIST (Continued)

D. Obedience to Instructions 1. Exact_____ 2. With Deviations_____	
III. *ATTITUDE TOWARD PERFORMANCE* A. Notices Mistakes_____ a. In process_____ b. At end_____ c. Sporadically_____	
B. Mistakes Unnoticed_____	
C. Shows Feeling_____ a. Pleasure_____ b. Vexation_____ c. Not clear_____	
IV. *CONDUCT AFTER TEST*	
A. Silent and Watchful_____	
B. Announces Result_____	
C. Asks Evaluation_____	
D. Expresses Feelings_____ a. Satisfaction_____ b. Vexation_____	
E. Leaves Materials a. In order_____ b. In disorder_____	

significance of such behavior, and because it is useful in training psychometrists, counselors, and personnel workers to get more than a test score from the administration of a test. In actual practice, however, such elaborate forms are rarely used; instead, the examiner who has learned to observe behavior in testing simply makes note of anything which he believes may be significant and includes it in his test report. Beginners do well to use a form such as this for some time, in order to learn what to look for and to get the habit of noting it; once the habit has been acquired the simpler method can effectively be adopted instead. Examples of notations of behavior in taking tests and of their use in interpreting test scores are given in Chapters XXI and XXII, in which methods of reporting test results are discussed in some detail and the content of test reports is illustrated.

One word of caution should be said at this point. Some clinicians delight in telling how much is learned about a subject from the way in which he attacks a problem, from his procedure in putting together a set of Wiggly Blocks or from his persistence in working on a difficult mechanical problem. These symptoms are extremely interesting, and it is easy to be carried away by the tendency to build an ambitious account of a personality upon them. They are, however, minute segments of behavior observed in a limited situation, and there is no real evidence that the behavior so manifested is typical of behavior in other situations. The possible insights which may be gained from watching a person solve arithmetic problems while taking a standard test should not be missed, but it should be remembered that it is the *score* which has been proved reliable and which is known to be related to behavior in other situations, not the *method of approach* or *the reaction to frustration*. At the same time, a knowledge of these latter helps one to understand how and why the obtained score was obtained, and provides data which may, with many other items from other situations, help in the construction of a picture of the counselee's personality.

Condition of the Examinee

Those who take objective tests sometimes claim that they are too nervous at the time of testing to do themselves justice, or that they were not in good health at the time and were therefore handicapped. In certain extreme cases these claims are no doubt warranted, as for example in that of a married man who took a test the morning after a violent quarrel with his wife and a subsequent resort to alcohol; he was in the second decile of the comparison group in that testing, but on a retake three months later, after a divorce and when clear-headed, he was in the highest decile. Despite these occasional rather obvious and verified cases, there is a good deal of skepticism concerning most such claims. Oddly enough, there has been very little research on these problems, although the concept of "test anxiety" is commanding increasing attention (Sinick, 1956).

The influence of tension on the intelligence test scores of children was investigated by Yager (1946) with a group of forty boys from ten to twelve years old. They were first tested under normal conditions, then under tension presumably produced by threats and evidenced by physiological changes. Thirty of the boys made better scores, but ten showed losses. The tendency to improve or to break down under tension was related to emotional stability. This experiment appears to confirm the belief that only a few persons, and those the neurotically inclined, suffer appreciably from the tension-creating conditions of testing.

The effects of health were investigated by British army psychologists in a study referred to by Vernon (1947). Standard selection tests were taken a second time by women recruits, and differences were related to menstrual phase. The effects of menstrual cycle on test scores were found to be negligible. Another group of over 1000 were asked at test and retest whether or not they felt able to do themselves justice; less than four percent claimed not to be able to do themselves justice, but their scores were not significantly different from those of the others. Those suffering from colds showed a slight, but not significant, drop in scores.

Another study which may have some bearing on this problem is a report by Glick (1940) that freshmen who took the college intelligence tests during the New England hurricane of 1938 made scores 20 percent higher than those of other years. When subsequently retested, they were shown to be a normal group. Glick suggests that their "hurricane intelligence" may have been the result of stimulating effects of ozone in the air at the time of the hurricane.

These studies, like those of the effect of distractions on test scores, suggest that the minor ailments can be dismissed as having no appreciable effect on test scores when examinees are well motivated, but that the more serious impairments are sufficient justification for questioning a test score.

Scoring Tests

The methods of scoring the tests which are widely used in vocational guidance and selection are objective and generally quite simple. The tests in which scoring involves judgment and training on the part of the examiner are used largely in clinical work; exceptions to this statement are the clinically interpreted Wechsler scales, which are quite frequently used as a special check in cases of adults who may be verbally handicapped, and the Rorschach Psychodiagnostic and Thematic Apperception Test, which are used in connection with executive selection. Both of these require extended special training. Most of the tests discussed in this book are scored by means of stencils or keys which can be used by a clerk or by clerically operated scoring machine; the others have simple time scores. For this reason only two points need to be made concerning the scoring of vocational tests.

The first of these is, again, familiarity with the directions. Persons scoring tests must first be sure that they understand the procedure. A routine can then be established that fits the immediate situation. If hand scoring is in order, clear and durable keys or stencils should be made, and scores should be systematically calculated and entered on record blanks. If machine scoring is done (it should be in any large-scale operations) this work will either be performed by a commercial scoring organization or by an especially trained scorer who is competent to set up procedures.

The second point has to do with checking. Even the best of scorers make errors, as illustrated at the beginning of this chapter. For this reason all scores should be checked by another person, at all stages, if hand scoring is utilized. If machine scoring is used, all manual steps should be checked. If an accurate instrument is worth using, its accurate use is worth insuring.

REFERENCES FOR CHAPTER IV

Baumgarten, Franziska. "Behavior in taking tests," *Occupations,* 14 (1935), 115-122.

Bingham, W. V. *Aptitudes and Aptitude Testing.* New York: Harper, 1937.

Bordin, E. S., and Bixler, R. H. "Test selection: a process of counseling," *Educ. Psychol. Measmt.,* 6 (1946), 361-374.

Glick, H. M. "Hurricane intelligence," *Science,* 91 (1940), 450.

Sinick, D. "Encouragement, anxiety, and test performance," *J. Appl. Psychol.,* 40 (1956), 315-318.

Super, D. E. "Testing and using test results in counseling," *Occupations,* 29 (1950), 95-97.

————, Braasch, W. F., and Shay, J. B. "The effect of distractions on test results," *J. Educ. Psychol.,* 38 (1947), 373-377.

The Question of Allowing Two Days for the Examinations of the College Entrance Examination Board. Princeton, N. J.: College Entrance Examination Board Report (mimeographed), 1947.

Traxler, A. E., and Hilkert, R. N. "Effect of type of desk on results of machine-scored tests," *School and Soc.,* 56 (1942), 277-279.

Vernon, P. E. "Research on personnel selection in the Royal Navy and the British Army," *Amer. Psychol.,* 2 (1947), 35-51.

Viteles, M. S. *Industrial Psychology.* New York: Norton, 1932.

Wilson, J. W., and Carpenter, E. K. "The need for restandardization of altered tests," *Amer. Psychol.,* 3 (1948), 172-173.

Yager, J. L. "The influence of emotional tension on the intelligence test scores of children," *Amer. Psychol.,* 1 (1946), 464 (abstr.).

V

THE NATURE OF APTITUDES AND APTITUDE TESTS

Definitions

THE term "aptitude" is generally used loosely both by laymen and by vocational psychologists and counselors. Its meaning varies not merely from one user to another, but even from one time to the next in the speaking or writing of a given psychologist or educator. It is used in either of two ways, as when we say that a man has a great deal of aptitude for art, meaning that he has in a high degree many of the characteristics which make for success in artistic activities, or when we say that a person lacks spatial aptitude, meaning that he lacks this one specialized aptitude which is of importance in a number of occupations. In the former instance the word is used to denote a combination of traits and abilities which result in a person's being qualified for some type of occupation or activity. In the latter case the word "aptitude" is intended to convey the idea of a discrete, unitary characteristic which is important, in varying degrees, in a variety of occupations and activities.

Both the popular concept of *aptitude for a vocation* and the scientific concept of *aptitude important in vocations* are essential; it is important, however, that the meaning intended be clear. In general, counselors and personnel men tend to think in terms of vocations and jobs, and therefore to use the term in the broad popular sense, while psychologists tend to think in terms of individual differences and traits, and therefore to use the term in the narrow scientific sense. As most of the literature on tests is written by psychologists, and most of the tests are constructed by psychologists, the counselor or personnel man needs to learn the scientific term. Similarly the psychologist, if his report of test results is to be meaningful and useful to the counselor, social worker, personnel man, or teacher, must translate trait data into vocations.

Various combinations of traits and abilities may make for success in a given field. One teacher, for example, may be successful because of scholarly ability, interest in his subject, and a desire to share it with others which result in a clarity of presentation, a wealth of material, and a warmth of manner which more than make up for a relative lack of interest in people as individuals and a dislike of the routines and details of classroom management. Another teacher may be equally successful because of his genuine interest in students, his warm and friendly manner, and his skill in classroom management, even though his scholarship and academic ability are mediocre. Similar differences could be pointed out among successful lawyers, salesmen, and foremen, occupations in which there is sufficient flexibility of role to permit varying patterns of success. It has been shown by Michael (1949) that flying success in white cadets is primarily a matter of interest, spatial ability, and coordination, while in Negro cadets it is dependent largely on kinesthesis, perceptual speed, and spatial ability.

Because of the varying combinations of special aptitudes and traits which make for success in a given occupation, it is desirable to continue the scientific use of the word aptitude in testing and test research. For this reason, the term will be used in its narrower sense in this book, except when expressly defined otherwise, as in the phrase "aptitude for the medical profession."

Even in its narrower scientific sense, however, the word aptitude is by no means consistently and clearly used in the literature on tests. In Warren's *Dictionary of Psychology* (1934) it is defined as a *condition* or *set of characteristics* indicative of ability to learn. This implies that an aptitude is not necessarily an entity, but rather a constellation of entities; the set of characteristics which enables one person to learn something may even be different from that which enables another person to learn the same thing; in this case, we arrive back at the popular definition. According to the dictionary by English and English (1958), aptitude is capacity to acquire proficiency, without specifying its composition. But the scientific study of an aptitude or of any other entity requires that one be able to name it, describe it, and locate it in a variety of individuals and situations. This means that it must be relatively constant in its nature and composition. The Warren, and the English definitions are therefore useless to a scientist or to a counselor. A scientific definition of aptitude would provide for *specificity, unitary composition,* and the *facilitation of learning* of some activity or type of activity.

In practice, the requirement of unitary nature is frequently disregarded without ill effects. The Minnesota Clerical Test or number- and name-checking test is, for example, a test of about as simple an entity as one could expect to find, and yet factor analysis shows that the names test includes not just a speed and accuracy of discrimination factor identical with that in the numbers test, but also an intelligence factor not found to any appreciable degree in the numbers test (Andrew, 1937). The Bennett Mechanical Comprehension Test, and others like it, are generally assumed to measure a special aptitude, and yet the mechanical information and ability to visualize space relations play major parts in it (see Ch. X). In our present state of knowledge and with current techniques, it seems wiser to be satisfied if the aptitudes measured are relatively distinct and have some validity, than to devote much time to obtaining pure traits. The quick success of this global approach in Binet's work with intelligence tests, discussed in Pintner (1931, Ch. 2), has been borne out in aptitude studies such as the Minnesota Mechanical Abilities Project (Paterson et al., 1930) and in interest research such as Strong's (1943), and even more recently in the slow rate of progress which has characterized the pure trait approach as used in Thurstone's work on primary mental abilities (1938) and Kuder's work on primary interests (see Ch. XVIII). In Thurstone's work the development of sufficiently refined and reliable instruments has been time-consuming and the results in terms of educational or vocational validity disappointing (see below, Ch. VI), and in Kuder's it required two decades to develop an instrument with vocational significance. This is not to decry the importance of such studies of primary abilities and interests, nor of the resulting tests; on the contrary, they undoubtedly launched a new approach to aptitude and interest measurement and foreshadow more refined and more valid tests than any we now have. Guilford's work (1947, Ch. 28; Guilford et al., 1954; Guilford and Zimmerman, 1947) has demonstrated this. But for most practical purposes it is still true that the most valid current tests are those which do not stress the unitary nature and purity of the aptitudes or traits measured.

A fourth and final characteristic of an aptitude should probably be added to our definition, namely, that it is relatively *constant*. If behavior or success is to be predicted, the entity upon which the prediction is based should be relatively stable. An aptitude which varied irrationally from one day, month, or year to the next would not provide a sound basis for predicting achievement at some future date. To put it statistically, an aptitude which is itself unreliable could be neither reliably measured nor significantly correlated with anything else. This question of the constancy of traits has, as the literature makes amply evident (Tyler, 1956), been a prime source of disagreement among psychologists. The attending controversies are too involved for adequate discussion to be possible here. It seems wiser simply to state the conclusion that, whether largely innate or largely acquired, the aptitudes about which we know something appear to become crystalized in childhood and that after that they mature in a predictable way and are generally relatively constant.

They may be affected by drastic experiences, but can otherwise be thought of as not being appreciably affected by education, special training, or experience. Specific practice on the test itself will raise the subject's *test score,* but that does not indicate a change in the degree of aptitude. As demonstrated in a number of different studies, interests and personality traits are crystalized later than aptitudes, in adolescence (Newman et al., 1937; Strong, 1931, 1943). The evidence for specific aptitudes and traits will be viewed later, as each test and the work done with it is studied in detail.

Two other terms need brief definition. One of these is the word *skill.* It is used here, and in most discussions of abilities, as synonymous with *proficiency,* to denote the degree of mastery already acquired in an activity. Thus a typing test is a test of skill, and a trade test is a test of proficiency. The other term is *ability,* which Bingham (1937, p. 19) uses to denote either aptitude or proficiency or both, leaving it to the context to indicate the meaning, and which English and English (1958) reserve for present proficiency. In view of the convenience of having a general term the writers prefer to use ability to include both aptitude and proficiency, using one of the latter terms when clarity and specificity require. The term *trait,* it might be noted, is used as comparable, in the field of interest and personality, with the term *aptitude* in the field of abilities.

The Basic Aptitudes

E. L. Thorndike once suggested that there are probably three types of intelligence: abstract, mechanical, and social. Since that time there has been a great deal of speculation and research on the nature and number of special aptitudes. T. L. Kelley used factor analysis and a variety of tests in order to study the question (1928), concluding from his data that aptitudes may be classified as verbal, numerical, spatial, motor, musical, social, and mechanical. His scheme provided also for various types of interests. Spearman made another analysis (1927) using other tests and a quite different method of factor analysis; since then he and his followers in England, Spearman and Wynn-Jones (1950), and Vernon (1950), have modified and elaborated his position, concluding that there are one general or intelligence factor "g," a number of group factors such as word fluency, perseveration, and goodness of character, and many specific factors which are found only in one test or situation. Thurstone's work (1935, 1938, 1941) in factor analysis and the organization of special aptitudes has probably had more influence in America than has any other. Using the centroid method of factor analysis he isolated the following special aptitudes: number, visualization, memory, word fluency, verbal relations, perceptual speed, and induction. This research has borne fruit in the Chicago Tests of Primary Mental Abilities (see Ch. VI) , which measure six factors, number, verbal meaning, space, word fluency, reasoning, and memory.

Other factor analyses of aptitudes have followed Thurstone's, each of them using a greater variety of tests and therefore isolating more factors than its predecessor. One of these was made by the United States Employment Service, under the direction of Shartle (Staff, Div. of Occ'l Analysis, 1945) , and another by the Army Air Forces, under Guilford's supervision (1947, 1948) . The lists of factors arrived at by each of these investigators are combined in Table 2, in order to show how the list of presumably unitary human abilities lengthens as the investigations become more thorough-going. It will be noted, for example, that what Thurstone thought was one single aptitude, perceptual speed, was broken down into two factors, perception of symbols and perception of spatial forms, in the USES study, and into two apparently similar aptitudes in the AAF investigation. What Thurstone's study isolated as one factor, memory span, did not appear at all in the USES research because no memory tests were used, but was broken down into three distinct types of memory factors in the AAF analysis. As might be expected in the case of a program which devoted considerable time and talent to the development of new types of tests, the Aviation Psychology Program battery revealed, when analyzed, far more primary traits than were isolated by the other investigations. Thurstone's list included only eight factors, Shartle's 11, and Guilford's as many as 28. The list continues to grow, as evidenced by the 28 percent of the variance in pilot success which was not, but might be, predicted, if suitable tests were used, and by French's list of 59 factors (1951) .

Other factors have been or may in time be isolated and added to our list of human abilities. In the meantime, the lists in Table 2 provide a good basis for job analysis and test selection or construction.

Thurstone's method of factor analysis provides for the isolation of independent factors or aptitudes. For this reason, most of the aptitudes named above are relatively independent of each other. Some, such as those normally included in the concept of general intelligence, are more closely related, but the intercorrelations are still lower than reliability coefficients, that is, too low to make a test of one aptitude or factor a good index of the score on the test of another factor. Tests of spatial visualization frequently have moderately high correlations with tests of intelligence, but this is sometimes an artifact arising from the fact that tests of intelligence often include tests of spatial judgment (e.g., Army Alpha and the Army General Classification Test) . Furthermore, factor analysis of these factors reveals the existence of a general, more fundamental reasoning factor (see Tyler, 1956, pp. 92–105). Tests of manual dexterities, not included in most factor analysis studies, have been analyzed to show that the concrete abilities which they measure are more discrete and have lower intercorrelations than do the more abstract aptitudes.

TABLE 2

THE EXPANDING LIST OF PRIMARY ABILITIES

According to Thurstone (1938), Shartle (Staff, 1945), and Guilford (1947)

Thurstone 1938	USES (Shartle 1945)	A.A.F. (Guilford 1947)
Spatial	Spatial	Spatial Relations I
		Spatial Relations II
		(Right-Left Discrimination)
		Spatial Relations III
		(Unknown)
		Visualization
		Mechanical Experience
Perceptual Speed	Symbol Perception	Perceptual Speed
	Spatial Perception	Length Estimation
Number	Numerical	Numerical
		Mathematical Background
Verbal Relations	Verbal	Verbal
Word Forms		
Memory Span		Paired Associates Memory
		Visual Memory
		Picture-Word Memory
Induction		
	Intelligence	General Reasoning
Reasoning or	Logic	Analogic Reasoning
Deduction		Sequential Reasoning
		Judgment
		Planning
		Simple Integration
		Complex Integration
		Adaptive Integration
	Speed	
		Psychomotor Speed
	Aiming	
		Psychomotor co-ordination
	Finger Dexterity	Psychomotor Precision
	Manual Dexterity	
		Kinesthesis
		Carefulness
		Pilot Interest
		(Active-Masculine)
		Social Science Background

Despite the relative independence of special aptitudes, there is a tendency for groups of people who score high on a measure of "general aptitude" to make good scores on other tests, whether of special aptitudes or of personality traits. As Terman pointed out (1930), the good things tend to go together, a statement amply borne out by psychological and social data on more than one thousand gifted children followed into adulthood (Terman and Oden, 1948, 1959). It is therefore not surprising that, in counseling practice, one encounters persons who make high scores on tests of academic aptitude and on almost any other test, and others who not only make low scores on tests of general mental ability, but distress one by making low scores on any other instrument used in the search for some "hidden talent" which might be capitalized and built upon. It is well not to be overimpressed by such cases, however, as it has been demonstrated (Piéron, 1945) that they are outnumbered by those whose aptitudes and personality traits vary considerably, giving them some assets and some liabilities.

Methods of Measurement

The most valid method of measuring an aptitude, that is, a unitary factor in the ability to learn something, would be to find out what part of the activity or skill to be learned is most heavily saturated with that factor, have the subject learn it, and compare his rate of learning with that of other persons with comparable backgrounds. This is in most cases an inordinately expensive method, although so-called teaching machines may in due course be programmed as tests of rate of learning. Selection on the basis of success or failure in an initial learning period is still the method used by many colleges and professional schools which admit two or three times as many beginning students as they expect to graduate and flunk those who make the lowest grades during the first year. It is the method used by many businesses and industries even now, despite interest in taking advantage of the possibilities of scientific personnel selection and great strides made in this direction by some life insurance companies, manufacturing concerns, banks, and retail establishments. Experience as well as theory has demonstrated that it is less expensive to analyze the task in which success is to be predicted, develop and validate tests for predicting achievement in that task, and select on the basis of test and other personal data than to do less initial screening and depend more on selection on the job. In the same way, it is less expensive, less discouraging, and less difficult for a high school or college student, unemployed man or woman, or adult considering a transfer or change of work, to take a series of tests and analyze his experiences in order better to ascertain his ability to learn a new task or to adjust to an occupation than it is for him to try it out as a probationist or actual employee.

There are different types of tests of aptitudes, each having its advantages and disadvantages. The user of tests should be familiar with these. They will be briefly described here in terms of contrasting types or dichotomies.

Miniature tests may be contrasted with tests of *abstract traits* or aptitudes. In the former, the task in which learning or success is to be predicted is reproduced in miniature and perhaps simplified form, as, for example, in the familiar lathe-type or two-hand spatial judgment and co-ordination test. This miniature test, used successfully in selecting shop students, duplicates on a smaller scale both the apparatus and the arm and hand movements of a lathe. In the test of abstract aptitudes the job has been analyzed and one or more of its essential characteristics has been abstracted and put into test form. Thus in the MacQuarrie Test of Mechanical Ability there are a series of tests of eye-hand co-ordination and of spatial judgment, one of which involves tapping three times in each of a series of small circles, another tracing a line through the variously placed small apertures in a series of barrier lines, and still another judging the number of blocks touching others in a series of piles of blocks. In this case the test bears no superficial resemblance to the original task or activity, let us say lathe operation, but some of the essential aptitudes seem to be measured.

The miniature type of test has a number of advantages. Its face validity or obvious similarity to the task in question makes it appeal to the examinee who is interested in such work. Being a small scale task, it is very likely to involve the same aptitudes and skills that are required by the criterion task and therefore to be highly correlated with it, that is, to be quite valid. One of the more valid tests used in the selection and classification of Air Force pilots is the Complex Co-ordination Test, a life-size but simplified stick and rudder test which, with its airplane controls and rows of red and green lights, appeals to aspirants to pilot training and involves some of the ability to co-ordinate arm and foot pressures with each other and with visual stimuli involved in controlling the plane in flight. That its validity is not greater than it is (about .40 with pass-fail in pilot training [DuBois, 1947]) is due partly to the fact that response to kinesthetic stimuli, that is to the "feel" of the plane through what fliers call the "seat of the pants," is not required by the test, and partly to the fact that many other factors are important in good flying, especially when the criterion is not *flight* but *completing flying training*.

The advantages of the miniature test suggest some of its disadvantages. A test which seems to have a bearing on an activity which is repugnant to the examinee will motivate him in the wrong manner, as did any test in aviation cadet classification testing which seemed to the would-be pilots to have special bearing on the work of a bombardier. One may be able to get a more nearly true measure of the examinee's aptitude or interest with a test the significance of which is not so obvious. This has been demonstrated with Strong's Vocational Interest Blank (Longstaff,

1948; Steinmetz, 1932; and others), which is not a miniature test but which contains a number of items of obvious vocational significance.

Another defect lies in the miniature test's unknown elements. Since it is a small-scale edition of the task, one has no objective way of knowing what psychological factors it measures. This may be very well in selection testing, when the important thing is to get the highest possible validities with the least possible effort, but in testing for vocational counseling it would necessitate another miniature test for each occupation or at least for each family of occupations to be considered in counseling. This would require an inordinate amount of test development and actual testing time. It is more practical to analyze each occupation or activity into its important component factors, develop relatively independent tests of each factor or aptitude, validate each of these, and weight each test for each occupation according to its importance in that occupation. This makes possible testing for a large number of occupations with a relatively small number of tests. In the Army's aviation cadet classification program, one test was weighted heavily for pilot, moderately for bombardier, and not at all for navigator, whereas another might be weighted heavily for navigator, moderately for bombardier, and slightly for pilot, according to the demonstrated relationship between each test and the criteria of success in each activity. The same technique is used by the Occupational Analysis Division of the United States Employment Service in the GATB (Ch. XIV). What the abstract aptitude test loses in validity as a single test of one factor, it seeks to make up as part of a battery of tests of known aptitudes combined to predict the same criterion. Its principal defect lies in its lack of appeal to the less intelligent examinee, who is not challenged by an abstract task but who may be challenged by a test which resembles an everyday activity. For the theoretical case for factorially pure tests, see Guilford (1948); the evidence on their validity is summarized in Ch. XIV.

Much of what has been written about miniature and abstract trait test applies also to *performance* and *paper-and-pencil* tests. A performance test is one involving doing something with materials or apparatus, whereas a paper-and-pencil test requires only marking responses to written or pictorial questions on a sheet of paper. The former may be abstract and the latter miniature type, as in the case of the Minnesota Spatial Relations Test and the O'Rourke Mechanical Aptitude Test. In the Minnesota Test the examinee places pieces of wood cut in the form of circles, crescent moons, oblongs, and various other shapes in the appropriate holes cut in a board; the assembly has no meaning, other than that of matching different shapes and sizes of objects and holes. In the O'Rourke test the subject marks blank spaces to indicate which mechanical objects, tools, etc., are used together or for specific purposes; the task has meaning, in that the objects and processes are taken from real life, are more or less familiar, and serve important practical purposes. But in general performance tests have the advantage of being more concrete and therefore seeming to be more meaningful to most people. Thus the Minnesota Spatial Relations Test, the real formboard, appeals to some examinees who rebel at the "unreality" of the Revised Minnesota Paper Formboard, a similar although not identical task in paper-and-pencil form. The reason for this is suggested by the relationship between the two tests, expressed by a correlation coefficient of .59 obtained by Super in an unpublished study of 100 NYA youths, and by the correlations of the two tests with measures of academic aptitude, the formboard having a correlation with the Otis S.A. Test of .25 and the paper formboard having one of .43 in the same study. The paper-and-pencil test requires more abstract mental ability than the performance test, probably because all spatial manipulations in the former must be made mentally rather than with actual materials. Paper-and-pencil tests are, because of the ease of group administration, cheaper than performance tests once they have been developed, and are cheaper to develop because of the materials involved.

Another dichotomy is that of *tests* as contrasted with *inventories*. The former are objective in that they require no judgments of self by the examinee, while the latter are subjective in that they ask the subject to judge or describe his interests, traits, or abilities. It is frequently stated that tests have right or wrong answers, whereas inventories have no right or wrong answers; what is right or wrong in the latter depends on what is true of the examinee. This definition is correct when applied to tests of intelligence and to inventories of personality or interests, but it is not correct when applied to tests of personality such as the Rorschach and Murray tests, which are objective (i.e., not self-descriptive), but which have no right or wrong answers. It is also not true of a type of personality test developed in military aviation (Guilford, 1947), which is objective but in which the correct answer is sometimes the "wrong" one and a wrong answer is sometimes the "right" one, right, that is, for one who is likely to succeed in certain types of occupations. Tests have the advantage of being less affected by the desire to make a good impression and by lack of insight than inventories, but are sometimes more expensive in administration and scoring than inventories. This is especially true in the field of personality and interest, although the developments in information tests of interests in military aviation testing mentioned above, and some comparable civilian work once suggested that this might cease to be true in the field of interests.

A fourth dichotomy into which tests may be classified is that of *speed* tests as opposed to *power* tests, illustrated in the intelligence field by the

Otis and the Ohio State Tests. The importance which should be attached to each of these was long a subject of debate in psychological testing, and also fortunately of research. Baxter (1941, 1942), for example, has shown that the Otis Self-Administering Test of Mental Ability, administered as a speed test, is a good measure of what will be done by the same subjects when the test is administered as a power test. Tinker (1944) analyzed the Revised Minnesota Paper Formboard as a measure of speed, power, and level, and found that the first two are highly correlated. Lorge (1936) has shown that older persons do as well as younger subjects on power tests, but are handicapped on speed tests. The advantages of briefer and uniform timing suggest the use of speed tests with younger persons, and power tests with persons in their forties or above. But since speed is often less important than power in life situations, and even some younger persons are handicapped on speed tests, power tests are generally preferred.

Finally, there is the dichotomy of *individual* versus *group* tests, illustrated in intelligence testing by the Wechsler and the Otis or American Council Tests. In the former one has the advantage of being able to observe individual reactions and to adapt directions to the intent of the test, rather than having to follow their letter because a modification which would be fairer to one might handicap another subject in the group. In the latter social stimulation, competition, the safety of numbers, the group example, and externally standardized conditions facilitate good results.

In vocational testing the optimum conditions vary with the circumstances and with the personality of the examinee. Sometimes it is better to test an individual alone, whether with group or individual tests; sometimes it helps to have him take tests as one of a group. In school situations the latter is more often the case; in a consultation service for adults the former is frequently better policy, although small groups are acceptable. In vocational selection, candidates actively seeking employment are probably just as well tested in groups, except in the case of applicants for higher level jobs who feel that they deserve individual treatment. Group testing requires either small groups or a large group divided into sections each with its own proctor who can observe it, supervise it, and give attention to special cases.

In view of the frequent psychological (and financial) superiority of group testing it is desirable for vocational tests to be suitable for use in groups; they can just as easily be administered individually when that is preferable. There are no inherent qualities in either group or individual tests which make one type generally better than the other; they must, rather, be considered on the basis of their own validity and of the situation in which testing is to be done. Sometimes a test can be so constructed as to be either a group or an individual test in every sense of the term:

the two forms of the Minnesota Multiphasic Personality Test are an example. The opinion of the test's authors (Hathaway and McKinley, 1951) is that when it is administered as an individual test the subject considers each item (printed on a separate card) more carefully and responds more truthfully than when it is administered in the group form (printed in booklets) and one item closely follows another. However, they now recognize that when administered to normal groups of people there is no difference in the results of the two forms, Wiener (1948) and Cottle (1950) having demonstrated this.

REFERENCES FOR CHAPTER V

Andrew, Dorothy M. "An analysis of the Minnesota Vocational Test for Clerical Workers: I, II," *J. Appl. Psychol.*, 21 (1937), 18-47, 139-172.

Baxter, B. "An experimental analysis of the contributions of speed and level in an intelligence test," *J. Educ. Psychol.*, 32 (1941), 285-296.

———. "On the equivalence of time-limit and work-limit methods," *Amer. J. Psychol.*, 55 (1942), 407-411.

Cottle, W. C. "Card versus booklet form of the MMPI," *J. Appl. Psychol.*, 34 (1950), 255-259.

DuBois, P. H. (ed.). *The Classification Program.* ("AAF Aviation Psychology Report," No. 2.) Washington, D. C.: Government Printing Office, 1947.

English, H. B., and English, Ava C. *Comprehensive Dictionary of Psychological and Psychoanalytical Terms.* New York: Longman's, Green, 1958.

French, J. W. "The description of aptitude and achievement tests in terms of rotated factors," *Psychometric Monog.*, 5 (1951).

Guilford, J. P. (ed.). *Printed Classification Tests.* ("AAF Aviation Psychology Report," No. 5.) Washington, D. C.: Government Printing Office, 1947.

———. "Factor analysis in a test development program," *Psychol. Rev.*, 55 (1948), 79-94.

———, Christensen, P. R., Bond, N. A., and Sutton, M. A. "A factor analysis of human interests," *Psychol. Monog.*, 375 (1954).

———, and Zimmerman, W. S. "Some AAF findings concerning aptitude factors," *Occupations*, 26 (1947), 154-159.

Hathaway, S. R., and McKinley, J. C. *Manual for the Minnesota Multiphasic Personality Inventory.* New York: Psychological Corp., 1951.

Kelley, T. L. *Crossroads in the Mind of Man.* Stanford: Stanford University Press, 1928.

Longstaff, H. P. "Fakability of the Strong Interest Blank and the Kuder Preference Record," *J. Appl. Psychol.*, 32 (1948), 360-369.

Lorge, I. "The influence of the test upon the nature of mental decline as a function of age," *J. Educ. Psychol.*, 27 (1936), 100-110.

Michael, W. B. "A factor analysis of tests and criteria: a comparative study of two AAF pilot populations," *Psychol. Monog.*, 298 (1949).

Newman, H. H., Freeman, F. N., and Holzinger, C. J. *Twins: A Study in Heredity.* Chicago: University of Chicago Press, 1937.

Paterson, D. G., et al. *The Minnesota Mechanical Abilities Tests.* Minneapolis: University of Minnesota Press, 1930.

Piéron, H. "L'hétérogéneité normale des aptitudes," *Année Psychol.*, 41-42 (1945), 1-13.

Pintner, R. *Intelligence Testing.* New York: Holt, 1931.

Spearman, C. *The Abilities of Man*. New York: Macmillan, 1927.
————, and Wynn Jones, L. *Human Ability*. London: Macmillan, 1950.
Staff, Division of Occupational Analysis, WMC. "Factor analysis of occupational aptitude tests," *Educ. Psychol. Measmt.*, 5 (1945), 147-155.
Steinmetz, H. C. "Measuring ability to fake occupational interest," *J. Appl. Psychol.*, 16 (1932), 123-130.
Strong, E. K. *Vocational Interests of Men and Women*. Stanford: Stanford University Press, 1943.
Terman, L. M., et al. *Genetic Studies of Genius: The Promise of Youth*. Stanford: Stanford University Press, 1930.
————, and Oden, Melita H. *The Gifted Child Grows Up*. Stanford: Stanford University Press, 1948.
————, and Oden, Melita H. *The Gifted Goup at Mid-life*. Stanford: Stanford University Press, 1959.
Thurstone, L. L. *The Vectors of Mind*. Chicago: University of Chicago Press, 1935.
————. "Primary mental abilities," *Psychometrika Monog.*, 1 (1938).
————, and Thurstone, Thelma G. *Factorial Studies of Intelligence*. Chicago: University of Chicago Press, 1941.
Tinker, M. A. "Speed, power, and level in the Revised Minnesota Paper Form Board Test," *J. Genet. Psychol.*, 64 (1944), 93-97.
Tyler, Leona E. *The Psychology of Human Differences*. New York: Appleton-Century-Crofts, 1956.
Vernon, P. E. *The Structure of Human Abilities*. London: Methuen, 1950.
Warren, H. C. *Dictionary of Psychology*. Boston: Houghton-Mifflin, 1934.
Wiener, D. N. "Differences between the individual and group forms of the MMPI," *J. Consult. Psychol.*, 11 (1947), 104-106.

VI

INTELLIGENCE

Nature and Role

INTELLIGENCE has frequently been defined as the ability to adjust to the environment or to learn from experience. As Garrett (1946) has pointed out, this definition is too broad to be very helpful in practical work. One might therefore resort to an operational definition and say that intelligence is the ability to succeed in school or college; such a definition would be justified by the fact that the criterion used in standardizing intelligence tests has generally been one of school placement and progress. This line of thought is illustrated by the tendency of many school and college officers to talk in terms of scholastic aptitude and scholastic aptitude tests, thereby implicitly limiting the application of such tests to the situations in which they have been proved valid and dodging the issue of their role in other types of situations.

An equally operational, but more scientific and therefore more generally applicable, definition is suggested by Garrett in the paper referred to above. "Intelligence . . .," he states, "includes at least the abilities demanded in the solution of problems which require the comprehension and use of symbols" (1946, p. 372). This definition is operational in that it is based on an analysis of the task involved in solving the problems presented by an intelligence test. It is broader than some test-based definitions because it applies not only to the tasks presented by the test, but also to the tasks presented by the school or college courses, success in which it is designed to predict. It is broader even than this, because it allows for the value of such tests in predicting success in certain types of occupations, namely those in which job analysis shows that it is necessary to comprehend and use symbols. And it has the additional advantage of taking into account the important work of the past ten or fifteen years which demonstrates that intelligence is not one aptitude but a constellation of aptitudes. As these components of intelligence apparently vary in importance in different occupations according to the type of symbol most

83

frequently used in that occupation, this advantage is of great practical significance.

Two closely related questions, in addition to that of the definition of intelligence, normally come up for discussion at this stage: those of the innateness and the constancy of intelligence. During the 1930's they were the subject of much debate and disagreement among psychologists, an excellent overview of which is provided by the 39th Yearbook of the National Society for the Study of Education (Whipple, 1940) ; reference should also be made to a paper by Stoddard (1939) expounding the environmentalist point of view, and to papers by Burt (1958), McNemar (1940), Thorndike (1940), and Wellman et al. (1938, 1940), in which detailed questions of the methods and results of nature-nurture studies are examined at length. The topic is much too complex for treatment in a handbook on vocational testing. The reader who has not studied sources such as those referred to, or who has not sufficient time to do so, must rest content with the general conclusion reached by the writers. This is that whereas both nature and nurture play a part in the development of intelligence, mental ability as indicated by the intelligence quotient is relatively constant from the time a child enters elementary school until late adulthood. It is true that the obtained I. Q. will vary some after the age of six, but this is generally less a function of the individual than of the tests, which are often not strictly comparable at different age levels and which are in any case subject to errors of measurement. Some changes which are too great to be explained by these causes are the result of emotional conditions which invalidate the score of one test, or of organic changes resulting from disease or injury. That there are other changes, not explained by any of these factors and attributable to changes in the environment which modify the functioning intelligence, has not been demonstrated to the satisfaction of all competent judges with persons of elementary school age or older.

Intelligence and Educational Success.   The role played by intelligence in educational achievement has been frequently studied. Comprehensive reviews of the research are available in Pintner (1931, Ch. 10–12) and in Tyler, (1956, Ch. 4). Our attention will be focused on certain points, an understanding of which is needed in the use of intelligence tests in educational and vocational guidance, and on some data illustrating those points.

Different *curricula* have been found to require or to attract different degrees of intelligence, whether at the high school or at the college level. In general, students in scientific and liberal arts courses have the highest intelligence test scores, with those in commercial subjects coming next and trade courses last. In one nation-wide study (Kefauver, 1932) the median I. Q. of high school boys in different courses was as follows:

TABLE 3

MEDIAN I.Q.'S OF BOYS IN HIGH SCHOOL COURSES

Course	Md. I. Q.
College Preparatory (Technical Schools)	114
Scientific (General Schools)	108
Academic	106
Commercial	104
Trade	92

The figures vary from one community to another and from time to time. It is therefore necessary to have local norms in actual counseling; in fact, not only the trends, as indicated by averages, are necessary, but even more needed are minimum critical scores which show what score a student should make in order to be a good risk in each type of training. The importance of local norms is further illustrated by the fact that in some cities there are trade schools which offer such attractive training that entrance is quite competitive, whereas some of the general high schools attract students of less ability who, for reasons such as the prestige of academic training, want the traditional education. It should be remembered, too, that if general intelligence were broken down into its component factors, the group which ranked highest on one might well rank lower on another.

Differences in the intelligence scores of students in different *institutions* have been found which, like curricular differences, are in line with popular expectation. Some of these can be expressed in generalizations: liberal arts college students tend to be intellectually superior to teachers college students, those in small rural colleges tend to be inferior to those in large urban universities, and those in highly endowed private institutions tend to be more able than those in state universities (at least when freshmen classes are compared) or in denominational colleges. The documentation for these statements is provided by the periodic analyses of the results of nation-wide testing programs such as that of the Educational Testing Service, in which some 350 colleges and universities of all types usually participate. After World War I studies made in a number of universities with the Army Alpha Intelligence Test gave results for a larger group of identified institutions than more recent publications, which generally use code numbers rather than names. The data were collected by Pintner (1931, p. 296) ; converted into Otis I. Q. equivalents, these show that some thirty years ago the median I. Q. at Yale was 131, at Oberlin 124, at Ohio State 120, at Penn State 117, and at Purdue 115. The overlapping of scores was no doubt considerable, but the ranges and quartiles are not reported. More recent data, largely unpublished, suggest that the averages are about the same today.

The American Council, Educational Testing Service, and College Entrance Examination Board data are for entering freshmen, which means that the normal elimination as a result of academic failure has not yet taken place. This is especially important at state institutions which are obliged to admit great numbers of high school graduates who subsequently fail to keep up with their classes, and which therefore have freshman attrition rates as high as 50 and 60 percent. In colleges using more stringent selection standards the differences in the average intelligence of freshmen and seniors is much smaller. Really adequate data on intelligence and college success would, as in the case of curricula, provide minimum critical scores for each college. Individual colleges, as will be seen shortly, have such data for their own use. The published material, however, is simply in terms of freshman averages and variations. In 1938, for example, the 355 colleges using the A.C.E. Psychological Examination (Thurstone et al., 1939) reported freshmen medians which, when converted into Otis I. Q. equivalents, range from 94 to 122, the median college having a median freshman I. Q. of 108. The interquartile deviations were such that the college with a median freshman I. Q. of 94 had a freshman class in which one fourth of the students had I. Q. equivalents of less than 90, and only one fourth exceeded 100.

Data for one liberal arts college, Oberlin, were reported in some detail by Hartson (1941, 1945), who set an example which, followed by other college officials, will be of general benefit in improving the college counseling done in the high schools. (The University System of Georgia has now set an example by publishing a manual of probability tables for state and private colleges in Georgia, using College Board scores; see Hill et al., 1960). At Oberlin some students with Otis I. Q. equivalents of less than 100 managed to graduate, but Hartson found that 65 percent of the entering freshmen who were below 110 failed academically. In another college of approximately the same academic but lower social standing, it was found that there were practically no freshmen with I. Q.'s of less than 110, indicating that the latter institution was admitting students on a more selective academic basis. Attrition data also showed a higher mortality rate among the lower intelligence levels at the latter college. Obviously, the former institution would be a better choice for a student with an I. Q. equivalent of about 110. At Franklin and Marshall the mean I. Q. was 111, but here also 65 percent of those below 110 failed (Marshall, 1943). Data on the Wechsler-Bellevue have been summarized by Plant and Richardson (1958), showing that the average liberal arts college *freshman* has a Wechsler-Bellevue I. Q. of 116, the average *student* one of 120.

Despite the relationship between intelligence and educational achievement revealed by data such as the above, the correlation between intelligence tests and *grades* is not especially high. The numerous summaries of the subject show that in high school it tends to range from .30 to .80, and in college from .20 to .70, the modal r's being .40 and .50 in the former and between .30 and .50 in the latter. The relationship in college seems lower than in high school because the selection procedures in colleges cut down the range of ability in their populations, and this in turn makes the correlation coefficients shrink artificially. The relationships are high enough to make them useful in studying groups, but the margin of error when working with an individual student is so great as to make considerable caution necessary in test interpretation and to require that the counselor or admissions officer give considerable weight to other indices such as high school marks, family educational achievement (as an indicator of what his intimate social group expects of him), personality adjustment and motivation. None of these, taken by itself, is any more valid than the score of a good intelligence test for predicting college marks, but, taken together, they yield a better prediction than any single index (Strang, 1934, p. 123). To cite the Oberlin studies once more, the fact that 65 percent of the freshmen who were admitted with I. Q.'s of less than 110 failed academically is a legitimate reason for questioning the choice of that college with an I. Q. of 110; on the other hand, it should be remembered that 35 percent of such students graduated. The counselor must ask himself, and get the student to ask himself, what reasons there are for expecting him to be in one group rather than in the other, and whether a less competitive situation might be more conducive to his fullest all-round growth.

The relationship of intelligence test scores to educational achievement has been demonstrated in one other type of study, in which a genetic approach has related intelligence to *amount of education* obtained. These studies make it clear that, on the whole, those who are most able obtain the most education. Proctor (1935) made a follow-up study in 1930 of persons who had been tested while in school in 1917 and found that those who, in 1930, had gone no further than the 9th grade had an average I. Q. in 1917 of 105, whereas those who had graduated from high school had a mean of 111 and those who went to college had averaged 116. This should not, of course, be taken as proof that students who have the ability to do college work manage to go to college; the Pennsylvania Study demonstrated that the bright students who actually get to college are matched by an equally able but economically less fortunate group who do not obtain that much education. What Proctor demonstrated is that those who get more education are, on the whole, more able than the much larger group who obtain less education.

Terman and Oden's long-term studies of gifted persons (1947, 1959), provide more data demonstrating the importance of intelligence in completing an education. Almost all of his group of 1300 children with I. Q.'s of more than 140 graduated from college (helped, be it said, by the fact that they lived in a state which provides more low-cost higher education than any other for its residents).

The studies mentioned so far have all dealt with the relationship between intelligence and educational achievement, none with the role of the former in *satisfaction* in one's studies. It is generally assumed that the placement of a student at the proper educational level, one on which he can compete with his peers without undue strain and on which he will be challenged by the need to exert himself in order to master the subject-matter, results in better adjustment and greater satisfaction on his part. The assumption seems reasonable. Every experienced teacher can cite instances in its support. The literature of clinical psychology abounds in references to cases illustrating it. But oddly enough there are no studies involving objective measures and carefully quantified data to prove the validity of the assumption. In one investigation Berdie (1944) correlated intelligence test scores and measured satisfaction in the study of engineering, finding an r of .02. This is disappointing, but is probably more a defect in the experiment than in the hypothesis; the scale used for the measurement of satisfaction may not have been sensitive to what it attempted to assess, or the relationship may be such that it would manifest itself in a study of many curricula without being revealed in a study of one type of curriculum. The latter, it will be seen, is true of the relationship between intelligence and success in occupations. Although one is justified in generally being skeptical of clinical experience and professional opinion unsupported by experimental evidence, this would seem to be one instance in which it is best, pending the carrying out of adequate objective studies, to accept the evidence of subjectively analyzed experience. This would lead one to conclude that students who are placed in courses which are difficult enough to make them work but not so difficult as to discourage them are most likely to be satisfied with and interested in their studies.

Intelligence and Vocational Success.   Because intelligence supposedly affects vocational success in a number of different ways, tests have been correlated with a variety of criteria. These include wisdom of vocational choice, success in training, ability to secure a job of a particular type, adjustment in the world of work as shown by placement on the occupational ladder, status in the occupation as indicated by criteria ranging from tenure to earnings, and satisfaction in one's work. Each of these will be discussed in the following paragraphs.

Vocational Choice.   In a number of studies (Grace, 1931; Sparling, 1933; Wrenn, 1935) the more intelligent individuals have been found to have more appropriate occupational objectives. This is what one would expect on *a priori* grounds, not only because the more able should have better insight into their own abilities and into job requirements, but also because, in a society which encourages people to aspire to the higher levels, they have more of the abilities which are required for success in the prestige occupations. The factors considered in these studies have usually been limited in number. Sparling (1933), for example, compared the tested intelligence of the student with the intelligence considered necessary for success in his chosen field on the basis of an analysis of intelligence test data gathered from soldiers in World War I, while Wrenn (1935) compared the correspondence between measured and self-estimated interests at different intelligence levels. Atomistic as they are in their approach to these problems, the investigations justify one in concluding that the more intelligent are more likely, other things being equal, to make wise vocational choices.

Success in Training. This topic has been dealt with under the heading of intelligence and educational success, as most formal training is under educational auspices and bears an educational label. But, since one cannot succeed in medicine or flying, for example, without first succeeding in medical or flying school, success in training is the first step in vocational success. It is frequently much easier to obtain criteria of success in training than in the practice or pursuit of the vocation itself. For these reasons training success is a commonly used criterion of vocational success, and needs to be mentioned in this section.

Securing employment. Studies of the relationship between intelligence and ability to secure employment have been made in depression years, as those are the times when attention is focussed on the problem of what it takes to obtain a job and on the differences between employed and unemployed workers.

Few of the youth studies of the 1930's used measures of intelligence, presumably because they were large scale surveys in which accurate testing was impractical. In several studies confined to more accessible subjects, however, testing was carried out with what at first appear to be surprising results. Dearborn and Rothney (1938) analyzed the relationship between tested intelligence and success in securing employment in a large sample of youth who were subjects of the Harvard Growth Study and lived in communities adjacent to Cambridge, Massachusetts. They found no relationship. Lazarsfeld and Gaudet (1941) studied a small but carefully matched sample of youth in Essex County, New Jersey. They also reported no relationship between tested intelligence and success in finding employment.

In contrast to these and similar studies of young persons stand the investigations dealing with adults in the depression. Morton (1935) and Paterson and Darley, in their summary of the psychological work of the Minnesota Employment Stabilization Research Institute (1936), reported that, in a variety of occupational groups in Montreal and in Minneapolis, the early unemployed were less able than those who were released later in the Depression. At least in retaining their jobs, then, the more intelligent fare better than the less intelligent. This suggests that in employing young people the average business man either does not have access to or does not utilize data revealing the abilities of the employment applicants, but relies instead on other and, as Dearborn and Rothney showed, less relevant indices, whereas the employer who is considering releasing employees does depend more on indices of ability. In the case of a worker already in his employ this need not be, and generally is not, an intelligence test, but is simply the employer's judgment of the relative value to the company (efficiency, versatility, etc.) of each of the persons in question. No such ability data, which frequently correlate with intelligence test scores (see below), are available to the employer of relatively inexperienced youth, although school experience should be such as to provide employers with data of the same type, and intelligence tests can be used in selection. Personnel men should be able to make considerable improvement in their work by bringing their practices in employing new workers up to the level of their practices in releasing workers when staffs must be cut.

Attainment on the Occupational Scale. In a culture in which material success and ability to rise to or maintain a high socio-economic level are valued as highly as in ours, the question of the relationship of intelligence to attainment on the occupational scale is one of vital importance. If the relationship is close, then the ambitions of many persons are unrealistic; if the relationship is not close then there is some justification for the widespread encouragement of youth to aspire to the higher levels.

The first large-scale studies of this question were made possible by the mass of data accumulated as a result of the use of intelligence tests in the Army of the United States in World War I. These were analyzed and published in the *Memoirs of the National Academy of Sciences* (1921), and were subsequently reworked by Fryer (1922) and by Fryer and Sparling (1934) to make them more usable in vocational counseling. Similar data for World War II, based on a sample of some 90,000 white men, have been organized in a similar table by Stewart (1947), reproduced (Table 4) by permission of *Occupations*.

A table such as this is useful in ascertaining approximately the occupational level at which an individual is most likely to be able to compete without undue strain and, at the same time, with sufficient challenge to make the work interesting. To know that a student with a score of 125 has the general ability to compete with men and women who have been successfully engaged in the lower professional and managerial occupations, but somewhat less than that which characterizes those who have made good in the higher level occupations of the same type, is of value.

But the apparent simplicity of the chart is deceptive because it does not bring out the great overlapping of the various occupational intelligence levels. A given occupation actually includes within itself a great variety of levels; a chemist, for example, may supervise routine tests on the one hand or do highly creative experimental research on the other, or, more commonly, something in between these two extremes. This means that there are opportunities in most occupations for some persons at relatively low levels who are not likely, if their mental ability is appropriate to these levels, to rise appreciably in the field, and for others with greater ability who should, other things being equal, rise to higher levels. Thus some chemists really belong in the highest occupational level in Table 4, where the majority are placed, but others should be in the second group of occupations. Other factors which play a part in occupational success need, of course, to be taken into account, but are not in the chart: Lack of motivation may disqualify a person from competing effectively at his appropriate intellectual level; or an unusually effective personality may enable another to compete above that at which he might otherwise be expected to make an optimal adjustment.

The overlapping of occupations when classified according to intelligence is well brought out by Stewart, who reports the median and adjacent quartiles for a number of different occupations in the Army sample. For example, a man with an AGCT score of 115 might, in so far as *mental ability* is concerned, be a high-average stock-keeper, average general clerk, low-average bookkeeper or below-average accountant—all in the clerical field, not to mention an average draftsman or a low-average reporter in other fields. Clearly, the extent and nature of the overlapping is so great that, while occupational intelligence levels provide a rough guide, they must be used as that and cannot be applied in a mechanical or arbitrary way.

Another limitation to the value of World War II data is imposed by the nature of the sample. Some occupations were not adequately represented in the Army. The War having been a total war, and Selective Service having operated according to written directives and on the basis of studies by the War Manpower Commission, we know a good deal how the occupations represented in the Army were affected by sampling problems. As lawyers had a type of training which was at a premium in neither war industries nor military service during the early years of the war, it

TAB

OCCUPATIONAL GROUPS WHOSE AGCT MEDIANS LIE IN EACH

Based on 88,907 White Enlisted Men in

−2.5 σ 85.3	−2.0 σ 89.9	−1.5 σ 94.5	−1.0 σ 99.1	−.5 σ 103.7	Mean 108.3
Teamster	Marine	Tractor Driver	Welder, Electric		Not Elsewhere Classified
Miner	Fireman	Painter,	Arc		Machinist's Helper
Farm	Laundry	General	Plumber		Foreman, Labor
Worker	Machine	Foundryman	Switchman,		Locomotive Fireman
Lumber-	Operator	Animation	Railway		Entertainer
jack	Laborer	Artist	Machine		Meat Cutter
	Barber	Hospital	Operator		Student, High School
	Shoe Repair-	Orderly	Hammersmith		Vocational
	man	Baker	Student, High		Cabinetmaker
	Jackhammer	Packer,	School, Agri-		Airplane Engine
	Operator	Supplies	cultural		Mechanic
	Groundman,	Sewing	Automotive		Heat Treater
	Telephone	Machine	Mechanic		Fire Fighter
	Telegraph,	Operator	Blacksmith		Engineering Aide
	or Power	Truck Driver,	Welder,		Construction Equipment
	Section Hand,	Heavy	Acetylene		Mechanic
	Railway	Painter, Auto-	Bricklayer		Optician
		mobile	Blaster or		Packer, High Explosives
		Hoist Operator	Powderman		Petroleum Storage
		Construction	Small Craft		Technician
		Machine	Operator		Pattern Maker, Wood
		Operator	Lineman, Power		Electrician, Automotive
		Horsebreaker	Packing Case		Coppersmith
		Tailor	Maker		Ship Fitter
		Stonemason	Carpenter,		Sheet Metal Worker
		Crane Operator	General		Electroplater
		Upholsterer	Pipe Fitter		Instrument Repairman,
		Cook	Electric Truck		Electrical
		Concrete-Mixer	Driver		Steam Fitter
		Operator	Highway Main-		Diesel Mechanic
		Truck Driver,	tenance Man		Carpenter, Ship
		Light	Automobile		Bandsman, Snare Drum
		Stationary	Serviceman		Lithographic Pressman
		Fireman	Rigger		Electric Motor Repair-
		Warehouseman	Woodworking		man
		Gas and Oil	Machine		Shop Maintenance
		Man	Operator		Mechanic
		Forging-Press	Chauffeur		Job Pressman
		Operator	Motorcyclist		Riveter, Pneumatic
		Longshoreman	Burner,		Power Shovel Operator
		Well Driller	Acetylene		Photographic Technician,
					Aerial
					Brakeman, Railway
					Automobile Body
					Repairman
					Tire Rebuilder
					Utility Repairman
					Boilermaker
					Foreman, Automotive
					Repair Shop
					Salvage Man
					Structural Steel Worker
					Welder, Combination
					Welder, Spot
					Seaman
					Engineman, Operating
					Foreman, Construction
					Millwright

TABLE 4

HALF-SIGMA INTERVAL FROM THE MEAN OF ALL THE MEDIANS
Machine Records Survey Taken June 30, 1944

$+.5\,\sigma$ 112.9	$+1.0\,\sigma$ 117.5	$+1.5\,\sigma$ 122.1	$+2.0\,\sigma$ 126.7	$+2.5\,\sigma$ 131.3
Carpenter, Heavy Construction	Switchboard Installer, Telephone and Telegraph, Dial	Bookkeeper, General	Writer	Accountant
Dispatcher, Motor Vehicle	Cashier	Chief Clerk	Student, Civil Engineering	Student, Mechanical Engineering
Gunsmith	Stock Record Clerk	Stenographer	Statistical Clerk	Personnel Clerk
Musician, Instrumental	Clerk, General	Pharmacist	Student, Chemical Engineering	Student, Medicine
Tool Maker	Radio Repairman	Typist	Teacher	Chemist
Nurse, Practical	Purchasing Agent	Draftsman	Lawyer	Student, Electrical Engineering
Photographer, Portrait	Survey and Instrument Man	Chemical Laboratory Assistant	Student, Business or Public Administration	
Photolithographer	Physics Laboratory Assistant	Draftsman, Mechanical	Auditor	
Rodman and Chainman, Surveying	Stock Control Clerk	Investigator	Student, Dentistry	
Airplane Fabric and Dope Worker	Manager, Production	Reporter		
Multilith or Multigraph	Boilermaker, Layer Out	Tool Designer		
Shipping Clerk	Radio Operator	Tabulating Machine Operator		
Printer	Linotype Operator	Addressing-Embossing Machine Operator		
Steward	Student, Mechanics	Traffic Rate Clerk		
Foreman, Warehouse	Salesman	Clerk-Typist		
Bandsman, Cornet or Trumpet	Athletic Instructor	Postal Clerk		
Instrument Repairman, Non-electrical	Store Manager	Bookkeeping Machine Operator		
Boring Mill Operator	Installer Repairman, Telephone and Telegraph	Meat or Dairy Inspector		
Projectionist, Motion Picture	Motorcycle Mechanic	Photographic Laboratory Technician		
Dental Laboratory Technician	Dispatcher Clerk, Crew	Teletype Operator		
Laboratory Technician, V-mail or Microfilm	Tool Dresser	Student, Sociology		
Foreman, Machine Shop	File Clerk			
Stock Clerk	Embalmer			
Painter, Sign	Brake Inspector, Railway			
Machinist	Airplane and Engine Mechanic			
Photographer, Aerial	Shop Clerk			
Engine Lathe Operator	Artist			
Parts Clerk, Automotive	Band Leader			
Cook's Helper	Photographer			
Railway Mechanic, General	Geologist			
Office Machine Serviceman	Airplane Engine Service Mechanic			
Student, High School, Commercial	Cable Splicer, Telephone and Telegraph			
Electrician, Airplane	Surveyor			
Student, Manual Arts	Student, High School, Academic			
Policeman	Blueprinter or Photostat Operator			
Sales Clerk				
Electrician				
Lineman, Telephone and Telegraph				
Watch Repairman				
Receiving or Shipping Checker				
Car Mechanic, Railway				
Toolroom Keeper				
Refrigeration Mechanic				
Cameraman, Motion Picture				
Telephone Operator				
Hatch Tender				

seems likely that the drafted lawyers are fairly representative of the young lawyers of that time. Psychologists, on the other hand, were at a premium in both military and industrial personnel work, and as the Army commissioned many who were aged thirty or more, and the Navy many who were under thirty, directly from civilian life early in the war, it is probable that the drafted psychologists who held the Ph.D. degree at the time of being drafted were not really representative of young psychologists in mental ability and *savoir faire*. A thorough-going study of data obtained during World War II would have been worth making, relating occupational intelligence findings to known policies of Army, Navy and Selective Service. Stewart did not do this.

A final possible defect in intelligence test data obtained under military auspices which must be mentioned is the fact that the testing conditions are often not optimal. Many new draftees were not well oriented to psychological tests; they often resented the tests as so much mumbo-jumbo. Others were negativistic in their attitude toward military service and vented their feelings in not cooperating in the testing—often to their later regret when they found that they needed a higher score in order to qualify for officer candidate school (an error many remedied by retaking the test and making qualifying scores). Still others, heeding rumors that men who made high scores were being assigned to a type of training they did not want (for example, to Link trainer instruction when they wanted to be aerial gunners), made low scores in order to avoid it. But draftee attitudes were not the only problem. Some were created by "efficiency" minded or routine-bound officers who sent men to testing after a night of duty in the kitchens or after they had had only a few hours sleep subsequent to a long trip by troop train. This should not, however, lead to the conclusion that all military testing was conducted under poor conditions or that the results should be entirely disregarded. On the contrary, much of it was well done, and many, probably most, of those who took the tests tried to do their best. It is easy for a few dramatic cases to create a false impression in such a situation.

The trends revealed by military studies have been confirmed not only in studies abroad by Cattell (1934) and Awaji (1928), but also in civilian studies made in this country by Scott and Clothier (1926) and Pond (1933). These last are unfortunately not based on large numbers from all parts of the country, but their tendency to agree with each other and with the Army data gives one greater confidence in their trends. Proctor's study (1935, 1937) is perhaps as good an illustration as any since it is longitudinal and covers one community. He tested 1500 students in 1917-18 and ascertained the occupations of 945 who were followed up thirteen years later. When classified according to the occupational levels of their 1930 jobs, the results in Table 5 were obtained.

TABLE 5

INTELLIGENCE IN HIGH SCHOOL AND OCCUPATIONAL LEVEL THIRTEEN YEARS LATER

Occupational Level	Mean I.Q.	N
I Professional	115	130
II Managerial	108	565
III Clerical	104	228
IV Skilled	99	12
V Semi-Skilled	97	10

A final approach to the topic of occupational levels which should be mentioned is that in which the minimum intelligence required for success in the simplest type of employment has been investigated. Most frequently referred to in this country is the study by Unger and Burr (1931), but Dunlop (1935) made a similar study in Canada, and Abel (1940), Beckham (1930), Channing (1932), Lord (1933), Fairbanks (1933), and others have also published on the subject in the United States. Table 6 lists typical occupations in which persons at the lower mental levels have successfully been employed after adequate induction on the job and when there were no serious personality problems to complicate things.

TABLE 6

MINIMUM MENTAL AGES FOR SIMPLE OCCUPATIONS

(From Unger and Burr)

Mental Age	Occupation
5 years	Packing, garden work, scrubbing floors, simple washing
6 years	Light factory work, light domestic work
7 years	Assembly work, errands, pasting, farm work
8 years	Cutting, folding, garment machine operation, laundry, cooking
9 years	Hand sewing, press operation, filing, stock work
10 years	Routine clerical, general housework, machine operation, electricians' helper, painter
11 years	Selling, millinery work, janitorial work

One advantage in employing mentally handicapped adults in jobs such as the above is that, after the first period of careful supervision while they are learning the job, they are more likely to be satisfied with routine work and to be dependable employees than are other persons whose mental ability is such that they can legitimately aspire to more challenging work and are impelled to do so by boredom.

Status within an occupation. The multiplicity of occupations and the variety of criteria applicable to them have prevented any systematic study of the importance of intelligence for success *within* occupations, as contrasted with success *among* occupations or placement on the occupational scale. But there have been a number of studies of the relationship between tested intelligence and success in certain specific occupations. An examination of a few typical studies, of their results, and of the reasons for these results, is important to the user of intelligence tests in counseling and selection.

Although occupational level studies have shown that executives tend to make relatively high scores on intelligence tests, attempts to correlate intelligence and success in executive positions met with so little success during the 1920's that they fell into disrepute. One such study was published by Bingham and Davis (1924). Using the army type intelligence test with 102 business executives, the correlation between test score and business success as indicated by a composite rating based on information contained in personal history records (salary, investments, debts, clubs, theatre attendance, etc.), was —.10. Their conclusion that "superiority in intelligence, above a certain minimum (all were above the Army median), contributes relatively less to business success than does superiority in several non-intellectual traits of personality" has been generally accepted, and since the late '20's intelligence tests have generally been used only as a rough screening device for executive positions. However, Thompson (1947) found a small group of top-rated executives superior to others on the Wonderlic Personnel Test.

As in the case of executives, so in that of salesmen: The studies of the relationship between intelligence and sales ability have yielded negative results. Most such studies have not been published, as they have been conducted by or for companies interested in their own personnel problems rather than by investigators with a more general interest. Experience with salesmen of tangibles and of intangibles has led to an emphasis on work with tests of other types (largely interests, personality, and personal history). One classical study is reported by Anderson in his book on personnel work at Macy's (1929). After administering the Otis Self-Administering Test of Mental Ability to 500 sales clerks, Anderson found that the distribution of intelligence scores clustered in the 80 to 110 range (75 percent), while 20 percent were below I. Q. 80 and 5 percent were above 110. This led to the conclusion that intelligence tests were of no value in selecting sales clerks, a conclusion reiterated by Anderson's successor (Moore, 1941, p. 46). Actually, this approach seems too gross to be conclusive; a more refined analysis might, for instance, show that rug salesmen are and need to be more able than packaged food salesmen or girls who sell perfumes. But this would be classification of sales jobs according to level; one would still need to ascertain whether the more intelligent rug salesman is more successful than the less intelligent rug salesman who also is above the critical minimum. Such studies have not been published, partly for the reasons given, partly because of the difficulty of obtaining enough comparable subjects in any one specialty for statistical study. Perhaps they are not worth making, in view of what we know of the role of intelligence in occupations in which personality factors are of importance.

Attempts to predict success in teaching, generally as evidenced in practice teaching while still a student, by means of intelligence tests have met with the same lack of success as investigations of executives and salesmen. Seagoe (1945) made a study correlating success in practice teaching, as rated on a specially constructed scale, with scores on a variety of tests, including the American Council on Education Psychological Examination for College Freshmen. She found no relationship between measured intelligence and rated teaching performance, although she did find some positive results in the area of personality. Earlier studies found equally disappointing results with intelligence tests, but two more recent investigations, discussed in connection with ACE, below, suggest that the situation may be more complex than this. Apparently the occupation "teacher" is too broad a category for psychological study.

Results with intelligence tests and clerical employees have been somewhat different, even though clerical workers are not, on the whole, as able intellectually as executives or teachers. Some of the most convincing studies of this occupational group have been made by Bills of the Aetna Life Insurance Company, in collaboration, at times, with Pond of the Scovill Manufacturing Company (Pond and Bills, 1933). In the early study Bills tested 133 clerical employees at different levels of responsibility and found a correlation coefficient of .22 with difficulty of the job. Two and one-half years later the correlation was .41 for those who were still employed, the more intelligent having left the low grade jobs, often for advancement in the company, and the least able in the higher grade jobs having left them. Aetna classified its office positions in categories from A, low, to H, high. Employees were classified also according to their intelligence test scores. The results for a study of 903 employees in 1933 showed that a clerical worker with a score above 100 had twice as good a chance of being promoted to a "responsible" position as an employee with a score of less than 80. At the same time they pointed out that almost as many employees with scores above 100 remain at the lowest levels as rise to the highest.

Another study has shown that intelligence is related not only to promotability in clerical work, but also to efficiency in the performance of clerical duties in a single job. Hay gave a battery of tests to machine

bookkeepers at the Pennsylvania Company, a Philadelphia bank (1943).
The operation was a routine, bimanual job; the criterion was production,
that is, the number of debits and credits posted and of balances extended
in a given amount of time, a criterion which had a reliability of about
.80. Hay points out that *amount* rather than accuracy is to be stressed,
as inaccurate operators cannot keep their jobs. The correlation between
amount produced and Otis scores was .56 for 39 women operators. This
was higher than the coefficient for any other test in the battery, which
included the Minnesota Vocational Test for Clerical Workers, Army
Alpha, and several manual dexterity tests, although some of these had
values independent of intelligence. These results are reported to have
been consistently obtained over a five-year period. Unfortunately such
studies are rare, and none are known to the writers which throw light on
the applicability of the conclusion concerning intelligence and this one
type of routine clerical work to other types of routine clerical work. But
one would assume that success in semiautomatic tasks such as filing would
correlate even more highly with intelligence than does production in a
practically automatic machine operation task.

Pintner once wrote: "The lower down the scale of industry we go, the
less valuable do our present intelligence tests appear to be for the selection of workers" (1931, p. 489). He cited two studies, one by Otis (1920)
with a performance test administered to 400 silk mill workers, many of
them foreign born or illiterate, and a study by Viteles (1925) with motormen, in support of this statement. Since that time a number of other
studies have been made, in which more adequate statistical methods and
better experimental design have been possible, with somewhat different
results. Blum and Candee (1941) administered the Otis Self-Administering Test to 372 department-store packers and wrappers, while Forlano and
Kirkpatrick (1945) gave it to 20 radio-tube mounters. The former found
that, although there was no relationship between test scores and production or supervisors' ratings for employees who had been on the job for
some time, there was a suggestion of a relationship for new male employees. The latter reported that test scores were related to success only
in the case of the less able learners; the additional increment of intelligence was of no value to superior beginners in learning a routine job.
Sartain (1945) reported a correlation of .64 between refresher course
ratings (reliability .77) and 46 aircraft factory inspectors' Otis intelligence
test scores. Shuman (1945, 1945a) administered the Otis to inspectors,
engine testers, machine operators, job setters, various types of supervisors,
and other aircraft engine and propellor factory workers, the groups ranging in numbers from 25 to 99 each. The correlations between Otis scores
and supervisors' ratings (reliability .70 to .91) ranged from .39 to .57,

depending upon the skill and responsibility required by the job. In view of results such as these, Pintner's conclusions from the earlier studies no longer seem correct. Instead, the following conclusions concerning intelligence and success within an occupation seem warranted:

1. People tend, in so far as circumstances permit, to gravitate toward jobs in which they have ability to compete successfully with others.

2. Given intelligence above the minimum required for learning the occupation, be it executive work, teaching, packing, or light assembly work, additional increments of intelligence appear to have no special effect on an individual's success in that occupation. This conclusion may be subject to revision as better criteria of success are developed, and *may not apply to more strictly intellectual jobs such as those in research or to some kinds of teaching,* but only to those in which personality and interest are peculiarly important. Moreover, it may be valid only for the company concerned, since it is possible the more intelligent workers leave to get better jobs elsewhere.

3. In routine occupations requiring speed and accuracy, whether clerical or semiskilled factory jobs, intelligence as measured by an alertness rather than a power test is related to success in the learning period and, in some vocations, after the initial adjustments are made.

It should be noted that nothing has been reported on intelligence and success in the higher professions, in skilled trades, or in unskilled occupations. This is because no research on these problems has been located by the writers. It seems likely that a positive relationship would be found in the first two, and none in the last, but this is still an unverified hypothesis.

Job Satisfaction. It has long been assumed that, even though a person might be able to do the work required by a job in which most of the workers are more able than he, the strain involved in keeping up with the competition would be such as to produce dissatisfaction in the worker. It has similarly been widely held that ability considerably in excess of that required by a job causes dissatisfaction because of lack of challenge and consequent loss of interest in the work. There is considerable clinical evidence to this effect, concerning both educational and vocational activities. Pruette and Fryer (1923) analyzed a number of case studies, confirming these beliefs for employed persons. Scott, Clothier, and Mathewson (1926) presented charts showing the relationship between amount of school retardation upon leaving school (as a rough index of intelligence) and desire to change jobs in employees engaged in several different types of work in one company. For 52 men employed in a repetitive, monotonous inspection job the curve indicating per cent desiring a change of job increased sharply with intelligence; in the simple but physically demanding foundry jobs the curve was bell shaped, the peak for the 42 men in

question being at two or three years of retardation, with those more retarded or less retarded more likely to be satisfied; while in the assembly
department, which offered a variety of somewhat more complex work, the
curve for 86 men decreased with intelligence, for in this situation the
abler men had more opportunity to use their ability and the less able felt
the strain of difficult work. Anderson (1929, pp. 88-89) reported similar
results in a study of labor turnover in the packing department at Macy's,
where the brighter employees were found to leave their jobs sooner than
the duller, seeking better outlets for their abilities.

The studies referred to above were all made in the 1920's, when attention was focused on the use of the then new intelligence tests in personnel
work. Although such tests are still widely, but more discriminatingly, used
for placement in business and industry, newer studies of the relationship
between intelligence and job satisfaction do not appear in print. This may
be an indication of the widespread acceptance of the relationship, but it is
also due to the increased recognition of the fact that intelligence is only
one among many complex factors in job satisfaction. It would seem desirable, however, to supplement norms which show the relationship between
intelligence and type of occupation with data on the relationship between
intelligence and *satisfaction* in each occupation. This would make possible
the establishment of more adequate critical scores than would otherwise
be possible. Guidance and placement in terms of prospective ability to
compete with satisfaction as well as in terms of ability to hold a job has
been shown to result in less instability; clinical evidence suggests that it
also results in less irritability, aggression, self-recrimination, and escape
into fantasy.

Specific Tests

There is need for a systematic review of the research which has been
carried on with some of the widely used and more promising tests of intelligence, in order to provide the user with a clear picture of what has been
done with these tests and with an understanding of their demonstrated
values and limitations in vocational guidance and personnel work. It is
only upon such a foundation that tests can be used with maximum effectiveness. Thorough coverage of a few representative instruments should
provide the user of tests with insight into the nature and usefulness of the
types of tests in question and enable him to make his own evaluation of
other tests in which he is especially interested. The selection of tests included in this book, then, should be taken simply as an indication that
they have been used in enough investigations for some facts concerning
them to accumulate, and as evidence of the authors' preferences, rather

than as a sign that these particular tests are necessarily intrinsically superior to others not treated in detail. In deciding to use some other test, one should summarize all relevant data in a manner comparable to that of this book.

The intelligence tests now used, whether individual or group, fall into three categories, which might be characterized as old type, new type, and factorial tests. A brief discussion of these types should provide a useful orientation to the tests which are to be discussed in the following pages.

Old type tests of intelligence consist of a variety of items arranged either in the spiral omnibus form, according to increasing degrees of difficulty, or grouped according to type with a time limit for each type and yield only a total score or I. Q. The Stanford-Binet is an individual test of this type; the Ohio State University Psychological Examination, the Henmon-Nelson Test of Mental Ability, the Pressey Classification and Verification Tests, the Terman-McNemar Test of Mental Ability, the Pintner General Ability Tests, the various Otis Tests, the Wonderlic Personnel Test, the Army Alpha Test, and the Army General Classification Test are group tests of the old type. Although it is possible to analyze some of these tests so as to obtain more refined estimates of the mental abilities of the persons tested, the tests were not designed for this purpose, and they have no norms for the interpretation of such scores. To point this out is not to deny the value of the overall score provided by any of these tests. Of these, appreciable amounts of vocational validation data are available only for Army Alpha, the Army General Classification Test, the Pressey, and the Otis and Wonderlic Tests.

New type tests include the same general type of items, but they are either arranged according to type in the test blank or rearranged in this way in the scoring process. These grouped items provide a total score, as in the old type tests, but also part scores based on the type of item. These part scores are generally *verbal* or linguistic and *performance* or quantitative. The Wechsler-Bellevue Intelligence Scale is an individual test of this type; the American Council on Education Psychological Examinations, the School and College Ability Test, and the California Mental Maturity Tests are group tests embodying the same features. Norms are provided for linguistic and quantitative parts with the objective of making it possible to study the special mental abilities of the subject and to predict success in verbal or academic subjects, on the one hand, and quantitative or technical subjects, on the other. Differential occupational predictions were expected to be made possible by this type of special, as opposed to general, mental ability score. A number of studies have been made of differential educational prediction on the basis of the A.C.E. with conflicting results; these will be taken up in connection with this test. Occupational evidence is still practically not available on these tests, their use having been largely clinical and educational.

Factorial tests of intelligence are still in an experimental stage, although the new type tests just described are based on the factor analysis work which preceded the development of factorial tests. The subtests which constitute a test of this type are included because they are heavily saturated with statistically isolated factors which seem to be fundamental components of intelligence. Although, in combination, they measure what is commonly called general intelligence, factorial studies have shown that they are relatively independent of each other and unitary in nature. Scores based on these subtests are therefore used as indices of special, or primary, mental abilities. These are not as coarse as verbal or quantitative ability, which factor analyses have shown to be constellations of abilities rather than unitary traits, but are more refined and include such verbal aptitudes as word fluency and verbal comprehension, and such quantitative aptitudes as spatial visualization and number facility. The best-known tests of this type are the Thurstone Tests of Primary Abilities. These and others will be discussed later; they have found the most wide-spread use in standard batteries of multifactor tests.

Two group tests of intelligence will be taken up in some detail in rounding out this chapter, and briefer discussions of three other tests will follow. The two treated at length are the Otis Self-Administering Test of Mental Ability and its derivatives, and the American Council on Education Psychological Examination for college freshmen and its successors, the Cooperative School and College Ability Tests. The three to which less space is given are the Army General Classification Test, the Thurstone Tests of Primary Mental Abilities, and the Wechsler-Bellevue Intelligence Scale and its revision, the Wechsler Adult Intelligence Scale.

The Otis Self-Administering Tests of Mental Ability (World Book Co., 1928). The Otis Self-Administering Test was designed for use with senior high school and college students and with adults. Another form is suitable for elementary and junior high school students. These have been revamped by Otis for special answer sheet and stencil scoring as the Otis Quick-Scoring Test of Mental Ability and by Wonderlic as the Personnel Test, both essentially the same as the Otis S.A. with improved scoring techniques, improved time limits in the case of the Wonderlic, but less adequate norms in each case. All three are widely used; the S.A. tests are described here as there are more data for them than for the other two tests.

Applicability. The Otis should not be relied upon with older college students and superior adults, as it is probably too easy. As Otis' manual indicates, a number of investigations agree that when high school seniors and other persons are tested, it is preferable to use the twenty instead of the thirty-minute time limit in order to correct for this weakness. Older (1942) has demonstrated, however, that the standing of persons tested with a twenty-minute time limit should not be compared with that of persons tested with a longer limit.

Contents. There are 75 mixed items arranged in order of difficulty, some verbal, some arithmetical, and others spatial; they involve vocabulary, sentence meaning, proverbs, number series, analogies, etc. A study by Hovland and Wonderlic (1939) showed that the arrangement of the items is no longer the best possible and that as many as 25 percent of the items are correctly answered by 90 percent of a large sample of adults ($N=8300$); for this reason the newer revisions would be preferred if adequate norms are available. Crooks and Ferguson (1941) found the items less suitable for college students than for adults, in both validity and difficulty level.

Administration and Scoring. There are no subtests to time, no special directions to give during the examination. The time required is 20 or 30 minutes (see above). Scoring is by means of printed keys, and the score is the sum of the right answers.

Norms. The norms for the test are based on the distributions of scores for about 120,000 persons. Raw scores may be converted into Binet mental ages derived from a combination of Herring Binet scores and true mental ages as calculated from the distribution of raw scores by age groups. This correction of Otis' data was deemed necessary because of the selective nature of the high school groups used in standardizing the test.

Bingham (1937, p. 338) has pointed out that Otis' college median is lower than that obtained by the College Entrance Examination Board. That the Otis norms do not err greatly on the easy side is shown by the fact that the average freshman makes an Otis I. Q. equivalent on the A.C.E. Psychological Examination of 109. Otis' median college *student* I. Q. of 111 is equivalent to the 57th college *freshman* percentile on the A.C.E. norms, probably a little lower than it would be if the lower-ranking freshmen had been eliminated. Differences between colleges are great, so that local norms should be used in both counseling and selection; Otis' manual reports median I. Q.'s for twenty-one colleges which range from 95 to 123.

Factors Influencing Scores. Baxter (1941) administered the Otis to 48 college students and found that time and work-limit scores had an intercorrelation of .85, demonstrating that at that age level a *speed* score measures the quality of the work the subject can do. Evidence has also been reported by Blair and Kammam (1942) indicating that college students who read poorly, as shown by the Iowa Silent Reading Test, are not underrated by the Otis Test; this was ascertained by comparing their Otis scores with their Army Beta (non-verbal) Test scores, a comparison which is vitiated by the important common speed factor. Scores have a very low negative correlation (—.03 to —.30) with age in adulthood (Lefever, 1946).

Standardization and Initial Validation. Otis' manual gives unusually complete and detailed information concerning standardization and initial, but little on subsequent, validation. Many of the items in the tests were taken from existing instruments. Preliminary editions were tried out on high-school groups of about 1000 each. Items were retained if they distinguished clearly between superior young students and inferior older students in a given grade; the criterion of validity was therefore rapidity of school progress. This suggests that the test, being academically standardized, might not be a very valid one for non-academic purposes. Only occupational validation, and studies such as Hovland and Wonderlic's, can provide the answer. The age and grade norms are based on large samples from various sections of the United States, neither a random nor a stratified sample, but one large and varied enough so that to assume its adequacy seems sound: the number for grade six, for instance, is 15,715; for grade twelve it is 24,724; for college students, 2516 from 21 colleges. These norms are those provided since publication of the test, utilizing additional data supplied by other investigators. Strictly adult norms have not been published, despite widespread use at that age level.

Reliability. Forms A and B have an intercorrelation of .92. Reported reliability coefficients range from .90 to .97 with the 20-minute time limit (Copeland, 1936). A coefficient of .86 has been reported for adults with the 30-minute limit (Otis, 1922).

Validity. Otis suggested in his manual that the method of standardization is the best indication of validity in an intelligence test. This has already been described. He also attempted validation through correlation with various criteria such as tests and grades.

Correlations with grades in several high schools were .55, .57, and .59, the numbers in the samples ranging from 157 to 249. Segel (1934) summarized six studies with nine coefficients ranging from .20 to .43 with a median of .38, while Hartson (1941, 1945) found correlations with scholarship of .39 in high school and of .56 to .58 in college. Miller (1924) found a correlation of .69 with high school grades, and Turney and Fee (1933), in a junior high school study, reported that the Otis test was the most useful of five tried. The test clearly has a substantial relationship with educational achievement, one which varies as one might expect with the practices of the school, the marking systems of the teachers, and the range of ability and attitudes of pupils.

Correlations with other tests are as follows: the Otis had correlations of more than .70 with Army Alpha, the CAVD, and other tests (Otis, 1922); Otis-Terman Group and Otis-Binet coefficients equal about .55 and .50

(Miller, 1924; Otis, 1922), the Otis I. Q. being 6 to 8 points lower than that obtained on the 1916 Stanford-Binet (Cattell, 1931; Traxler, 1934). Otis I. Q.'s tend to differ from Binet I. Q.'s, especially at the higher extreme. These results are typical for this type of test; the Terman Group Test being anchored to the Binet is most like it, while the Otis, standardized without this base, is more closely correlated with group tests such as the Army Alpha. It is generally agreed that the use of the term I. Q. for converted Otis scores is not strictly justified. Otis pointed this out in his manual, but used the term I. Q. because it is the standard method of measuring brightness, cautioning users of the test always to specify "Otis I. Q." Despite the statistical impossibility of an adult I. Q., the chronological age factor in the ratio of MA to CA having ceased to change after mid-adolescence, it is often convenient for test users to think in terms of I. Q. equivalents.

Correlation with Success on the Job. This topic has been dealt with at some length earlier in this chapter in connection with intelligence as measured by various tests. A substantial number of the studies referred to in that section involved the use of the Otis Self-Administering Test which, together with Army Alpha in its various revisions, was probably the most widely used test in business and industry during the 1920's and 1930's, especially at the clerical, skilled, and semiskilled levels. In this section, therefore, only specific findings which may aid in the understanding and use of the Otis test will be mentioned.

Hay and his associates used the Otis in selecting bank clerks and calculating machine operators over a number of years at the Pennsylvania Company (Hay and Blakemore, 1942). There it was found desirable to use 36 as a critical minimum raw score for clerical workers, with a 20-minute time limit; this is equal to a 30-minute raw score of 46, and an I. Q. of 104. Correlation of Otis scores with the production of machine bookkeepers (Hay, 1943) yielded a coefficient of .56 (N equaled 39), a correlation which was substantiated by subsequent experience.

Shuman (1945, 1945a) has reported studies dealing with success in skilled employment. He studied supervisors and skilled workers such as toolmaker learners and job setters, correlating Otis scores with ratings by supervisors. The ratings had a reliability ranging from .70 to .91; the validity coefficients ranged from .39 to .57, increasing with the skill and degree of supervision exercised in the job. Critical scores were established for each supervisory job, the minimum ranging from a raw score of 30 to one of 33 for foremen on the Otis Quick-Scoring, the I. Q. equivalent being 88 to 91, whereas that for inspectors in the same plants was 51 (I. Q. equals 109). Shuman calculated that the use of the Otis test would have improved the selection of excellent skilled and supervisory workers by from 15 to 20 per cent. Sartain (1946) correlated Otis S.A. scores of groups of 40 foremen and 85 assistant foremen with supervisors' ratings, the reliability of which was as high as .79 or as low as .48 depending upon the comparison. The validity coefficients were .04 and .16; other tests were no better.

Studies of semiskilled jobs have been more numerous. Forlano and Kirkpatrick (1945) analyzed the Otis test scores of 20 radio tube mounters, whose work requires considerable finger and hand dexterity. Each worker was a new employee, tested upon application for work; each was rated "good" or "fair" by a supervisor after one month of employment. There were as many fair as good employees among the group making above average or average scores on the Otis (I. Q. 95 or above), but six out of the seven employees who made below average scores (I. Q. 94 or less) on the Otis were considered fair and only one was considered good. As the ratings were based on the induction and learning period, this suggests that in semiskilled work having more than the critical minimum of intelligence is desirable for rapid adjustment to the job, but that additional increments of ability are of little value. It will be remembered that this was the sole positive finding of Blum and Candee (1941, 1941a) in their study of the role of intelligence in another semiskilled job, packing and wrapping: in this instance there was no relationship between Otis scores and production or supervisors' ratings for regular employees (those who had passed the learning period) and no relationship between intelligence and production in seasonal employees (whose brief employment period makes them learners for most of their period of employment), but the supervisors' ratings of the latter group did show a slight tendency for the superior male workers to be more intelligent than the inferior male workers. The authors suggest that the failure to find a similar tendency among the women seasonal workers may be due to rating on a different basis. In a project of the Office of Scientific Research and Development, Satter (1946) found no relationship between Otis scores and submarine officers' ratings of enlisted men's performance.

The Wonderlic Personnel Test, a revision of the Otis, was administered to 769 applicants for ordnance factory work, together with other tests, by McMurry and Johnson (1945). The criterion of success in this study was supervisors' ratings of 587 employees still working when the follow-up was made. Although some of the tests did have rather high validity for some jobs, there were no significant correlations between intelligence and any of the ratings. Tiffin and Greenly (1939) administered the Otis to women electrical fixture and radio assembly workers, with similar results: although scores on other tests were positively correlated with production, there was no relationship ($.23 \pm .11$) between intelligence and production. As there was no analysis of the relationship during the learning period, it is impossible to draw any conclusions concerning the role of intelligence during induction into the job, but it is clear that, in these and in many other semiskilled jobs, intelligence is unrelated to success once the worker has made the initial adjustments.

Success in skilled and semiskilled jobs has been correlated with Otis scores in training situations by Paterson and associates (1930) and by Sartain (1945). The former worked with junior high school boys, using a variety of criteria, several of which were occupational rather than educational in nature. The Otis was administered, together with a variety of other tests, to 217 seventh and eighth grade boys; it was correlated with instructors' ratings of the quality of work done in producing standard samples or projects in mechanical drawing and sheetmetal courses, in addition to an over-all rating of the quality of their shop operations (N equalled 100 in this instance). These ratings were shown to have reliabilities of .87, .56, and .68, using the odd-even technique, and .93, .72, and .81 corrected by the Spearman-Brown formula. The correlations with Otis scores were, respectively, .25, .16 to .19, and .21; although not high enough for use in counseling individuals, their relationships were statistically significant and indicate that intelligence plays some part in shop operations.

Sartain's study (1945), unlike Paterson's, used adult subjects in an industrial situation, but unfortunately his criterion was more educational than vocational in nature, and a number of important details are not supplied. He gave the Otis and other tests to 46 employees of the inspection department of an aircraft factory who were taking a refresher course for inspectors. The sex and age of the employees are not described, although it is stated that many had considerable experience and some were relatively new in the department. No information is provided as to the type of inspection work done; failure of a given test to predict success in inspecting engine assemblies would, for example, mean something quite different from failure of a test to predict success in inspecting fuselages. The two instructors rated each employee independently, their agreement being indicated by the unusually high correlation of .77; when the subsequent merit ratings of 20 of these employees who were on the job a year later were averaged, the correlations between instructors' ratings and merit ratings was .42. This suggests that the immediate criterion was not only fairly reliable, but also related to job success, even though based on performance in a refresher course rather than on the job. The correlation between Otis scores and instructors' ratings was .64, higher than that for any other test except the MacQuarrie Test for Mechanical Ability; other mechanical aptitude tests yielded coefficients of from .24 to .47. In another study of three groups of foremen ($N=40$, 53, 85) the criterion was supervisors' ratings (reliability=.79) , but the validity of the Otis was only .04 to .16.

Differentiation between Occupations. Despite its widespread use with employed adults, no studies of intellectual differences between occupa-tions have been made with the Otis test. Shuman's study (1945a) estab-lished critical scores for certain jobs in one company, but these are of limited applicability. Presumably occupational differentiation has been so well established with other tests, from which conclusions may be drawn for the Otis, that it has not seemed worth while to make such investiga-tions. It would certainly be impractical to try to improve upon the sam-pling of the Army testing in both World Wars, defective though it is in some respects.

Job Satisfaction. No studies have been located in which Otis scores have been related to satisfaction either in the current job or in the usual occupation. The general paucity of work on this topic has already been discussed.

Use of the Otis Tests in Counseling and Selection. The evidence con-cerning the use of the Otis tests in educational counseling and selection clearly points to the conclusion that it is of value in estimating a given student's prospects of success in school or college. Although many other factors need to be taken into account, and although the relationship be-tween Otis scores and grades varies from school to school and from college to college, an individual's performance on such a test is one factor which should be known by that individual and by the counselor or admissions officer.

Concerning its value in vocational guidance and selection, the evidence is not so clear. But this is only to be expected, in view of the greater com-plexity of the occupational world and of the greater variety of demands made upon the worker by the various jobs in which he might engage. Despite this fact, it has proved possible to establish critical minimum Otis scores for employment in clerical, in skilled, and in semiskilled jobs, below which a disproportionately large number of workers fail and above which a reasonable proportion succeed; research with other tests indicates that this could also be done for executive and professional jobs.

It has also been demonstrated that, at least in some semiskilled jobs, the Otis is valuable in predicting the speed and ease with which the new worker will make his initial adjustments to the job demands.

Once the new worker has made the initial adjustment to a routine job, the Otis score has no value in predicting success either in terms of produc-tion or in terms of supervisory judgments. At least one exception to this generalization is provided by machine bookkeeping, in which the work is routine but mental as well as manual and demands great accuracy.

No other generalizations concerning the Otis tests and vocational adjustment are warranted by the research. However, certain other generalizations based on work with other intelligence tests which correlate reasonably well with the Otis are possible. These have been discussed with the supporting evidence earlier in this chapter.

Even if the results of studies of all intelligence tests and vocational adjustment are thus taken into account, there is a dearth of longitudinal studies of their predictive value in vocational guidance as contrasted with selection. The vocational counselor must rely largely upon deduction and generalization from validation studies in selection programs and from cross-sectional studies such as those of the Army intelligence test data, and upon cautious insights which use a thorough understanding of the available research as a springboard for establishing working hypotheses. More will be said on this subject in Chapter XX on the interpretation of test results.

The American Council on Education Psychological Examination (The American Council on Education). For a number of years the American Council on Education published each fall a new form of its Psychological Examination for College Freshmen, used by more than 300 colleges and universities. L.L. and T.G. Thurstone of the University of Chicago were responsible for the technical work on the tests, and the constant revision of forms which were used each year with thousands of entering college students resulted in a superior series. But the Educational Testing Service has now substituted in its place the Cooperative School and College Ability Test, a series of measures of scholastic aptitude at the lower as well as the college levels. Several forms of the A.C.E. continue to be available. For this reason, and because of its demonstrated usefulness in counseling and educational selection, the test is reviewed in the sections which follow.

Applicability. Designed for and standardized on entering college freshmen, the test may also be used with high school seniors, but studies by Barnes (1943) and Hunter (1942) concerning changes in scores with increasing age have demonstrated a need for caution in making comparisons of high school students, older college students, or adults with the normative group. In the latter investigation 87 of 105 college girls gained an average of 31 percentile points by their senior year, 75 percent of this change occurring during the first year. The fact that published norms are in terms of college freshmen has tended to limit the use of the tests to that group; no tables are yet available to make possible the accurate interpretation of scores made by high school juniors or by college graduates.

Contents. Various editions of the test have included five or six sections such as sentence completion, artificial language, same-opposites (vocabulary), arithmetic reasoning, analogies (symbols, spatial), and number series, all grouped more recently into two parts to give a quantitative (arithmetic and spatial) and a linguistic as well as a total score. The items are probably less affected by knowledge than those in most group tests, for the emphasis in selecting items was to choose those which measure ability to manipulate symbols rather than mastery of previously learned facts. Thus in the artificial language test the subject is given a new vocabulary into which he must make translations, and in the analogies test he must pick out similarities and differences in unfamiliar symbols and forms. As these tests and items have been selected and modified from earlier tests and tried out over a period of nearly twenty years on large numbers of subjects, with adequate funds for necessary research, they constitute an unusually valid and reliable instrument.

Administration and Scoring. Each subtest is preceded by a practice exercise, and both are closely timed. The test requires about one hour all told. Scoring is simple, machine-scoring methods being applied even in hand scoring.

Norms. Norms consist of percentiles for freshmen in liberal arts, teacher training, and junior colleges, a type of norm more helpful in the guidance of high school seniors planning further education than comparison with freshmen in colleges in general. The numbers in each group tend to be about 60,000, 12,000, and 12,000 respectively. College admissions officers use local norms for such tests as the A.C.E. in evaluating doubtful candidates for admission. The Thurstones have not supplied I. Q. equivalents because of the artificiality of adult mental ages; such equivalents are provided by the Educational Records Bureau and are helpful in interpreting A.C.E. scores in terms useful in generalizing from college to vocational competition.

In the absence of norms for specific institutions, the next best type would be norms for clearly defined and homogeneous groups of institutions. The classification of colleges into four-year, junior, teachers, and technical and professional colleges might seem at first glance to provide these, but as Crawford and Burnham (1946, p. 92-94) pointed out this is not the case. The four-year liberal arts colleges, for example, cover a range of scholastic aptitude which is almost as great as that of all four types of institutions (90 percent). They are, therefore, an extremely heterogeneous group; while the norms may be typical of colleges in general, the range is so great as not to be very helpful in counseling an individual about the choice of a specific institution. Crawford and Burnham point out that the average Yale freshman is at the 90th percentile on the general norms, and nearly 80 percent of these freshmen exceed the national 75th percentile. Norms should be provided for various classes of liberal arts colleges, adequately defined, or, as is now done for the College Board's Scholastic Aptitude Test, for specific colleges.

Studies of sex differences reveal negligible differences in total scores, but indicate masculine superiority in quantitative parts and feminine superiority in linguistic parts (Thurstone et al., 1939). This checks with data on interests reported by workers with Strong's interest inventory.

Factors Influencing Scores. Smith (1943) reported finding higher scores among urban than among rural students, as have other studies of urban-rural differences. Whether this is primarily the long-term result of selective migration or the effect of environment and urban-constructed tests is still a question. Barnes (1943a) found that two years of college mathematics had no appreciable effect on the Q scores of an experimental group of 40 students, when compared with 75 controls who had equal Q scores as entering freshmen but took no college work in mathematics.

Standardization and Initial Validation. New forms of the A.C.E. tests were constructed so as to resemble earlier forms, although there were differences in details, and innovations were gradually introduced as new types of items were tried and adopted. Each new form was thus based on extensive previous work which proved its validity; in addition, it was administered for tentative standardization to 1000 or more students who have also taken the preceding form. The scores of some 60,000 college freshmen who took the test each fall provided final norms. Studies have occasionally been made to determine the academic predictive value of the examination and to establish its reliability. The assumption was usually made, however, that since the new edition was anchored to the preceding editions and had similar norms it would be approximately as reliable and valid as they. A report was published each year in the *American Council on Education Studies,* giving data on the form published the preceding fall.

Reliability. The reliability of the A.C.E. tests has been consistently high. One study by the test authors reported odd-even reliabilities of .95 for the total score, and of .87 and .95 for the Q and L scores respectively, for the 1938 college edition (Thurstone et al., 1939). Votaw (1946) found a correlation of .74 between Otis scores in 7th grade and A.C.E. scores six years later ($N=70$).

Validity. It is generally accepted that one indication of the validity of an intelligence test is the carefulness of its standardization. The care used in this series of tests is illustrated by subtest intercorrelations for the 1938 form which range from .30 to .65 with a median of .39 in an attempt to measure relatively distinct components of intelligence (Thurstone et al., 1939). The high reliability of part scores mentioned above is another illustration. Another illustration is provided by the specific college norms reported by the authors and by Traxler (1940) who converted A.C.E. scores to I. Q. equivalents and ascertained the median I. Q.'s of the freshmen in 323 colleges. These ranged from 126 in a private liberal arts college to 87 in one junior college. The median for liberal arts colleges was about 110, for teachers and junior colleges it was about 107. Schneidler and Berdie (1942) have reviewed similar data. As has been shown in numerous earlier studies, there is a college for almost every I. Q. level. It is regrettable that they cannot be identified by professional counselors.

Correlation with Other Tests. The A.C.E. test has frequently been correlated with other intelligence tests. With the 1916 Binet a correlation of .69 (Kohn, 1938) has been reported, while for the 1937 Revision it is .58, .62 (Anderson et al., 1942) and .67 (Manuel et al., 1940). With the Otis S.A. Higher Form, coefficients of .78 and .82 were found by Traxler (1945). Hildreth found that the A.C.E. gave approximately the same percentile ranks in the senior year of high school as the Binet had given previously to the same children in elementary school (1939). Anderson and others (1942) reported correlations of .48 and .53 between two different forms and the Wechsler-Bellevue; the two verbal scales are about as closely related (.49, .51), but the performance and quantitative scales have less relationship (.31, .39), a fact needing further investigation to make it clear just what types of concrete mental ability each of these scales measures. Certainly it would be dangerous to interpret Wechsler-Bellevue performance I. Q.'s in terms of the validity of A.C.E. Q-scores, or vice-versa.

The use of performance or quantitative scores in educational and vocational guidance is in any case still largely hypothetical, although in some selection programs specific evidence has been collected which makes possible the use of part scores. Super (1940) administered the 1938 college edition of the A.C.E. to 123 high school juniors and seniors, together with the Nelson-Denny Reading Test, the Minnesota Vocational Test for Clerical Workers, and the Co-operative Survey Test in Mathematics. The results, shown in Table 7, indicate that A.C.E. linguistic scores are more closely related to reading ability than are either quantitative or total scores; that linguistic scores predict achievement in mathematics as well as do quantitative scores; that linguistic scores are more closely related to name-checking scores than are quantitative, but that they are equally related (or unrelated) to number-checking scores. Traxler (1943) found *r*'s of .26 between Bennett Mechanical Comprehension scores and Q scores and of .34 between the same test and L scores. Apparently the latter are a better measure of general ability than the former, and neither is a superior measure of special aptitudes. It will be seen later that there is some evidence to support the belief that quantitative and linguistic scores have differential predictive value for college courses, but the evidence is conflicting, and data such as those just presented suggest that they are actually comparable in predictive value except for the closer relationship of linguistic scores and reading ability.

TABLE 7

RELATIONSHIP OF A.C.E. PART-SCORES TO OTHER ABILITIES
$(N = 123)$

A.C.E.	Reading	Mathe-matics	Name-Checking	Number-Checking	T	Q	L
Total	.66	.65	.62	.26	—	.75	.92
Q	.37	.56	.41	.18	.75	—	—
L	.80	.56	.58	.22	.92	.47	—

Bryan (1942) and Estes (1942) have reported correlations of .05 to .36 and .45 between Q scores and the Minnesota Paper Form Board (Revised). In the former study, the spatial subtests correlated .55 with the Paper Form Board. This is a lower correlation than is generally found between intelligence tests and the Paper Form Board, perhaps because of the homogeneous population.

A totally different line of investigation was opened up by Munroe in a study of the relationship between A.C.E. scores and Rorschach indices (1946). She administered both tests to 80 students at Sarah Lawrence College and ascertained the difference between the Q and L percentiles for each girl. These difference scores were distributed, and the top and bottom quartiles were selected for further study. This gave Munroe one group of "higher L's" and one of higher "Q's." The Rorschach patterns of each of these groups were then analyzed and contrasted, with the following conclusions:

There were no differences in general adjustment as measured by the Rorschach Inspection Technique;

There were no differences in the number of responses nor in the number of words in the protocols of the two groups;

The *higher* Q's gave a significantly larger percentage of responses in which form was the determinant;

The *higher* L's gave significantly more movement responses.

The personality picture obtained from the above data, which has received support in a study by Pemberton (1951), is one of a subjective, imaginative, *higher* L syndrome, and a more objective, literal, outer-reality-bound *higher* Q syndrome. The latter type (if persons at the extreme of a continuum may be called that) resembles that found in paleontologists by Roe (1946) and described in Chapter XVIII. In pointing this fact out, Roe also states that the *higher* Q's were found to choose more scientific courses than the *higher* L's. Di Vesta's (1954) research pursued this line of investigation one step further by relating *higher* L and *higher* Q patterns to educational and occupational differences. The criteria used in a sample of 418 Air Force officers (average age = 32 years) were the following: the rating of the officer (flying or ground) ; service status (regular or reserve) ; career field; and college major. The results indicated that pilots tend to make *higher Q* scores whereas non-pilots tend toward *higher L*; officers in maintenance and comptroller jobs obtained *higher L* scores; reservists and regulars cannot be differentiated; and, officers with college majors in the arts and sciences had *higher L* scores as compared to the *higher Q* scores of those who majored in engineering and business administration. Contrary to the findings of Munroe and Roe, higher Q scores were not found characteristic of science majors. If these findings for engineers (and Munroe's and Roe's for scientists) are confirmed by other studies it would seem that differences in quantitative and linguistic scores may be indicative of differences in the utilization of intelligence arising from differences in personality, as well as, or perhaps even rather than, differences in primary mental abilities. Such a radical conclusion would be compatible with the findings that Q and L scores are not differentially related to success in quantitative and linguistic subjects, but are related to the choice of some types of curricula.

Correlation with Grades. The relationship with achievement has been most intensively studied, academic prediction being the purpose of the test. Studies from various earlier editions yielded validity coefficients ranging from .17 to .81 for grade-point averages (Gerberich, 1931) and from .34 to .60 with freshmen marks, and correlations of .43 to .54 (Gerberich, 1931; Laycock and Hutcheon, 1939; McGehee, 1938; Rigg, 1939; Segel and Profitt, 1937) with long-term averages. Subsequent studies reported correlations of .39 to .60 with grades in various colleges (Anderson et al., 1942; McGehee, 1943; Munroe, 1946; Fredericksen and Schrader, 1952) the mode being about .55. Modal correlations with first semester grades are about .45 for engineers and .50 for art students. For grades over four years the correlations are about .45.

Weintraub and Salley (1945) found that, at Hunter College, 14 percent of the upper half of a freshman class of 1064 students were dropped for poor scholarship over the four-year course, as contrasted with 24 percent in the lower half on the A.C.E. The range of intelligence in this group was of course limited.

At the University of Chicago (Thurstone et al., 1939) correlations with introductory biology marks ranged from .43 to .47; humanities, .46 to .53; physical science, .39 to .46; social science, .46 to .51 ($N=200$ to 2000). Slightly (2 to 6 pts.) higher results were reported by Shanner and Kuder (1941). The correlation with marks for students of agriculture in another institution was .49; engineering, .45; general, .49 (Mosier, 1935). This appears contrary to the suggestion of some that the test should be more valid in liberal arts than in other colleges.

Part-scores have been related to achievement in specific subjects and fields by several investigators. Segel and Gerberich (1933) correlated part-scores with marks in English, foreign languages, and mathematics, with the results shown in the left-hand column of each pair in Table 8. Co-efficients for variables which should theoretically be highly correlated are shown in italics.

Part scores were correlated with Iowa Placement Test scores in the

TABLE 8

CORRELATION BETWEEN A.C.E. PART-SCORES AND ACHIEVEMENT

A.C.E.	English Marks	Test	Foreign Languages Marks	Test	Mathematics Marks	Test
Completion	.41	.44	.19	.55	.33	.31
Art. Lang.	.54	.65	.38	.75	.43	.38
Analogies	.38	.38	.26	.44	.31	.41
Arithmetic	.20	.28	.14	.38	.38	.62
Same-Opposites	.51	.52	.32	.70	.36	.35

same subjects. The results appear in the right hand member of each pair of columns in Table 8. The discrepancies would be surprising were it not for the unreliability of marks; nevertheless, patterns of ability and achievement seem to exist, the verbal tests being more closely related to the verbal subjects, the quantitative tests (in one case) to the quantitative subjects. Similar curricular relationships were later found at the University of Florida (Mosier, 1935). Work such as this, combined with Thurstone's factor analysis (Thurstone et al., 1939), led to the use of Q and L scores in more recent editions. Evidence which indicates a need for caution (Super, 1940) shows that whereas the total scores on the A.C.E. test correlate .65 with the Co-operative Survey Test of Mathematics, both the Q and L scores correlate .56 with the same test, Q scores giving a prediction of achievement in mathematics in no way superior to that yielded by L scores. On the other hand, while the total score has a correlation of .66 with the Nelson-Denny Reading Test, that for Q is .37 and that for L is .80, indicating a genuine difference in Q and L scores. Generally similar results have been obtained by four other investigators using grades as criteria (Anderson et al., 1942; Barnes, 1943; MacPhail, 1942; Stopher, 1941). MacPhail's study involved analyses of data at both secondary and collegiate levels; the latter were treated in terms of both curriculum and courses. Representative data from two of his tables are reproduced in Table 9.

Of the courses for which data are not reproduced here, only psychology among the "quantitative" subjects showed a possibly significant difference between the correlations, and that was in favor of the L score; there were no significant differences among the other "linguistic" courses. MacPhail's conclusion is that data of this type must be obtained by each institution if it wishes to use Q and L scores for selection and guidance; certainly any blanket use of such scores in counseling is now unwarranted, and, if one

TABLE 9

CORRELATION OF GRADES IN QUANTITATIVE AND LINGUISTIC COURSES WITH Q AND L
SCORES ON THE A.C.E., AFTER MACPHAIL.

N	Courses (Quantit.)	Q	L	C.R.	N	Courses (Linguistic)	Q	L	C.R.
49	Descriptive Geom.	.39	.13	2.10	95	French (Intermed.)	−.02	.45	5.26
64	Chemistry (Elem.)	.665	.50	2.06	53	German (Elem.)	.13	.20	0.54
31	Chemistry (Qual. An.)	.19	.01	1.09	27	History (U.S.)	.14	.50	2.24
82	Mathematics (Trig., Cal.)	.31	.21	0.98	48	History (Europe)	.38	.44	0.49

were to generalize from his study (as adequate as any now available), it would be to the effect that L scores are as satisfactory as Q scores for predicting success in mathematical and scientific courses, and perhaps slightly more satisfactory for predicting achievement in some linguistic and verbal courses.

Estes (1942) correlated A.C.E. scores with grades in analytic geometry for 76 engineering freshmen with the following results: r between Q and grades$=.33$, r between L and grades$=.15$. This agrees with MacPhail's findings. Bryan (1942) found correlations between A.C.E. scores and art grades varying from .02 to .37 for various types of art students ($N=1008$), those for the quantitative parts tending to be slightly lower than those for the verbal, but the trends are not significant.

Part scores on tests such as this presumably measure constellations of primary abilities, as Thurstone has shown. These *may* be related to achievement in special fields as reported by some investigators, but it is obvious that more clear-cut evidence is needed before A.C.E. Q and L scores are relied on in differential prediction or counseling.

Correlation with Success on the Job. It is regrettable, in view of its excellent construction, widespread use and the extensive information on hand concerning it, that the A.C.E. test has not been adequately validated for vocational guidance and selection at the business and professional levels. There are practically no validation studies of this test using strictly vocational criteria, although several studies have shown that its total scores are related to success in some types of professional training, e.g., engineering (McGehee, 1943), and, in some institutions, nursing (Rainier, 1942). Seagoe (1945) found that well-adjusted student-teachers, and maladjusted student-teachers of average or low intelligence in one college, tended to remain in training, whereas the bright but maladjusted students dropped out—perhaps because they recognized the misfit and saw other more appropriate opportunities. Ratings of success in practice teaching did not correlate significantly with A.C.E. scores. Rolfe (1945) found no relationship ($r = -.10$) between A.C.E. scores and the teaching success of 52 Wisconsin one- and two-room school teachers, the criterion being tested pupil progress. Rostker (1945), however, applying similar techniques to 28 teachers of 375 seventh and eighth grade pupils found a correlation of .57. Perhaps teaching in larger schools is a more intellectual activity. Low positive (.10 to .28) but significant correlations with grade point ratio were obtained by Borg (1950) for 427 men and women art students. Bransford and others (1946) found a correlation of .64 between A.C.E. scores and ratings of the administrative effectiveness of 20 civil servants at the top management level. These findings suggest that intelligence as measured by the A.C.E. plays a part in the intellectual aspects of some vocations, including those important in training, but that in other occupations, whether in training or in practice, other factors are more important.

Differentiation between Occupations. Two studies have found the usual relationship between parental occupation and student intelligence. Byrns and Henmon (1936) found significant differences between adjacent occupational levels, except the business and clerical and the skilled and semiskilled. Smith's study (1942), based on 5487 students, found similar differences.

Job Satisfaction. No studies with this test have been located which bear, directly or indirectly, on job satisfaction although Berdie (1944) showed that A.C.E. scores were not related to satisfaction with training in engineering.

Use of the A.C.E. Psychological Examination in Counseling and Selection. This review of the A.C.E. Psychological Examination shows that it has been studied in most of the ways in which other tests have been tried, although rarely in investigations of vocational adjustment. There is probably more material concerning its educational significance than there is for any other single test. It is a reliable and valid test of scholastic aptitude or general intelligence at the college level. The test goes beyond this, however, in attempting to break down the concept of "general intelligence" by providing part-scores for what logical and statistical analysis indicate may be special aspects of intelligence. As Thurstone (1939) has shown in a factor analysis of the 1938 edition, these aspects of intelligence are not primary abilities or factors, but constellations of related factors. This breakdown is thus a compromise attempt to take advantage of the findings of factor analysis and yet to provide a practical measure for administrative and guidance use. It is promising because it represents a step in advance in group testing technique without departing so far from proved techniques as to make it a purely research instrument, but its part-scores are still of limited value in appraisal and prediction.

The freshman college norms were until recently the most adequate available. It is unfortunate that the same forms are not standardized at other educational and age levels, and that its vocational significance is not better established (deficiencies which will hopefully be corrected by the SCAT). However, the high correlation with other intelligence tests, together with the equivalent scores which have been made available, make it possible cautiously to use occupational and educational norms established for other tests. It should be remembered in so doing that Otis I. Q.'s are not the same as Binet I. Q.'s because of different methods of calculation, that I. Q.'s are artificial equivalents and not true ratios of mental to chronological age at older adolescent and adult levels, and that equivalent scores are based on averages and may therefore be distorted in extreme cases.

The Cooperative School and College Ability Tests (Educational Testing Service, 1955). These tests are the successors to the American Council on Education Psychological Examinations. Developed through the cooperation of an advisory board of educators and psychologists, and based in large part upon their recommendations, the SCAT series was designed "to aid in estimating the capacity of a student to undertake the next higher level of schooling." In contrast to the A.C.E., which supposedly measured more abstract and special scholastic aptitudes, the SCAT was constructed to assess "school-learned abilities," such as reading skills and proficiencies in arithmetic computation and problem-solving. This change in emphasis was recommended by the Advisory Committee on the development of the SCAT for three reasons: first, the best single predictor of future academic performance is past achievement; second, verbal and quantitative skills which are acquired in school are prerequisites for advancement to the higher grade levels; and, third, scores based upon measures of these abilities, rather than tests of general intelligence or mental ability, are more easily interpreted to and discussed with students and parents because they relate directly to school subjects. Supposedly, then, the SCAT is more a measure of skill or proficiency, whereas the A.C.E. was predominantly a measure of aptitude or capacity to learn.

The item content of the SCAT does not clearly reflect this distinction between the measurement of past achievement and the evaluation of aptitude to learn, for the test content is similar to that of other academic intelligence tests. Each form of the test at the various grade levels contains four subtests which measure different kinds of school-learned abilities traditionally used to assess capacity to learn: sentence completion, in which the task is to select one of five words that best fits the meaning of the sentence; vocabulary, in which knowledge of word meanings is tested by the selection of synonyms; arithmetic computation, in which numerical calculations involving addition, subtraction, multiplication, and division are made; and, numerical reasoning, in which problems involving quantities are solved. Perhaps the term "developed abilities" is overworked in an attempt to avoid the problems of overemphasis on the innate basis of intelligence at the expense of cultural contributions. These tests, which yield verbal, quantitative, and total scores based upon 60, 50, and 110 items respectively, were chosen from a larger experimental battery which was administered in the initial standardization. There were nine tests in this group, which included measures of resourceful computation, reading comprehension, sentence completion, analogies, routine computation, data sufficiency, vocabulary, mixed computation, and arithmetic reasoning. To identify the best combination of four of these tests they were correlated with total grade averages and senior year English grades in samples ranging in number from 113 to 404, each of which represented a different level of "per pupil investment in education by the community."

The validity coefficients with the grade criterion indicated that the optimum set of predictors was comprised of sentence completion, routine computation, mixed computation, and analogies. For the latter two tests, however, substitutions were made in the final battery: arithmetic reasoning replaced mixed computation, because it provided greater variety of item content with only minimal loss of validity; and vocabulary replaced analogies for essentially the same reason, although it was also thought that a word meaning test, which has more items per unit of testing time, is more reliable than a word reasoning test. This may or may not be so, since the Verbal Reasoning sub-test of the DAT, which is quite similar to analogies tests, has high reliability. Inclusion of the vocabulary test seems better justified on other grounds: it is a good measure of general intelligence as well as a required scholastic skill; and it provides greater range in the battery as a whole, since analogies items measure much the same reasoning functions as arithmetic problem-solving tasks.

After the four item types—sentence completion, vocabulary, arithmetic computation, and numerical reasoning—were selected, they were pretested at a number of grade levels to determine the relative difficulty of items for students in adjacent grades and to evaluate the validity of the items in discriminating between high and low scoring students. This preliminary work yielded data which were used in the construction of alternate forms of the SCAT for five different grade levels: grades four, five, and six; junior and senior high school; college freshmen; and college sophomores. Administration of the SCAT follows standard procedures for other paper-and-pencil ability tests with the possible exception that the tests are not highly speeded. They require approximately 70 minutes of actual testing time in addition to the reading of instructions, etc. Extensive grade norms based upon school and college testing in a number of states during the fall of 1956, and instructions and tables for construction of local norms, are published in the Manual, along with school mean norms by grade, which are useful to school administrators in the evaluation of grade and school differences. The adequacy of the college norms may be an issue: these norms are based upon only 12 students per class (freshman and sophomore) in each of 100 colleges. The logic of this variation from usual norming methods is that the reliability of norms depends upon the number of schools sampled rather than the number of students tested. If this is true, it is difficult to understand why the procedure was used only at the college level and not at the lower educational levels, where the traditional, large-sample type norms were constructed. The Manual provides no answer to this apparent contradiction in establishing norms for the SCAT.

Although alternate forms for SCAT are available, only split-half reliability coefficients are reported in the Manual, and, consequently, they are estimates of internal consistency rather than stability of scores over periods of time. For large samples ($N=612$ to 2880) of subjects in grades five, seven, nine, eleven, and thirteen the trend of the reliabilities was in the low 90's, with only a few exceptions. When the coefficients were less than .90, they were for the Quantitative score; at the fifth and ninth grade levels they were .88 and .89, respectively. These are quite adequate for individual prediction, but, as the Manual notes, they are based upon large N's from a number of schools; within one school the reliabiliites are lower, but not significantly so, since they are only from .01 to .03 less than the average for the complete grade groups. Standard errors of measurement ranged from 2.71 to 4.34 for the two part and total SCAT scores, indicating that the precision with which the abilities are measured is fairly high. Nevertheless, in recognition of the unreliability of the tests, the Manual lists percentile rank *intervals,* rather than points, for the interpretation of scores. These percentile bands provide a more accurate estimate of the range within which an individual's true score falls and hence increase the confidence which can be placed in a person's standing relative to the norm group.

The *validity* of the SCAT is restricted to the educational setting as yet, since its relationship to criteria of vocational success has not been determined. Estimated correlations between SCAT and A.C.E., at both the high school and college levels, based upon scores derived from the DAAQ (a half-length form of SCAT), ranged from .75 to .89, which is only slightly less than the reliabilities of the various tests.

The Army General Classification Test (The Adjutant General's Office, War Department, 1940; Science Research Associates, 1947). This test was devised by the Adjutant General's Office when Selective Service was adopted in 1940, as a substitute for the widely used Army Alpha of World War I. The two original forms designated by the Army as AGCT-1a and AGCT-1b were used from October 1940 and April 1941, respectively, to October 1941. The two final forms, AGCT-1c and AGCT-1d, were equated with the first two and were used in the testing of all men and women who were inducted into the Army between October 1941 and April 1945. AGCT-1 was administered to a total of well over 9,000,000 persons. It was so widely used that more than 4000 persons were tested daily. With the introduction of a completely revised classification test, based on more modern principles of intelligence test construction and yielding separate scores for verbal, numerical, and spatial aptitudes, forms 1c and 1d became obsolete. The large number of men and women who had been tested with these forms, and the vast amount of educational and occupational validation data which had been accumulated for them, made them unique in the history of psychological or vocational testing. Two forms were therefore released for civilian use, the first civilian edition appearing as forms AH (hand scored) and AM (machine scored). This, it should be noted, is AGCT-1a, which is a little used Army form, predecessor of the widely used forms, 1c and 1d.

Applicability. The AGCT was designed for use with draftees, that is, with young men between the ages of 18 and 36, with widely varying amounts and types of education and with even greater differences in general cultural background. In order to make the test applicable to this group, an attempt was made to avoid items which might be greatly influenced by schooling beyond the first few grades and by other cultural inequalities. Information items were not used. Instead, vocabulary, everyday arithmetic, and spatial items were included. A special effort was made to make the items seem sensible to young men from all walks of life. The data on distributions of test scores, for example the occupational norms, indicate that the objective of getting a wide-range intelligence test of reasonable brevity was achieved. It was used also with young women who volunteered for the Army, and the data on such groups give no reasons for questioning its applicability to women. Observation of the use of the test with both men and women suggests that they find the types of items acceptable, although the block-counting sections apparently make a special impression; the test is often referred to by examinees as "that test with block counting in it."

As military experience showed that young men and women with widely varying amounts of education seemed to be able to manage this test, it can be used also in the last years of high school. However, no objective evidence on this point has as yet been published. Its use with older people might be questioned, for although the correlation with age in a representative enlisted population was only .02, it was —.33 and —.20 for two groups of officers which included many men who were older than most draftees (Staff, Personnel Research Section, A.G.O., 1945, 1947). As pointed out in the official report, this is probably due to the influence of the speed factor, although an attempt had been made to minimize that by a time limit in which all examinees could, if not finish, at least show their power.

Content. The test consists of three parts: vocabulary, arithmetic problems, and block counting. Three practice parts introduce the test to insure familiarity with the procedure. A sample vocabulary item is "To permit is to, a) demand, b) thank, c) allow, d) charge." The arithmetic problems involve real life situations, such as dividing rounds of ammunition among a group of men, finding out how many more cows one man has than his neighbor, and computing the amount of money each man on a baseball team would have to contribute in order to supplement the club's treasury in buying uniforms. The block-counting items are of the familiar type, like those used in the MacQuarrie.

There are 30 practice items in the civilian edition, and 150 test items, in contrast with 10 practice items and 140 test items in Army editions 1c and 1d. The manual does not indicate which Army form was used, but it is one of the older forms, Form 1a (letter from John Yale of Science Research Associates, dated April 14, 1948). AGCT-1a was standardized on 2675 men aged 20–29. Form 1b was standardized on 3856 men who also took Form 1a, in 1941. The correlation between scores on the two tests was found to be .95, and their means and standard deviations were practically identical. Forms 1c and 1d were prepared immediately after 1b, administered to 1782 men, and compared with 1a. The two new forms were found to be somewhat more difficult than 1a, and somewhat more discriminating in the upper ranges (Staff, Personnel Research Section, AGO, 1945, p. 763); no comparisons were made with form 1b, but presumably the same would be true of it.

Administration and Scoring. The testing time is 40 minutes. Directions in each booklet are complete, making the test self-administering. The civilian edition uses the step-back format, in which each page is slightly narrower than the one before it and the answers are recorded on successively exposed columns of the answer sheet. This has the great advantage of making a manageable booklet and answer sheet and of minimizing recording errors. The hand-scored form provides the examinee with a pin with which to prick holes in the answer sheet instead of marking it. The holes which appear in marked areas of the back of the answer sheet are counted and indicate the number of right answers. Scoring takes only about one minute per test. Raw scores are converted into standard scores known as Army standard scores, for which the mean was intended to be 100 and the standard deviation 20. These can also be converted into percentiles, a table in the manual being provided for this purpose.

Norms. As the extensive Army norms are for AGCT-1c and 1d (more than 8,000,000 men), it is to be regretted that the civilian form is one of the preliminary editions. As they are very similar, even though not identical, it may be safe to use the general norms.

The manual provides a table for the conversion of raw scores into Army standard scores and percentiles. There is no indication as to what size or type of group this table is based on. It is military, but whether or not it is the standardization group for the same form, or a much larger group tested with equated forms, is uncertain. A sentence elsewhere in the manual indicates that it is based on 160,000 (undescribed) inductees. The mean raw score of the standardization group used with Form 1a was 78, which gives a standard score of 102 and a percentile of 45 according to the manual; the percentile would be the 50th if the standardization group were the norm group. As the manual's norms are for a larger number of persons than were tested with this form, data from other forms which had been calibrated with this one must have been used. Such matters should be made clear in the manual or in accompanying publications.

Occupational norms, in the form of bars representing the middle 50 and 80 percents of each of 120-odd occupations, are also included in the manual. Again, it is not clear what forms of the test were administered to these groups. If 1c and 1d were used, the norms may not be strictly applicable to the civilian form (AGCT-1a), which was found to be easier and less discriminating at the upper levels. Persons of average or high-average ability would seem more able to compete in executive and professional work than they actually are. The means in the manual's occupational norms are almost identical with those of the longer list of occupations covered by Stewart's analysis (1947), but the numbers of cases are in some instances smaller, and in some larger, than hers.

Standardization. The standardization of the various forms of the AGCT has been described in readily available journals by the staff which developed it (Staff, Personnel Research Section, AGO, 1945, 1947) and need not be repeated here. Steps which should be noted include the fact that a large item-pool was developed, and the seemingly most appropriate items were selected from it; each successive form was equated with the previous forms (but as noted previously 1a and 1b were somewhat easier than 1c and 1d); the estimated mean of the first form proved to be too low, so that when the calibrated scores of later forms were standardized the actual mean standard score was between 100 and 110 rather than 100, one sample of more than 91,000 men having a mean of 105 (Stewart, 1947, p. 34).

The *reliability* of the various forms was ascertained, the retest reliability with varying intervals between tests being .82, the alternate-form reliability between .89 and .95, the Kuder-Richardson reliability between .94 and .97, and the corrected odd-even reliability .97 (Staff, Personnel Research Section, AGO, 1945, p. 765). These are quite satisfactory.

Validity.   As the AGCT was devised as a measure of learning ability and routinely administered to all enlisted men and women in the Army, it was used as a predictor of success in training for many types of specialties. But it was also possible to relate scores on this test to certain criteria from the previous civilian experience of the persons tested, such as the amount of education they had obtained (it having been well established by other studies that brighter people tend to get more education) and civilian occupation (it has been seen that occupations can be ranked according to their intellectual requirements).

Education, as measured by the highest grade attained, was correlated with the AGCT scores of 4330 men, the coefficient being .73. This may be unduly high, because socio-economic status is correlated with each of these variables, but it is an indication that the test has some of the validity which has generally characterized good intelligence tests.

Tests of intelligence which have been correlated with the AGCT include Army Alpha, Otis S. A., and the American Council on Education Psychological Examination. The most representative populations for which such data have been published ranged in numbers from 750 to 1646. The correlations were .90 for Army Alpha, .83 for the Otis, and .79 for the A.C.E.

Other tests with which the AGCT has been correlated include those used in the selection of aviation cadets (DuBois, 1947); see Table 10. The correlation with a test of *reading comprehensions* was .53, *mechanical comprehension* .32, and *mathematics* .45. The correlations with tests of *manual dexterity, co-ordination,* and similar capacities were generally below .20. These data were obtained from a group of more than 1000 unselected applicants for cadet training.

Success in training was the most commonly used criterion for the validation of the AGCT. A summary of such results was compiled by the Staff of the Personnel Research Section of the Adjutant General's Office (1945), and is reproduced here with additional data from DuBois (1947). The means and sigmas of the various military training groups are given, together with the correlations with the criteria. As the authors point out, preselection of students, sometimes on the basis of this test, makes the relationship seem lower than it actually is, in some instances, whereas in others the true relationship is shown. Motor mechanics, for example, were not preselected, and r equalled .69; teletype maintenance students were preselected, and in their case r equalled .20. It would be necessary to sort these data into at least two groups, according to whether or not they had been preselected, in order to generalize concerning the types of training in which the test best predicted success. Even then, it would be necessary to be cautious, because of the presumably academic nature of much of the training, even for specialties which were very concrete and practical. The example of Navy aerial gunnery training has already been cited as evidence of the fact that intelligence tests sometimes predict success in training because the training is unnecessarily abstract, and that when the training is made more life-like intelligence tests lose their predictive value.

It is worthy of note, as the AGO authors pointed out, that the correlations between AGCT and grades in Army Specialized Training (college courses) and also in most West Point courses, tend to be low. They range from .12 to .40. The authors point out that this is no doubt partly due to the extreme preselection which had taken place in both programs. Despite this, however, the correlations with grades in English and Mathematics at West Point were .40 and .43. Another reason for the poorer predictions in specialized training lies in the fact that a substantial number of men were sent to training in which they had little genuine interest, either because they thought it would be a pleasant type of assignment or because quotas had to be filled. With motivation undermined in this latter way, the correlation between ability and grades would be definitely lowered. Some confirmation of this reasoning is provided by Chappell (1955) in a study of college students; correlations between the AGCT and grades were generally higher than those reported above, ranging from .36 to .47.

The value of the AGCT as a predictor of success in pilot training can be ascertained by comparing it with the tests of the Aviation Cadet Selection program. It is obviously not relevant to compare it with tests of special aptitude, interest, or temperament, but it may legitimately be compared with the general qualifying examination administered to applicants for preliminary screening, in order to ascertain the relative value of general intelligence tests and of custom-built tests of ability to adapt to the learning requirements of a specific training program. Table 10 has shown that in the experimental group of more than 1000 cadets sent to pilot training regardless of test scores the AGCT had a validity of .31 with a pass-fail criterion. For this same group, with the same criterion, a test of learning ability designed with flying training specifically in mind had a validity of .50 (DuBois, 1947, p. 191). The pilot stanine (weighted combination of special aptitude test scores) had a validity of .66. Obviously, although the general intelligence test had some value for predicting success in pilot training, it did not measure certain factors which were of considerable importance and which were tapped by the more specialized tests.

TABLE 10

VALIDITY COEFFICIENTS OF THE AGCT

Population	Criterion	N	Mean	SD	r
Administrative Clerical Trainees, AAF	Grades	2947	121.7	11.1	.40
Clerical Trainees, AAF	Grades (weighted)	123	125.9	9.9	.44
Clerical Trainees, Armored	Grades	119	125.3	8.3	.33
Clerical Trainees, WAAC	Grades	199	116.8	12.0	.62
Airplane Mechanic Trainees	Grades	99	104.8	10.6	.32
Airplane Mechanic Trainees	Grades	3081	118.1	10.7	.35
Motor Mechanic Trainees	Grades	318	88.3	24.4	.69
Tank Mechanic Trainees	Grades	237	116.6	11.3	.33
Aircraft Armorer Trainees	Grades	1907	117.3	10.9	.40
Aircraft Armorer Trainees	Ratings	449	112.7	12.1	.27
Aircraft Welding Trainees	Grades	583	114.8	10.3	.26
Bombsight Maintenance Trainees	Grades	195	129.1	10.5	.31
Sheetmetal Trainees, AAF	Grades	764	115.6	10.3	.27
Teletype Maintenance Trainees, AAF	Grades	487	123.5	12.1	.20
Radio Operator & Mechanic Trainees, AAF	Grades	1055	122.4	11.1	.32
Radio Operator & Mechanic Trainees, AAF	Code Rcg. Speed, WPM	217	117.4	11.7	.24
Radio Operator Trainees, WAAC	Grades	152	116.2	11.7	.38
Radio Mechanic Trainees, AAF	Grades	419	108.0	13.0	.49
Gunnery Trainees, Armored	Grades	66	120.0	12.1	.50
Field Artillery Trainees, Instrument and Survey	Grades	68	102.7	6.5	.33
Motor Transport Trainees, WAAC	Grades	269	111.4	13.6	.31
Tank Driver Trainees	Ratings	330	87.7	19.5	.16
Truck Driver Trainees	Road Test Ratings	421	95.5	20.1	.13
Bombardier Trainees, AAF	Grades, Academic	40	111.5	18.6	.62
Aircraft Warning Trainees, Plotter-Teller	Grades, Theory	119	107.1	15.6	.73
Aircraft Warning Trainees, Plotter-Teller	Grades, Performance	119	107.1	15.6	.26
Intelligence Trainees, AAF	Grades, Academic	104	118.9	10.6	.51
Photography Trainees, AAF	Grades	431	123.0	11.9	.24
Cryptography Trainees, AAF	Grades, Phase 1	417	129.9	9.7	.31
Weather Observer Trainees, AAF	Grades	1042	130.2	12.5	.43
Aviation Cadets, Experimental Group	Pilot training, Pass-fail	1080	113.0	13.8	.31*
Officer Candidates, Infantry	Grades, Academic	103	123.0	10.8	.30
Officer Candidates, Ordnance	Grades, Academic	190	128.2	9.6	.41
Officer Candidates, Signal Corps	Grades, Academic	213	128.6	10.1	.36
Officer Candidates, Tank Destroyers	Grades, Academic	52	125.8	10.7	.44
Officer Candidates, Transportation Corps	Grades, Academic	314	126.4	9.8	.38
Officer Candidates, WAAC	Grades, Academic	787	128.4	11.3	.46
Officer Candidates, Infantry	Leadership Ratings	201	122.6	10.8	.12
Officer Candidates, Ordnance	Leadership Ratings	190	128.2	9.6	.09
Officer Candidates, 13 Arms & Services	Success vs. Failure	5186	128.7	10.0	.28*
AST Trainees, basic engineering	Grades, Inorganic Chemistry	222	126.6	7.8	.21
AST Trainees, basic engineering	Grades, Math. (Trig.)	222	126.6	7.8	.16
AST Trainees, personnel psychology	Ranks in Statistics	132	134.2	10.4	.25
AST Trainees, personnel psychology	Ranks in Tests & Measurements	130	134.0	10.3	.29
West Point Cadets, 4th Class	Grades, English**	932	131.3	10.9	.40
West Point Cadets, 4th Class	Grades, Mathematics**	932	131.3	10.9	.43
West Point Cadets, 4th Class	Grades, Military Topography	932	131.3	10.9	.40
West Point Cadets, 4th Class	Grades, Tactics	932	131.3	10.9	.29
West Point Cadets, 4th Class	Grades, French**	167	130.2	11.0	.22
West Point Cadets, 4th Class	Grades, German**	164	132.4	10.9	.20
West Point Cadets, 4th Class	Grades, Spanish**	932	131.3	10.9	.19
West Point Cadets, 4th Class	Grades, Portuguese**	168	130.0	10.3	.12

* Biserial Correlation.
** First Term.
After Staff, AGO (1945) by permission of the American Psychological Association and DuBois (1947).

Occupational differences have been studied with the AGCT as with the Army Alpha, but only for a one percent sample of the tested population. Some of the data for this test are presented in Table 4, on pages 92-93. Stewart's paper (1947) has shown that, as in the case of World War I data, occupations can be ranked according to a hierarchy of intelligence, there is considerable overlapping of occupational groups, and the spread of intelligence is greater in the lower-level (less selective) than in the higher-level (more selective) occupations. It is worth noting that although 90 percent of the highest ranking occupational group in either sample, accountants, made scores of 114 or better, more than 10 percent of the men in the least able occupational group, lumberjacks, made equally high scores. The overlapping is even greater among the occupations which are nearer to the middle of the distribution. Scores on this, as on other, intelligence tests can therefore give only a very general indication of the occupational level at which a person might best aim, notwithstanding the great variety of available occupational norms which seem to indicate the contrary.

Stewart's analysis compares occupational ranks in World War II with those found in World War I data. She found that only gunsmith, toolmaker, machinist, telephone and telegraph lineman, locomotive fireman, meat cutter, and boilermaker had made appreciable gains in position relative to other occupations. Occupations which had lost status were draftsman, file clerk, electrician, auto mechanic, pipe fitter, auto serviceman, chauffeur, and motorcyclist. As Stewart points out, it is difficult to know just how to interpret these differences, or the relative lack of differences, between the two sets of norms. The sampling of occupations during the two wars may have been different; certainly selective service did not operate on the same principles, and some occupations may have been granted deferments more liberally in one war than in the other because of differing industrial needs. This would result in inferior members of an occupation being its representatives in the war in which their group was considered essential to the civilian war effort. In the absence of detailed information on the basis of which corrections in the occupational means and deviations can be made, one can use the Army occupational intelligence data only as a very rough guide.

A seemingly sound form in which AGCT occupational norms have been presented for this type of use is Table 4 prepared by Stewart. In this table will be found broad groupings of occupations on the basis of the AGCT scores characterizing their members. This arrangement minimizes the likelihood that undue emphasis will be placed upon insignificant differences within a level; but at the same time it risks overemphasizing the importance of differences between top and bottom occupations in adjacent levels.

One wonders, for example, whether the differences between chemists and lawyers are as great as the fact that one falls in Stewart's highest group and the other in her next highest group implies. The difference is, actually, one of three AGCT score points, or less than one-fifth sigma. Although the writers have used such tables, it now seems wiser to work from a graph such as that provided in the manual. The scaled arrangment permits the counselor and client to study broad groupings by drawing lines wherever they may wish, and at the same time encourages the realistic consideration of overlapping and of relative standing in a variety of occupations. Data for a longer list of occupations will be found in the Stewart reference (1947, Table I).

Use of the AGCT in Counseling and Selection. It is clear from the relationship between the AGCT and other standard tests of intelligence that this instrument is a measure of learning ability. This conclusion is reinforced by the consistently significant correlations between AGCT scores and success in administrative, clerical, mechanical, electrical, academic and other more specialized types of training in the Army, even though the nature of the data did not permit generalization concerning its relative importance in each of these types of training.

Although no evidence is available concerning the relationship between AGCT scores and occupational success, the data on differences between occupational groups confirm the opinion that persons with higher AGCT scores are likely to make good in higher level occupations. The details are in general agreement with the findings of studies made with other tests, so that generalizations to the effect that those with high scores are most likely to master new jobs rapidly, to rise to positions of responsibility, and to be satisfied in high level occupations, can probably be made from this test as from other standard tests of intelligence.

The test can be used in high schools, colleges, guidance centers serving adolescents and adults, employment offices, and business and industrial establishments. It is perhaps unfortunate that the name "Army" has been kept on the test booklets (although it should be identified correctly among professional users) , as this may injure rapport with some subjects. Experience will no doubt throw more light on this problem. The contents and form are quite appropriate despite some items dealing with military objects or situations. The occupational norms make the test useful for vocational counseling, and for selection in the absence of local norms. The lack of college student norms makes it less useful than the A.C.E., Otis, and certain other tests for educational guidance, but this defect is to some extent remedied by the availability of means for certain special types of college students and by the substantial correlations found with grades in various types of training courses.

The Thurstone Tests of Primary Mental Abilities (American Council on Education, 1938, 1941; Science Research Associates, 1947). The Tests of Primary Mental Abilities were developed by the Thurstones in an attempt to provide practical batteries of tests implementing their work in the isolation of primary mental abilities. The "Chicago" (long-form, two hours) and "SRA" (short-form, 45 minutes) Tests were designed for use primarily at the high school level (Thurstone, Thelma, 1941); another battery was added for the lower age levels. Only the long experimental and "Chicago" forms are discussed here, as there are very few data concerning the rather unsatisfactory short forms, and Super (American Personnel and Guidance Association, 1957) has evaluated these elsewhere.

Description. The *Chicago* tests were standardized on children in the higher grades and in high school and are therefore designed to be applicable to children aged through 17. Approximately 1000 children were tested at each half-year in Chicago schools. While this means that the norms are not truly national, they do represent the school population of one of our largest cities and provide useful norms; it would still be desirable to have national norms, but even more important is the accumulation of local norms by other school systems, colleges, and organizations using the tests. The battery consists of 11 tests, selected from the 60 tests tried out experimentally on 1154 pupils and subjected to factor analysis, and a second experimental battery of 21 tests tried out on 437 subjects and factorially analyzed. These 11 tests measure six primary mental abilities, named Verbal Meaning (V), Space (S), Number (N), Memory (M), Word Fluency (W), and Reasoning (R). These are measured by tests such as vocabulary and opposites (V), flags and cards (S), addition and multiplication (N), and letter grouping (R). Two tests are used to measure each of the six abilities except memory, assessed by one test. They are arranged in booklets which can be administered in two school periods. Each test is accurately timed, with a practice exercise preceding it. They can be scored by hand or by machine, perforated stencils being provided for the former.

Evaluation. The success of the Thurstones in constructing a practical battery of tests of primary mental abilities is obviously an important question. An easily administered and scored, reliable, and valid battery would represent a major advance in aptitude testing, as it would make possible the measurement of a number of aptitudes which are widely used and which are of varying importance in different types of activities. Recognition of the importance of this possibility is shown by the fact that, although Thurstone's experimental tests were published in 1938 and the definitive battery only in 1941, there have appeared since then almost a score of studies of their reliability and validity. The short forms should be subjected to even closer scrutiny.

Influence on Current Test Construction. The influence of Thurstone's factorial analyses of mental abilities has not been limited to these attempts to validate his tests; it has manifested itself in the verbal and quantitative scores of the American Council on Education Psychological Examinations which he developed (see above), in the performance and verbal I. Q.'s of the Wechsler-Bellevue (see below) and of the California Test of Mental Maturity, in the Arithmetic Reasoning, Verbal Comprehension, and other similar tests of special mental abilities used in the Engineering and Physical Sciences Aptitude Test, the Navy's Basic Classification Test Battery (Staff, Test and Research Section, 1945), in the United States Employment Service's General Aptitude Test Battery (see below), the Psychological Corporation's Differential Aptitude Tests (see below), and the Aviation Cadet Classification Tests (DuBois, 1947) of the Army Air Forces. Test batteries such as the last four yield no I. Q.'s but, instead, yield part scores which, in a given selection program, are weighted according to their differential predictive value, in accordance with a concept of constellations of abilities needed in various occupations rather than of general ability required in varying amounts in different occupations. We have seen that the use of quantitative and verbal scores is still somewhat problematical in the case of the A.C.E. tests, and even more so in those of the California and Wechsler-Bellevue Tests. The GATB and DAT, we shall see below, have turned out better but must be used with caution for differential prediction. The Aviation Psychology Program used tests of this type to good effect for selection purposes (a simpler matter than counseling), as demonstrated by the correlations in Table 11, which indicate the differential prognostic value of some of the factorial-type tests for pilot and navigator training. Multiple correlations for batteries which also include tests of other types were in the .60's.

TABLE 11

COMPARATIVE VALIDITIES OF FACTOR-TYPE TESTS FOR AIRCREW TRAINING

Test	r Pilot Training	r Navigator Training
Reading Comprehension	.19	.32
Arithmetic Reasoning	.09	.45
Numerical Operations	.04	.26
Mechanical Principles	.32	.13
Number of Cases	300 to 1,500	8,100 to 10,500

In view of the widespread influence of Thurstone's work, and the important role which it is playing in shaping the intelligence test construction work now being done, it seems essential to discuss in some detail the practical work which has so far been done with the Primary Mental Abilities Tests.

Studies of the Tests as Such. Traxler (1941) ascertained that the *reliabilities* of the original Primary Mental Abilities Tests were high, judging by both the split half and the retest techniques, but attributed this to the importance of speed in all of the tests. Results for 673 freshmen at the University of Chicago were analyzed by Stalnaker (1939), in order to evaluate both the reliability and the adequacy of the standardization of the adult tests. He reported that the tests used to measure a given factor had intercorrelations of .20 to .79, the mean being .49. Goodman (1944) reported slightly lower coefficients. These seem rather low, but the intercorrelations of tests not used to measure the same factor range from —.17 to .49, most of them being under .20 More serious than this, perhaps, is the fact that the items were found not to be in the order of difficulty, and that some items were ineffective. His conclusion was that the tests were not yet ready for use with individuals.

Adkins and Kuder (1940) administered the original Primary Mental Abilities Tests and the Kuder Preference Record to more than 500 freshmen at the University of Chicago and found relatively little overlapping between the two sets of measures. What overlapping there was seemed reasonable in view of the nature of the tests in question. Shanner (1939) reported a study made at the secondary school level at about the same time. He concluded, from evidence generally similar to Stalnaker's, that the tests were reliable and had sufficiently low intercorrelations to indicate independence of the traits measured. Although concluding that the tests need more research for refinement and interpretation, he stated that they are a valuable addition to the field of aptitude testing. Crawford (1940) took issue with this conclusion, presenting the test intercorrelations by frequencies rather than averaging them and concluding that they were not sufficiently independent. He also pointed out that the correlations between PMA tests and Co-operative Achievement Tests were low and concluded that the tests do not have demonstrated diagnostic value. Fortunately, more satisfactory evidence is now available, to take the issue out of controversy and into the realm of fact.

Applications to Education and Vocations. The experimental edition of the PMA Tests was given to 501 University of Chicago freshmen by Shanner and Kuder (1941), together with a number of other tests, and correlated with grades on comprehensive examinations taken to secure exemption from freshman courses. Results are presented in Table 12.

It can be seen from Table 12 that the two especially constructed aptitude tests yield the highest validities for the appropriate subjects, and

TABLE 12

CORRELATION BETWEEN TESTS OF GENERAL, SPECIAL, AND PRIMARY MENTAL ABILITIES
AND FRESHMAN EXAMINATION GRADES, UNIVERSITY OF CHICAGO

Test	Biological Sciences	Humanities	Physical Sciences	Social Sciences	Average Exam Grades
A.C.E. Psychol. Exam.	.48	.48	.48	.57	.52
Physical Sciences Apt.	—	—	.65	—	.52
Social Sciences Apt.	—	—	—	.65	.575
PMA: Perception	.08	.13	.17	.135	.12
Number	.21	.265	.27	.30	.31
Verbal	.38	.47	.38	.435	.415
Spatial	.225	.07	.14	.13	.18
Memory	.145	.13	.18	.16	.20
Induction	.22	.03	.25	.20	.23
Deduction	.42	.19	.485	.43	.38
Multiple R	.50	.54	.56	.57	—

validities at least as high as any other test for average grades. It would seem probable, in view of the multiple correlations between PMA tests and subject grades, that these tests would predict average grades about as well as the A.C.E. and the special aptitude tests, were it not for the tendency of multiple correlation coefficients to shrink. For special subjects these last have the advantage of being based on job analysis and of being basically miniature situation tests; the presumably greater versatility of the PMA tests makes them more desirable for selection in institutions which do not have large test construction staffs and for general vocational and educational counseling. When the PMA Tests are compared with the A.C.E., it is notable that no single PMA factor is as good a predictor as the test of general scholastic aptitude (although the verbal and deduction factors do about as well for certain courses), and that the multiple correlations between PMA Tests and grades in specific courses, while generally higher than those of the A.C.E., are not usually sufficiently greater to justify the additional time and effort in test administration and scoring.

Using a battery of academic achievement and reading tests as the criteria, Shaw (1949) obtained correlations with the V, R, W, S, N, and M Primary Mental Abilities which were somewhat higher than those reviewed above. For 591 entering ninth grade students in two school systems in Iowa the correlations ranged from .061 (S vs. Reading Time) to .793 (V vs. Composite Iowa Tests of Educational Development), the highest relationships being between Verbal and the achievement measures. Reasoning ability had moderately high correlations with the criteria, but the other PMA tests showed little relationship to achievement scores. However, optimum combinations of the primary mental abilities by multiple correlational techniques accounted for a considerable amount of the total variance in the achievement criterion. The multiple correlation coefficients were mostly in the 50s, 60s, and 70s.

In a study by Yum (1941), also of University of Chicago freshmen, somewhat less promising results were obtained. He computed one relationship not reported by Shanner and Kuder, namely a multiple correlation between PMA Tests and semester average. More important still, he used actual grades for students taking the courses, rather than grades based on examinations taken to obtain exemption from the courses. The correlation was .42, which is considerably lower than that obtained by Shanner and Kuder for any single subject, and lower than their multiple correlation would presumably have been had it been computed. A similar finding has been reported by Ford (1950) who obtained a correlation of .48 between PMA total score and grade point average in three schools of nursing (N—146).

Ellison and Edgerton (1941) used the experimental tests first published by Thurstone with 49 liberal arts students at the Ohio State University. Only the Verbal and Memory Tests had moderately high correlations with point-hour averages (.44 and .31 respectively), but the multiple correlation for weighted scores was .64. The results for grades in specific courses were most promising, for Verbal, Spatial, and Deductive Tests gave better predictions of English grades than did the Ohio State Psychological Examination (.75, .44, and .44 as opposed to .42), the Verbal Test predicted Science grades better than the general examination (.68 vs. .42), and similar results were reported for foreign language grades and for psychology grades. The numbers in each case were, however, between 25 and 30, and the results seem almost too good.

Most helpful is a series of studies conducted at the Pennsylvania State College under the direction of Robert G. Bernreuter. Ball (1940) administered the older Thurstone battery to 147 freshmen women and 159 men in the liberal arts college. The correlations with semester point average ranged from .04 for the Spatial Tests to .35 for the Verbal. The multiple correlation for Memory, Number, Verbal, Induction, and Deduction Tests and semester point average was .46, which is no better than what one would expect from a much briefer scholastic aptitude test. Some of the tests of specific factors correlated substantially with appropriate college marks, the coefficient for Number and Mathematics being .41, and Verbal and English Composition .40. The Verbal Tests, however, tended to have moderately high correlations (.20 to .40) with all courses. Hessemer (1942) analyzed PMA Test scores for 147 freshmen women, using first semester point average and grades in inorganic chemistry as her criterion. The Verbal Tests were again the best predictor, with a correlation of .44

with semester point average; Deduction followed closely with one of .40. There were no satisfactory correlations, however, with chemistry grades, that for the Verbal Tests being .13, and the two highest being —.25 for the Spatial Tests and .18 for the Deduction Tests, the irreconcilability of which relationships suggests their chance nature.

Bernreuter and Goodman (1941) obtained data for 170 freshmen engineers. In this instance the correlations between PMA Tests and semester point average ranged from .04 (Perceptual) to .38 (Deduction), the multiple correlation being .51 for Number, Verbal, Space, Induction and Deduction or Reasoning Tests. Again the Verbal Tests yielded significant correlations with all courses (except Drawing); the correlation between Verbal Test and English Composition grades was .44, and that between Number and Mathematics grades was also .44. Unfortunately this study, like the others just summarized, provides no validity data for tests of general intelligence, which might enable one to decide whether or not the extra time required by the PMA battery is justified by higher validities. This defect is remedied by another Penn State study by Tredick (1941) who tested 113 freshmen women students of home economics with the PMA battery, the Otis, and several other tests. The results, shown in Table 13, are in line with the trend of those so far reported, in that the Verbal Tests tend to give moderately high predictions of grades in all courses and especially in English (.55), the Number Tests have a substantial correlation with chemistry grades (.46), and Induction and Deduction are also good predictors. Most interesting, perhaps, is the fact that the multiple correlation coefficient of .61 for four PMA Tests (NVID) and semester point average is substantially higher than that of .53 between the Otis and the same criterion, but the R was apparently not corrected for the shrinkage which usually takes place with a second group.

It is interesting to note, in passing, the correlations between PMA Tests and the tests of general and special aptitudes used by Tredick. All of the former have moderate or high correlations with the Otis (.29 to .68), only the coefficients for the Number and Memory Tests being below .40. The perceptual factor is important in the Otis ($r = .53$) (presumably because of the emphasis on speed), the Minnesota Vocational Test for Clerical Workers (.57, .51) and the Minnesota Spatial Relations Test (.55), but much less so in the Minnesota Paper Form Board (.39). The number factor is highly correlated not only with the Minnesota Clerical Numbers (.59), but also with the Names (.58) Test. The verbal factor is very important in the Otis (.68) and of moderate importance in the Clerical Names (.40) and Art Judgment Tests (.39). The spatial factor plays a moderately important part in all of the tests in the study except, interestingly, in the Art Judgment Test, where its role is of only slight importance

(.20) . It is most closely correlated with the Minnesota Spatial Relations Test, but only to the extent of .49, and its relationship to the Minnesota Paper Form Board is no closer than to the other non-spatial tests (.37

TABLE 13

CORRELATIONS BETWEEN PMA TESTS, OTHER TESTS, AND GRADES FOR
113 HOME ECONOMICS FRESHMEN (TREDICK)

	Sem. Pt. Average	Art	Engl. Comp.	Chem-istry	P	N	V	S	M	I	D
PMA Tests: Combined NVID	.61										
P	.28	.15	.19	.20							
N	.41	.11	.22	.46							
V	.51	.24	.55	.28							
S	.28	.25	.10	.23							
M	.20	−.02	.08	.25							
I	.40	.26	.19	.37							
D	.42	.21	.21	.43							
Otis	.53	.17	.54	.37	.53	.33	.68	.40	.29	.60	.61
Minn. Paper Form Board	.31	.24	.13	.24	.39	.21	.24	.37	.06	.48	.45
Minn. Clerical Names	.23	.07	.07	.26	.57	.58	.40	.41	.24	.44	.46
Minn. Clerical Numbers	.36	.08	.27	.31	.51	.59	.06	.36	.20	.28	.28
Minn. Mechanical Assembly	.11	.17	−.01	.16	.23	−.12	.11	.34	.07	.26	.30
Minn. Spatial Relations	.23	.20	.02	.22	.55	.15	.16	.49	.06	.47	.33
Meier Seashore Art Judgment	.23	.20	.29	.03	.33	.11	.39	.20	.18	.23	.15

as contrasted, e.g., with .41 and .36 for Clerical Names and Numbers) . This suggests that the so-called spatial factor measured by the PMA Tests may be more general than strictly spatial. The memory factor is moderately correlated only with the Otis (.29) ; other coefficients are about .20 or below. Induction plays important parts in the Otis (.60) and in the spatial tests (.48 and .47) , is moderately important in Clerical Names (.44) , and of some importance in the other tests used. The deduction or reasoning factor plays a similar role, but is somewhat less important in the Minnesota Spatial Relations Test than in the Paper Form Board (r's of .33 and .45 respectively) .

Goodman (1944) reviewed the work done by other investigators at Penn State and reported further research of his own with engineering freshmen. The correlations between PMA Tests and first year semester point averages ranged from .08 (P) to .34 (V) and .36 (D). The Number Factor, which one might logically expect to yield one of the highest *r*'s with engineering grades, had a correlation of only .36 and the spatial factor only .18. This tends to support the conclusion drawn earlier from work with the A.C.E. part scores, to the effect that verbal and "general" intelligence tests are at least as effective predictors of success in technical courses as are more quantitative tests. Goodman also obtained the inter-correlations between specific tests in the PMA battery and between these tests (as contrasted with combinations of tests which measured specific factors) and the criterion. This analysis showed that the intercorrelations of tests measuring the same factors ranged from .01 to .72, with a median of .33, which suggests that the measurement of specific or primary factors still leaves much to be desired; it also revealed that some of the specific tests had higher correlations with the criterion than did the factor scores to which they contributed. This last finding is not surprising, as a test of mixed factors might predict success in a task involving some of those same factors better than a score representing more adequately one "pure" factor which is only one contributor to success in the activity in question.

A few other studies which have been reported show results similar to those just reviewed. Wolking (1955) found that the corresponding sub-tests of the PMA and DAT show moderate to substantial intercorrelations, but that, regardless of sex, the DAT yields generally higher validities with high school grades as the criterion. Stuit and Hudson (1942) admin-istered the PMA Tests to students in engineering, medical, and journal-ism schools, and reported characteristic profiles. Engineers were high on S and D, low on V and M; journalists were high on P, N, and V, but low on M and D; medical students were high on P and I. In a similar approach Berdie (1955) analyzed extensive longitudinal data on 219 men and 252 women who were originally tested in 1939 and subsequently graduated from the University of Minnesota. Profiles for business, medical, medical technology, and nursing students showed distinctive PMA patterns but also reflected considerable individual differences within each group. For the men the verbal and reasoning subtests and for the women the verbal, reasoning, and perception primary mental abilities differentiated students in various curricular programs in the Science, Literature, and Arts College, but none of the PMA tests correlated higher than .20 with total grades. This suggests that the battery should be useful in guiding students into curricula in which their abilities resemble in type those of the majority of students, but should not be used as a basis for prediction of success in these curricula. More work should be done along these lines, as the predictive as well as differential use of the tests needs further validation. This type of standardization, however, has merely been begun.

Perhaps the nearest thing to validation in terms of vocational criteria has been carried out by Harrell and Faubion (1941), who administered the experimental PMA Tests to 105 men in aviation maintenance courses in an Air Forces Technical School. The multiple correlation of Verbal, Spatial, Induction, and Deduction Tests with average grades was .63, which contrasted with a correlation of .45 between Army Alpha scores and grades. The Number Tests correlated most highly with grades in shop mathematics (.37, contrasted with .31 for Army Alpha and .46 for the combined PMA Tests); the Verbal Tests correlated most highly with grades in Electricity (.51, compared to .47 for Army Alpha and .57 for the combined PMA Tests); and the Deduction or Reasoning Tests predicted grades in blue-print reading and mechanical drawing most effectively (.54, compared with .30 for Army Alpha, .36 for the Spatial Tests, and .60 for the combined PMA battery)

Use of the PMA Tests in Vocational Counseling and Selection. The studies reviewed in the preceding pages make it clear that the long forms of the Thurstone Tests of Primary Mental Abilities, while sufficiently perfected to make possible important research into the nature and organization of human abilities, still need to be improved before they become a practical instrument for use in guidance and selection. The defects in the tests have been summarized by Crawford and Burnham (1946, p. 213). The measures of specific factors are still somewhat impure, as shown by the moderate rather than high intercorrelations of tests used to measure a given factor. Speed plays too important a part in all the tests. The relationships between specific factors and other tests or criteria with which they might be expected to be related are often low enough to make one question the adequacy of the measurement of the factor (e.g., the spatial factor). On the other hand, there are a number of findings which are extremely encouraging. Among these are the generally higher multiple correlations between PMA Tests and criteria than among general intelligence tests and criteria, which suggest that in selection work especially it will be advisable to use this more refined type of measure, to obtain differential occupational weights, and to score accordingly. In time, accumulated data may make these differential weights useful in counseling. In the meantime, it should be remembered that these tests are still a promising device for research rather than a practical tool for counselors or personnel managers, and that the short forms have been found inadequate (American Personnel and Guidance Ass'n, 1957).

The Wechsler-Bellevue and Wechsler Adult Intelligence Scales (Revised book: Williams and Wilkins, 1958. Manual and test materials: Psychological Corporation.) Although the Wechsler Adult Intelligence Scales (WAIS), published in 1955, are gradually supplanting the older forms of the Wechsler-Bellevue tests, studies of their vocational significance are practically nonexistent. In fact, only one study has been found on the use of the WAIS in guidance or personnel activities (Balinsky and Shaw, 1956). Consequently, in the discussion which follows, reference is made only to the Wechsler-Bellevue scales, for which there are considerably more research data. It should not be inferred, however, that these findings are therefore applicable to the WAIS. They pertain only to the earlier edition. For a detailed comparison of the Wechsler-Bellevue and WAIS consult Wechsler's (1958) monograph.

The publication, in 1939, of the Wechsler-Bellevue Scale of Mental Ability as an individual intelligence test designed for use with adults, rather than with children, immediately focussed the attention of the more clinically minded psychologists and counselors on this instrument, even when the nature of the counseling problem was largely vocational and educational. The aura surrounding individual testing, as opposed to the supposedly less sensitive measurements obtained from group tests, alone was a sufficient cause of such interest in the Wechsler-Bellevue. To this appeal was added, however, that of a test which yields two types of scores, one based on verbal and one on performance items. The fact that the scale was developed in a mental hospital, primarily for the diagnosis of mental defects and mental impairment in adolescents and adults, and that all the original material on the test was directed toward these uses (Wechsler, 1944), resulted only in greater confidence on the part of the clinically minded who proceeded to use the scale in vocational and educational guidance. Because of their widespread use in guidance centers some aspects of the Wechsler-Bellevue Scales are considered here, more as a caution to users than as a guide to use in vocational counseling.

The question of the clinical usefulness of the scales is clearly quite independent of the question of its usefulness in vocational counseling and selection. When considering the use of such a test in vocational guidance and personnel work, three questions are relevant. First, what advantages, if any, does an individually administered test of mental ability have over a group-administered test in vocational guidance or selection? Secondly, how good is the instrument as a test of general mental ability? Thirdly, what evidence is there concerning the occupational significance of total and part scores, particularly the latter? Each of these questions will be dealt with briefly in the following paragraphs.

Individual vs. *Group Tests.* The relative advantages and disadvantages of group and individual, performance and paper-and-pencil tests were discussed in Chapter V. But for the sake of convenience a few especially pertinent points should be made here. Tests designed for group administration can also be administered individually, and therefore have the advantage of being more flexible in their use. On the other hand, they are generally paper-and-pencil tests, which do not have the flexibility that orally administered individual scales such as the Wechsler-Bellevue possess. In the former, the examinee reads and answers questions by himself without the examiner being able to judge his reactions by anything more than expression and gestures and with no possibility of modifying the questions to suit the background of the subject. In the latter, the administrative procedure is more conversational; therefore the examiner has much more opportunity to judge the reactions of the subject and to modify procedures in such a way as to be completely fair. In clinical work the desirability of the latter type of technique is obvious, for then one is working with cases whose background or condition is unusual in some respects; it is important that the test situation permit the examiner to observe these abnormalities and to modify the test procedure accordingly in some instances and to note them for diagnostic use in others. But in vocational and educational counseling or selection the examiner is dealing with persons whose condition is approximately normal and whose background is such as to make standardized techniques appropriate. For each normal counselee or employment applicant there is a suitable group test of mental ability, developed for use with and standardized on subjects such as he; modification of test procedures is therefore generally unnecessary if the examiner has background data on his subjects and chooses his tests well. Furthermore, the normality of the examinee means that the purpose of the test is to get an overall measure of mental ability, not to study peculiarities of mental functioning. For this reason also the group test, which provides a suitable series of standardized tasks and obtains a measure of performance on those tasks, yields all of the types of data which can legitimately be expected from intelligence testing for vocational or educational purposes.

The Wechsler-Bellevue as an Intelligence Test. Studies of the Wechsler-Bellevue published prior to 1956 have been summarized by Rabin (1945), Watson (1946), Rabin and Guertin (1951), and Guertin et al. (1956). The trends revealed in these summaries are for the Wechsler-Bellevue scores and Revised Stanford-Binet to correlate from .78 to .93 when the groups are heterogeneous in age or mental ability, and about .62 when they are more homogeneous (e.g. college freshmen). The verbal scale is uniformly more highly correlated with the Revised Stanford-Binet than is the performance scale. The correlations with group tests are, as has generally been the case with individual tests, lower than those with other individual tests; for Army Alpha a coefficient of .74, for the Otis SA .425, and for the A.C.E. .48, .53, and .61 are reported. [One exception has been reported by Tamminen (1951), a correlation of .91 with the AGCT when the sample was corrected for range of talent.] Wechsler-Bellevue I.Q.'s of superior individuals were found to be lower than those obtained on the Revised Stanford-Binet, while persons of little mental ability made higher scores on the Wechsler than on the Binet Scales, because the Wechsler has a smaller standard deviation. The reviews also deal with the clinical significance of part scores, but that topic is not relevant to our purposes. From the trends reported above one can conclude that the results of the Wechsler-Bellevue Scales agree with the results of other intelligence tests as well as can be expected.

Occupational Significance of Total and Part Scores.   From the point of view of the vocational psychologist, counselor, and personnel manager, the crucial question concerning this or any other intelligence test is: What evidence is there to help me interpret the test scores in terms of prospects of success in various types of work? The answer, for the Wechsler-Bellevue Scales, is in 1960 as in 1949: Practically none. Some data have been collected by Simon and Levitt (1950), who provide medians and interquartile ranges for sixteen broad, mostly professional, occupational groups (N's equal to 50 or more). Unfortunately, this information is not reported by sex. Frandsen (1950) computed zero-order correlations between Full Scale, Verbal, Performance, and individual subtest scores and three-year average grade-point ratios for 83 high school seniors (both sexes). The most efficient predictor ($r = .76$) was an abbreviated scale based upon all but the Picture Arrangement, Picture Completion, and Object Assembly subtests. Altus and Mahler (1946) reported significant differences in the Wechsler Mental Ability Scale (Form B) verbal scores of 2476 Army illiterates who had been employed in skilled or semiskilled occupations, on the one hand, or in unskilled occupations, on the other. One can, of course, use the total or verbal scores in a general way, by analogy. A person who has very superior intelligence on these scales would also have very superior intelligence on Army Alpha or AGCT, and such people, we know from research with these tests, tend to succeed in the higher professional and managerial occupations; similarly for dull, normal, average, and other levels. But the possibility of such interpretations does not constitute a special advantage of the Wechsler-Bellevue in vocational and educational guidance. It is, rather, a means of salvaging and making useful the results of a test which would otherwise be useless in vocational guidance and selection. There are other tests of mental ability whose vocational significance is based on more direct evidence; they are therefore subject to less error in interpretation.

For the part scores, or verbal and performance I. Q.'s, the answer concerning the vocational and educational significance of the scales is even less equivocal. Guertin, Frank, and Rabin (1956) cite a study by Ladd

(1950) in which students with higher Verbal I.Q.'s were found in academic teacher-preparation areas, whereas those with higher Performance I.Q.'s were majoring as teachers of non-academic subjects. Anderson and his associates (1942) reported a correlation of .41 between the full scale and the first semester grades of 112 college women, while the Verbal and Performance I. Q.'s yielded correlations of .50 and .19 respectively. These compared with correlations for 1941 A.C.E. total, linguistic, and quantitative scores of .54, .54, and .39 (the data for the 1940 form of the A.C.E. were .48, .48, and .36). Obviously, the Wechsler-Bellevue Performance I.Q. is of no value in predicting success in the first semester of a liberal arts college, and the performance items lower the validity of the verbal items in the total score. The Verbal I.Q. itself is no more adequate a predictor of success in the liberal arts than is a group test of intelligence such as the A.C.E.

With such a paucity of evidence the use of the Verbal and Performance I.Q.'s in the differential diagnosis of vocational and educational aptitudes is clearly unwarranted. To reason by analogy and interpret Wechsler-Bellevue scores on the basis of data on the American Council Psychological Examination or on primary mental abilities scores on the Thurstone tests is also unwarranted, although this seems to have become a rather widespread practice among psychometrists and counselors. It is true that Balinsky's (1949) factor analysis isolated verbal and performance factors, the former consisting, at age 25–29, of digit symbol, comprehension, and information items, and the latter of spatial items such as picture completion, object assembly, and block design. But Anderson and others (1942) have shown that, although there is a moderate correlation between Wechsler Verbal and A.C.E. Linguistic scores $(r = .49$ or $.50)$, the relationship between Performance and Quantitative scores is too low $(r = .31$ or $.39)$ to justify interpreting one in terms of the other. No such data are yet available for the Wechsler and PMA Tests. And we have seen that differential educational diagnosis on the basis of either A.C.E. or PMA Test part-scores is still in the experimental stages.

Use of the Wechsler-Bellevue Scales in Counseling and Selection. As the Wechsler Scales are used in more and more studies, evidence upon which to base judgment concerning the vocational and educational significance of part scores will presumably be forthcoming. In the meantime the objective psychologist, counselor, or personnel officer can only recognize that the use of anything more than the total or verbal score as a rough index of the educational and occupational level which the person in question may attain is unwarranted, and that, for most persons, this can be done at least as well and more economically by means of paper-and-pencil tests.

REFERENCES FOR CHAPTER VI

Abel, T. M. "A study of a group of subnormal girls successfully adjusted in industry and community," *Amer. J. Ment. Def.*, 45 (1940), 66-72.

Adkins, D. C., and Kuder, G. F. "The relation between primary mental abilities and activity preferences," *Psychometrika*, 5 (1940), 251-262.

Altus, W. D., and Mahler, C. A. "Significance of verbal aptitude in the type of occupation pursued by illiterates," *J. Appl. Psychol.*, 30 (1946), 155-160.

American Personnel and Guidance Association. *The Use of Multifactor Tests in Guidance*. Washington, D. C.: American Personnel and Guidance Association, 1957.

Anderson, E. E., et al. "Wilson College studies in psychology: I. A comparison of the Wechsler-Bellevue, Revised Stanford-Binet, and American Council on Education tests at the college level," *J. Psychol.*, 14 (1942), 317-326.

Anderson, V. V. *Psychiatry in Industry*. New York: Harper, 1929.

Awaji, Y. "Intelligenz pruefung in Japanischer Heere," *Zeitsch. fur Angew. Psychol.*, 30 (1928), 81-118.

Balinsky, B. "An analysis of the mental factors of various age groups from nine to sixty," *Genet. Psychol. Monog.*, 23 (1941), 191-234.

———, and Shaw, H. W. "The contribution of the WAIS to a management appraisal program," *Pers. Psychol.*, 9 (1956), 207-209.

Ball, F. J. "A Study of the Predictive Values of the Thurstone Primary Mental Abilities as Applied to Lower Division Freshmen." Unpublished M.A. thesis, Pennsylvania State College, 1940.

Barnes, M. W. "Relationships of the study of mathematics to Q-scores on the A.C.E. Psychological Examination," *Sch. Sci. Math.*, 43 (1943), 581-582.

———. "Gains in the A. C. E. Psychological Examination during the freshman-sophomore years," *Sch. and Soc.*, 57 (1943), 250-252.

Baxter, B. "An experimental analysis of the contribution of speed and level in an intelligence test," *J. Educ. Psychol.*, 32 (1941), 285-296.

Beckham, A. S. "Employment and guidance: minimum intelligence levels for several occupations," *Pers. J.*, 9 (1930), 309-313.

Berdie, R. F. "Prediction of college achievement and satisfaction," *J. Appl. Psychol.*, 28 (1944), 239-245.

———. "Aptitude, interest, and personality tests: a longitudinal comparison," *J. Appl. Psychol.*, 39 (1955), 103-114.

Bernreuter, R. G., and Goodman, C. H. "A study of the Thurstone Primary Mental Abilities Tests applied to freshman engineering students," *J. Educ. Psychol.*, 32 (1941), 55-60.

Bingham, W. V. *Aptitudes and Aptitude Testing*. New York: Harper, 1937.

———, and Davis, W. T. "Intelligence test scores and business success," *J. Appl. Psychol.*, 8 (1924), 1-22.

Blair, G. M., and Kammam, F. F. "Do intelligence tests requiring reading ability give spuriously low scores to poor readers at the college level?" *J. Educ. Res.*, 36 (1942), 280-283.

Blum, M. L., and Candee, B. "The selection of department store packers and wrappers with the aid of certain psychological tests," *J. Appl. Psychol.*, 25 (1941), 78-85.

———, and Candee, B. "The selection of department store packers and wrappers with the aid of certain psychological tests: study II," *J. Appl. Psychol.*, 25 (1941), 291-299.

Borg, W. R. "Some factors relating to art school success," *J. Educ. Res.*, 43 (1950), 376-384.

Bransford, T. L., et al. "A study of the validity of written tests for administrative personnel," *Amer. Psychologist*, 7 (1946), 279 (abstr.).

Bryan, A. I. "Grades, intelligence, and personality of art school freshmen," *J. Educ. Psychol.*, 33 (1942), 50-64.

Burt, C. "The inheritance of mental ability," *Amer. Psychologist*, 13 (1958), 1-15.

Byrns, R., and Henmon, V. A. C. "Parental occupation and mental ability," *J. Educ. Psychol.*, 27 (1936), 284-291.

Cattell, Psyche. "Why Otis 'IQ' cannot be equivalent to the Stanford-Binet I.Q.," *J. Educ. Psychol.*, 22 (1931), 599-603.

Cattell, R. B. "Occupational norms of intelligence," *Brit. J. Psychol.*, 25 (1934), 1-28.

Channing, A. *Employability of Mentally Deficient Boys and Girls*. Washington, D. C.: Government Printing Office, 1932.

Chappell, T. L. "Note on the validity of the Army General Classification Test as a predictor of academic achievement," *J. Educ. Psychol.*, 46 (1955), 53-55.

Copeland, H. A. "Some characteristics of three tests used to predict clerical success," *J. Appl. Psychol.*, 20 (1936), 461-470.

Crawford, A. B. "Some observations on primary mental abilities battery in action," *Sch. and Soc.*, 51 (1940), 585-592.

————, and Burnham, P. S. *Forecasting College Achievement: A Survey of Aptitude Tests for Higher Education. Part I. General Considerations in the Measurement of Academic Promise*. New Haven: Yale University Press, 1946.

Crooks, W. R., and Ferguson, L. W. "Item validities of Otis Self-Administering Tests of Mental Ability for colleges," *J. Exp. Educ.*, 9 (1941), 229-232.

Dearborn, W. F., and Rothney, J. W. M. "Scholastic, economic, and social backgrounds of unemployed youth," *Harvard Bull. in Educ.*, 20 (1938).

Di Vesta, F. J. "Subscore patterns on A. C. E. Psychological Examination related to educational and occupational differences," *J. Appl. Psychol.*, 38 (1954), 248-252.

Du Bois, P. H. (ed.). *The Classification Program*. ("AAF Aviation Psychology Report," No. 2.) Washington, D. C.: Government Printing Office, 1947.

Dunlop, F. S. "Subsequent careers of non-academic boys," *Teachers College Contributions to Education*, 1935.

Ellison, M. L., and Edgerton, H. A. "The Thurstone Primary Mental Abilities Tests and college marks," *Educ. Psychol. Measmt.*, 1 (1941), 399-406.

Estes, S. G. "A study of five tests of 'spatial' ability," *J. Psychol.*, 13 (1942), 265-271.

Fairbanks, R. E. "The subnormal child—seventeen years after," *Ment. Hyg.*, 17 (1933), 177-208.

Ford, A. H. "Prediction of academic success in three schools of nursing," *J. Appl. Psychol.*, 34 (1950), 186-189.

Forlano, G., and Kirkpatrick, F. H. "Intelligence and adjustment measurements in the selection of radio tube mounters," *J. Appl. Psychol.*, 29 (1945), 257-261.

Frandsen, A. N. "The Wechsler-Bellevue Intelligence Scale and high school achievement," *J. Appl. Psychol.*, 34 (1950), 406-411.

Fredericksen, N., and Schrader, W. B. "The A. C. E. Psychological Examination and high school standing as predictors of college success," *J. Appl. Psychol.*, 36 (1952), 261-265.

Fryer, D. "Occupational intelligence standards," *Sch. and Soc.*, 16 (1922), 273-277.

————, and Sparling, E. J. "Intelligence and occupational adjustment," *Occupations*, 12 (1934), 55-63.

Garrett, H. E. "A developmental theory of intelligence," *Amer. Psychologist*, 1 (1946), 372-378.

Gerberich, J. R. "Validation of a state-wide educational guidance program for high-school seniors," *Sch. and Soc.*, 34 (1931), 606-610.

Goodman, C. H. "Prediction of college success by means of Thurstone's Primary Mental Abilities Test," *Educ. Psychol. Measmt.*, 4 (1944), 125-140.

Grace, A. G. "The relationship of mental ability to occupational choices of adults," *Voc. Guid. Mag.*, 10 (1931), 354-358.

Guertin, W. H., Frank, G. H., and Rabin, A. I. "Research with the Wechsler-Bellevue Intelligence Scales: 1950-1955," *Psychol. Bull.*, 53 (1956), 235-257.

Harrell, T. W., and Faubion, R. "Primary mental abilities and aviation maintenance courses," *Educ. Psychol. Measmt.*, 1 (1941), 59-66.

Hartson, L. D. "Influence of level of motivation on the validity of intelligence tests," *Educ. Psychol. Measmt.*, 5 (1945), 273-283.

———, and Sprow, A. J. "Value of intelligence quotients obtained in secondary school for predicting college scholarship," *Educ. Psychol. Measmt.*, 1 (1941), 387-398.

Hay, E. N. "Predicting success in machine bookkeeping," *J. Appl. Psychol.*, 27 (1943), 483-493.

———, and Blakemore, H. M. "Testing clerical applicants," *J. Appl. Psychol.*, 26 (1942), 852-855.

Hessemer, M. "The Thurstone PMA Tests in a Study of Academic Success with School of Engineering Chemistry and Physics." Unpublished M.A. thesis, Pennsylvania State College, 1942.

Hildreth, G. "Comparison of early Binet records with college aptitude test scores," *J. Educ. Psychol.*, 30 (1939), 365-371.

Hill, T. H., et al. *Counselor's Guide to Georgia Colleges*. Atlanta: Regents of the University System of Georgia, 1960.

Hovland, C. I., and Wonderlic, E. F. "A critical analysis of the Otis Self-Administering Test of Mental Ability," *J. Appl. Psychol.*, 23 (1939), 367-387.

Hunter, E. C. "Changes in scores of college students on the A. C. E. Psychological Examination at yearly intervals," *J. Educ. Res.*, 36 (1942), 284-291.

Kefauver, G. N., et al. "The horizontal organization of secondary education," *U. S. Office of Educ. Bull.*, 17 (1932).

Kohn, H. A. "Achievement and intelligence examinations correlated with each other and with teacher's rankings," *J. Genet. Psychol.*, 52 (1938), 433-437.

Ladd, A. H. "The differential predictive value of the W-B Scale for certain areas of teacher preparation," In *Indiana Univer., Sch. Educ., Stud. Educ. 1950.* Bloomington, Ind., 2 (1951), 62-68.

Laycock, S. R., and Hutcheon, N. B. "A preliminary investigation into the problem of measuring engineering aptitude," *J. Educ. Psychol.*, 30 (1939), 280-289.

Lazarsfeld, P. F., and Gaudet, H. "Who gets a job?" *Sociometry*, 4 (1941), 64-77.

Lefever, D. W., et al. "Relation of test scores to age and education for adult workers," *Educ. Psychol. Measmt.*, 6 (1946), 351-360.

Lord, A. B. "A survey of four hundred forty-nine special class pupils," *J. Educ. Res.*, 27 (1933), 108-114.

McGehee, W. "Freshman grades and the American Council Psychological Examinations," *Sch. and Soc.*, 47 (1938), 222-224.

———. "Prediction of differential achievement in a technological college," *J. Appl. Psychol.*, 27 (1943), 88-92.

McMurray, R. N., and Johnson, I. L. "Development of instruments for selecting and placing factory employees," *Adv. Mgt.*, 10 (1945), 113-120.

McNemar, Q. "Critical examination of the University of Iowa studies of environmental influences upon the I.Q.," *Psychol. Bull.*, 37 (1940), 63-92.

MacPhail, A. H. "Q and L scores on the A. C. E. Psychological Examinations," *Sch. and Soc.*, 56, (1942), 248-251.

Marvel, H. T., et al. "The new Stanford-Binet at the college level," *J. Educ. Psychol.*, 31, (1949), 705-709.

Marshall, M. V. "What intelligence quotient is necessary to success?" *J. Higher Educ.*, 14 (1943), 99-100.

Memoirs. The National Academy of Sciences, XVI (1921). Ch. 15.

Miller, W. S. "Variation and significance of intelligence quotients obtained from group tests," *J. Educ. Psychol.*, 15 (1924), 360.

Moore, H. "Experience with employment tests" ("Natl. Indust. Conf. Bd., Studies in Pers. Policy," No. 32.) 1941.

Morton, N. W. *Occupational Abilities*. New York: Oxford University Press, 1935.

Mosier, C. I. "Group of factors in college curricula," *J. Educ. Psychol.*, 26 (1935), 513-522.

Munroe, R. L. "Rorschach findings on college students," *J. Consult. Psychol.*, 10 (1946), 301-316.

Older, H. J. "A note on the twenty-minute time limit of the Otis S-A tests when used with superior students," *J. Appl. Psychol.*, 26 (1942), 241-244.

Otis, A. S. *Manual for the Otis Self-Administering Tests of Mental Ability*. Yonkers, N. Y.: World Book Co., 1922.

———. "The selection of mill workers by mental tests," *J. Appl. Psychol.*, 4 (1920), 339-31'

Paterson, D. G., et al. *The Minnesota Mechanical Abilities Tests*. Minneapolis: University of Minnesota Press, 1930.

———, and Darley, J. G. *Men, Women, and Jobs*. Minneapolis: University of Minnesota Press, 1936.

Pemberton, Carol L. "Personality inventory data related to A. C. E. subscores," *J. Consult. Psychol.*, 15 (1951), 160-162.

Pintner, R. *Intelligence Testing*. New York: Henry Holt, 1931.

Plant, W. J., and Richardson, H. "The I. Q. of the average college student," *J. Counsel. Psychol.*, 5 (1958), 229-231.

Pond, M. "Occupations, intelligence, age and schooling," *Pers. J.*, 11 (1933), 373-382.

———, and Bills, M. A. "Intelligence and clerical jobs," *Pers. J.*, 12 (1933), 41-56.

Proctor, W. M. "Intelligence and length of schooling in relation to occupational levels," *Sch. and Soc.*, 42 (1935), 783-786.

———. "A 13-year follow-up of high school pupils," *Occupations*, 15 (1937), 306-310.

Pruette, L., and Fryer, D. "Affective factors in vocational maladjustment," *Ment. Hyg.*, 7 (1923), 102-118.

Rabin, I., and Guertin, W. H. "Research with the Wechsler-Bellevue test: 1945-1950," *Psychol. Bull.*, 48 (1951), 211-248.

Rabin, I. "The use of the Wechsler-Bellevue Scales with normal and abnormal persons," *Psychol. Bull.*, 42 (1945), 410-422.

Rainier, R. A. "Use of tests in guiding student nurses," *Amer. J. Nurs.*, 42 (1942), 679-682.

Rigg, M. C. "Relation of college achievement tests to grades and to intelligence. *J. Educ. Psychol.*," 30 (1939), 397-400.

Roe, Anne. "A Rorschach study of a group of scientists and technicians." *J. Consult. Psychol.*, 10 (1946), 317-327.

Rolfe, J. F. "The measurement of teaching ability: study number two," *J. Exp. Educ.*, 14 (1945), 52-74.

Rostker, L. E. "The measurement of teaching ability: study number one," *J. Exp. Educ.*, 14 (1945), 6-51.

Sartain, A. Q. "The use of certain standardized tests in the selection of inspectors in an aircraft factory," *J. Consult. Psychol.*, 9 (1945), 234-235.

———. "Relation between scores on certain standard tests and supervisory success in an aircraft factory," *J. Appl. Psychol.*, 30 (1946), 328-332.

Satter, G. A. *An Evaluation of the Personal Inventory and Certain Other Measures in the Prediction of Submarine Officers' Evaluation of Enlisted Men.* Washington, D. C.: U. S. Department of Commerce, 1946.

Schneidler, G. G., and Berdie, R. F. "Educational hierarchies and scholastic survival," *J. Educ. Psychol.,* 33 (1942), 199-208.

Scott, W. D., Clothier, R. C., and Spriegel, W. P. *Personnel management.* New York: McGraw-Hill, 1954.

Seagoe, M. V. "Prognostic tests and teaching success," *J. Educ. Res.,* 38 (1945), 685-690.

Segel, D. "Prediction of success in college," *U. S. Office of Educ. Bull.,* 75 (1934).

———, and Gerberich, J. R. "Differential college achievement predicted by the American Council Psychological Examination," *J. Appl. Psychol.,* 17 (1933), 637-645.

———, and Proffitt, M. M. "Some factors in the adjustment of college students," *U. S. Office of Educ. Bull.,* 12 (1937).

Shanner, W. M. "Report on Thurstone Tests for primary mental abilities," *Educ. Rec. Bull.,* 27 (1939), 54-60.

———, and Kuder, G. F. "A comparative study of freshman week tests given at the University of Chicago," *Educ. Psychol. Measmt.,* 1 (1941), 85-92.

Shaw, D. C. "A study of the relationships between Thurstone Primary Mental Abilities and high school achievement," *J. Educ. Psychol.,* 40 (1949), 239-249.

Shuman, J. T. "The value of aptitude tests for supervisory workers in the aircraft engine and propeller industries," *J. Appl. Psychol.,* 29 (1945), 185-190.

——— "Value of aptitude tests for factory workers in the aircraft engine and propeller industries," *J. Appl. Psychol.,* 29 (1945), 156-160.

Simon, L. M., and Levitt, E. A. "The relation between Wechsler-Bellevue I. Q. scores and occupational area," *Occupations,* 29 (1950), 23-25.

Smith, M. "University student intelligence and occupation of father," *Amer. Sociol. Rev.,* 7 (1942), 764-771.

Sparling, E. "Do college students choose vocations wisely?" New York: *Teachers College Contributions to Education,* 561 (1933).

Staff, Personnel Research Section, AGO. "The Army General Classification Test," *Psychol. Bull.,* 42 (1945), 760-768.

Staff, Personnel Research Section, AGO. "The Army General Classification Test, with special reference to the construction and standardization of forms 1a and 1b," *J. Educ. Psychol.,* 38 (1947), 385-420.

Staff, Test and Research Section, Bureau of Naval Personnel. "Psychological test construction and research in the Bureau of Naval Personnel: the Basic Test Battery," *Psychol. Bull.,* 42 (1945), 561-571, 638-644.

Stalnaker, J. M. "Primary mental abilities," *Sch. and Soc.,* 50 (1939), 868-872.

Stewart, Naomi. "AGCT scores of Army personnel grouped by occupation," *Occupations,* 26 (1947), 5-41.

Stoddard, G. D. "The I. Q.: its ups and downs," *Educ. Rec.,* 20 (1939), 44-57.

Stopher, E. C. "The freshman testing program." *J. Higher Educ.,* 12 (1941), 159-162.

Strang, Ruth. *Personal Development and Guidance in College and Secondary School.* New York: Harper, 1934.

Stuit, D. B., and Hudson, H. H. "The relation of primary mental abilities to scholastic success in professional schools," *J. Exp. Educ.,* 10 (1942), 179-182.

Super, D. E. "The A. C. E. Psychological Examination and special abilities," *J. Psychol.,* 9 (1940), 221-226.

Tamminen, A. W. "A comparison of the Army General Classification Test and the Wechsler-Bellevue Intelligence Scales," *Educ. Psychol. Measmt.,* 11 (1951), 646-655.

Terman, L. M., and Oden, Melita H. *The Gifted Child Grows Up*. Stanford: Stanford University Press, 1947.

———, and Oden, Melita H. *The Gifted Group at Mid-life*. Stanford: Stanford University Press, 1959.

Thompson, C. E. "Selecting executives by psychological tests," *Educ. Psychol. Measmt.*, 7 (1947), 773-778.

Thorndike, R. L., "Constancy of the I. Q.," *Psychol. Bull.*, 27 (1940), 167-186.

Thurstone, L. L., Thurstone, Thelma G., and Adkins, Dorothy C. "The 1938 Psychological Examination," *Educ. Rec.*, 20 (1939), 263-300.

Thurstone, Thelma G. "Primary mental abilities of children," *Educ. Psychol. Measmt.*, 1 (1941), 105-116.

Tiffin, J., and Greenly, A. J. "Employee selection tests for electrical fixture assemblers and radio assemblers," *J. Appl. Psychol.*, 33 (1939), 240-263.

Traxler, A. E. "Reliability, constancy, and validity of the Otis I. Q.," *J. Appl. Psychol.*, 18 (1934), 241-251.

———. "Stability of scores on the Primary Mental Abilities Test," *Sch. and Soc.*, 53 (1941), 255-256.

——— "Correlation between 'mechanical aptitude scores' and 'mechanical comprehension' scores," *Occupations*, 22 (1943), 42-43.

———. "The correlation between two tests of academic aptitude," *Sch. and Soc.*, 61 (1945), 383-384.

Tredick, V. D. "The Thurstone Primary Mental Abilities Test and a Battery of Vocational Guidance Tests as Predictors of Academic Success." Unpublished thesis, Pennsylvania State College, 1941.

Turney, A. H., and Fee, Mary. "The comparative value for junior high school use of five group mental tests," *J. Educ. Psychol.*, 24 (1933), 371-379.

Tyler, Leona E. *The Psychology of Human Differences*. New York: Appleton-Century-Crofts, 1956.

Ungar, E. W., and Burr, E. T. *Minimum Mental Age Levels of Accomplishment*. Albany: University of State of New York, 1931.

Viteles, M. S. "Research in the selection of motormen," *J. Pers. Res.*, 4 (1925), 100-115, 173-199.

Votaw, J. F. "Regression lines for estimating intelligence quotients and American Council Examination scores," *J. Educ. Psychol.*, 37 (1946), 179-181.

Watson, R. I. "The use of the Wechsler-Bellevue Scales: a supplement," *Psychol. Bull.*, 43 (1946), 61-68.

Wechsler, D. *The Measurement of Adult Intelligence*. Baltimore: Williams and Wilkins, 1944.

Weintraub, R. G., and Salley, R. E. "Graduation prospects of an entering freshman," *J. Educ. Res.*, 39 (1945), 116-126.

Wellman, B. L. "Our changing concept of intelligence," *J. Consult. Psychol.*, 2 (1938), 97-107.

———, Skeels, H. M., and Skodak, M. "Review of McNemar's critical examination of Iowa studies," *Psychol. Bull.*, 37 (1940), 93-111.

Whipple, G. M. (ed.). "Intelligence: its nature and nurture," *39th Yrbk. Nat. Soc. of Educ.*, 1940.

Wolking, W. D. "Predicting academic achievement with the Differential Aptitude and the Primary Mental Abilities tests," *J. Appl. Psychol.*, 39 (1955), 115-118.

Wrenn, C. G. "Intelligence and the vocational choices of college students," *Educ. Rec.*, 16 (1935), 217-219.

Yum, K. S. "Primary mental abilities and scholastic achievement in the divisional studies of the University of Chicago," *J. Appl. Psychol.*, 25 (1941), 712-720.

VII

PROFICIENCY

Promise and Proficiency

IN COUNSELING young people concerning the choice of careers one is generally concerned with *promise,* that is, with prospects of success in a field in which the youth has as yet had no substantial training or experience. In selecting employees, on the other hand, the concern is more likely to be with *proficiency,* that is, with present ability to perform the tasks involved in a given job. Proficiency, achievement, or trade tests are therefore generally thought of as instruments for the selection of personnel or for the evaluation of the outcome of training, whether in school or on the job. However, past achievement is often one of the best indices of future accomplishment, so that achievement tests can frequently be used as tests of aptitude for related types of activity.

The difference between an aptitude and an achievement test therefore lies more in its use than in its content. An achievement or proficiency test is used to ascertain what and how much has been learned or how well a task can be performed; the focus is on evaluation of the past without reference to the future, except for the implicit assumption that acquired skills and knowledge will be useful in their own right in the future. A test of achievement in arithmetic is therefore a measure of mastery of the essential processes of arithmetic and of ability to make certain types of computations. A measure of proficiency in typing is an index of ability to copy typewritten material with speed and accuracy and therefore of ability to perform certain types of clerical duties to an employer's satisfaction. An aptitude test is used to judge the speed and ease with which skills and knowledge, that is, proficiency, will be acquired. But, obviously, proficiency in a given task may be an index of promise in a related task, and knowledge of certain types of facts may be indicative of facility for the learning of other types of facts.

Therefore a test of arithmetic achievement may be a good index of aptitude for algebra or for engineering, a test of typing proficiency may be a good measure of aptitude for stenography, and a test of information concerning recent developments in science may be a good predictor of success in medical training. Each such relationship is of course strictly hypothetical until experimentally checked and found to be true, for even a good achievement test cannot be assumed to be a good aptitude test until it has been validated in the same manner as any other aptitude test. Achievement in arithmetic may prove to predict success in algebra, but have no relationship to engineering grades; one cannot take the relationship for granted, since what may seem like perfectly legitimate assumptions in the field of prediction often prove unwarranted. An achievement test (or test of any type) can be used as an aptitude test only when there is a known relationship between the performance tested and the performance in which success is to be predicted. This is the essence of aptitude testing, the understanding of which takes all the mystery out of the subject. As it becomes more generally realized that aptitude testing is nothing more than the prediction of success in one performance by means of a measure of success in another performance known to be related to it, people in need of guidance will have more reasonable expectations from tests, business and industrial men will be more inclined to see their possibilities and limitations, and professional users of tests will have more freedom to make legitimate use of them.

Educational Achievement Tests

Educational achievement tests are of interest to us here only as indices of promise in vocational activities. Treatises of their use in evaluating the results of instruction, as measures of educational progress, in predicting educational success, and related topics are numerous (Lindquist, 1951; Thorndike and Hagen, 1961; Traxler et al., 1953); unfortunately there has been less study of their value in predicting vocational success.

In the prediction of educational success, educational achievement tests have been effectively used in the admissions programs of colleges and professional schools. In most investigations they have been tried in combination with tests of scholastic aptitude and with high school averages, in order to determine the relative value of each type of predictor. In one such study at the University of Minnesota (Williamson and Bordin, 1942), it was found that high school rank was the best single predictor of sophomore achievement, but that a combination of the three types of indices was better than any single index. They may be similarly used by counselors in guiding students concerning the choice of college or professional school, the counselee's standing on a test in comparison with typical candidates for admission being used as an index of the possible wisdom of the choice.

It would be desirable also to have data which would make it possible to counsel concerning the wisdom of the choice of a major field of study such as premedical, engineering, business, and related courses, but unfortunately the data which are needed for such applications of achievement test results are available for only a few institutions. Although the assumption that a *weakness* in science after high school should be taken as a negative indication for a college major in science has some justification, it should not be concluded that the *lack* of a given high school subject will mean a weakness in a related college subject (provided the student can take a beginning course in college), for too many studies of the importance of high school prerequisites in college admissions (Bolenbaugh and Proctor, 1927) have demonstrated that one may do superior college work regardless of lack of background in specific high school subjects. On the other hand, as Super and Bachrach's review of studies of science and engineering (1957) points up, the quality of work done in a high school subject, whether measured by the grade obtained or by score on an achievement test, is a good predictor of the quality of work that will be done in a college course in the same subject. What is known concerning the actual predictive value of achievement tests will be examined in connection with the specific tests discussed below, but for detailed treatment reference is made to texts on educational measurement and to Buros' Yearbooks (1959). Experience has shown that achievement tests not only yield predictions of college averages which are about as good as those provided by intelligence tests, but also give better differential predictions of success in specific subjects than do intelligence tests (Segel, 1934).

The Co-operative Achievement Tests (Educational Testing Service, periodically). The Co-operative Test Service began the publication of annual editions of achievement tests in the major school subjects early in the 1930's, sponsored by the American Council on Education and operated under the leadership of Ben D. Wood and John C. Flanagan during the first decade of its existence. It is now part of the Educational Testing Service.

Applicability, Content, Administration, Scoring, and Norms. Each test is designed for use at a specified educational level, which may include a range of as many as three or four years. The content is kept up to date by the periodic publication of new editions, but earlier editions are also available and are generally usable for several years (an important point, as examination of the content of some older social studies or science tests will reveal). Norms are provided for large groups of students, and are made national and kept up to date by the large-scale testing programs in which the annual editions are used. The content varies with the field covered by the test and with the level for which it is designed, the method of construction (discussed below) providing for adequate coverage.

Of special interest in vocational and educational guidance and selection are the Co-operative General Achievement Tests (Natural Sciences, Social Studies, and Mathematics), designed for use with high school students and college freshmen; the Co-operative General Culture Test (History and Social Studies, Literature, Science, Mathematics, and Fine Arts) designed for college students; the Co-operative Contemporary Affairs Test for College Students, which measures familiarity with recent developments in Public Affairs, Science and Medicine, and Literature and Art; the Co-operative Achievement Tests in English, Mathematics, Social Studies, Science, and Foreign Languages, designed to evaluate achievement in junior high school, senior high school, and lower division college courses; and the Sequential Tests of Educational Progress, designed to measure critical skills in the application of learning in seven major fields from elementary school through the sophomore year of college. These tests have the advantage of providing not only comparisons of the achievement of the person being studied with that of other persons with similar backgrounds, but also a picture of the relative strengths and weaknesses of the counselee in the subjects tested. The General Achievement Tests, being only generally related to high school courses, are useful in counseling high school seniors and entering college freshmen concerning the choice of college majors; the General Culture Test and the STEP, less anchored to specific courses, are useful in helping students understand their special strengths and can be used as both interest and aptitude tests, for they reflect to a considerable extent the subjects in which the student has been interested and in which his aptitudes have found outlets; the Contemporary Affairs Test functions as an information test of interest and aptitude.

Administration is simple, and scoring can be done either by hand or by IBM test-scoring machines; in either case, the use of special answer sheets makes for economy of materials and ease of scoring.

Standardization and Initial Validation. As in the case of most such tests, the Co-operative Achievement Tests are developed by subject-matter experts who work with test technicians; test outlines are based on analyses of courses of study and textbooks, or of other relevant materials, and items are checked by both types of experts. The first type of validity achieved is, therefore, content validity. Further validation is occasionally carried out by correlating test scores with high school or college grades; these correlations have generally been moderately high (.30 to .50) for appropriate subjects.

Reliability. The reliability coefficients vary slightly with the test and form, but have generally been .90 or higher, as one would expect in the case of subject-matter tests constructed by experienced technicians.

Validity. It has already been stated that the validities of the Co-operative Achievement Tests for the prediction of grades in related subjects range from about .30 to about .50. When scores made on a battery of achievement tests such as the Co-operative General Culture Test are combined, higher correlations are reported.

More striking still are the mean General Culture scores made by students in different major fields, which show that students of journalism, religion, and law made above average total scores, probably reflecting their broader interests, whereas engineers have apparently a much more restricted range of interests and make significantly low general culture scores. More important than pre-occupational differences in total general information are, of course, the differences in patterns of scores on the various subtests. Analyses (Schneidler and Berdie, 1942) of these show that students who later became medical students had made generally high scores as freshmen. Dentistry students had excelled in mathematics and science but not in other areas. Journalism students reversed this pattern. Library Science students were high in English but mediocre in other fields. Business students were characteristically high in mathematics but low in English.

It would be desirable to have data showing the relationship between patterns of achievement on tests such as the STEP and General Culture Tests, and choice, achievement, and satisfaction in different types of work. One would expect, for example, that social workers would be persons who, in college, made their highest scores on tests of the social studies, and that successful engineers are those who, on entering college, showed special strength on tests of achievement in natural sciences. Studies with miscellaneous tests reviewed by Super and Bachrach (1957) support this, but data for these specific tests are needed.

Use of the Co-operative Tests in Counseling and Selection. In view of the moderately high relationship between scores on these subject-matter achievement tests and grades in appropriate courses, they may well be used in helping students evaluate their prospects of success in various major fields in high school and college, in placing students in sections for which their background qualifies them, and in selecting students for courses of training which emphasize mastery at a higher level, of the same type of subject matter as that covered by the test. There are as yet no direct, objective data to justify counseling concerning the choice of an occupation on the basis of educational achievement test scores, but insofar as achievement on a test is related to grades in a professional or vocational school, and grades in such a school are related to entry into or success in the occupation for which it prepares, it should be safe to deduce that some educational achievement tests do have at least indirect predictive value for some occupations.

The Iowa Tests of Educational Development (Science Research Associates). The Iowa Tests of Educational Development, prepared under the direction of E. F. Lindquist, follow the pattern established by the USAFI Tests of General Educational Development during World War II and used widely in evaluating the readiness of veterans for admission to college. Like the GED Tests, the ITED attempt to measure broad intellectual skills and interests, understanding of, and ability to use what has been learned, rather than mastery of standard subject matter or knowledge of specific facts. They thus resemble the Sequential Tests of Educational Development in their basic philosophy. It is worth noting, therefore, that these achievement tests tend to resemble intelligence or scholastic aptitude tests, and are something of a cross between the two types. They tend to measure the functioning of intelligence in the use of academic skills and data, and they are designed to predict success in college.

Applicability, Content, and Administration. The ITED are designed for use in grades 9 through 12. They consist of nine parts, the first eight of which are combined into a composite score for a total of ten scores. The specific tests are: Understanding Basic Social Concepts, General Background in the Natural Sciences, Correctness and Appropriateness of Expression, Ability to Do Quantitative Thinking, Interpretation of Reading Materials in the Social Studies, Natural Sciences, and Literature, General Vocabulary, and Use of Sources of Information. Total testing time is about eight hours, divided into briefer sessions. Scoring may be done either by machine or by hand-scoring stencils.

The norming of these tests represents a real advance over practices that have tended to prevail in test development: national norms are based on large numbers of schools; the publisher assists individual schools in compiling local norms; and expectancy tables are provided to College Entrance Examination Board Tests and to freshman grades in three types of colleges. Average profiles of students tested in high school and attending college, graduating from college, and graduating with majors in eleven different fields ranging from mathematics and science to the fine arts, are supplied.

Standardization and Initial Validation. Standard test construction methods were used in developing this battery, building on earlier experience with similar tests. The result is an efficient test, as shown in the specificity of the norms and in the excellent expectancy tables which constitute a meaningful way of reporting validity data.

Validity. Technical details are reported in a research manual, containing considerable evidence on the predictive value of the battery for college achievement. No data on the validity of the battery for occupational prediction are presented, but the tests are not designed for that purpose. It is obvious, however, that the prediction of academic success is a first step in the prediction of success in occupations which require college preparation. The validities tend to run from .46 to .79 for grades in the liberal arts subjects.

Use of the ITED in Counseling and Selection.   The established predictive validity of this battery for college grades makes it clear that it is a useful tool for counseling concerning the choice of college and of college major, functioning as a combination aptitude and achievement test. It can similarly be used in selection, but is somewhat lengthy unless part scores are to be used. The part scores have value in counseling students concerning strengths and weaknesses, identifying areas in which remedial work may be called for and skills which can be capitalized in further study.

The Essential High School Content Battery (World Book Co.).   As the title indicates, this battery measures achievement in the core subjects of high school education: mathematics, science, social studies, and English. The content is based on textbooks, courses of study, and expert opinion in the various fields. It is thus probably most appropriate for students in academic or college preparatory programs. The norms are very complete, and are broken down by type of program, including commercial. They cover grades ten to twelve and college freshmen. The required testing time is about three hours and 45 minutes, or five school periods. Validity data, in the form of correlations with college grades and expectancy tables, are still sparse, but should be equal to that of other subject-matter tests. No data on vocational validity are available, making the test useful primarily in evaluating school achievement and predicting further academic success.

Vocational Proficiency Tests

Unlike tests of educational achievement, vocational achievement tests cannot well be used as measures of aptitude in students; vocational proficiency tests measure skills or knowledge already acquired, rather than ability to acquire them. The degree of skill or knowledge in one occupation cannot often be used to predict the degree of skill which will be acquired in another occupation, even when the latter can be considered a higher level occupation of the same general type. Skill as a machinist is an inefficient index for the prediction of success in engineering, for training in the one occupation takes as long as training in the other, and the varying degrees of aptitudes needed in each can be more easily measured by other types of tests. On the other hand, vocational proficiency tests can be used as indices of the prospects of success in a job when dealing with trained candidates for a job. Such tests are therefore widely useful in selection, but in counseling only with marginal workers who may need to be encouraged to change their field of endeavor. Because they are largely a selection technique, and because companies with good selection devices of their own prefer to keep them from becoming known to others, there is little published material concerning specific vocational proficiency tests. Apart from a few stenographic tests, the trade tests developed by the U.S. Armed Forces and Employment Service are the most generally known. Others, like typing tests, are often informally given and evaluated, as samples of work.

The Blackstone Stenography Test (World Book Co., 1932). This test is designed to measure more than ability to take and transcribe dictation; it includes English, office practice, and related abilities.

Applicability, Content, Administration, Scoring, and Norms. This test was designed for use at or above the high school level. The English test measures knowledge of grammar, punctuation, capitalization, and spelling by means of sentences in which the type of error made is to be indicated; three tests measure proficiency in hyphenating, alphabetizing, and abbreviating; two tests cover knowledge of office practice and business organization; and one test measures ability to take dictation at a fixed rate and to transcribe two letters on the typewriter. This is a group test, but the two letters to be dictated are to be chosen from the manual on the basis of appropriateness to the persons being tested. Dictation time ranges from one to three minutes, transcription time is twelve minutes, and other parts require 33 minutes. Norms are based on students with varying amounts of training and on employed stenographers.

Standardization and Initial Validation. Correlations of .62 and .79 with efficiency ratings for groups of 37 and 49 stenographers are reported in the manual. These seem remarkably high, but the data do not permit evaluation of the adequacy of this phase of the work with the test.

Reliability. The inter-form reliability reported in the manual is .88 for 1000 subjects.

Validity. No validity data have been located in the literature, although they would be even more desirable in the case of a test such as this than in the case of the typing test, since it purports to measure more than one phase of stenographic work.

Use of the Blackstone Stenography Test in Selection. In the case of this test as with other selection tests, local critical minima should be established with the aid of employee evaluation techniques. Such minima must, of course, vary with the available supply of workers.

The Seashore-Bennett Stenographic Proficiency Tests (Psychological Corporation, 1943). The Seashore-Bennett tests are a current series of phonographically recorded stenographic proficiency tests, two forms designed for use in employee selection by business firms. The use of recordings of business letters was resorted to as a method of standardizing the voice and rate of dictation.

Applicability, Content, Administration, Scoring, and Norms. These tests have, like others in this category, been designed for use at the high school level or above, with persons who have had some training in shorthand and typing. They consist of phonographically recorded letters, five letters (four discs or one LP side) to each form of the test. Two letters are short and slow, two are of medium length and average speed, and one is long and rapid. Administration requires about fifteen minutes, with another half hour for transcription. Complete scripts and reproductions of good and poor transcriptions are provided for use in scoring. Norms were at first not provided, as it was expected that they would vary considerably from company to company, and nation-wide norms could not be collected. Distributions of scores for several companies are provided by Seashore and Bennett (1948).

Standardization and Initial Validation. In one sense, this test can depend on internal evidence of validity, for it involves shorthand and transcription. It is virtually a life-situation test. Preliminary validation studies have been reported, however, showing correlations of .49 and .61, respectively, with supervisors' ratings of general value (combined ratings) and stenographic ability (Seashore and Bennett, 1948).

Reliability. When scores on two of the letters were correlated with scores on the other three, the reliability coefficients were .80, .83, and .91.

Validity. No other validation studies have been completed and published. In this type of test validity seems self-evident.

Use of the Seashore-Bennett Tests in Selection. The availability of alternate forms of these tests makes possible their use both in initial selection and in the evaluation of progress for promotion. Local norms for both purposes should be developed, as job requirements vary both within an organization and among organizations. It may be desirable, for example, to start new stenographers in certain departments but not in others, transferring them to these latter positions after promotion tests demonstrate that they have attained the proficiency needed in the more demanding positions.

The SRA Typing Skills Test (Science Research Associates). The SRA Typing Skills Test consists of two parts, requiring fifteen minutes for administration and yielding two scores, one for accuracy and one for speed. Two forms are available, suitable for high school and employment use. The tests are standard typing tasks. Although normative and validation data are scarce, one study has reported validities of .40 and .64 for the respective parts, using validation and cross-validation groups of about 100 typists in a two-week induction training course given to new insurance company employees, with completion of that course as the criterion (Skula and Spillane, 1954) . The test therefore shows promise as a selection test for typists.

Interview Aids and Trade Questions. During both World War I and World War II extensive use was made of trade tests in the rapid classification and assignment of military personnel. The first trade tests were described in detail by Chapman (1921) ; those developed by the United States Employment Service have yet to be described in detail. Between the two World Wars the technique of trade testing was further developed at the Cincinnati Employment Center (Thompson, 1936) , where the trade questions were revised and brought up to date. Subsequently the United States Employment Service recognized the value to this approach, and developed trade questions for use in its work, as described in Stead and Shartle (1940, Ch. 3 and pp. 156-162) . Because of its general availability, Thompson's Cincinnati work is described here in order to illustrate the technique; it should be stressed, however, that occupational changes which have taken place since the mid-thirties make local and up-to-date revisions such as those of the USES, and custom-built tests developed as outlined by Stone and Kendall (1956, Ch. 13) , essential.

Applicability, Content, Administration, Scoring, and Norms. These trade questions were designed for use in employment offices and standardized on experienced craftsmen, but they may also be used with high school students who have had some trade training and are seeking their first employment. The book consists of questions concerning the tools, materials, and methods of 131 trades ranging from Ammonia Pipefitter and Armature Winder to Wood Finisher and Woodmill Worker. Each test contains from 15 to 25 questions, such as: "What kind of weld has a boiler tube?" (for Boilermaker), the correct answer to which is "lap or nobble." The examiner reads the questions aloud, and they are answered orally. The examiner notes the answers. This procedure has the advantage of appealing to manual workers more than would a paper and pencil test. The number of right answers is converted into a decile rating and a proficiency rating ranging from novice to expert. Norms are occasionally based on small groups, the work having been published while in process of completion.

Standardization and Initial Validation. Because of the tendency to rely on internal validity in achievement and proficiency tests, and because of early publication of the book, statistical evidence of validity is lacking. However, the fact that questions were developed with the aid of specialists in each field, and their ability to differentiate novices from journeymen and experts, constitute evidence of a sort.

Reliability. Data are not presented on the reliability of these trade questions. Stead and Shartle (1940) reported reliabilities of .79 to .93 for the USES tests.

Validity. No later studies casting light on the validity of Thompson's questions in selecting workers have come to the writers' attention.

Use of the Interview Aids and Trade Questions in Selection. Experience has repeatedly shown that a few well selected questions concerning the tools, material, and methods of his claimed trade are likely to weed out the ill-trained or inexperienced worker who wants to bluff his way into a desirable job (a very real problem in military classification) and command the respect of the expert who knows his craft. The use of trade questions in employment offices therefore seems amply justified, even though controlled experiments and quantitative data are lacking.

The Purdue Vocational Tests (Science Research Associates various dates since 1951) . Several tests developed at Purdue University for proficiency testing in the skilled trades have been published by Science Research Associates. These include the Purdue Test for Electricians, the Purdue Test for Machinists and Machine Operators, and the Purdue Blueprint Reading Test. The second test, for example, can be scored for six operations such as lathe and grinder operation. The tests take from 35 to 55 minutes to administer, and they are designed for use in trade schools but can be used with applicants for skilled employment whose work records are too limited for good evaluation of proficiency. Since they are school oriented, they may seem somewhat academic to older and more experienced workers. They have the obvious advantage of being more up-to-date than the published trade questions, but their applicability to any local situation needs to be investigated before they are put to use, and as usual local norms and validation data should be collected.

REFERENCES FOR CHAPTER VII

Bolenbaugh, L., and Proctor, W. M. "Relation of the subjects taken in high school to success in college," *J. Educ. Res.*, 15 (1927), 87-92.

Buros, O. K. (ed.). *Mental Measurement Yearbook.* New Brunswick, N. J.: Rutgers University Press, 1938, 1939, 1940, 1949, 1953, 1959.

Chapman, J. C. *Trade Tests.* New York: Henry Holt, 1921.

Lindquist, E. L. (ed.). *Educational Measurement.* Washington, D. C.: American Council on Education, 1951.

Schneidler, G. C., and Berdie, R. F. "Educational ability patterns," *J. Educ. Psychol.*, 32 (1942), 92-103.

Seashore, H. G., and Bennett, G. K. "A test of stenography: some preliminary results," *Pers. Psychol.*, 1 (1948), 197-209.

Segel, D. "Prediction of success in college," *U. S. Office of Educ. Bull.*, 75 (1934).

Skula, Mary, and Spillane, R. F. "Validity information exchange," *Pers. Psychol.*, 7 (1954), 147-148.

Stead, W. H., and Shartle, C. L. *Occupational Counseling Techniques.* New York: American Book Co., 1940.

Stone, C. H., and Kendall, W. E. *Effective Personnel Selection Procedures.* Englewood Cliffs, N. J.: Prentice-Hall, 1956.

Super, D. E., and Bachrach, P. B. *Scientific Careers and Vocational Development Theory.* New York: Teachers College Bureau of Publications, 1957.

Thompson, L. A., Jr. and Associates. *Interview Aids and Trade Questions for Employment Offices.* New York: Harper, 1936.

Thorndike, R. L., and Hagen, Elizabeth. *Measurement and Evaluation in Psychology and Education.* New York: Wiley, 1961.

Traxler, A. E., et al. *Introduction to Testing and the Use of Test Results in Public Schools.* New York: Harper, 1953.

Williamson, E. G., and Bordin, E. S. "Prediction of success in the College of Science, Literature, and the Arts." *University of Minnesota Stud. Predict. Schol. Ach.,* 1 (1942), 1-32.

VIII

CLERICAL APTITUDE: PERCEPTUAL SPEED

Is There a Special Clerical Aptitude?

A COMMONLY used classification of clerical jobs (Bingham, 1935) describes three phases of clerical work: doing the work, checking it, and supervising it. Job analysis has shown that these are levels as well as types and that each of these levels of clerical work requires the making of more decisions than the level immediately below it. But planning and decision making imply intelligence—aptitude for abstract thinking—a requirement by no means confined to clerical work. This being the case, one might well ask whether there is actually such a thing as clerical aptitude. Material discussed in the chapter on intelligence shows that general intelligence is indeed a factor in success in clerical work, the minimum desirable I. Q. being 95 to 100, and the minimum requirements rising with the level of responsibility. When promotability is a factor to be considered in the counseling or selection of potential clerical workers, intelligence should be heavily weighted; when, on the other hand, success in a routine clerical job is in question, intelligence exceeding the minimum requirement is all that is needed, other factors then being the decisive ones. What these other factors are will be seen below.

Job analysis suggests other aptitudes which should be important in clerical work. In routine clerical work, at least, one would expect speed and accuracy in checking numerical and verbal symbols to be a characteristic of the successful worker. Bookkeeping, typing, filing, and other record-keeping jobs involve constant checking or copying of words and numbers, calling for perceptual speed and accuracy on the part of the employee. It will be seen below, in the discussion of the Minnesota Clerical Test, that this hypothesis is borne out by research; it will also be seen that speed in perceiving numerical and verbal similarities is so much more important in clerical than in other occupations that there is some justification for referring to this ability as clerical aptitude.

Another aptitude which job analysis suggests should contribute to success in clerical activities is motor skill or manual dexterity. Standard works on aptitude testing such as that by Bingham (1937, p. 152) list motor skill as one of the aptitudes required in clerical work, with the obvious justification that such work involves frequent and rapid manipulation of papers, cards, pencils, typewriters, and other office tools and machines. As will be seen in the next chapter, the only evidence from aptitude tests to support this claim lies in the superior scores made by clerical workers on fine manual dexterity tests. No studies of the relationship of such tests to clerical success are known, and gross manual dexterity has actually been demonstrated to be unrelated to clerical success. It seems that other aptitudes such as intelligence and perceptual speed are so much more important that anyone who has average or better manual dexterity has enough motor skill for success. To put it in other terms, the critical score for manual dexterity in clerical work is so low that almost everyone of average intelligence surpasses it.

Finally, analysis of the work of office clerks has suggested that proficiency in language and in arithmetic is essential to success. These are of course not aptitudes in the strict sense of the term, but only in the sense that such proficiency may be prognostic of success on the job. However, it has been seen that the validity of clerical proficiency tests has not actually been demonstrated against external criteria, legitimate though the assumption may appear.

The answer to our initial question is, then, that two or more aptitudes contribute to success in clerical work, and that one of these appears to be peculiarly important, partially justifying referring to it as clerical aptitude. Although perceptual speed as measured by other techniques is important in other occupations (Harrell, 1940), it has been shown that there are two perceptual factors, one involved primarily in the perception of space relations, the other primarily in clerical (numerical and verbal) tasks (Staff, WMC, 1945:152). The latter's importance in clerical work is such as to warrant its treatment as clerical aptitude. The balance of this chapter will therefore be devoted to a survey of perceptual speed as clerical aptitude.

Typical Tests

Tests measuring perceptual speed by means of numerical or verbal symbols have long been a standard part of the armamentarium of the psychologist, a number of them having been included in the grandfather of measurement tests, Whipple's Manual (1910). It was not until the days of more refined statistical procedures and validation against occupational success, however, that the peculiar value of these tests in vocational guidance and personnel selection became obvious. The idea was tried out and validated as the Minnesota Vocational Test for Clerical Workers at the Minnesota Employment Stabilization Research Institute by Paterson and Andrew (see below). The Psychological Corporation's General Clerical Test and the O'Rourke Clerical Test incorporate items of the same type, together with others which measure numerical and verbal abilities more complex than mere perceptual speed. The Minnesota test is the only clerical aptitude test which has been subjected to widespread and careful study and validation. It is therefore the only instrument in this category to be discussed in detail.

The Minnesota Clerical Test (Psychological Corporation, 1933, 1946, 1959). This test was the one test construction project carried out by the Minnesota Employment Stabilization Research Institute, which found that its needs for tests of intelligence, manual dexterity, mechanical aptitude, spatial visualization, and personality were fairly well met by the then available instruments. It was so easy to administer and score and so thoroughly studied that it immediately became one of the most widely used aptitude tests. It was originally called the Minnesota Vocational Test for Clerical Workers.

Applicability: Effects of Age, Training, and Experience. The Minnesota Clerical Test was designed and standardized for adult use, the adult group including girls of 17 and above and boys aged 19 and above. It was then assumed that the test would be equally applicable to boys and girls of high school age, but data for age and grade norms were subsequently compiled (Schneidler, 1941). These show an increase in scores with age and grade, the median Number-Checking scores for 14, 15, 16, 17, and 18 year-old boys being 89, 94, 100, 104, and 102. As Schneidler points out, the sample is not perfect for age norms, as it includes only those who happened to be in grades eight through twelve; the duller 14 year-olds were therefore not included, and the brighter 18 year-olds had already been graduated from school. However, the age and grade norms resemble each other enough to give one some confidence in both sets.

Unfortunately, Schneidler's analysis is not sufficiently refined to answer the important question concerning the applicability of the test, namely, that concerning the influence of age on scores. Her data reveal an increase in the mean scores of increasingly higher age groups, but they do not indicate whether this increase is due to the selection which normally operates in high schools to eliminate the less intelligent as they get older, to the maturation of clerical aptitude with age, or to the effects of training and experience in high school which involve practice in speed and accuracy of perception. She does provide intelligence test data for her sample, but these are in terms of scores which are insufficiently described to permit interpretation. If they are intelligence quotients, then there was no selection on the basis of intelligence, for the scores remained relatively constant throughout the four years of high school. This would indicate that the increase in clerical scores with age is due either to maturation or to experience. While it would be surprising to find so simple a skill maturing as late as the last two years of high school, it would be still more surprising, in view of data to be presented below, to find that experiences as dissimilar to that of the test as high school work affect the test scores. There are clearly some important problems for further investigation here before this simple-appearing test is really understood. In the meantime it must be used with caution at the adolescent level.

Klugman (1944) attempted to ascertain the effect of a year of schooling on the test. His subjects were a group of 207 commercial high school girls, who showed significant gains in scores on both parts of the Minnesota Clerical Test after a year of high school commercial education. As the 30 oldest did not differ significantly from the 30 youngest, Klugman concluded that the increase was due to training rather than to maturation. This conclusion does not seem warranted, in view of Schneidler's prior finding that scores increased with age in all types of high school students. It is regrettable that Klugman used no control groups.

The problem of the effect of experience, as distinct from maturation, is not confined to the use of the test with adolescents. Andrew (1937) investigated it in the original studies with the test, administering it to 155 clerically experienced women aged 17 to 29 and correlating scores with amount of experience. The correlations for the Numbers and Names Tests were .30 and .31, respectively. This might be taken as indicating that clerical experience has some effect on Minnesota Clerical Test scores, were it not for one problem of sampling: The less experienced group could normally be expected to include some relatively unselected workers of low aptitude who are normally weeded out during the first year or so of experience and who shift to light factory, sales, or other non-clerical employment. If this group could have been sifted out, in retrospective analysis, it might have left a group in which "true" clerical aptitude was equally distributed and in which the correlation between Minnesota Clerical Test scores and length of experience was zero. In another study Andrew and Paterson (1934) administered the test to 28 clerically inexperienced adults before they embarked upon a five-month training program in clerical work, and readministered it again at the end of the training period. The difference between pre-training and post-training scores was not significant, leading to the conclusion that training in clerical work had no effect on the scores of the Minnesota Vocational Test for Clerical Workers.

A further study of the effects of experience was made by Hay and Blakemore (1943) in a large bank. They tested 229 inexperienced and 241 experienced women applicants for clerical employment. The experienced group averaged 7 points higher on the Names, and 7.5 points higher on the Numbers Test, the equivalent of less than .25 sigma or 7 percentile points at the mean. These differences are statistically significant, but in practice they are not likely to prove vital, especially if the reasoning applied to Andrew's first study is valid and applicable here. Indeed, it is highly likely that Hay's inexperienced applicants included some women of little true clerical aptitude who would in due course be weeded out and who would not subsequently be in the market as experienced applicants for clerical employment. If this is so, then it would be all the more legitimate to consider the small but statistically significant difference reported by Hay and Blakemore as psychologically and practically insignificant. The authors found negligible correlations between scores and length of experience in clerical work, further supporting this conclusion.

In summary, it seems necessary to conclude that it has not been demonstrated that training or experience affect scores on the Minnesota Clerical Test. The preponderance of evidence from several ambiguous studies, together with the clear-cut findings of one study of the effect of training on scores, indicates that the test result is relatively independent of training and experience in clerical work.

Sex differences have been found to be significant (Andrew and Paterson, 1934; Englehardt, 1950; Schneidler and Paterson, 1942). This means that although the test is usable with both sexes, separate norms are needed. Women tend to be superior to men in general, although in the same job men and women are found to be equal in clerical aptitude, indicating the effects of selection. Age, however, has no effect on scores according to evidence compiled with adult groups by the same authors.

A defect in the format of the Numbers Test, which should be corrected although it is not serious, has recently been noted by Kirkpatrick (1957). Whereas in the Names Test the dissimilar parts in item pairs which are not identical are distributed evenly throughout the test, in the Numbers Test 77 per cent of the elements which are different are located in the last half of the numbers. Consequently, an examinee who reads these numbers backwards (if indeed any such exist) saves time in his search for dissimilar sets of numbers and may receive a higher score.

Administration and Scoring. The test is designed for group administration and requires fifteen minutes working time. Examiners need to make sure that subjects are working on the proper part of the test, and that they draw a line, as directed, under the last pair at which they looked before the direction to stop was given. Scoring is by means of a stencil and involves a correction for wrong answers. Scores are thus a combination of speed and accuracy and have been criticized as such by Candee and

Blum (1937), who developed a scoring system which yields separate scores for speed and accuracy. Their contention is that accuracy is more important than speed in clerical work, a slow accurate worker being preferable to a fast inaccurate worker. Such a scoring method might be desirable when the criteria permit evaluation of the relative importance of each factor, but in most situations they are not so refined. It seems probable that the combined score provided by the test authors is generally to be preferred for occupational use, giving as it does some weight to each factor. The great majority maintain a fair degree of accuracy, knowing that it counts together with speed, and the important individual differences revealed in the test are differences in speed (Copeland, 1936). If an examinee lowers his accuracy level in order to increase his speed, the wrong-penalty minimizes the gain.

Norms. The manual (1959) provides norms for various male and female occupational groups, according to experience or lack of experience, and for junior and senior high school students. In the case of men, for example, there are norms for 2188 inexperienced applicants for clerical employment in banks; these are divided into those who are employed as general clerks ($N=835$) and those who were hired as machine operators ($N=101$) after testing. There are also norms for 579 experienced male applicants, and for comparable groups of women. Although the separation of experienced from inexperienced groups may not be necessary, in view of the data on the effects of training and experience, the precaution does no harm in view of the sizable numbers involved.

Although the numbers are small and the data were not presented to serve as norms, the USES figures published by Stead and Shartle (1940) and reproduced in Figures 4 and 5 provide useful indications as to the perceptual speed and accuracy of various specific occupations. The data agree reasonably well with the original local norms for the test (also based on small groups).

The adolescent norms provided by Schneidler, and discussed elsewhere in this chapter, are also included in the 1959 manual, as are norms (eleventh and twelfth graders) from a number of New England high schools. These last are divided by curricular groups, with numbers ranging from 89 to 170, and seem, in their current presentation, to be a much more adequate sample than appeared to be the case in the earlier editions of the manual.

One other problem stemming from the age differences which have already been considered remains to be discussed in connection with the norms. There is a very real question as to which norms to use when counseling high school students, a problem which Barnette (1940) has also encountered with business college students. This may best be illustrated

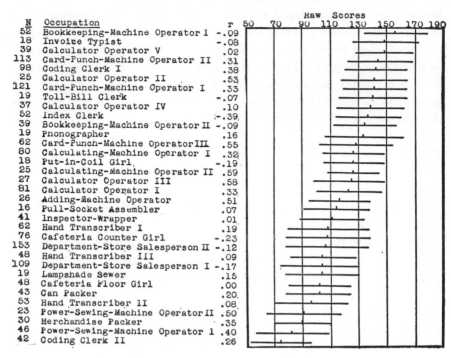

N	Occupation	r
52	Bookkeeping-Machine Operator I	-.09
18	Invoice Typist	-.08
39	Calculator Operator V	.02
113	Card-Punch-Machine Operator II	.31
98	Coding Clerk I	.38
25	Calculator Operator II	.53
121	Card-Punch-Machine Operator I	.33
19	Toll-Bill Clerk	-.07
37	Calculator Operator IV	.10
52	Index Clerk	-.39
39	Bookkeeping-Machine Operator II	-.09
19	Phonographer	.16
62	Card-Punch-Machine Operator III	.55
80	Calculating-Machine Operator I	.32
18	Put-in-Coil Girl	-.19
25	Calculating-Machine Operator II	.59
27	Calculator Operator III	.58
81	Calculator Operator I	.33
26	Adding-Machine Operator	.51
16	Pull-Socket Assembler	.07
41	Inspector-Wrapper	.01
62	Hand Transcriber I	.19
76	Cafeteria Counter Girl	-.23
153	Department-Store Salesperson II	-.12
48	Hand Transcriber III	.09
109	Department-Store Salesperson I	-.17
19	Lampshade Sewer	.15
48	Cafeteria Floor Girl	.00
43	Can Packer	.20
53	Hand Transcriber II	.08
23	Power-Sewing-Machine Operator II	.50
30	Merchandise Packer	.35
46	Power-Sewing-Machine Operator I	.40
42	Coding Clerk II	.26

FIGURE 4

OCCUPATIONAL DIFFERENCES ON THE MINNESOTA CLERICAL NUMBERS TEST
Means and Standard Deviations after Stead and Shartle (1940).

by a specific example. An 18-year-old high school senior, let us say, is considering taking training to be an accountant, has taken the Number-Checking Test, and made a raw score of 106. This puts him at the 50th percentile for his grade, the 58th for his age, and the 74th when compared to employed adults (old norms). So far, then, the picture is one of average or superior clerical aptitude, although one might suspect that the superiority of an average high school senior when compared to employed adults is the result of the selectivity of high schools. However, when compared to accountants and bookkeepers (original norms), the group with which he is to compete, his percentile rank drops to the first. The counselor must ask himself whether this is his true and ultimate standing when compared with accountants and bookkeepers (in which case he should certainly be encouraged to consider other possibilities), or whether the poor standing is the result of immaturity and therefore subject to modification by age and maturation. If the latter is the case, then he and all of his fellow seniors will improve in score, making them even more superior to adults-in-general, although it does not seem likely that they should actually exceed more than 75 or 80 percent of the employed adult population in

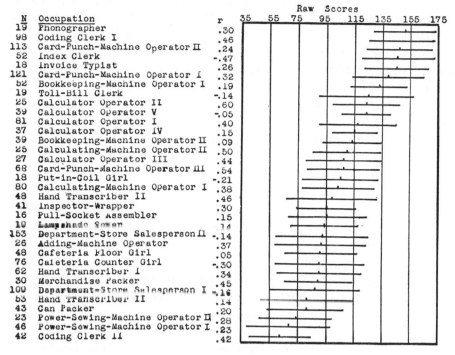

N	Occupation	r
19	Phonographer	.30
98	Coding Clerk I	.46
113	Card-Punch-Machine Operator II	.24
52	Index Clerk	-.47
18	Invoice Typist	.26
121	Card-Punch-Machine Operator I	.32
52	Bookkeeping-Machine Operator I	.19
19	Toll-Bill Clerk	-.14
25	Calculator Operator II	.60
39	Calculator Operator V	-.05
81	Calculator Operator I	.40
37	Calculator Operator IV	.15
39	Bookkeeping-Machine Operator II	.09
25	Calculating-Machine Operator II	.50
27	Calculator Operator III	.44
68	Card-Punch-Machine Operator III	.54
18	Put-in-Coil Girl	-.21
80	Calculating-Machine Operator I	.38
48	Hand Transcriber II	.46
41	Inspector-Wrapper	.30
16	Pull-Socket Assembler	.15
10	Lampshade Sewer	.14
153	Department-Store Salesperson II	-.14
26	Adding-Machine Operator	.37
48	Cafeteria Floor Girl	.05
76	Cafeteria Counter Girl	-.30
62	Hand Transcriber I	.34
30	Merchandise Packer	.45
100	Department-Store Salesperson I	-.16
53	Hand Transcriber II	.14
43	Can Packer	.20
23	Power-Sewing-Machine Operator II	.28
46	Power-Sewing-Machine Operator I	.23
42	Coding Clerk II	.42

Raw Scores: 35 55 75 95 115 135 155 175

FIGURE 5

OCCUPATIONAL DIFFERENCES ON THE MINNESOTA CLERICAL NAMES TEST
Means and Standard Deviations after Stead and Shartle (1940).

clerical aptitudes. In view of this last consideration, it seems wise to assume that there will not be much change in the raw scores of high school seniors after graduation (assumption supported also by the lack of relationship between age and scores among persons aged 17 to 19). The adult occupational norms should therefore be used, cautiously, even for high school juniors and seniors, rather than the age or grade norms made available by the manual.

When in due course more light is thrown on the role of maturation, it may prove necessary, and it may become possible, to provide conversion tables which will show the probable adult score of an adolescent who has made a given raw score; by converting the adolescent raw score to the adult equivalent, and this to the specific occupational percentile, one will then be able to make a fair evaluation of an adolescent's prospects of successful competition in a specific clerical occupation. This procedure has now been adopted by the GATB, but needs to be used with caution (Super, 1960).

Standardization and Initial Validation. The manual for the Minnesota Clerical Test, which has been revised several times, is more complete than most in the presentation of data concerning the standardization and initial validation of the test, and has gone somewhat beyond that in summarizing subsequent findings—a pattern now fortunately being followed to an increasing extent by the more responsible publishers and authors of tests. The data which follow concerning the standardization of the test are therefore also found in the manual.

The correlation between Number-Checking and Name-Checking was found by Andrew (1937) to be .66, indicating that the tests have a great deal in common but that, since their intercorrelation is lower than their individual retest reliabilities of .76 and .83 (Darley, 1934), at least one of them is measuring something not so well measured by the other.

This was shown by other correlational data to be intelligence, which plays a more important part in Name-Checking than it does in Number-Checking; in homogeneous groups the correlation between the former and the Pressey Senior Classification and Verification Tests (of intelligence) was found to be .37, whereas the same figure for the latter was .12. In heterogeneous groups these correlations rose to .65 and .47. These data bring out another fact important to an understanding of the nature of clerical aptitude: In a group of persons of the same general level of intelligence, such as one normally finds in a class in a large high school and in a business office, clerical perception is an aptitude which is unrelated to intelligence; on the other hand, in a group of persons with a wide spread of intelligence, such as one finds in a class in a smaller high school where sectioning has not been possible or in a group of unsorted applicants for clerical employment, those who are more intelligent tend to have more clerical aptitude than those who are less intelligent. The relationship is far from perfect, but it is real.

Since the test involves reading words and numbers, Andrew correlated it also with tests of reading speed, spelling, and arithmetic. Using homogeneous groups, the correlations between reading on the one hand and Numbers and Names on the other were respectively .09 and .45; the correlation between Names and spelling was .65; that between Numbers and arithmetic was .51. Holding intelligence constant, since it plays a part in reading and in the Names Test, the correlations between reading and the Numbers and Names Tests changed to .18 and .30. Since reading and arithmetic are proficiencies and perception an aptitude, one would be inclined to assume that clerical aptitude explains the reading and arithmetic scores, were it not for the fact that skill in reading affects the speed of perception of symbols such as those used in the Minnesota Clerical Test. Leaving the riddle of the hen and the egg unsolved, it is still possible to conclude that, in homogeneous groups, the relationship between reading skill and clerical aptitude is relatively low. In the case of arithmetic the riddle is more solvable, for the Numbers Test requires no computation and is therefore not affected by proficiency in arithmetic; the relationship reported must therefore be causal from Number-Checking to computation rather than vice-versa. This may perhaps justify the conclusion, by analogy, that speed of reading is affected by perceptual speed as measured by Name-Checking.

The relationship between clerical aptitude and success in clerical training was ascertained (Andrew and Paterson, 1934). More than 100 commercial high school students were rated for prospects of success in training by their teachers; the ratings correlated .58 with total Minnesota Clerical scores and .43 with intelligence test scores. The correlations with college accounting grades were found to be .47 for Numbers and .49 for Names. These results seem extraordinarily good; unfortunately, it will be seen that subsequent field validation has not tended to confirm them

The validity of the test for selecting clerical employees was ascertained by correlating supervisors' ratings with Minnesota Clerical Test scores. The groups involved ranged in size from 22 to 97 workers; the reliability of the ratings was not checked. Even with this presumably imperfect criterion, the test validities ranged from .28 to .42. Subsequent studies of the same type, discussed below, have yielded similar results.

Employed and unemployed clerical workers were compared in order to ascertain whether or not there were measurable differences in clerical aptitude between such groups. The critical ratios were 3.32 for Numbers and 4.49 for Names, showing that the employed clerical workers were significantly superior to the unemployed clerical workers on these tests. Further analysis showed that the early unemployed were inferior to those who had been released later in the depression, as well as to the still employed, but that the late unemployed were not inferior to the still employed. As it seems logical that the first to be released would be those whose services were least valued by employers, and the last those whose services were difficult to dispense with, this would seem to be a validation of the Minnesota Clerical Test against employers' ratings of essentiality—an efficiency rating made much more carefully than the average rating.

A final type of preliminary validation of the test carried out by the Minnesota Employment Stabilization Research Institute was the evaluation of the ability of the Minnesota Clerical Test to differentiate clerical from non-clerical workers. This involves the hypothesis that the trait measured is truly an aptitude, one which is supported by research evidence, and the further hypothesis that the aptitude is not so widely or generally distributed that people in general possess it in a degree equal to that characterizing those in the occupation, a supposition which is automatically checked in this type of validation; see Figure 6.

Figure 6 reproduces data from the MESRI studies (Andrew and Paterson 1934) which graphically portray the ability of the Minnesota Clerical Test to differentiate between workers in general and workers employed in various clerical occupations. The distribution of scores for men in general

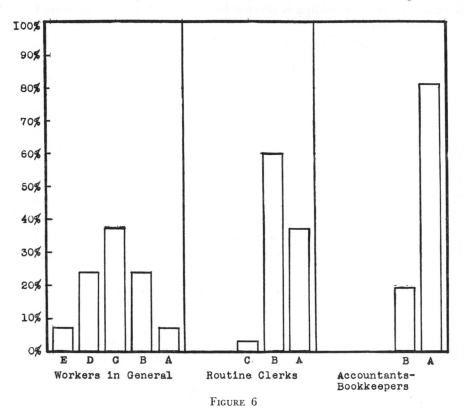

FIGURE 6

OCCUPATIONAL DIFFERENCES ON THE MINNESOTA CLERICAL (NUMBERS) TEST
Showing the percentage of each type of worker making a given letter
grade. After Andrew and Paterson (1934).

is normal, whereas the higher one goes in the scale of clerical occupations the more skewed the distribution becomes. Approximately 7 percent of the worker-in-general group received letter ratings of E on the Numbers Test, while no routine clerical workers received a grade of E; in fact, none of the latter group received ratings of D, and only 3 percent received a grade of C. Accountants and bookkeepers, on the other hand, in no case received a rating as low as C; in fact, more than 80 percent of them rated A on the Numbers Test, as contrasted with about 37 percent of the routine clerks and 7 percent of the workers-in-general.

Although the differentiation between clerical and non-clerical workers shown above is striking, it should not be taken as indicating that no non-clerical occupational groups excel in what has for convenience been labelled clerical aptitude. As the Minnesota norms bring out, miscellaneous minor executives, life insurance salesmen, retail salesmen, and draftsmen are all above the 80th percentile on the Numbers Test. This is perhaps only to be expected, in view of the fact that in all of these occupations there is a great deal of record keeping or work in which minute details must be accurately and quickly checked. Even policemen rate at the 66th percentile. But these scores seem less impressive when it is noted that the only male clerical group whose median is below the 91st percentile when compared to the general population is the shipping and stock clerk category at the 77th percentile.

Reliability. The corrected split-half reliabilities were found to be .85 for the Numbers Test and .89 for the Names Test (manual), while the retest reliabilities were somewhat lower, .76 and .83 respectively (Dailey, 1934). Hay (1943) found retest reliabilities of .61, .69, and .56 for the Numbers Test, and .75, .62, and .81 for the Names Test after intervals as long as 54 months.

Validity. Because of its rapid and widespread adoption, a number of validation studies have been carried out and published by workers in the field. These studies have included the usual variety of correlations with other tests, one-factor analysis and correlations with educational and vocational criteria.

The relationship between Minnesota Clerical Test scores and intelligence was checked by Copeland (1936) and Super (1940). In the former study, correlations with the Otis S.A. Test were found to be .34 for Numbers and .51 for Names; in the latter study the A.C.E. Psychological Examination was used, and the correlations were .26 and .62 respectively. The range of intelligence and clerical aptitude was probably greater in the latter group, which consisted of high school juniors and seniors, than in the former, which was made up of unemployed clerical workers. This would explain the closer relationship between intelligence and the Names Test in Super's study, but not the slightly lower relationship with the Numbers Test, which may be due to chance. Both of these relationships are in between those reported by Anderson and Paterson for more strictly homogeneous and heterogeneous groups. Tredick (1941) correlated the Numbers and Names Tests with Thurstone's Primary Abilities Tests. The former had low r's with verbal, memory, induction, and reasoning tests (.06 to .28); the latter with only the memory test (.24). Other r's were above .36. Both tests are heavily loaded with perceptual and numerical factors, while the Numbers Test is weak in the verbal and reasoning factors.

Only one investigation of the relationship between clerical aptitude and *clerical interest* has been found. Brayfield (1953) correlated scores on the Kuder Preference Record (Form BB) and the two sub-tests of the Minnesota for a group of 231 female clerical workers employed by a large wholesale drug company in the following positions: stenographer, general clerk, typist, high level machine operator, low level machine operator, and entry clerk. Only eight of the product-moment correlation coefficients were significant at either the five or one per cent levels. Scientific interest correlated .46 and .39 with Number and Name Checking, respectively, in the entry group, and .35 with the Name test in the group of high level machine operators. Among general clerks the literary scale correlated .44 with Number and .47 with Name Checking. In this same group, social service interest was negatively related to the Minnesota tests, the *r*'s being .62 and .38 respectively for Number and Name tests. For stenographers there was a —.37 correlation between clerical interest and Name Checking. Whether these data support the absence of real trends in the relationship of clerical aptitude to interest is difficult to ascertain for a number of reasons. As the author of the study pointed out the correlations may have been attenuated by the homogeneity, and thus restricted score range, of the group. However, it may be that, whereas linear regression coefficients were not significant in many instances, measures of nonlinear relationships might have indicated real covariation between clerical aptitude and interest. Crites (1957) found, for example, that intelligence, which is related to the Names test, was curvilinearly related to interest in technical occupations, with individuals of average intelligence scoring higher than those of either above or below average intelligence. The same relational form may exist between clerical aptitude and interest: The more intelligent individual with greater clerical aptitude and the less intelligent person with less clerical aptitude would be expected to have less clerical interest than the individual whose average intelligence and clerical aptitude are more consistent with the average difficulty and complexity of the routine activities which comprise the bulk of clerical work and represent sources of pronounced clerical interest. The possibility of nonlinear relationships between aptitude and certain interest areas should be explored further before the conclusion is drawn that no relationships exist, especially since few (if any) investigations of this problem in which correlational analysis has been used have tested the assumption of linearity of regression.

The relationship between the clerical test and the Co-operative Survey Test in Mathematics was computed in an unpublished study of high school juniors and seniors, with negligible relationships resulting (— .07 and — .10). This does not seem to agree with Andrew's finding of .51 for Numbers and arithmetic, but may be due to the more advanced mathematical content of the Co-operative test, which requires reasoning more than routine computation.

The relative validity of the Minnesota Clerical Test and the General Clerical Battery of the United States Employment Service was ascertained by Ghiselli (1942), who administered both to a group of 562 workers. His analysis showed that the latter added nothing to the former, which was adequate for counseling use.

A factor analysis of a battery of clerical tests, including the Minnesota Clerical Test, was conducted by Bair (1951), using 194 high school commercial students (sex unspecified). Three factors were extracted from the intercorrelation matrix. Factor I, which accounted for approximately 17 per cent of the total variance, was identified as composed primarily of perceptual analysis, with span and accuracy dominating speed of movement. About 14 per cent of the variance was attributable to Factor II, which appeared to be more heavily loaded with speed of movement, particularly in making simple discriminations. Factor III (11 per cent of total variance) was tentatively described as comprehension of relationships, with verbal ability assuming a more important role than in the other factors. The Minnesota Clerical Test was more highly related to the other tests than they were to each other, accounted for more of the total variance than the other tests, and had high loadings on all three factors. These results indicate that the Minnesota is evidently measuring what has been termed clerical aptitude, but they also suggest that this aptitude is apparently multidimensional and, since only 41 per cent of the total variance was accounted for by three factors, may be related to factors other than those measured adequately by clerical tests (such as intelligence discussed above).

Teachers' ratings of written work were used as a criterion by Swem (1945). His subjects were 35 boys and 39 girls enrolled in high school courses. For the former the correlations with Numbers and Names Tests were .30 and .49 respectively; for the latter they were .05 and .34. Only the correlations for the Names Test were statistically reliable. These findings contrast unfavorably with those reported in the original studies.

The relationship between Minnesota Clerical scores and grades in typing and shorthand was analyzed by Barrett (1946), working with groups of 96 and 75 college students. Unfortunately her analysis was not made in terms of correlations or similar statistics, but inspection of her data shows a tendency for those who made higher scores on the Minnesota test to make higher grades in both typing and shorthand. Tredick (1941) found correlations of .08, .31, and .27 between grades in Art, Chemistry, and English Composition on the one hand and Numbers on the other; the figures for Names were .07, .26, .07. Correlations with average grades were .36 and .23. The subjects were 113 freshmen women in Home Economics.

An examination in machine calculation was used as a criterion with 51 women students of office practice by Gottsdanker (1943), whose battery of tests included a slightly modified version of the Numbers Test. The correlation between his Number-Comparison Test and the criterion was .29; when combined with the Tapping Test of the MacQuarrie Mechanical Ability Test, a Number-Dot Location Test (a "paper keyboard") , and an Arithmetic Computation Test, the multiple correlation coefficient was .57.

Output on the job (speed of posting) served as criterion in a study of 39 bookkeeping machine operators by Hay (1943) . The reliability of the production trials was found to vary around .90 for any one trial period; when inter-trial reliability was checked, it was somewhat lower, but in no cases lower than .72. With this carefully studied criterion the correlations for Numbers and Names Tests were .51 and .47, respectively. When these two tests were combined with the Otis S.A. Test a multiple correlation of .65 was obtained. Hay used this battery in a large bank for a number of years with cut-off scores of 130 for the Minnesota tests (Hay and Blakemore, 1942) .

Supervisors' ratings of the efficiency of clerical workers were used as criteria in another study (Davidson, 1937) , in which the validity of Numbers and Names Tests was found to be .27 and .29. When promotability was estimated by job level attained after five or more years of service and correlated with the same tests, the coefficients were .07 and .34. The Thurstone Examination in Clerical Work (a proficiency test) , and a test of the same type by O'Rourke, had validities ranging from .40 (efficiency) to .77 (promotability) . This is not the reflection on the Minnesota test that it might seem at first glance, because the former instruments are tests of mixed functions, comparable to a battery, whereas the Minnesota is a purer test of two factors only, perceptual speed and, to a lesser extent, intelligence. It is to be expected that tests of clerical tasks would correlate more highly with efficiency ratings than a test of perceptual speed, and that tests as heavily loaded with intelligence factors as the Thurstone and O'Rourke would correlate more highly with promotability. When selecting new workers, however, there are important advantages in using a battery of purer tests, one of intelligence, one of perceptual speed, and one of arithmetic or language usage, depending upon the type of clerical work. In Hay's work (1943) , for example, the first two proved sufficient, because in that case neither arithmetic nor language was of special importance.

In the USES study (Stead and Shartle, 1940), data from which are reproduced in Figures 4 and 5, a battery of tests including the Minnesota Clerical Test was administered to various groups of clerical workers. For two samples totaling 234 card-punch machine operators (sex unspecified but presumably female) the criterion was the average number of cards punched per hour, with each incorrectly punched card counted as an error, combined into an "errorless production" score. The reliabilities of the two components, cards punched per hour and number of errors, were about .95 for the former and .90 for the latter. Coding clerks ($N =$ 96), bookkeeping-machine operators ($N = 52$) and hand-transcribers ($N = 62$) were studied with a similar battery and criterion; for calculating-machine operators ($N = 80$) and adding-machine operators ($N = 26$) the criterion was a worksample. For card-punch machine operators the validities were .31 and .33 for Numbers, and .24 and .32 for Names; these were among the most valid tests in the battery, only a letter-digit substitution test being as good and the McQuarrie subtests having no consistent validity. The validities for coding clerks were .38 and .46 for Numbers and Names, validities equaled by a number-writing test and exceeded by a personal-data test. In the case of the bookkeeping-machine operators the validities were — .09 and .19, although, as will be seen later, this group tended to make high scores on the tests and Hay (1943) found validities of .51 and .47: perhaps the difference lies in the criteria, the USES having used an error criterion while Hay used a speed criterion which he considered more valid. That Hay's criterion was superior is suggested by the relatively low validity of the other tests in the USES battery, none of which exceeded .28. For the hand-transcribers the coefficients were .20 and .34, again among the best of the battery, sentence-completion, vocabulary, and number-writing tests being in the same range. Validities for calculating-machine operators were .34 and .38 for Numbers and Names; for adding-machine operators, they were .51 and .37. For the former group MacQuarrie Tracing and Location, and a number-finding test were also valid; for the latter, all of the MacQuarrie subtests except Tapping and Dotting had some validity, as did vocabulary, number-finding, and an arithmetic test.

Data for other clerical groups, including some comparable to those just discussed, and for a number of semiskilled jobs in which it was assumed clerical perception would be important, are reproduced in Figures 4 and 5. Worthy of note are the substantial negative correlations between Numbers (—.39) and Names (—.47) and the ratio of errors to the production of index clerks, whose average scores are more than one sigma above the women's mean. These relationships suggest that in this occupation a high level of perceptual ability is desirable, but that those who are too much above the critical minimum are likely to be the poorer workers; whether or not this is because their rate of work is too fast for the precision requirements of the job is not shown by the data. Also noteworthy, in view of the Blum and Candee study cited below, are the correlations of .015 and .30 between Numbers and Names, on the one hand, and ratings of inspector-wrappers, on the other, and those of .35 and .45 between the same tests and production records (ratio of time required to standard time per unit) of merchandise packers. Another non-clerical job for which the test had some validity was power-sewing-machine operator (.40 to .50, and .23 to .28).

Blum and Candee (1941) tested 317 seasonal and 55 permanent packers and wrappers in a department store. In the permanent group the Numbers Test had a correlation of .57 with packers' production, and the Names Test an r of .65 with wrappers' production. In the seasonal group only manual dexterity was important. The authors' conclusion that the initial job adjustment of packers is somewhat affected by speed of gross arm-and-hand movement, while long-term superiority is more dependent upon clerical speed and accuracy, seems legitimate. But the differential results for Numbers and Names, packers and wrappers, need further investigation before the matter is closed; the USES study showed that both were valid for packers.

In the study of pharmaceutical inspector-packers Ghiselli (1942) worked with 26 young women who were rated by their forewoman and supervisor. The correlation between the two sets of overall ratings was .72, which was considered adequate reliability and justification for combining the two to serve as criterion. The correlations with Minnesota Numbers and Names Tests were respectively .29 and .26.

Apparently packing work of both gross (department store) and fine (pharmaceutical) types requires speed and accuracy of perception such as is measured by the Minnesota Clerical Test. Just why the gross type should require it more consistently than the fine is difficult to see. It will probably not become clear until other studies of these and other packing jobs are made with the same tests, in combination with detailed job analyses. It would be illuminating, for example, to know whether it is speed in recognizing numbers and names, as in the Minnesota test and in clerical activities, which is important in packing and wrapping, or whether it is general perceptual speed and accuracy such as might be measured by other speed of discrimination tests. If the former, the Minnesota test is perhaps truly a test of clerical aptitude; if the latter, it is more probably a perceptual test measuring something of value in a variety of occupations. The data on power-sewing-machine operators suggest that it is the latter.

Two studies have checked the ability of the Minnesota Clerical Test to differentiate between persons in clerical and non-clerical occupations. In one investigation Barnette (1940) found that business college students were superior to general adults, but inferior to clerical workers, on both Numbers and Names Tests. One would expect this of a student group, some of whom were likely to be weeded out before establishment in the occupation, unless they were preparing exclusively for the higher levels of clerical work.

The other study is from the United States Employment Service studies in occupational analysis, previously discussed, and cited by Stead and Shartle (1940, Ch. 8 and pp. 217–225) . As the sex composition of the occupational groups is not specified, comparing them with general population norms involves the probably legitimate assumption that most of the clerical workers studied were women. When comparing one clerical group with another the procedure is made more justifiable by the fact that men and women in a given clerical job are found to be equal in clerical aptitude. As Figures 4 and 5 show, there is a definite tendency for clerical workers to make higher scores on the Numbers Test than workers in the semiskilled occupations to whom the same test was administered. The mean scores of almost all of the clerical jobs tested were above the mean of the MESRI standard sample of employed adults, hand transcribers and one sample of coding clerks being the only clerical workers whose average is lower than the adult average. A cut-off score of 122 (about one sigma above the adult women's mean) would include all of the clerical workers above the mean of their group except those just mentioned and ten-key-adding-machine operators; of the 12 non-clerical jobs included in the list, only the put-in-coil girls have a mean score as high as this. If Hay's critical score for bookkeeping-machine operators (also his mean) of 130 were used, all of the above-average bookkeeping-machine operators and other comparable clerical workers would surpass the critical score.

The data for the Names Test show similar trends, although Hay's cut-off score of 130 appears to be too high for this test; 105 or 110 would be comparable to that used for the Numbers Test, although the latter is about the mean for adult women. The differentiating power of the Minnesota Clerical Test revealed by these data is greater than it at first seems, because the non-clerical jobs in the occupational sample were included on the assumption that perceptual speed as measured by the Minnesota test would be important in them too, a hypothesis which was proved valid for some by the reported validity coefficients. It is noteworthy, however, that these non-clerical jobs in which clerical perceptual speed is important almost invariably rank lower in the amount typical of their workers than do the clerical jobs themselves.

One of the objectives of vocational counseling and selection is the attainment of *satisfaction in his work* by the worker. This being the case, one would expect to find studies of the relationship between clerical aptitude and job satisfaction. No such studies have been located, however; the emphasis has so far been entirely on success.

Use of the Minnesota Clerical Test in Counseling and Selection. The preceding discussion has brought out the fact that the Minnesota Clerical Test has value for distinguishing those who have promise for clerical work from those who do not, and that the higher the score made by a person the higher, other things being equal, he may rise in the field of clerical work. Even though persons in the highest level clerical jobs are characterized by more perceptual ability than those in lower-level clerical work, one is not justified in assuming that this is all that need characterize the aspirant to high-level clerical work. We have seen also that while perceptual speed is more important in routine clerical work than is intelligence, intelligence is probably more important in promotion to the higher levels than is perceptual speed.

When appraising clerical promise it is well, therefore, to use tests of both perceptual speed and intelligence. If a battery can be used, it should include the Minnesota Test (Numbers and Names) and an intelligence test such as the Otis. If time is at a premium, the Minnesota Numbers Test and the Otis will do. If only one test can be used, and it must be brief, then the Minnesota Names Test, as a combination of perceptual speed and intelligence, may suffice. In selection programs, if the selection is to be made from a wide range of ability, an intelligence test may suffice as a screening instrument, because of the correlation between the two aptitudes in heterogeneous groups. But if the selection is to be made from groups with a limited spread of general intelligence, the Minnesota Numbers Test is preferable as a purer measure of the important variable. Although the differences between experienced and inexperienced workers on the Minnesota Clerical Test were slight, and probably due to selective factors rather than to experience, it is worth noting (until more conclusive evidence is available), that at least one personnel worker (Hay) has thought it advisable to use separate norms in selecting experienced and inexperienced clerical workers.

In counseling the principal problem which is raised by the research is that of age and occupational norms. Although increase in scores with high school grade and age has been demonstrated, it is not clear to what extent this is due to maturation and to what extent to the elimination of the less able students as they reach the higher grades. In view of the fact that there is no change in scores with age from ages 17 to 29, and since the age changes in mid-adolescence are open to some question, it seems wise to use adult norms even with high school juniors and seniors until more adequate evidence is available on the effects of maturation. When the test is being used at the junior high school level for curricular guidance purposes, grade norms are to be preferred; maturation may play a significant part at that age, and school work can provide an exploratory experience which supplements the test scores. Obviously, students who take commercial courses in high school should have appropriate mental ability and more than average clerical aptitude. Since directional guidance is all that is needed at that stage, the more specific decisions can be postponed until a later age when tests and experience yield more specific evidence.

In using the adult norms, emphasis should be on the occupational rather than on the general norms. It only confuses the issue to know that a man is at the 74th percentile in accounting (Number) ability compared to men-in-general, when in reality he exceeds only 1 percent of accountants in that type of ability, for it is against accountants rather than men-in-general that he must match his accounting aptitude. However, these occupational norms must still be used with considerable caution, since they are based on small and relatively nondescript groups whose representativeness is unknown except for the rough correspondence of MESRI, USES, and Hay's norms. Most guidance centers should be able to develop norms of their own which are more adequate for local use than the original Minnesota occupational norms, but these should be *occupational* norms, not norms for all clients locally tested.

In administering the Minnesota test for non-clerical purposes as in the counseling or selection of semiskilled workers, it is well to supplement the directions with a statement that the test is a measure of the speed with which details are noticed, and that this is an important characteristic in a number of assembly, inspection, and other jobs. This helps to counteract the antipathy of some examinees to anything with a clerical label.

Finally, a word concerning speed and accuracy. We have seen that as a rule speed on this type of test is a good measure of accuracy. But there are occasional exceptions, and one subject will make a given score by working rapidly with errors, whereas another will make the same score by working more slowly without errors. For this reason the psychometrist or counselor should examine the responses to each test, and take the error score into account in making his interpretation. While it may not help as much in judging prospects of success as the total corrected score, it will help considerably in understanding the person being evaluated or counseled.

REFERENCES FOR CHAPTER VIII

Andrew, D. M. "An analysis of the Minnesota Vocational Test for Clerical Workers. I. II." *J. Appl. Psychol.*, 21 (1937), 18-47, 139-172.

———, and Paterson, D. G. "Measured characteristics of clerical workers," *University of Minnesota Bulletin of the Employment Stabilization Research Institute*, 1 (1934).

Bair, J. T. "Factor analysis of clerical aptitude tests," *J. Appl. Psychol.*, 35 (1951), 245-249.

Barnette, W. L. "Norms of business college students on standardized tests: intelligence, clerical ability, English," *J. Appl. Psychol.*, 24 (1940), 237-243.

Barrett, D. W. "Prediction of achievement in typewriting and stenography in a liberal arts college," *J. Appl. Psychol.*, 30 (1946), 624-630.

Bingham, W. V. "Classifying and testing for clerical jobs," *Pers. J.*, 14 (1935), 163-172.

———. *Aptitudes and Aptitude Testing*. New York: Harper, 1937.

Blum, M. L., and Candee, B. "The selection of department store packers and wrappers with the aid of certain psychological tests: Study II," *J. Appl. Psychol.*, 25 (1941), 291-299.

Brayfield, A. H. "Clerical interests and clerical aptitude," *Pers. Guid. J.*, 31 (1953), 304-306.

Candee, B., and Blum, M. L. "A new scoring system for the Minnesota Clerical Test," *Psychol. Bull.*, 34 (1937), 545 (abstr.).

Carruthers, J. B. "Tabular summary showing relation between clerical test scores and occupational performance," *Occupations*, 29 (1950), 40-50.

Copeland, H. A. "Some characteristics of three tests used to predict clerical success," *J. Appl. Psychol.*, 20 (1936), 461-470.

Crites, J. O. "Intelligence and Adjustment as Determinants of Vocational Interest Patterning in Late Adolescence." Unpublished Ph.D. dissertation, Columbia University, 1957.

Darley, J. G. "Reliability of tests in the standard battery." (In "Research studies in individual diagnosis.") *University of Minnesota Bull. Empl. Stab. Res. Inst.*, 4 (1934).

Davidson, C. M. "Evaluation of clerical tests," *Pers. J.*, 16 (1937), 57-64, 95-98.

Englehardt, O. E. de Cillis. "The Minnesota Clerical Test: sex differences and norms for college groups," *J. Appl. Psychol.*, 34 (1950), 412-414.

Ghiselli, E. E. "Comparison of the Minnesota Vocational Test for Clerical Workers with the general clerical battery of the U.S.E.S.," *J. Appl. Psychol.*, 26 (1942), 75-80.

——— "Tests for the selection of inspectors-packers," *J. Appl. Psychol.*, 26 (1942), 468-476.

Gottsdanker, R. M. "Measures of potentiality for machine calculation," *J. Appl. Psychol.*, 27 (1943), 233-248.

Harrell, T. W. "A factor analysis of mechanical ability tests," *Psychometrika*, 5 (1940), 17-33.

Hay, E. N. "Predicting success in machine bookkeeping," *J. Appl. Psychol.*, 27 (1943), 483-493.

———, and Blakemore, A. M. "Testing clerical applicants," *J. Appl. Psychol.*, 26 (1942), 852-855.

———, and Blakemore, A. M. "The relationship between clerical experience and scores on the Minnesota Vocational Test for Clerical Workers," *J. Appl. Psychol.*, 27 (1943), 311-315.

Kirkpatrick, D. L. "The Minnesota Clerical Test," *Pers. Psychol.*, 10 (1957), 53-54.

Klugman, S. F. "Test scores for clerical aptitude and interest before and after a year of schooling," *J. Genet. Psychol.*, 65 (1944), 89-96.

Schneidler, G. G. "Grade and age norms for the Minnesota Vocational Test for Clerical Workers," *Educ. Psychol. Measmt.*, 1 (1941), 143-156.

———, and Paterson, D. G. "Sex differences in clerical aptitude," *J. Educ. Psychol.*, 33 (1942), 303-309.

Staff, Division of Occupational Analysis, WMC. "Factor analysis of occupational aptitude tests," *Educ. Psychol. Measmt.*, 5 (1945), 147-155.

Stead, W. H., and Shartle, C. L. *Occupational Counseling Techniques.* New York: American Book Co., 1940.

Strong, E. K., Jr. "Norms for graduate school business students on the Minnesota Vocational Test for Clerical Workers," *J. Appl. Psychol.*, 31 (1947), 594-600.

Super, D. E. "The A.C.E. Psychological Examination and special abilities," *J. Psychol.*, 9 (1940), 221-226.

——— "The critical ninth grade: vocational choice or vocational exploration," *Pers. Guid. J.*, 39 (1960), 107-109.

Swem, B. R. " 'Accounting aptitude' and 'home work'," *Occupations*, 23 (1945), 218-219.

Tredick, V. D. "The Thurstone Primary Mental Abilities Test and a Battery of Vocational Guidance Tests as Predictors of Academic Success." Unpublished thesis, Pennsylvania State College, 1941.

Whipple, G. M. *A Manual of Mental and Physical Tests*. Baltimore: Warwick and York, 1910.

IX

MANUAL DEXTERITIES

Nature and Role

Singular or Plural? Personnel men, vocational counselors, and psychologists have long been in the habit of referring to manual dexterity as though it were a unitary ability. If this were so, then it would be legitimate to conclude that a person who is adept at one manual activity has the aptitude to become equally adept at any other manual activity. It would also be true that one good test of manual dexterity would be sufficient in a battery used to survey the assets of a student or employment applicant.

The plural form has been used in the title of this chapter in order to stress the fact that the research of the past two decades has demonstrated the existence of a number of manual dexterities. Whether these aptitudes range on a continuum from gross (arm-and-hand) to fine (wrist-and-finger) dexterities or whether they are relatively distinct and unrelated, representing separate abilities, has not been firmly established. There is some evidence, however, that the latter is probably more nearly the case, at least as measured by the tests now available, although it will be seen below that low to moderate interrelationships between some of the manual factors which have been identified do exist.

A factor analysis study of 59 different aptitude tests conducted by the United States Employment Service (Staff, W.M.C., 1945) revealed two dexterity factors, one of which was common to the Placing and Turning Tests of the Minnesota Rate of Manipulation Test and to the Peg Board Apparatus of the USES (both of which require relatively gross movements), and the other important in tests requiring fine assembly work. Relevant studies by Seashore et al. (1940) and Buxton (1938), using laboratory tests, in which factors which appear to consist of manipulative, wrist-turning, arm-and-shoulder, ballistic (uncontrolled), steadiness, and one unidentifiable motor skill were isolated, further support the multidimensionality of manual ability, as does a more recent study by Fleishman and Hempel (1954). In the latter investigation 400 basic airmen were administered a battery of 15 performance and pencil-and-paper dexterity tests, including the Minnesota, O'Connor, and Peg Board, in counterbalanced order to control for the effects of practice. The factorial structure which was obtained was clearly oblique in certain instances, but since alternative orthogonal and oblique solutions yielded the same five common factors they were considered as relatively independent. As might be expected on the basis of previous findings, two of the factors represented the *gross* and *fine* manual dexterities, the former being defined by the Minnesota Turning and Placing and Peg Board Assembly tests and the latter by the grasping, releasing, or manipulation movements involved in the Peg Board Assembly, O'Connor, and Minnesota Turning tasks. A third factor, *wrist-and-finger speed,* involving either rapid rotary or bending wrist movements in which speed rather than coordination seemed crucial, was composed of the Minnesota Turning and other apparatus and printed tests including measures of pin sticking and tapping. An *aiming* factor, reflecting the ability to perform quickly and precisely a series of movements requiring eye-hand coordination, was distinguished from *wrist-and-finger speed,* which does not involve the same high degree of speed and accuracy, but seemed somewhat related to a fifth factor tentatively identified as *positioning.* The relationship between aiming and positioning was not clear, however, as the authors of the study point out: ". . . both appear to involve the terminal accuracy of movements to a designated position in space. It is true that the Aiming factor is most restricted to printed tests and the Positioning factor is restricted to certain apparatus tests (Minnesota Placing and Peg Board-Right Hand). However, the precise distinction between the two factors in terms of some more basic underlying functions needs to be determined. At present, the Aiming factor seems to involve more precision in moving the hand *from one position to the other,* where the Positioning factor seems to involve precision of single, more localized discrete responses" (p. 27). The extent to which these additional manual dexterities are more or less distinct and can be more adequately defined operationally is a matter for further research. It can be concluded, however, that at least two anatomically based manual dexterities, gross and fine, are well-established by present empirical knowledge.

What is Manual Work? Further distinctions which need to be made early in the discussion of manual dexterities are those between manual work and mechanical work, manual dexterities and mechanical aptitude. White-collar workers and professional people who have not had intimate contact with industry often confuse manual and mechanical work and skills, taking note only of the fact that both involve use of the hands. Aware that some factory and shop work is skilled, some semiskilled, and some unskilled they assume that these distinctions in the degree of skill characterizing the work are distinctions in degree of manual skill. Hence the unwarranted conclusion that the higher the level of skill in industrial employment, the greater the need for manual dexterity.

As experienced industrial men and personnel psychologists have long known, nothing could be further from the facts. The independence of measures of manual dexterity and of mechanical comprehension or spatial visualization will be brought out in subsequent parts of this chapter and in the two which follow, as will the different degrees to which manual (unskilled and semiskilled) workers on the one hand and mechanical (skilled) workers on the other hand tend to possess these aptitudes. It should suffice to point out here that "manual" work is essentially semiskilled or unskilled; semiskilled work relies primarily on the manual skill of the worker in assembling objects, packing them, or in other ways manipulating them with fingers or arms and hands, and unskilled work depends primarily upon the strength of back and legs and body co-ordination rather than eye-hand co-ordination; skilled work, on the other hand, is more dependent on the understanding and planning of the worker than upon mere manual dexterity. To put it in everyday industrial parlance, the skilled worker needs "know-how," the semiskilled worker skillful hands and fingers, and the unskilled worker a strong back.

A unique contribution to the understanding of manual skill and the nature of semiskilled work was made by Cohen and Strauss (1946) in a study of 21 experienced women employed in a highly repetitive operation. The task consisted of folding an 18 x 18-inch gauge sheet of metal six times to a size approximately 4 x 4 inches. Motion pictures were taken of the operatives at work, and operation analysis was made. It was found that, in general, the more skilled operatives (so classified by a standard time-and-motion study technique) performed their work more simply. This greater simplicity of technique was illustrated by several differences in methods. Better operatives have fewer limiting grasps and releases, in that they grasp and release as a part of transport operations rather than as separate movements; their movements are more global, less discrete, than those of inferior operatives. The more proficient operatives make the movements of their two hands overlap more than the less proficient workers, thus performing two operations at once instead of one after the other. The Purdue Pegboard, described later in this chapter, is almost unique in testing this type of two-hand co-ordination. Poorer operatives make more extra moves because of fumbles, faultily performed operations, and superfluous operations than do the better operatives; the latter therefore have a shorter work cycle than the former, and a higher rate of production.

Superior skill manifested itself not only as greater speed of performing basic operations but, the above makes clear, as improvement in the series of basic operations performed. The authors therefore asked, "Is method independent of skill?" Their answer is an affirmative for general method, but a tentative negative for the basic operations. An illustration helps to make the point: "One operator releases a part during a motion rather than after it has been made, but if the less skilled operator attempts to do so, the part may not be placed correctly and an adjustment may be necessary. Therefore the first operator can perform without the occurrence of 'Release' as a limiting operation, but the second cannot" (p. 152). It is the accumulation of such small differences which differentiates operatives. Cohen and Strauss feel (without evidence) that the problem is primarily one of selection rather than of training, and suggest that dexterity tests are needed which can measure the ability to eliminate limiting motions or to merge them into more global movements. Although no available dexterity tests yield scores of this type, Test IV of the Purdue Pegboard (see below) provides an excellent opportunity to observe this type of skill, and other dexterity tests give some clues.

Typical Tests

The best known test of arm-and-hand dexterity is the Minnesota Manual Dexterity Test, better known as the Minnesota or Ziegler's Rate of Manipulation Test. No other test of this type has been widely studied or used. Wrist-and-finger dexterity tests include O'Connor's Finger and Tweezer Dexterity Tests and the Purdue Pegboard, the latter also a measure of arm-and-hand dexterity. Both are dealt with in this chapter. Other tests of this type are the Pennsylvania Bimanual Worksample (Educational Test Bureau) and the pegboard and plier-dexterity tests of the United States Employment Service. These and others like them are not treated here, because they are newer and less well validated or not generally available.

The Minnesota Rate of Manipulation Test (Educational Test Bureau, 1931). The Minnesota Rate of Manipulation Test was originally developed by Ziegler as the Manual Dexterity Test, in connection with a study of the role of manual dexterity in performance on the Minnesota Spatial Relations Test. For this reason it was not, unfortunately, included in the Minnesota Mechanical Abilities Project (Paterson et al., 1930), although several other tests designed to measure dexterity were used. It was, however, available in time for inclusion in the research of the Employment Stabilization Research Institute (Paterson and Darley, 1936). It has been published in two editions, one by the Mechanical Engineering Department of the University of Minnesota, the other by the Educational Test Bureau. The latter version differs from the former in the arrangement of parts at the beginning and the end of the test, in the number of parts (60 vs. 58), and in the colors used on the movable parts; as the university version was used in the extensive normative work of the MESRI only it should be used with the employed-adult and special occupational-group norms gathered by the Institute. This fact appears to have been disregarded by the publishers of the other version, who give norms for 500 unidentified adults which seem to be those of the Minnesota project. The Educational Test Bureau version is more widely used despite this fact, probably because of a more finished manufacturing job which includes a tray to hold the formboard and parts, combined with more aggressive marketing methods. Supplementary norms for this form of the test are available, in the literature, as will be seen below, but the manual has not been revised in the necessary detail.

Applicability. The Minnesota Rate of Manipulation Test was designed for use with and standardized on adults. It has generally been assumed that it is applicable at any age level between 13 and 50 (Bingham, 1937), dexterity being a characteristic which matures relatively early. However, the old Educational Test Bureau norms show that men and women are faster than boys and girls, and Tuckman (1944) found even greater differences between adults and adolescents. According to his data, for example, a raw score of 232.5 is equal to the 50th percentile for boys, but the 27th percentile for men. The question is raised as to whether these differences are due to the selection of the samples (clients of a guidance center may come for different reasons, from different backgrounds, at different ages), to differences in the motivation of the two age-groups (the boys may consider manual tasks beneath them while the adults are more realistic in their vocational objectives), or to the role of maturation (manual dexterity may still be developing in the boys). The study was not so planned as to throw light on these various alternatives. Seashore (1947) has shown that college men do substantially better than the norms. Perhaps in the future more persons planning test research will recognize the futility of merely compiling normative data for relatively undescribed groups, and so set up their research as to provide for answers to questions such as these. As in the case of the Minnesota Clerical Test, the applicability of this test to adolescents is still in doubt.

Content. The test consists of a formboard in which there are four rows of identical holes, with fifteen holes in each row. Sixty identical discs, each somewhat larger than a checker, fit into these holes, the thickness of the discs being greater than that of the formboard so that they may be readily grasped while in place. The flat sides of the discs are differently painted, so that they contrast with the board and so that a ready check may be made in the Turning Test (Educational Test Bureau form only). This test consists of administering the test with the discs in place, but to be turned over and returned to their places by the examinee; the Placing Test (both forms) involves moving the discs from the table-top to the holes in the formboard.

Administration and Scoring. The test is administered individually, with the subject standing at a table of normal height. The examiner places the board with discs on his own side of the table, leaving a little more room between the board and the examinee's edge than is required to accommodate the board. The formboard is then raised, leaving the discs on the table and undisturbed. The formboard is then placed between the discs and the examinee, about one inch from the edge of the table. All this is as recommended in the manuals; administration is further simplified if the psychometrist uses a light board or tray open on one side as a base for the formboard, sliding the latter off the base or tray to place the discs and putting the base back under the formboard when placing it in front of the subject for testing. This makes it possible to lift and remove the formboard without losing discs, and has them in place for the next administration. The test is administered in four trials, requiring from six to eight minutes all told.

The scoring used in the original MESRI studies added all four trials; Darley (1934) has shown, however, that greater reliability is achieved by using the first trial as practice and adding the time required in the last three as the score. The revised Minnesota manual gives appropriate norms.

Variations have been tried also by Jurgensen (1943) and Wilson (1945). In the former study Jurgensen used nine methods of administration, some involving use of one hand, some the other, and some both. (When both hands are used, blocks are picked up from the same *row,* in adjacent *columns,* except in the last, odd, column.) Although he concluded that his revision is more valid and more reliable, and that the part scores are more independent than in the standard version, this method has not been widely taken up. It nevertheless merits consideration, along with other variations, when the test is to be validated as part of an employee-selection program, for some variations will almost certainly be more valid for some jobs and less so for others, because of the operation of specific factors. Wilson's modification consisted of using only the lowest of three trials rather than the total time, but he gives opinion rather than evidence, convenience rather than validity, as justification for the procedure.

Norms. As was previously indicated, norms for the University of Minnesota form are available, for the Placing Test only, for the MESRI standard sample of 500 adult workers, and for about a dozen occupations such as butter-wrappers, food-packers, bank tellers, typists, and garage mechanics, represented by from 14 to 164 persons each. Although these small occupational groups were sufficiently large to supply answers to some of the questions studied at the Minnesota Institute, and are more varied than those upon which most aptitude tests antedating World War II were based, they are not satisfactory for vocational guidance or selection. Data based on them throw a great deal of light on the nature of the traits tested, but it is altogether possible than norms based on larger and more representative groups would differ considerably from these. The best test-construction projects of the war and post-war era have recognized the need for larger as well as more varied norm groups; as these projects are completed and become better known the better norming of tests such as this will become a necessity, from a marketing as well as from a professional point of view. It might be added, parenthetically, that this relatively new recognition of the need for large-scale occupational norms is virtually taking test construction out of the hands of individual psychologists, who will still originate test ideas, and is putting it in the hands of consulting organizations and test publishers who have the financial resources to subsidize the extensive standardization research which must precede publication. It will also take test publication out of the hands of publishers who merely print and sell tests without carrying on or subsidizing test standardization.

The Educational Test Bureau form supplies norms for both Placing and Turning Tests, and for the three additional variations developed by Jurgensen (1943). As pointed out above MESRI norms which are included in the Bureau norms in some unspecified manner should not be used with this different form until evidence is produced to show that the difference in the formboards does not affect performance. Subsequent studies by Teegarden (1942, 1943), Tuckman (1944), Jurgensen (1943), Seashore (1947) and Cook and Barre (1942) have used this form, and make available other sets of norms. Teegarden's are perhaps the most useful, for she sampled a dozen jobs represented by applicants at the Cincinnati Employment Center, a white group ranging in age from 16 to 25. As they were a young group, their experience was somewhat limited and their occupations in many cases as yet unsettled. In her first two papers (1942) Teegarden gives norms for this group of 500 young men and 360 women taken as a group; in the last paper (1943) she gives data on occupational differences. The fields represented include such entry jobs as helpers in skilled trades, operatives of factory machines, factory operatives (hand), packers and wrappers, restaurant workers, and assemblers, inspectors, and testers, together with more adult occupations such as manual laborers, truck drivers and chauffeurs, and sales clerks. The numbers in these occupational groups, as in the MESRI samples, were small, ranging from 26 (truck loaders and helpers) to 123 (women domestics). Like the MESRI norms, they give one an understanding of the test and of the significance of arm-and-hand dexterity in various types of work (topic dealt with below), but they are neither large enough nor well-enough selected to serve as norms in the usual sense of the word.

Tuckman's norms are for 1117 subjects aged 18 to 58, tested at the Jewish Vocational Service in Cleveland. This group was interested in all types of work and had varying amounts of education and mental ability, but as clients of a guidance and placement office they were not representative of adults-in-general: 365 were high school students, 407 adult men, and 345 women, and the mean age was 22. The Cleveland boys' and girls' Placing norms were approximately the same as those provided by the Educational Test Bureau, but the adults were faster than the original norm group; on the Turning Test, all of the Cleveland groups were faster. Men excelled most in Placing.

Jurgensen tested 212 male paper-mill operatives aged 18 to 31. These norms were combined with MESRI and other data in a way not indicated by the 1946 manual. Seashore's data are for two groups of 96 and 48 college men. They did much better than the norm group.

Cook and Barre tested 468 men and 2007 women applicants for manufacturing employment, providing new norms for 18 to 25 year-olds. This group differs from Teegarden's and Tuckman's in that it was a factory population, at least temporarily; Teegarden's subjects were willing to accept "anything," but some were clerical, sales, and service workers by background; and Tuckman's included many from the professional and managerial levels, the median Otis percentile being 74 for men and 52 for women. As might be expected under the circumstances, Cook and Barre's norms differ from the old, being higher. Like Tuckman, they found that sex norms were needed for the Placing, but not for the Turning Test. The writers are inclined to believe that Teegarden's norms are the most helpful to the user of the Educational Test Bureau form in counseling, since, like the MESRI norms for the university form, they make possible some differential interpretation; but they should not, for reasons given above, be used mechanically. In selection, local norms should be developed, using the available occupational norms only as a source of ideas as to situations in which the test may prove useful.

Standardization and Initial Validation. The original work with the Minnesota Manual Dexterity Test (apart from the study of its role in spatial visualization tests) having been carried out as part of the operations of the Employment Stabilization Research Institute, the standardization and initial validation data have to do only with the reliability and occupational differentiation of the test. Its reliability is taken up below. Its ability to differentiate workers in various occupations was demonstrated by the occupational norms discussed above. Highest scores were made by women butter packers and wrappers and by women food packers, who stood at the 94th, 92nd, and 88th percentiles respectively, while semi-skilled workers in general stood at the 64th. Apparently arm-and-hand dexterity is important especially in packing and wrapping jobs.

Bank tellers were at the 85th percentile, ranking highest among clerical workers, with men office clerks at the 77th, which suggests that, although there is no correlation between manual dexterity and success in office work, office workers are a somewhat select group in dexterity. Since the 164 women office clerks were only at the 60th percentile when compared to general adults, and since the male office clerks were only 66 in number, this may be partly a result of sampling. It is probably wise to suspend judgment concerning the importance of manual dexterity in clerical work, operating on the conclusion that the critical minimum is rather low, a conclusion which is in accord at least with the data concerning women clerks.

Finally, it should be noted that the skilled groups tested in the Minnesota project did not differ greatly from the mean of the general adult population. Skilled workers in general averaged at the 60th percentile, while garage mechanics, to cite a specific example, were at the 55th when compared to employed adults. This bears out the statement, made at the beginning of this chapter, to the effect that skilled workers depend not on their manual skill, but on other aptitudes and upon technical knowledge.

Reliability.   Darley reported that the reliability of the Placing Test was above .90 for the standard sample (1934). Tuckman also used the odd-even method (1944), reporting corrected reliabilities of more than .90 for his samples. He obtained retest reliability coefficients which were slightly lower, probably because of practice effect. In this connection, he confirmed Darley's finding that it is best to use the first trial for practice: the mean score for the first trial was at the 52nd percentile, while that for the 4th trial was at the 79th, a substantial improvement. Jurgensen (1943) found reliabilities of .87 and .91 for 212 adult men.

Validity.   The first step to be taken in ascertaining the validity of the Minnesota Rate of Manipulation Test would seem to be to determine how *independent* the two parts are. This was done by Blum and Candee (1941), Jacobsen (1943), Jurgensen (1943), Seashore (1947), Teegarden (1942) and Tuckman (1944). The first obtained a correlation of .55 based on 120 women packers and wrappers, which compares very favorably with that of .57 reported in the test manual. Jacobsen's intercorrelation was only .27, for 90 aircraft industry trainees. Jurgensen's intercorrelation was .52 for 212 adult male paper-mill operatives. Seashore reported correlations of .46 and .58 for two samples of college men. Tuckman's figures were higher, being .60 for 345 women and .66 for 407 men. Teegarden's were still higher, at .65 for 171 women and .73 for 230 men. Presumably the true correlation is about .60 for women, and somewhat higher for men (only Jacobsen's study is out of line), indicating that the two tests are measuring the same basic aptitude manifesting itself in two slightly different ways, or that they have an important factor in common but one or more others peculiar to one and not to the other. The factor analysis study carried out by the United States Employment Service (Staff, W.M.C., 1945), referred to early in this chapter, showed that the former hypothesis is correct, and that the Placing and Turning Tests have practically identical factor composition: they are almost pure tests of arm and hand dexterity.

The Manual Dexterity Test has been correlated with tests of *intelligence* by Tuckman (1944), Jacobsen (1943), and Super (unpublished study). Tuckman administered the A.C.E. Psychological Examination to high school students and adults, finding correlations of .18 and .17 for Placing, and .29 and .26 for Turning. Job analysis of the tests suggests that the closer relationship between Turning and intelligence may be due to the slightly more complex manual task in that test, which requires bimanual co-ordination of a rudimentary sort. But Jacobsen found correlations of .16 and .12, using 90 adult subjects. Administering the Otis S.A. Test to 100 NYA youth, Super obtained a correlation of .11 with the Placing Test. In any case, the role of intelligence is negligible.

The similarity of fine-manual to gross-manual dexterity was ascertained by Roberts (1943), Jacobsen (1943) and by Blum and Candee (1941). Roberts found correlations of .46 and .40 between Placing and Turning, on the one hand, and his Pennsylvania Bimanual Worksample (Assembly) Test, on the other, the latter being a nut-and-bolt assembly task somewhat finer than the Minnesota Test but grosser in its requirements than the O'Connor Tests ($N = 473$). Jacobsen tested 90 wartime aircraft industry trainees and found correlations of .20 and .06 between O'Connor Finger Dexterity and Placing and Turning Tests, and of .26 and .20 between Tweezer Dexterity and the two Minnesota subtests. Only the highest of these correlations was statistically significant. Blum and Candee tested 130 women packers and wrappers in a department store with the O'Connor Finger Dexterity Test, finding correlations of .42 and .335 with the Placing and Turning Tests. The correlations were reliable. With only two studies available, one with negative findings and one with positive, we are faced with a dilemma. But poor testing conditions and other defects of procedure are more likely to produce negative findings than positive, and the negative study was the work of a beginner while the positive was that of two experienced investigators. It therefore seems necessary tentatively to conclude that there is some relationship between arm-and-hand dexterity on the one hand, and wrist-and-finger dexterity on the other. That the relationship is not high is indicated not only by these data, but also by the USES factor analysis which isolated two relatively independent manual factors: one gross and one fine.

The role of arm-and-hand dexterity in tests of *mechanical comprehension* was studied by Jacobsen (1943) and Super (unpublished study). The latter found a correlation of only .05 between Minnesota Mechanical Assembly Test scores and the Placing Test, the subjects being 100 boys and girls aged 16 to 24 employed on NYA projects. This is noteworthy, as the Assembly test involves the putting together of a variety of mechanical objects such as a spark plug, a mechanical bottle-stopper, and an old-fashioned lock. It is confirmed by Harrell's (1940) factor analysis of the Minnesota Mechanical and other tests, which showed no manual dexterity factor in the Minnesota Mechanical Assembly Test. Jacobsen found correlations of .21 and .14 between Placing and Turning, on the one hand, and the Bennett Mechanical Comprehension Test on the other. The latter is a paper-and-pencil test measuring a somewhat higher order of mechanical comprehension than the assembly test; that it has no significant relationship to manual dexterity is therefore not surprising.

Tests of spatial visualization have been correlated with the Minnesota Rate of Manipulation Test by Jacobsen (1943), Teegarden (1942) and Super (unpublished study). The Minnesota Paper Form Board had correlations of .06 and .00 with Placing and Turning in Jacobsen's study, as compared with one of .23 with the Placing Test in Super's investigation. In the latter study there was a correlation of .05 between the Minnesota Spatial Relations Test and the Placing Test, a relationship which has not been located in the literature although it was to study it that Ziegler constructed the latter test. Jacobsen supplied the correlations between the Crawford Spatial Relations Test and the Placing and Turning Tests: .19 and .11. As none of the above relationships were statistically significant it is clear that manual dexterity and spatial visualization tests are independent.

Ratings on success in training were used as a criterion in only one published study with the Minnesota Rate of Manipulation Test. This was Jacobsen's investigation of the relationship between success in training in aircraft mechanics and scores on various aptitude tests (1943). These war-industry trainees were rated by their instructors after the first two weeks of training, and periodically each month thereafter for the two or three months of training. Ratings on a five-point scale were for seven traits such as learning, speed and coordination, workmanship, and personal fitness for the occupation. As the specific traits had correlations with total fitness ratings which ranged from .84 to .97, the latter only were used as a criterion, all fitness ratings being combined for a given individual. Apparently no attempt was made to ascertain the reliability of the ratings, although the data would have permitted it. Correlations between the ratings and tests ranged from —.03 to .17, none of them being reliable. Either gross-manual dexterity as manifested in aircraft engine, aero repair, machine shop, and other similar courses has no bearing on instructors' evaluations of mechanical promise, even though they rated the subjects for speed and co-ordination, or the Minnesota Rate of Manipulation Test does not measure the type of manual dexterity sought by instructors. As will be seen later, fine-manual dexterity as measured by the O'Connor tests had unreliable and low correlations with these same ratings, the only tests which give reliable predictions of instructors' ratings in these courses being mechanical comprehension, arithmetic, and intelligence tests, in that order.

Success on the job has been studied with electrical worksamples, production in department-store packing and wrapping, supervisors' ratings of efficiency on these same jobs, ratings of efficiency in pharmaceutical inspecting and packing, and ratings of success in ordnance factory and paper-mill employees.

The electrical *worksample* developed by O'Rourke (connecting a push-button, bell, and dry-cell) was used with 49 boys and 37 girls aged about 18, employed on NYA projects, by Steel, Balinsky, and Long (1945). Tests were administered to one-half of the subjects before the projects were initiated and to the others after the worksample. The worksample was carried out individually in order to permit careful observation by the examiners, who recorded care in the use of directions, facility in handling tools and materials, initial adjustment to the task, and reaction to difficulties. Brief interviews were held after the project in order to elicit further reactions, but only the time score on the worksample was used in the correlations. Neither of these was statistically significant for boys (—.02 and .10 for Placing and Turning), but both were for girls (.50 and .35). Other data throw light on the reasons for these discrepancies. The boys took significantly less time to complete the worksample than the girls, although this was not true of the tests; the boys had had more experience with electrical equipment and tools. Apparently it was amount of experience with electrical equipment which determined the boys' time scores, rather than gross-manual dexterity or any of the abilities measured by the other tests (fine-manual dexterity, spatial visualization, and vocabulary), but unfortunately no test of electrical information was used to provide a quantitative check on this explanation. The girls, on the other hand, had had so little experience with such equipment that vocabulary (ability to understand and follow the directions), spatial visualization, and both types of manual dexterity determined the amount of time they required to complete the task. Mechanical comprehension, had it been tested, might also have played a part in the case of the girls, since the other relevant aptitudes were important to their success. These conclusions suggest that manual dexterity and other aptitude tests are most likely to be valuable when selecting inexperienced workers for semiskilled jobs, or for counseling inexperienced persons, whereas careful evaluations of experience are likely to be more valuable with those who have had relevant experience. This conclusion applies only to *initial job adjustments* in semiskilled work, however, for that is what the worksample tested; as Blum and Candee's second study of packers and wrappers (1941) showed, skills that are important in initial adjustment sometimes play no part in long-term success, other aptitudes emerging as the important ones after some experience has been acquired.

In their first study of department store *packers and wrappers* Blum and Candee (1941) tested 38 permanent employees of one department store, together with 52 employment-service applicants subsequently employed by the store for whom criterion data became available. The criteria used were production records and supervisors' ratings. For the former, the average daily number of packages wrapped during the month of December, when employees work most nearly at their capacity, was used; its split-half reliability was .88. The supervisors' ratings were those routinely made on a four-point scale and consisted of an overall efficiency rating phrased in terms of recommended continued employment and seasonal rehiring. No data are presented concerning the reliability of the ratings, which included none in the "inefficient" or lowest category.

The correlations between production records and Placing and Turning Tests were .35 and .27 for seasonal employees, and .21 and .06 for permanent employees. Evidently arm-and-hand dexterity plays some part in initial job adjustment in packing, but the skill requirements are actually low enough so that experience erases the effect of differences in aptitude. When supervisors' ratings were used as a criterion no significant differences were found between superior and inferior seasonal nor between superior and inferior permanent employees, although the permanent employees were rated superior to the seasonal employees and made higher test scores. As the seasonal employees were considered especially good that year, although not actually superior to the general population, Blum and Candee concluded that experience must affect test performance. While this is perhaps true, it cannot be considered as having been proved, for there was no pre-employment testing of the experienced group and no post-employment testing of the inexperienced group. Furthermore, the higher scores of the experienced group may have been due to self-selection, through the quitting of satisfactory experienced workers who found that relative lack of manual dexterity required them to put forth a disproportionate and unsatisfactory amount of effort in order to keep up.

In their second study (1941), Blum and Candee tested comparable groups in another department store, and used similar criteria, but the Turning Test was omitted. Again there was a moderate but significant relationship between arm-and-hand dexterity and production in the case of packers who handle large items (.37), but not in the case of wrappers who handle small items and make change. Again there was no relationship between test scores and supervisors' ratings of permanent employees, but seasonal employees given the highest ratings tended to make slightly higher test scores than those given lower ratings. For packers the general conclusion is the same as for the first study: Arm-and-hand dexterity plays a part in initial job adjustment when movements are gross in nature, but practice minimizes its effects. In the case of wrappers, whose work involves somewhat finer but still gross movements, neither arm-and-hand dexterity as measured by the Minnesota test played a part. Nor finger dexterity as measured by O'Connor's test. Perhaps a new test of an intermediate degree of fineness, involving wrist-and-finger movements with objects the size of the Minnesota Rate of Manipulation Test's discs, would have produced positive results.

Another study of the same type was made by Ghiselli (1943) with 42 seasonal wrappers who were rated for both quality and quantity of output. The ratings were combined, and proved to have no significant relationship to Placing and Turning Test scores (—.10 and —.02). Data for finger dexterity were approximately the same. Ghiselli (1942) also worked with pharmaceutical inspector-packers, whose tasks consisted of filling, stoppering, examining, labeling, cartoning, and packaging containers of fluids, powders, and pastes. Job analysis suggested that arm-and-hand dexterity and eye-hand co-ordination should be among the important characteristics in performing the work. The Minnesota Rate of Manipulation Test was therefore among those included in the battery. Production being difficult to measure because of variations in the nature of the work, a rating scale was devised to measure the traits suggested by the job analysis, and the forewoman in charge of the work rated each of the 26 girls. In addition, the supervisor of the finishing room rated each on overall value to the organization. Reliability of the ratings was checked by correlating the composite forewoman's ratings with the supervisor's overall rating: the coefficient was .72. The two ratings were therefore combined to serve as criterion. The correlations between criterion and Placing and Turning Tests were —.24 and —.40 (negative because the scores are in terms of seconds used to perform the task). Of the other factors measured spatial visualization was the most important, more so than manual dexterity; clerical perception was important, but less so than manual dexterity; and some of the spatial and eye-hand co-ordination parts of the MacQuarrie were also valid. Ghiselli's preliminary job analysis therefore proved to be a sound one. It is interesting that the specific factors in the Turning Test made it more valid than the Placing, even though they measure the same basic factor. These findings, then, provide further evidence of the desirability of using custom-built test batteries, and even custom-built tests, for selection purposes.

It is also noteworthy that, although the manual operations in the pharmaceutical job appear to have been more like those of the wrappers than those of the packers in Blum and Candee's studies, the dexterity test had less validity for wrapper selection than for packer selection, and less for packers than for pharmaceutical inspector-packers. In Blum and Candee's studies manual dexterity had some predictive value for initial job adjustment, but no validity for experienced workers; but in Ghiselli's pharmaceutical study no distinction on the basis of experience was made. Herein perhaps lies the explanation of the apparent discrepancy: Ghiselli's group is not described in terms of specific experience, but the general statement is made that both the rate of turnover in the department and company morale were high. If the group contained as great a range of experience as these facts suggest, and if manual dexterity is a selective factor on the job, then the range of manual dexterity was probably greater in Ghiselli's sample than in Blum and Candee's (the published data do not permit comparisons). A difference in aptitude sampling such as this would result in a higher correlation coefficient for Ghiselli's study, even though the role of manual dexterity were really identical in the two occupations. The final judgment would seem to be that Blum and Candee's conclusions are correct, but that the role of manual dexterity is somewhat greater than they found it to be.

A final study of the role of manual dexterity in packing jobs is that carried out by the United States Employment Service and cited by Stead and Shartle (1940, pp. 217–227). They administered the Minnesota test to 43 can packers, 30 merchandise packers, and 41 inspector-wrappers (the jobs are not further described). A production criterion was used for the first two jobs: average number of cans packed per hour, and ratio of time needed to complete a unit of work (estimated by time-and-motion study men) to time actually used to complete the unit; a rating was used for the last-named job. The correlations for the Placing Test were .35, .14, and —.09; for the Turning Test, .22, .11, and .01 respectively. Only for the can packers are the correlations high enough to be significant, and the relationship is the opposite of that anticipated (true also for finger dexterity): The slower or less dextrous tended to have the greater output. For the inspector-packers, whom Ghiselli had considered most likely to resemble his group, no relationship was found. The merchandise packers closely resembled Blum and Candee's department store packers in operations performed, but the correlations are lower in this study than in theirs. Failing more detailed data on the USES study, reconciliation of its findings with the others seems impossible; if enough facts were available, good reasons for the discrepancy would no doubt be found. Perhaps the USES study merely reversed signs. It therefore seems wise to abide by the conclusions drawn from the studies which have been reported in more detail. The USES study also included pull-socket assemblers, put-in-coil girls, and cafeteria counter and floor girls, for none of whom the test had validity (r's $= -.15$ to .19).

A different type of occupational group was studied by McMurry and Johnson (1945), who administered the Minnesota dexterity test to 768 women being hired by an ordnance factory. Scores were validated against ratings of 587 who remained long enough to be rated. The reliability of the ratings was apparently not checked. Distribution among jobs is illustrated by the fact that there were 97 welders, 140 assembly workers, and 33 inspectors. No validities were reported, however, for the Rate of Manipulation Test.

The *paper-mill employees* studied by Jurgensen (1943) were men hired as converting-machine operators, whose work consisted mostly of removing a specified number of tissue-paper sheets from the machine, raising the top sheet to insert advertising material, and placing the package of sheets on a conveyor. All 60 were right-handed high school graduates between the ages of 18 and 31. The criterion was a combination of three supervisors' ratings, the reliability of which was .75. Placing and Turning Tests were both administered, plus some variations which included placing and turning with both hands simultaneously. Validity coefficients were: Placing .325, Turning .455, Right-Hand Placing-Turning .57, Simultaneous Placing-Turning .33. These findings indicate not only that the Minnesota test has predictive value for this type of semiskilled factory work, but also that motion study can be valuable in suggesting variations in the test which increase its validity for specific operations. It is regrettable that Jurgensen did not also utilize an output criterion, the greater objectivity of which (if not affected by slow-down, poor morale, etc.) would provide a better index.

Occupational differentiation by means of the Minnesota Rate of Manipulation Test has been checked by a number of investigators and for a variety of jobs. Blum and Candee (1941) found that satisfactory experienced department store packers and wrappers made better scores than the general population on the Placing Test, but the seasonal workers who were considered an exceptionally good group did not. Ghiselli (1942) reported that pharmaceutical inspector-packers stood at the 96th percentile on the Placing and at the 91st on the Turning Tests when compared to the general population. In the USES study (Stead and Shartle, 1945) pull-socket assemblers, put-in-coil girls, and can packers exceeded the 75th percentile of the general adult population in Placing; in Turning the merchandise packers displaced the can packers. Merchandise packers, cafeteria counter and floor girls, and inspector-wrappers were in the normal range in Placing, with can packers taking the place of the merchandise packers in Turning. Teegarden provided data for groups of from 26 to 123 semiskilled workers in a study previously cited. Of these occupational groups only the assemblers, inspectors, and testers stood at about the third quartile, with women packers and wrappers slightly below it, on both the Placing and Turning Tests. Male packers and wrappers, helpers in skilled trades, factory hand operatives, machine operators, and women clerks were about one sigma above the adult mean in Placing, the women machine operators and packers and wrappers scoring similarly on the Turning test. Truck drivers and chauffeurs, truck loaders and helpers, male sales clerks, restaurant workers, domestic workers, and manual laborers were all in the normal range. It has already been noted that in the MESRI studies butter and food packers and wrappers, bank tellers, and male office clerks ranked higher than the third quartile on the Placing Test, while women office clerks, minor bank officials, minor executives, semiskilled workers, stenographers, typists, and garage mechanics, were in the average range. From these findings it seems legitimate to conclude that arm-and-hand dexterity as measured by the Minnesota test is important is packing, wrapping and inspection jobs and in gross-manual assembly and machine-operation jobs; however, the predictive value of the test depends somewhat upon the specific factors in the job and the degree to which they are also tapped by the test. For this reason sometimes the Placing Test, sometimes the Turning Test, and sometimes other variations such as those tried by Jurgensen (1943) with the Minnesota materials and by others with custom-built pegboards, will have the most predictive value and so be most helpful in selection or counseling.

Job satisfaction, in the case of the Minnesota Manual Dexterity Test as in that of the Minnesota Clerical Test, has apparently not been a subject of investigation.

Use of the Minnesota Rate of Manipulation Test. The Minnesota Manual Dexterity or Rate of Manipulation Test has been found to be useful primarily in connection with semiskilled occupations in which skill in arm-and-hand movements seems, in job analyses, to be important. It has not been found valuable in skilled trades, in which understanding of the processes involved is more important than individual differences in the manual dexterity with which they are executed. Even in the grosser manual jobs such as packing and the assembly of large parts, differences in skill which are found to exist before employment play a part primarily in initial adjustments to the work rather than in long-term adjustments; practice in the specific job operations appears to reduce the effect of pre-employment differences to the zero point. It may be that these differences nevertheless play a part after job experience which current studies have not brought out, perhaps by making the maintenance of adequate production so easy as to render the work satisfying, or by producing such a strain that it becomes subtly unbearable and makes the worker quit or continue in a state of undiagnosed dissatisfaction. In the light of present knowledge, however, this test seems likely to be useful in counseling inexperienced persons concerning the choice of packing and assembly jobs. It is even more likely to find use in selection, when quick adjustment to routine work is desired, than in counseling.

In *selection* programs local norms should be used, and in the initial studies of the test with a given job in a given plant variations in the technique of the test-task should be tried. The test then taps specific factors in the job along with the basic or group factor which should be its principal source of validity. The nature of these variations is suggested by job analysis. The validity of the test is increased by this method, for the initial job-adjustment period; but its long-term adjustment validity may be decreased by the emphasis on developed rather than on latent skills. At this stage of our knowledge, however, this is only a subject for speculation and investigation.

It is doubtful whether this type of test has any place as a directional instrument in a *school counseling* program. If experience erases the effects of normal individual differences in this type of dexterity, then it is the function of education to provide such experience in appropriate cases (those of persons who may enter such work, as suggested by intelligence, interest, and socio-economic status). The test will not be useful in providing data for the making of decisions concerning the choice of semiskilled occupations. It may, on the other hand, give some insight into the assets and liabilities with which a student enters upon new experiences.

In *employment counseling,* whether at the end of an educational program, in an adult guidance center, or in an employment service, the test should be of more value, for the question of initial job adjustments of workers inexperienced in jobs requiring arm-and-hand dexterity is both more common and one on which the Minnesota test throws some light. Since the occupational norms are based on small groups they must be selected with a full understanding of the particular sample and employed tentatively, but some facts cautiously used are better than none at all when decisions have to be made. When the University of Minnesota's form is used, the MESRI norms are still the best; when the Educational Test Bureau's form is used, then Teegarden's data will probably be found most helpful. In either case the norms should be thought of as merely suggestive.

Finally, it is pertinent to ask whether both Placing and Turning Tests should be used, or only one of them; and if the latter, which one. In a specialized battery for semiskilled jobs both should be used, because of the higher correlation of the Placing Test with some gross-movement jobs such as department-store packing, and of the superior validity of the Turning Test for some finer-movement jobs such as packaging drugs. In more comprehensive test batteries, in which there is not sufficient testing time for the refined investigation of each area, the fact that the factor composition of the two tests is identical means that one of the tests should be sufficient for survey or screening purposes. In such situations the test to be used should depend upon which is likely to be more closely related to jobs the examinee may consider or be considered for; in the absence of data for the making of such judgments, the Placing Test can probably best be used, together with a wrist-and-finger dexterity test to tap the other extreme of fineness.

The O'Connor Finger and Tweezer Dexterity Tests (C. H. Stoelting and Co., 1928). The O'Connor Finger and Tweezer Dexterity Tests were developed in the middle 1920's while O'Connor was employed in the West Lynn works of the General Electric Company (Hines and O'Connor, 1936). He was concerned with the selection of women for electric-meter and instrument assembly work, and devised these tests for that purpose. Similar tests had previously been described by Whitman (1925), who used them with children. They have since been tried out on various types of workers, particularly in the Minnesota Employment Stabilization Research Institute.

Applicability. The tests were designed for use with adults and with older adolescents of post-high school age; they were standardized on such groups, and restandardized on similar groups by the MESRI project. They are widely administered to adolescents, but the writers have seen no studies of their applicability to these younger groups. The fact that physical maturity comes somewhat earlier than mental has seemed to warrant the use of this dexterity test from age 13 or 14 on (Bingham, 1937), but it has not actually been demonstrated that this specific type of dexterity matures early. We have seen that the assumption of early maturation proved misleading in the case of the Minnesota clerical and manual dexterity tests; it may be equally misleading in the case of this instrument. In the absence of data on this question, one should proceed cautiously with the use of the O'Connor tests with high school boys and girls, but there is probably not much danger of being misled as a result of age-changes after the last two years of high school.

Candee and Blum (1937) have reported that age in adulthood and work experience have no effect on the scores of the O'Connor tests.

Content. The Finger Dexterity Test consists of a shallow tray beside a metal plate in which there are 100 holes arranged in ten rows of ten holes each (the only readily available form, Stoelting's, is made of different materials). Each hole is large enough to hold three metal pins one inch long and .07 inches in diameter; the holes are spaced one-half inch apart. The Tweezer Dexterity Test is sometimes the opposite side of the boards used for the Finger Dexterity Test; again the metal plate has 100 holes in it, but these are only slightly larger than the pins, allowing one to be placed in each hole. A pair of oo gauge tweezers are used in this test to pick up the pins.

Administration and Scoring. The Dexterity Test is administered with the subject seated at a table of standard height (30 inches), with the pinboard about a foot from the edge of the table, the tray on the side of the favored hand, placed at an angle of about 90 degrees to the subject. The directions are clear except for one point. The O'Connor tests are incorrectly given by many psychometrists because they do not read the instructions carefully enough to realize that if a right-handed subject were to start in the top-left corner and fill the holes toward himself he would fill *columns,* which go *vertically,* up-and-down, rather than *rows.* The examinee should actually begin at the far corner (top-left for a right-handed person) and fill the holes of the top *row across* to the other (top-right for a right-handed person) corner, then begin to fill the holes in the second row in the same manner as the first, then the holes of the third row, etc.

In the Finger Dexterity Test the subject picks up three pins with his preferred hand and places them in each hole; in the Tweezer Dexterity Test he picks up one pin at a time and places it in its hole. The score is normally on the basis of time, with a small correction of the second half for practice on the first half; some recent studies, including those of the USES, use simply the total time required, which is probably sufficiently refined for practical purposes. The time required varies from 8 to 15 minutes for the Finger Dexterity Test, and up to about 10 minutes for the Tweezer Test. Accurate timing is important and requires either a stop watch or a watch with a sweep-second hand.

Norms. Although O'Connor presented adult norms in his original report of his work with Hines (1936), the most representative and generally used norms are those of the Minnesota Employment Stabilization Research Institute (Green et al., 1933). These are for the standard sample of 500 employed adults, supplemented by averages for small groups of persons in a variety of occupations, most of which are unfortunately not the types for which these tests can be expected to be useful. Means and sigmas are available for more pertinent occupations in other studies (Blum, 1940; Stead and Shartle, 1940) discussed below, but unfortunately the scores in these are given in terms of total number of seconds used rather than in terms of O'Connor's correction. Perhaps in due course the work of the USES will make it advisable to use the total time score and their norms; in the meantime, the corrected score and the MESRI norms are best. As no published manual is available, the Minnesota norms are reproduced in Table 14.

TABLE 14

NORMS FOR THE O'CONNOR FINGER AND TWEEZER DEXTERITY
TESTS, MESRI STANDARD SAMPLE EMPLOYED ADULTS

Raw Score: Men		Raw Score: Women			
F.D.	T.D.	F.D.	T.D.	Standard Score	Percentile
183	—	166	—	8.0	99.9
194	255	175	249	7.5	99.4
207	271	186	263	7.0	97.7
221	289	197	279	6.5	93.3
238	309	211	297	6.0	84.1
257	333	226	318	5.5	69.1
280	360	244	342	5.0	50.0
307	393	265	369	4.5	30.9
340	432	290	401	4.0	15.9
382	479	319	440	3.5	6.7
434	539	356	487	3.0	2.3
503	615	402	544	2.5	.6
598	—	462	—	2.0	.14

Means for occupational groups which might be expected to make high scores on these tests, together with those of certain others included for sake of contrast, are given in Table 15 and can serve as a suggestive guide in the use of O'Connor test results.

It should be noted that women tend to do better than men on this as on other types of dexterity tests, and that the only occupations for which these tests have been shown to have any clear-cut value are women instrument assemblers, bank tellers, office workers, manual-training teachers, and draftsmen. As will be brought out below, these data help one to understand the test, but they are hardly enough to serve as norms.

TABLE 15

AVERAGE FINGER AND TWEEZER DEXTERITY SCORES OF
SELECTED OCCUPATIONAL GROUPS

No.	Sex	Occupations	F.D. Mean Score	F.D. Md. Centile	T.D. Mean Score	T.D. Md. Centile
17	M	Bank Tellers	243	80	325	76
113	M	Office Clerks	255	70	323	76
170	M	Manual Training Teachers	258	67	327	74
21	M	Draftsmen	259	69	335	70
61	M	Ornamental Iron Workers	271	57	341	65
102	M	Garage Mechanics	278	51	352	56
31	M	Machine Operators	331	18	385	34
228	M	Casual Laborers	385	7	370.9	1
*	F	Instrument Assemblers	219	76	*	*
180	F	Stenographers-Typists	230	65	333	57
21	F	Office-Mach. Operators	231	64	*	*
15	F	Food Packers	235	59	345	48
19	F	Butter Packers	248	47	340	50
317	F	Graduate Nurses	252	42	334	55

* Data not available

Standardization and Initial Validation. O'Connor standardized the test on 2000 women applicants for factory employment and an equal number of men in the General Electric plant at West Lynn, Massachusetts. The Finger Dexterity Test was administered a number of times to the same workers, with the finding that the second trial was somewhat better than the first, and the fifth trial showed little further improvement over the fourth. Retest reliability for the first and second trials was .60 on the Finger Dexterity Test, considerably lower than coefficients obtained by others. The original validation of this test was on a group of 36 women applicants who were tested when interviewed for employment and hired for assembly work. Hines and O'Connor (1936) reported that 36 percent of those in the lowest quarter left the company before 8 months had elapsed, as compared with only 6 percent of those in the top quarter; this seems impressive until it is realized that 36 percent of one-quarter of 36 (the total number of cases) is slightly more than one-third of 9, that is, three-and-a-fraction persons, and that 6 percent of one-quarter of 36 is approximately 1/17 of 9, or a little more than one-half of one person. Just how three-and-a-fraction persons, and a little more than one-half a person, can fail is something that even some eminent test-construction specialists have failed to ask (Paterson et al., 1938). The report does not exactly strengthen one's confidence in the original work with the test, however ingenious the test idea. No data were published by O'Connor dealing in specific detail with the Tweezer Dexterity Test.

Reliability. As we have seen, Hines and O'Connor (1936) originally reported the retest reliability of the Finger Dexterity Test as .60. Blum (1940) retested 64 employment applicants, obtaining a much higher coefficient of .89; he also reported an uncorrected split-half reliability of .77. Split-half reliabilities for the same test have been reported by Darley (1934) : these are (corrected) .93 and .90 for samples of 475 men and 215 women. Apparently the test is reliable even according to the retest method. No reliability data have been located for the Tweezer Dexterity Test, the above investigators having made the seemingly warranted assumption that the two tests cannot differ much in this respect.

Validity. Because of their early publication the O'Connor dexterity tests have been used in a number of studies. Even though many of these had only an indirect or very partial interest in the nature and validity of the test, they do, taken as a whole, throw considerable light on its validity.

Correlations with other tests have been computed for the usual variety of measures. The Finger and Tweezer Dexterity Tests have been found to have intercorrelations of .17 by Jacobsen (1943) with 90 war-industry trainees as subjects, .19 by Blum (1940) who tested 119 women factory-employment applicants, .47 by Thompson (1942) with 35 dental freshmen, .33 by the Minnesota project (Darley, 1934) with a heterogeneous group of women and .56 for a similar group of men, and .57 by Harris (1937) with a group of 66 dental students 59 of whom completed the four year course. As Blum's and Jacobsen's results are based on factory workers, the others' on professional or mixed groups, it is probably safe to conclude that the correlation is approximately .50 in heterogeneous groups and less than .20 in homogeneous groups.

Correlations between O'Connor dexterity tests and *intelligence* tests have been reported by Harris (1937) for dental students, using the Otis S.A. Test. The coefficients are —.01 and .015.

The relationship with *arm-and-hand dexterity* is perhaps of most interest. Finger Dexterity was found to correlate to the extent of .21 and .42 with the Minnesota Placing Test by Jacobsen (1943) and, by Blum and Candee (1941), .06 and .335 with the Turning Test. For Tweezer Dexterity, correlations of .26 and .20 with Placing and Turning Tests were reported by Jacobsen (1943). With one exception, Jacobsen's correlations are not high enough to be significant, whereas Blum and Candee's are. As was brought out in the discussion of arm-and-hand dexterity, it seems likely that the latter's results should be accepted until more conclusive studies are made. The two types of dexterity should be thought of as related but distinct aptitudes.

Correlations with tests of *spatial visualization* are more numerous, Andrew (1937) reported correlations of .28 and .31 between the Minnesota Spatial Relations Test and the Finger and Tweezer Dexterity Tests, which had been administered to 200 women clerical workers. For the Revised Minnesota Paper Form Board Jacobsen (1943) and Thompson (1942) reported correlations of less than .15 in groups of war-industry trainees and dental students. Jacobsen also found no significant relationships with the Crawford Spatial Relations Test (.22 and .11), although in a more heterogeneous group they might be higher. Harris (1937) reported correlations of —.02 and .15 with the Wiggly Block. Evidently ability to visualize space relations plays no part in wrist-and-finger dexterity.

Wrist-and-finger dexterity has rarely been correlated with *mechanical comprehension,* probably because of the anticipated low relationship. Jacobsen (1949) confirmed expectations with coefficients of — .08 and .14 with the Bennett Mechanical Comprehension Test.

Success in training has been investigated for an electrical worksample, aircraft mechanics, power-sewing-machine operation, machine-tool operation, fine arts, and dentistry.

The study of the electrical worksample (Steel et al., 1945) has already been described (see p. 193) in connection with the Minnesota Rate of Manipulation Test. In it the Finger Dexterity Test had validities of .08 for boys and .35 for girls, while those for the Tweezer Dexterity Test were .18 and .42 (other data show that the signs should be negative, being for time scores).

The investigation of factors in success in *aircraft mechanic* training was also discussed in the section on the Minnesota Rate of Manipulation Test. Jacobsen (1943) found only two significant relationships between O'Connor dexterity tests and instructors' ratings of fitness for the occupation: these were between Finger Dexterity and ratings in aircraft electricity (.31) and Tweezer Dexterity and ratings in aircraft instruments (.32). As the other eight coefficients ranged from —.02 to .22, and there is no apparent logic underlying the different results, the writers are inclined to consider the two statistically significant correlations the products of chance. In any set of correlation coefficients some will appear significant simply as a result of chance factors. Such a conclusion is forced also by the illogic of those who take most time to complete a speed test being the best students (unless Jacobsen reversed signs).

High school girls learning *power-sewing-machine operation* were studied by Otis (1938), who used time taken to complete a series of worksamples and quality-ratings of the same tasks as criteria. The two criteria had an intercorrelation of —.17±.13, from which it might be concluded that there was no relationship between speed and quality, but which may, in the absence of reliability data, only prove that one or both of the criteria were unreliable. The speed criterion had a correlation of .27 with Finger and .46 with Tweezer Dexterity, and the quality criterion was correlated .20 and .07 with the two tests, but neither of these latter coefficients were statistically significant. These results suggest that at least the speed criterion was reliable, and show that those who were fastest on the test tended to be most rapid on the task.

In the study of *machine-tool trainees* Ross (1943) administered the O'Connor Finger Dexterity, Minnesota Spatial Relations, and O'Rourke Mechanical Aptitude Tests and related them to grades in training, establishing critical scores but not obtaining any indices of degrees of relationship.

Students of *fine arts* ($N=50$) were tested with the O'Connor dexterity tests and the Minnesota Paper Form Board by Thompson (1942). Correlations with point-hour ratios were .21 for Finger and .08 for Tweezer Dexterity, neither of which was clearly significant. This finding can perhaps be discounted, however, since grades in fine arts are probably not the most appropriate of criteria; a study using ratings of the quality of artistic craftsmanship, made by experts and checked for reliability, might yield quite different results.

Students of *dentistry* have been studied by Douglass and McCullough (1942), Harris (1937), Jones (unpublished study), and Thompson (1942). In the first-named study a variety of tests were tried at the University of Minnesota over a period of several years, with average grades in dental school as the criterion. The results varied somewhat from one sample to another, but in a typical group of 83 students the correlations between grades and Finger and Tweezer Tests were —.40 and —.30. In Harris' preliminary study of 50 dental freshmen at Tufts first year grades were the criterion, and the correlations with Finger and Tweezer Dexterity Tests were —.395 and —.36. These are the only studies reporting validity for *grades* in dentistry; it seems rather surprising that so specific an aptitude should show a substantial relationship to such a multi-factorial criterion as college grades, especially since the first two years of dental training are more academic than manual or practical. And Harris' more definitive study, in the same school and with the same tests, based on 66 students with both first- and four-year grades as criteria, yielded validities of only —.10 and —.17 for first-year grades and .15 and —.10 for four-year grades (for the numbers in question, the coefficients would need to equal .31 to be significant at the 1 percent level). The Otis S.A. Test, on the other hand, had validities of .55 and .35. Thompson also correlated O'Connor's tests with freshman and four-year grades, for one group of 35 freshmen and another of 40 seniors in dentistry, finding validities of .01 and .01 for Finger and —.07 and .13 for Tweezer Dexterity. E. S. Jones, in a personal communication, has also reported obtaining negligible correlations between O'Connor tests and dental grades at the University of Buffalo. The evidence is now very strongly in favor, therefore, of a lack of predictive value in the O'Connor tests for grades in dental school, despite the statements of O'Connor (1928) and the guarded suggestions of Bingham (1937, pp. 284 and 286). However, their logic seems so good that it would not be surprising to see substantial validities for these tests when correlated with a practical criterion, e.g., reliable ratings such as might be made by patients, of skill in clinical dental work. Douglass and McCullough's (1942) correlations with laboratory grades, —.43 and —.35, are promising. Other studies of this type, and consistent validities, have as yet not been reported; it will be seen that other evidence of the validity for dental training exists.

Success on the job has been the subject of investigation with watch assemblers, electrical fixtures and radio assemblers, department store packers and wrappers, pull-socket assemblers, put-in-coil girls, and can packers.

In a preliminary study of *watch assemblers* Candee and Blum (1937) administered the Finger and Tweezer Dexterity Tests to 20 women workers selected as superior and 17 selected as mediocre by their foremen. The difference between scores of the two groups on the Finger Dexterity Test approached significance $(D/\sigma d = 3.18)$; no such difference was found for the Tweezer Dexterity Test $(D/\sigma d = 1.01)$, but this latter test differentiated employees from a group of applicants better than did the former. Critical scores of 7'30" and 5'30" were established for Finger and Tweezer Dexterity Tests. Two years later these workers were followed up by Blum (1940). None of those who had been rated superior had been discharged, as contrasted with 18 percent of the mediocre workers; the critical ratio was 2.00. The salary ratios (average weekly piece-rate earnings over a three-month period divided by the average for all employees and expressed as an index with $20 per week equal to 100) of the two groups were 110 and 93, which gave a critical ratio of 3.7; apparently the foremen's judgment of superiority was generally good. Although the groups were so small as to make conclusions necessarily tentative, the trend was clearly for superior workers to make better scores on the two tests.

In a subsequent study Blum (1940) used length of employment, foremen's ratings, and salary ratio as the criterion. The salary ratio was that described above; length of employment was divided into "less than one week" (failure group), one week to four months (unsatisfactory group), four months to one year (a moderately proficient group), and more than one year (permanent and effective employees); foremen's ratings were on a five-point scale ranging from "excellent" to "terrible." The first two criteria are objective and hence reliable; the last had a reliability coefficient of .60 for 49 workers re-rated after the lapse of more than one year, which is quite high in view of changes in the worker during such a period. The subjects were women applicants for factory work at a branch of the New York State Employment Service; 137 constituted the tested group, and another 84 who also were selected solely on the basis of an interview, but were not tested, were used as a control group. Most of the group had had industrial experience but none had worked in watch factories; all were white, and 90 percent were between 20 and 25 years of age, with a range from 18 to 40. The factory at no time had knowledge of the women's test scores. The Finger and Tweezer Tests were administered before hiring; scores obtained were time in seconds, quality ratings (reliability for Finger Dexterity equaled .89), and absolute and relative improvement (reliabilities of .13 and .26). It is worth noting that time and quality scores had intercorrelations of .14 for Finger and .71 for Tweezer Dexterity Tests, and that the two quality ratings had an intercorrelation of .26. In view of the reliability of the Finger Dexterity quality ratings and the restricted range of Tweezer quality ratings this is difficult to explain.

Quality ratings yielded no significant relationships with length of employment or salary ratio, with the exception of Tweezer Dexterity and the former; whereas 64 percent of those who received above-average quality ratings worked for four months or longer, only 39 percent of those rated below average on quality of Tweezer Dexterity remained on the job that long $(D/\sigma d = 3.6)$. On the other hand, both Finger and Tweezer dexterity quality ratings yielded reliable contingency coefficients with foremen's ratings (.50 and .24, with .84 the maximum possible).

Time scores on both tests showed significant differences between less-than-seven-day employees and those who remained on the job for more than a year $(D/\sigma d = 4.3$ and $2.5)$, with differences approaching significance when the former group were compared with the four-month-to-a-year group. Correlations between the two tests and salary ratio were .26 and .32 (other data show that the signs should be negative, being time scores;) when the two tests were combined, the validity was .39. All three have some statistical significance. The relationships with foremen's ratings were not reliable.

A further step consisted of applying the previously established critical scores (1937) to this new group of workers and to the 84 controls who were not tested. There was again no relationship with foremen's ratings. Of the group who "passed" both tests when the critical score was applied, only 7 percent were discharged in less than one week, while 57 percent were employed for more than a year; for the no-test group the percentages were 23 and 41; for the group who "failed" one or both tests they were 24 and 28. Appropriate critical ratios were clearly significant. Salary ratios were 91, 88, and 73 for the three categories just utilized, with the differences again significant.

Finger and Tweezer Dexterity Tests are clearly useful in selecting successful watch assembly workers when criteria such as turnover and output (salary ratio) are used.

Electrical assembly workers and one type of packer were tested by the USES Division of Occupational Analysis (Stead and Shartle, 1940) : *pull-socket assemblers, put-in-coil girls,* and *can packers.* The groups were 16, 18, and 43 in number, presumably all women although sex is not specified for two groups. The criteria were number of pull sockets assembled per hour, ratio of time consumed to complete a unit of work to standard time set by time and motion study men for put-in-coil girls, and average number of cans packed per hour. Only the Finger Dexterity Test was administered to all three groups, with validities of —.09, —.25, and .26 Put-in-coil girls also took the Tweezer Dexterity Test, the validity being —.57. It is interesting to note that the can packers, for whom the correlations of time scores with the Minnesota Manual Dexterity Test and the USES Pegboard were negative, have a positive correlation with time scores on the tests of wrist-and-finger dexterity. This suggests that some types of assembly work tend to retain workers who are fast in gross movements but slow in fine, whereas others retain workers who are dextrous in both types of operations; presumably the latter types of assembly work tend to pay more and to be more selective. But the finding may be a reflection of a less selective employment policy rather than of less stringent work requirements, for the numbers are small and the workers may have been employed in only one company. Also, the spread of scores is much greater for the can packers than for the other assembly workers (sigma equals approximately 30 as opposed to 18 seconds). For one of these assembly jobs the O'Connor dexterity tests do clearly have predictive value, apparently that requiring the finest wrist-and-finger movements; for another, somewhat grosser, assembly job it seems to have none (neither did the Minnesota Manual Dexterity Test) ; for the third and grossest manual job it has low validity of a negative sort, slow test workers tending to be fast task workers. The last two relationships may be the result of the operation of chance factors, but the first is too consistent to be the result of chance.

Blum and Candee used the O'Connor Dexterity Tests in their two studies (1941) of *department store packers and wrappers,* described under the Minnesota test, finding negligible relationships between these tests and output or supervisors' ratings.

Occupational differentiation on the basis of wrist-and-finger dexterity is brought out by MESRI data presented earlier in Table 15. Office workers, particularly those using machines, tend to make scores approximately one sigma above the average employed adult. Men who must use their hands skillfully in certain crafts and professions (manual-training teaching, drafting, and ornamental iron work) stand approximately as high. Women who assemble small objects (electric meters and instruments) also excel. On the other hand, skilled workers to whom technical information and understanding are more important than manual precision (garage mechanics), and assembly workers and operatives whose operations are gross in nature, score no better than the average worker.

It would be highly desirable to compare the means of the USES, Blum, and other more recent and more relevant occupational groups with these, but unfortunately this is made impossible by differences in the scoring methods or by doubt concerning the scoring methods, and by mean scores which seem quite out of line with MESRI norms (e.g. Blum's mean Finger-Dexterity time of 417 seconds for successful women watch assemblers compared to the mean of 244 seconds for MESRI adult women). Only one comparison seems clearly legitimate, that between Harris' dental students (1937) and the MESRI norms. This shows that the former group stood at the 84th percentile on Finger Dexterity and at the 89th on Tweezer Dexterity, higher than any of the occupational groups for which norms were obtained by the Minnesota project. Such a vindication of the clinical judgment of many users of and writers about a test is, unfortunately, all too rare.

Job satisfaction has not been related to the O'Connor dexterity tests in any published studies. Presumably the tendency is to focus on the worker's need to make a living and on the employer's desire for efficiency, rather than on the mutual need for emotionally adjusted citizens who find satisfaction in their work.

Use of the O'Connor Finger and Tweezer Dexterity Tests in Counseling and Selection. The studies which have been made with the O'Connor dexterity tests have, like the original investigation in which they were used, been concerned almost exclusively with their use in the selection of vocational or professional students and employees. While data from such sources are not only valuable but essential for tests which are to be used in vocational and educational counseling, they are not sufficient. We have repeatedly seen that one must also have information concerning the development and maturation of the aptitude or trait in question, in order to be able to apply the test to adolescents, and that information must be available which in other ways throws light on the nature of the characteristic being measured. For the O'Connor dexterity tests fairly adequate data are available to help understand the *nature of the trait:* It is distinct from others which we are able to measure, and it plays a part in certain types of vocational activities (summarized below). But little is known specifically about its *development and maturation,* apart from the fact that such aptitudes generally mature earlier than intellectual traits. This means that caution is necessary in interpreting the test scores of adolescents, although those of 17 and 18-year-olds can probably be used with some assurance of stability.

In general, experience with the tests suggests that wrist-and-finger dexterity is likely to be important during the period of *initial adjustment to fine manual jobs,* and that it is likely to be related to success on the job when people with approximately equal amounts of *technical understanding* or trade knowledge are being compared. When the latter vary considerably among applicants or employees, differences in them are likely to outweigh the importance of differences in finger dexterity.

Commenting on the earlier studies of tests of manual dexterity, Wittenborn (1945, p. 406) has pointed out that the common failure of such tests to prove valid probably lies in the nature of the criteria that have been employed. He states:

"Most of the criteria which have been employed in the prediction of mechanical ability have been work samples prepared under unusual competition and other atypical conditions which appear to call for a much higher order of spatial visualizing judgment than manipulative ability, e.g., the criteria used in the Minnesota study (of mechanical abilities). The so-called motor aspects of mechanical ability cannot be assumed to be of limited significance simply because their significance has not been rigorously demonstrated by suitable studies. If investigators employed such criteria as satisfaction in work, duration of employment in routine operations, speed of work, quality of specific operations, piece work output, breakage, fatigability and other factors . . . it might well be demonstrated that the motor abilities, particularly manipulative ability could . . . be granted a significant role in guidance and selection procedures."

Although his paper was written after the publication of most of the studies reviewed in this chapter, Wittenborn apparently based his remarks almost entirely on the Minnesota mechanical abilities study, for while the gist of his remarks is true, some studies have been made which conform to his suggestions. We have seen that some craftsmen whose work requires manual precision and probably some interest in using one's hands excel in fine manual dexterity (ornamental iron workers, manual-training teachers, draftsmen, and dentists), while others whose work requires trade knowledge and insight but no special manual skill (garage mechanics) do not. We have seen that watch assembly workers who stand high in fine manual dexterity tend to keep their jobs longer and to produce more than do those who make lower scores on the O'Connor tests. We have seen that those whose fine manual skills impress a psychometrist as above average tend to be rated as better workers by their foremen. But these fine dexterities are not important in gross manual work such as packing. Wittenborn's insights were excellent, although the state of research was not as lamentable as he thought it.

Although Wittenborn was correct in claiming that (fine) manual dexterity is important in some mechanical occupations, its primary importance lies in certain types of semiskilled jobs. The principal reason for the apparent uselessness of tests of manual dexterity in guidance and selection lay, not so much in the criteria taken by themselves, as in the types of jobs which were first studied by means of manual dexterity tests, e.g., those in the MESRI norm group. Other studies discussed in this section have shown that fine manual dexterity is important in simple manual jobs which require rapid wrist-and-finger movements, e.g., power-sewing-machine operation and the assembly of small electrical parts; in more complex assembly work requiring both speed and precision, e.g., watch assembly; and in other occupations in which rapid manipulation of small objects such as office machines, cash, and the like are involved, e.g., office machine operator, bank teller, and typist.

The O'Connor dexterity tests can therefore make a contribution to diagnostic and prognostic work in *high schools* and *colleges,* at least for students in their late teens and above. In such work they are helpful with students who are considering entering or preparing for professional, mechanical, or office work in which skill with the hands is important, and with others who may enter types of semiskilled factory work in which speed or precision of wrist-and-finger movements is related to stability of employment, earnings, and, probably, satisfaction.

In *guidance centers* the tests are useful for the same purposes, and have additional value in employment counseling when initial adjustments are likely to be important; Steel and others demonstrated this with their electrical worksample, and Blum with the watch assemblers who remained on the job for less than a week.

In *business and industry,* the Finger and Tweezer Dexterity Tests are most useful in the selection of persons who will adapt themselves most readily to speedy or precise semiskilled work. They have little to contribute to the selection of skilled, clerical, and professional workers, as those who have completed appropriate training and chosen to continue in the field are likely to be above the crtical minimum needed in such occupations.

Since there are two O'Connor wrist-and-finger dexterity tests it is in order to ask, finally, whether both should be used or only one will do, and if so, which one. In *heterogeneous groups,* and when rough screening is the objective, one of the tests suffices because of the substantial correlation in such groups. Normally the Finger Dexterity Test is to be recommended as a measure of a more commonly used degree of dexterity, but in some situations the Tweezer Test will be more appropriate. The Finger Test also has the advantage of having been more thoroughly studied. *In homogeneous groups,* and when more refined judgments need to be made concerning manual skill, both tests should normally be used, although local norms and validities will sometimes make possible the omission of one test. In any case, it will generally be wise also to use a test of gross manual dexterity, such as the Minnesota, in testing for counseling; in selection testing both should be used in the research stages, dropping the test or tests which prove not to have predictive value in the local situation.

The Purdue Pegboard (Science Research Associates, 1943). The Purdue Pegboard was developed by the Purdue Research Foundation, Purdue University, and published in 1943 as a test of two types of manual dexterity: arm-and-hand dexterity of a finer type than the Minnesota Test, and finger dexterity manifested in a more realistic way than in the O'Connor tests. Although still new and relatively little studied, both motion study of the test and preliminary data suggest that it merits detailed consideration. As pointed out early in this chapter, it appears to tap ability to perform global movements and to eliminate non-essential operations to a degree greater than other manual dexterity tests.

Applicability. The Pegboard was designed as a group test for and standardized upon adult industrial workers. It has since been standardized upon veterans counseled in guidance centers and upon college students, but, like other manual dexterity tests, the development of the skills it measures from adolescence to adulthood has not been studied. As dexterities generally mature early, it is probably safe to use the adult norms with older high school boys and girls.

Content. The Purdue Pegboard consists of a 12x18 inch rectangular board with four shallow cups of trays at one end, and two rows of ⅛ inch holes perpendicularly down the middle. Fifty easily fitting metal pins are provided, together with 20 metal collars and 40 metal washers made to fit the pins.

Administration and Scoring. The test is administered with the subject seated at a 30-inch table on which the board is placed with the cups away from the subject. If the psychometrist sits opposite the subject, he must be careful not to let his own hands get near enough to the cups to seem to interfere with the testing. The first part tests the right hand, putting the pins in the holes one at a time; the second repeats with the left hand; the third tests both hands simultaneously; the fourth score consists of the first three combined; and a final sequence consists of assembling pin, washer, collar, and washer using right, left, right, and left hands. Thus dexterity is tested for each arm and hand, with fingers playing a simple grasping role; ability to perform the same operation with both hands simultaneously is measured; and ability to perform different operations in a coordinated way with the two hands simultaneously is assessed. As Cohen and Strauss (1946) point out, if the worker can effectively merge the two sets of operations in a task such as the assembly test he saves time in the total task; if he must work first with one hand and then with the other, he adds to the time required. The assembly test also seems to require finer finger movements than the other parts, which appear to resemble the O'Connor tests. The score is the number of pins placed in 30 seconds (sequences 1 to 3) and the number of assemblies made in 60 seconds.

Norms. The revised one-trial norms (1948 Manual) are for 4138 women applicants for factory employment, 392 college women, 2439 college men and veterans, and 865 male industrial applicants, treated separately, but the numbers are not given in the manual as finally printed. Three-trial norms are based on data from 500 college students which made possible the extrapolation of norms for all groups. Analysis of data for 900 subjects by previous employment, regional origin, and race failed to reveal any group differences. But norms for veterans published by Long and Hill (1947) tend to be somewhat lower, particularly the total scores. Although these norms are helpful for general interpretation, they throw no light on the vocational significance of the test scores. Occupational norms, especially for semiskilled workers, are badly needed.

Standardization. The test authors stated in the original manual that considerable data had been gathered concerning the test's validity, but that government (wartime) regulations made impossible their publication. They added that comparable studies were being made elsewhere, results of which were made available in the revised manual and are described below, under validity.

Nothing is said, in the manual, concerning the process of developing the test. Reliability data are given: .71 for the total score of the combined pin-placing tests, and .68 for the assembly test, one trial each ($N = 175$ to 434). Three-trial reliabilities are estimated to be .88 and .86.

These data led to a suggested modification of the Pegboard, to increase its reliability, which was made by Super (in the earlier edition of this book) and which has recently been studied by Bass and Stucki (1951). The proposed modification was that the board should be reconstructed to provide three rows of holes at each side of the board, more pins, washers and collars, and 90 seconds of working time for each of the pin-placing tests rather than 30 seconds. The modifications made by Bass and Stucki took into consideration Super's suggestion. The board consisted of four rows of twenty-five holes each, the rows being equidistant from each other and centered on a board the same size as the original. Double the number of pins, washers, and collars were placed in the four cups, as in the unmodified test. Sixty industrial education college students were then first given two administrations of the unmodified board followed by two administrations of the modified test one week later. Sixty seconds of working time were allotted for each of the pin-placing tests and 120 seconds were allowed for the assembly test. All directions were the same for the modified as for the unmodified test, with the exception that in the administration of the former the subjects were instructed to use the two right rows first when placing pins with both hands and then proceed to the top of the two left rows. In each comparison of the modified with the unmodified tests on the various operations performed the test-retest reliabilities were considerably greater for the modified form of the board. These results are reproduced in Table 16. With the exception of the Assembly subtest, doubling the length of the Pegboard had the effect of raising the reliabili-

TABLE 16

TEST-RETEST RELIABILITY COEFFICIENTS FOR THE
UNMODIFIED AND MODIFIED PURDUE PEG BOARD SUBTESTS
($N = 60$)

| | Test-retest Reliability Coefficients | | | |
| | Obtained | | Expected | |
Subtest	Unmodified Board	Modified Board	2 Unmodified Administrations	3 Unmodified Administrations
Left hand	.66	.82	.80	.85
Right hand	.67	.85	.80	.86
Both hands	.71	.87	.83	.90
L + R + B	.79	.90	.88	.91
Assembly	.72	.76	.84	.90

After Bass and Stucki (1951)

ties sufficiently for use in individual counseling and placement. Since the correlations between the modified and unmodified boards were approximately as high as their reliabilities would permit, it was concluded that the two forms were measuring essentially the same thing.

Reliability. As indicated above, the reliability of the standard one-trial test leaves something to be desired. Surgent (1947) has confirmed the test author's data with a group of 233 women factory workers.

Validity. The test being relatively new, only one field validation study has as yet been published (Surgent, 1947). Table 17 gives the results of the validity studies reported in the manual, by permission of Science Research Associates. It should be noted that numbers were very small (and the *r*'s therefore not very reliable) in all groups except the last. For this group of 233 radio tube mounters, with ratings as a criterion, the validity of the three-trial assembly test was .64. The trend of the other correlations is encouraging but more adequate data are clearly needed.

It should be noted that the suggestions for interpretation on the Score Sheet provided by the publisher include artists, chauffeurs, mechanics, musicians, pilots, and others, as well as assembly workers, as groups for which the test should prove useful. But no data support these claims, and while pilots, at least, might conceivably make high assembly (co-or-

TABLE 17

RESULTS OF VALIDITY STUDIES WITH THE PURDUE PEGBOARD

Test	No. of Trials	Job	Criterion	N	r
Right Hand	1	Light machine operation	Make-up pay while learning	17	.56
Left Hand	1	" " "	" " " "	17	.23
Both Hands	1	" " "	" " " "	17	.21
R + L + B	1	" " "	" " " "	16	.31
Assembly	1	" " "	" " " "	16	.38
Right Hand	1	" " "	Earnings after learning	17	.52
Left Hand	1	" " "	" " "	17	.20
Both Hands	1	" " "	" " "	17	.07
R + L + B	1	" " "	" " "	16	.33
Assembly	1	" " "	" " "	16	.38
Assembly	1	Textile quilling	Production Index	28	.15
Right Hand	1	Simple assembly, small parts	" "	15	.76
Assembly	1	" " " "	" "	15	.76
Assembly	3	Radio tube mounters (807)	Pooled overall ratings	233	.64

dination) scores, there definitely is no relationship between manual dexterity and success in flying (DuBois, 1947).

Use of the Purdue Pegboard in Counseling and Selection. Until further validation data are provided, there is only one kind of situation in which this test can now be used for *counseling*: that in which the counselor, or a psychometrist who writes detailed test reports, has a first-hand knowledge of factory jobs acquired by job-analysis experience. Such a user of the test may obtain from it clinical insights into the manual dexterities of his clients, which he then subjectively translates into occupational terms. Unless this translation is based on intensive job-analysis information it is likely to be dangerously misleading. The observer will want to look for efficient use of hands, particularly for global co-ordinated movements in the assembly test. The nature of the test is such that the writers are confident that specific occupational norms and good validity data can be made available in due course, although disappointingly few have accumulated to date.

In *selection,* the test may similarly be used in situations in which decisions have to be made before validation and local norming can be completed. Again, job analysis data are needed. On the other hand, it is possible and wise, more frequently than most so-called practical men admit, to make immediate decisions on other bases, and to use tests at first only to gather research data which will provide a better basis for similar decisions as the need recurs in the future. If research data are not gathered the first time, but the tests are put to intuitive use, then judgmental errors, comparable to those which the tests were adopted to do away with, are perpetuated. One type of intuition replaces another.

The Purdue Pegboard, modified as suggested in the discussion of reliability, seems to be an extremely promising test for assembly, packing, machine-operation, and other fairly precise manual jobs. The analysis of manual work by Cohen and Strauss, discussed in the opening section of this chapter, and the nature and validity of other manual and finger dexterity tests, suggest this. It should be valid for a greater and manually more demanding variety of jobs than the Minnesota Rate of Manipulation Test, and should have higher validities than the O'Connor dexterity tests for jobs such as those for which these have proved valid. But evidence should be assembled and published.

REFERENCES FOR CHAPTER IX

Andrew, D. M. "An analysis of the Minnesota Vocational Test for Clerical Workers. I, II," *J. Appl. Psychol.*, 21 (1937), 18-47, 139-172.
Bass, B. M., and Stucki, R. E. "A note on a modified Purdue Pegboard," *J. Appl. Psychol.*, 35 (1951), 311-313.
Bingham, W. V. *Aptitudes and Aptitude Testing.* New York: Harper, 1937.
Blum, M. L. "A contribution to manual aptitude measurement in industry," *J. Appl. Psychol.*, 24 (1940), 381-416.
———, and Candee, B. "The selection of department store packers and wrappers with the aid of certain psychological tests," *J. Appl. Psychol.*, 25 (1941), 78-85.
———, and Candee, B. "The selection of department store packers and wrappers with the aid of certain psychological tests: Study II," *J. Appl. Psychol.*, 25 (1941), 291-299.
Buxton, I. "Application of multiple factorial methods to the study of motor abilities," *Psychometrika*, 3 (1938), 85-93.
Candee, B., and Blum, M. L. "Report of a study done in a watch factory," *J. Appl. Psychol.*, 21 (1937), 572-582.
Cohen, L., and Strauss, L. "Time study and the fundamental nature of manual skill," *J. Consult. Psychol.*, 10 (1946), 146-153.
Cook, D. W., and Barre, W. F. "Effect of specialized industrial norms on the use of the Minnesota Rate of Manipulation Test as a selective instrument," *J. Appl. Psychol.*, 26 (1942), 785-792.
Darley, J. G. "Reliability of tests in the standard battery." (In "Research studies in individual diagnosis.") *University of Minnesota Bull. Empl. Stab. Res. Inst.*, 4 (1934).
Douglass, H. R., and McCullough, C. M. "Prediction of success in the School of Dentistry," *Univer. Minn. Stud. Predict. Schol. Ach.*, 2 (1942), 61-74.
Du Bois, P. H. (ed.). *The classification program.* ("AAF Aviation Psychology Report," No. 2) Washington, D.C.: Government Printing Office, 1947.
Fleishman, E. A., and Hempel, W. E., Jr. "A factor analysis of dexterity tests," *Pers. Psychol.*, 7 (1954), 15-32.
Ghiselli, E. E. "Tests for the selection of inspectors-packers," *J. Appl. Psychol.*, 26 (1942), 468-476.
——— "Use of the Minnesota Rate of Manipulation and O'Connor Finger Dexterity Tests in the selection of package wrappers," *J. Appl. Psychol.*, 27 (1943), 33-34.
Green, H. J., et al. "A manual of selected occupational tests for use in public employment offices," *University of Minnesota Bull. Empl. Stab. Res. Inst.*, 3 (1933).
Harrell, T. W. "A factor analysis of mechanical ability tests," *Psychometrika*, 5 (1940), 17-33.

Harris, A. J. "Relative significance of measures of mechanical aptitude, intelligence, and previous scholarship for predicting achievement in dental school," *J. Appl. Psychol.*, 21 (1937), 513-521.

Hines, M., and O'Connor, J. "A measure of finger dexterity," *J. Pers. Res.*, 4 (1936), 379-382.

Jacobsen, E. E. "An evaluation of certain tests in predicting mechanic learner achievement," *Educ. Psychol. Measmt.*, 3 (1943), 259-267.

Jurgensen, C. E. "Extension of the Minnesota Rate of Manipulation test," *J. Appl. Psychol.*, 27 (1943), 164-169.

Long, L., and Hill, J. "Additional norms for the Purdue Pegboard," *Occupations*, 26 (1947), 160-161.

McMurry, R. N., and Johnson, I. L. "Development of instruments for selecting and placing factory employees," *Adv. Mgt.*, 10 (1945), 113-120.

O'Connor, J. *Born That Way*. Baltimore: Williams and Wilkins, 1928.

Otis, J. L. "Prediction of success in power sewing machine operating," *J. Appl. Psychol.*, 22 (1938), 350-366.

Paterson, D. G., et al. *The Minnesota Mechanical Abilities Tests*. Minneapolis: University of Minnesota Press, 1930.

————, and Darley, J. G. *Men, Women, and Jobs*. Minneapolis: University of Minnesota Press, 1936.

————, Schneidler, G., and Williamson, E. G. *Student Guidance Techniques*. New York: McGraw-Hill, 1938.

Roberts, J. R. *Manual for the Pennsylvania Bimanual Worksample Test*. Minneapolis: Educational Test Bureau, 1943.

Ross, L. W. "Results of testing machine-tool trainees," *Pers. J.*, 21 (1943), 363-367.

Seashore, H. G. "The superiority of college students on the Minnesota Rate of Manipulation Test," *J. Appl. Psychol.*, 31 (1947), 249-259.

————, Buxton, C. E., and McCollum, I. N. "Multiple factorial analysis of five motor skills," *Amer. J. Psychol.*, 53 (1940), 251-259.

Staff, Division of Occupational Analysis, WMC. "Factor analysis of occupational aptitude tests," *Educ. Psychol. Measmt.*, 5 (1945), 147-155.

Stead, W. H., and Shartle, C. L. *Occupational Counseling Techniques*. New York: American Book Co., 1940.

Steel, M., Balinsky, B., and Long, H. "A study on the use of a work sample," *J. Appl. Psychol.*, 29 (1945), 14-21.

Surgent, L. L. "The use of aptitude tests in the selection of radio tube mounters," *Psychol. Monog.*, 61 (1947), Whole of No. 283.

Teegarden, L. "Manipulative performance of young adult applicants at a public employment office. Pts. I, II," *J. Appl. Psychol.*, 26 (1942), 633-652, 754-769.

———— "Occupational differences in manipulative performance of applicants at a public employment office," *J. Appl. Psychol.*, 27 (1943), 416-437.

Thompson, C. E. "Motor and mechanical abilities in professional schools," *J. Appl. Psychol.*, 26 (1942), 24-37.

Tuckman, J. "A Comparison of norms for the Minnesota Rate of Manipulation Test," *J. Appl. Psychol.*, 28 (1944), 121-128.

———— "A study of the reliability of the Minnesota Manipulation Test," *J. Appl. Psychol.*, 28 (1944), 388-392.

Whitman, E. C. "A brief test series for manual dexterity," *J. Educ. Psychol.*, 16 (1925), 118-123.

Wilson, G. M., and Staff. "Adapting the Minnesota Rate of Manipulation Test to factory use," *J. Appl. Psychol.*, 29 (1945), 346-349.

Wittenborn, J. R. "Mechanical ability, its nature and measurement. I. II. Manual dexterity," *Educ. Psychol. Measmt.*, 5 (1945), 241-260, 395-409.

X

MECHANICAL APTITUDE

Nature and Role

THE TITLE of this chapter, and indeed the writing of a separate chapter on this subject, are a concession to practical considerations and to popular usage, rather than an organization of materials dictated by the nature of aptitudes. Counselors, personnel men, and vocational psychologists have long been accustomed to thinking in terms of mechanical aptitude. They have not defined the term in any strict sense, but have used it operationally to refer to the characteristic or set of characteristics which tends to make for success in mechanical work. Tests have been developed which have proved to be reasonably valid for various types of mechanical occupations. In one sense, then, there has been some justification for using the term mechanical aptitude. But while these practical developments were taking place, psychologists were also studying mechanical aptitude in order to ascertain whether it was in fact one trait or aptitude in the limited sense of the term, or whether it was really a combination of aptitudes.

The first significant attempts to study, rather than simply measure, mechanical aptitude were carried out by Cox (1928) in England and by Paterson and associates (1930) at the University of Minnesota. Using especially constructed mechanical apparatus which did not lend itself well to scoring, Cox applied factor analysis to his data according to Spearman's two-factor method. He isolated a factor which seemed to be of special importance in the mechanical tasks, and therefore might be called "mechanical aptitude"; but it was an eductive factor of the spatial relations type, rather than something peculiarly mechanical which might be called "mechanical comprehension."

At about the same time Paterson and his colleagues were carrying out the Minnesota Mechanical Abilities Project, in which they first tried out a number of existing tests, then revised and selected from these to make a definitive study of mechanical aptitude in junior high school boys. As Harvey (1931) points out, the Minnesota project was superior in test ideas and construction to the Cox, but was somewhat weaker in theory, for Cox utilized factor analysis theories and procedures which were not yet in use by American psychologists. He consequently had not only superior statistical methods but also somewhat more clear-cut hypotheses to guide him in planning his project. In the Minnesota project the Minnesota Mechanical Assembly, Spatial Relations, and Paper Form Board Tests were administered, together with the Otis, an interest inventory, and the Stenquist Mechanical Aptitude or Picture Tests (resembling the O'Rourke). Data on cultural status, recreational interests, mechanical operations or activities around the home, father's mechanical operations, tools owned by the subject and by his father, mechanical ability required in the father's occupation, and similar factors were obtained. The subjects were 150 junior high school boys in Minneapolis. Validity aspects of the study will be considered in connection with specific tests; at this point our interest is in the nature of the factors measured by the tests which were selected to appraise mechanical aptitude.

Information on this subject comes from studies by Harrell (1940) and by Wittenborn (1945). Harrell applied Thurstone's centroid method of factor analysis to the Minnesota battery, which he had administered to 91 cotton-mill machine fixers together with more than 30 other tests. Five factors emerged, of which two, perception of detail and visualization of space relations, were important in the Minnesota tests. The former was demonstrated by repetitions of the tests to be a routine type of ability, whereas the latter played a part only in the earlier administration of the test to a given subject; Harrell therefore described the spatial factor as the equivalent of mechanical ingenuity. Wittenborn applied the same factorial method to the data of the original study. In this case the intercorrelations between the Minnesota Mechanical Assembly Test (described later and cited here as the prototype of "mechanical aptitude" tests) and the Minnesota Spatial Relations Test and Paper Form Board were respectively .56 and .49. This suggests that spatial visualization plays an important part in "mechanical aptitude," but does not explain entirely performance on such a test. Wittenborn isolated four factors, of which only one, spatial visualization, played an important part in the Mechanical Assembly Test. Spatial visualization accounted for 37 percent of the variance in the Assembly Test; this is to be compared with 55 percent of the variance in the Spatial Relations Test, 49 in the Paper Form Board, and 56 of ratings of the quality of shop work, showing in another way that spatial visualization is important but still only one of the factors which play a part in such instruments as the Minnesota Mechanical Assembly Test.

Neither Harrell's nor Witttenborn's studies raise the question, or throw any light on the nature of the factor or factors which account for the remaining 63 per cent of the variance of the Minnesota Assembly Test. Neither does another analysis of Cox's mechanical assembly tests by Slater (1940), although the last-named investigator agreed with the others in finding no special mechanical factor over and above general intelligence and spatial visualization. But this inability to isolate any other factors is in part a function of the types and varieties of tests which are used in the factor analysis; one can locate only the factors which are important in several of the tests, and if a factor is important in only one or two tests it may not emerge as significant.

Bingham (1937: Ch. 11) suggests that factors in mechanical success are mechanical aptitude, measured by tests such as the Minnesota Assembly and Spatial Relations Tests, manual dexterity (demonstrated to be unimportant), perceptual acuity (confirmed), and mechanical information. The Minnesota study included a measure of mechanical information ("the shop operations information criterion") which had a correlation of .35 with the Assembly Test, but this item was omitted in Wittenborn's analysis, and nothing comparable to it was included in Harrell's data. Both authors included the Stenquist Picture Tests which are generally thought to measure mechanical information and which correlate .40 and .46 with the Minnesota Mechanical Assembly Test. Although only 22 and 18 percent of the variance in the Stenquist tests is accounted for by the spatial factor (Wittenborn, 1945), and perceptual speed and accuracy plays some part in them (Harrell, 1940), they are virtually unanalyzed by Wittenborn and Harrell's studies.

Guilford's analysis of a greater variety of tests tried out in the Army Air Forces' Aviation Psychology Program (1947, 1948) provides the answer to the question of what other factors play a part in tests of mechanical aptitude. In this analysis, thanks to the inclusion of a test of mechanical information, an aptitude test patterned after the Bennett Mechanical Comprehension Test (described below) was found to be heavily saturated with two factors: spatial visualization and mechanical information.

What has commonly been thought of as mechanical aptitude, what vocational psychologists have for twenty years known to be partly spatial visualization, and what some authorities (Bingham, 1937) erroneously thought to be also partly manual dexterity, finally emerges in Harrell's and Guilford's studies as a composite of spatial visualization, perceptual speed and acuity, and mechanical information. As in the case of Binet's global approach to the problem of measuring intelligence, this lumping together of several aptitudes in one test has had its advantages, for in days when factor analysis was in its infancy, reliable and valid tests were developed, effective even though impure, for the prediction of success in mechanical activities. With the information and techniques now available purer tests can be developed which provide us with a better understanding of both aptitudes and activities, and which are more versatile in their applicability. The evidence on multifactor batteries, reviewed in a later chapter, shows that the advantages of face validity and the inclusion of specific factors which characterize factorially impure tests depending heavily on job analysis and job content for their items are important. Impure tests of so-called mechanical aptitude or comprehension are among the most valid tests available. For this reason they are dealt with as such in this chapter, and purer tests of spatial visualization are treated separately in the next, just as tests of manual dexterity were taken up in the preceding chapter.

Specific Tests

One of the earliest tests of mechanical aptitude was the Stenquist Mechanical Assembly Test (1923), consisting of a long narrow box, each compartment of which contained a mechanical contrivance to be assembled by the examinee. The ten items consisted of a mouse trap, a push button, and similar everyday objects. Stenquist also developed two picture tests designed to measure the same type of aptitude; but since manipulation and trial of the parts is impossible in a printed test, it has generally been thought of as being more heavily saturated with information than the apparatus tests. As a result of work with Army trade and mechanical aptitude tests during World War I, O'Rourke (Fryer, 1931, p. 265) developed a graphic and verbal test of the same type. Paterson and associates (1930) modified and lengthened Stenquist's Assembly Test as the Minnesota Mechanical Assembly Test for their intensive study of the nature and measurement of mechanical aptitude. More recently, Bennett (Bennett and Cruikshank, 1940) developed his Test of Mechanical Comprehension in order to tap a higher level of mechanical aptitude and Owens (1950) constructed a still more complex modification. A totally different type of composite test was constructed by MacQuarrie (1927), who combined subtests of spatial visualization and manual dexterity in a test of so-called mechanical aptitude.

Of these and other tests like them, the Minnesota Mechanical Assembly Test, the O'Rourke Mechanical Aptitude Test, the Bennett Mechanical Comprehension Test, and the MacQuarrie Test of Mechanical Ability have been selected for detailed treatment. The assembly test has been chosen as the most adequate of its type, because of the insights which studies using it give into the nature and organization of aptitude for mechanical work, even though it is no longer widely used. The O'Rourke has been as thoroughly studied as the Stenquist and other picture tests, and has the advantage of more recent and more extensive norms than most; it is still widely used, although there is room for a well-constructed and up-to-date test of the same type. The Bennett is one of the newest but most thoroughly studied and widely used graphic tests of mechanical aptitude, and taps a higher level of aptitude than the other mechanical aptitude tests. And the MacQuarrie is not only unique as to content, but widely used and studied; although it could just as well be dealt with under tests of manual dexterity or spatial visualization, it is included in this chapter as a composite test of mechanical aptitude. The Purdue Mechanical Adaptability Test is also treated, more briefly, as a possible alternate for the O'Rourke.

The Minnesota Mechanical Assembly Test (Marietta Apparatus Co., 1930). This test was developed as a part of the University of Minnesota's study of mechanical aptitude, in the preliminary work of which it was found that Stenquist's ten-item test had a reliability of only .72. Three boxes, or a total of 36 mechanical items, were used with a resulting reliability of .90. Three of these items have since been omitted, making a total of 33. The Stenquist test having been one of the first fairly good tests of mechanical aptitude, and the Minnesota being a demonstrated improvement upon that, the latter came rapidly into widespread use in clinics and guidance bureaus doing individual testing with adolescent boys; it has not been so extensively used in other situations, because of administration time, wear and tear, and the effects of experience.

Applicability. Like the Stenquist, the Minnesota Mechanical Assembly Test was designed for use with junior high school boys, and particularly for the prediction of success in shop courses. It was recognized that experience or familiarity with mechanical objects might well play an important part in scores on such a test, even at this age; the Minnesota study therefore analyzed the relationship between a number of environmental factors which reflect or constitute differences in experience, either direct or vicarious, with mechanical objects and processes. Two experience items showed positive correlations with the assembly test: recreational interests (.23) and mechanical household tasks such as electrical repairs performed by the boy (.40). On the other hand, ratings of the mechanical ability required by the father's occupation, the tools owned by the boy, and the tools owned by the father, had no relationship with the assembly test scores of the 150 boys of the study (r's$=$ —.11, .14, and .03).

Two other relationships are of interest here, one being that with age which is understandably negligible (.13) in a group as relatively homogeneous as seventh and eighth grade boys, and the other that with scores on a test of shop information which is moderately high (.35). It is noteworthy that the three experience items with which substantial correlations were found probably involve both cause and effect: Boys with more mechanical aptitude could be expected to choose mechanical hobbies, seek to do household repairs, and learn a good deal about shop processes. At the same time, boys who have such hobbies, perform such chores, and learn well in shop courses could be expected to acquire the knowledge to do better than others on a test of mechanical assembly. On the other hand, the items which are more strictly environmental, i.e., not within the control of the boys but affecting them nonetheless, show negligible relationships with assembly test scores; boys do not choose their fathers' occupations nor decide how many tools their fathers will have, and economic factors and parental ideas probably determine the boys' own tools more than do their desires; but one would expect mechanically inclined fathers who have and use their own tools to have some effect on the mechanical information possessed by boys in their early teens. More important, perhaps, than mere possession of mechanical tools and hobbies by the father may be the extent of identification of the son with the father and of father acceptance of the son. If this is so, the continua are not experience *vs.* no-experience, but mechanical-father-identification, and non-mechanical-father-rejection, each of which must be combined with son-acceptance and son-rejection in order to describe the emotional as well as material environment which shapes the boy's interests and information. Unfortunately, no such refined studies have as yet been attempted. That the mechanical activities of the fathers do not affect the sons seems to indicate that at this age the Minnesota Mechanical Assembly Test is more a measure of differences in mechanical insight (spatial visualization) than of mechanical information.

Perhaps this is why Wittenborn's factor analysis (1945), cited in the opening section of this chapter, and using the original Minnesota data, failed to isolate any other important factors in this test. Harrell (1937) reported a correlation of $-.22$ between inexperience and assembly test scores in his study of mechanical aptitudes in adult cotton-mill machine fixers. Adults who had had mechanical experience did better than those who lacked it (Harrell also showed that practice on the assembly test reduced it to a measure of perceptual speed and accuracy). We have already seen that Guilford (1947, 1948) found an experience factor in another mechanical comprehension test used with aviation cadets. These data lead to the conclusion that in early adolescence tests such as the Minnesota Mechanical Assembly Test are primarily measures of mechanical comprehension (spatial visualization), whereas in late adolescence and adulthood they also tap mechanical information (experience).

Clinical experience with the assembly test has led to the generally accepted conclusion that it is unsuitable and too easy for use with older adolescents and adult men, and too difficult for most women. The first is perhaps verified by the AAF study (Guilford, 1947) cited above, but none of them have actually been objectively confirmed with the assembly test itself except through data on age differences in the reliability of the test (see below). The most objective evidence, apart from Harrell's data, lies in the norms for various age and occupational groups, which show increasingly higher scores from age 12 to age 19 (raw scores of 232 to 299, the former median being at approximately the 10th percentile for 19-year-olds). But the available data do not tell us whether these increases with age are the result of maturation of spatial visualization or of increased familiarity with mechanical objects. As manual training teachers and ornamental iron-workers in the Minnesota Employment Stabilization Research Institute fell midway between the average 18- and 19-year-old boy in the original norms, auto mechanics were slightly lower, and the average employed adult was little more than midway between the average 17- and 18-year-old, the implication is that either the sampling in the adolescent group was skewed toward the upper limits or maturation of spatial visualization plays a greater part in assembly test scores than experience in mechanical activities. If this were not so, miscellaneous boys would not surpass skilled mechanical workers. It seems more probable that the adolescent sample is not adequate at the upper limits (due to elimination in high school) and that skilled workers surpass 19-year-olds about as much as they do 17-year-olds: that is, by more than one sigma. Lacking adequate objective evidence concerning the effects of experience on the assembly test scores of adults it seems wise for practical purposes to agree with Bingham (1937, p. 308) and with Paterson, Schneidler and Williamson (1938, p. 222) that the varied amounts of mechanical experience which characterize adults make it unwise to use this test with that age group; the theoretical question remains open until better evidence is accumulated.

Content. The Minnesota Mechanical Assembly Test consists of three boxes containing 33 mechanical objects such as an expansion nut, a hose-pinch clamp, a wooden clothespin, a push-button door bell, a spark plug, an inside caliper, and a petcock.

Administration and Scoring. A fixed amount of time is allowed for work on each object, these being presented unassembled in their compartments. Scoring is on the basis of proportion of possible connections made in the allotted time. The psychometrist needs to be thoroughly familiar with the assembly and disassembly of the objects, both from studying the directions and from actually practicing with the materials, especially the latter. He must know not only how to put the parts together, but what condition they should be in when new, for many boxes actually in use contain bent or broken parts and non-standard replacements which change the nature of the task. In fact, one problem brought out by World War II testing operations, and not adequately realized when investigations such as the University of Minnesota's study of 150 boys was planned, is the drastic effect on apparatus tests of the wear and tear of large-scale testing. In the Air Force program, for example, it was found necessary to assign an officer and several enlisted men to an apparatus control unit at each testing center, their sole function being to make statistical studies of the effects of differences in supposedly identical pieces of apparatus on test scores and to establish correction formulas for raw scores on each apparatus. Most of these differences were due to wear and tear through use, as many as 100 men per day being tested by a given piece of equipment.

Norms. Norms for boys aged 11 to 21 were published by Paterson and associates (1930) as a result of the Minnesota Mechanical Abilities Project, and for general adults and specific occupations by Green and others (1933) after the test was used in the Minnesota Employment Stabilization Research Institute. Paterson does not make clear the number of cases used in the original norms, which included at least 150 boys in 7th and 8th grades, but unknown numbers at the higher levels. Since the test is most useful at the junior high school level this is not a serious limitation. The adult norms are based on the Minnesota standard sample of 500 employed adults; the specific occupational groups are small, ranging from 18 draftsmen to 169 manual-training teachers. In view of the presumed effects of experience and the suitability of other tests for adult use, the adult norms are of questionable value; they do show the expected group differences, as will be seen below, but these are not as great as one would expect in a good aptitude test, perhaps because of the leveling effects of experience and information with items such as these.

Standardization and Initial Validation. As has already been indicated, the Minnesota Mechanical Assembly Test was developed as a more reliable edition of Stenquist's test. As a part of the intensive study of mechanical abilities carried out by Paterson and associates (1930) it was correlated with a variety of other tests and with a number of experience variables in order to throw light on its nature and validity. Some of these have already been discussed in connection with the question of the applicability of the test; others remain to be considered.

In the relatively restricted age, but somewhat greater intellectual, range of the 7th and 8th grades the correlation between assembly test scores and Otis I. Q. was .06. Spatial visualization as measured by the Minnesota Spatial Relations and Paper Form Board Tests, on the other hand, had correlations of .56 and .49 respectively, showing the important role of the spatial factor in mechanical assembly work at this age. Correlations with the Stenquist Picture Tests were .46 and .40, as might be anticipated with paper-and-pencil tests of mechanical comprehension.

There was no relationship between assembly test score and average academic grades ($r = .13$), but the correlation with ratings of the quality of shop operations was .55, and that with a test of shop information was .35. The higher correlation with operations, as opposed to information, suggests that the test was accomplishing its objective of measuring aptitudes for mechanical work. Certainly it predicted success in that much better than in academic work.

Two other relationships are of interest, one a correlation of .02 with preference for mechanical occupations, the other a correlation of .42 with scores on a mechanical interest inventory. The discrepancy suggests that the expressed occupational preferences of junior high school boys may not be valid indicators of interest, whereas inventory scores may be, a conclusion confirmed by other studies reviewed in the chapter on interests. In view of the confirmation of this deduction, it may be concluded that mechanical interests and mechanical aptitude tend to be associated, although the relationship is far from perfect. Perhaps the relationship is due to the role of interest in the acquisition of information, and the role of information in so-called mechanical aptitude.

Reliability. In the original study of the Minnesota Mechanical Assembly Test its reliability was found to be .94 when computed by the odd-even method and corrected by the Spearman-Brown formula, based upon 217 junior high school boys (Paterson et al., 1930). In the MESRI project the corrected odd-even reliability was only .79 for 444 adult men, and .68 for 127 adult women (Darley, 1934), the difference presumably being due to the effects of experience in adolescence and adulthood. Brush (1941) found a corrected reliability of .65 with engineering freshmen. For this reason only extremely high and extremely low scores are likely to have any significance for adults. In another study using deaf children as subjects, Stanton (1938) found retest reliabilities of .74 for boys ($N = 57$) and .60 for girls ($N = 36$) after a period of two years; in view of the probability of experience with mechanical objects at that age, and of the known effects of maturation on spatial visualization, these may be taken as not out of line with the other report based on children.

Validity. The Minnesota Mechanical Assembly Test was correlated with *intelligence* tests in the MESRI project (Green et al., 1933), where with adult subjects and the Pressey Classification and Verification Tests the coefficients ranged from .10 to .26, and by Super in an unpublished study with the Otis and NYA youth, in which the correlation was .24.

While these coefficients are slightly higher than those reported in the original work with the test, they are low enough to be negligible.

No published data on the correlation between widely used *manual dexterity* tests and assembly test scores have been located, but several less used tests in the Minnesota battery yielded low or negligible correlations. In his factor analysis of these data, Wittenborn (1945) found that manual dexterity did not have an appreciable loading in the assembly test, and Harrell (1940), using the same tests and new subjects, confirmed the absence of a manual dexterity factor in this test. In an unpublished study of 50 junior high school boys Super found a correlation of only .05 between assembly test and Minnesota Placing Test scores. Apparently manual dexterity is subordinate to other factors in the task of assembling mechanical objects such as those in the Minnesota test.

Although the assembly test was correlated with the Stenquist Picture Tests in the original study, it has apparently not been related to other tests of *mechanical comprehension,* except in an unpublished study by Super, in which it and the O'Rourke Mechanical Aptitude Test were administered to fifty junior high school boys with a resulting correlation of .65. This is higher than that of .46 reported with the Stenquist in the original study and confirmed by Harrell (1937) with adults, although Super used a similar group of subjects; it is not, however, contrary to what one might expect in apparatus and paper-and-pencil tests designed to measure the same type of aptitude. Perhaps it indicates that the O'Rourke more closely approximates a graphic version of the Minnesota than does the Stenquist.

The important role of *spatial visualization* in mechanical assembly tests seems to have also been accepted virtually unchecked as a result of the Minnesota project, in which the correlation was .56 between assembly test and Minnesota Spatial Relations Test. In the unpublished study of junior high school boys referred to above Super found the expected correlation of .48 between the assembly test and the Revised Minnesota Paper Form Board, but one of only .25 with the Minnesota Spatial Relations Test. In view of the other data, this may be only a chance lack of relationship, which might prove to be higher in other similar samples of the same population. Harrell (1937) reported a somewhat higher correlation of .35 between Minnesota assembly and spatial relations tests administered to adult factory workers. However, the results of his factor analysis agreed with Wittenborn's (1945) in describing spatial visualization as the principal factor in the assembly test, and Tredick (1941) found its highest correlation among Thurstone's PMA Tests to be with the spatial factor (.34; Reasoning was .30, Induction .26, Perception .23).

The correlation between mechanical assembly test and mechanical *interest* inventory scores, reported as .42 for junior high school boys by the original study, was found to be only .10 when the same tests (Minnesota Assembly and Minnesota Interest Analysis) were used with adults by Harrell (1937). Whether this is a result of the effects of experience on the test scores, giving them different meaning for adults, or a direct contradiction of the Minnesota findings is not shown by the data; it seems likely that it is to be explained by age differences in experience and its effects on assembly scores.

Grades have been used as a criterion by Stanton (1938), Tredick (1941) and Brush (1941). Stanton administered Minnesota Battery A (Assembly, Spatial Relations, and Paper Form Board) to 121 deaf boys aged 12 to 14. The battery validity was .50, and that for the assembly test was .12, using *amount of time spent in shop work* as a criterion. This finding is not as favorable as the original .55 reported by the test authors, and the shrinkage seems greater than that normally found between first and subsequent validities, but this may be due to the substitution of a time for a quality criterion.

Tredick's study involved 113 freshmen students of home economics at Pennsylvania State College. She used the Minnesota Mechanical Assembly Test together with an extensive battery of other tests. Her criteria were *semester-point average* and grades in first semester courses in art, chemistry, and English composition. The correlations were respectively .11, .17, .16, and —.01, none of which are high enough to be of value.

Brush administered the assembly test to 104 freshmen *engineering students* at the University of Maine, correlating results with grades for the first year and for all four years. The two coefficients were .28 and .27, both of them reliable. Apparently the test has sufficient value for the prediction of success in engineering training to justify its inclusion in a battery, despite the effects of experience by the end of high school. In view, however, of the cumbersomeness of administration and scoring, and of the high correlations with paper-and-pencil tests of the same type, it is doubtful whether the increased predictive value of a well-selected battery would warrant the time and trouble to include it.

Success on the job has not been used as a criterion with the Minnesota assembly test, judging by the lack of such reports in the journals. In view of its greater suitability for use with junior high school students than with adults this is perhaps not surprising; it is to be regretted, however, that no follow-ups have been made, to ascertain the relationship between assembly test scores in junior high school and choice of and success in subsequent mechanical employment.

Differentiation of occupational groups by the Minnesota Mechanical Assembly Test was demonstrated at the Employment Stabilization Research Institute (Dvorak, 1935), where machinists scored at the 80th percentile, manual-training teachers, ornamental ironworkers, and garage mechanics at the 68th, and draftsmen at the 65th percentiles. Workers in less mechanical occupations such as office clerks, machine operators, retail salesmen, and policemen, generally make scores less than one sigma above the mean of the general population. These trends are in the expected directions, although, as pointed out earlier, the mean scores of manual-training teachers and certain other mechanically inclined groups are not as much above the mean as one would anticipate, perhaps because universal experience with the items in the test tends to minimize differences in mechanical comprehension among adults.

Occupational satisfaction would seem to be a logical criterion against which to validate mechanical aptitude, on the hypothesis that those who are relatively lacking in it would find their work uncongenial and perhaps a strain, while those who are relatively high in mechanical comprehension would solve new problems and master new techniques readily and with zest. As an aptitude which is also somewhat related to interest this should perhaps be more true of mechanical comprehension than of most purer "aptitudes." Despite these facts, no known studies have correlated scores on the Minnesota Mechanical Assembly Test with job satisfaction.

Use of the Minnesota Mechanical Assembly Test in Counseling and Selection. The evidence which has been reviewed in the preceding paragraphs is more adequate concerning the standardization and validation of the Minnesota Assembly Test than are comparable data for most tests, the authors having systematically studied it in a variety of respects. Unfortunately it has not been so thoroughly studied since that time, despite Wittenborn's and Harrell's factor analyses. One reason for this is the cumbersomeness of the test, not only in administration and scoring, but also in maintenance; another is the proved adequacy of paper-and-pencil tests designed to measure the same factors.

Despite these defects the assembly test is useful with early adolescents whose significant experiences with mechanical items such as those in the test are still largely dependent upon aptitude and interest. The effects of maturation upon the principal component, spatial visualization, make the use of adult occupational norms impossible with adolescents. The leveling effects of experience, suggested by the decreasing reliability coefficients with increasing age, further complicate the picture and render the scores of older adolescents and adults difficult to interpret.

Occupational groups distinguished by high scores on this test include machinists, manual-training teachers, ornamental ironworkers, garage mechanics, draftsmen, and presumably other workers in mechanical occupations, job analysis of which suggests a need for ability to visualize space relations and interest in the acquisition of knowledge about the nature and operation of mechanical contrivances. Whether the superior scores made on this test by adult workers in these fields are due more to aptitude than to experience, or vice versa, does not appear to be important when early adolescents are being counseled, for at that stage the test is largely a measure of aptitude which apparently leads to experience; nor is it especially important when selecting adults for a related type of work, for in such a case present ability to do the work is important, regardless of its basis. It is only when long-term adjustments and present ability to learn are important that it is necessary to distinguish between experience and aptitude as causative factors in assembly test scores.

School and college use of the assembly test has proved feasible, the test having predictive value in junior high school, high school, and engineering college courses. In view of the equally high validities of other tests, and the little added to battery validity by this test at any save the junior high school level, it is doubtful whether the time and trouble required for its use are justified. The test may be of considerable value, however, in the clinical study of the aptitudes and experiences of special cases.

Guidance centers and clinics are most likely to find the test valuable in this type of case. When a client's experience with mechanical objects is in need of further study because of lack of mechanical outlets, or when his aptitudes as measured by other tests of spatial visualization, mechanical information, and manual dexterities seem out of line with his experience, then administration of the assembly test by a skilled examiner may prove fruitful. The ease with which the subject approaches the apparatus, the familiarity displayed by his examining and assembling of them, his confidence in his ability to complete the assemblies in time, his reactions to difficulties and failure, his incidental comments concerning the test and related matters during and after testing, all provide material in addition to the actual score which a skilled psychologist can piece together in order to obtain a truer picture of the client's aptitudes, interests, and experiences.

Business and industrial use of the Minnesota assembly test is probably unwise because of its unreliability with adults, the leveling effects of experience, and difficulties in administration. It is true that it can have some value in indicating present mechanical skill in job applicants, but if these are in a skilled category trade tests are more appropriate and valid, and if they are semiskilled manual and spatial tests will prove more economical and more valid.

In summary, then, the Minnesota Mechanical Assembly Test is important primarily for historical reasons and for the insight the studies with it give into the nature of mechanical aptitude; its practical use is limited primarily to the clinical study of special cases, especially in adolescence.

The O'Rourke Mechanical Aptitude Test, Junior Grade (Psychological Institute, 1926, 1940, 1957). The O'Rourke Mechanical Aptitude Test was developed after World War I, as a result of the test author's experience with the Army Mechanical Aptitude and Army General Trade Tests, incorporating essentially the same items (Fryer, 1931, pp. 265 ff.). According to Fryer, the original work by Rice was carried further by O'Rourke and Toops in the Army, and the former continued to work with the test during the early 1920's. It was subsequently restandardized in three forms with Tennessee Valley Authority workers (Pritchett, 1937). Unfortunately none of the work done by O'Rourke has been published, leaving us entirely dependent for our understanding of its development upon Fryer's brief account of its origin, Toops' dissertation, O'Rourke's and Pritchett's unpublished dissertations, and the sketchy data published on the test form and scoring key.

Applicability. The civilian edition of the test prepared by O'Rourke was first used with boys in their late teens who were interested in entering "mechanical" occupations. Just which occupations were included under this heading is not indicated, but the fact that his contemporary, E. L. Thorndike, classified wrestlers as mechanical workers (1931, p. 24) suggests that a word of caution in accepting the designation may be warranted. The group on whom the military form had been standardized were draftees, therefore mostly young men; the civilian group were aged 15 to 24, were no longer in school, and none of them had completed more than one year of high school. The second standardization of the civilian form was on workmen who applied for mechanical jobs with the Tennessee Valley Authority. Again the term "mechanical" is not specifically defined, but a list of occupations for which mean scores are provided includes apprentices as well as journeymen, in such fields as automobile mechanics, boilermaking, carpentering, machine-shop, painting, and even textile manufacturing. This suggests that O'Rourke's definition of the term mechanical is as broad when applied to occupations as it is when applied to the types of information which make up the content of his test.

Most important, from the point of view of the applicability and use of the test, is the fact that the means and standard deviations for older adolescents without mechanical training (the original norm group), for adult men with mechanical and other skilled and semiskilled training (TVA), and a group of 785 adult men in a WPA education program in California (Hanman, 1942) are approximately the same. This suggests that the test is probably equally applicable to older adolescents and to adults. In view of the evidence which suggests an effect of experience on the Minnesota Mechanical Assembly Test this seems surprising, but it is perhaps due to the fact that by their middle teens boys who have mechanical aptitudes and interest learn as much about the tools and processes tested as they ever will. It is conceivable that the additional trade knowledge gained after that time is in specialized fields and of an advanced type which does not affect general "mechanical" information such as is tapped by this test. As age differences have not been studied as such, it is not possible to give an adequate answer to the question of the effect of age and experience on this test.

Content. The test consists of two parts. The first is pictorial; the subject matches pictures in order to show which tools and other objects are used together. The second part is verbal; it is a multiple-choice test concerning tools, materials, and processes. As stated above, the term "mechanical" is broadly conceived to include mechanics, electricity, carpentry, cabinet-making, painting, printing, surveying, and other activities, the items being of a type which might be learned in everyday activities, without actual technical training. No rationale is offered for the proportions allocated to each field, although these vary greatly. Table 18 shows, for example, that Form A includes 19 auto mechanics items, 16 carpentry, and 19 electrical, only 1 drafting, 1 brick laying, and 1 painting, and no plastering or shoe repairing items. At the same time, Form B contains 24, 16, 9, 4, 0, 0, 1, and 1 items in each of these categories. This seems likely to lessen the equivalence of the three forms, although no notice seems to have been taken of the fact.

Administration and Scoring. The two parts require 30 and 25 minutes of working time, respectively, with a brief practice period at the beginning. Both parts must be used, no norms being available for the subtests. The test requires somewhat more supervision than the average group test, because it is arranged in folder form which confuses many examinees, and because the time limits are excessive for many high school students who finish Part I and proceed to work on Part II before instructed to do so. The test is frustrating to girls and boys without mechanical inclinations who feel that it is unreasonable to require them to sit for an hour over questions they cannot answer in any amount of time. Scoring is by means of an old-fashioned stencil which is placed against the answer spaces in the test booklet. The test should be revised for special answer sheets and punched stencils, and its contents should be balanced and brought up to date.

Norms. The original norms, published in 1926, were based on 9000 boys aged 15 to 24 who were "entering mechanical occupations." The individuals in question may have been mere applicants, many of whom were

TABLE 18

O'ROURKE MECHANICAL APTITUDE TEST

Number of Items in Each Form of the Test by Different Occupational Activities

Occupational Activity	Form A			Form B			Form C		
	Part I	Part II	Total	Part I	Part II	Total	Part I	Part II	Total
1 Auto Mechanics	10	9	19	13	11	24	10	15	25
2 Carpentry	9	7	16	10	6	16	6	7	13
3 Electrical	7	12	19	1	8	9	2	8	10
4 Mechanical	4	9	13	5	3	8	5	5	10
5 Plumbing	5	7	12	2	5	7	5	3	8
6 Machinist	2	4	6	4	5	9	1	—	1
7 Mechanical Comprehension	—	2	2	1	4	5	2	4	6
8 Drafting	1	—	1	1	3	4	3	2	5
9 Metal Working	1	—	1	2	3	5	—	3	3
10 Cabinet-Making	1	2	3	1	2	3	—	2	2
11 Wood-Cutting	—	—	—	2	2	4	1	1	2
12 Forge Work	2	—	2	—	—	—	2	1	3
13 Foundry	—	2	2	—	3	3	—	—	—
14 Surveying	1	1	2	—	2	2	1	—	1
15 Pick and Shovel Work	—	—	—	1	—	1	2	1	3
16 Painting	—	1	1	—	—	—	1	2	3
17 Plastering	—	—	—	—	1	1	1	2	3
18 Welding	—	1	1	—	2	2	—	—	—
19 Bicycle Repairing	1	—	1	—	—	—	—	1	1
20 Glazing	—	—	—	1	—	1	1	—	1
21 Printing	—	2	2	—	—	—	—	—	—
22 Shoemaking	—	—	—	1	—	1	—	1	1
23 Stationary Engines	—	1	1	—	—	—	1	—	1
24 Steel Construction	—	—	—	—	—	—	—	2	2
25 Brick Laying	1	—	1	—	—	—	—	—	—
26 Farming	—	—	—	—	—	—	1	—	1
Total	45	60	105	45	60	105	45	60	105

rejected, or they may have been successful trainees; the occupations may have been semiskilled, or they may have required considerable insight and knowledge. That their educational level was not high is shown by the fact that none had gone beyond the first year of high school, but in 1926 that meant only that they had as much education as the average adult male.

The TVA norms were based on 70,000 men who applied for so-called mechanical jobs, an unusually large standardization group. These norms differ little from the earlier set, the mean of the adolescent group being a raw score of 198, that of the adult group 190 (equivalent to the 54th percentile in the early norms). The lowest quartiles are 162 and 137, respectively, and the third quartiles are 245 and 242. The adult group includes more low-scoring cases than the adolescent group, perhaps because of loss of speed with age, perhaps because of regional differences in populations. The age distribution of the adult group is not given, but the rural southern localities from which the latter of the two groups came, as described by Pritchett (1937), suggest that at least the latter reason may apply. Hanman's (1942) study was based on California men aged 20 to 65, with a mean age of 40, and found a distribution of scores like that of the original norms, which suggests that age differences are probably not the cause.

O'Rourke's manual also provides norms for 33 specific occupations in the TVA population, ranging from auto-mechanic apprentices and journeymen, through foundrymen and plasterers, to textile worker journeymen (just which of the Dictionary of Occupational Titles' more than 1800 different textile workers is not specified), welders, and woodworkers. This is an unusually large number and variety of occupations for which to provide norms, and in this respect O'Rourke has set an example for other test authors. Unfortunately, however, there are serious hidden defects. One of these, poor and at times even meaningless occupational classification, has just been pointed out; it is impossible, without more data on some of the jobs, or without reference to a standard classification system such as the Dictionary of Occupational Titles, to know what the norms mean. A second defect is the provision of only means and sigmas; this is much less serious, but if the numbers are adequate, more specific norms could easily have been provided. With no indication of the numbers in each category, it is impossible for the test user to know whether, as in the case of the MESRI occupational norms, the data are merely suggestive, or whether they can really be used for norms. The importance of this point is brought out by the fact that the means are sometimes very close together, and sometimes even in the reverse of the expected order. For example, millwrights make a mean of 199 whereas for machinists the mean raw score is 211, and truck and tractor operator apprentices score three points higher than journeymen. Differences such as the former probably reflect in part the composition of the test which, as pointed out in the discussion of content, is very unevenly weighted for the various fields it taps; the latter type of difference is presumably due to sampling errors. Both lessen one's confidence in the value of the norms, which may be useful as a rough indication of validity for the directional counseling of adolescents (see below under Occupational Differences) but which can hardly be used for the counseling or selection of individual adults without more descriptive data and detail.

Standardization and Initial Validation.   According to Fryer (1931), in work with the Army Mechanical Aptitude and General Trade Tests, and in subsequent dissertations with these instruments, O'Rourke found correlations between the two Army tests and ratings of the mechanical ability of high school boys of about .30, and O'Rourke and Toops found correlations with school grades which ranged from .16 to .41. Correlations with Army Alpha were .30 for the Army Mechanical Aptitude Test and .42 for the Army General Trade Test, based on a group of 208 eighth grade boys. Correlations of the same tests with the Stenquist Mechanical Assembly Test were .41 and .33, with the Stenquist Picture Test I .44 and .27, and with the Stenquist Picture Test II .46 and .33, based on 145 eighth grade boys.

The two Army tests were validated on student-soldiers awaiting return to civilian life after World War I and on junior high school groups studied by O'Rourke and Toops, data from whose dissertations are provided by Fryer (1931, Ch. 8). The former were rated for achievement after the completion of courses, the numbers ranging from 24 to 61 per course. For the automotive course the validity coefficient for the Aptitude Test was .05, but in electrical and machine-shop courses they were .50 and .43. Comparable validities for the Trade Test were .20, .53, and .47. For the 208 junior high school boys the two tests had correlations of .33 and .41 with grades; for the 100 boys who subsequently entered high school the validities were .16 and .32 when only the reliable grades were used.

Work dealing specifically with the standardization and validation of the final published version of the O'Rourke test has not been published. Fryer (1931, p. 270) states that the O'Rourke is a modified version of the Army Mechanical Aptitude and General Trade Tests. Part II, for example, consists of 60 multiple-choice questions rather than 50 one-word completion items as in the Trade Test from which it originated. In view of these changes, considerable restandardization must have been done. All O'Rourke tells us, however, is that the published form is based on 9000 fifteen- to twenty-four-year-old males no longer in school and entering mechanical occupations. There is nothing on reliability. Concerning validity, the manual states that "correlations reported between test scores and ratings in vocational courses are as high as .84; between test scores and ratings in school vocational classes .83." These are, it should be noted, cited as maximum validities obtained; they are considerably higher than the best validities reported for the two Army Tests; they are also considerably higher than the validities of single tests generally prove to be when they are cross-validated. They cannot therefore be taken as indices of the actual validity of the O'Rourke test. Judgments concerning its validity must be based solely on inferences from the Army tests and on the published reports of subsequent investigators.

Reliability. The reliability of the O'Rourke Mechanical Aptitude Test has apparently never actually been established. Bingham (1937) estimates that the standard error of measurement does not exceed 18 raw-score points, or less than one-half sigma, but this is just an estimate. As the 40 item Army General Trade Test had a reliability of .98 (Fryer, 1931, p. 268) it seems probable that the longer O'Rourke is also reliable.

Validity. The intercorrelation of Parts I and II of the O'Rourke is .52 (1944). The O'Rourke has been correlated with *intelligence* in an unpublished study by Super, who administered it and the Otis S.A. Test to 108 high school junior and senior boys, the resulting coefficient being .23. Sartain (1945) reported a correlation of .16 for the same tests administered to 46 aircraft factory inspectors.

Other mechanical comprehension tests with which the O'Rourke has been correlated include the Stenquist (Scudder and Raubenheimer, 1930), data having been obtained from 114 seventh and eighth grade boys: $r = .375$; the Minnesota Mechanical Assembly Test (Super, unpublished data) administered to 50 seventh grade boys: $r = .65$; and the Bennett Mechanical Comprehension Test (McDaniel and Reynolds, 1944), used with 147 high school and defense-training students: $r = .55$. Sartain (1945) also reported an r of .55 between the O'Rourke and the Bennett. McDaniel and Reynolds (1944) found a correlation between the O'Rourke and the Mac-Quarrie Test of Mechanical Aptitude as high as .51, but in Scudder and Raubenheimer's study (1930) of junior high school boys the correlation was only .01, a difference which it is difficult to explain without more data. Sartain's data tend more toward a lack of relationship with the Mac-Quarrie ($r = .20$).

The only *spatial visualization* test with which the O'Rourke has been correlated is the Revised Minnesota Paper Form Board, in studies by Tuckman (1944), Sartain (1945), and Super (unpublished data). These coefficients were .40, .09, and .44, the subjects of the first study being clients of a Jewish Vocational Service, those of the second experienced factory inspectors, those of the last high school boys in the junior and senior classes. The differences in degrees of relationship are probably due to differences in mechanical experience.

Interests were related to the O'Rourke by Leffel in an unpublished master's thesis (1939). The subjects were 121 boys in the junior and senior years of high school. The correlations with Strong's Vocational Interest Blank were .42 for the Chemist key, .46 for the Engineer key, .27 for Mathematics and Physical Science Teacher, and approximately —.25 for keys for Social Science Teacher, Lawyer, and Certified Public Accountant.

Grades were used as criteria in a study of 114 seventh and eighth grade boys by Scudder and Raubenheimer (1930), with a reported correlation of .15 between the O'Rourke test and grades in shop courses. McDaniel and Reynolds (1944) used instructors' ratings of 149 high school and defense-training-course students. The multiple correlation coefficient between the battery and ratings was .47; the validity of the O'Rourke alone was .26, no other test having a closer relationship with the criterion. In a third study, Ross (1943) tested an unspecified number of machine-tool trainees in the Parker Defense Training Program at Greenville, South Carolina. He established critical scores for the tests used, that for the O'Rourke being 175; this score would have eliminated 67 percent of the failing trainees, together with only 7 percent of the successes. The criterion of success was grades in the training courses. The correlation with scores on the O'Rourke was not ascertained. A study conducted in an aviation machinists school by the U.S. Navy during World War II (Stuit, 1947, p. 247) used grades as a criterion. The validity was .65. Other Navy studies used custom-built tests of similar type. It should be noted that, although the O'Rourke Test of Mechanical Aptitude is thus shown to have some validity for predicting the quality of work done in mechanical courses, and about as much validity as other available tests, it gives a considerably less accurate estimate of achievement than is suggested by O'Rourke's partial data.

Success on the job was studied with aircraft factory inspectors by Sartain (1945) and with Tennessee Valley Authority workmen by Pritchett (1937). Sartain's report is unfortunately very brief: He provides no information as to the type of inspection or materials inspected, although there are probably very important differences in the psychological and technical demands made upon inspectors of fuselages on the one hand and of engines on the other; the sex and ages of the workers are not specified; and representativeness of the sample is assumed without evidence other than the facts that "some of them" were relatively new and "many" were among the most experienced in the department. Two criteria were used: ratings (we are not told of what) in a refresher course (subject-matter not specified), the two instructors of which were in most cases familiar with the job performance of the inspectors, and merit ratings made by supervisors during the year following the refresher training. There were 46 employees in the early group, and 20 still on the job one year later. The correlation between ratings by the two instructors was .77, which compares favorably with the reliabilities of ratings in general. When correlated with the combined merit ratings made during the subsequent year, the coefficient was .42. In one sense this is a reliability coefficient, because both sets of ratings were based partly on job performance; in another sense it is a validation of the ratings given in refresher training, for it shows that they were positively related to ratings of subsequent job performance. Sartain did not report the correlations between tests and merit ratings one year later, perhaps because the number of cases was by then reduced to 20. With ratings in refresher training the correlation for the O'Rourke test was .24, as compared with .32 for the Bennett Test of Mechanical Comprehension, .47 for the Minnesota Paper Form Board, and .64 for the Otis.

In view of all the unknowns in this investigation, ranging from the nature of the work, through the characteristics rated, to the similarity between refresher training and the job itself, it is difficult to evaluate Sartain's findings. It may be safe to assume, in view of the findings of other studies, that the high correlation between intelligence and ratings was due to intellectual factors which are more important in training than on the job: Moderately high correlations between spatial relations tests and ratings suggest that the inspection job, or at least the refresher training related to it, required ability to visualize spatial relations; and the lower validity of the O'Rourke suggests that, at this stage of experience, general mechanical interest and information are less important than spatial visualization and intelligence in this type of work. Generalization to possible use of the O'Rourke in the selection or guidance of inexperienced workers is impossible, however, not only because the type of inspection work and training was not described, but also because the role of the factors measured by the O'Rourke may be quite different at the novice as contrasted with the journeyman stages. This was seen to be the case, for example, with manual dexterity tests and department-store wrappers.

Pritchett's dissertation (1937) might be expected to deal more directly with job success. His data are based on the administration of the O'Rourke to 70,000 applicants for skilled jobs with the TVA. The criteria were efficiency ratings, promotions, demotions, and lay-offs. But no evidence is given, beyond a brief statement to this effect.

Occupational differences in scores on the O'Rourke Mechanical Aptitude Test are shown in the manual by data obtained in administering the test to applicants for TVA employment. High-scoring occupations include journeyman electricians, machinists and sheetmetal workers with mean raw scores equal to approximately one standard deviation above the general mean (209 to 228); apprentices in each of these fields are generally somewhat lower than journeymen. Low-scoring occupations include watchmen, foundrymen, textile workers, and plasterers, all more than one sigma below the general mean (raw scores from 140 to 147). It is noteworthy that auto mechanics, mechanic-millwrights, plumbers, and carpenters make mean scores not significantly higher than the general average. This is presumably a reflection of the fact that the items in the O'Rourke test sample a variety of skilled trade subjects, some fields being more heavily weighted than others. We have seen that mechanical and electrical items are most numerous in Part II, and that foundry and cabinetmaking are barely represented; it is only logical, then, to find carpenters and machinists making higher scores than foundrymen and carpenter-finishers. As a trade test for selecting skilled workers the O'Rourke is, therefore, inadequate; there are too many irrelevant items for most trades, and not enough relevant for others. As a test for measuring underlying aptitude in experienced workers it leaves much to be desired, since an electrician's score, for example, is heavily weighted by his experience with many items, whereas a foundryman's score is relatively little affected by his training and experience, only one item in Part II being directly relevant. As a general mechanical aptitude test for untrained adolescents, on the other hand, the test seems much more appropriate, for this group has more opportunity to follow up interest in and aptitude for mechanics and electricity than for foundry work, and differences in general information in these areas may more legitimately be taken as indicative of differences in aptitude and interest. It would seem worthwhile, however, to develop a mechanical or technical information test which sampled each of the major fields adequately enough to yield part scores which would be diagnostic of special aptitude or proficiency (depending upon the age of the examinee) in the various fields.

Leffel (1939) classified 121 high school juniors and seniors according to the occupational fields which they named as their objectives. The boys who planned to enter technical professions or semi-professions made significantly higher scores on the O'Rourke than did those who planned to enter other fields, while those who planned to enter social science occupations made significantly lower O'Rourke scores.

Job satisfaction has not, so far as the writers have been able to determine, been used as a criterion for the O'Rourke test. It would seem logical to expect those who have a high degree of mechanical aptitude to be dissatisfied without outlets for it, and to expect those whose work requires more such aptitude than they have to be dissatisfied with their too-demanding work situations.

Use of the O'Rourke Mechanical Aptitude Test in Counseling and Selection. The findings discussed in the preceding sections show that the O'Rourke Mechanical Aptitude Test is only slightly correlated with intelligence, and that it has a moderately high correlation with other mechanical comprehension tests, with tests of spatial visualization, and with measured interest in mechanical and scientific activities. It is therefore possible that the acquisition of mechanical information such as is measured by this test is the result of spatial aptitude, technical interest, and presumably opportunity; unfortunately, no studies have been made which prove causation. From the practical point of view, however, the relationships between the O'Rourke and tests of these other factors is low enough to warrant using it in a battery of tests for appropriate persons and for suitable purposes.

Changes in scores with age after mid-adolescence have not been brought out by the norms, but this may be due to failure to make a refined analysis of age differences; the only data are the similarity of the means of older adolescent and adult groups. This seems surprising in an information test, but it could be due to the fact that the items in the test tap a low level of information which is generally acquired from miscellaneous sources during adolescence, rather than the higher level of technical information which is learned in training or on the job. That this is so has not been demonstrated, but the existence of two such levels of information has frequently proved to be a good working hypothesis in test construction, and O'Rourke's use of it is implied in the sub-title, "Junior Grade."

The occupational significance of the O'Rourke test can only be broad, because of the unbalanced heterogeneity of the so-called mechanical items it contains and because of the resulting dislocation of the occupational norms. Evidence with both adolescents and adults indicates that the test has some value in distinguishing those who have some aptitude for technical work from those who have little such aptitude; it does not, however, make possible differential diagnosis or prediction within the field of technical work.

In schools, technical institutes, and colleges, the O'Rourke test should prove most useful with those who have had no training and no systematic experience in technical fields. In such instances it will reveal the extent to which the person in question has sought and utilized opportunities for the exercise of technical aptitudes and interests. It will not help in determining in which of the various technical fields he is likely to do best or find most satisfaction, but it does have value in general directional guidance. It can normally be expected to improve the selection of high school students who will do well in technical courses, but is not likely to predict success as well as the test manual implies.

In guidance centers and employment the possible uses of the test are about what they are in educational institutions. It can be useful in selecting promising young trainees or entry workers for industrial employment, supplementing the history of mechanical and related interests and activities.

In industry the O'Rourke test is also useful in selecting young people for entry jobs and for training opportunities, as a measure of previous exposure to and profit from incidental technical experiences. Although it cannot properly be used as a trade test, it has been shown to have some value as a screening device even for experienced workers on technical jobs, when large numbers have to be employed and the evaluation of experience is difficult. In any case, the O'Rourke should be supplemented by purer and less easily contaminated tests of aptitudes such as intelligence and spatial visualization, and, in the case of experienced workers, by trade tests; and it should go without saying that personal data should also be utilized.

The Bennett Test of Mechanical Comprehension (Psychological Corporation, 1940, 1941, 1947, 1949). This test of mechanical aptitude was developed after a survey of existing tests of mechanical aptitude led the author to the conclusion that there was a need for a test which would measure a higher order of mechanical aptitude than that assessed by available tests. The facts concerning the Minnesota and O'Rourke tests, summarized and discussed in the preceding sections of this chapter, partially substantiate that conclusion, as would those concerning other tests of mechanical aptitudes were they similarly treated.

Applicability. There are four forms of Bennett's test: AA, designed for high school students, engineering school applicants, and other relatively untrained and inexperienced groups, most widely used and therefore selected for detailed treatment in this chapter; BB, more difficult and designed for use with engineering school applicants, candidates for technical courses, and applicants for mechanical employment; CC, the Owens-Bennett, still more difficult and suitable for use with engineering students; and W1 (developed in collaboration with Dinah E. Fry), designed for use with high school girls and women. An attempt was made to devise items appropriate to the aptitude and experience of each of these types of groups. In the case of the women's form, for example, items used embody what seem to be the same types of physical principles, but the objects and situations are such as are more commonly encountered by women than those in the men's forms; they involve the kitchen and the sewing room more than the shop and the garage. That this goal of devising items suitable to the group in question was reasonably well attained is illustrated by the fact that ninth grade boys make raw scores which range from 5 to 54, with a mean of 31, whereas twelfth graders' make scores ranging from 11 at the first percentile to 57 at the 99th, the mean being 39. As the total number of items is 60 in Form AA, most of the items are actually working at this age range. The improvement which takes place with age in adolescence does not make the test too easy. Freshmen engineers, on the other hand, make raw scores of 56, 57, and 59 at the 90th, 95th, and 99th percentiles, and a raw score of 47 at the 50th percentile, showing that that test is so easy for freshmen engineers that the most able cannot show the true extent of their ability. Form AA is suitable for engineering school applicants, as the author states, for in such a selection program the principle objective is to screen out those who are too weak rather than to locate those who are unusually able; in a scholarship program, however, it would be better to use Form BB, thus achieving discrimination at the top and locating the most able. Another indication of the suitability of the special forms lies in the fact that women's scores average about 12 points lower than the scores of comparable men on the men's form (1942).

The question of the effect of having studied physics upon scores on a test such as Bennett's is frequently raised, since the items measure understanding of and ability to apply physical principles. Two studies have investigated this problem, both reported in the manual. In one study 315 applicants for defense-industry training answered a question concerning previous training in physics. The 220 persons who had had such training made a mean score of 41.7, while the 95 reporting no training made a mean score of 39.7, difference which was in the expected direction but not great enough to be *statistically* significant. Expressed in percentiles, one group was at the 60th and the other at the 50th percentile, both of which can be thought of as average. As two raw-score points (equal to less than one-fourth sigma) generally make less difference than this in percentiles, the difference can be thought of as *practically* insignificant also. A similar analysis was made of data obtained from 1471 candidates for positions as firemen and policemen in New York City; the biserial r between having had training in physics and score on Bennett's tests was .26, and the difference in the means was four points or less than one-half of one standard deviation. This is equally true of Owens' form (1950).

Content. The items of the Bennett Test of Mechanical Comprehension, unlike those of the O'Rourke, are objects which are almost universally familiar in American culture: airplanes, carts, steps, pulleys, windlasses, see-saws, and cows. In this respect the test is presumably less subject to the effects of differences in experience and environment than is the O'Rourke. This is probably also true of what the examinee must do with the objects in order to take the test, for the tasks require comprehension of the nature, operation, and effects of various physical principles rather than knowledge of specific tools or items of equipment and their uses. To put it concretely, in Bennett's tests it is not a matter of what to use a pulley for, but rather one of how weight is distributed on pulleys when they are used. The only knowledge needed for the latter type of item is an idea of the general nature and use of pulleys; the answer can be found by logical analysis of the problem, that is, by mechanical comprehension. There are a total of 60 such items. The existence of a sex difference equal to one and one-half sigma (manual) shows that cultural factors affect even this test, but it seems likely that, for a given sex, they are less important, as witness the data on physics training.

Administration and Scoring. The test has no time limit, being designed as a power rather than as a speed test. The majority finish in less than 25 minutes, and a 30-minute time limit is ample for almost any group. Booklets are used a number of times, a special answer sheet being provided for responses. Sample problems help orient the examinee to the methods and forms. Scoring is by means of stencils, either by hand or in the IBM scoring machine. Both administration and scoring are simple and expeditious.

Norms. For Form AA three sets of norms are available, one for educational groups, one for occupational groups, and one for women. For Form BB they consist of data for technical educational groups and applicants for mechanical work. Form CC has norms for engineering students at various year levels and several institutions. The women's form has educational and occupational norms.

The educational norms (Form AA) are for each of the four years of high school, each year being based on from 300 to 833 boys; for technical-high school seniors; for introductory engineering school freshmen, there being from 402 to 613 cases in each of these last groups. The means increase from year to year, and from less selected to more highly selected groups.

The so-called industrial norms are in some cases more truly educational, as when they are based on candidates for WPA mechanical courses or on clients of a veterans guidance center (veterans are not an occupational group, but a cross-section of young men). In other cases they are marginally occupational, being based, for example, on candidates for positions as policemen and firemen (occupational norms could have been obtained by excluding those not actually appointed), candidates for apprentice training, candidates for engineering positions (as their average education equalled two years of college they could not be considered engineers without substantial appropriate experience), and applicants for jobs as mechanics' helpers, unskilled laborers, and leadmen. Only two groups are truly occupational, the paper-factory workers and bus and street-car operators. The numbers in each of these categories range from 145 candidates for engineering positions to 2217 applicants for employment as mechanic's helper. The two strictly industrial or occupational groups number respectively 1637 and 734.

While the numbers are generally sufficiently large, there is no way of knowing how representative they are: The schools and colleges from which the educational norms were obtained are not specifically identified, although some can be guessed from the list of acknowledgments in the manual; and the pre-occupational and occupational norms are not described as to location, number of companies, age, or other variables, although here again one can identify some groups by deduction and obtain further information from the original studies. The defense-course trainees, for example, appear to be Moore's (1941) cases, while the paper-factory workers are a group tested in a Savannah, Georgia plant but not described in any detail (Bennett and Wesman, 1947).

Women's norms for Form AA are based on one small group of college freshmen $(N = 111)$, a moderately large group of wartime applicants at an employment agency $(N = 238)$, and 1090 trainees in an airplane factory. With no other information concerning the college and employment agency groups their norms are of little value, for other colleges may have different types of students and women job seekers are not the same in peace and in war. The airplane factory workers constitute a large and, judging by other information about women workers in wartime airplane factories, heterogeneous enough group so that they can be of some use. The limited norms for women are perhaps not too important in any case, since women do not ordinarily compete for mechanically demanding jobs in peacetime and, when they do, must hold their own with men. In a period of industrial mobilization for war production the opposite is, of course, true, and an instrument which can select mechanically apt even though inexperienced women is of great value.

As the manual has been revised by its author in order to keep it up to date (in less detail than one might wish) and he and his associates have continued to publish new studies involving the test, it can probably be assumed that the defects in the norms will be progressively minimized, and that in due course both more representative samples and more adequate descriptions of the samples will be made available.

Standardization and Initial Validation. As described in the manual preliminary work with this test consisted of preparing rough sketches of proposed items and trying them out on various types of persons. After elimination and revision of items, 75 were tried out in booklet form. As a readily available criterion for the retention of items in the test, scores on three existing tests of mechanical aptitude were combined with the Bennett scores: the MacQuarrie, the Detroit, and the Revised Minnesota Paper Form Board. The responses of the highest and lowest scoring 27 percent of a group of 283 applicants for skilled technical training were used for item analysis—just as in an item analysis of one test by itself, but with the advantage of additional items designed to measure the same trait to help differentiate the most able from the least able candidates. This is therefore neither an internal consistency validation nor a validation against existing tests, but rather a mixture of the two. As a result of this procedure the number of items was reduced to 60, plus two easy items which were retained as practice questions; having survived such an analysis, these items can be presumed to be measuring the same trait or constellation of traits; to be measuring something resembling what others have called mechanical aptitude; and, if these other tests have some validity for measuring promise in mechanical work (as they do), to have some validity as a test of mechanical aptitude. Such indirect proof of validity is not satisfactory in and of itself, but it suffices as a first step, the successful taking of which then justifies the labor of validating against occupational criteria.

Reliability. The only reported reliability coefficient located by the writers is that given in the manual, .84 for a group of 500 ninth grade boys, calculated by the split-half method. This is sufficiently high, especially for such a homogeneous group; it would presumably be higher if the age and ability range were greater.

Validity. Because of the strength of its rationale and the consulting activities of its author, the Bennett Test of Mechanical Comprehension has been used in a large number of studies, including several in the Army, Navy, Air Force and industry which have not been reported in the general literature. Criteria used have included not only other tests, but grades and supervisors' ratings; output and other objective vocational criteria have not, however, as yet been utilized as criteria, perhaps partly because the test was designed and used primarily for jobs above the semiskilled level in which success cannot often be judged by production records.

Tests of intelligence which have been correlated with Bennett's have been summarized in a table in the manual. Of special interest are the correlations of .25 and .45 with the Otis S.A. Test based on 156 high school and on 292 defense-training students. The manual does not indicate the age or grade range of the high school students, but the low correlation may be due to homogeneity; the higher correlation for the defense-industry trainees is presumably due to greater ranges of education and age. Other correlations with the Otis test have been reported by Sartain (1945, 1946), who found a relationship of only .175 between the two tests with a group of 46 inspectors in an aircraft plant (presumably a homogeneous group) and one of .37 for 40 aircraft factory foremen and assistant foremen. The relationship with the A.C.E. Psychological Examination reported in the manual for 212 technical-high school seniors (apparently in Springfield, Mass.) is .55; working with 230 Merchant Marine Cadets, Traxler (1943) found a correlation of .37. For the L score the coefficient was .34, and that for the Q score was .26. This tendency for verbal intelligence to be at least as closely related to mechanical comprehension as quantitative intelligence is confirmed by Carnegie Mental Ability Test data reported in the manual: $r = .54$ for the L score, .52 for the Q score, the subjects being 131 defense trainees. Owens' (1950) form correlated .39 with the A.C.E. at Iowa State College. It seems that in fairly heterogeneous groups abstract mental ability is moderately related to mechanical comprehension (as indeed the term implies), whereas in homogeneous groups it is quite distinct. This makes its measurement in technical training institutions which select largely on an intellectual basis especially pertinent, assuming that the test actually has predictive value.

Manual dexterity tests which have been correlated with Bennett's include the Psychological Corporation's Large Hand-Tool Dexterity Test (disassembly and assembly of nuts, washers, and bolts with wrench and screw driver), the Minnesota Manual Dexterity Test, and the O'Connor Finger and Tweezer Dexterity Tests. The first study is reported in the manual, the subjects being 89 veterans in a guidance center and 1109 paper-bag factory workers; the correlations equalled .39 and .28. The Minnesota Manual (Placing and Turning) Tests and the O'Connor tests were used by Jacobsen (1943) in a study described in an earlier chapter; for 90 mechanic learners he found correlations of .21 and .14 with Placing and Turning Tests, and of —.04 and .14 with Finger and Tweezer Dexterity, respectively. It seems surprising that there should be a relationship between mechanical comprehension and gross manual dexterity as measured by the hand tool test but not as measured by an arm-and-hand movement test. It would seem more logical that there be no relationship at all between dexterity and comprehension, as suggested by Jacobsen's data. More evidence is needed.

Mechanical aptitude has been measured by other tests and correlated with the Bennett in several studies reported in the manual and in two other studies by Sartain (1945) and by McDaniel and Reynolds (1944). The test reported on in the manual is the MacQuarrie, administered to 136 applicants for WPA mechanical courses and to 220 applicants for apprentice courses, with correlations of .40 and .48. Sartain's correlation coefficient was .44 for aircraft factory inspectors; McDaniel and Reynolds' was .55 for 147 defense-training students. These correlations are only to be expected, in view of the use of the MacQuarrie as part of the internal consistency criterion in selecting items for the Bennett test.

Spatial visualization tests used with Bennett's which throw some light on what it measures are the Revised Minnesota Paper Form Board and the Crawford Spatial Relations Test. Correlations reported for the former in the manual are consistent, ranging from .44 for 206 technical high school seniors to .59 for 136 applicants for WPA mechanical courses; Traxler (1943) reported one of .39, but Sartain (1945, 1946) found relationships of .27 and .31, and Jacobsen (1943) reported a coefficient of .00. These inconsistencies are difficult to explain, but Jacobsen's finding is so unlike the others that it may perhaps be disregarded. The trend then rather clearly is for the two tests to be moderately closely related, as they should be in view of the use of the Paper Form Board in selecting Bennett items. Jacobsen is the only author who has reported on the relationship of the Bennett to the Crawford test, his r being only .18.

Interest was correlated with Bennett scores by Moore (1941) who used Strong's Vocational Interest Blank as a measure of interest. His subjects were two groups of engineering defense-training students, numbering 205 and 292 respectively. The correlations between the Bennett and Strong's Engineering key were .30 and .35 for the two groups; for the Aviator key they were .21 and .26; for the Production Manager key they were .12 and .08; and for Carpenter they were .06 and .12. These findings suggest that the higher the level of mechanical comprehension, the higher the level of technical interest, for the higher correlations are for the technical occupations. This is not confirmed by the somewhat different mechanical and scientific keys of the Kuder Preference Record (Sartain, 1946), the correlations with which are only .15 and .15 for a more homogeneous group of foremen. Jordaan (1949) has shown that high social status appears to prevent the development of technical interests in mechanically gifted boys, while at other socioeconomic levels he, like Moore, found the two related.

Grades in technical courses, standing on examinations in technical subjects, ratings of students and learners by instructors, and ability to complete technical training courses have been used as criteria in training situations. Grades made by 1834 defense industry trainees in a chemistry course were correlated with Bennett scores by Moore, *r* being .36. For 137 shop trainees of Pan-American Airways the correlation with shop grades was .62. Moore also obtained correlations of .39 with final examination scores in defense-training chemistry courses, and .52 with final examinations in the physics course. The latter examination was a Cooperative Test Service physics test; the manual also reports a correlation of .42 between the Bennett and College Entrance Board Physics Examination scores of 275 applicants for an engineering school.

Not reported in the manual are two studies of the test's value in predicting ratings of the mechanical promise of war industry trainees. McDaniel and Reynolds (1944) used a group of high school students and defense industry trainees, 147 in number. Their criterion was instructors' ratings of learning aptitude, speed and accuracy in acquiring muscular and manipulative skills, quality and precision of work, and eagerness in getting at the job and staying with it, combined into one overall rating of promise. Ten-point scales (too refined for use by non-psychologically trained raters) with behavior descriptions were used for each of the four traits. No data are presented as to the reliability of the ratings; their correlation with Bennett scores was .24, approximately that for the O'Rourke and slightly higher than those for various parts of the MacQuarrie Mechanical Aptitude Test.

Owens (1950) correlated scores on his form with the engineering grades of groups of students ranging from 107 to 260 in size. The coefficients ranged from .28 to .49, the biserial *r* with passing-failing being .59. Halliday, Fletcher and Cohen (1951) used Owens' form with 105 Ohio State engineering freshmen, obtaining an r of .40 with first year averages, compared with one of .59 for the Ohio State Psychological Examination. They suggest a cutting score of 30 to 35.

Jacobsen's study (1943) has been described in connection with other tests. He found that the correlations between Bennett scores and ratings of fitness for mechanical work as judged in courses in aircraft instruments, airplane engines, aeronautical repair mechanics, machine shop, and aircraft electricity were .35, .11, .30, .35, and .41 respectively (*P.E.* equalled .07 to .09). When combined with other tests the multiple correlations ranged from .46 (repair mechanics) to .64 (instruments), except for ratings in the course in aircraft engines; perhaps this was due to defects in the ratings in this course, rather than to differences in the psychological demands which it made on the learners.

Bennett points out in his manual that many validity coefficients were obtained for his test or for very close copies of it in the armed forces. One part of the Army Air Force Qualifying Examination (Davis, 1947), consisted of from 15 to 60, generally 30, Bennett-type items; validity coefficients for various forms correlated with success failure in primary pilot training ranged from .14 to .38; for graduation-elimination in navigator training the validities ranged from .22 to .45; and for bombardier training, the criterion of success for which was not satisfactory, the one validity coefficient reported was .13. In an experimental group of 1080 cadets sent to pilot training regardless of test scores (DuBois, 1947), the validity coefficient for the mechanical comprehension part of the Qualifying Examination was .47 (graduation criterion); the Mechanical Principles Test of the regular cadet test battery had a validity coefficient of .43 for this group; only two tests had higher predictive values, one entitled Instrument Comprehension II ($r = .48$) and the other a Test of General Information scored for pilots ($r = .51$).

The test was used by the Army and Navy, in various forms, for the selection of trainees in other specialties. The Army Mechanical Aptitude Test included 22 items from Bennett's Form AA, plus others resembling it; the Navy had its own forms also. Validity data for some of these are reported by Fredericksen (1946) and by Stuit (1947), but will not be cited in detail here, as the Air Force data illustrate them. As Bennett's manual puts it, whenever the ability to understand machines is important the test and its derivatives are likely to have fairly high validity. Navy technical courses for which the Bennett-type tests were validated are listed in Table 19, with validities.

Art grades are somewhat correlated with Bennett scores, Borg (1950) reporting a coefficient of .31, significant at the .01 level, for 96 advanced art students.

TABLE 19

RELATIONSHIP BETWEEN BENNETT SCORES AND NAVY GRADES

Submarine School

Course	r
Torpedoes	.23
Communications	.23
Submarines	.23
Engineering	.39

Indoctrination School	
Seamanship	.28
Ordnance	.29
Navigation	.36
Final Average	.35

Success on the job as measured by ratings of supervisors has been correlated with Bennett scores by Bennett and Fear (1943), McMurry and Johnson (1945), Sartain (1945, 1946), Shultz and Barnabas (1945), Shuman (1945, 1945), Poe and Berg (1952), Wolff and North (1951), Barnette (1952), Littleton (1952), and Cuomo and Meyer (1955). In Bennett and Fear's study 60 machine-tool-operator trainees were tested prior to training and were rated by their supervisors for performance on the job several months later. The reliability of the criterion was apparently not checked. Test scores and ratings of job performance had a correlation of .64, an unusually high validity for one test which would need to be confirmed in other similar studies before being accepted (Shuman's study, discussed below, found an r of .44 for machine operators). As a result of this finding only applicants who rated A or B on a combination of this and one other test were employed, the group as a whole making good employment records, as evidenced by the fact that, "of all new men hired since tests were installed 76 percent were rated as 'excellent' or 'good' on the job. Only 8 percent were rated 'below average.' None were rated as 'poor.' Not a single new man, hired since tests were introduced as part of the selection procedure, has had to be dismissed because of lack of ability to do the job." Perhaps this conclusion needs to be qualified by a reminder of the facts that supervisors are generally reluctant to use the "poor" rating, and that during the war employers were reluctant to release employees.

Further confirmation is provided by McMurry and Johnson, who tested 769 ordnance factory employees at the time of selection with a battery including the Bennett test. Supervisors' ratings of 587 of these were obtained after they had been on the job some time. Validity coefficients were computed for occupationally homogeneous subgroups. For a group of 33 cranemen the Bennett test had a validity of .65; other occupational groups were also tested, but validities are not reported for the Bennett alone.

Littleton (1952) found validities of .62 and .57 in using the Bennett to predict composite ratings by instructors of auto body workers and mechanics, numbering 85 and 105 respectively. And, with turbine floor assembly workers ($N = 90$), Cuomo and Meyer (1955) found a correlation of .42 with speed of promotion.

Sartain's first study has been discussed elsewhere. The correlation between Bennett scores and this mixed training-job criterion was .32, lower than those of .65, .64, and .47 for the MacQuarrie, Otis, and Minnesota Paper Form Board. In his second study, the subjects of which were 40 aircraft factory foremen and assistant foremen rated by their supervisors, the correlation between Bennett scores and ratings was —.15. This may prove that foremen in this plant were judged more by success in handling employees than by success in coping with mechanical problems, and is probably no indication of the validity of the test for mechanical and technical work. Shuman's study, discussed below, suggests that in some situations the mechanical comprehension of foremen is considered by raters; Schultz and Barnabas' investigation also bears on this point.

Employee relations and "budget-control efficiency" of 30 foremen and assistant foremen were rated by supervisors in the study reported by Shultz and Barnabas. The foremen were tested with a battery made up of the Bennett Mechanical Comprehension Test, the Strong Vocational Interest Blank (scored for Production Manager and Occupational Level), and the Bernreuter Personality Inventory (combined scores). The reliability of the ratings was determined by re-rating at the end of a five-month period. The correlation between the combined ratings on "employee relations" and "budget-control efficiency" for the first and second ratings was .85. When T scores for the three predictors were combined a correlation of .52 with combined ratings was obtained. The correlation between Bennett scores and the criterion was .11.

In Shuman's study of aircraft-engine and propeller factory workers the criterion of success was supervisors' ratings of efficiency of the job. Workers were rated as good, average, or poor, in consultation with rating experts. In two departments the ratings thus made were correlated with ratings made by a departmental instructor trained in rating techniques. The reliabilities thus obtained were .91 for 42 production engine testers and .705 for 36 inspectors; the former correlation is so high as to make one wonder about possible contamination of data through discussion by supervisor and instructor. Tests were administered to operators who had been on the job for six months or more; ratings were secured after testing. New applicants were also tested at the time of application, and those employed were followed up six months later and rated. These two groups were combined, the possible differential effects of pre- and post-hiring testing apparently not being investigated. The numbers in each occupational group varied from 25 (job setters) to 99 (foremen). Biserial coefficients of correlation were computed between the tests used (Otis, Minnesota Paper Form Board, and Bennett) and supervisors' ratings, by occupation. Data for the Bennett Test are presented in Table 20.

TABLE 20

BISERIAL CORRELATIONS BETWEEN JOB RATINGS AND BENNETT SCORES

Job	N	r bis	Critical Scores Male	Critical Scores Female	Percent Improvement Male	Percent Improvement Female
Inspectors	49	.665	34	19	12	28
Engine testers	45	.17	33		10	
Machine operators	81	.44	27	18	22	12
Foremen	99	.465	30		10	
Job setters	25	.73	36		47	
Toolmaker learners	64	.46	36		5	
Mean	363	.52			18	

We have already seen, in the discussion of the Otis test, that the latter had substantial validity for all of these jobs ($r = .39$ to $.57$); it is interesting that the validities for the Bennett are lower in some cases (engine testers) and higher in others (inspectors and job setters). It would be helpful, in such a case, to have job descriptions which would throw light on the reasons for these differences, but presumably in the engine tester's work there is no advantage in having more than the minimum required degree of mechanical comprehension (perhaps it is more a matter of manual dexterity in making connections and perceptual ability in reading dials), while in the job setter's and inspector's work higher degrees of understanding of mechanical principles make for greater worker efficiency (which is understandable if the inspectors were *engine* inspectors).

Critical scores were set for each of the tests used, those for the Bennett being shown in the next-to-the-last column of Table 20. In jobs utilizing both men and women sex differences made special minima necessary, in other jobs men only were employed. The difference between these minima indicate that the machine operators' work requires least mechanical comprehension (it also requires the least mental ability), and that job setters and toolmaker learners are the most highly selected groups in mechanical comprehension; this is what one would expect, and can be taken as a sign of the validity of the test. Foremen, for whom supervision of personnel is more crucial than mechanical aptitude, also have a lower critical score than the more technical workers, although in this situation, unlike Sartain's, mechanical comprehension does play some part in foreman success as judged by the supervisors. As the final column of Table 20 shows, the hiring of workers on the basis of the established critical minimum scores would be improved by from 5 percent in the case of toolmaker learners to 47 percent in the case of job setters, with a mean hiring improvement of 18 percent for all the jobs in question. The Bennett test contributed more to the improvement of selection than either of the other tests used, except possibly in the case of inspectors and toolmaker learners.

Supervisory workers in three factories were studied in another investigation in which Shuman used the same battery of tests. Foremen, group leaders, and job setters were rated as to production, handling of workers, housekeeping, and overall opinion by their superiors, the total usable group numbering 208. The mean correlation between Bennett scores and ratings of several groups of foremen was .55. Minimum critical scores were established for each job, that for foremen being 30, and that for group leaders 26. When data for all supervisors were combined, the percent improvement in selection of excellent workers which would have been effected by use of the Bennett test was 18, exceeded only by the Otis 19 percent.

Poe and Borg's subjects were 33 production supervisors, the ten highest rated being contrasted with the ten lowest rated. Since the former were 11 years younger and had five years more education, the results cannot well be interpreted.

In the Wolff and North study, however, 144 firemen, rated by their officers, were significantly differentiated by the Bennett. Barnette compared engineers who stayed in that field for two years after counseling with those who changed or planned to change occupations or never entered it—the subjects were all counseled veterans. The successes, thus defined, were lower on the Bennett than were the failures, but their mean was still moderately high.

Occupational differences in mechanical comprehension as measured by the Bennett test are shown by Shuman's studies (1945a, 1945b) and by the industrial or occupational norms reported in the manual. As Shuman's basis for establishing critical scores is not described, and as he does not present data on means and sigmas, it is not possible to integrate his published findings with the industrial norms of the manual. However, we have seen that according to him, job setters and toolmaker learners require more mechanical comprehension than do other skilled and semiskilled workers in airplane-engine and propeller factories, and that machine operators require least. The critical scores (apparently close to Q 1) for toolmaker learners and job setters are at the 30th percentile for trainees in an airplane factory, and at the 50th for candidates for police and fire department appointments, as shown in the manual. The critical score for inspectors was at about the 23rd and 43rd percentiles when compared to the same groups. That for machine operators was at the 17th and 20th. These data suggest that the most skilled jobs in an airplane factory require only a modicum of such ability. In the norms provided by the manual, it is the candidates for engineering positions (average education equalled two years beyond high school) who ranked first, trainees in an airplane factory second, and men in defense training courses and applying for leadman jobs third, while candidates for WPA mechanical training courses, working in a paper-bag factory, and applicants for employment as mechanics' helpers made the lowest mean scores. These data are still limited to too few occupations, in too few plants, to be more than suggestive. Norms for other skilled and also for professional-technical jobs should have been provided by this time.

Job satisfaction has not yet been used as a criterion for the validation of the Bennett Mechanical Comprehension Test, except in Barnette's study, as a means of separating successes from failures.

Use of the Bennett Mechanical Comprehension Test in Counseling and Selection. The reported relationships between the Bennett and other tests make it clear that, when the group being tested is homogeneous, there is little relationship between mechanical comprehension and intelligence; since they are both abstract functions, however, it is only natural that they should appear to have some relationship when the groups concerned represent considerable spread in mental ability. This test has been seen to be closer to spatial visualization, a finding which is not surprising in view of the studies which have shown that mechanical aptitude is in reality a combination of ability to judge spatial relations, perception, and information. Similarly, we have seen that Bennett scores and technical interests as measured by Strong's Blank are moderately correlated, although the relationship was found to be negligible in a more homogeneous group of men in whom interest was measured with Kuder's inventory.

The effects of age and experience on Bennett scores have not been adequately studied, although we have seen that partial data throw light on some important aspects of these problems. There are no data on the development of mechanical comprehension, but this is natural enough in a composite trait. It has been brought out that the easier of the male forms is too easy for brighter and more mature men, that presumed cultural influences handicap women somewhat on the men's form, but that such specific and pertinent environmental influences as training in physics do not appreciably affect men's scores; apparently older boys' and men's opportunities to become familiar with the objects and principles involved are sufficiently uniform in urban American culture to make the test "universally" applicable. In this respect the test is probably superior to O'Rourke's.

Occupational significance of Bennett's test has been made clear in a variety of ways, even though the occupational groups included in the published norms are in too many instances really pre-occupational or at best marginal. As Bennett puts it in the manual, the test is likely to be of value in jobs in which understanding machines is of fundamental im-portance; when dealing with people or with abstract problems other tests will have greater validity. Thus engineers and toolmaker learners are characterized by a high degree of mechanical comprehension as measured by this test; good machine operators tend to have more than the general population; and foremen in some situations (presumably the more technical) are found to be superior in mechanical comprehension while those in others (presumably those in which human relations are important) do not excel in this trait but are superior in other ways.

In schools and colleges the test can tentatively be used with the published educational norms, but local norms should be developed as soon as possible in view of reported differences between colleges. The test should prove valuable in *counseling* students concerning the choice of technical curricula and occupations; it may be safe to generalize from the validity data and norms that those aiming at semiskilled machine work might be expected to make scores above the 15th percentile of their high school class on Form AA, those considering skilled trades above the 25th or 45th depending upon the trade, and those aspiring to engineering and related professions above the 50th percentile for their high school grade. These suggested critical scores, it should be emphasized, have not been proved appropriate for these purposes; they are merely those which the normative data on hand indicate might prove valid. The test can also be used in the *selection* of students for technical courses, for we have seen that the test has some validity for training in such varied courses as machine shop, mechanics, physics, chemistry, and military flying. In selection programs, of course, critical scores should be established on the basis of local experience and validities.

In guidance centers and employment services the four forms can be used as in schools and colleges, discussed above. The main problem in such centers will be the choice of the appropriate form in the case of male clients; it should be made on the basis of an appraisal of the education and experience of the client, with regard to levels and quality of both intellectual and mechanical content.

In business and industry the value of the Bennett Test of Mechanical Comprehension should be greatest in the selection of trainees for skilled technical jobs, and for semiskilled jobs in which fairly complex equipment is used and the induction period is longer than usual. Local norms and cut-off scores should be developed, as conditions and requirements vary not only from job to job but also from plant to plant. The findings reported in Shuman's studies indicate the value the test can have when so used. Even when experienced skilled workers are being selected, the test can probably be of some value if jobs beings filled require versatility of skills and ability to apply them to constantly changing situations. In industrial work, as in counseling, due consideration should be given to other measurable and less tangible factors, for we have seen that intelligence, interest, and personality traits also play a part in success in skilled work— sometimes, as in some foremen's jobs, a more important part than mechanical comprehension.

The MacQuarrie Test for Mechanical Ability (California Test Bureau, 1925). The MacQuarrie Test for Mechanical Ability was developed in 1925 as a rough measure of promise for mechanical and manual occupations. It is not a test of mechanical comprehension as such, but a battery of subtests each of which was designed to measure some factor which was believed to be important to success in mechanical and manual occupations. Subtests were designed to measure spatial visualization, manual dexterity, and perceptual speed and accuracy, on the assumption that a test made up of such items would measure mechanical aptitude. The test might well be treated in the chapter on manual dexterities, insofar as some of the subtests are concerned, or in the chapter on spatial visualization, when dealing with other subtests; it is considered here because it, like mechanical comprehension tests, is an attempt at an overall measure of mechanical aptitude. It has been widely used and, despite defects related to its early origin and insufficient subsequent editorial work, has held its own as a useful test of mechanical aptitude.

Applicability. The MacQuarrie Test was designed for use with adolescent boys and girls, apparently as a tool for selection in trade training. Subsequent work has found that the items are equally applicable to adults, and adult norms and validity data have been accumulated. The original norms (MacQuarrie, 1927), only part of which are in the current undated manual, show that scores increase each year from age 10 to age 19 or 20, the mean raw score at age 10 being 26, age 15, 57, and ages 19 and 20, 67 and 68 respectively. Mitrano (1942), it is true, reported that scores decreased with age in adolescence, a surprising finding until it is noted that his sample of 13- to 16-year-olds were all in eighth grade and that the oldest pupils were therefore probably the dullest members of the class and the least well motivated. On the other hand, Goodman's (1946) finding that scores decreased with age in a group of 329 women radio assemblers aged 16 to 64 years is not surprising: r's for subtests and age ranged from —.21 (Location) to —.34 (Tracing); r for the total score and age was —.38 (P.E. = .03). As one might expect, younger adult subjects tend to do better on a speed test. Use of appropriate norms, discussed below, is important in view of the age differences which the original adolescent norms make quite clear.

Content. The MacQuarrie is a booklet made up of seven subtests, the first three of which (Tracing, Tapping, and Dotting) seem on inspection to be measures of manual dexterity or eye-hand co-ordination, the next three (Copying, Location and Blocks) spatial visualization, and the last one (Pursuit) perceptual speed and accuracy. Because of these differences in content most users of this test in validation studies have preferred to treat each part separately, a judgment which will be seen to be justified by the results.

Administration and Scoring. This is a group test requiring about one-half hour for administration. The only special precaution required is making sure that examinees turn the page when so directed at the end of each subtest, rather than working beyond the time limit. This is easily controlled by beginning at once with the directions for the next practice test, but when groups of more than 25 are tested assistance is especially important. Scoring is more complex than for most paper-and-pencil tests, as the scorer must, for example, examine each opening in the lines of the Tracing Test to make sure that the pencil has gone through the opening without touching the sides; a little practice soon makes it possible to make these inspections very rapidly. It might be noted in passing, however, that a somewhat greater degree of mechanical aptitude on the part of the test author could have resulted in machine- or stencil-scoring for the Tracing, Dotting, Location, Blocks, and Pursuit Tests, at least when the test was slightly revised at some unspecified date after 1943.

Norms. The norms provided in the manual show the scores made by an unknown number of adolescents of unspecified sex at ages 10 through 16, and for "average adults" of 17 and above. These are abbreviated norms, showing only the means and critical percentiles rather than the total distributions. In view of the continued increase in scores from age 16 to 19 or 20 the lumping together of all persons over 16 might be questioned, unless other data showed that the sample of older adolescents was inadequate as a result of elimination in the last years of high school. This has not apparently been actually demonstrated for this test, but the fact that the mean average adult score reported in the manual's table of norms is only 62, as compared with those of 63 and 68 for 17- and 20-year-olds reported in the original norms, suggests that the latter two groups may have been somewhat highly selected rather than representative. More debatable, in view of the data, is the lumping together of the two sexes in these general norms, for the norms for part scores, to be discussed below, show sex differences for some subtests. Finally, the failure to specify the number of cases involved in these norms is to be deplored, although it may perhaps be deduced from the old manual that the adolescents number 1000 minus the number of 17- to 20-year-olds, and from the new manual that the adults number 2000 or more. In view of the paucity of descriptive data by which one might judge the nature and adequacy of the adolescent sample it is necessary to use these norms with extreme caution.

The adult norms supplied in the current manual remedy three defects of the adolescent norms: They are specific as to sex, indicate the number of cases involved (1000 of each sex), and, equally important, are arranged according to subtests. The significance of the sex differences is not reported, but the trend is for women to be superior in the spatial subtests and in total scores; that the women are not superior in manual dexterity is surprising, but the significance of failure to find such a difference is not clear. One detail concerning age grouping raises a question: Although in the table of adolescent norms 16-year-olds were not included in the average adult group and made lower scores than the latter, in the table of adult norms they are included with the adults. Presumably the age differences justify one treatment or the other, but not both. Finally, as in the case of the adolescent norms, the sampling is not described. One thousand men and an equal number of women might be reasonably representative of adults *in general;* they might represent some *one segment* of adults, such as routine clerks, quite adequately; or they might be a hodge-podge which can be considered a sample of *no particular universe.* In view of the very real difficulties which complicate the establishing of adult norms, the user of psychological tests is, in the absence of detailed descriptive data concerning normative groups, justified only in assuming that the norms are based on the last-named type of sample, i.e., a meaningless hodge-podge of adults. Such norms can be used only with extreme caution.

More meaningful but specialized norms are provided by Bingham (1937, p. 316), based on data for 124 apprentice toolmakers from 16- to 22-years-old and employed by the Scovill Manufacturing Co. early in the 1930's. Bingham points out that these norms, reproduced in Table 21, correspond fairly closely to the 16-year-old norms of the original manual at the mean but include relatively fewer high and low scores; they were, in fact, a more homogeneous group such as one might expect to find working on one job in a plant with a well-tried selection program.

Norms for a miscellaneous group of 334 14- to 16-year-olds in a sectarian guidance center and high school in Cleveland, Ohio, have been published by Tuckman (1946). As he points out, these agree rather well with MacQuarrie's, and they supplement the latter by providing norms for subtests and for each sex. In the absence of national or local norms, these should prove useful.

TABLE 21

MACQUARRIE NORMS FOR APPRENTICE TOOLMAKERS $(N = 124)$
(After Bingham, by permission)

1 Tracing	2 Tapping	3 Dotting	Subtests 4 Copying	5 Location	6 Blocks	7 Pursuit	Total Score	Standard Scale	Letter Grades
59	52	28	72	39	26	38	89	7.5	
									A+
55	49	26	65	37	24	34	83	7.0	
									A−
51	46	24	58	34	22	31	78	6.5	
									B+
47	43	22	51	30	19	27	72	6.0	
									B−
43	40	20	44	25	16	24	67	5.5	
									C+
39	37	18	37	21	13	20	61	5.0	
									C−
35	34	16	30	17	10	16	56	4.5	
									D+
31	31	14	23	12	7	13	50	4.0	
									D−
27	28	12	16	7	4	9	45	3.5	
									E+
23	25	10	13	3	1	6	39	3.0	
									E−
19	22	8	12	1	0	2	34	2.5	

Standardization and Initial Validation. There is relatively little available on the standardization and initial validation of the MacQuarrie test. As pointed out in connection with the norms, the manual is quite inadequate in the provision of detailed information concerning the test, the recent revision reading as though it had been written for untrained and unsophisticated users of tests rather than for persons who are familiar with psychometrics. The original article by MacQuarrie (1927) gives little on the actual development of the test, although data on the reliability and validity of the final form are provided. The total score was found to have correlations with intelligence which equalled .20 and .002 as measured by unidentified intelligence tests. Teachers of shop courses rated the mechanical ability of their pupils, the correlation between these and the MacQuarrie scores being as high as .48. Other such correlations were obtained but not reported, as the reliability of the ratings was not satisfactory.

Pupils also did some undescribed mechanical work which was rated by judges who did not know the pupils' identity; the correlations with these criteria were .32 and .81 for two different groups, but not enough detail is supplied to make possible the judging of these quite different and in one case almost unbelievable validities. This report must, of course, be viewed in the light of the methods and standards of work current at the time of publication; at that time recognition of the importance of studying the criterion was much less widespread, and it was not generally realized to what extent supporting detail is needed for the interpretation of personnel studies. Despite its defects, it makes amply clear the fact that this test is one of considerable promise, worthy of the further study which it has fortunately subsequently received at the hands of others.

Reliability. MacQuarrie (1927) reported that the reliability of the subtest scores was as follows: Tracing .80, Tapping .85, Dotting .74, Copying .86, Location .72, Blocks .80, and Pursuit .76. The retest reliability of the total score was more than .90. The number of cases used in computing the total reliability was 34, 80, and 250 in three different groups; the groups on which the part-score reliabilities were based are not described. The manual makes no mention of reliability.

Validity. We have seen that the initial validation data published by the author leave much to be desired insofar as detail is concerned, but appear promising in a general way. Fortunately, a number of studies have supplemented MacQuarrie's findings.

Intercorrelations of the MacQuarrie subtests have been computed by Goodman (1947) in a factor analysis study, to be described in more detail below. The coefficients range from .29 between Tapping on the one hand, and Location, Blocks, and Pursuit on the other, to .55 between Tracing and Dotting. The manual dexterity subtest intercorrelations range from .47 to .55 and the spatial relations intercorrelations from .52 to .54, while these two types of subtests are intercorrelated with each other to the extent of from .29 to .44. Correlations between dexterity and perceptual tests are of the same order, but the spatial and perceptual tests intercorrelate between .44 and .48, which suggests that the distinction may be arbitrary. The factor analysis throws more light on this, by revealing indeed three factors, one called visual inspection (our perceptual ability), another spatial visualization, and the third manual movement (our manual dexterity). This last factor is important in the Tracing, Tapping, and Dotting Tests; the spatial factor in the Copying, Location, and Blocks Tests, to a lesser extent in the Pursuit Test, and to a still lesser extent in the Tracing and Dotting Tests; and the perceptual or visual inspection factor is important in the Tracing, Dotting, and Pursuit Tests. In a later motion analysis and factor analysis of the Tracing, Dotting, Tapping, and Copying Tests Goodman (1950) identified factors which appear to be visual, spatial and manual. Harrell (1940) found the Dotting Test saturated with a dexterity factor, the Copying, Blocks, and Pursuit Tests saturated with a spatial factor. The subtests are not particularly pure tests, although the three spatial tests are relatively unweighted by other measured factors; at

the same time, the classification into *Spatial* (Copying, Location, Blocks) ,
Manual Dexterity (Tapping) , *Manual-Visual* (Tracing and Dotting) ,
and *Visual-Manual* (Pursuit) seems warranted for interpretative purposes.

   Intelligence tests have been found to have correlations with the Mac-
Quarrie which vary from .02 to .62. Horning (1926) tested 25 pupils aged
12 to 15, finding a correlation of only .02 with intelligence as measured
by the Terman Group Test. Murphy (1936) worked with 143 ninth grade
boys, finding no relationship between MacQuarrie and Terman Group
Test scores. Holcomb and Laslett (1932) , using the A.C.E. Psychological
Examination with 50 engineering freshmen, found an r of .305. Morgan
(1944) administered the MacQuarrie and Army Alpha to boys aged 13
through 16, each age-group including from 35 to 159 members, and obtained correlations of .33, .35, .39, and .16 respectively; it should perhaps
be noted that the low coefficient is that based on the smallest group. Pond,
as reported by Bingham (1937, p. 317), found a correlation of .38 between
MacQuarrie and Otis, her subjects being 83 apprentice toolmakers. Finally, both Sartain (1945) and Babcock and Emerson (1938) obtained
correlations of .62 between MacQuarrie and intelligence tests, the former
using the Otis with 46 aircraft factory inspectors and the latter a vocabulary test with 300 subjects ranging in age from 14 to 28. The last-named
study found that, contrary to expectation, the correlation between intelligence and MacQuarrie scores increased with age.

   At first glance, it seems almost hopeless to attempt to rationalize such
divergent findings. But if these studies are grouped according to the homogeneity of the subjects the differences in the findings seem more reconcil-
able. The two studies reporting no relationship, it should be noted, are
probably those in which the subjects were most homogeneous: pupils in
a shop course and ninth grade boys. Those reporting moderately high
correlations also tend to be those which were fairly homogeneous: engineering freshmen, high school boys by age groups, and apprentices in one
company. One of the investigators who reported high correlations worked
with an extremely heterogeneous group of cases: Babcock and Emerson's
subjects not only ranged in age from 14 to 28, but, more important still,
were reached as clients of a counseling service and students in public
schools. In the other study, Sartain's, the heterogeneity of the adult workers studied is shown by a mean Otis score of 28.61 and a standard deviation
of 9.48, equivalent (20-minute time limit) to a mean Otis I. Q. of 95,
minus one sigma being I. Q. 82 and plus one sigma being 108; this suggests
that, although the adult group was small and occupationally homogeneous, it was heterogeneous in aptitudes. Since it has frequently been demonstrated that the greater the heterogeneity of the group the greater the
correlation between their scores on any two psychological tests, it may

probably be concluded that the MacQuarrie Test of Mechanical Ability is relatively independent of intelligence in persons of similar status, but somewhat associated with it in groups of varied individuals.

Mechanical comprehension tests which have been correlated with the MacQuarrie include the O'Rourke and the Bennett. Scudder and Raubenheimer (1930) found no relationship (.01) between O'Rourke and MacQuarrie scores, using data from 114 seventh and eighth grade boys. Sartain's study (1945) showed a correlation of .20 between the two tests, his subjects being 46 inspectors. McDaniel and Reynolds (1944) reported a correlation of .51 based on 147 students in high school and defense-training courses. The differences in results again appear to be due to degrees of heterogeneity in the groups, the first being probably the most homogeneous and the last undoubtedly the most heterogeneous. Similar data are available for the Stenquist Mechanical Assembly Test, Scudder and Raubenheimer (1930) reporting a correlation of .01 and Harrell (1937) one of .61. For Bennett's test the results are more consistent. Bennett and Cruickshank (1940) report correlations of .40 and .48 based on 130 WPA and 220 apprentice training applicants. McDaniel and Reynolds also found a correlation of .48 with 147 high school and defense-training students, while Sartain's (1945) factory inspectors yielded a correlation coefficient of .44 for the same two tests. Underlying these more consistent findings is the fact, discussed elsewhere, that the MacQuarrie was a part of the criterion used to determine the selection of items for the Bennett test.

Spatial visualization tests correlated with the MacQuarrie include the Revised Minnesota Paper Form Board. Morgan (1944) and Sartain (1945) agreed in reporting correlations of about .30 to .40, although the use of total scores somewhat obscures the relationship shown in Harrell's (1940) factor analysis, previously discussed. The correlation between MacQuarrie Copying and the Minnesota Paper Form Board, for example, is .49 (Murphy, 1936), showing the greater importance of spatial visualization in the Copying than in some of the other subtests.

Interest in technical subjects as measured by Strong's Engineering key was related to MacQuarrie scores in one study, in which Holcomb and Laslett (1932) tested engineering freshmen. The relationship was lower than in the case of experienced-affected mechanical comprehension tests, being only .22.

Grades have been used as a criterion of the validity of the MacQuarrie in junior high schools, technical schools, engineering colleges, dental and nursing schools, and commercial schools and colleges. Horning (1926) had 25 boys aged 12 to 15 graded on the basis of a project completed in a shop course, and on the basis of time taken to complete the project; the correlations with test scores were respectively .79 and .72, both remarkably high. Scudder and Raubenheimer (1930) made a study using the grades of 114 seventh and eighth grade boys as a criterion which did not, however, agree with this: their validity coefficient was only .08. Unfortunately, both studies are so sketchily reported as to make evaluation difficult.

Class standing achieved in technical and *industrial schools* by boys 13 to 16 was the criterion employed by Morgan (1944), with from 35 to 159 boys in each age group. His multiple R was .60; that for the MacQuarrie alone was not given. The 147 high school and defense-training students studied by McDaniel and Reynolds (1944) were rated for mechanical aptitude by their instructors and subtest validity coefficients were calculated. These were as shown in Table 22.

TABLE 22

CORRELATION BETWEEN MACQUARRIE SUB-
TESTS AND INSTRUCTORS' RATINGS

MacQuarrie	*Ratings*
Tracing	.22
Tapping	−.17
Dotting	.22
Copying	.21
Location	.10
Blocks	.22
Pursuit	.12
Total	.14

These are certainly not impressive; that this may be due to defects in the criterion rather than in the test is a truism which the authors seem to have forgotten, for there is no discussion in the paper of the reliability of their criterion, and such ratings are notoriously unreliable. That this may be the explanation in this case is suggested by the equally low validities of the other tests used, although the multiple correlation coefficient based upon the MacQuarrie and O'Rourke subtests and the Bennett total score was .45.

Grades in courses taken by aviation mechanic trainees in the Army Air Forces prior to World War II were correlated with MacQuarrie and other test scores by Harrell and Faubion (1940). The correlation between this one test and grades in drafting and blueprint reading was .47.

Engineering grades during the freshman year and over the whole four years of college were correlated with the MacQuarrie by Brush (1941) in a study of more than 100 men at the University of Maine; the correlations were respectively .25 and .22, with probable errors of .06. The best subtest correlations were, as might be expected, those which measure spatial visualization, but these also were low, ranging from .24 to .265 for freshmen grades and from .18 to .27 for four-year marks. Revised Minnesota

Paper Form Board scores, on the other hand, had validities of .42 and .43. Brush cites an unpublished study by Horton in which the MacQuarrie yielded a correlation of .44 with engineering drawing grades, subtest scores ranging from .13 to .40. Equally good results were obtained by Holcomb and Laslett (1922), who found a correlation of .48 between MacQuarrie scores and grades of 50 freshman engineers. The discrepancies are difficult to explain; however, Brush's numbers were greater and his criterion went beyond first-year grades.

Grades in *dental* schools were correlated with MacQuarrie scores in studies by Thompson (1942) and by Robinson and Bellows (1941). In the latter the correlations were .35 and .48 for two different groups of freshmen, .40 for sophomores. In the former, the correlation with freshman theory grades was .05 ($N = 158$) and with practicum grades it was .11. For seniors ($N = 66$) the coefficients were .17 and .13. Correlations between part scores and criterion were no better for theory courses, but that between manual dexterity subtest scores of seniors and practicum grades was .32 and that between spatial subtest scores and senior practicum grades was —.27. It is noteworthy that the same trend held for freshman practicum grades (.22 and —.23), and that the correlations were reliable even though slightly lower. Just why the spatial parts of the test should be negatively correlated with laboratory grades is difficult to understand, although Thompson considers it logical, and the failure to confirm Robinson and Bellows' results for grades in general is also a topic for further investigation. It is perhaps relevant that Sartain (1945) obtained results rather like Thompson's for manual dexterity and spatial parts of the MacQuarrie and average grades during the first six months of *nursing* training, with the difference that both coefficients were positive (.26 and .36), as logical analysis of the test and of the tasks involved would lead one to expect, for spatial judgments are important in both theoretical and practical aspects of the sciences.

The predictive value of the MacQuarrie for *clerical* training in which manual dexterity might be considered important has been ascertained in several studies. Using 124 entering commercial high school girls as his subjects, 37 of whom graduated three years later, Klugman (1943) found the latter superior on MacQuarrie Blocks and Tapping subtests, with somewhat better scores on other subtests the differences for which were not clearly significant. Gottsdanker (1943) tested 51 women students in a business college, and used examinations in work with machine calculators as his criterion of success. The three dexterity tests had the following validities: Tapping .25, Dotting .21, and Tracing .08. The validities are such as might be expected from the nature of the tests. Barrett (1946) also worked with college age women, but hers were liberal arts students, 96 of whom were studying typing and 75 shorthand. Final grades were the criterion. No correlation coefficients were computed, but instead the effectiveness of the tests in differentiating superior from inferior students was ascertained. For typing the best subtests and their critical scores were the Tracing 50; Dotting 22; and Pursuit Tests 22; for shorthand, the Pursuit Test 24. It seems odd that the Tapping Test was not also valid for typing, but it did not differentiate between good and poor typing students; the Tapping, Dotting, Copying, and Blocks Tests also had some discriminating value for shorthand, but not sufficient to justify using them in addition to the other tests which had proved more useful. On logical grounds, the Pursuit Test should have the most validity, for it seems to involve to a high degree the smooth-flowing and precise co-ordination of hand and eye which is required in writing shorthand.

Success on the job, it is interesting to note, was not used as a criterion of the validity of the MacQuarrie Test for Mechanical Aptitude until more than ten years after its publication. Harrell administered it to loom fixers (1937); then the United States Employment Service used it in its studies of occupational ability patterns (Stead and Shartle, 1940); subsequent studies have been published by Blum (1943), Sartain (1945), and Goodman (1946, 1947, 1947, 1950).

In his study of loom fixers Harrell used 45 subjects employed in one Southern plant, with ratings by supervisors as the criterion of success. Each employee was rated by three or four persons on a six-point scale for mechanical ability. The reliability of the ratings was not ascertained, and no validity coefficient was published for this test.

Sartain, as has been seen in another context, worked with 46 aircraft-factory inspectors in a refresher training course, using ratings as a criterion. The correlation between MacQuarrie scores and ratings was .65, and was this high partly, no doubt, because of the greater importance of abstract abilities such as spatial visualization in training courses than in actual work. Ghiselli (1942) studied another group of 26 inspectors, but these were girls who inspected and packed pharmaceutical products. In this case the criterion was ratings of performance on the job, and the correlation with the MacQuarrie test was only .19, the lowest r obtained.

Sewing-machine operators were tested by Blum (1943), who selected the 25 highest-earning and 25 lowest-earning workers on piece work, using a combination of ratings and earnings as a criterion. The Tracing Test was the best single subtest (not confirmed by Stead and Shartle, as discussed below), better than any other and better than the total score. A critical score of 30 was established for this subtest, and would have eliminated 76 percent of the poor and 40 percent of the good operators when applied to this same group of workers. Failure to cross-validate was a defect in this study, as there would certainly be some shrinkage in discriminating power. Although the percentage cited would, if it remained the same in future samples, improve selection appreciably, the critical score eliminated so many successful workers that it could be applied only in an employer's market. (It would have elimniated about 55 and 70 percent of two USES samples, discussed below.) Other tests should be added in such a program, in order to cut down the percentages of false-positives and false-negatives.

In a thorough study Goodman (1946) administered the MacQuarrie to 329 women radio assembly operators immediately after they were hired. Their age range was 16 to 64, with a mean of 27, 34 percent being under 19 years of age and only 15 percent over 50 years old. The job was described as follows in the job summary: "Assembles radio components such as tube sockets, transformers and capacitors on chassis to form a complete set; assembles terminal boards and other small assemblies using hand tools; mounts subassemblies on chassis and secures them in place using nuts and bolts or soldering iron and rosincore solder; removes insulation from wires using sandpaper and emery cloth, and tins stripped leads; may specialize in one phase of assembly details."

The criterion was a rating of each new employee by the vestibule-training-school instructor after the construction of three models; ratings were based on the amount of work done during a fixed period of time, and on qualitative factors such as excess or deficiency of solder and looseness of joints. No check was made on the reliability of the ratings, perhaps because of operating problems, but the distribution of ratings was found to be normal after proper statistical treatment. Validity coefficients for the part scores of the MacQuarrie are shown in Table 23.

TABLE 23

CORRELATIONS BETWEEN THE MACQUARRIE
TEST AND RATINGS OF ASSEMBLY WORK
($N = 329$)

MacQuarrie Subtest	Ratings
Tracing	.32
Tapping	.18
Dotting	.13
Copying	.31
Location	.35
Blocks	.32
Pursuit	.27
Total	.42

It will be noted that the validity of the total score is greater for this job than is that of any subtest, although this is not true of certain other jobs or training courses. The reason for this is made clear by the fact that five of the subtests have moderate validities; apparently the work is of a type which requires manual, spatial, and perceptual aptitudes rather than just one of these abilities. It is because of its tapping of these three widely applicable aptitudes that the MacQuarrie has so often proved to have some validity, although other and better measures of any one of these aptitudes usually prove more valid when relevant. It is worth noting that when the most effective combination of the subtests was made, the multiple R (all subtests) was .46, only four points higher than the zero-order correlation of the total score.

Unlike most publishers of such studies, Goodman went further in order to ascertain the efficiency of this test in employee selection. His R of .46, evaluated by means of the coefficient of alienation, shows that use of the MacQuarrie would improve the selection of radio assembly operators in that plant by about 12 percent over and above what it would be without the test. The company then planned to apply the Taylor-Russell (1939) selection-ratio tables, selecting for employment only the top 30 percent of the distribution on the MacQuarrie. It was estimated that the old method resulted in the selection of employees, 50 percent of whom were satisfactory. With an R of .46, the selection ratio set at 30 percent, the Taylor-Russell Tables indicated that 71 percent of those selected with the aid of the MacQuarrie should be satisfactory. At this point the wartime shortage of personnel became so acute that every applicant seeking work had to be hired; it was still possible to make such a study in retrospect, however, using procedures which it had been planned to apply to future employees. The results were reported in a third article (1947). Of the original 329 employees, 193 or 58 percent had left the company; 35 of these were discharged, largely for "inability to do the work." An attempt to establish critical scores was considered a failure, but those who left of their own accord made significantly better scores than those who were discharged ($M = 48$, 40), and those who remained made intermediate scores which tended to be better than those of the dischargees ($M = 44$, $C.R. = 1.41$). If the Taylor-Russell ratio had been used, significantly fewer dischargees would have been selected, but almost proportionately fewer long-tenure workers also would have been accepted. The test did not, therefore, contribute materially to selection.

The Division of Occupational Analysis of the United States Employment Service used the MacQuarrie test in its test development work, including it in the research batteries for a variety of occupations according to hypotheses suggested by analysis of the test and of the job (Dvorak in Stead and Shartle, 1940, Ch. 6). The result was the finding that some of the subtests are valid for clerical occupations as well as for some mechanical jobs, just as one might expect in the case of tests of manual dexterity and of perceptual ability. A group of 227 clerical workers were compared with 78 manual workers (not otherwise described), and were found to equal or exceed Q3 of the latter group on the Tapping, Dotting, Copying, Location, and Blocks subtests. The last three may have been due to differences in mental ability, since spatial visualization is an abstract function, but the first two have been seen to be primarily dexterity tests. Validity coefficients for the occupations concerned are presented in Table 24; data on occupational differences are discussed subsequently.

TABLE 24

VALIDITY COEFFICIENTS AND CUITERIA FOR THE MACQUARRIE SUBTESTS

(After Stead and Shartle)

Occupation	N	Criterion				r Subtest			
			I	II	III	IV	V	VI	VII
Clerical Occupations									
Card-Punch-Machine Op.	121	Output	.16	.12	.27	.05	.03	—.03	.13
Card-Punch-Machine Op.	113	Output	.05	.25	.19	.24	.07	—.04	.10
Index Clerk	52	Error ratio	—.09	—.29	—.05	—.08	—.14	.07	—.25
Toll-Bill Clerk	19	Output	—.10	—.27	—.24	—.04	.02	.07	—.28
Calculator Operator	80	Worksample	.42	.13	.07	.38	.33	.36	.43
Adding-Machine Operator	26	Worksample	.38	.29	.18	.06	.31	.06	.12
Manual Occupations									
Pull-Socket Assembler	16	Output	.38	—.01	.22	.30	.02	—.14	.14
Put-in-Coil Girl	18	% effic.*	.20	—.29	—.28	—.24	—.40	—.06	—.09
Power-Sewing-Machine Operator	46	% effic.	.27	.09	.29	.00	.17	.32	.10
Power-Sewing-Machine Operator	23	Unknown	.17	.12	.05	.20	.15	.36	.51
Lamp-Shade Sewer	19	Output	.16	—.25	—.19	—.08	.33	.37	.01
Merchandise Packer	30	% effic.	—.18	.26	.31	—.01	.21	.15	.12
Can Packer	43	Output	.18	.24	.33	.20	.09	—.11	.09

* Ratio of time set by time study to complete work to actual time required by worker in question to complete work.

Outstanding in this table are three facts: The validity of some of the subtests for occupations in both clerical and manual fields; the unreliability of even some high correlation coefficients when checked on another sample of workers in the same job; and the different validities of tests saturated with identical factors. Illustrative of the former point is the Tracing Test, moderately valid for calculating and adding-machine operators and also for pull-socket assemblers, and the Location Test, which has positive validity for the two business-machine operator groups and for lamp-shade sewers but negative validity for put-in-coil girls. Illustrative of the fluctuation of validity coefficients when the samples are small are the correlations of .51 and .10 for two groups of power-sewing-machine operators, differences which might, however, be due to differences in the criteria, one of which is not specified. The third fact is illustrated by the validity of the first dexterity test (Tracing) for three occupations and the doubtful validity of the second test of manual dexterity for any of the fields in question, and also by the validity of the first spatial test (Copying) but not of the second (Location) for pull-socket assemblers.

Despite these discrepancies, inspection of the table suggests that there is a tendency for the Tapping and Dotting Tests, and for the Copying and Location Tests, to agree. The dexterity tests tend to have some validity for various types of office-machine operators and for packers, both of which agree reasonably well with logical analysis of the tasks; the latter, or spatial tests, tend to have some validity for office-machine operators and for machine and hand-sewers. It is unfortunate, since the test was designed as a test of mechanical aptitude, that no mechanical occupations were included; the differential validities for other types of occupations are helpful as indicators of possibly worthwhile groups on which to try the test for selection purposes; they are not, however, clear-cut enough to provide very helpful data in counselling. This fact will be brought out especially by the data on occupational differences, for some of the high-scoring occupations are those for which low validities were reported, and some of those for which the subtests have moderately high validities are fields, the mean scores of which are relatively low—an apparent paradox which will be discussed in subsequent paragraphs.

Occupational differences have apparently not been studied as such by means of the MacQuarrie Test for Mechanical Ability, but data on differences between a few jobs have been reported in Stead and Shartle (1940, pp. 232-235) in the form of graphs which show the approximate means and standard deviations. The groups of workers making high scores on the manual dexterity subtests include index clerks, put-in-coil girls, card-punch-machine operators, and toll-bill clerks; power-sewing-machine operators, can packers, and adding and calculating-machine operators tend to make low scores on one or more dexterity tests. On the spatial tests those tending to make high scores were card-punch-machine operators, index clerks, and toll-bill clerks, although the can packers included many high scorers on the one three-dimensional subtest (Blocks), as did also the merchandise packers. Low scores on the spatial tests were most frequently made by power-sewing-machine operators. The Pursuit Test, which is both perceptual and spatial, is one on which card-punch-machine operators and electrical-assembly workers tend to make high scores, the power-sewing-machine and adding and calculating-machine operators being low.

It is interesting to note that the data on occupational differences do not always agree with those on the correlation between scores on these tests and output. For example, the correlation between Location Test scores and card-punch-machine operation has been seen to be .03 and .07 for two samples, while in contrast with this negligible relationship we have also seen that card-punch-machine operators make higher scores on the Location Test than most of the other groups of workers tested. At first this seems inconsistent, but on second thought it is not illogical for a job to require a fairly high degree of a given aptitude, natural selection discouraging or eliminating those who lack it, and yet not to be so dependent on it that those who possess it in a high degree excel in the work. We have already seen this in connection with intelligence tests; the data show that in many occupations the workers must have more than a critical minimum of mental ability and that additional increments do not affect success, other factors then becoming much more important. So, apparently, it is in the case of other aptitude tests. This means that evaluations of the effectiveness of tests in personnel selection and guidance should not be based on correlation coefficients alone.

It is also true that in some low-scoring groups the correlation with success is moderately high. Can packers, for example, made a relatively low mean score on the Dotting Test, but the correlation with output in their case was found to be moderately high (.33). To make this point in another way, a high correlation between test scores and success does not necessarily mean a high critical minimum for employment; and a high critical minimum for employment does not necessarily mean that a high correlation will be found between the scores of unselected *workers* and success, although it would mean a substantial correlation between test scores and success in an unselected group of *applicants* for work.

Job satisfaction, in the case of the MacQuarrie as in that of most other tests, has not been used as a criterion of success.

Use of the MacQuarrie Test of Mechanical Ability in Counseling and Selection.   The evidence reviewed in the preceding pages makes it clear that the MacQuarrie Test of Mechanical Ability measures three different aptitudes: manual dexterity, spatial visualization, and perceptual speed and accuracy. Although some of the subtests appear to be relatively pure measures of one single factor (the Copying, Location, and Block Tests measure spatial visualization and Tapping measures dexterity), others are measures of combinations of factors (Tracing and Dotting are manual-perceptual, and Pursuit is perceptual-manual). This being the case, it is not surprising that the educational and occupational significance of the test is sometimes obscured by the use of total scores, and the significance of the subtests varies with the occupation.

The effects of maturation on the MacQuarrie Test appear to be an increase in scores during adolescence, followed by the decrease with later adulthood which is usually found in scores on tests in which speed is a factor. Although these tendencies have been made sufficiently clear to be considered in counseling, they have not been studied in great enough detail to make possible the establishment of special norms for use in counseling either in early adolescents or older adults in terms of status in comparison with adult workers. In such cases it is possible only to use age norms (adolescents) or general adult norms (making allowances for age on a rule-of-thumb basis).

Occupations for which the test has validity include business-machine operators (calculating machines, adding machines, card-punch machines, etc.), small-assembly workers (radios, electrical pull-sockets, etc.), and packers (merchandise and cans), although some subtests are valid for some and not for others of these. Superior aircraft factory inspectors tend to make higher total scores than less successful inspectors, and efficient radio-assembly operators surpass less efficient operators on the total score, because both jobs seem to require the combination of aptitudes represented by high total scores. On the other hand, good can packers excel on some of the manual dexterity and on the three dimensional tests, but not on others, and good power-sewing-machine operators make higher scores on the Blocks Test than do inferior operators while the Copying Test has little validity for this group.

School and college use of the MacQuarrie can be varied. The test is useful in counseling students concerning the choice of trade, technical, and dental curricula, although its validity is not as great as some studies suggest and part-scores should be used in fields such as dentistry, with recognition of the fact that other factors are of considerably more importance than those assessed by the MacQuarrie. The dexterity and pursuit subtest scores also have bearing on success in training in typing and shorthand. Because of the specificity of its part-scores, the MacQuarrie is likely to be more valuable in selection for training than in counseling concerning fields of endeavor.

In *guidance centers and employment services* this test can be useful in counseling clients concerning training in the fields just listed, and in screening employment applicants who are most likely to prove successful in office-machine operation and assembly jobs.

In *business and industry* the MacQuarrie can be a useful screen for the selection of the business-machine operators and assembly workers who have the manual dexterities and spatial aptitude which make for success in such work. Because of the specific factors measured by the test and the great variations in the psychological requirements of machine-operation and assembly jobs it is important that local validities and cut-off scores be established for each subtest, rather than depending on data from other studies. As Stead and Shartle's data have shown, subtest validities sometimes vary even from one sample to another, as when the Pursuit Test yielded a validity of .51 for one sample of power-sewing-machine operators and .01 for another.

The Purdue Mechanical Adaptability Test (Div. of Applied Psychology, Purdue University, 1946). The Purdue Mechanical Adaptability Test was published in 1946 as a result of work designed to produce a brief test which could be used by industrial personnel workers to measure "knack" for mechanical, electrical, and related activities. It was assumed that the most effective way to do this was to measure the amount of information acquired concerning mechanical, electrical, carpentry, plumbing, and related tools, materials, and processes. The test is, therefore, very similar in approach and content to the O'Rourke Mechanical Aptitude Test, previously discussed in some detail. It differs in that it uses only verbal rather than both graphic and verbal items, and in that it is much briefer, consisting of only 60 items. Although only two studies of the test are known to be in print at the time of writing and one the original study by the test's authors (Lawshe et al., 1946), the instrument is briefly treated because it is a widely used and valuable type of instrument.

Description. The 60 items in the test are divided as follows: woodwork and finishing, 10 items; automotive, 17; electricity and radio, 18; machine shop, 4; plumbing, 4; sheetmetal, 2; miscellaneous, 5. These items were selected from 400 which were written to tap first-hand contact rather than principles, and to utilize eighth grade vocabulary except for technical terms. The 100 best items were selected on the basis of lack of relationship to an intelligence test and internal consistency and tried out on 439 high school and college students, revised on the basis of their answers and criticisms, and administered to 364 men applying for steel mill jobs and to 98 men employed in foundries and metal products manufacturing concerns. Again lack of relationship to intelligence test items and internal consistency were the criteria for evaluating items, the 60-item Form A for Men being the result. The weighting of the different fields of "mechanical" work was therefore based not on judgment of the appropriate representation of the types of activity in which boys and men engage, but on the proved usefulness of various types of items in consistently measuring familiarity with tools, materials, and procedures in a variety of fields in which men and boys are customarily active. The result is an empirical rather than an *a priori* weighting which takes into account the very factors which *a priori* judgment might have considered.

The test takes 15 minutes to administer, and scoring is simply a matter of counting the correct responses, doubling this sum, and adding the sum of the "don't knows." Norms given in the manual are for 667 industrial applicants, not described. The article by Lawshe, Semanek, and Tiffin (1946) provides norms for 1015 "industrial" men, 103 non-engineering college men, 54 engineers in non-mechanical fields, and 71 mechanical engineers. The latter groups are sufficiently well described for the norms to be of some value, despite the small numbers; almost all were underclassmen at Purdue, the non-engineers being majors in science, pharmacy, and physical education. The industrial group is not described, although it presumably includes groups mentioned in the paper, namely industrial applicants in a steel mill and industrial applicants in an optical manufacturing plant. These groups are not, however, well enough defined as to intellectual or trade level for one to be able to use them as general norms. They may, for example, have been applicants for skilled jobs, or applicants for unskilled employment, or, more likely, an unknown mixture of applicants for unskilled, semiskilled, and skilled jobs. Norms for applicants for time-study training have been published by Rothe (1950) on 278 persons in seven plants.

The reliability of the test, determined by the odd-even method and corrected by the Spearman-Brown formula, was found to be .84 and .80 with groups of industrial and college men. This is not as high as is desirable and possible in aptitude and achievement tests, although it is not too low for use; lengthening the test to 80 items with a 20-minute time limit might well prove worth while.

Validity of the test has been checked in a variety of ways. The correlation with *intelligence* tests was demonstrated to be low by coefficients of .32 (487 industrial employment applicants) and .17 (173 college men) with the Purdue Adaptability Test. When correlated with the Otis S.A. scores of 25 mechanics, presumably a somewhat homogeneous group like the college students, the coefficient was .08. Although its correlation with the California Capacity, Non-Language, Test was .41, that with the Language Test was only .12 (40 apprentices). Correlation with the Bennett Mechanical Comprehension and Minnesota Paper Form Board Tests were .71 and .18 for some 30 unidentified subjects, which suggests that, as one would expect, the Purdue Test measures the informational component of mechanical comprehension rather well but does not tap spatial visualization to any great extent. These findings need, however, to be confirmed by other studies with well described samples before they can be considered conclusive.

The authors report no relationships with *grades,* their interest having been primarily in the industrial use of the test. Correlations with *occu-*

pational criteria are mostly rank-order coefficients based on very small groups, and so can be considered only as preliminary indications of the test's possible significance. These data need to be followed by more comprehensive validation studies. A group of 14 experienced mechanics in an ice company were rated by their supervisors. The scatterdiagram showing ratings and scores is long and narrow, suggesting a rather high correlation (.81) and a rather effective cut-off score of 90. Six time-study men in a musical instrument factory were ranked by their supervisor, the rank-order correlation with the Mechanical Adaptability Test being .75 ± .18. Twelve steel mill apprentices were tested at the time of hiring and ranked by their supervisor after they had been on the job, the rank-order correlation being .39 ± .24. Data for several other groups are reported, but as they were used in standardizing the test they are not meaningful. The one later study (Rothe, 1950), using 278 time-study applicants as subjects, yielded such differing validities for the very small groups in each of seven plants that it has little meaning, or, perhaps, shows no validity for this occupation.

Although no data on *occupational differences* are as yet available, the authors report differences between pre-occupational college groups which are rather informative. The mean scores for 71 mechanical and aeronautical engineering students were 103, civil, metallurgical, and electrical engineering students 96, and science, pharmacy, and physical education majors 92. The critical ratios between these groups were 3.8 (mechanical vs. non-mechanical engineers), 6.3 (mechanical engineers vs. non-engineers), and 2.1 (non-mechanical engineers vs. non-engineers). These significant differences suggest that this test is indeed a mechanical rather than a scientific, or even physical science, information test, and that it should be most useful in the counseling and selection of persons considering mechanical work.

As more studies are made it will be helpful to have comparisons of this test's effectiveness with that of the O'Rourke, as the most nearly similar test available, and with that of the Bennett, as one which differs from this in that it attempts to measure comprehension of principles rather than familiarity with tools and processes. More detailed and specific industrial norms will be helpful in counseling, although in selection local norms must always be developed. And validation studies based on larger groups with refined criteria of success are needed so that the occupational significance of the test may be known. In view of the simplicity of the vocabulary, educational validation for trade and technical courses should not be neglected. If such evidence is forthcoming the Purdue Mechanical Adaptability Test will probably become a widely used and useful diagnostic and prognostic instrument; it should have been available by now.

REFERENCES FOR CHAPTER X

Babcock, H., and Emerson, M. R. "An analytical study of the MacQuarrie Test of Mechanical Ability," *J. Educ. Psychol.,* 29 (1938), 50-56.

Barnette, W. L., Jr. "An occupational aptitude pattern for engineers," *Educ. Psychol. Measmt.,* 11 (1951), 52-66.

Barrett, D. W. "Prediction of achievement in typewriting and stenography in a liberal arts college," *J. Appl. Psychol.,* 30 (1946), 624-630.

Bennett, G. K., and Cruikshank, R. M. *A Summary of Manual and Mechanical Ability Tests.* New York: Psychological Corporation, 1940.

———, and Cruikshank, R. M. "Sex differences in the understanding of mechanical problems," *J. Appl. Psychol.,* 26 (1942), 121-127.

———, and Fear, R. A. "Mechanical comprehension and dexterity," *Pers. J.,* 22 (1943), 12-17.

———, and Wesman, A. G. "Industrial test norms for a Southern plant population," *J. Appl. Psychol.,* 31 (1947), 241-246.

Bingham, W. V. *Aptitudes and Aptitude Testing.* New York: Harper, 1937.

Blum, M. L. "Selection of sewing machine operators," *J. Appl. Psychol.,* 27 (1943), 35-40.

Borg, W. R. "Some factors relating to art school success," *J. Educ. Res.,* 43 (1950), 376-384.

Brush, Edward N. "Mechanical ability as a factor in engineering aptitude," *J. Appl. Psychol.,* 25 (1941), 300-312.

Cox, J. R. *Mechanical Aptitude.* London: Methuen, 1928.

Cuomo, Sylvia, and Meyer, H. H. "Validity information exchange: floor assembler," *Pers. Psychol.,* 8 (1955), 270.

Darley, J. G. "Reliability of tests in the standard battery," (In "Research studies in individual diagnosis.") *University of Minnesota Bull. Empl. Stab. Res. Inst.,* 4 (1934).

Davis, F. B. (ed.). *The AAF Qualifying Examination.* ("AAF Aviation Psychology Report," No. 6) Washington: Government Printing Office, 1947.

DuBois, P. H. (ed.). *The Classification Program.* ("AAF Aviation Psychology Report," No. 2.) Washington, D. C.: Government Printing Office, 1947.

Dvorak, B. J. "Differential occupational ability patterns," *University of Minnesota Bull. Empl. Stab. Res. Inst.,* 8 (1935).

Fredericksen, N. *Validity of Navy Aptitude Tests in Service Schools at the Great Lakes Naval Training Station.* Washington, D. C.: Department of Commerce, 1946.

Fryer, D. *Measurement of Interests.* New York: Henry Holt, 1931.

Ghiselli, E. E. "Tests for the selection of inspectors-packers," *J. Appl. Psychol.,* 26 (1942), 468-476.

Goodman, C. H. "The MacQuarrie Test for Mechanical Ability: 1. Selecting radio assembly operators," *J. Appl. Psychol.,* 30 (1946), 586-595.

——— "The MacQuarrie Test for Mechanical Ability: II. Factor analysis," *J. Appl. Psychol.,* 31 (1947), 150-154.

——— "The MacQuarrie Test for Mechanical Ability: III. Follow-up study," *J. Appl. Psychol.,* 31 (1947), 502-510.

——— "The MacQuarrie Test for Mechanical Ability: IV. Time and motion analysis," *J. Appl. Psychol.,* 34 (1950), 27-29.

Gottsdanker, R. M. "Measures of potentiality for machine calculation," *J. Appl. Psychol.,* 27 (1943), 233-248.

Green, H. J., et al. "A manual of selected occupational tests for use in public employment offices," *University of Minnesota Bull. Empl. Stab. Res. Inst.,* 3 (1933).

Guilford, J. P. (ed.). *Printed Classification Tests.* ("AAF Aviation Psychology Report," No. 5.) Washington, D. C.: Government Printing Office, 1947.

———— "Factor analysis in a test-development program," *Psychol. Rev.,* 55 (1948), 79-94.

Halliday, R. W., Fletcher, F. M., Jr., and Cohen, Rita M. "Validity of the Owens-Bennett Mechanical Comprehension Test," *J. Appl. Psychol.,* 35 (1951), 321-324.

Hanman, B. "Performance of adult males on the Minnesota Paper Form Board Test and the O'Rourke Mechanical Aptitude Test," *J. Appl. Psychol.,* 26 (1942), 809-811.

Harrell, T. W. "Validity of certain mechanical ability tests for selecting cotton mill machine fixers," *J. Soc. Psychol.,* 18 (1937), 279-282.

———— "A factor analysis of mechanical ability tests," *Psychometrika,* 5 (1940), 17-33.

————, and Faubion, R. "Selection tests for aviation mechanics," *J. Consult. Psychol.,* 4 (1940), 104-105.

Harvey, O. L. "Mechanical 'aptitude' or mechanical 'ability'?" *J. Educ. Psychol.,* 22 (1931), 517-522.

Holcomb, G. W., and Laslett, H. R. "A prognostic study of engineering aptitude," *J. Appl. Psychol.,* 16 (1932), 107-115.

Horning, S. D. "Testing mechanical abilities by the MacQuarrie Test," *Ind. Art. Mag.,* 15 (1926), 348-350.

Jacobsen, E. E. "An evaluation of certain tests in predicting mechanic learner achievement," *Educ. Psychol. Measmt.,* 3 (1943), 259-267.

Jordaan, J. P. "The Relationship between Socioeconomic Status and the Vocational Interests of Mechanically Gifted Boys." Unpublished Ph.D. dissertation, Teachers College, Columbia University, 1949.

Klugman, S. F. "Test scores and graduation," *Occupations,* 21 (1943), 389-393.

Lawshe, C. H., Semanek, I. A., and Tiffin, J. "The Purdue Mechanical Adaptability Test," *J. Appl. Psychol.,* 30 (1946), 442-453.

Leffel, E. S. "Students' Plans, Interests, and Achievement." Unpublished M.A. thesis, Clark University, 1939.

Littleton, I. T. "Prediction in auto trade courses," *J. Appl. Psychol.,* 36 (1952), 15-19.

McDaniel, J. W., and Reynolds, W. A. "A study of the use of mechanical aptitude tests with selection of trainees for mechanical occupations," *Educ. Psychol. Measmt.,* 4 (1944), 191-197.

McMurray, R. N., and Johnson, I. L. "Development of instruments for selecting and placing factory employees," *Adv. Mgt.,* 10 (1945), 113-120.

MacQuarrie, T. W. "A mechanical ability test," *J. Pers. Res.,* 5 (1927), 329-337.

Mitrano, R. J. "Relationship between age and test performance of applicants to a technical-industrial high school," *J. Appl. Psychol.,* 26 (1942), 482-486.

Moore, B. V. "Analysis of tests administered to men in engineering defense training courses," *J. Appl. Psychol.,* 25 (1941), 619-635.

Morgan, W. J. "Some remarks and results of aptitude testing in technical and industrial schools," *J. Soc. Psychol.,* 20 (1944), 19-79.

Murphy, L. W. "The relation between mechanical ability tests and verbal and non-verbal intelligence tests," *J. Psychol.,* 2 (1936), 353-366.

Owens, W. A., Jr. "A difficult new test of mechanical comprehension," *J. Appl. Psychol.,* 34 (1950), 77-81.

Paterson, D. G., et al. *The Minnesota Mechanical Abilities Tests.* Minneapolis: University of Minnesota Press, 1930.

————, Schneidler, G., and Williamson, E. G. *Student Guidance Techniques.* New York: McGraw-Hill, 1938.

Poe, W. A., and Berg, I. A. "Psychological test performance of steel industry production supervisors," *J. Appl. Psychol.,* 36 (1952), 234-237.

Pritchett, C. N. "The Tennessee Valley Authority." Unpublished Ph.D. thesis, University of Chicago, 1937.

Robinson, J. B., and Bellows, R. M. "Characteristics of successful dental students," *Assn. College Registr.,* 16 (1941), 109-122.

Ross, L. W. "Results of testing machine-tool trainees," *Pers. J.,* 21 (1943), 363-367.

Rothe, H. F. "Normative and validity data for the Purdue Mechanical Adaptability Test," *Pers. Psychol.,* 3 (1950), 187-192.

Sartain, A. Q. "The use of certain standardized tests in the selection of inspectors in an aircraft factory," *J. Consult. Psychol.,* 9 (1945), 234-235.

——— "Relation between scores on certain standard tests and supervisory success in an aircraft factory," *J. Appl. Psychol.,* 30 (1946), 328-332.

Scudder, C. L., and Raubenheimer, A. S. "Are standardized mechanical aptitude tests valid?" *J. Juv. Res.,* 14 (1930), 120-123.

Shultz, I. T., and Barnabas, B. "Testing for leadership in industry," *Trans. Kans. Acad. Sci.,* 48 (1945), 160-164.

Shuman, J. T. "Value of aptitude tests for supervisory workers in the aircraft engine and propeller industries," *J. Appl. Psychol.,* 29 (1945), 156-160, 185-190.

Slater, P. "Some group tests of spatial judgment or practical ability," *Occup. Psychol.,* 14 (1940), 39-55.

Stanton, M. B. "Mechanical ability of deaf children." *Teachers College Contributions to Education,* 751 (1938).

Stead, W. H., and Shartle, C. L. *Occupational Counseling Techniques.* New York: American Book Co., 1940.

Stenquist, J. L. "Measurement of mechanical ability." *Teachers College Contributions to Education,* 130 (1923).

Stuit, D. B. *Personnel Research and Test Development in the Bureau of Naval Personnel.* Princeton: Princeton University Press, 1947.

Taylor, H. C., and Russell, J. T. "The relationship of validity coefficients to the practical effectiveness of tests in selection: discussion and tables," *J. Appl. Psychol.,* 28 (1939), 565-578.

Thompson, C. E. "Motor and mechanical abilities in professional schools," *J. Appl. Psychol.,* 26 (1942), 24-37.

Thorndike, E. L. *Prediction of Vocational Success.* New York: Commonwealth Fund, 1931.

Traxler, A. E. "Correlation between 'mechanical aptitude scores' and 'mechanical comprehension' scores," *Occupations,* 22 (1943), 42-43.

Tredick, V. D. "The Thurstone Primary Mental Abilities Test and a Battery of Vocational Guidance Tests as Predictors of Academic Success." Unpublished thesis, Pennsylvania State College, 1941.

Tuckman, J. "The correlations between 'mechanical aptitudes' and 'mechanical comprehension' scores: further observations," *Occupations,* 22 (1944), 244-245.

——— "Norms for the MacQuarrie Test for Mechanical Ability for high school students," *Occupations,* 25 (1946), 94-96.

Wittenborn, J. R. "Mechanical ability, its nature and measurement. I. II. Manual dexterity," *Educ. Psychol. Measmt.,* 5 (1945), 241-260, 395-409.

Wolff, W. M., and North, A. I. "Selection of municipal firemen," *J. Appl. Psychol.,* 35 (1951), 25-29.

XI

SPATIAL VISUALIZATION

THE ability to judge the relations of objects in space, to judge shapes and sizes, to manipulate them mentally, and to visualize the effects of putting them together or of turning them over or around, is generally referred to as spatial visualization. It is an aptitude which has long been considered important in such clearly similar activities as machine-shop work, carpentry, and mechanical drawing, in which the worker must judge shape and size and translate two-dimensional drawings into three-dimensional objects, and which has been considered likely to be important in certain other occupations, the principal activities of which were not quite so clearly similar, such as engineering and art.

Work in the measurement of spatial judgment began, however, as one aspect of the measurement of intelligence rather than as an attempt to measure a special ability of significance in certain occupations. Clinical psychologists, attempting to devise non-verbal or performance tests of intelligence which would be useful in appraising the mental ability of persons with limited formal education or whose linguistic development might in some other way have been handicapped, resorted to the familiar puzzle-type test in which the subject is required to put objects together in such a way as to make a pre-determined pattern. Sometimes the pieces to be assembled were parts of a picture, as in the Mare-and-Foal Test used in the Pintner-Paterson Scale of Performance Tests; in such cases the cues relied upon by the examinee are partly spatial (the shape of the curved outlines of the parts) and partly experimental (e.g., the head must fit at the end of the neck). In other tests experiential content was not utilized, as in the case of the Casuist Board, in which geometric figures are put together to form large wholes, also geometric. In such tests, the removal of cues based upon and requiring the analysis of experience was part of an effort to make the test truly a measure of mental ability rather than one of education. As subsequent work showed, it resulted in the measurement of a trait which is related to mental ability in childhood but relatively independent of it in adulthood.

When large-scale testing operations made it desirable to develop group tests of the performance type, Army psychologists in World War I produced Army Beta, a paper-and-pencil version of a performance scale. The subtests, like those of the apparatus tests, involved completing incomplete figures of people and other familiar items in which analysis of content could help the examinee, and judging the relations of geometric figures, in which it was hoped that abstract reasoning alone would play a part. As such paper-and-pencil tests of spatial judgment were made available for adult use, form boards were also developed for use with normal adults. Link developed a Form Board which subsequently developed into the Minnesota Spatial Relations Test, and Kent and Shakow devised a series of Form Boards which has models for clinical use with mental patients and for industrial use with normal adults.

Because of the emphasis on the measurement of the intelligence of special groups which pervaded early work with tests of spatial relations, and the subsequent application of such tests to industrial use, students of testing are often confused by what seems to be a serious inconsistency in the use of such tests by psychologists. They find tests of spatial judgment figuring prominently in intelligence tests such as Army Beta, the Army General Classification Test, and the American Council on Education Psychological Examination, and also masquerading as tests of a special aptitude as in the case of the Minnesota Spatial Relations Test, the Minnesota Paper Form Board, the Kent-Shakow Form Boards, and the Blocks Test of the MacQuarrie Test of Mechanical Ability. The question arises, is it possible that the same type of item can measure both intelligence and a special aptitude not related to intelligence?

The theoretical explanation of what actually seemed to be the case was slow in coming, but it was implicit in data familiar to most psychologists, for it had long been known that performance tests of intelligence (i.e., form boards, tests heavily saturated with spatial visualization) did not correlate well with other tests of mental ability and gave poor predictions of school achievement—increasingly so with increasing age. This suggested that spatial judgment might be a special aptitude which develops at approximately the same rate as other mental abilities, and therefore provides a fair measure of mental age in childhood, but that, being a special aptitude, the degree of spatial judgment possessed in middle adolescence or adulthood is not a good indicator of the amount of any other mental ability possessed by the individual. This has since been confirmed by Thurstone's work (1938), in which it was demonstrated that what is thought of as intelligence is, in fact, a number of special aptitudes. In this analysis spatial visualization emerges as a special aptitude, distinct from the verbal, numerical, perceptual, memory, and other aptitudes which are relatively independent of each other in homogeneous groups but tend to be associated in heterogeneous groups. A spatial relations test is therefore effective in classifying people according to "general" ability when wide ranges of ability are in question, and so has a part in a test such as the AGCT; on the other hand, when a group of fairly similar general ability is being studied, whether they be factory workers or college students, scores on tests of spatial relations are found to vary considerably and to be related to success in certain types of activity without being good predictors of success in others. We have already seen, for example, that verbal scores on the A.C.E. Psychological Examination give equally good predictions of success in social studies and in mathematics, whereas quan‧ titative scores, which are partly based on spatial items, give substantially better predictions of success in mathematics than in social studies.

Of the tests which have been developed for the measurement of spatial visualization, the most widely used in vocational counseling and selection have for some years been the Minnesota Spatial Relations Test and the Likert-Quasha Revision of the Minnesota Paper Form Board. These will be discussed in this chapter; it will be seen that the tests are impure, for they measure certain other factors to a lesser degree. Other tests somewhat like the Paper Form Board have been made available, but have not been the subjects of much investigation. In addition to these special tests of spatial judgment the user of tests should keep in mind the spatial subtests of composite tests or test batteries such as the Blocks Tests of the Mac-Quarrie Test of Mechanical Ability, the Surface Development Test of the Chicago Tests of Primary Mental Abilities, and the Space Relations Test of the Psychological Corporation's Differential Aptitude Tests, all of which are discussed elsewhere in this book.

Another very well-known test of spatial visualization is Johnson O'Connor's Wiggly Blocks (Keane and O'Connor, 1927; Remmers and Scholl, 1933), the past widespread use of which would justify discussion in this chapter if it were not so unreliable as to make it useless. Mellenbruch (1946) developed a series of similar blocks at about the same time but did little with them, and Uhlaner (unpublished study) has developed a reliable series of curved blocks. Although attempts to demonstrate that two- and three-dimensional spatial visualization are distinct have failed, there is considerable evidence to show that spatial visualization can be broken down into even more refined factors. Michael, Guilford, Fruchter, and Zimmerman (1957) have reviewed this work, concluding that these factors are three in number: spatial relations and orientation, visualization, and kinaesthetic imagery.

Specific Tests

   The Minnesota Spatial Relations Test (Marietta Apparatus Co. and Educational Test Bureau, 1930).   The Minnesota Spatial Relations Test was developed by the Mechanical Abilities Research Project of the University of Minnesota because of the promise of the Link Form Board (Paterson et al., 1930). The latter test had a reliability of only .72 as determined in the preliminary work of the project; by using four boards instead of one, the new test achieved satisfactory reliability. It has since been used in the Minnesota Employment Stabilization Research Institute which added valuable normative material, and in several other studies to be discussed below, but the administrative expense of apparatus tests and the fact that it has a rather good paper-and-pencil equivalent have kept it from being as widely used and studied as some other tests. It is discussed here because it is a purer test of spatial judgment than the paper-and-pencil tests, as will be seen later, and therefore contributes materially to our understanding of the trait and has special value in testing for the less abstract or academic types of technical training and employment.

   Applicability.   Like the other tests of the Minnesota Mechanical Abilities Project, the Spatial Relations Test was first used with junior high school boys taking trade courses, but was designed with the objective of making it usable with older adolescents and adults. Use of the test with boys as young as 11 years old and with adults of all ages has confirmed the belief that the nature of the task is such as to make it applicable to a wide range of ability, spatial judgment beginning to mature early enough for the items to be meaningful even before adolescence. As the aptitude is still maturing during adolescence age norms are of course needed, and here as elsewhere a problem is encountered in the vocational counseling of adolescents. If one uses age norms in interpreting the test scores of high school students, one runs the risk of encouraging a student who is superior to his class or age group in spatial judgment to enter an occupation for which he may actually be lacking in the aptitude in question, because those who enter the occupation may be so highly selected. Age norms are available, as are some occupational data, but developmental conversion tables are lacking which would enable a counselor of high school students to determine how able a given boy or girl will be when adult to compete with persons engaging in various occupations. Judging by the age norms, spatial visualization increases until age 14 and remains constant at ages 15, 16, and 17; there is a suggestion of an increase at age 18, the mean score for which is somewhat higher than that for the three preceding years, but the difference is not great and may be due to elimination of some of the less able in the older sample; the 80th and 90th percentiles are about the same for ages 15 through 18, which fits in with the explanation of the difference on the basis of sampling.

Content. The Minnesota Spatial Relations Test is made up of four form boards, of which A and B use the same pieces and C and D have common parts. The arrangement of the parts differs, however, in the two members of each pair, so that having placed them in Board A presumably helps one in doing Board B only by orienting one to the task and materials; it does not teach one where the parts go. The parts themselves are cut from a rectangular board about three feet long by one wide; there are three pieces of each shape, but of varying sizes, arranged close together but not adjacent to each other in the board. The shapes include crescents, squares, angles, and odd-shaped geometrical forms.

Administration and Scoring. The test is administered individually and requires from 15 to 45 minutes, the average adult finishing all four boards in 20 or 25 minutes. Although it is not stated in any of the publications or manuals dealing with the development or administration of the test, the subject stands while taking the test. (Personal communication from the test author).

Apart from these questions of the examinee's position and the nature of the test materials, administration of the test is straightforward. Scoring, in the original work of the mechanical ability project, involved obtaining the total number of seconds required to complete all four boards; the norms for boys are based on this procedure. This is the method described in the manual published by the Educational Test Bureau, publisher of the green-topped inserts and black-painted boards. The Minnesota Employment Stabilization Research Institute experimented with methods of scoring the test and found, however, that its reliability was increased by treating the first board as a practice trial and scoring only Boards B, C, and D (Darley, 1934). The general adult and occupational norms obtained in the MESRI work were therefore published in terms of the last three boards (Green, et al., 1933) and this is the recommended method of scoring.

Norms. The boys' norms provided by the Mechanical Ability Project cover ages 11 through 18, in grades 7 to 12, the numbers in any given group ranging from 55 to 150. All of them were boys in Minneapolis and St. Paul schools, and while they may have been a good local sample there are no data to enable one to judge the applicability of these norms in other localities. Norms are also available for 57 arts and 201 engineering college students at the University of Minnesota, all freshmen. These norms are based on time for all four trials; if it is desired to use them, time for Board A should be recorded and included in the total. The Board A score will not be used, however, if the norms compiled at the MESRI are utilized.

These are based on the now familiar standard sample of 500 employed men and women, and on various occupational groups of from 20 to 489 persons each. They are available in abbreviated form in the Educational Test Bureau Manual, recomputed for all four boards, but this is an inferior method. In view of the paucity of data about the norm groups in the Educational Test Bureau manual, the inferiority of its scoring system, and the relative unavailability of the Minnesota bulletins in which the better type of norms are published, general adult norms are provided in Table 25 and occupational median scores, also from the MESRI, are provided in Table 26.

TABLE 25

ADULT NORMS FOR THE MINNESOTA SPATIAL RELATIONS TEST

Raw score (in seconds) Sum for Boards B, C, and D Men	Women	Standard Score	Centile Rank	Letter Grade
				} A+
608	605	7.0	97.7	
				} A−
652	648	6.5	93.3	
				} B+
726	758	6.0	84.1	
				} B−
814	838	5.5	69.1	
				} C+
916	933	5.0	50.0	
				} C−
1047	1037	4.5	30.9	
				} D+
1218	1156	4.0	15.9	
				} D−
1442	1354	3.5	6.7	
				} E+
1583	1571	3.0	2.3	
				} E−

Standardization and Initial Validation. When existing tests were being surveyed for possible use in the research of the Minnesota Mechanical Ability Project, Link's Form Board seemed one of the most promising. Included in the preliminary research, it proved to have less reliability than that needed for its scores to be usable in individual diagnosis. It was therefore lengthened by making a total of four boards with the same type of items, and a satisfactory reliability was obtained.

Like the other tests in the Mechanical Ability Project, the Spatial Rela-

TABLE 26

MEDIAN SCORES FOR VARIOUS OCCUPATIONAL GROUPS

(Minnesota Spatial Relations Test)

Number	Group	Median Percentile
102	Garage mechanics	85
170	Manual training teachers	75
62	Ornamental iron workers	69
113	Men office clerks	66
20	Draftsmen	59
29	Minor bank officials	59
84	Retail salesmen	55
47	Life insurance salesmen	55
489	Occupationally unselected men	50
26	Minor executives	46
69	Janitors	30
124	Policemen	27
33	Casual laborers	2

tions Test was subjected to rather thorough study and validated against success in mechanical activities. It was found to have a low correlation with intelligence as measured by the Otis $(r = .18)$; the group was a fairly homogeneous one of 100 seventh and eighth grade boys. It had a rather high correlation with the Minnesota Mechanical Assembly Test, based on the same group $(r = .56)$ and with the Stenquist Picture Test $(r = .42)$. When correlated with a mechanical interest inventory a relationship was again found, r being .46. Scores were not, however, related to the father's occupation, the household chores engaged in by the boys, and similar environmental data.

Validation in this early stage was done against ratings of the quality of shop work done by the boy; the work was a standard task carefully rated by the instructor. The group were the same 100 seventh and eighth graders. The correlation of .53 showed that this was one of the most valid tests in the Minnesota battery for the prediction of success in mechanical activities.

Reliability. Using all four trials in computing the score, the original study of the Minnesota Spatial Relations Test yielded a reliability of .84 based upon scores of 100 seventh and eighth grade boys (corrected for attenuation). When the last three boards only were counted, with Board A serving as a practice trial, the reliability for 482 adult men in a selected sample of the employed population was .91 (Darley, 1934).

Validity. Criteria used in studying the validity of the Minnesota Spatial Relations Test include the usual variety of tests of other abilities, grades in school and college courses, ratings of work samples, and differentiation between persons in various occupations. Ability of the test to yield predictions of success in employment has not been studied, perhaps because of the difficulty of administering an apparatus test to large numbers of employment applicants and the availability of a paper-and-pencil version of the same test (the Revised Minnesota Paper Form Board, discussed in the next section) .

We have seen that the original work with the spatial relations test yielded a correlation of .18 between spatial scores and scores on the Otis Self-Administering Test of Mental Ability. In an unpublished study of 100 NYA youths aged 16 to 24 Super obtained a correlation of .25 between the same two variables. Andrew (1937) correlated spatial relations test scores with scores on the Pressy intelligence tests, finding r's of .43 and .36 for groups of 334 unselected men and 131 unselected women in the MESRI project and an r of .25 based on 200 women clerical workers. The higher coefficients were obtained with more heterogenenous groups such as unselected adults, and the lower figures with less heterogeneous groups such as seventh and eighth grade boys; it seems legitimate to conclude that in homogeneous groups there are variations in ability to visualize spatial relations which are quite independent of general mental ability, and that in heterogeneous groups the relationship between the two is positive but not high enough to make one useful by itself as a predictor of the other.

Manual dexterity has been studied in relation to spatial judgment by Andrew (1937) and by Super in an unpublished study. The former investigator correlated scores on the Minnesota spatial test with scores on the O'Connor Finger and Tweezer Dexterity Tests; her subjects were 200 women clerical workers. The correlations of .28 and .31 showed that the two types of aptitude overlap slightly, but are virtually independent. In Super's study of 100 NYA youths aged 16 to 24 the Minnesota Manual Dexterity Test (Placing) yielded a correlation of .05 with the spatial test, confirming the findings of the original unpublished study of the placing test which was developed in order to ascertain the role of manual dexterity in the Minnesota Spatial Relations Test. The conclusion that differences in manual dexterity do not affect scores on the spatial test therefore seems warranted.

Mechanical comprehension was seen in the preceding chapter to be composed of spatial judgment and mechanical information. The correlations between scores on spatial visualization tests and tests of mechanical comprehension were reviewed and discussed in some detail, and are therefore not repeated here.

Spatial visualization has been measured by other instruments, the scores of which have been correlated with those on the Minnesota apparatus test. The original, free-response, form of the Minnesota Paper Form Board was reported by Paterson et al. (1930) to have a correlation of .63 with the apparatus test. In Super's unpublished study of NYA youths, the correlation between the Revised Minnesota Paper Form Board (multiple-choice form) and the apparatus test was found to be .59; Harrell (1940) found it to be .65. No data have been seen concerning relationships between scores on this two-dimensional test of spatial relations and such presumably three-dimensional tests as the Wiggly Block and the Crawford Spatial Relations Test, although it would seem to be very important to ascertain the relationship between ability to judge relationships of two-dimensional objects and ability to think in terms of three-dimensional space. It may be that, in working with two-dimensional objects, one actually works in three dimensions, mentally turning objects around and over, so that there is no real difference between the two types of tests; but this has not yet been demonstrated to be the case.

Factor analysis studies including the Minnesota Spatial Relations Test have been carried out by Andrew (1937), Harrell (1940), Wittenborn (1945) and the Staff of the Occupational Analysis Division of the United States Employment Service (1945). Andrew's study focused on the Minnesota Clerical Test, but her factor analysis confirmed the existence of a distinct spatial factor. Harrell worked with a total of 37 variables, including the Minnesota Spatial Relations and Mechanical Assembly Tests, the MacQuarrie, the Stenquist Picture Test, and Thurstone's Primary Mental Abilities Tests. He located five factors, including spatial visualization, perceptual ability, and manual agility; the first-named factor was the important one in the Minnesota Spatial Relations Test, although when *accuracy* was scored rather than *time* the perceptual factor also played an important part. Wittenborn's analysis of the definitive Minnesota battery isolated only a spatial factor in the Minnesota Spatial Relations Test; this factor was found to be the only one of importance in the Paper Form Board, the Assembly Test, the Mechanical Interest Analysis Blank, and, most significant of all, the shop operations quality criterion, thus further confirming the conclusion that spatial visualization is a distinct factor and the principal factor underlying aptitude for mechanical work.

The USES study, of which only a summary report has been published, found that the Minnesota Spatial Relations Test is heavily saturated with a spatial factor, and that two other factors play a part in it. One of these was a space-perception factor, isolated in this study and in Harrell's but not in Andrew's or Wittenborn's, presumably because of the smaller number of tests used in the last two studies. The other was difficult to define; it has a wider significance than Thurstone's induction factor, and seemed to have some of the properties of Spearman's general factor; since they used a multi-factor method of analysis the authors hesitate to call it general intelligence, but consider it more likely to be that than anything else. Since the subjects used were adults, aged 17 to 39, the finding of a general intelligence factor would be important, not only because it would explain why spatial tests can be used as measures both of general ability and of a special aptitude, but also because it would contradict the theory of group factors which, in the United States, has been accepted to the exclusion of Spearman's two-factor theory. Obviously, the USES data must be reported in more detail, and confirmed by other studies, before conclusions of such major importance can be drawn. In the meantime, it can be concluded that there is a distinct spatial factor which is the most important element in the Minnesota Spatial Relations Test and in mechanical success, and that perceptual ability does also play a part in this test.

Another approach to this question is available through an unpublished thesis by Tredick (1941), reported by Goodman (1944). In this work Tredick correlated scores on the Minnesota Spatial Relations Test with factor scores derived from Thurstone's Primary Mental Abilities Tests administered to 113 freshman college women. Significant correlations were found with the perceptual, spatial, and reasoning factors (.55, .49, .47), and with the other reasoning or deductive factor (.33). These data tend to confirm the USES findings in so far as components in the Minnesota test are concerned.

Grades and ratings of performance in mechanical tasks were used as criteria by Brush (1941), Tredick (1941), Stanton (1938), and Steel, Balinsky, and Lang (1945). Brush used 104 engineering students at the University of Maine as his subjects, correlating spatial relations scores with freshman and four-year grades; the results were disappointing, the r's in both cases being .06. It should be noted here that the Revised Minnesota Paper Form Board yielded validity coefficients of .42 and .43, which suggests that the heavier loading of intelligence in the paper version of the test makes it superior for predicting success in technical activities which are as abstract as college engineering courses. Tredick also found this to be the case in a different college curriculum. The students studied by Tredick were 113 freshman students of Home Economics at the Pennsylvania State College, her criteria being grades in several courses and semester-point-average for the first semester. Correlations between test scores and grades were .20 for Art, .22 for Chemistry, .02 for English Composition, and .23 for semester-point-average. The relationships are in the expected directions, but not high enough to make the test usable by itself; it might have some value in a battery of unrelated tests.

The nearest approach to a repetition of the original validation of the Minnesota tests was made by Stanton (1938), who correlated scores on Minnesota Battery A against ratings of shop work performed by deaf boys and girls. She worked with 121 boys and 36 girls, aged 12 to 14. The battery as a whole had correlations of .48 and .46 with the ratings; the validity of the spatial test alone was not given. While not as high as the coefficients reported by Paterson et al. (1930) these are high enough to make the test useful in counseling and selection when combined with other data. The work sample approach was used also by Steel and associates, in a study already discussed elsewhere in this book. For boys the correlation was .25; for girls, .39; as pointed out in a previous discussion, experience may have counteracted the effect of individual differences in aptitude in the boys more than in the girls, but in both cases the test had some validity.

Success on the job, it has already been pointed out, has not been used as a criterion of the validity of the Minnesota Spatial Relations Test. Ross (1943) established a critical score for machine-tool trainees, setting it at the 30th percentile. There were approximately 40 trainees. But the criterion was grades in on-the-job training.

Occupational differentiation on the basis of spatial relations test scores was studied first by the Minnesota Employment Stabilization Research Institute (Green et al., 1933) and then by Teegarden (1943). In the former study garage mechanics were found to make a median score equal to the 85th percentile of the general population, while manual training teachers stood at the 75th; ornamental ironworkers and men office clerks were also one sigma or more above the median (69th and 66th percentiles). Draftsmen were, surprisingly, at only the 59th percentile; the middle range included also such groups as retail salesmen, bank clerks, minor executives, and life insurance salesmen, while the lower ranges included janitors (30th percentile), policemen, and casual laborers (27th and 2nd percentiles). These differences are about as might be expected, except for the fairly high standing of the office clerks and the lower standing of the draftsmen; perhaps the latter would show up better on a paper-and-pencil test such as the Minnesota Paper Form Board, which would seem to approximate the medium in which they work more closely than does an apparatus test.

The group studied by Teegarden was younger and less experienced, and her general adult norms were locally established, which makes impossible the merging of her occupational norms with those of the MESRI project without going back to the raw scores. Within the limitations of her sample, it is instructive to note that there were no groups which make significantly high scores, with the exception of male operatives performing hand work in factories, who stand at the 74th percentile, and female assembly workers at the 72nd percentile. But women hand operatives stand at the 55th, leading one to question the data for men; the numbers were not large, ranging from as few as 22 to 123 workers per group. Women packers and wrappers were at the 67th percentile, men at the 62nd. All other groups of men and women were between the 44th and 65th percentiles. As none of the occupations studied were skilled or technical occupations, the failure to find clear-cut differentiation is not surprising. The MESRI occupational norms are much more helpful; we have seen that they revealed a tendency for technical and skilled workers to make high scores, and for others to make average or low scores, depending upon the intelligence level.

Job satisfaction may be related to having a modicum of the ability required to perform the tasks which constitute the job, but the role of spatial visualization in vocational satisfaction has not been investigated.

Use of the Minnesota Spatial Relations Test in Counseling and Selection. Data reviewed and discussed in the preceding paragraphs make it clear that the Minnesota Spatial Relations Test measures at least three factors, the most important of which is ability to visualize and judge spatial relations. Ability to perceive spatial differences is also tapped by the test, and indeed it is difficult to imagine a test of ability to judge spatial relations which would be entirely independent of ability to perceive spatial differences and similarities. The third factor is reasoning ability, something approaching general intelligence, which plays a part in this test but is less important than the first two factors. Because of the common rate of maturation and because of the fact that abstract reasoning plays a part in the test used to measure spatial judgment, some relationship is found between the spatial relations and intelligence test scores of heterogeneous groups; despite this, the spatial relations test can be thought of as measuring something distinct from intelligence when working with homogeneous groups.

In working with college students this means that one can expect a large percentage of average and moderately high scores, while in less able groups one will encounter more low average and low scores; these must be seen in perspective, the counselor realizing that a moderately high spatial score in a very able person does not mean special aptitude for professional-technical work and that a high average spatial score in a person of low average intelligence may well indicate promise for the skilled trades.

Changes with age were seen to take place up to about age 14, after which it appears that the aptitude is relatively stable. More work needs to be done before this can be considered conclusively demonstrated, but it seems a safe working principle.

Occupationally viewed, the Minnesota Spatial Relations Test measures an aptitude which is found in a higher degree in workers in skilled trades and professions such as automobile repair work, manual training, and ornamental iron. This is true also of workers in semi-skilled occupations in which job analysis suggests that spatial judgment should be important; these have been found to include hand-working operatives in factories, assembly workers, and packers and wrappers. Although one would expect draftsmen to excel on a test such as this, the one study which included such workers found that they were only high average in spatial ability as measured by this test. This seems somewhat anomalous and indicates a need for caution in making assumptions concerning the test; further studies should be made of the relationship between drafting success and scores on this test. Most office and minor executive groups make moderate scores on the test, presumably because they tend to be of moderate intelligence. Semi-skilled and unskilled workers in occupations not requiring spatial visualization tend to score average or below on this test, because of selection and because they tend to have less general intelligence than other workers.

In schools and colleges the Spatial Relations Test is useful for selecting students who are likely to do well in shop courses, although it is of less value for the more abstract types of technical training than for the more concrete.

In Guidance Centers and Employment Service Offices the test can be helpful in cases of clients considering the choice of technical occupations, especially at the semiskilled and skilled levels for which a paper form board is sometimes too abstract. It has value in helping in the choice of trade and technical training, and in determining a client's prospects of making a quick adaptation to the demands of certain semiskilled jobs for which training is offered during the induction period; these latter include especially work such as assembly of vari-formed parts, machine operation, and packing objects of different shapes and sizes.

Business and industrial personnel workers should find the test useful in selection of the type just described above. As an aptitude test it is most useful, obviously, in selecting people for training in skilled occupations; this will happen most often in schools, but also to some extent in industry in connection with apprenticeships. It can have much greater value in industry in the selection of semiskilled employees who can quickly adapt to new jobs, who can readily master procedures of machine operation or assembly, and who, because of the speed and accuracy with which they judge size and shape, will produce more per hour of work and do it with less waste of materials.

The Minnesota Paper Form Board, Likert-Quasha Revision (Psychological Corporation, 1934, 1948). The first form of the Minnesota Paper Form Board, used in the Minnesota Mechanical Ability Project (Paterson et al., 1930), was a completion test based on the Geometrical Construction subtest of Army Beta, the non-verbal intelligence test developed by the U.S. Army during World War I. Since the scoring of completion items is laborious and subjective, requiring that the scorer scrutinize each response and make judgments as to its adequacy, it seemed highly desirable to find some way of converting the Minnesota Paper Form Board into a multiple-choice test. This was done by Likert and Quasha, unfortunately not early enough to be included in the MESRI studies (Quasha and Likert, 1937). However, the early Minnesota studies of the completion test are probably indicative of the nature of the validity of the revised test, and a variety of validation studies have been made with the revision.

Applicability. Army Beta was designed for and standardized upon unselected adults, the completion form of the Paper Form Board was developed for a study using early adolescent subjects, and the multiple-choice revision was designed for use with and standardized upon adolescents and adults. The directions are simple enough for children in the upper grades; the range of difficulty of the items is such that 10-year-old boys make a median score of 22 compared with the adult male median of 31, the 5th percentile in each case being 6 and 16, indicating that individual differences are revealed at both age levels. The items seem to have a reasonable amount of challenge at all age levels, despite their abstract form.

The effects of maturation can be studied in two of the sets of data provided by the 1941 test manual. One of these consists of the age norms for 9, 12 and 15-year-olds in the schools of Kearney, New Jersey, the other of data for grades four and five in the Bronx. In the former instance a 25-minute time limit was used, instead of the usual 20-minute limit. The median scores for the three age levels (boys) were 18, 32, and 38, revealing a more rapid increase in the six years from 9 to 15 (three points per annum) than in the three years from 12 to 15 (two points per annum). This suggests that the growth of this ability begins to level off early in the teens, although it does not indicate the age at which the plateau begins. The grade data confirm the changes in pre-adolescence, but go no further. Lefever and others (1946) found no relationship ($r = -.14$) with age in adults. As in the case of the MacQuarrie, Mitrano (1942) has drawn some conclusions concerning age changes which are based on spurious factors in his data, and are therefore unwarranted. Studies should be made which would throw more light on the question of the age of levelling-off, to make possible the construction of developmental conversion tables such as are needed when the scores of growing individuals are to be compared to those of mature persons established in an occupation. The grade norms in the 1948 manual throw no more light on age differences.

Content. The test consists of 64 items. Each item is made up of a "stem" and five possible choices from which to select an answer. The stems are the disarranged parts, from 2 to 5 in number, of a geometric figure. The responses are assembled geometric figures, only one of which could be made by putting the parts of the stem figure together. The problem is in each case to select the figure which corresponds to the assembled parts, which must sometimes merely be mentally pushed together in order to make an appropriate whole, and sometimes mentally turned around or even over. The items therefore resemble those of the real form board, except that there can be no trial-and-error work with the Paper Form Board; all the matchings of shapes and sizes must be done mentally.

Administration and Scoring. The test is preceded by practice problems, with 20 minutes of working time allowed for the test proper. It is necessary to demonstrate how the booklet opens, and to be sure that the many examinees who prefer to follow their own visual cues rather than the psychometrist's spoken directions do actually observe the demonstration. If this is not done correctly, some booklets will be turned in with a page of easier problems skipped and some more difficult problems attempted, making scoring impossible. Scoring, done by matching marked spaces with a key, is objective and simple. Forms adapted to machine scoring have been published, with special norms.

Norms. Because of piecemeal standardization of the Likert-Quasha revision the norms for the test are rather unsatisfactory. Series AA and BB grade norms for ninth, tenth, and twelfth grades are based on guidance center clients in the first two instances and on students applying for admission to the arts and engineering colleges of New York University in the last, certainly not a typical group of high school seniors since it omits the 80 to 90 percent who do not go to college. The college freshmen were students at New York University; the freshmen engineers were at New York University and Northeastern University, no significant difference having been found between engineers in the two institutions. These norms are of local value, but can be no more than a rough guide to counselors or admissions officers in other communities and institutions.

Series MA and MB norms are considerably better, the ninth grade norms representing three large cities, and the twelfth grade norms, 60 New England schools.

Stephens (1945) administered the Revised Minnesota Paper Form Board to 2936 seniors and 3332 juniors, male and female, in all curricula in New England high schools, publishing norms based on them. As he points out, these are higher than the old national norms, which we have seen to be strictly local. The 1948 manual includes these norms, expanded by additional cases from subsequent samples.

Hanman (1942) tested 785 men in the educational program of the WPA in California, ranging in age from 20 to 65 with a modal age of 40. Their education varied as greatly, from none to the doctorate, with mode at 8 to 9 years. The author concluded from his data that the old so-called national norms were too high (they were then based on 76 cases) , failing, apparently, to take into account the fact that his was a selected, although large, sample, heavily weighted toward the lower end of the scale of education and ability. Such heterogeneous and skewed norms do not have the values and uses of homogeneous and skewed or of heterogeneous and representative norms.

The sample studied by Baldwin and Smith (1944) consisted of 975 women employed by the Eastman Kodak Co. The group was divided into 16 to 25-year-olds and 26 to 60-year-olds, norms for the younger group being somewhat higher than the original norms and those for the older group being somewhat lower. Although this is in no sense a cross-section of adult women, and the norms are not general adult norms, they are useful in that they depict a large occupational population of varying skills. The jobs to which they were assigned included unskilled repetitive jobs such as lens wrapping and highly skilled precision jobs such as final assembly and inspection of optical and mechanical equipment. The 1948 manual includes these and other local but useful industrial norms, each set of which needs to be carefully studied by users.

Standardization and Initial Validation. The completion form of the Minnesota Paper Form Board was one of the best tests in the Minnesota Mechanical Ability Battery; it had a correlation of .63 with its apparatus counterpart, and a validity coefficient of .52 against ratings of quality of shop work. In revising the test and making it more objective the multiple-choice form was used, practice problems were included to insure understanding of the task, stencil scoring was utilized, and three time limits were tried out, the intermediate limit proving to be the best. The test went through two revisions, and was standardized on college students. High-school norms were then added. It yielded a correlation of .40 with the Otis S.A. Test based on college students, and a correlation of .75 with scores on the original completion form. Validity of the test was assumed to be demonstrated by the correlation with the original form and by the validity of that form; it was also ascertained by correlations of .49 with the mechanical drawing grades of engineering students and .32 with grades in descriptive geometry (Quasha and Likert, 1937). In 1948 the revised manual provided more standardized directions and better norms for the machine scored forms, which can also be hand scored.

Reliability. The uncorrected reliability based on the intercorrelation of the two revised forms of the test was found to be .79, while the split-half reliability was, corrected, .92 (Quasha and Likert, 1937). This latter figure is made spuriously high, however, by the speeded nature of the test. The retest reliability after periods of one or more years had elapsed was ascertained by Ebert and Simmons (1943) with children aged 10 to 14, the age groups varying in number from 73 to 210. For 10-year-old children retested at age 11 the reliability coefficient was .87, at age 12, .86; for 12-year-olds tested again at ages 13 and 14 the reliabilities were .87 and .80. It can safely be assumed, then, that the reliability is actually in the .80s and sufficiently high for individual diagnosis.

Validity. A criticism of time-limit tests such as this which is occasionally made by examinees or observers is that the imposition of a time limit makes the test a measure of speed and prevents it from measuring adequately the trait which it is designed to measure. We have already seen that Baxter demonstrated the independence of speed (the time required to attempt every item once) and level (the number of items correctly answered in unlimited time), in the Otis intelligence test. Tinker (1944) studied the roles of speed and level in the revised Minnesota Paper Form Board, confirming the finding that they vary independently. Scores obtained in a standard time limit were found to consist primarily of speed, with level of difficulty at which the subject could work playing a lesser part. Apparently tests would generally be improved if they were administered as level tests, making possible the more nearly pure measurement of the trait being assessed, but the mixed speed and level scores now obtained for most tests are useful despite their impurity.

Intelligence having been measured by tests which included spatial judgment items, one of the first steps in validating the Minnesota Paper Form Board has been to correlate its scores with scores on tests of general mental ability. Sartain used two groups, one consisting of 46 inspectors in an aircraft factory (1945) and the other 40 foremen also employed in an aircraft factory (1946). Both groups took the revised Paper Form Board and the Otis S.A. Test, the correlations being .62 and .39; the reasons for the great difference are not clear, although the foremen may be a more homogeneous group. Super's intercorrelation of tests administered to 100 NYA youth yielded a relationship of .43 for the same two tests, which agrees not only with Sartain's foreman data but also with the relationship reported by Quasha and Likert (1937). The NYA group was rather heterogeneous.

The American Council on Education Psychological Examination was correlated with Paper Form Board scores in a study by Traxler (1943), with 230 Merchant Marine Cadets as subjects. The correlation of total scores was .42; for the linguistic scores it was .34 and for the quantitative it was .41. Bryan (1942) tested art-school freshmen, correlating A.C.E. part scores and Paper Form Board scores; for the spatial subtest of the A.C.E. the correlation was .55. Army Alpha has been found (Morgan, 1944) to have intercorrelations with the Revised Minnesota Paper Form Board which ranged from .35 and .31 at ages 14 and 15 ($N = 159$ and 109) but fell, unaccountably, at ages 13 and 16 to only .11 and .17 ($N = 86$ and 35). When the Revised Paper Form Board was correlated with the parent test (Geometrical Construction) of Army Beta (1936) the coefficient was found to be .57, considerably lower than that of .75 between the original and re-vised forms of the Minnesota Paper Form Board referred to earlier. The subjects were ninth grade boys in the Army Beta study, but college students in that of the two forms, which suggests that the larger correlation may have been obtained with the more homogeneous group. If this is so, then the revised test is more like the original Minnesota test than like the part of Army Beta from which they both originated.

Manual dexterity is not an aptitude which one would expect to find playing a part in a spatial test as abstract as this is, but two studies have provided evidence concerning the degree of relationship. Thompson (1942) found no relationship between either the Finger or the Tweezer Dexterity Test and the Revised Paper Form Board (—.08 and —.15); Super obtained a correlation of .23 with the Minnesota Manual Dexterity (Placing) Test. The true relationship is presumably about zero.

Mechanical comprehension has been seen in Chapter 10 to include spatial visualization among its components. For this reason there is little to be gained here by repeating the data concerning the relationship as shown in various studies reviewed there and cited in the manual. It should suffice to summarize by stating that the correlation with the O'Rourke is generally found to be about .40, with the Bennett about .35, with the Minnesota Mechanical Assembly Test about .48 (one study only), and with the Mac-Quarrie about .35. This means that a test of so-called mechanical aptitude may contribute materially to the prediction of success even when a good measure of spatial relations is used, for the score on the latter only partly accounts for the score on the former.

Spatial Visualization as measured by apparatus tests such as the Minnesota Spatial Relations Test, the Crawford Spatial Relations Test, and the Wiggly Block should be correlated with the same ability as measured by the Paper Form Board, in order that the instruments and the trait may be better understood. Super found the correlation for the Minnesota test to be .59, his subjects being 100 NYA youths, but Morrow (1938) reports it as .33, with 80 subjects. Jacobsen (1943) found that for the Crawford to be .20, based on data from 90 mechanic learners. Estes (1942) reported that for the Crawford as .26 and that for the Wiggly Block as .31, with data obtained from 76 engineering freshmen. Jacobsen's study, it will be remembered, reported a number of deviant results; disregarding it, there-fore, we find only a moderate agreement among these rather different-appearing tests of spatial relations. The fact that the Paper Form Board is more heavily saturated with general intelligence or inductive reasoning than the apparatus test explains at least a part of the failure to agree more closely. It is also possible that there are differences between two- and three-dimensional spatial judgment, as the Crawford and Wiggly Block attempt to measure it; and it is true that when a test is as unreliable as the Wiggly

Block it cannot often yield significant correlations with anything.

Interest in mechanical and scientific activities as measured by Kuder's Preference Record was correlated with Paper Form Board Scores by Sartain (1946), who found it to be negligible ($r = .13$ and $.19$). As the group consisted of foremen in an aircraft plant, who might be assumed to be homogeneous as to mechanical and scientific interests (high on the former but low on the latter), this probably does not tell us much concerning the relationship between technical aptitude and interest.

Three factor analysis studies involving the Revised Minnesota Paper Form Board threw further light on the subject of the traits measured by this test. Morris (1939) analyzed the intercorrelations of scores made by 56 9-year-olds to whom the Pintner-Paterson Scale of Performance Tests, the Porteus mazes, and Henmon-Nelson intelligence test, and others were administered, together with the Paper Form Board. He found three group factors, which he called spatial relations, perceptual ability, and ability to discover patterns or a rule of procedure (induction). These resemble those found in the studies of the Minnesota Spatial Relations Test. Murphy (1936) used the Paper Form Board together with the Terman Group Test of Mental Ability, the Revised Army Beta, the Detroit Mechanical Aptitude Test, the MacQuarrie, and others, testing 143 ninth grade boys. Three factors emerged from this analysis: mental manipulation of relations expressed symbolically (presumably induction), speed of hand and eye co-ordination (in the MacQuarrie particularly), and mental manipulation of spatial relations (in the Paper Form Board, parts of the MacQuarrie and Detroit, and part of Army Beta). Estes (1942) gave the Paper Form Board, Crawford Spatial Relations, Wiggly Block, and A.C.E. Psychological Examination (L and Q scores) to 76 engineering freshmen. A factor analysis revealed one common factor, but this may be due at least partly to the small number of tests. The implication, if correct, is that two- and three-dimensional tests of spatial judgment measure the same spatial factor, although imperfectly because of the different media. Until further evidence is available, it seems legitimate to conclude that the Revised Minnesota Paper Form Board measures spatial relations, perceptual ability, and inductive reasoning, in that order, and that although it measures spatial judgment by means of two-dimensional media this ability is the same as that measured by three-dimensional means.

Grades and ratings of promise in training have been used as criteria in a dozen studies with this test. Stanton (1938) administered the original form to deaf boys and girls and obtained a correlation of .50 between scores and ratings of shop performance. Jacobsen (1943) used it with between 80 and 90 mechanic learners in a war industry, found that it correlated between .18 and .22 with fitness ratings, but the probable errors were so large as to make the relationships insignificant. Ross (1943) administered the Paper Form Board to 41 machine-tool trainees, but published no correlations. Apprentice pressmen were studied by Hall (1930), with ratings of skill as a criterion; the correlation was .58. An attempt was made to differentiate between "good" and "poor" classes in an industrial and technical high school by means of the Paper Form Board, but Morgan (1944) reported failure to discriminate; his subjects were 319 eighth grade boys applying for admission to a technical high school. Littleton (1952) used the test with students of auto mechanics and body work, N being 105 and 85, finding correlations of .35 and .42 with instructors' ratings. In a similar study of tool and die makers' and machinists' apprentices, N being 47, correlations of .34 to .49 were obtained with grades, .48 with overall ratings.

Several studies have used engineering students as subjects. Berdie (1944) obtained a low but significant correlation (.33) between test scores and honor-point ratios of 154 engineering students. At the University of Maine, Brush (1941) studied a group of more than 100 students, obtained correlations of .42 and .175 with first-year and .43 and .21 with four-year grades. Physics grades at the University of Iowa were found to have a correlation of .26 by Stuit and Lapp (1941). Coleman (1953) found correlations of .22 to .30, all significant at the .05 level or better, with freshmen grades. But Schmitz and Holmes (1954), with 275 subjects, found no relationship between the MPFB and freshmen engineering average, although the Bennett and ACE did predict ($r = .36$ to .45). It can be concluded that the Revised Minnesota Paper Form Board does in some institutions have some value in selecting students for or guiding them in the consideration of engineering training; Brush found it one of the best aptitude, as contrasted with achievement, tests in his extensive battery, and it found a place in some of his best regression equations, as have others, but Schmitz and Holmes found it valueless.

Dental students were tested by Thompson (1942), correlations with combined grades and ratings of 35 freshmen and 40 seniors being respectively .24 and .61; the difference is surprising, even when allowance is made for the fact that more professional work is included in the senior than in the freshmen year.

Art students have been studied with the Revised Minnesota Paper Form Board, on the assumption that spatial judgment is important in layout and related work. Barrett (1945) found that 40 art majors at Hunter College were significantly superior to 40 control students in spatial judgment, although the actual difference in scores was small. Thompson (1942) obtained a correlation of only .18 between the test scores and point-hour ratio for 50 fine-art students. Bryan (1942) used art grades as a criterion, reporting a validity of .19.

Success on the job has been studied more frequently with this test than with its apparatus counterpart, thanks to its group procedure. Aircraft factory workers were studied by Sartain and Shuman in studies already described. The former (1945, 1946) tested 46 inspectors and 40 foremen, the latter (1945a, 1945b) 263 engine and propeller workers, both skilled and semi-skilled, and 297 supervisors of several grades; ratings were the criterion in all instances. Validity for Sartain's inspectors was .47, for his foremen only .10 (as high as any in this study). For Shuman's workers it ranged from .16 to .59, depending upon the job: moderately high correlations (.38 or above) were found for inspectors, machine operators, foremen, job setters, and toolmaker apprentices; the only low coefficient was for engine testers, for whom the Bennett Mechanical Comprehension Test had equally low validity, and for whom the critical scores on both tests were low, which suggests that the job may have been more clerical than mechanical. In Shuman's other study the validity of the Paper Form Board for supervisors was found to be .33. The test would have improved selection by approximately 15 percent in each of Shuman's studies.

Inspector-packers in a pharmaceutical concern were subjects of a study by Ghiselli (1942), already described. Ratings served as a criterion of the success of the 26 girls, for whom the Paper Form Board had a validity of .57. Stead and Shartle (1940) report a correlation of only —.01 between scores on this test and ratings of 41 inspector-wrappers, but as they do not describe the job it is impossible to determine whether or not this finding is in conflict with Ghiselli's. For can packers and merchandise packers they found validities of .28 and .48, for two groups of power-sewing-machine operators .31 and .48, and for put-in-coil girls the astonishing figure of —.52. This last group made the highest mean score of any tested by the USES research program as reported by Stead and Shartle. Perhaps they were an able group who, bored by their routine jobs, actually tended to produce less than the less able girls. The criteria in the jobs mentioned were based on output, and the numbers of subjects ranged from 18 to 46. For lamp-shade sewers and pull-socket assemblers, also tested in this investigation, the validities approached zero.

Policemen ($N = 129$) were tested by DuBois and Watson (1954), using police academy grades, achievement test scores, marksmanship, and service ratings on probation as criteria: the validities were respectively .38 and .29, .30, .26, and .04.

Speer (1957) tested 69 inland waterway pilots, with pooled ratings by at least three judges as his criterion; the MPFB had zero validity.

Occupational differences in spatial visualization as measured by the Revised Minnesota Paper Form Board are suggested by Barrett's study of Hunter College art majors (1945) which showed slight but significant differences between these students and control students in other fields, and by that of Stead and Shartle (1940), which found that put-in-coil girls and lamp-shade sewers were high average when compared to clients of the Adult Guidance Bureau of New York, and that the other workers listed in the preceding paragraph clustered around the 35th percentile. The norms in the manual indicate, rather more helpfully, that engineering freshmen, at least in New York University, tend to score about five points higher than liberal arts freshmen, and that upper classmen in engineering curricula score about three points higher than freshmen. Barrett's art majors made an average score equal to that of the engineering upper classmen (raw score = 47), her controls an average equal to that of the engineering freshmen (raw score = 43) rather than the liberal arts freshmen, but the Hunter students were all upper classmen. More comprehensive and varied occupational norms are badly needed for this test.

That occupational level attained is somewhat related to MPFB scores was shown by Cantoni (1955), who followed up 97 boys tested in ninth and twelfth grades 10 years after graduation from high school. The correlation, significant at the .05 level, was only .21, which might disappear if intelligence were partialled out.

Satisfaction in a professional curriculum, if not in the occupation itself, has been studied with the Minnesota Paper Form Board. Berdie (1944) gave the revised form to 154 engineering students and obtained curriculum satisfaction data by means of a modification of Hoppock's Job Satisfaction Questionnaire. The correlation between spatial visualization and curricular satisfaction was only .06. The study can probably not be considered definitive, because a curriculum is something abstract and, unfortunately, often somewhat unreal to the student, whereas a job is usually something rather tangible. Engineering students in particular are likely to be critical of the academic, despite ability and interest in technical matters. A study of vocational or job satisfaction might therefore yield different results.

Use of the Revised Minnesota Paper Form Board in Counseling and Selection. Although the Minnesota Paper Form Board is found to have a moderately high correlation with tests of general intelligence, more refined analyses have demonstrated that it is primarily a test of spatial relations, a special aptitude or distinct factor, and that the test is also somewhat saturated with quantitative perception and inductive factors. It is the presence of this last, combined with the fact that some intelligence tests include spatial items, which makes the test correlate significantly with general intelligence tests. A spatial relations test may therefore make a distinct contribution to some test batteries.

Maturation of ability to judge spatial relations seems to come in the early teens, with little if any increase after age 15 or 16. This suggests that adult occupational norms should be usable with high school juniors and seniors, and perhaps even with sophomores.

Occupations for which the test has been found to have significance include professions such as engineering, art, and dentistry; skilled trades such as toolmaking, job setting and aircraft engine inspection; and semiskilled jobs such as inspection and packing of merchandise, cans, and other objects, power-sewing-machine operation, and electrical assembly. Supervisors and foremen of both skilled and semiskilled workers also tend to make superior scores on this test.

In schools and colleges the test should be found useful for counseling concerning the choice of trade courses, engineering curricula, dental training, and the professional study of art. Presence of the trait in a high degree cannot be considered a good prognosticator of success, because of the importance of other aptitudes and traits, but its relative absence in an individual can be considered a danger signal. Despite the importance of spatial visualization in tests of so-called mechanical comprehension, the correlation between these two types of tests is low enough to prevent the use of both from being a duplication.

In guidance and employment centers the use of the test can be comparable to that in educational institutions when choice of training is involved. It can be of value also in selecting individuals who are likely to adapt quickly to the demands of assembly work and machine operations in new jobs in which they might be placed.

In industrial personnel work the Minnesota Paper Form Board can be valuable in the selection of adaptable workers for semiskilled and skilled employment, for the evaluation of workers on the job whose skills may be most readily utilized in new assembly or machine operations, and also in the selection of apprentices for training in the skilled trades. In any such selection or evaluation program other indices should also be obtained, and here too a good mechanical comprehension test, an intelligence test, oral trade tests, and evidence concerning leisure-time activities which throw light on aptitudes and interests may be important data.

REFERENCES FOR CHAPTER XI

Andrew, Dorothy M. "An analysis of the Minnesota Vocational Test for Clerical Workers. I, II," *J. Appl. Psychol.,* 21 (1937), 18-47, 139-172.
Baldwin, E. F., and Smith, L. F. "Performance of adult female applicants for factory work on the Revised Minnesota Paper Form Board Test," *J. Appl. Psychol.,* 28 (1944), 468-470.
Barrett, Dorothy W. "Aptitude and interest patterns of art majors in a liberal arts college," *J. Appl. Psychol.,* 29 (1945), 483-492.
Berdie, R. F. "Prediction of college achievement and satisfaction," *J. Appl. Psychol.,* 28 (1944), 239-245.

Brush, E. N. "Mechanical ability as a factor in engineering aptitude," *J. Appl. Psychol.*, 25 (1941), 300-312.

Bryan, A. I. "Grades, intelligence, and personality of art school freshmen," *J. Educ. Psychol.*, 33 (1942), 50-64.

Cantoni, L. J. "High school tests and measurements as predictors of occupational status," *J. Appl. Psychol.*, 39 (1955), 253-255.

Coleman, W. "An economical test battery for predicting freshman engineering course grades," *J. Appl. Psychol.*, 37 (1953), 465-467.

Darley, J. G. "Reliability of tests in the standard battery." (In "Research Studies in Individual Diagnosis.") *University of Minnesota Bull. Employ. Stab. Res. Inst.*, 4 (1934).

DuBois, P. H., and Watson, R. I. "Validity information exchange: policeman," *Pers. Psychol.*, 7 (1954), 414-417.

Ebert, E., and Simmons, K. "The Brush Foundation study of child growth and development. I. Psychometric tests," *Monog. Soc. Res. Child Development,* 2 (1943).

Estes, S. G. "A study of five tests of 'spatial' ability," *J. Psychol.*, 13 (1942), 265-271.

Ghiselli, E. E. "Tests for the selection of inspector-packers," *J. Appl. Psychol.*, 26 (1942), 468-476.

Goodman, C. H. "Prediction of college success by means of Thurstone's Primary Mental Abilities Test," *Educ. Psychol. Measmt.*, 4 (1944), 125-140.

Green, H. J., Berman, I. R., Paterson, D. G., and Trabue, M. R. "A manual of selected occupational tests for use in public employment offices," *University of Minnesota Bull. Employ. Stab. Res. Inst.*, 3 (1933).

Hall, O. M. "An aid to the selection of pressman apprentices," *Pers. J.*, 8 (1930), 77-81.

Hanman, B. "Performance of adult males on the Minnesota Paper Form Board Test and the O'Rourke Mechanical Aptitude Test," *J. Appl. Psychol.*, 26 (1942), 809-811.

Harrell, T. W. "A factor analysis of mechanical ability tests," *Psychometrika,* 5 (1940), 17-33.

Jacobsen, E. E. "An evaluation of certain tests in predicting mechanic learner achievement," *Educ. Psychol. Measmt.*, 3 (1943), 259-267.

Keane, F. H., and O'Connor, J. "A measure of mechanical aptitude," *Pers. J.*, 6 (1927), 15-24.

Lefever, D. W., et al. "Relation of test scores to age and education for adult workers," *Educ. Psychol. Measmt.*, 6 (1946), 351-360.

Littleton, I. T. "Prediction in auto trade courses," *J. Appl. Psychol.*, 36 (1952), 15-19.

Mellenbruch, P. L. "Preliminary report on the Miami-Oxford Curve-Block Series," *J. Appl. Psychol.*, 30 (1946), 129-134.

Michael, W. B., Guilford, J. P., Fruchter, B., and Zimmerman, W. S. "The description of spatial visualization abilities," *Educ. Psychol. Measmt.*, 17 (1957), 185-199.

Mitrano, A. J. "Relationship between age and test performance of applicants to a technical-industrial high school," *J. Appl. Psychol.*, 26 (1942), 482-486.

Morgan, W. J. "Some remarks and results of aptitude testing in technical and industrial schools," *J. Soc. Psychol.*, 20 (1944), 19-79.

——— "Scores on the Revised Minnesota Paper Form Board Test at the different grade levels of a technical-industrial high school," *J. Genet. Psychol.*, 64 (1944), 159-162.

Morris, C. M. "A critical analysis of certain performance tests," *J. Genet. Psychol.*, 54 (1939), 85-105.

Morrow, R. S. "An analysis of the relations among tests of musical, artistic, and mechanical abilities," *J. Psychol.*, 5 (1938), 253-263.

Murphy, L. W. "The relation between mechanical ability tests and verbal and non-verbal intelligence tests," *J. Psychol.*, 2 (1936), 353-366.

Paterson, D. G., et al. *The Minnesota Mechanical Abilities Tests.* Minneapolis: University of Minnesota Press, 1930.

Quasha, W. H., and Likert, R. "Revised Minnesota Paper Form Board," *J. Educ. Psychol.*, 28 (1937), 197-204.

Remmers, H. H., and Scholl, J. W. "Testing the O'Connor Wiggly Block Test," *Pers. J.*, 12 (1933), 155-159.

Ross, L. W. "Results of testing machine-tool trainees," *Pers. J.*, 21 (1943), 363-367.

Sartain, A. Q. "The use of certain standardized tests in the selection of inspectors in an aircraft factory," *J. Consult. Psychol.*, 9 (1945), 234-235.

———— "Relation between scores on certain standardized tests and supervisory success in an aircraft factory," *J. Appl. Psychol.*, 30 (1946), 328-332.

Schmitz, R. M., and Holmes, J. L. "Relationship of certain measured abilities to freshman engineering achievement." In Layton, W. L. (ed.). *Selection and Counseling of Engineering Students.* Minneapolis: University of Minnesota Press, 1954.

Shuman, J. T. "Value of aptitude tests for factory workers in the aircraft engine and propeller industries," *J. Appl. Psychol.*, 29 (1945a), 156-160.

———— "The value of aptitude tests for supervisory workers in the aircraft engine and propeller industries," *J. Appl. Psychol.*, 29 (1945b), 185-190.

Slater, P. "Some group tests of spatial judgment or practical ability," *Occ. Psychol.*, 14 (1940), 39-55.

Speer, G. S. "Validity information exchange: ship pilot," *Pers. Psychol.*, 10 (1957), 201.

Staff, Division of Occupational Analysis, WMC. "Factor analysis of occupational aptitude tests," *Educ. Psychol. Measmt.*, 5 (1945), 147-155.

Stanton, M. B. "Mechanical ability of deaf children." *Teachers College Contributions to Education*, 751 (1938).

Stead, W. H., and Shartle, C. L. *Occupational Counseling Techniques.* New York: American Book Co., 1940.

Steel, Marion, Balinsky, B., and Long, H. "A study on the use of a worksample," *J. Appl. Psychol.*, 29 (1945), 14-21.

Stephens, E. W. "A comparison of New England norms with national norms on the Revised Minnesota Paper Form Board," *Occupations*, 24 (1945), 101-104.

Stuit, D. B., and Lapp, C. J. "Some factors in physics achievement at the college level," *J. Exp. Educ.*, (1941), 251-253.

Teegarden, L. "Occupational differences in manipulative performance of applicants at a public employment office," *J. Appl. Psychol.*, 27 (1943), 416-437.

Thompson, C. E. "Motor and mechanical abilities in professional schools," *J. Appl. Psychol.*, 26 (1942), 24-37.

Thurstone, L. L. "Primary mental abilities," *Psychometrika Monog.*, 1 (1938).

Tinker, M. A. "Speed, power, and level in the Revised Minnesota Paper Form Board Test," *J. Genet. Psychol.*, 64 (1944), 93-97.

Traxler, A. E. "Correlation between 'mechanical aptitude scores' and 'mechanical comprehension scores'," *Occupations*, 22 (1943), 42-43.

Tredick, V. D. "The Thurstone Primary Mental Abilities Test and a Battery of Vocational Guidance Tests as Predictors of Academic Success." Unpublished thesis, Pennsylvania State College, 1941.

Wittenborn, J. R. "Mechanical ability, its nature and measurement. I, II. Manual dexterity," *Educ. Psychol. Measmt.*, 5 (1945), 241-260, 395-409.

XII

AESTHETIC JUDGMENT AND ARTISTIC ABILITY

OVER a substantial part of the past thirty years artistic ability has been studied most thoroughly by N. C. Meier and his students at the State University of Iowa. The analytic procedures used by these investigators in the study of artistic ability were partly biographical and partly mensural and hence should not be confused with the more objective procedures of factor analysis. Nevertheless, in the absence of analyses utilizing completely objective methods Meier's long-standing conclusions after years of research provide the best available insights into the nature of artistic ability. It is odd that no substantial recent work exists with which to verify or supplement them.

According to Meier (1926) artistic ability can be broken down into six factors. Some of these, such as aesthetic intelligence, most likely are complexes which can or will be subdivided into underlying unitary traits of the Thurstone variety; others, like aesthetic judgment, probably are basic and unitary and consequently are not capable of further refinement. *Aesthetic intelligence,* one of the more complex factors, is defined operationally by a combination of scores on the spatial and perceptual aptitude subtests of the Thurstone battery. In contrast, *aesthetic judgment,* considered to be the most important single factor in artistic ability, is defined as the ability to recognize unity of composition and is believed by Meier to be not the application of a series of rules, but rather something which is innate in the neuro-physical constitution yet modifiable by experience. *Creative imagination,* which has not been satisfactorily established with research evidence [with the possible exception of the aesthetic product itself and the uniqueness of ink blot interpretations (Dreps, 1933) that may actually indicate personality deviation], is defined as the ability to organize vivid sense impressions into an aesthetic product. *Perceptual facility,* which is difficult to distinguish clearly from aesthetic intelligence, is the ability to observe and recall sensory experiences and was identified through biographical material on artists and a test of recall of observed material after intervals of 10 days and 6 months (Dreps, 1933). Similarly, the last two factors, *manual skill* and *energy output and perseverance,* which are defined in their usual ways, were evidenced in studies of the family histories and biographies of artists.

As in any occupation, success in art may be due to various combinations of the abilities and traits just described. The artists whose lives Meier has studied are believed to have excelled in some of the abilities listed, although not necessarily in all. Meier developed his Art Judgment Test first, because of his conviction of the primary importance of this aptitude; his plans for subsequent work, financed by the Spelman and Carnegie Foundations, called for the development of tests for the two other abilities in his list which are not presently mensurable, namely, perceptual facility and creative imagination. The writers are unaware of any practical tests, however, resulting from this work. Of the three other traits, the manual and intellectual factors are currently well measured by existing tests, already described in other chapters, while the emotional characteristics, as we shall see, have so far not lent themselves to satisfactory measurement.

In appraising artistic promise it would therefore seem well to use: a) tests of intellectual ability, particularly those tapping spatial factors, since Tiebout and Meier (1936) found that 50 outstanding artists selected from 5,500 listed in the Biography of American Artists had an average Otis I.Q. of 118, with their successes predominantly in the verbal and spatial items; b) tests of manual dexterity, although, as we have seen in that chapter, there is little in the way of normative material to assist one in test interpretation (presumably an average score or better would be desired); and c) tests of aesthetic judgment, discussed in detail in this chapter. Other data must be gathered by means of techniques other than tests. These might include the expert appraisal of the counselee's sketches, paintings, or other art products; the summarization of experience in artistic avocations and activities; and the evaluation of motivation to persevere in art as shown in discussions of artistic activities and aspirations.

Aesthetic Judgment

Aesthetic judgment emerges as the one trait in Meier's list of six which may be considered a candidate for discussion as a mensurable special aptitude not dealt with in this book under some other heading. It is for this reason that it is singled out for treatment toward the end of our list of special aptitudes, and before batteries of aptitude tests and measures of interest and personality are taken up.

There are two well-known tests of aesthetic judgment: the *Meier Art*

Judgment Test (a revision of the Meier-Seashore Art Judgment Test) and the *McAdory Art Test,* the original editions of which were both published in 1929. The graphic material used by Meier was more or less timeless, for it included masterpieces of art which appear to be able to withstand temporary shifts of fashions and schools; the subject-matter used by McAdory was more transitory, for it included textiles, clothing, furniture, and architecture which were in vogue in the late 1920's but which no longer seem to represent the best in composition. McAdory has done virtually no further work with her test, whereas Meier maintained his interest and production of research over a long period. The McAdory is for the present of purely historic interest; and since a summary of work with it can be found in Kinter (1933), it will not be reviewed here. Other similar tests are too new to have been studied. Therefore, as the only art judgment test of practical significance for the psychometrist or counselor, the Meier alone will be dealt with in this book. In addition, two tests of so-called creative artistic ability, both of which are essentially worksamples, are briefly treated in this chapter for lack of a more appropriate place.

The Meier Art Judgment Test (Bureau of Educational Research and Service, 1940 Revision). The first edition of this test, published in 1929, was known as the Meier-Seashore Art Judgment Test. It was revised and published as the Meier Art Judgment Test in 1940. During the intervening years Meier and his students at the State University of Iowa conducted a number of important studies in the nature of aptitude for artistic work, summarized in the 1941 Yearbook of the National Society for the Study of Education (1941), in a brief monograph chapter (Saetveit et al., 1940), and in Meier's broader treatise on *Art in Human Affairs* (1942). Meier's perseverance in the study of artistic ability gave his institution a leading place in this field.

Applicability. The revised form of the Meier Art Judgment Test, like its predecessor, was standardized on junior and senior high school students and on college students. As Greene (1941) points out, however, the grade norms for the Meier-Seashore Test show nearly chance success at the eighth grade level, and he refers to other studies which demonstrate that not only are the choices of pictures by 10-year-olds similar to those of average adults but by the age of 7 there is considerable agreement between the preferences of young and old. Since the studies with the unrevised test were based upon different materials, it is not possible to draw precise conclusions from a comparison; however, it seems probable that the judgments required by the revised test are more refined than those involved in the other studies, and that this more refined type of aesthetic judgment matures later. The median score for junior high school students on the revised form is 88, whereas that for senior high school students is 99. This difference is presumably due in part to selection, but, as the test has a very low correlation with intelligence, it may be concluded that it is due primarily to developmental differences. Meier seems to attribute this increase in median score with age largely to experience in his book (1942, p. 131) but not in the test manual (pp. 15–16). Apparently aesthetic judgment is still developing during the middle teens, making age norms necessary. As in the case of so many other tests, tables making possible the conversion of age-group percentiles into occupational percentiles would be highly desirable. It is noteworthy that training in art has been found to have little effect on scores (Carroll, 1932).

Content. The Meier Art Judgment Test, 1940 revision, consists of 100 pairs of pictures, printed in booklets with one pair per page on one side of the sheet only. The pictures are largely paintings, sketches, etc., which are generally recognized as works of permanent merit; others are vases and other *objets d'art;* all were included because of agreement concerning their merit by a group of established artists and because of high biserial *r*'s with total scores. In each pair, one member is the unaltered reproduction of the original work, whereas the other member is a slightly modified version. The modifications are designed to make the composition, form, etc., less pleasing to the eye; the nature of the difference is pointed out to the examinee. His task is to decide which picture he prefers in each pair, with no knowledge of which is the original picture (the paintings are not so well known that subjects are likely to recognize the original).

Administration and Scoring. The Meier test can be administered either individually or in groups, but, as there is no time limit and there is great variation in the amount of time required to complete it, it is not a convenient test for group administration at any time other than the end of a test battery. It is usually completed in less than one hour. Scoring is by means of a stencil and is simple and objective.

Norms. The 1942 manual for the revised test provides norms for 1445 junior high school, 892 senior high school, and 982 college art school students. The students were "interested in art" "for the most part," thus making the norms representative of neither general population nor art students, except at the college level. The 25 schools represented were scattered throughout the whole United States.

Standardization and Initial Validation. In the initial standardization work for the earlier form of the test nearly 600 pairs of items were tried out on over 2000 pupils in various types of schools and colleges. The 125 which were then retained were those which had the most discriminating values and those which were most favored by a group of experts. The current revision includes 100 items selected in a similar way during the eleven years intervening between the two forms of the test.

Reliability. The earlier form of the test had retest reliabilities which ranged from .61 to .65 for non-art students, and from .69 to .85 for art students (Meier, 1926; Leighton cited by Kinter, 1933; Carroll and Eurich, 1932) . These are lower than is desirable in a test used in individual diagnosis, making caution necessary in its use. The reliability of the 1940 revision ranges from .70 to .84, the two lowest coefficients being based on students of Pratt Institute and a junior high school and the two highest on students in an art school and a senior high school (grades not specified) . It is to be regretted that they were not increased for more accurate diagnosis, but as Meier points out the test is really only a screening device, which makes the reliability adequate.

Validity. All but a few of the published studies of the Meier Art Judgment Tests are based on the older edition. Because of the similarity of the two revisions they are briefly discussed here, together with the little new material available.

Items in the early form were analyzed by Brigham and Findley, reported by Kinter (1933) , who calculated the biserial coefficient of correlation between items and total score; the correlations ranged from —.02 to .53. Perhaps this partly explains the relative unreliability of the first edition of the test, which clearly contained dead wood. The revision used Brigham and Findley's data (Meier and Seashore, 1929) to select the 100 best items, thereby correcting this defect. When old records were rescored with the new key, greater differentiation was found. The method of selecting the items may therefore be considered evidence of validity, for the answers scored "right" are those which are chosen by high scorers on the test as a whole, and they are those which are chosen by established artists. That no established artists made low scores, and that some untrained persons made high scores, was taken by Meier as an indication that the test measured an aptitude rather than the effects of specific training (Meier and Seashore, 1929), although he has since modified his point of view to allow a somewhat more important role for experience (Meier, 1942) .

Intelligence test scores, correlated with scores made on the original form by art students (Carroll and Eurich, 1932) and by college students (Farnsworth and Misumi, 1931) , were only slightly if at all related to aesthetic judgment. These findings agree substantially with those of Meier, who found correlations with intelligence test scores (Terman Group, Stanford Binet, Thorndike) which ranged from —.14 to .28. Comparable data for the new form have not been published, but it seems reasonable to conclude that the test is not a measure of general intelligence. Indirectly, then, these findings support the validity of the test as a measure of artistic ability by reducing the probability that it is a measure of verbal ability.

Spatial visualization test scores might logically be expected to be related to art judgment scores, since the aesthetic judgments involve the arrangement of objects in space. Brigham and Findley (in Kinter, 1933) found a correlation of .37 with the College Entrance Examination Board spatial test, showing that the two aptitudes do have something in common. Unfortunately, no other intercorrelations of such tests have been located, although the data for their computation have been available (Barrett, 1945). A factor analysis of a battery of tests of these two types, plus others of art information, perceptual ability, etc., might throw considerable light on the nature of art judgment.

Artistic judgment as measured by the McAdory test correlated only .37 (Wallis, 1930) and .27 (Carroll, 1933) with the Meier-Seashore Test, a difficult finding to explain. The Lewerenz Test of Fundamental Abilities in Visual Art is related only to the extent of .53, but this is not surprising in an *ability* test; it is, in fact, rather gratifying as an index of validity.

Art grades were related to scores and the first edition by Brigham and Findley, who found the surprisingly high validity of .46 for a group of 50 students at Cooper Union but concluded, according to Kinter (1943, p. 61), that the test did not have sufficient discriminating value—perhaps because of the inclusion of poor items. One study (Barrett, 1949) with the revised form yielded a correlation of .35 with an art ability criterion based upon the classroom work of ninth grade students and an *r* of .37 with general grade average.

Ratings of creative artistic ability have been somewhat more extensively used as a criterion of the validity of the Art Judgment Test. Carroll (1933) found a correlation of .40 between these two variables; Morrow (1938) found a validity of .48, and cited one by Jones of .69. Apparently the test has considerable value in selecting the students who manifest promise in their art courses.

The differentiation of occupational groups by means of the Art Judgment Test has been demonstrated, primarily with students, but to a lesser extent with artists and art teachers. The manual for the first edition shows that art teachers made higher scores than art students or students in general, but no critical ratios were computed. Eurich and Carroll (1931) found that art majors ranked 8.14 points higher than other college students on the old form, which seems especially important in view of their finding that training had no effect on scores; the difference was statistically significant and the groups were large. Barrett (1945) confirmed this finding with the revised test: art majors at Hunter College scored six points higher than non-majors on the average, a difference which was significant at the one per cent level. More helpful than any of these data would be correlations between pre-training scores and success in art work, but no such data are available. There are data, however, on sex and racial differences with the new form. Protho and Perry (1950) found, in contrast to Eurich and Carroll, that male and female non-art college students did not differ on the Meier, but that whites did better than Negroes, evidently because of marked differences in background, a fact which would support Meier's more recent contention that artistic judgment may be affected by the individual's experiences.

Vocational satisfaction has not, apparently, been related to art judgment in any studies.

Use of the Meier Art Judgment Test in Counseling and Selection. The evidence concerning the Meier Art Judgment Test indicates that it measures an ability which varies from person to person, is found in a higher degree among artists than among non-artists, is possessed by some untrained persons in a very high degree, is distinct from intelligence and only moderately related to spatial visualization, is not much influenced by training in late adolescence, and is related to success in art training. This ability therefore seems to be an aptitude in the narrower sense of the term.

Development of aesthetic judgment appears to continue well into adolescence, making age norms desirable. Just when development begins to level off, however, is not clear. Since the ability is a relatively complex one, it may be safe to assume that maturity is reached in the late teens or early twenties. But further work is needed to clarify the developmental characteristics of artistic aptitude.

Occupations in which aesthetic judgment may be important have unfortunately not been extensively investigated. That artists excel in it has been demonstrated, but the writers know of no data which show the role which it plays in other fields.

In schools and colleges the Art Judgment Test should be useful as a means of locating students who may have special talent and deserve special opportunities for artistic training, special attention in art courses, and encouragement to capitalize on extra-curricular opportunities for the development of their talent, whether for vocational or for avocational purposes. It can also be useful as a selection instrument in art schools, although at this stage, as in counseling to a lesser extent, the evaluation of artistic production often yields more helpful information. In judging a client's or applicant's art work it is necessary that the judge be not only an artist, but an artist who has appraised the work of beginners in the light of the amount of training they have already had. When, for special reasons, samples of a counselee's work are not available, it may be desirable to administer a worksample test of artistic ability such as the Lewerenz Tests in the Fundamental Abilities of Visual Art or the Knauber Art Ability Test, both of which were designed to measure creative ability in art (described below).

In guidance centers the use of the test is similar to that in schools and colleges, whether for counseling purposes or for selection in connection with training programs. It has little place in the evaluation of employment applicants, since they are usually already trained in art and can better be judged by their work, unless an especially important position is to be filled and it is desired to have a comprehensive study of the applicant.

The business and industrial use of the Art Judgment Test is extremely limited, for the reasons just given. It may, however, prove quite valuable at times when non-artistically trained personnel are to be selected or transferred to work in which ability to judge good form and composition are important, for example, in certain retail trade jobs of a merchandising type.

Creative Artistic Ability

As was mentioned earlier in this chapter, tests of so-called creative artistic ability are in reality worksamples devised to measure the subject's ability to construct a good artistic design or to utilize the concepts, vocabulary, and tools of the artist. As such they hardly belong in a discussion of aptitudes in the narrower sense of the term, but logically should be taken up in connection with custom-built tests or, if there were enough of their kind to warrant such a classification, with worksamples. In this case it seems more practical, however, to treat these tests in the chapter dealing with another special aptitude, the importance of which is seemingly limited to the same occupations.

The two worksample tests dealt with here are the Lewerenz and the Knauber. Because of the similarity of content and the lack of subsequent studies of their validity, both are discussed briefly, the Lewerenz being given more space since it is a more manageable test.

The Lewerenz Tests in the Fundamental Abilities of Visual Art (California Test Bureau, 1927).

Applicability. The test was designed as a measure of creative artistic ability for use in school systems. It was standardized on children in grades 3 through 12. It can also be used with young adults who have had no further artistic training.

Contents, Administration, and Scoring. Because of the independence of the separate parts of the test, they are best described in detail individually.

Test 1. Fifteen sets of drawings with four pictures to a set (multiple-choice), including bowls, friezes, cornices, etc., varying from good to bad in proportion and balance. Two parts, recognition of proportion in standard forms, and problems of abstract proportion and balance. Time, 10 minutes. Score equals number right.

Test 2. Ten sets of dots in varying numbers. The subject is told to draw any subject he chooses, using all the dots in each space with straight or curved lines, then to write one word in the space to indicate what he has drawn. The arrangement of dots varies, to permit formal and fanciful interpretations. Time, 20 minutes. Score is obtained by comparing drawings with six graded rating sheets.

Test 3. Ten drawings ranging from simple to complex. The subject is required to indicate omissions of shades and shadows, the light being considered as coming from the left. Time, 5 minutes. Score is the number right.

Test 4. A vocabulary test, utilizing the matching method in five ten-word sections dealing with materials, craft processes, graphic processes, drawing terms, and pictures. Time, 20 minutes. Score is the number right.

Test 5. A black vase form mounted on a white background is exposed to the subject for two minutes. After it is removed the subject is instructed to draw it from memory, on a test blank which shows the top and bottom of the vase with a vertical line through the center. Time, 5 minutes. Scoring is by a stencil.

Tests 6, 7, and 8 deal with ability to analyze problems in perspective· cylindrical, parallel, and angular. The subject may use a ruler in correcting incorrectly drawn lines in each of the three tests. Time, 5 minutes for each test. Score is the number of correct responses.

Test 9. A color chart with six known colors at the top; below are 46 "unknown" variations divided into four sections. The initial letter of the known six colors is used to indicate the one predominant known color in each of the unknowns, by means of a six-response type multiple-choice technique. Time, 20 minutes. Score is the number correct.

Norms. Norms are available for elementary grades, junior high school, and senior high school, based on an unselected group of 1100 pupils. Separate norms may be used for part scores.

Standardization and Initial Validation. As has just been stated, the tests were standardized on a supposedly typical group of school children. Various comparisons were made by the test author with art students, the correlation with art grades being .40 and the rank correlation between performance and predicted ability being .63. In subsequent studies, summarized long ago by Kinter (1933), Lewerenz found a correlation of .155 between his tests and a test of intelligence for a group of over 1000 children. Sex differences were also reported, girls being superior to boys in all but originality and ability to analyze.

Reliability. A retesting of 100 pupils in grades 3 to 9 after an interval of one month yielded a reliability coefficient of .87 (manual). No other such data have been located.

Validity. Few studies of the Lewerenz tests have been made by persons other than the test author, who seems to have ceased work with it years ago, which is to be regretted in view of the fact that it is the more manageable of the two well-known tests designed to measure creative artistic ability. Wallis (1930) correlated the test with the Meier-Seashore and McAdory tests, finding correlations of .53 and .58, both of which were higher than the correlation (.37) between the two art tests.

Use of the Lewerenz Tests in Counseling and Selection. From the above material it is clear that the Lewerenz tests are measuring, with considerable reliability, various factors which are rather distinct from intelligence, which have a substantial relationship with achievement in art, and which vary with age and sex. An analysis of the content suggests that these factors have to do with visual and creative artistic abilities, but too few relationships with other variables have been determined, and no factor analyses have been carried out upon which to base adequate conclusions. On the basis of the available evidence, however, it may be tentatively concluded that the tests have practical value in selecting students with sufficient promise for further training in art.

Because comparatively little is as yet known about it, scores on this test must clearly be supplemented by a variety of other information, such as Meier scores, data on art training and interests, intelligence, ratings of art work, etc.

The Knauber Art Ability Test (Distributor: Psychological Corporation; 1927, revised 1935). *Applicable* at or above the junior high school level. *Contents* are drawings in which the subject creates or completes drawings or locates errors. They yield seven measures of presumed components of art ability, such as long and short-time memory, observation, accuracy, creative imagination, ability to visualize and to analyze, etc. *Administration* involves no time limit, but the test normally takes about three hours. Drawings are rated on a three-point scale. *Norms* are based on 1366 students from seventh grade to university sophomore and are in terms of grade percentiles. *Standardization and validation* are described in the manual and in an article by Knauber (1935). After trials of other forms on 300 art students and then 550 art students, the present form was standardized on 1366 cases. Art students make a median score of 95 compared to that of 52 for non-art students; art teachers make a median score of 123 contrasted with 61 for other teachers. With 42 art students as subjects, the correlation with the Meier-Seashore Test was .57; with the Lewerenz, which it should resemble more closely on a priori grounds, the correlation was .64. *Reliability.* Retest reliability after one year was

.96 (Knauber, 1934); by the split-half method it was .95. *Use in counseling and selecting* seems justified by the fact that the test distinguishes between the various levels of artistic ability as shown in the group differences reported. With the exception of evidence which shows high reliability over a period of one year, no data are available on the effects of training, which might account for these differences. The test does appear to measure creative ability, if the nature of the items may be taken as evidence of validity. However, in view of the present limited knowledge of the test, scores must be used with considerable caution. Individuals making high scores may, if other evidence such as art judgment tests, intelligence, interests, and ratings of art work, is favorable, be encouraged to continue training in art; persons making low scores should be investigated further before recommendations are made.

REFERENCES FOR CHAPTER XII

Barrett, Dorothy W. "Aptitude and interest patterns of art majors in a liberal arts college," *J. Appl. Psychol.*, 29 (1945), 483-492.

———— "An examination of certain standardized art tests to determine their relation to classroom achievement and to intelligence," *J. Educ. Res.*, 42 (1949), 398-400.

Carroll, H. A. "What do the Meier-Seashore and the McAdory Art Tests measure?" *J. Educ. Res.*, 26 (1933), 661-665.

————, and Eurich, A. C. "Intelligence and art appreciation," *J. Educ. Psychol.*, 23 (1932), 214-221.

Dreps, H. F. "Psychological capacities and abilities of college art students of high and low standing," *Psychol. Monogr.*, (1933).

Eurich, A. C., and Carroll, H. A. "Group differences in art judgment," *Sch. and Soc.*, 34 (1931), 204.

Farnsworth, P. R., and Misumi, Issei. "Notes on the Meier-Seashore Art Judgment Test," *J. Appl. Psychol.*, 15 (1931), 418-420.

Greene, E. B. *Measurements of Human Behavior*. New York: Odyssey Press, (1941), 395.

Kinter, M. *The Measurement of Artistic Abilities*. New York: Psychological Corporation, 1933.

Knauber, A. J. "Testing for art ability," *Education*, 55 (1934), 219-225.

———— "Construction and standardization of the Knauber Art Tests," *Education*, 56 (1935), 165-170.

Meier, N. C. "Aesthetic judgment as a measure of art talent," *University of Iowa Studies, Series on Aims of Research*, 19 (1926).

———— "Factors in artistic aptitude." *Psychol. Monog.*, 231 (1939).

———— "Recent research in the psychology of art." *Yrb. Nat. Soc. Stud. Educ.*, 40 (1941), 379-400.

———— *Art in Human Affairs*. New York: McGraw-Hill, 1942.

————, and Seashore, C. E. *The Meier-Seashore Art Judgment Test*. Iowa City: Bur. of Res. and Service, University of Iowa, 1929.

Morrow, R. S. "An analysis of the relations among tests of musical, artistic, and mechanical abilities," *J. Psychol.*, 5 (1938), 253-263.

Protho, E. T., and Perry, H. T. "Group differences in performance on the Meier Art Test," *J. Appl. Psychol.*, 34 (1950), 96-97.

Saetveit, J., Lewis, D., and Seashore, C. E. "Revision of the Seashore measures of musical talent," *University of Iowa Stud., Series on Aims of Research,* 65 (1940).

Tiebout, C., and Meier, N. C. "Artistic ability and general intelligence," *Psychol. Monog.,* 213 (1936).

Wallis, N. "A Study of Tests Designed to Measure Art Capacities." Unpublished M.A. thesis, Florida State College for Women, 1930.

XIII

MUSICAL TALENT

TO TURN our attention to musical aptitudes in this chapter, as to artistic in the preceding chapter, is to risk abandoning the logic of the organization of the book as a whole. For in this text the focus is first on psychological characteristics, whether they be aptitudes, skills, or traits, then on the means of measuring them, and finally on the vocational and educational significance of the ability or trait being measured. The use of the terms "artistic" and "musical" implies an orientation which is primarily occupational. Useful as this latter approach is when judging a person's fitness for a specific occupational field or when devising or selecting a battery of tests for a single area, it is not, on the whole, as helpful as the psychological approach is to the counselor who seeks an understanding of the person with whom he is working and who hopes, through a sharing of that understanding with the client, to help him to make appropriate vocational plans. In this chapter as in the preceding, however, the focus on the occupational field is brief and introductory to the discussion of specific aptitudes which happen to be important primarily to one family of occupations. The aptitudes, in this instance, are physical capacities which have been found to be fundamental to success in music; they include such abilities as sense of pitch, sense of rhythm, and sense of time. They are treated in some detail below, in connection with the Seashore Measures of Musical Talent.

Music being a creative aesthetic occupation, it seems likely that many of the traits which have been shown or are presumed to be of importance to success in artistic occupations would also play a part in musical success. Seashore has studied these in an early monograph (1919) and discussed them in his more recent general treatise of the psychology of music (1939); the list does indeed tend to parallel that of his colleague Meier in the field of art. Manual skill is considered necessary for instrumental work in music, as for the use of tools in art; energy output and perseverance are deemed important in music too, with its requirement of hour after hour of routine practice; creative imagination is presumed to play a part, not only in the composition of new works but also in the interpretation of existing works; and emotional sensitivity may be thought to be important in both creative and interpretative work, if the musician or the artist is effectively to portray feeling and to play upon the emotions of others. Intelligence may be assumed to be increasingly important at the higher levels of musical endeavor; while it may not be important in a blues singer, Stanton's studies at the Eastman School of Music (1935) showed that intelligence is important in mastering the more abstract aspects of music. And, finally, Seashore's investigations (Saetveit, Lewis, and Seashore, 1940), confirmed by those of Stanton and others, have shown that the physical capacities measured by his tests are basic to musical success.

As the preceding paragraph implies, the only factors presumed to be important to success in music which have satisfactorily been demonstrated to be related to achievement in that field are intelligence and Seashore's measures of psychophysical capacities. The writers have seen no investigations other than the tentative early study by Seashore (1919) which demonstrated that musicians are superior to the general population in manual skill, energy output, or creative imagination, or that scores on measures of these factors are correlated with musical success. There is some evidence which suggests that musicians may be more sensitive emotionally than the general population, for Super (1940) found that male amateur musicians who played in symphony orchestras were significantly more likely to be unmarried, dissatisfied with their social life, and dissatisfied with their occupations than were other men of the same age and socio-economic status. If maladjustment is a sign of emotional sensitivity, then the hypothesis is perhaps validated; but it is possible that there is such a thing as emotional sensitivity without maladjustment, and that it is sensitive persons who are not maladjusted who make the best musicians. In any case, Super's subjects were amateur, not professional, musicians. It cannot therefore be said that it has been demonstrated that emotional sensitivity plays a part in success in music.

In view of the demonstrated importance of Seashore's physical capacities in musical success, the infrequency with which they play a part in other fields, the lack of evidence concerning the significance of other abilities in music, and the general rather than specifically musical nature of the other characteristics which are presumed to affect success in music, it seems legitimate to discuss Seashore's tests and the capacities which they measure under the heading of musical aptitude or talent. Other similar tests, described by Greene (1941, pp. 425–438), are not dealt with here because they have not been so thoroughly studied.

The Seashore Measures of Musical Talent (RCA Manufacturing Co.,

1939; since 1949, Psychological Corporation). The initial work on the measurement of physical capacities which might be important to success in music was begun by Seashore before World War I. As in the case of other psychologists who were then developing new measuring instruments, he continued his work during the war, applying it successfully to the selection of submarine dection men in the Navy. The first edition of the test for general use in musical guidance and selection was published soon afterwards, in 1919. As a pioneer in the study of the psychology of music, and aware, apparently, of the value of focusing his research energies on one promising field, Seashore continued to work with his tests, attracted graduate students who carried out additional studies, and found financial support to further his and his students' investigations. As a result, his laboratory at the State University of Iowa became the most active center for research in the psychology of music and in the prediction of musical success in the United States, and his tests are, together with the Stanford-Binet and Strong's Vocational Interest Blank, among the best known, most widely used, and most thoroughly understood instruments in the field of psychological measurement. The tests were revised and a second edition published in 1939 (Saetveit, Lewis, and Seashore, 1940).

For these reasons, the tests are treated here in some detail, even though the frequency of their use in counseling is somewhat limited because of the relatively few persons in musical occupations. Were it not for this fact, they would be dealt with at much greater length, as an illustration of the thorough work and multiple approaches which are needed in making vocational tests useful.

Applicability. The first edition of the Seashore tests was designed for use at any grade level, from the first grade to adulthood. Because of the effects of motivation and attention on the test scores, however, the revised manual recommends that the tests be used beginning with the fifth grade, that is, with children of about ten years old. This is acceptable to Seashore as a minimal age because it is also early enough to make possible serious planning for musical training if it seems warranted.

The norms for the revised tests indicate that scores tend to increase somewhat with age, for there is a steady increase in the means from grades 5 and 6 to adulthood. Although these differences are slight, amounting to only one or two points, they might conceivably be interpreted as showing that the abilities in question are still maturing. The ranges of scores are the same, however, at the different age levels, and the reliabilities are somewhat higher in adulthood than in adolescence (median $r = .82$ in adulthood, .78 in adolescence), facts which suggest the validity of Seashore's contention that the lower means of younger people are due to problems of concentration, attention, and similar administrative factors. If this is so, it becomes important to take especial pains to establish good rapport when testing school-age children and to test in two or three sessions. Seashore (1919) and Stanton (1935) have shown that training and experience, e.g., three years in a school of music, do not influence scores. The tests are therefore as applicable to adults as to children, and vice versa.

Content. The tests consist of two series of three double-faced twelve-inch phonograph records each. Series A is made up of wide-range tests suitable for survey or screening purposes with heterogeneous groups, while Series B has a higher base and "ceiling" in order to make it more diagnostic at the higher ability levels and with music students. The six capacities measured by either series are Pitch, Loudness (formerly called Intensity), Time, Timbre, Rhythm and Tonal Memory. The 1919 edition contained a test of Consonance, for which Timbre was substituted. No verbal description can convey an adequate idea of the specific content, but it may help those who do not have access to the tests to describe the Pitch Test, for purposes of illustration, as a series of pairs of musical notes. One member of each pair of notes is higher than the other; sometimes the higher note comes first, sometimes last. In later pairs the two notes are of more nearly the same pitch than in the first, the notes becoming more and more alike in pitch as the test progresses. As a result, a point is reached at which it is virtually impossible to decide which note is higher. This point comes early in the test for those lacking in pitch discrimination, late in the test for those who excel in it. The other five tests are built on similar principles.

Administration and Scoring. The manual for the 1939 edition gives quite adequate directions for administering the tests, which require about one hour. Several points deserve special emphasis, however, because of the unusual nature of the medium. The records used must be in good condition, neither scratched nor warped. So also should be the record player, adjusted to play loud enough to be heard throughout the room, at the speed of 78 r.p.m. As the records are monotonous, capturing the interest and retaining the co-operation of the subjects is especially important; in a paced test such as this a little wandering of the attention can spoil a test score. The manual recommends that examinees lean slightly forward in a poised position which facilitates concentration. Most unusual in the testing procedure is the desirability of demonstrating the tests by playing parts of each record before testing; the examiner gives the directions, then plays a few items near the beginning of the record, asking all examinees to respond orally, and permitting time for questions. He plays a few more items nearer the end of the record, again asking for group responses and allowing questions. This is to familiarize all subjects with the unusual type of test item, and to make it truly a measure of capacity. It might be objected that the test is spoiled by familiarization with the specific contents, but experimentation has shown that practice does not vitiate the test if the excerpts from the records are not consecutive (Allen, 1941; Farnsworth, 1931). Responses, in terms of "high, low," "strong, weak," or similar terms, are recorded on simple answer sheets which can be purchased or mimeographed; scoring is done by comparing responses with a key or a homemade stencil and counting the number of correct answers. The tests can be given more than once for the sake of greater reliability, and the scores averaged, a fact which more than any other brings out the fundamental difference between this and other aptitude tests!

Norms. Decile norms are provided for fifth and sixth grade pupils, seventh and eighth graders, and adults, for Series A tests, and for adults only for the Series B tests. No separate high school norms were deemed necessary, because of the small differences between eighth graders and adults. The normative tables do not indicate the number of cases on which the standardization was based, but the table of reliabilities in the manual makes it clear that the numbers in each grade group varied from about 1000 to 1700 pupils, depending upon the test, and from 600 to 1100 adults, the smaller numbers of cases being for Series B. There is no indication as to how the samples were selected; as Series A is designed as a survey test it should be a cross-section of school children and adults in general for that series, and, for Series B, the diagnostic test, a group of adults studying music. The manual is defective in not making the nature of the samples explicit.

Standardization and Initial Validation. To describe adequately the extensive and intensive standardization and validation studies carried out with the Seashore music tests by Seashore, his students, and other psychologists interested in music would require far more space than is merited in a text such as this. In fact, even the full-sized volume in which Seashore discusses his twenty-five years of work with the tests is tantalizing to a scholar because of its generality and lack of specific data on what was done and with what results. For present purposes, it seems best to survey a few of the studies of the validity of the tests, referring those interested in their standardization to the monographs by Seashore and his colleagues (Saetveit et al., 1940; Seashore, 1919, 1937).

Reliability. Farnsworth (1931) reviewed the studies of the reliability of the old form of the tests in 1931, 88 in all, and concluded that only the tests of pitch and tonal memory were sufficiently reliable for use with individuals. Drake (1939), for example, found that the better tests had reliabilities of about .86; these were odd-even reliability coefficients, corrected by the Spearman-Brown formula, and might be spuriously high in a test which is paced and therefore somewhat speeded. However, Larson (1930) retested children and adults with substantially the same results. The revised battery has higher reliabilities, on the whole: for Series A they range from .69 to .84 at grades 5 and 6, from .69 to .87 for seventh and eighth graders, and from .62 (the next higher is .74) to .88 for adults. The median reliabilities at the same levels are .78, .785, and .82. For Series B the coefficients are somewhat lower: .70 to .89, with a median of .735. Tonal Memory is the most reliable test in the new battery, with pitch and loudness about equally good, while Timbre, which replaced the unsatisfactory test of Consonance, is the least reliable. It seems surprising that what appear to be immutable physical capacities are measured with less reliability than some more strictly psychological factors; perhaps this is due to the large number of fine discriminations which must be made, and to vagaries of attention, rather than to the nature of the trait or defects in the tests.

Validity. Most studies of the validity of the Seashore tests have been concerned, as one might expect, with the relationship between scores and variables such as intelligence, music grades, and success as a musician. In the revised manual and related publications (Saetveit et al., 1940), however, Seashore has taken a new and different position. Although the validation studies have tended to demonstrate a considerable degree of predictive and occupational differentiating power, he now seems to feel that the validity of the tests lies in their accurate measurement of basic capacities which are utilized by musicians, rather than in the degree to which they are correlated with success in musical training or performance. The difference may seem a fine one, but it may be made clearer by explaining that in the latter approach one correlates test scores with grades or ratings, whereas in the former one analyzes the performance of musicians in order to ascertain to what extent they reveal high degrees of pitch discrimination, sense of timbre, etc. To the writers, this seems like a reversal of the natural order of things, for surely one should analyze the job to ascertain what factors seem to be important in it, construct tests to measure them, and then, as validation of both the job analysis and of the tests, correlate scores on the tests with criteria of success on the job. If there is no relationship between the measures and success, it matters little what the analysis showed. Perhaps Seashore did not intend to convey the impression that he had thus reversed his approach, or perhaps it was simply that, having found objective methods of analyzing the performances of musicians (Seashore, 1937), his interest in the technique caused him to lose sight of its place in the prediction, as opposed to the analysis, of musical performance. Be this as it may, there are a number of helpful studies of the predictive value of the musical aptitude tests in their older form; comparable studies of the essentially similar new form have yet to be published.

Intercorrelations of the original six tests were reviewed by Farnsworth (1931), who found them to have a median intercorrelation of .48 for college students and .25 for elementary and junior high school pupils. This suggests that the capacities measured by these tests are not as completely independent and basic as Seashore believes them to be, suggestion apparently confirmed by Drake's factor analysis (1939) of the five best Seashore tests, the Kwalwasser-Dykema tonal movement test, and two new tests, one of memory and one of retentivity, which revealed one common factor and three group factors underlying them. It may be, for example, that senses of pitch and rhythm underlie tonal memory. McLeish's (1950) factorial analysis of the unrevised tests also revealed a general factor, probably composed of appreciation and performance, but indicated that over a third of the total variance was attributable to specific factors associated with each of the measures. He concluded that, although there was evidence of a general musical ability, it was evidently highly complex and somewhat atomistic. Whether musical talent reflects an underlying dimension of aptitudes or a loosely interrelated constellation of more specific abilities is difficult to ascertain on the basis of present information. It is possible that neither explanation is sufficient to depict accurately a capacity which may become more differentiated with increasing age. Cross-sectional studies of musical ability at different age levels or, more desirably, longitudinal investigations of the development of musical talent, and its relation to the maturing of other aptitudes, are sorely needed.

Intelligence has repeatedly been found to have little relationship to Seashore scores. Farnsworth's review (1931) covered the earlier studies of this topic, sixteen in all, with a median correlation of .10, the range being —.08 to .45.

Grades in music courses have less often been used as a criterion of success, perhaps because they have not seemed sufficiently representative of musical ability. Larson's finding of a correlation of .59 between composite Seashore scores and grades in the first course in music theory at the Eastman School of Music seems rather high; a correlation of .31 between Seashore tests and grades in a college of music was reported by Highsmith (1929), which seems more in line with expectation. Intelligence tests were found more useful in this latter study ($r = .42$), and were included in the Eastman School battery (Stanton, 1935).

Ratings of musical ability have not yielded such satisfactory results. Mursell (1937) reviewed such studies and drew the conclusion that the tests were invalid. In view of studies such as Stanton's (see below), which have utilized objective procedures and have demonstrated considerable validity in the tests, it hardly seems justifiable to make such drastic judgments on the basis of data as subjective as ratings. Not only have ratings frequently been proved unreliable, but in studies such as those in question the subjects rated were all sufficiently able in music to be active students, a select group, thereby narrowing the range of both ratings and scores and artificially attenuating the relationship. In such circumstances the making of ratings is more difficult and the product therefore less reliable than ever.

Completion of musical training seems a much more objective criterion of success than rating, even when the effects of financial factors are recognized. Stanton (1935) made a ten-year study of the Seashore tests at the Eastman School of Music in Rochester. More than 2000 entering students were tested, and the test results were not used but simply filed until criterion data were available four years later. An analysis was then made of the relationship between test scores and the completion of training in music. The results of Seashore tests were combined with intelligence (Iowa Comprehension) test scores and teachers' ratings to provide a "cumulative key" or overall predictor. It was found that 60 percent of those who were rated "safe" risks on this basis had graduated in the normal amount of time, 42 percent of those who were classified as reasonably good risks and 33 percent of the fair risks graduated, in contrast with 23 percent of the poor and 17 percent of the very poor risks. The case histories of the high-scoring drop-outs were studied, in order to ascertain why the predictions based on test scores were not even better than they were; in these cases financial need, family pressures, and other non-aptitudinal factors seemed to be sufficient cause.

This study has been criticized by Mursell (1946, p. 233) because the predictive value of the Seashore tests has generally been assumed to have been demonstrated by it, whereas the often-referred-to evidence is actually not based solely on the Seashore tests. As Mursell pointed out, the data were not presented in a way which made possible a definite evaluation of the predictive value of the Seashore tests, although this could easily have been done. The value of the "cumulative key" may have been due largely to the intelligence test or to the ratings of previous music teachers. There is implicit in Stanton's report, however, evidence to the effect that such data were available (1935: 68), and while it is true that if they were available they should have been reported, statements to the effect that the "lowest musical talent students were very short-lived in the school" should be taken into account. No correlational data have been located, but in an earlier study (1929) it was reported that in the four years, 1923–26, the percentage of students making grades of A, B and C on the music tests rose from 79 to 92, and teachers' estimates of student talent rose from 67 to 88 percent in the same categories. The indication is that the higher level of talent revealed by the tests was confirmed by teacher evaluation. While the reports are to be criticized for their lack of details from which generalization would be possible, it seems that the findings are not to be dismissed as completely as Mursell suggested they should be.

Occupational differences were also studied by Stanton in a comparison of the scores of professional and amateur musicians with those of beginning students of music and non-musicians. The former were found to be significantly higher than the latter, result which, in view of other findings already mentioned which showed that the test scores are not affected by training or experience, demonstrates the ability of the tests to differentiate the more talented from the less talented musicians.

Preferences for different types of music were ascertained by Fay and Middleton (1941), working with 54 college students. Twelve musical selections were played to this group, and were rated by them for preferences. They found that those who preferred classical music made higher scores on the pitch and rhythm tests than did those who preferred light classical music or swing, and that they also scored higher on the time test than did the swing fans. If confirmed by other studies with larger groups and more extensive sampling of musical tastes this would be an indication of the role of musical aptitudes in the development of musical preferences, for apparently the most "high-brow" music does appeal more to those who are best endowed. It would be interesting to know what the relationship is between scores on the Seashore tests and satisfaction with employment as a member of dance and symphony orchestras, assuming that extraneous factors such as working hours, rates of pay, and employment stability could be controlled.

Use of the Seashore Measures of Musical Talent in Counseling and Selection. From the preceding discussion it is apparent that the Seashore tests measure aptitudes which are relatively independent of mental ability and of each other, and that these are physical capacities which mature by about age 15 and are not affected by training or experience. Although it is possible that one or two of them are in reality a combination of some of the others, the conclusion concerning their physical basis still holds. Seashore's recommendation that the scores be used separately, and never combined, should be followed if musical capacities are to be meaningfully studied.

The occupational significance of the Seashore tests is primarily musical, although they have been found to have some value in selecting persons for other jobs in which ability to make auditory discriminations seemed important. It is doubtful whether they will ever have guidance values, however, outside of the field of music. In this area, however, it has been demonstrated that those who make high scores are more likely to complete training and to achieve professional status than those who make low scores.

In schools and colleges these tests can be used to advantage to screen out students who have musical talents which are often unsuspected or undetected, thus making it possible for them to develop their abilities for their own enjoyment and that of others, if not actually as a means of earning a living. If the training and experience in music is found to hold a challenge, and if the skill acquired by the student seems equal to his promise, then it may be appropriate to consider vocational possibilities in music. In schools of music the tests can well be used as a selection device, with due recognition of the fact that what a student has done with his musical ability by that time is at least as important a predictor of success as the ability itself. Talents may be a *sine qua non,* but they cannot be sufficient in and of themselves.

In guidance and employment centers the tests probably have value only in cases in which the prospect of further training is to be considered. Job seekers who are already trained can best be judged on the basis of performance. Those with some training but seeking more should also have auditions in which the amount of previous training is taken into account by experienced teachers of music; but in such cases the talent tests should be of value in checking up on the trainability of the candidate. It should probably be kept in mind, in such instances, that there are hierarchies in music as in other fields, and that some persons of lesser aptitudes may find ways to use them whereas others with more aptitude may find doors closed. For example, the potential night-club crooner may succeed with a modicum of talents assisted by good looks and a smooth manner, whereas a more gifted person who aspires to symphonic work may find himself outclassed in that field.

Business and industry have so far apparently failed to find, or to attempt to find, any uses for these tests. Perhaps certain types of machine tenders, inspectors, and mechanics, who need to judge the operation or defects of machinery by pitch or other auditory senses, could be selected partly by these means. The hypothesis would first need to be validated, and then experimentation might actually find that thresholds are low enough so that selection on this basis is unnecessary. When accident rates are relatively high in such jobs, however, it might well be worth experimenting with some of these tests. A good automobile driver, for example, drives partly by ear, and responds at once to any change in the pitch of the customary noises of his machine, thereby forestalling some types of mechanical failure.

A development in the construction and validation of a set of musical ability tests, and their relationship to the Seashore measures, is worthy of note in concluding this chapter. Although not published and therefore not generally available for appraisal and guidance purposes, the battery of five tests devised by Lundin (1949) not only represents some departure from Seashore's approach to the measurement of musical talent, especially with respect to underlying rationale, but shows considerable promise for the more accurate prediction of success in musical endeavors. Rather than attempting to measure specific, relatively independent musical abilities as did Seashore, Lundin assumed that musical behaviors are interrelated to a great extent and proceeded to design items which would differentiate musicians as well as unselected groups of individuals on behaviors which successful instrumentalists, vocalists, or composers share, such as ". . . writing melodies and harmonies correctly after they have been produced audibly, harmonizing single melodic lines correctly following the rules set down by the older masters, ability to play and write rhythms correctly, and ability to detect changes in sequential patterns" (Lundin, 1949, pp. 2–3).

The tests which resulted from preliminary research (1944) involving an item analysis for internal consistency and degree of difficulty, included measures of interval discrimination, melodic transposition, mode discrimination, melodic sequences, and rhythmic sequences. Split-half reliability coefficients for the separate sub-tests and total scores ranged from .60 to .89, for a group of 167 music majors, and from .71 to .85 (with the exception of mode discrimination, .10), for an unselected group of 196 college freshmen. Using instructors' ratings of melodic and harmonic dictation, written harmonization, general ability in theory, and general performance ability, validity coefficients for those studying music were obtained which varied from .10 to .66 for sub-tests and from .43 to .70 for total scores. The multiple correlation coefficient for the various tests with the sum of ratings was .71, only slightly higher than the .69 with unit weights. Comparisons of the mean subtest scores of the musicians and an unselected group yielded highly significant critical ratios, indicating the superior ability of the musicians, but there were also considerable differences in the variabilities of the two groups. The unselected group was far more heterogeneous than the musicians in their performance on the tests, suggesting that marked individual differences in musical talent exist in groups of individuals who are not preparing for a career in music but who potentially may have a level of musical ability comparable to neophyte musicians.

Since Seashore scores for the musicians were available, an opportunity was provided to compare the validities of the Seashore and Lundin tests using the same criterion, instructors' ratings. In general, the Seashore measures of pitch, rhythm, and tonal memory correlated much lower with the ratings than did the Lundin tests. Only one coefficient was as high as .45, and the others ranged from .13 to .40. From these data Lundin (1949, p. 15) concluded that the validities of his tests were superior to ". . . those reported by previous investigators for other tests, when similar external criteria are used", an evaluation which seems unjustified since the criterion used was much more closely related in content to the abilities measured by the Lundin than the Seashore tests. As a consequence the validity coefficients for the Lundin tests may have been spuriously increased. An independent criterion of achievement in music is needed before accurate conclusions can be drawn concerning the relative merits of the different measures of musical talent. The Lundin tests represent, however, progress in the direction of more adequate coverage of the domain of musical abilities, since, as their author (1949, p. 3) points out, they ". . . measure directly and in an objective fashion some of the kinds of musical behavior not heretofore considered by previous investigators, and which we believe are important constituents of a musical personality".

REFERENCES FOR CHAPTER XIII

Allen, A. T. "Cogs in the occupational wheel," *Occupations,* 20 (1941), 15-18.

Drake, R. M. "Validity and reliability of tests of musical talent," *J. Appl. Psychol.,* 17 (1937), 447-458.

———— "Factor analysis of music tests," *Psychol. Bull.,* 36 (1939), 608-609.

Farnsworth, P. R. "An historical, critical, and experimental study of the Seashore-Kwalwasser test battery," *Genet. Psychol. Monog.,* 9 (1931), 291-389.

Fay, C. J., and Middleton, W. I. "Relationship between musical talent and preferences for different types of music," *J. Educ. Psychol.,* 32 (1941), 573-583.

Greene, E. B. *Measurements of Human Behavior.* New York: Odyssey Press, 1941.

Highsmith, J. A. "Selecting musical talent," *J. Appl. Psychol.,* 13 (1929), 486-493.

Larson, R. C. "Studies in Seashore's measures of musical talent," *University of Iowa Studies,* 6 (1930).

Lundin, R. W. "A preliminary report on some new tests of musical ability," *J. Appl. Psychol.,* 28 (1944), 393-396.

———— "The development and validation of a set of musical ability tests," *Psychol. Monog.,* 305 (1949).

McLeish, J. "The validation of Seashore's Measures of Musical Talent by factorial methods," *Brit. J. Psychol., Stat. Sec.,* 3 (1950), 129-140.

Mursell, J. L. "What about music tests?" *Music Educ. J.,* 24 (1937).

———— *Psychological Testing.* New York: Longmans, Green, 1946.

Saetveit, J., Lewis, D., and Seashore, C. E. "Revision of the Seashore measures of musical talent," *University of Iowa Stud., Series on Aims of Research,* 65 (1940).

Seashore, C. E. *The Psychology of Musical Talent.* New York: Silver, Burdett, 1919.

———— "Objective measures of musical performance," *University of Iowa Studies in the Psychol. of Music,* 4 (1937).

———— *Psychology of Music,* New York: McGraw-Hill, 1939.

Stanton, H. M. "Prognosis of musical achievement," *Eastman School of Music Studies in Psychology,* 1 (1929), 1-89.

———— "Measurement of musical talent," *University of Iowa Studies in Music,* 1935.

Super, D. E. *Avocational Interest Patterns: A Study in the Psychology of Avocations.* Stanford: Stanford University Press, 1940.

XIV

STANDARD BATTERIES WITH NORMS
FOR SPECIFIC OCCUPATIONS

THE characteristics, advantages, and disadvantages of standard batteries consisting of generalized items which can be validated and weighted as tests rather than as items, and for which norms can be developed for a great variety of occupations, have been well publicized during the past decade, and have been reviewed in a monograph sponsored by the American Personnel and Guidance Association (1957).

The principle underlying this type of test battery is that, since each mensurable aptitude is usable in a number of occupations, standard instead of custom-built test batteries can be constructed and normed in such a way as to yield scores for a number of specific occupations. This is fundamentally the same concept as that underlying the Primary Mental Abilities Tests, but the approach is different. Instead of beginning with a series of tests designed to primarily measure the currently known and isolable aptitudinal factors and proceeding to ascertain their vocational significance, as in Thurstone's work, the procedure has been to develop tests which are fundamentally the same as those which have been demonstrated to have occupational significance, and then to obtain occupational norms for this uniformly developed and standardized series of tests. Since mechanical comprehension tests have proved valid for some occupations but not for others, such a test is likely to be included in such a battery and given a weight in the score for a given occupation which is proportionate to its correlation with success in that occupation. Sometimes, as in the case of the USES battery, the tests are parts of well-known tests or close approximations of them; in other batteries, as in that of the Psychological Corporation, they utilize somewhat more original types of items designed to measure the same factors or constellations of factors as existing tests; in neither case is the main goal to measure pure factors, as in Thurstone's batteries, although factorial purity is considered desirable. The USES does not use all of the tests in its battery for each occupation, selecting, instead, the few which have the most predictive value for any one occupation; the Psychological Corporation, on the other hand, has planned its work around the battery as a whole.

The multi-occupational approach of the last two test batteries represents a major trend, different from that of the professional aptitude tests discussed in the next chapter. It results in one relatively brief series of tests with many applications, rather than in a collection of diverse test batteries, each usable only for one occupational field. It is potentially much more valuable to vocational and educational counselors than is the professional aptitude test, for, with one battery of tests, it becomes possible to explore a great variety of occupational possibilities. It takes time to accumulate occupational norms for such a battery of tests (the General Aptitude Test battery came into tentative practical use by the USES only in 1947, after nearly a decade of work, and the Differential Aptitude Test Battery has barely begun to develop occupational norms); it takes even more time to develop special batteries for a number of occupations. But it is also true that special occupational batteries are likely to have greater immediate validity for selecting students or employees than general aptitude test batteries, because of their miniature-situation elements and their custom-built character; these advantages are soon lost by the changes which take place in specific details, outmoding many miniature-type items, and by the variations from one employing agency to another unless continuous research maintains the tests. For example, Super (1947) developed a personality inventory for the selection of Air Force pilots during World War II which had more validity than the standard personality inventories and tests which were tried out at the same time; it was truly custom-built, with items phrased in the language of aviation cadets and content drawn from their wartime experiences, both actual and anticipated. But changes connected with the end of the war made this test currently useless as a personnel instrument. The obvious conclusion is that tests with *custom-built items* are best for *selection programs* in which conditions are relatively stable and investments are great enough to warrant the continuous validation of existing tests and the constant construction of new instruments, but that for *counseling* purposes tests consisting of *generalized items* with occupational norms are the only practical choice.

Specific Tests

In this chapter we describe and discuss the two such batteries which are now in general use: the General Aptitude Test Battery of the United States Employment Service, and the Differential Aptitude Tests of the Psychological Corporation. Other such batteries have, of course, been published, notably by Guilford and by Flanagan, all of which have been described and evaluated in the American Personnel and Guidance Association (hereafter APGA) monograph (1957); as yet they do not have substantial amounts of validity data.

The General Aptitude Test Battery (United States Employment Service, 1947, 1953, 1958). This battery is the product of a score of years of research in worker characteristics and test development by the Occupational Analysis Division of the United States Employment Service, described most completely in journal articles by the Staff, Division of Occupational Analysis (1945), by Dvorak (1947), and in the excellent series of manuals published in 1958. This comprehensive program of research in vocational aptitudes was itself the outgrowth, insofar as principles and technical matters are concerned, of the Employment Stabilization Research Institute of the University of Minnesota (Paterson and Darley, 1936), the work of which has been frequently encountered throughout this book. With such a long and fruitful background, it is natural to expect that this battery should prove a landmark in the history of the appraisal of vocational promise.

The objective of the General Aptitude Test Battery is to measure the factors that have been found to underlie the most valid aptitude tests and to develop occupational norms and validity data for these factors, thus making it possible to test virtually all significant aptitudes in one test session and to interpret a person's score in terms of a wide range of occupations. Some 59 different tests were thus reduced in number to 15 and then to 12, measuring what first appeared to be 10 factors but have now been reduced to nine. Some 500 occupations have been grouped in a total of 23 occupational ability patterns [one was added in the 1958 manual to the 22 cited by Dvorak in the 1956 article which forms part of the booklet on the Multifactor Tests (APGA, 1957)], using both test results and job analysis as a guide to grouping.

The first edition of this text was both enthusiastic about the promise of this batttery and critical of the paucity of data made available in the manuals and in other publications to justify the battery's proposed use. In two revisions of the manuals and in a large number of journal articles, Dvorak and her collaborators have since provided the empirical evidence needed for the evaluation and use of the test battery; in their current form they are a model of completeness and of clarity.

Applicability. The GATB was developed for use with older adolescents and adults who are in need of vocational counseling and seeking employment through the public employment service. While some of the tests have been standardized and validated for selection purposes, the objective battery is to make possible a better evaluation of the aptitudes of those whose experience and insights do not provide sufficient evidence to guide them in seeking employment.

Because of developing cooperation between schools and employment services the question of the applicability of the battery to high school boys and girls has aroused considerable interest. The tests having been standardized and validated on adults, scores of adolescents cannot be interpreted unless one knows what the effects of maturation may be. Considerable evidence has now been accumulated on this matter, presented in the manual and in supplementary technical reports, and more definitive data are being accumulated. The data show that the aptitudes in question change significantly until age 16 or Grade 11, but that changes in and after those years are not great. Conversion tables have been made available in the technical reports which enable the counselor to estimate the probable adult status of a ninth or tenth grader on the battery, and thus to compare him with adults with whom he will compete if he chooses one of the occupations for which norms are available. The wisdom of making a choice at that age is, as Super (1960) has pointed out, a real question. It was found, further, that long range prediction is possible, for the retest reliabilities over the three years from ninth to twelfth grade are about as high as those over three months in twelfth grade, and the correlations of ninth grade scores with three years' high school grades are about the same as those of twelfth grade scores with high school average.

Contents. The battery now consists of 12 tests, the scores of which are combined to yield scores for 9 factors. The paper and pencil tests are printed in three booklets; the apparatus tests consist of a rectangular manual dexterity box or pegboard and a small rectangular board for the finger dexterity test. The subtests in the booklets of the revised battery are as follows: Tool Matching, a test for perception of similarities and differences in the black and white shading of simple pictures of familiar tools; Name Comparison, resembling the Minnesota Clerical (Names) Test; Computation, consisting of addition, subtraction, etc.; Three-Dimensional Space, a metal or paper-folding test; Arithmetic Reasoning, verbally expressed arithmetic problems; Vocabulary, a same-opposites test; Mark-Making, a manually more complex dotting test; and Form Matching, like the analogies tests of the A.C.E. Psychological Examination. The Pegboard yields two scores, one for placing and one for turning, as in the Minnesota Manual Dexterity Test, but the pegs are smaller than the disks of the latter test, and both hands are used in placing. The Finger Dexterity Board is administered for both assembly and disassembly. The USES policy appears to have been to construct items as much as possible like those of earlier standard tests which had proved valid.

Administration and Scoring. Administration of the General Aptitude Test Battery requires about two hours. The booklets of paper-and-pencil tests are designed for group testing; this is true also of the apparatus tests, which are so constructed that in taking one part of the test the examinee automatically sets them up for the next test. Answers to paper-and-pencil tests are recorded in the test booklets in the old forms, on separate answer-sheets for the revised battery. Raw scores for each part are changed to "converted scores" by means of a conversion table; these are summated by groups to provide "aptitude scores" for each of the 9 factors measured by the 12 tests. These are standard scores, with a mean of 100 and a standard deviation of 20.

The 9 aptitude scores obtained from the 12 tests are described as follows:

G—Intelligence: general learning ability, ability to grasp instructions and underlying principles. It is often referred to as scholastic aptitude, and is measured by three tests.

V—Verbal Aptitude: ability to understand the meaning of words and paragraphs, to grasp concepts presented in verbal form and to present ideas clearly. One test.

N—Numerical Aptitude: ability to perform arithmetic operations quickly and accurately. Two tests.

S—Spatial Aptitude: ability to visualize objects in space and to understand the relationships between plane and solid forms. One test.

P—Form Perception: ability to perceive pertinent detail in objects or in graphic material, to make visual comparisons and discriminations in shapes and shadings. Two tests.

Q—Clerical Perception: ability to perceive pertinent detail in verbal or numerical material, to observe differences in copy, tables, lists, etc. It might also be called proofreading. One test.

K—Motor Co-ordination: ability to co-ordinate hand movements with judgments made visually; speed and precision. One test.

F—Finger Dexterity: ability to move the fingers and to manipulate small objects rapidly and accurately. Two tests.

M—Manual Dexterity: ability to move the hands easily and skillfully, a grosser type of movement than finger dexterity, involving the arms and even the body to a greater extent. Two tests.

It can be seen from the above that the General Aptitude Test Battery measures most of the aptitudes which have so far been isolated and proved occupationally significant. There is no measure of mechanical comprehension, but we have seen that this is not a factorially pure aptitude, but rather a composite of aptitude and experience, of which spatial comprehension is the major component. Artistic judgment and the musical capacities are not tapped, but they are of very specialized significance and perhaps wisely omitted from a general aptitude battery. Interests and personality are not assessed, but these are not aptitudes. The GATB therefore includes all of the aptitudes discussed in this book, all of those isolated in earlier factor analyses of abilities except memory (if Thurstone's Reasoning and Induction factors may be considered subsumed in G), and some more recently isolated factors.

Norms. The number of persons in each occupation is generally 50 or more, the range being from 30 to about 200. The occupational ability groups, consisting of several occupations with similar patterns on three tests, are thus based on samples of from 60 to 900 persons. The manual states that "it is desirable for the final sample to include at least 50, preferably more, workers who are all performing the same kind of work and who have survived the training period on the job" (Sect. III, 1–1–8), referring to specific occupational norms. No evidence is cited to support this judgment; the desirable number is actually very likely to vary from one occupation to another, depending upon the size and homogeneity of the population from which samples are drawn; thus a small occupation drawing exclusively from college graduates in biology who continue with graduate work (e.g., paleontologists) may be very well represented by 50 persons, but a large occupation such as general accounting, with its many means of entry and its diverse sources of supply, probably requires a much larger sample.

The GATB norms are expressed in terms of occupational aptitude patterns. Cutting scores are established for each of the three most important aptitudes found to characterize a group of related occupations, related in that they have the same aptitude requirements. Pattern 3, which is denoted only by a code number, might be called the applied science (professional) field; it is characterized by cutting scores of 125 for General Aptitude and 115 for Numerical and Spatial Aptitudes, and includes two sub-groups. One of these is called the Laboratory Science Work group (D.O.T. Code 0–X7.0), but, consisting of practitioner occupations such as physician and public health officer, might better be called the medical practitioner group; the other is made up of Engineering and Related Occupations such as the various kinds of engineers and designers.

Some of the occupations included in these groups are placed there because of the similarity of their known test profiles, each having its own cutting scores which resemble those of the others. Other occupations are included because job analysis data (the *Dictionary of Occupational Titles*) seem to justify this placement. As Super has pointed out in the APGA booklet (APGA:1957), this latter kind of grouping is judgmental, and can be validated by collecting relevant test data. Some of the occupations which were included in groups in the second edition of the manuals have been dropped in the third; for instance, OAP (Occupational Aptitude Pattern) 4 formerly had 39 occupations, six of which had their own test data, but now includes only 22 occupations, 16 of which are drafting occupations and only one of which (chiropractor) seems like an odd bedfellow in this group. Obviously, more caution is called for when the grouping is based on job analysis than on test scores.

The establishment of the cutting scores is based on the finding that the bottom third of the distribution of workers in most occupations is not very successful. As pointed out in the manual, this generalization provides only a rough guide, for the screening out of poor workers varies in severity from one occupation to another, from one period of time to another, and from one company to another, with supply and demand, risks involved, etc. The cutting point is therefore moved up or down, after consultation with foremen and supervisors, and after examining turnover and production data which may throw light on the matter.

Standardization and Initial Validation. The General Aptitude Test Battery has no mean history. The genesis of the idea was in the Minnesota Employment Stabilization Research Institute, written up by Paterson and Darley (1936) and by Dvorak (1935); early work by the USES is described by Stead, Shartle, and others (1940); but this work was still partly with published tests and did not concern the General Aptitude Test Battery; a factor analysis of these and other tests was published by the Staff of the Occupational Analysis Division (1945) and the Dvorak articles (1947, 1947), and the manual now adequately describes the battery and procedure of standardization and validation, giving results.

In the Staff (1945) paper data are given on the USES's factor analysis study. The GATB was included, along with 44 other tests. Based on this total of 59 different tests, administered in various combinations to groups of from 99 to 1079 persons, or a total of 2156 individuals in 13 different communities scattered across the country, this is one of the most thorough factor analyses of aptitude tests which has been made.

Despite limitations the report is helpful. It gives some idea of the empirical justification for using the tests which are in the battery and especially for combining them to yield factors or aptitude scores. This is fortunate, as it is in this respect more than in any other (except its occupational norms) that this battery differs from the Psychological Corporation's Differential Aptitude Test Battery. There is, for example, the justification for grouping three of the GATB tests (Three-Dimensional Space, Arithmetic Reasoning, and Vocabulary) to yield a score for general intelligence. One's first reaction might be to assume that this was merely a catering to the layman's desire to think in terms of "intelligence" because tests have yielded such scores for a generation; on the contrary, the report of the factor analysis makes it clear that this step was made necessary by the evidence. As the authors state: "it appears to have some of the properties of Spearman's G (sic), but the two-factor theory has no place for group factors like V, N, or S (which also were isolated) . On the other hand, this factor has a wider significance and is more persistent than either Thurstone's R or I. It appears to possess many of the properties that teachers, test examiners, and clinical psychologists would attribute to 'intelligence' . . . this factor has been designated, noncommittally, as Factor O." In the manuals it has been designated as G, and is uncompromisingly called intelligence. It is interesting that this finding of a general intelligence factor was accomplished, not with Spearman's two-factor statistical procedures, but with the use of Thurstone's centroid method of factor analysis, which has not on other occasions revealed a general factor. Furthermore, the sample was one of young adults, aged 17 to 39, rather than one of children in whom maturation rates would tend to produce a seemingly general factor.

The standardization procedure began with job analysis, to identify the job and define the sample population. Persons were then included in the sample if they were performing the same type of work, had passed the learning stage, and were rated satisfactory by their supervisors. Care was taken to make the sample all-inclusive or representative.

Validity criteria were then considered. Sometimes these were subjective, when supervisors' ratings appeared to be the best criterion; sometimes they were objective, as when production records were available and appeared to reflect the ability of the worker rather than other extraneous factors. When possible and desirable, both types of criteria were used, to get a better balanced picture of the varied aspects of success. Unfortunately, sometimes training, sometimes job criteria were used; both are important, but it is necessary to remember, for example, that the cutting scores for physicians have to do with success in medical school, not with the practice of medicine. In the case of engineers, both student and employee success can be studied, academic and industrial criteria having been used. As Ghiselli's summary (1955) of validities shows that aptitude tests tend to be valid for training but not for performance, this distinction is important, and users should not confuse validity for training with validity for the job. Sometimes longitudinal studies were made, applicants being tested before hiring and followed up in employment, giving data on the predictive validity of the battery. Sometimes only concurrent validity data are available, students or workers having been tested in school or on the job. This is clearly a second-best procedure.

Reliability. Extensive reliability data are supplied in the 1958 edition of the manual, the data being quite satisfactory (retest reliabilities are above .80) for most of the factors measured by paper and pencil tests, but barely acceptable (.65 to .79) for the perceptual, coordination, and dexterity factors.

Validity. One section of the manual for the GATB is devoted to validity and related data, and frequent reports of additional studies appear in the Validity Information Exchange of the journal, *Personnel Psychology.* The decentralized nature of the Employment Service results in the conduct of studies by a variety of organizations with a variety of subjects and criteria; the results sometimes appear somewhat chaotic as a consequence, but as more and more studies are completed the end result becomes rather impressive; the tables in the manual (Sect. III, J) , listing 145 occupations and describing the samples and criteria, reflect a vast amount of work. Dvorak (APGA, 1957) sums up the validity data by the statement that the coefficients tend to be around .60: this too is impressive, until one begins to wonder how the USES has achieved this when in most instances test authors are quite satisfied if they obtain validities of .40 and .50. We shall come back to this question after considering first some aspects of the sample and criterion questions.

The subjects tested may be students, apprentices, applicants, trainees, or employees. Validity data in all of these types of situations are useful, and the Employment Services cooperate with schools, colleges, and industries in making studies of all of these kinds of groups. But, as we have seen in the chapter on test construction, the most important kind of test validation for guidance purposes is that which is done with applicants as subjects. In such a study persons applying for training or for the job in question are tested as part of the application process, but the results are not used in hiring. Those who are admitted or employed are followed up in training or on the job, and data on their success are obtained. The correlation between test scores and criterion indicates the predictive validity of the test, and tells one how useful it is in selecting students or workers. This fact is of course known to the USES but since it has no control over the state employment services, and since in any case predictive validity studies are not always easily arranged, studies of the concurrent validity of the GATB are often made. The user of the GATB thus needs to pay particular attention to the type of occupational group used in validating the battery for a particular occupation. In the case of beauty operators, for example, all validity data are for students, while for billing machine operators they are employees; in the case of electricians, on the other hand, data are available for both apprentices and employees, the validity coefficients for these last two groups being respectively .50 and .37. This is as one would expect, for aptitude tests have generally (Ghiselli, 1955) predicted success in training better than success on the job; in the USES data, on the other hand, this is not the rule, the two generally being about equally effective (Dvorak, in APGA, 1957) . One wonders why this unusual trend.

Unavoidably, too, the criterion varies considerably from one study to another. For some occupations production criteria prove available and satisfactory, but for others ratings must be used. The user of a test battery needs to take these criterion variations into account, and ask himself, "Valid for what?" Whether or not he accepts the tests as valid will depend on what it is that he wants to predict. For example, the battery for the job of mounter had a validity of .24 when the criterion was supervisors' ratings, but of .52 for another group of employees for whom production records provided the criterion; if one seeks workers who satisfy the boss, the battery is of little practical value, but if one wants workers who can turn out the work the battery appears quite useful.

As was pointed out earlier, however, the size of the validity coefficients is often such as to make one wonder whether chance or some biasing factor may not have caused an unduly large number of large validity coefficients to be found. One possible explanation, as Super has pointed out elsewhere (APGA, 1957), lies in the use of tetrachoric correlations; these, Guilford (1954) notes, require large numbers of cases to reduce the sampling error which tends to be systematically great. Numbers should approach 400 in order to provide sound correlation coefficients. But the numbers in the GATB occupational samples range from 30 to 200, and are generally below 100. The data for the occupation of stenographer provide a good illustration, for with a validation group of 130 the correlation with work sample scores was .37, a quite reasonable and in fact rather low figure. But when the battery was cross-validated with other groups of stenographers, numbering 60, 50, and 58, the validities were respectively .68, .62, and .49, defying all precedent and the laws of regression and probability! The explanation undoubtedly lies in the small samples and in the sampling error of tetrachoric correlations.

It is relevant to ask, then, whether the large number of high validity coefficients, the high average of .60 cited by Dvorak, is likely to prove substantially smaller as data accumulate. Super (APGA, 1957, p. 30) has elsewhere reported an analysis of the sizes of the correlations in relation to the sizes of the samples, based on the second edition of the manual with data for 77 occupations. We have now analyzed the data for the first 100 occupations in the third edition of the GATB manual, for which 134 validity coefficients are reported, 108 of them validation (first sample) studies, and 26 of them cross-validation (additional samples, sometimes several for one occupation) studies. The data are reported in Table 27.

Table 27 shows that 40 per cent of the validity coefficients reported for the GATB are for occupational samples of less than 75 persons and are .60 or higher, whereas only 22 percent, about half as many, are for samples of that size but smaller than .60. In the occupational samples numbering

TABLE 27

SIZE OF VALIDITY COEFFICIENT AND SIZE OF SAMPLE IN THE GATB

	$N<75$				$N=75-99$				$N=100$ or More			
	Val.		Cross		Val.		Cross		Val.		Cross	
	<.60	.60+	<.60	.60+	<.60	.60+	<.60	.60+	<.60	.60+	<.60	.60+
Coefficient	29	53	11	11	2	9	2	1	13	2	1	0
Percent	22	40	8	8	1	7	1	1	10	1	1	0

100 or more persons, only 15 percent of the validity coefficients are to be found, 10 percent in the below .60 category and 1 percent in the .60 of above category. There is, clearly, a tendency for the small samples to have large validity coefficients, and for the large samples to have smaller (below .60 can still be substantial) coefficients. It is noteworthy that the cross-validation coefficients tend to appear about equally in the above and below .60 rubrics. Another way of expressing these trends is to state that when N is below 75 (77 percent of the validation samples), 75 percent of the correlations reported in validation studies are .60 or above; when N is 75 to 99 (10 percent of the validation samples), 80 percent of the validities are .60 or above, but that when N is 100 or above (15 percent of the validation samples) only 13 percent of the correlations are .60 or above.

It should be stressed that the fact that the validity coefficients thus far reported must clearly be inflated does not lead to the conclusion that the GATB validity data are false; it merely suggests that they are not as high as they appear to be. The validities for the occupational groups which are over 100 in size cluster around .50, a reasonable and useful figure. One can conclude that, even after one makes allowances for the as yet large number of small samples, the GATB has considerable utility as a battery of tests for occupational classification and guidance.

Use of the GATB in Counseling and Selection. The General Aptitude Test Battery has a distinguished history, is outstanding today for the unique extent to which it has both accumulated occupational normative and validity data and established its applicability to adolescents and adults, and shows promise of continuing to improve its research basis. Despite the fact that some of the normative groups are still small and some of its validity coefficients therefore too large and despite the use of concurrent as well as predictive validation criteria, there is no doubt but that this is the most adequately standardized and validated battery of tests now available for the vocational counseling and placement of inexperienced young persons and adults. The large and varied number of partly validated occupational aptitude patterns are equalled by no other battery.

But it should be recognized that a battery of aptitude tests measures only aptitudes. As the materials accompanying the GATB make clear, the battery is an aptitude, not an interest, personality, or proficiency battery. It needs to be supplemented by interest inventories, proficiency tests for learned skills, and other methods designed to yield data on other aspects of suitability for a type of employment.

In schools and colleges the GATB is often available to students through the local branch of the state employment service. Some schools arrange to have the employment service test all pupils about to enter the labor market, and to discuss the results with them. It is particularly useful, because of its norms, with the oft-neglected non-college students. The availability of conversion tables which permit comparing an adolescent's scores with adult occupational norms extends the usefulness of the battery to all age groups needing directional vocational guidance, although (Super, 1960) caution needs to be exercised and developmental trends understood. As the professional competence of counselors in both employment services and schools improves, greater use, and greater flexibility in the use, of the battery should become possible.

In guidance centers and employment services the GATB should prove to be one of the most useful tools available with inexperienced and untrained persons who need help in finding a focus for their efforts in securing training or beginning employment, particularly in the middle and lower level occupations. Few tests or test batteries have many normative data for skilled occupations, and fewer still have such for the semi-skilled occupations which make up the majority of employment opportunities for high school graduates and for those who drop out of high school. The GATB has such norms, and validity, for a wide variety of occupations, and keeps adding more.

In business and industry testing time and skills can be saved by the kind of screening which the employment service is in a position to do with the GATB, releasing the time and skills of the personnel department for supplementary testing of a more specialized type, and for other screening, employment, and classification function. Company norms and company validity data are, of course, likely to be preferable to the less appropriate general norms of a variety of industries; but by working with test-selected applicants a company can begin with part of the selection job done and devote its energies to doing the rest better.

The Differential Aptitude Tests (Psychological Corporation, 1947, 1952, 1959). This battery of tests was developed by Bennett, Seashore, and Wesman, in response to widespread feeling among vocational psychologists and counselors that a major defect in current testing programs is the lack of a uniform baseline for the various tests which are used with a given student or client. We have seen, for example, that the Revised

Minnesota Paper Form Board has norms which are based on differing groups in a few localities, and that the Bennett Mechanical Comprehension Test has a totally different and equally limited base. A student may be at the 65th percentile when compared to liberal arts college freshmen on one test, and at the 55th on another, but actually have more ability of the type measured by the second test; the seemingly lower score may be due to differences in the normative groups. It is only when the tests in a battery have been standardized on strictly comparable groups, if not the same group, that one can effectively study aptitude or interpret differences *within* individuals.

Other needs also contributed to the development of this battery. One was the improvement of statistical procedures which made possible the construction of tests which effectively measure narrower aspects of ability than general intelligence. The development of quantitative and linguistic scores for the A.C.E. Psychological Examination, the Wechsler-Bellevue Scale and other modern substitutes for the undifferentiated tests of the times of Binet and Otis, and the further development of factor scores by Thurstone in the Primary Mental Abilities Tests were the forerunners of a now general trend in the construction of general aptitude tests. Still another was the time factor, for it is important that a comprehensive battery be administrable in a reasonably brief period if educational and occupational norms are to be obtained for all tests from the same subjects. It was a sign of the times that both the United States Employment Service and the Psychological Corporation moved simultaneously to meet these needs. The American Institute for Research has prepared the Flanagan Aptitude Classification Tests, an integrated battery, also for use in guidance; Guilford has released a similar battery; and other test publishers have followed suit (APGA, 1957). Perhaps in due course even paper-and-pencil tests of manual dexterities and interest inventories can be developed which will be much more valuable if used as parts of an integrated battery.

Applicability. The battery was designed for use with high school students, including eighth grade boys and girls. Items were devised for and retained on the basis of their suitability for this age and ability range, and the time limits and norms are based upon the performance of samples of high school populations. They may therefore be considered extremely effective at these levels. No attempt was made to make the tests applicable to college students or adults, although use in personnel selection was envisaged and the items may well be suitable, but the fact that the grade norms increase annually from grade 8 through 12 shows that special *norms* would be necessary. As age norms have not yet been provided, and no analysis has been made of the effects of progressive elimination in high school on the sample, it is still impossible to draw any conclusions concerning the development of these abilities from the preliminary work with these tests; seniors may make higher average scores because they have lived and studied one year longer than juniors, or because they have lost their less able classmates by the wayside. Be this as it may, the development of college or adult norms has one drawback in the ceiling of the tests: Having been designed for high school students, they do not permit the most able college students and adults to show the full extent of their abilities.

Content. The Differential Aptitude Tests consist of eight tests designed to measure eight different abilities. Some of the abilities are aptitudes in the stricter sense of the term (Verbal Reasoning, Numerical Ability, Space Relations, and perhaps Abstract Reasoning); others are factorially less pure (Clerical Speed and Accuracy and Mechanical Reasoning) but can be treated as aptitudes; still others are proficiencies (Language Usage: Spelling and Sentences). The last-named are, however, sufficiently basic forms of achievement to be used effectively as indices of promise. Because of the excellent descriptions in the manual, the following paragraphs are in part abstracts of the manual.

The Verbal Reasoning Test attempts to measure ability to generalize, to think with words à la Thurstone (V). It consists of verbal analogies, in which the first member of the first pair and the second member of the second pair have been omitted from the stem and must be selected from two sets of items with four choices each, e.g., ———— is to x as y is to ————. Analogies were used because they have proved to be one of the best types of reasoning test items, and the form chosen is highly reliable, versatile, and lends itself to complexity without resort to esoteric terms. Because of this latter fact, the vocabulary is relatively simple, the content familiar, and complexity is a function of the reasoning processes involved.

The Numerical Ability Test is designed to measure understanding of numerical relationships and facility in handling numerical concepts, another of Thurstone's factors (N). As the manual points out, the items are cast in the form usually referred to as "arithmetic computation" rather than "arithmetic reasoning;" the reason given is that language problems are thus avoided, and that complexity was attained by the numerical relationships and the processes to be used in the problems.

The Abstract Reasoning Test attempts to measure reasoning without the use of words (Thurstone's R). Problems are of a spatial type made familiar by the A.C.E. Psychological Examination, and require finding the principle underlying a series of changing geometric figures.

The Space Relations Test (Thurstone's S) is the most ingenious in the series, although embodying familiar principles. These are ability to visualize a constructed object from a pattern (structural visualization in three dimensions) , and ability mentally to manipulate a form in order to judge its appearance after rotation in various ways. By combining these two principles in items which require the mental folding of cut or partly shaded patterns a test of spatial visualization has been developed which promises to be superior to any so far developed.

The Mechanical Reasoning Test is another form of the familiar Bennett Mechanical Comprehension Test. The mechanical principles are illustrated with pictures of familiar objects, but care was taken to avoid textbook illustrations.

The Clerical Speed and Accuracy Test is designed to measure speed of response to numerical and alphabetical symbols. Although presumably a substitute for the Minnesota Clerical Test, it differs considerably from the latter in its mechanics, and also seems to differ in its factorial composition, for letter and number-letter combinations are substituted for the names used in the older test. The examinee finds the underlined combination in each row of a block of symbols, then marks the same combination (differently placed) in the same row of the same block on the answer sheet. Intelligence plays a less important part in this task than in the Minnesota Names Test.

The Language Usage Test contains two parts, *Spelling* and *Sentences*. In the former, each word is marked as spelled either right or wrong; in the latter each sentence is divided into parts, to be marked according to their correctness. The types are familiar, the items chosen by established scientific procedures.

An attempt was made, in drawing and printing the items in these tests, to make them sufficiently large and clear so that visual acuity would play no part. Inspection of the items does suggest that they are free from some of the defects which can be noted in certain other tests involving mechanical objects, geometric figures, and other drawings in which details might be obscure or irrelevant differences slight and confusing.

Although the test authors point out that the Differential Aptitude Tests were designed, not to measure all known and mensurable aptitudes, but rather to measure a number of important variables which have meaning for vocational counseling and selection and which can be assessed in a reasonable period of time, one cannot help but check the aptitudes tapped by these tests against those assessed by the USES General Aptitude Test Battery and isolated by various factor analysis studies. The Verbal, Numerical, Spatial, Abstract Reasoning, and Clerical Speed and Accuracy Tests clearly correspond to the verbal, numerical, spatial, reasoning, and perceptual factors isolated by Thurstone (1938) and by the Staff, Division of Occupational Analysis (1945) , and measured by the General Aptitude

Test Battery. The Mechanical Reasoning Test has no counterpart in the GATB, presumably because it taps a composite of factors rather than one factor; neither do the Language Usage Tests, which are achievement measures. On the other hand, Thurstone isolated a memory factor (not reliably measured) and the GATB provides measures of eye-hand co-ordination, motor speed, finger dexterity, manual dexterity (the last two require apparatus tests), and distinguishes between form and clerical perception. This suggests that Bennett, Seashore, and Wesman have gone further in the direction of measuring what counselors look for and what has proved to have validity than did Shartle, Dvorak, and associates; and, conversely, that the latter have attempted more consistently to make useful the findings of the factor theorists. Given adequate norms and validation data, the USES policy may prove wiser in the long run; until then, the Psychological Corporation's policy of providing measures of types which have known occupational validities may be sounder.

Administration and Scoring. The eight tests are printed in seven booklets (the two Language Usage Tests are in one booklet), making possible administration of any of the tests in any order desired, and in combined booklets for convenience and economy in using the whole battery. Time limits are such that any test can be given in one class period; they vary from six minutes to 35 minutes. Total testing time is three hours and six minutes. The manual recommends that the tests be given in an order which will hold interest and avoid monotony, and suggests three arrangements which are not quite identical. This raises the interesting question of the possible effect on profile scores of testing some students with one sequence, some with another, and of testing some students in few sessions, some in several. The test authors do not mention this problem, which may not be an important one, but until it is demonstrated to have no effect it is probably wise to adopt a set sequence and spacing of tests and to follow it rigidly, thereby making all local scores comparable with each other if not actually with the national norms (it is not clear just what sequence and spacing were used in gathering norms, nor even that the procedure was standardized in this respect). Answers are recorded on IBM answer sheets, making possible either hand-stencil or machine scoring. The manual contains unusually complete suggestions for efficient test administration and scoring, from advance arrangements to a summary table of scoring information, incorporating the best experience of the large-scale testing programs of recent years.

Norms. Norms are available for each grade from eighth through twelfth, and for each sex, for both forms of the test, revised in 1952 on the basis of 47,000 students. They permit the conversion of raw scores into percentiles, which were adopted instead of standard scores because of their current widespread use; the profiles permit conversion into approximate standard scores, and such a system is to be made available in due course because of that system's more accurate representation of individual differences. The students on whom the tests were standardized were enrolled in more than one hundred school systems from all parts of the United States, 26 states in all. Industrial and business norms which were to be provided routinely to manual owners as research projects made them available have not so far materialized. In some communities all pupils in all five grades were tested; in others, representative samples (as judged by the local research director) were tested. Form A was standardized on the largest groups; these range in numbers from 2,100 for the twelfth grade boys to 6,900 for the ninth grade boys, and from 2,300 twelfth grade girls to 7,400 ninth grade girls. Such regional coverage and numbers are almost unique; they appear to be such as to make possible the use of the tests throughout the U.S.A. It is to be hoped that curricular norms will become available, and that college freshmen norms, based on homogeneous and well-described types of colleges, will also be compiled and published. If this is done, the lack of industrial or occupational norms for this battery will not hinder its general usefulness in schools.

Standardization and Initial Validation. What has previously been said concerning the content, the development of norms for this battery of tests, and data in the subsequent paragraphs on its reliability, conveys an adequate idea of the work which was done in standardizing these tests. The types of items to be included were decided upon on the basis of factor analysis and validation studies carried out by other psychologists with other tests. The test items were tried out in preliminary studies and the tests were administered for standardization purposes only when they seemed administrable. Care was taken to obtain large samples of students at each appropriate grade level and in representative communities. The reliability of each test was computed and found adequate for individual diagnosis (see below). Finally, the intercorrelations of the tests were obtained. These latter ranged, for Battery A (boys), from .06 (Mechanical Reasoning and Clerical Speed and Accuracy) to .62 (Verbal Reasoning and Language Usage: Sentences); data for girls, and for Battery B, were approximately the same. The median intercorrelation for Form A tests is .425. These intercorrelations are not much higher than those of the Primary Mental Abilities Tests, after allowance is made for the achievement (Language Usage) and composite (Mechanical Reasoning) tests, for which the two highest correlations with other tests were obtained. Knowledge of the educational and vocational predictive value of similar tests, which have already been discussed (the Primary Mental Abilities Tests, A.C.E. Psychological Examination, Minnesota Paper Form Board,

Bennett Mechanical Comprehension Test, Minnesota Clerical Test) , combined with the proved reliability and relative independence of these tests suggested that studies using external criteria should demonstrate considerable validity for these tests.

Reliability. Particular care was taken, in establishing the reliability of the Differential Aptitude Tests, to avoid the common defect of tests with part scores, that is, reliability of the total score but insufficient reliabilty of the part scores for individual diagnosis. Homogeneous groups were used, to avoid the spuriously high coefficients which are yielded by heterogeneous groups. Split-half reliabilities were computed for all but the Clerical Speed and Accuracy Test, for which, as a speed test, that technique is not suited; instead, alternate-form reliability was ascertained. The Form A reliability coefficients for 960 boys range from .85 (Mechanical Reasoning) to .93 (Space Relations) ; for 1064 girls they ranged from .71 (Mechanical Reasoning, a type of test which generally has little value for girls) or .86 (Numerical Ability, the second lowest for girls) to .92 (Language Usage: Spelling) . For boys, then, all of the tests in Battery A have quite adequate reliability; for girls, all those which are likely to be useful have equal reliability. Data for Battery B are about the same, this form of the Mechanical Reasoning Test having been revised and improved. The stability of DAT scores over time has also been reported; for ninth grade boys retested in twelfth grade they range from .62 to .87; for girls, .58 to 82.

Validity. The Differential Aptitude Tests' authors felt that the known significance of the abilities measured, combined with the internal evidence of validity, was sufficient to justify making the tests available early in their development, but they committed themselves to an extensive program for the validation of the battery against educational and occupational criteria. Supplements to the manual were made available including a large number of validity coefficients, based on the high school grades of norm groups, and the second and third editions of the manual have been models of reporting. In the current edition a particularly effective digest of a large number of validity studies is provided, making detailed reporting here unnecessary.

Intelligence (as operationally defined by most tests of that attribute) being essentially a combination of verbal and numerical factors, the correlations obtained between appropriate tests of the DAT battery and other measures of intelligence are worth noting. The Verbal Reasoning Test, as reported in the manual, correlates .74 (156 men) and .84 (204 women) with the L score of the ACE Psychological Examination, and .78 and .86 with the ACE Total score. The Numerical Ability Test has correlations of .67 and .69 with the ACE Q score, .60 and .69 with the Total.

When the Verbal and Numerical scores were combined (simple addition proved as good as regression methods) and correlated with the Wechsler Adult Intelligence Scale scores of youthful prisoners, the coefficients ranged from .79 for the 16 to 17 year-olds to .74 for the 20 to 24 year-olds. These correlations are like those typically found between group and individual tests of intelligence.

Grades obtained after the DAT was administered are the criteria used in a large number of studies summarized in the manual. Grades in high school English are best predicted by Verbal Reasoning, Language Usage, and (although the discussion in the manual does not mention it) Numerical Ability, these coefficients averaging from .44 to .50 for boys, .44 to .53 for girls. For Mathematics, Numerical Ability is clearly the best predictor ($r=.47$ and .52), but Verbal Reasoning is about equally important for girls, while it and other tests are of some value for predicting mathematics grades for boys. Science grades are correlated with Verbal Reasoning, Numerical Ability, Abstract Reasoning, Space Relations, Mechanical Reasoning, and Sentences Tests, most of the median coefficients being in the .40s or low .50s. Social Studies and History grades are best predicted by Verbal Reasoning, Numerical Ability, and Sentences Tests, with coefficients averaging .43 to .52. From these findings it seems clear that the tests do have some differential predictive value for high school subjects (e.g., Mathematics grades are best predicted by Numerical Ability), but that the differentiation is not very good (e.g., Numerical Ability is also one of the best predictors of English grades and Verbal Reasoning, good for predicting English grades, is also good for predicting Mathematics grades for girls).

Examination of the data for individual studies, rather than the medians cited here, shows that there are great variations from school to school; as the test authors point out in the manual, these variations are probably related to differences in the objectives, content, method and grading of these courses. One teacher of mathematics may stress computation, thus making Numerical Ability and Clerical Speed and Accuracy the best predictors of the grades he gives, whereas another may put the emphasis on mathematical processes, thereby making Verbal Reasoning the best predictor of grades in his course. Caution is therefore called for in making use of these generalizations, and, in particular, local studies are important for truly effective use of the DAT in differential prediction.

The data reported in the manual on the relationship between DAT scores and Mechanical Drawing grades in Gloucester, Massachusetts, and Independence, Missouri, well illustrate this point. In a study in Gloucester the only parts of the DAT which had significant correlations with Mechanical Drawing grades were the Abstract Reasoning and Clerical Speed and Accuracy Tests ($r=.43$ and .61, N being 46). But in Independence the valid tests were Verbal Reasoning, Numerical Ability, Space Relations, Spelling, and Sentences, although all of the other tests are correlated with Mechanical Drawing grades if one accepts the .05 rather than the .01 level of probability. Using the higher level of significance, one might hypothesize that in Gloucester, Mechanical Drawing was taught in a way which stressed perceptual speed and accuracy in the use of abstract symbols, whereas in Independence a greater variety of abilities was called for by the methods of instruction and evaluation, with verbal reasoning and spatial visualization emphasized and perceptual speed minimized. These inferences of course would have to be verified by analyzing the classroom and examination or grading methods which were actually used at that time.

Type and amount of education completed have also been used in criteria in several studies, discussed in some detail in the manual as well as in journal articles or special bulletins. The trends are in the expected directions: The more demanding types of higher education are pursued and completed by students who tend to make higher scores on appropriate tests than by those who make lower scores. Furthermore, the tests have some differential predictive value, liberal arts students and graduates doing somewhat better than science students and graduates on Abstract Reasoning (which seems surprising) while doing about the same on Verbal Reasoning and technical students and graduates surpassing others in Space Relations and Mechanical Reasoning but particularly on Numerical Ability. In Hall's (1957) study of 287 high school boys followed up after two years of work experience, verbal ability was the main discriminant, supplemented by conceptual speed in routine work.

Occupational differences of students tested in high school in 1947 and followed up at work in 1955 are also reported in the manual. The groups are, as the authors point out, small. In the DAT 1955 follow-up there were 22 engineers, whose scores on all of the tests surpassed those of every other occupational group (typically about the 85th percentile of high school seniors) and were particularly high on Numerical Ability, Abstract Reasoning, and Mechanical Reasoning. It should be noted, however, that occupations requiring graduate studies were excluded from this analysis, as the data were collected the year after the college-going subjects graduated from colleges; what the data indicate is that the engineers were the ablest of those who went to work with only a high school or four-year-college education. Those still in student status, however, were not as able. The 21 businessmen were slightly above the average high school graduate on most tests, but below average on Spatial and Mechanical Tests. Factory operatives, by contrast, were about average on these two aptitudes, and below average on others. Building trades workers tend to differ from factory operatives in being below average on Mechanical Reasoning but about average on Abstract Reasoning and Clerical Speed and Accuracy (perceptual speed).

Women teachers are generally superior to nurses except in Space Relations, nurses are superior to stenographers except on Clerical Speed and Accuracy, stenographers are superior to clerks on all tests (the numbers are from 126 and 198 respectively), and housewives are, as one might expect, an average (no doubt heterogeneous, wide-range) group.

It is clear that there is some occupational differentiation by the various tests, although the bulk of the occupational differences are a matter of general level of ability rather than of special aptitudes. Perhaps, as a larger number occupations are studied with larger samples, more special aptitude differences such as those which appear to exist between factory operatives and building trades workers will be established.

Auto mechanics and machine shop students were studied in another investigation reported in the manual. For the former group of students the tests had virtually no validity, whether because the criterion rating was poor or for other reasons. For the 130 machine shop students the Mechanical Reasoning, Space Relations, Numerical Ability, and Verbal Reasoning tests had correlations with total ratings by instructors of .47, .46, .36, and .35 respectively, making it possible to set up expectancy tables.

Use of the Differential Aptitude Tests in Counseling and Selection. These tests make use of item types which have been proved useful in older tests, and which in some instances gain in predictive validity what they sacrifice in factorial purity. They are therefore somewhat more highly intercorrelated than are the tests of certain other multifactor batteries. A great deal of evidence has now been accumulated and reported. Several of the tests are rather good predictors of academic success in school and college and of the occupational level attained after completing formal education; two of them can be combined to make a good test of general intelligence. Some of the tests appear to have differential predictive value for school grades and for occupational field, but the data are somewhat contradictory and at times surprising, making the carrying out of local validation studies necessary; carefully refined and well-defined criteria are essential before the full usefulness of the battery for differential prediction is established.

In schools and colleges, when the objective is the study of a counselee in terms of his psychological make-up and its general educational and vocational implications, the battery should prove useful. When, however, comparisons need to be made with pre-occupational or occupational groups, the paucity of occupationally differential norms greatly limits the usefulness of this battery. As there is every reason for believing that curricular and occupational norms will be provided in increasing numbers, counselors in schools and colleges may want to use this battery for counseling, developing their own curricular and vocational norms as part of their follow-up work. It should be noted, however, that the tests are too easy for students in selective colleges.

Guidance and employment centers which habitually carry on normative studies may also find it worth their while to use this battery of tests in counseling, supplementing it with others which have more adequate occupational norms when such data are really needed. Other tests, such as those of manual dexterity, may be needed in any case to round out the picture, together with personal data obtained in interviews. If the battery is used, it should be with a definite co-ordinate research program in mind. This can be materially aided when the center works co-operatively with business and industry in employee selection programs.

In business and industry, even more than in counseling, the gathering of local norms and validation against local criteria should precede the use of these tests for selection purposes. Validation for selection is so much easier than validation for counseling, and the accuracy of predictions is improved by so much greater a degree, that to adopt any other policy is to be guilty of gross negligence.

REFERENCES FOR CHAPTER XIV

American Personnel and Guidance Association. *The Use of Multifactor Tests in Guidance*. Washington, D. C.: American Personnel and Guidance Association, 1957.

Dvorak, Beatrice J. "Differential occupational ability patterns," *University of Minnesota Bull. Employ. Stab. Res. Inst.*, 8 (1935).

——— "The new USES. General Aptitude Test Battery," *J. Appl. Psychol.*, 31 (1947), 372-376.

——— "The USES. General Aptitude Test Battery," *Occupations*, 26 (1947), 42-44.

Ghiselli, E. E. *Measurement of Occupational Aptitude*. Berkeley: University of California Press, 1955.

Guilford, J. P. *Psychometric Methods*. New York: McGraw-Hill, 1954.

Hall, R. C. "Occupational group contrasts in terms of the DAT," *Educ. Psychol. Measmt.*, 17 (1957), 556-567.

Paterson, D. G., and Darley, J. G. *Men, Women, and Jobs*. Minneapolis: University of Minnesota Press, 1936.

Staff, Division of Occupational Analysis, WMC. "Factor analysis of occupational aptitude tests," *Educ. Psychol. Measmt.*, 5 (1945), 147-155.

Stead, W. H., and Shartle, C. L. *Occupational Counseling Techniques*. New York: American Book Co., 1940.

Super, D. E. "Validity of standard and custom-built personality inventories in a pilot-selection program," *Educ. Psychol. Measmt.*, 7 (1947), 735-744.

——— "The critical ninth grade: vocational choice or vocational exploration," *Pers. Guid. J.*, 39 (1960), 106-109.

Thurstone, L. L. "Primary mental abilities," *Psychometrika Monog.*, 1 (1938).

XV

CUSTOM-BUILT BATTERIES FOR SPECIFIC OCCUPATIONS

THE realization of the fact that tests are likely to give better predictions when designed and validated for a specific rather than for a general purpose has, for many years, led psychologists concerned with the selection of persons for professional training to devise batteries of tests for specific occupations. Some of these have been designated as tests rather than batteries, and they have in general been called tests of professional aptitudes, hence names such as the Moss Medical Aptitude Test and the Ferson-Stoddard Law Aptitude Examination. But they have actually been batteries of tests even when combined in one booklet, and they have generally, but not always, been designed for use in selecting professional students rather than in counseling students or selecting employees.

This latter point is an important one, for many school counselors lacking a sound foundation in psychological measurement expect, on hearing of the existence of an instrument such as the Medical Aptitude Test, that they will find it invaluable in counseling their students or clients. In general, those who press the matter are disappointed, for they often find that the desired test is used exclusively by the professional schools which developed it as a selection device, or that it is disappointingly like certain other familiar tests and therefore difficult to accept as a test of "medical," "nursing," or "teaching" aptitude.

Whether available for general use, like the Engineering and Physical Science Aptitude Test, or restricted to use in professional schools, like the Medical Aptitude Test, batteries of tests for specific occupations are nothing more than combinations of existing types of tests of special aptitudes, usually modified in order to give them some of the specific predictive and face validity which is characteristic of the miniature-situation test. Thus the Engineering and Physical Science Aptitude Test is made up of parts of the Revised Iowa Physics Aptitude Test, the Moore Test of Arithmetic Reasoning, the Bennett Test of Mechanical Comprehension, and the Moore-Nell Examination for Admission to Pennsylvania State College;

no special attempt was made to give the test face validity, presumably because mathematical and mechanical items have enough inherent face validity for technical fields. The Coxe-Orleans Prognosis Test of Teaching Aptitude, on the other hand, is made up of especially developed items, such as vocabulary, information, and judgment. But these items were selected or devised so as to have special bearing on education: The vocabulary deals with subjects with which people who are interested in teaching are presumed to be familiar; the information is of a type which a would-be teacher might well be expected to possess; and the judgment items deal with classroom situations, behavior problems, and other matters in the handling of which a prospective teacher should presumably have some ability. They certainly possess face validity, although whether they reproduce the life-situation on a small scale is an open question until experimentally demonstrated.

The tests discussed in this chapter are largely custom-built and were designed, sometimes for student, sometimes for personnel selection. Professional training institutions invest so much in their students as to make selection essential; in a few instances they have been developed for the selection of other types of trainees or employees, but here also the investment in the trainee or worker has generally been large, as in the Air Force pilot-training program. The tests have generally been kept confidential in order to prevent coaching, being made available only to member schools or official testing centers. Tests of this type are briefly described in this section, as the great majority of users of psychological tests need no more than a knowledge of their existence and nature. A few tests of this type are available for general use, and while these are discussed at slightly greater length they are not treated in detail because most of them have not been widely studied. Both types are taken up under the title of the occupation for which they were developed, the occupational titles being arranged in alphabetical order.

Accountants. A battery of custom-built aptitude and achievement tests, and occupational norms for the Strong and Kuder interest inventories, have been developed for the accounting profession, and described by North (1958).

Business Executives. A great deal of time and money is currently being spent on the application of psychological methods to the selection of executive personnel. General discussions of the executive selection and evaluation services offered by consulting organizations have been published, but evaluative studies are lacking on this very important phase of personnel psychology, particularly evaluations of clinical methods of appraisal. In general, there may be said to be five current types of work in executive selection and evaluation: 1) The development of custom-built batteries of tests such as the Cleeton-Mason Vocational Aptitude Examination and the U.S. Civil Service Commission's experimental battery, discussed below; 2) the validation of standard tests for this particular purpose, as in the University of Minnesota's College of Business Administration project also discussed below; 3) the development of single tests for executive interests or other traits, best illustrated by Strong's work with executives and public administrators, mentioned below, and discussed in connection with that inventory; 4) the clinical use of interviews and tests as commonly done by consulting psychologists, considered in this section; and 5) the use of clinically evaluated situation tests as developed by the British War Officer Selection Boards and carried further by the U.S. Office of Strategic Services for the selection of personnel for critically important assignments, also considered in this section despite the fact that little research has been done with it even by organizations following in that tradition, e.g., the Institute for Personality Assessment and Research at the University of California (Berkeley). Current research on executive selection undertaken by the Educational Testing Service, some of it in cooperation with Teachers College in a study of school administrators, may yield valuable results.

The Cleeton-Mason Vocational Aptitude Examination (McKnight and McKnight, 1947), is designed to measure aptitude for four types of business activity, clerical, accounting, administrative, and technical. It is one of the few tests which purport to measure aptitude for executive work; it consists of eight subtests, the contents of which measure general information, arithmetic reasoning, analogic reasoning, reading comprehension, interest (as in Strong's), personality (as in Bernreuter's), vocabulary, and ability to estimate such things as the number of cars in the United States. Although the authors have written a monograph on executive ability, in which they have analyzed the nature of the executive's task in a helpful manner, data on the validity of the *test* are so lacking as to make the test itself of little value. The purposes it might serve are probably better served at present by batteries of tests, such as the Otis Tests of Mental Ability, the Minnesota Clerical Test, and other tests of special aptitudes which have been rather thoroughly studied, except perhaps when the test items are completely tailor-made.

A battery for the selection of public administrators has been developed by Bransford (1946) and Mandell and Adkins (1946) of the U.S. Civil Service Commission, utilizing two standard tests of intelligence (the A.C.E. Psychological Examination and Thurstone's Estimating Test) and custom-built tests of current events, data interpretation, administrative judgment, and knowledge of agency organization and personnel. The criterion of success was a combined rating of administrative effectiveness, the average number of raters per employee being four. The top management ($6,200 to $10,000) group consisted of 20 persons; for this group, the correlations between criterion and A.C.E. were .64, Current Events .64, Interpretation of Data .65, and Administrative Judgment .68; other validities for this group were low. For the staff group (63 specialists at $2300 to $7500) the validities were .30, .26, .41, and .49. The multiple validity coefficient for the staff group (the only one large enough for computation) was .55. These data suggest that truly custom-built tests of executive ability may have considerable validity, but this battery cannot yet be considered to have been validated, in view of the fact that the persons tested were already on the job at the time of testing. Its validity can be considered established only after applicants for employment have been tested and followed up. This is especially true of custom-built batteries, some of the items of which may be more readily handled after one has worked in the situation than before. But, as the test authors concluded, this preliminary work with the battery suggests that it may have merit and that further validation should be carried out.

The validation of a battery of standard tests for the selection of students of business administration at the University of Minnesota was written up by Douglass and Maaske (1942). This battery was designed solely for local selection purposes, but the investigation does provide some suggestions as to what types of tests are likely to have predictive value. The tests which showed the closest relationship to success in the college of business administration measured knowledge of social terms (Wesley College Test of Social Terms) and of business mathematics, with correlations with first-year honor point ratios of .56 and .47, respectively, and an *R* of .64. It need hardly be pointed out that success in training may be much more dependent upon academic ability (the verbal factor) than success on the job, and that the selection or upgrading of executives might require a rather different battery of tests.

Strong's (1927, 1946) *attempts to develop scales of executive interests* have shown that executives are not a homogeneous occupational group, but actually an extremely heterogeneous one, drawn from a great variety of fields such as sales, accounting, engineering, clerical, and skilled occupations. Under these circumstances it seems probable that the traits which executives have in common are fewer and more difficult to isolate than those which subdivide the group. It might, for example, be easier to distinguish insurance executives from insurance salesmen, engineering executives from engineering technicians, or office managers from office clerks, than to distinguish executives as a group from a group of men-in-general which includes insurance salesmen, engineering technicians, and clerks. Strong's work has shown that, in the field of interests at least, what the salesmen, technicians, and clerks have in common is what the insurance executives and office managers have in common. The lines are drawn vertically rather than horizontally, the executive salesmen being the most able salesmen, the executive engineers bing the most able engineers, the executive office workers being the most able office clerks. In the field of aptitude, also, being an executive may be a matter of being superior in one's field, rather than having notable characteristics which are common to all types of executives (abstract intelligence would be an exception to this statement, in that executives in a given field and in all fields could be expected to excel in such a general ability). But some of the work with Strong's Blank suggests the existence of generalized executive interests, namely the ability of the Occupational Level Scale to differentiate men in executive positions from those in skilled and semi-skilled work (Strong, 1943), while work with forest rangers suggests that administrators differ from the specialist ranks from which they rise (Strong, 1945).

A battery of standard tests administered to 15 superior and 10 average executives of a firm of consulting management engineers by Thompson (1947) is of interest as one of the few published studies reporting positive results. The tests used included the Wonderlic Personnel Test, Michigan Vocabulary Profile Test, Cardall Test of Practical Judgment, Kuder Preference Record, Adams-Lepley Personal Audit, Beckman Revision of the Allport A-S Reaction Study, Guilford-Martin Personnel Inventory, and Root I-E Test. The criterion consisted of performance records (not described) and ratings by partners; how reliable these were is not stated. Differences between the superior and average groups, significant at or above the 5 percent level, were found with the Wonderlic, Michigan Vocabulary (Government, Physical Science, Mathematics, and Sports subtests), Kuder (Mechanical and Social Service), and Adams-Lepley (Firmness and Stability) tests. Both groups were found also to be above the 93rd percentile on the Kuder Persuasive scale. All of the reported differences favored the superior executives, except that on the Kuder Social Service scale: in this characteristic the average or less successful executives were at the 79th, while the more successful executives were at the 51st, percentile. These results portray the successful management engineer executive as superior to less successful partners in mental ability, technical and governmental vocabulary, sports vocabulary, mechanical interests, firmness, and stability, and inferior in interest in social service. As Thompson's groups were very small these conclusions are highly tentative; cross-validation might change the picture considerably. Further studies of this type appear, however, to be worth making.

The clinical use of interviews and tests is perhaps the most common method now used by consulting psychologists in the selection or evaluation of executive (and sales) personnel. Although it does not make use of a total score based on a test battery, this procedure is briefly described here because of its prevalence and because it constitutes one method of using tests.

Flory and Janney (1946) have listed five factors which experience has led them to believe must and can be appraised in executive evaluation: intelligence, both abstract and concrete; emotional control, defined as ability to maintain steady output without emotional tension under varying and trying circumstances; skill in human relations, or leadership in face-to-face situations; insight into human behavior, both one's own and that of other persons; and ability to organize and direct the activities of others. Some of these traits can be rather effectively measured, intelligence, for example, by means of standard tests and perhaps by certain Rorschach indices. But others, such as emotional control and insight into human behavior, have not as yet lent themselves to effective measurement. The judgment of such qualities is a much more complex and unreliable procedure than the statement by Flory and Janney implies.

The procedures used by these consultants consist of a detailed personal history secured in an interview lasting from twenty minutes to two hours, "suitable objective instruments" to probe areas of adjustment, and a clinical interview for the checking of symptoms revealed by the personal history and the tests. Fear, in part of another article in the same symposium (Achilles, 1946), mentioned comparable methods used by another organization, without going into details other than stating that they can be used only by a highly trained psychologist.

This procedure is nothing more than that used by any well-trained and balanced user of tests for selection purposes: It consists of selecting and interpreting the results of tests believed likely to throw light on significant aspects of the applicant's qualifications, gathering important supplementary data by other means, and synthesizing them into a meaningful picture. But, in contrast with test procedures for many other types of work, it is actually *less* than what is done in most personnel evaluation programs. For in the best use of tests in personnel selection and evaluation the tests have been previously subjected to experimental validation for the work in question, and are used because there is an objectively demonstrated relationship between the test score and success in that job, whereas in the procedure under discussion few if any such relationships have been established and the additional clinical work is an attempt to make up by subjective procedures for what has not been done by objective techniques. Flory and Janney's "suitable objective instruments" for probing personality may be objective in form, and suitable in the best judgment of a competent vocational psychologist, but the existence of a relationship between scores on such tests and success in executive work had not, at the time of their writing, been demonstrated. The personnel selection and evaluation procedure described by Flory and Janney, Fear, and others is a clinical procedure which uses tests *diagnostically* but not *prognostically;* the predictions are based on *clinical judgments* and not on the *known relationships* of *tests.*

To underline this fact is not to deny the value of current psychological methods of executive selection; as a matter of fact, they are probably superior to other presently available methods. It is merely to point out a major difference between the use made of tests in such programs and in most other selection or evaluation procedures. The reasons for this difference are clear: They lie in the elusiveness of personality factors, in the primitive state of development which characterizes our present methods of appraising personality, and in the fact that executive selection is so important that it justifies the time of the psychologists who must make the clinical judgments involved. Subjective and defective though these judgments may be, they represent the best available: Informed guesses are preferable to uninformed guesses, and better-informed to less-well-informed. In the equally complex problem of predicting success in pilot training, for example, it was found that judgments made in psychiatric interviews with aviation cadets had a correlation of only .27 with success in flying training, as contrasted with a validity of .66 for a custom-built and objectively scored test battery; the psychiatric interviews were of little more than chance value, and much less effective than the test battery, but if no such battery of valid tests had been available the weeding out of even a few failures would have justified depending upon the judgment of the psychiatrists. It would be well worth the while of organizations interested in the selection and upgrading of executives to finance whatever fundamental research is a prerequisite to the development of better tests for the measurement of characteristics which may affect success in administrative and top-managerial work. The fact remains, however, that most enterprises are more willing to pay for poor service in the present than to ensure better service in the future, and that some psychologists are willing to sell poor service without accompanying research programs, a fact exploited by certain popular writers.

Clinically evaluated situation tests used by the Office of Strategic Services have been described by Murray and MacKinnon (1946) and by the Assessment Staff (1948). In this work they were concerned with appraising "the relative usefulness of men and women who fell, for the most part, in the middle and upper ranges of the distribution curve of general effectiveness or of one or another special ability," and with assessing a number of "personality qualifications—social relations, leadership, discretion . . ."

As it seemed that none of the conventional screening devices tested good will, tact, teamwork, freedom from annoying traits, leadership, and other social qualifications, special procedures had to be devised. In other words, the project had to develop methods of appraising executive ability, since none were available; that the executive ability was to be applied in "cloak-and-dagger" work is incidental, and should not blind civilian personnel workers to the possibilities of the methods tried. That they are also being used in a number of corporations is evidence of widespread interest in assessment methods.

The O.S.S. procedure consisted essentially of bringing about 18 candidates to a house party for a period of three and one-half days. The activities of the house party were directed by a staff of psychologists, psychiatrists, and sociologists. Data were gathered by means of: casual observations; standard tests of intelligence, mechanical comprehension, etc.; projective tests such as Incomplete Sentences, Thematic Apperception, and the Rorschach used primarly to assess motivation and emotional stability; personal history interviews of an hour and one-half; group situation tests, one requiring working with a team to accomplish a feat of physical prowess, another a discussion, in both of which leadership might develop [see Bass (1954) for a summary of subsequent work along these lines], and some assigned leadership problems in which the examinee must lead his group; individual situational tests involving frustration-tolerance and a stress-interview; an obstacle course; tests of observing and reporting details; tests of propaganda skills as shown in the preparation of a pamphlet to disturb Japanese workers in Manchuria; psychodrama involving difficult social situations; debate in a convivial party; a sociometric questionnaire concerning fellow candidates; and judgment of others as revealed in sketches of the five men known best during the three and one-half days.

Data obtained by these methods were clinically evaluated by the staff subgroup responsible for the study of several candidates, and reworked in case conference by the whole staff. About 20 percent of the 5,500 men and women thus studied were not recommended for duty; 1,200 of those who went overseas were followed up and evaluated by supervisors and three or four associates. The choice and collection of criterion data was not undertaken until late in the war, and convincing quantitative validation proved especially difficult (Assessment Staff, 1948, Ch. 9). Despite these difficulties a validity coefficient of .39 was obtained for a sample of 31 candidates assigned to appropriate duties. The authors conclude, with some justification, that the true validity of their procedure was probably between .45 and .60. Two important points can now be made on the basis of this work:

First, the possibility of following up employees and obtaining evaluations under even the most difficult circumstances is rather conclusively demonstrated by the obtaining of evaluations of men and women who were appraised in this country and followed up in scattered combat areas.

Second, there are many devices for obtaining potentially significant and quantifiable personality data which psychologists have only begun to explore, making the field of personality measurement a rich one in which to carry on research. Since executives play crucial roles in their organizations, and represent considerable investment of company or public funds, the exploration of these possibilities should be well worth the while of business, industry, and government.

Dentists.   Early research in the selection of students for dental schools was summarized by Bellows (1940) and little has been done since. Most of the batteries used consisted of standard tests selected because it was thought they would have validity for this purpose, but two included tests which were developed specifically for dental selection. One was the *Iowa Dental Qualifying Examination* of the State University of Iowa (Smith, 1943), the other a battery developed at the University of Minnesota partly on the basis of the Iowa work (Douglass and McCullough, 1942). The Iowa tests were: information on the development of the teeth, reading comprehension (dental anatomy), memory for nomenclature, predental chemical information, predental zoological information, a worksample (trimming a plaster of Paris block to specification), and a paper-and-pencil test of spatial relations. The correlations between scores on the first five tests and theory grades in thirteen dental schools ranged from .11 to .74, the average being .53; for the worksample the correlation with grades in first-year technique courses was .62; that for the spatial test was .41. Several possible combinations of tests were used in the Minnesota studies, their validity varying somewhat not only from battery to battery but also from year to year, the numbers varying from 83 to 111. One battery consisted of predental grades ($r = .45$), a metal-filing worksample (.53), the Iowa Visual Memory Test for Nomenclature (.40), the O'Connor Finger Dexterity Test (—.40), and the Iowa Spatial Relations Test (.52); the multiple correlation with total grades in dental school was .78, even when only the filing, memory, and dexterity tests were used. When laboratory (Prosthesis) grades were used as a criterion, the Metal Filing Test (custom-built) had a validity of .60 while that of the Finger and Tweezer Dexterity Tests (standard) was —.35 and —.43 (high time scores are bad, hence the negative relationship).

These studies show that grades in dental school have been predicted with considerable success by means of batteries of tests, some of which were constructed especially for that objective. However, the value of this approach can be judged only by comparing its results with those of studies which have used standard tests weighted for dental selection on the basis of local validities. Only Harris' study (1937) permits such a comparison, made in a different school with a criterion (grades) which may have been more or less reliable than those in the Iowa and Minnesota studies; his multiple validity coefficient, using predental grades and intelligence test as predictors, was .67, which is substantially lower than the .79 obtained at Minnesota with a special battery. Whether or not the additional validity justifies the extra labor of constructing the special battery depends, of course, upon the expense of the mistakes which result from using an inferior selection procedure.

Engineers. Although various investigators and institutions have developed procedures for the selection of engineering students, no so-called tests of engineering aptitudes were published until the *Engineering and Physical Science Aptitude Test* (Psychological Corporation, 1943) followed by the Pre-Engineering Inventory of the Educational Testing Service. Oddly enough, the former was not developed as a test for selecting students for colleges of engineering. It was developed in connection with the war-industry training program at the Pennsylvania State College, and so has norms for miscellaneous young men and women, some of them not high school graduates, who applied for technical training at the trade and technician level in connection with war industries, and later norms for miscellaneous groups of engineering students. This test, or rather battery of tests, is not a test with custom-built items in the sense in which that term is used here. Instead, it consists of items from existing tests of special aptitudes, selected on the basis of item validities to constitute a new battery. The items were therefore custom-selected, but not custom-built; they are of possible general significance, rather than drawn from and restricted to the local situation. It is only the weights and norms which are custom built.

The tests from which the items were selected on the basis of local validities were the Iowa Physics Aptitude Test (revised), which provided the Mathematics, Formulation, and Physical Science Comprehension Tests; the Moore Test of Arithmetic Reasoning, which supplied the Arithmetic Reasoning Test; the Bennett Test of Mechanical Comprehension, from which came the Mechanical Comprehension Test; and the Moore-Nell Examination for Admission to Pennsylvania State College, vocabulary section, which provided the Verbal Comprehension Test. These are all tests which have been found to have some value in predicting success in technical and engineering courses, and since the items have all been twice selected on the basis of validity for predicting success in technical training at some level (in the original test and in this battery) the battery should be a very promising one on which to collect local data and to establish local norms. An engineering or technical school which cannot at once invest much money in test construction and validation would probably find that this battery provided a ready basis for establishing local selection criteria, although the results available so far show no outstanding validity for this test as compared to others.

As currently available information concerning the Engineering and Physical Science Aptitude Test is virtually limited to the original study and is contained in the manual and in the article by Griffin and Borow (1944), work with it is not discussed here in any detail. It should suffice to say that correlations between scores on this test and grades in technical courses ranged from .13 to .71, depending upon the course and the subtest, and that the correlation between total score and average grade was .73. Subtests showed higher correlations with grades in the types of courses with which one would expect them to be related than in others; the correlation of .71, for example, was between the Mathematics score and grades in mathematics, whereas a correlation of .14 was found for Mathematics score and grades in a course in manufacturing processes.

The Pre-Engineering Inventory (Educational Testing Service), developed specifically for the selection and guidance of engineering students, has not been as successful as custom-built tests tend to be; Pierson and Jex (1951) found it predicted grades in freshman engineering only slightly better than the Cooperative General Achievement Tests.

Attempts to develop batteries of tests for selecting engineering students, in which standard tests have been used as *tests* rather than as *sources of items,* are well illustrated by studies conducted by Holcomb and Laslett (1932), Laycock and Hutcheon (1939), Brush (1941), and Coleman (1953). Holcomb and Laslett used the MacQuarrie Mechanical, Stenquist Picture, and Stenquist Assembly Tests, and the Strong Vocational Interest Blank (engineer scale). They computed no multiple correlation coefficients, although they found validities of .48, .15, .43, .16, and .32 respectively.

Laycock and Hutcheon used the National Institute for Industrial Psychology (England) Form Relations Test, the Cox Mechanical Aptitude Tests (Models and Diagrams) , and the physical science score on the Thurstone Interest Inventory, together with high school grades and scores on the A.C.E. Psychological Examination. The best combination of this group consisted of marks in grade 12, A.C.E. score, Form Relations, and Physical Science Interest, the multiple R being .66.

Brush's study included the Minnesota tests, the Wiggly Block, the Cox Mechanical Aptitude Tests (Explanation, Completion, Models) , the MacQuarrie, the Thorndike Intelligence Examination, and the Columbia Research Bureau science tests; not all students took all tests, as he worked with two groups. The multiple correlations for all tests and four-year engineering grades were .54 for one group (no intelligence test included) and .61 for the other (including intelligence test). With the first group the best battery was probably that consisting of the Minnesota Paper Form Board and the Cox Models, with an R of .46. For the second group the best batteries were one consisting of the Thorndike, C.R.B. Algebra and Geometry, Cox Models and Completion, Minnesota Paper Form Board and Interest Analysis, with an R of .59. The highest correlations for single tests were for C.R.B. Algebra and Physics, and Thorndike Intelligence, respectively .51, .50 and .43.

Coleman used the A.C.E., Minnesota Paper Form Board, Bennett Mechanical Comprehension, and Cooperative English and Algebra Tests. Validities for various subjects tended to be from .30 to .50

Studies such as that by Pierson and Jex, referred to above, suggest that well-selected standard tests are about as effective as custom-built tests in predicting success in engineering training, presumably because education depends too heavily on verbal ability.

Lawyers. Tests and test batteries for the selection of law students have been developed at a number of universities, notably California, Columbia, Iowa, Michigan, Minnesota, and Yale, and by the Educational Testing Service; a review of early work with these and other tests in law schools was prepared by Adams (1943). The pioneer test in this field appears to have been the *Ferson-Stoddard Law Aptitude Examination* (no longer in print). It consists of four parts: a reading comprehension and recall (after the other parts) test based on a law case, a reading comprehension and reasoning test based on another case, a verbal reasoning test, and a reading comprehension test based on legal material. The test has been used only by law schools and has not been available to counselors. Ferson and Stoddard (1927) found that the Law Aptitude Examination had a correlation of .54 with the first-year law grades of 100 students at the University of Iowa; as summarized by Adams, subsequent studies of the test yielded validity coefficients of .54 at Tennessee, .34 at Newark, .42 at the New Jersey Law School, .46 at Illinois (first semester only), and .49 at Chicago. All of these studies agree, then, in showing considerable validity in the test, about that shown by scholastic aptitude tests in liberal arts colleges; since the populations of law schools are somewhat more homogeneous than those of colleges, the test presumably has somewhat more validity. It is therefore interesting to compare its validity, in the last study, with that of the A.C.E. Psychological Examination, which was found to be .56 in contrast with that of .49 for the Ferson-Stoddard Law Aptitude Examination As the combined tests yielded a correlation of .62 it seems that, although they were not measuring exactly the same thing, the contribution of the professional aptitude test was not great. In the Illinois study Welker and Harrell (1942) found that pre-law grades had much more predictive value than the aptitude test (.75 as compared to .46), and that the correlation for the combined indices was not much higher (.78). Only three of the six scores of the Ferson-Stoddard test (Part 2 of which yields three scores) were found to have any appreciable correlation with grades: these were Part 2C, Relevant Facts, Part 3, Logical Inferences, and Part 4, Matching; these validities were .17, .28, and .31, respectively; the validities of A.C.E. part scores were of the same order, but more consistently so. The implication is that a good general intelligence test is at least as useful as this professional aptitude test, especially when one notes, with Welker and Harrell, that the effective law aptitude subtests are the reasoning rather than the "legal memory" tests. Studies at the University of Minnesota (Douglass et al., 1942) obtained correlations of custom-built tests with law grades which were as good as those for intelligence tests, but multiple correlations permitting comparison were not reported.

In 1943 Adams published studies of a new *Iowa Legal Aptitude Test,* developed for use in the same institution as the Ferson-Stoddard nearly twenty years earlier. Its preliminary form consisted of eight subtests, the first three of which are not legal in content, while the last five are. Part 1 is a verbal analogies test, Part 2 is a mixed relations or more complex analogies test, Part 3 contains opposite items of a verbal type, Part 4 is a test of memory for material in a judicial opinion read before Part 1 or two hours earlier, Part 5 is a reading comprehension test stressing judgments of relevance, Part 6 is also a reading comprehension test adapted from Part 2 of the Ferson-Stoddard Test, Part 7 is a verbal reasoning test, and Part 8 is a legal information test. When the first-semester grades of 110 law students were correlated with part and total scores on the Legal Aptitude Test, the former were found to range from .36 (Part 5, reading comprehension for relevance) to .57 (Parts 3 and 7, verbal opposites and verbal reasoning), while the validity of the total score was .65. It was decided to use Parts 3, 7, and 8 (verbal opposites, verbal reasoning, and legal information) in the final form of the test; the multiple correlation of these subtests with the criterion was .67, higher than that of the total score on the preliminary form of the test. Although no comparisons were made with general intelligence tests, comparison with the predictive value of achievement tests and pre-law grades indicated that in this case the professional aptitude test had more validity than the non-specialized indices. This was presumably because the professional aptitude test was, itself, a highly refined test of general intelligence, couched in terms most appropriate to the field in question, to which was added an interest-achievement factor by the inclusion of a subtest of legal information.

Nurses. Batteries for the selection of nursing students have been developed by a number of university schools of nursing, and by independent organizations or individuals working on a consulting basis with nursing schools.

The George Washington University Series of Nursing Tests (Center for Psychological Service, George Washington University, 1944) was developed from the Moss-Hunt Nursing Aptitude Test, first published in 1931 and available to counselors. The series incorporates a modified form of the Nursing Aptitude Test, consisting of five parts, as follows: judgment in nursing situations, memory for anatomical diagram and nomenclature studied during the test, nursing information, scientific vocabulary, and following directions in filling out a nurse's report form. This test is, obviously, custom-built as to items, drawing heavily on the technical content of nursing as it might have been experienced before training or as presented in the test itself. A second test in the series is a Reading Comprehension Test, utilizing material from commonly used textbooks in nursing schools. The third test is an Arithmetic Test; the fourth is a General Science Test based on high school courses; and the fifth is an Interest-Preference Test somewhat resembling Strong's Vocational Interest Blank, the items of which were selected because they differentiated nurses from non-nurses. Norms based on high school graduates applying for admission to nursing schools are provided with the manual, together with suggested critical scores for interpretation, but it is recommended that local norms be developed because of differences in standards. No indication of the numbers on which the standardization was done is included, nor are there any data on the validity or reliability of the new series of tests. Although the test items look promising and have obviously been based on the best available experience in nurse selection programs, validation data such as have been provided by other investigators using the earlier form of the Aptitude Test for Nursing are needed. In these studies of the earlier form of the first subtest of the present series Douglass and Merrill (1942) found correlations ranging from .54 to .62 with grades in the first year of nursing school at the University of Minnesota, and Williamson and others (1938) found correlations of .34 and .37 with grades in twenty schools of nursing. As these grades were very unreliable in some schools the validity seems lower than it actually was; in one school with a better marking system the validity was .49. It seems clear that this one part of the present series is what the manual suggests: a "specialized intelligence test for prospective nurses." The other subtests appear to be specialized achievement and interest measures for prospective nurses, but need to be evaluated as such.

The Nursing Entrance Examination Program of the Psychological Corporation has developed another battery of tests for use in schools of nursing. This battery is administered periodically at various centers throughout the country, by arrangement with co-operating institutions; it is not available for general use. Like the battery developed by Hunt, the Nursing Entrance Examinations consist of custom-built tests constructed by the Psychological Corporation for schools of nursing. The program, described by Potts (1945), has since been modified and improved.

Other standard tests have been used in studies referred to above, conducted at the University of Minnesota and co-operating schools of nursing. In these it was found that standard tests of vocabulary (Co-operative Test Service), English, and General Science had substantial validities, as high as .44, .53, and .58 in one school where marking was reasonably reliable. Douglass and Merrill found a validity of .77 for the Moss-Hunt Test of Nursing Aptitude and the Co-operative General Science Test. Crider (1943) found that the Strong Interest and Bell Adjustment inventories added little to predictions based on the Otis Test of Mental Ability, confirming Douglass and Merrill's correlation of .20 for Strong's nurse scale and grades. Correlations with an occupational stability, rather than achievement, criterion might have yielded different results.

Pharmacists. Until recently little attention was paid to the scientific selection of students of pharmacy, and little was known concerning psychological factors related to success in this occupation. During World War II, however, members of the occupation became more self-conscious as a profession, even to the point of changing the status of pharmacists in the Army from enlisted to commissioned grade. After the war the American Pharmaceutical Association engaged in a co-operative study with the American Council on Education, one of the purposes of which was to develop better methods of selecting pharmacists, and Schwebel (1951) developed a pharmacist scale for Strong's Vocational Interest Blank.

Physicians. *The Moss Medical Aptitude Test* (Association of American Medical Colleges, 1930) was for many years the standard instrument for the selection of medical students, used by most medical schools in the United States and not available to others. New forms were provided periodically, but the content is rather like that of the Moss-Hunt Nursing Aptitude Test which has already been described and which was based in part on Moss's experience with the Medical Aptitude Test. Parts deal with comprehension and retention, logical reasoning, scientific vocabulary, etc., making the test one of intelligence measured by means of medical material. Some of the studies published in the Association's journal have shown that there is a tendency for high-scoring applicants to succeed in training and to be rated favorably as interns, whereas those who make low scores tend to do poorly. Moss (1942) reported that one percent of the top-decile students failed, as contrasted with 18 percent of the bottom-decile students.

Chesney (1936) found that refusing to admit anyone in the lowest decile would eliminate 25 percent of the failing students, 15 percent of the mediocre students, 7 percent of the fair students, and only 3 percent of the good students. But Douglass (1942) and Cavett and others (1937) found validities of only .12 to .34 for various classes at the University of Minnesota, compared to .40 to .57 for liberal arts grades. Moon (1938) found a closer relationship at Illinois, where the validity was .42 and liberal arts grades had a validity of .49. The Minnesota Medical Aptitude Test, another custom-built battery, had validities of only .14 to .40. Strong's Physician scale had a validity of only .16 for 131 students, using first-year honor points as criterion. Stuit (1941) obtained correlations of .23 and .32 between the Moss Test and first-year grades in medicine at the University of Iowa, as compared to correlations of .45 and .46 between college grades in liberal arts and science courses, on the one hand, and medical grades on the other. The Moss Test and science grades yielded a multiple correlation of only .49. These studies suggest that, although the Moss and Minnesota Medical Aptitude Tests have some value in selecting medical students, they do not add much to predictions made on the basis of undergraduate college grades. Apparently further study and development of new types of instruments is needed in this field. In the meantime, the standard measures of intelligence and achievement in appropriate areas will probably prove as useful as the professional aptitude test in appraising promise in this field. The Psychological Corporation now handles this admission-testing program for the A.A.M.C.

Pilots. Apart from embryonic efforts in the first World War, tests for the selection of aircraft pilots were first developed early in World War II by the Civilian Pilot Training Program of the Civil Aeronautics Administration, the work of which was summarized by Viteles (1945); were further developed for the U.S. Navy under Jenkins' leadership (1946); and especially by the Army Air Forces Aviation Psychology Program under Flanagan (1947, see also DuBois, 1947). The most far-reaching of these, both in the variety of tests used and in the extent of its validation procedures was the last named; as it included tests comparable to those originated by the other two programs, only it is described here.

The Aviation Cadet Classification Battery (U.S. Air Force, 1942, revised in 1943 and subsequently) consisted of a personal history questionnaire arranged in multiple-choice form and stressing experiences and background factors which had been found related to success in flying training; two spatial orientation (perceptual) tests utilizing aerial photographs and maps; a reading comprehension test; a dial and table reading test involving taking readings from airplane instruments and aeronautical tables; two instrument comprehension tests also based on flight instruments; a mechanical principles test based on the Bennett; a general information test presumably tapping interests and personality traits underlying the possession of information found to be related to success or failure in flying training; two mathematics tests; a rotary pursuit (eye-hand co-ordination) test; a lathe-type two-hand co-ordination test; a stick-and-rudder test in which controls are moved to match light signals appearing in a prearranged pattern; a rudder control test in which the examinee's seat is kept in equilibrium by movements of the rudder with the feet; a discrimination-reaction-time test requiring the selection of a switch to be moved in order to put out a series of lights; and a pegboard measure of finger dexterity (DuBois, 1947). Most of these, it may be noted, involved custom-built items: The biographical data items were written to tap aspects of experience which might be related to flying success; the perceptual items involved perception of the type used in pilotage; the eye-hand-foot co-ordination test used a stick and rudder; etc. Although correlational analysis techniques were used to insure relative independence of the tests, the miniature-situation element was strong in most of them.

As is necessary in a custom-built selection testing program in which conditions are constantly changing, these tests, their antecedents, and their successors, were continuously validated as data concerning new criterion groups were received. The most impressive of these validation studies (DuBois, 1947, Ch. 5; Flanagan, 1947) was made with a group of 1143 candidates for aviation cadet training who were sent to pilot training regardless of their scores on psychological tests. Analyses were made to reveal the comparative validity of the psychological tests, the cadet selection battery as a whole, the Adaptability Rating for Military Aeronautics (psychiatric examination), the Army General Classification Test, the Aviation Cadet Qualifying Examination (custom-built intelligence test used in preliminary screening), and years of education. Data are reproduced in Table 28.

The correlations given are with success in training through advanced flying school, that is, with ability to win wings and a commission. Outstanding in the above data are the following facts:

The three most valuable tests are paper-and-pencil tests;

The most valid tests are custom-built even in item content;

The battery has more predictive value than the best single test;

Objective tests have more predictive value than psychiatric judgment.

Later work with this battery has involved the factor analysis of these and certain other tests (Guilford, 1947, 1948), the refinement of the most promising, the addition of subsequently developed tests to the battery, and an ambitious joint project of the Air Force, Navy, and American Institute for Research in which a battery of paper-and-pencil tests was developed in an attempt to measure with maximum economy all of the characteristics found to contribute to flying success. Studies were also made which ascertained the predictive value of the wartime battery and its components for success in combat (Lepley, 1947); this was found to be significant, although attenuated by the relatively small and select group of pilots which reached combat and the complexity of the criterion. The number of planes shot down by a fighter pilot in England in 1942 cannot be compared, for example, to the number shot down in the same theater in 1945 when air superiority had changed hands and daylight bomber raids were unknown.

TABLE 28

RELATIVE PREDICTIVE VALUE OF CERTAIN CUSTOM-BUILT AND
STANDARD PSYCHOLOGICAL TESTS AND CERTAIN OTHER INDICES
FOR SUCCESS IN PILOT TRAINING (After DuBois)

	Test	Validity
	General Information	.51
Pilot	Instrument Comprehension II	.48
Tests	Mechanical Principles	.43
	Complex Co-ordination (Stick-Rudder)	.42
	Discrimination-Reaction-Time	.42
	Spatial Orientation II	.40
	Dial and Table Reading	.40
	Rudder Control	.40
	Two-Hand Co-ordination	.36
	Biographical Data	.33
	Stanine (Battery score)	.66
	Aviation Cadet Qualifying	.50
	Army General Classification	.31
	Education	.21
	Flying Adaptability Rating (Psychiatric)	.27

The American Institute for Research, established by Flanagan and other aviation psychologists on the basis of their wartime experience, has carried out a number of research projects for the Civil Aeronautics Administration and several of the commercial airlines, analyzing the work of the airline pilot and constructing a battery of tests for the evaluation of pilot proficiency which might be used in selecting personnel for commercial airlines. The Institute has established testing centers at which the current form of this battery is now being used in such selection, but evaluation studies have awaited the slow accumulation of objective criterion data.

Psychologists.   The post-war demand for clinical and vocational psychologists resulted in a great increase in the number of candidates for training in psychology and a strain on training facilities. Graduate departments of psychology, the Veterans Administration, the U.S. Public

Health Service, and the American Psychological Association worked together on the problem of improving the selection and training of psychologists. One result of this co-operation was a project carried out at the University of Michigan, by Kelly and Fiske (1950, 1951), for the development of a battery of tests for the selection of students for training in clinical psychology; another project provided for the study and revision by Kriedt (1949) of the psychologist scale for scoring Strong's Vocational Interest Blank at the University of Minnesota. The Kelly and Fiske study used grade, internship supervisors' ratings, and completion of the doctorate as criteria, finding validities in the forties for the Miller Analogies Test and Strong's Psychologist Keys, somewhat lesser but significant validities for the Allport-Vernon and Guilford-Martin inventories, and none for projective or interview material. Kriedt's Specialty Keys proved valid for success as well as for occupational differentiation.

Salesmen. More attention has been devoted by business and industry to the problem of selecting salesmen than to any other single group save possibly executives. Unfortunately too many business concerns have been so near-sighted that they have been willing to employ psychological consultants for actual selection work but have not been willing to finance the research which should precede the development of any new method or instrument, whether it be psychological, chemical, or mechanical. Even scientifically trained executives such as engineers often fail to realize that developmental work must be done in personnel selection just as in manufacturing. And there have too often been psychologists and pseudo-psychologists available who were willing, either through ignorance of the complexities of personnel testing, or through eagerness to supplement academic incomes, to attempt to meet the needs of business and industry on their own inadequate terms. So-called institutes for aptitude testing therefore flourish in most of our large cities, testing candidates for sales positions and making recommendations to referring employers which are based to an undetermined extent upon hunches and shrewd judgments made independently of the tests, and partly upon clinical evaluation of test scores, as described by Flemming and Flemming (1946) and discussed in connection with executives, above.

The Moss Test for Ability to Sell (Center for Psychological Service, George Washington University, 1929) is one of the few tests or batteries of tests marketed as a device for selecting salesmen. It consists of items designed to test memory for names and faces, judgment in sales situations, observation of behavior, comprehension and retention of selling points in reading material, following directions in making out sales records, and sales arithmetic, and has norms based on department store salespersons. Although it has been tried in numerous sales situations, the results have not generally been published in the journals. The prevailing opinion of it among department store personnel workers known to the writers is not favorable.

The majority of researchers who have experimented with test batteries for the selection of salesmen have utilized personal history blanks, interest inventories, and personality inventories, as well as intelligence tests. The first-named are generally custom-built, the second is usually Strong's Vocational Interest Blank as a source of either a score obtained from a standard key or of items for the development of a new key, and the personality measures have included the Bernreuter Personality Inventory, the Humm-Wadsworth Temperament Test, or other well-known inventories. For example, Bills (1938) reported on the use of the life insurance and real estate salesman's keys of Strong's Blank, personal data, the Bernreuter, and a mental alertness test, the last two were of little value, but the others, combined, significantly improved the selection of successful salesmen. Kurtz (1941) worked with life insurance salesmen, using personal history items and Kornhauser's personality inventory and obtaining correlations of .40 with production. Men who rated A had twice the chance of staying in the business for a year than men with E ratings had. Similar findings have been reported with salesmen of more tangible things than life or casualty insurance. Otis (1941) used personal data items, a combination of Strong's life insurance and real estate keys and the Bernreuter, with salesmen of a detergent company, finding that the first two were effective predictors of success while the last-named test was not. Building materials salesmen were studied by Ohmann (1941), who used only personal data; he found a correlation of .67 between a questionnaire of 13 items and his most reliable criterion, annual commission earnings. Viteles (1941) tried the Humm-Wadsworth Temperament Test with 59 appliance salesmen, but found that 12 of the 20 who had "desirable" patterns were discharged or resigned during the try-out period.

From studies such as these, more thoroughly reviewed by Schultz (1936) and by Kornhauser and Schultz (1941), the conclusion to be drawn is that, contrary to the expectation of many personnel consultants, personality inventories have little or no value in the selection of salesmen. The reasons for this will be discussed in a later chapter dealing with such instruments. The most effective batteries have consisted of the sales keys of Strong's Vocational Interest Blank and, especially, custom-built personal history questionnaires. The nature of the personal history items which prove valuable varies somewhat with the type of saleswork, but some consistent trends are revealed. In Ohmann's study the 13 valid items were as follows: height; age; marital status; number of dependents; amount of life insurance; debts; years of education; number of clubs and organizations belonged to; years on the last job; experience in the line of sales in question; average number of years on all jobs; average monthly earnings on the last job; and reasons for leaving the last job. It is notable that, although these salesmen were handling a tangible, building materials, the success of life insurance salesmen has also been found to be related to age, marital status, dependents, amount of life insurance, organizations belonged to, etc. (Bills, 1941). Stokes (1941), reviewing what experience has shown to be important in research in the selection of salesmen, has like others emphasized the need to take into account the job environment of the salesman, pointing up the fact that, despite the similarities which exist between sales jobs, and the more or less universal validity of Strong's sales keys, specific factors are found in any job which make custom-built batteries of tests more valid than standard tests. His second point then follows of necessity: Research in the selection of salesmen must be dynamic, for it must continue to take into account the changes which take place in the environment in which the salesman is working and therefore in the demands of his job. The fact that Strong's Vocational Interest Blank has been found to predict success in sales jobs, but in very few other occupations (see the discussion of Strong's Blank in Chapter 17), appears to confirm this point concerning the special importance of interest and motivational factors in selling.

Scientists.   The importance of scientific occupations was emphasized as never before during World War II and its aftermath, when some countries such as Great Britain kept their science students and scientists draft-exempt because of their potential contributions to the war effort, and when the various Allies engaged in a scramble for the talents of the scientists of the conquered countries, particularly Germany. Although there had been small scale attempts at the development of techniques for predicting success in science prior to the second World War, it was only during and after it that national efforts were organized to locate scientific talent and to encourage its training. With such ability at a premium it seems likely that its selection will receive even more attention in the future than medicine has in the past and than psychology has recently received. Studies of scientists have recently been summarized, in a study initiated by the National Science Foundation, by Super and Bachrach (1957); scientists are characterized by superior scores on intelligence tests, and on tests of spatial visualization and mechanical comprehension, and dexterity. They have distinctive interests on the Strong and Kuder blanks.

The Stanford (or Zyve) Scientific Aptitude Test (Stanford University Press, 1929) is probably the first published attempt to develop a measure of scientific aptitude, but little work has been done with it since either by its author or by others despite its continued use. The test attempts to measure the components of scientific aptitude, science being defined as organized knowledge based on experiment and observation. The test therefore consists of eleven parts, designed to measure experimental bent by: expressions of preference for experimental as opposed to bibliographical or other methods of obtaining information; clarity of definitions; suspended versus snap judgment as manifested in ability to state that answers to problems are not available; reasoning concerning physical problems (in four parts differing in content) ; caution and thoroughness as demonstrated in the solution of apparently easy problems; ability to select and arrange experimental data for the solution of a problem; comprehension of scientific reading matter; and perception of complex spatial detail. The items were developed and checked with the aid of established scientists, and were validated against grades in scientific courses. The correlation with intelligence tests, according to the manual, was found to be .51 with college students. The correlation with the grades of science students was .50, in contrast with that of .27 for the Thorndike Intelligence Examination; the correlations with grades of non-scientific students were respectively .02 and from .38 to .53, which strongly suggests that the test does measure intellectual factors which are important to success in scientific but not in literary endeavor.

The Stanford test was administered by Benton and Perry (1940) to 49 students (30 science majors, 13 others) at the College of the City of New York. They found correlations of .30 and .37 between this test and four-year grades, while intelligence as measured by the A.C.E. Psychological Examination had a validity of .31 with total grades, .27 with science grades, and .41 with non-science grades. The intercorrelation of the two tests was .45. Studies of this test have been so few and are so inconclusive that it is difficult to judge its validity, especially when the attenuation of validities usually noted in studies made after the original authors' are kept in mind.

The Science Talent Search administered by Science Service and financed by the Westinghouse Electric Corporation is a project in which one might expect to find a battery of tests for the selection of potential scientists being developed. The selection procedure consists of a series of five hurdles: a Science Aptitude Examination; high school grades; a recommendation by teachers; an essay on a scientific topic; and psychological and psychiatric interviews (1943) . The Science Aptitude Test first used was a reading test of scientific subject matter, but in later years what amounted to a battery of tests was utilized. A variety of types of items were used, including both scientific vocabulary and Bennett-type mechanical comprehension pictures; scores were independent of amount of mathematics and science studied; but validity data so far made available (Edgerton et al.,

1948) have focussed on the total process of selection, not on its specific instruments. Winners have been found to earn better grades, get more education, win more honors, and enter the professions more than do non-winners, but the award procedure may be in part a cause, as well as a predictor, of these events.

"Scientific aptitude" being presumably largely an intellectual matter, it seems likely that batteries of tests for the selection of promising scientists should stress such factors as reasoning, spatial visualization, and number ability; scientific vocabulary and mechanical comprehension are two less pure aptitudes which are significant; and inventoried interest may prove to have value for completion and occupational utilization of training if not for quality of work done.

Teachers. Tests of aptitude for teaching have been experimented with by a number of individuals and schools of education, in attempts to improve the selection of students of education. The New York State Department of Education and the Psychological Service Center of George Washington University, are among the institutions which have published custom-built tests of so-called teaching aptitude. Other institutions such as the University of Wisconsin and the University of California at Los Angeles have worked with batteries of standard tests in attempting to develop sound selection procedures. Tests for the evaluation of preparedness for teaching have been prepared by the Educational Testing Service as the National Teacher Examinations, administered annually to candidates for teaching positions who wish to have an objective record of their mastery of subject matter made available to possible employers (Flanagan, 1941).

The Coxe-Orleans Prognosis Test of Teaching Ability (World Book Co., 1930) is a good example of custom-built tests of aptitude for teaching. It consists of five subtests: general information; knowledge of teaching methods and practices; ability to learn the type of material included in professional texts; comprehension of educational reading matter; and judgment in handling educational problems. Validation of this instrument has been in terms of success in teacher training, but the data are not very helpful because they consist of correlations between the prognostic test and a comprehensive achievement test at the end of the first year of training. These coefficients range from .53 to .84 as cited in the manual; but in view of the highly academic nature and similar content of both tests the evidence is not convincing.

It has apparently not been validated against criteria of success on the job. In view of the difficulties commonly encountered in establishing criteria of success in teaching this is perhaps understandable. The validity coefficients will undoubtedly be much lower than those reported in the manual, since teaching is less exclusively dependent upon intellectual ability than is learning about teaching.

Seagoe's studies (1945a, 1945b, 1946) are a good illustration of work with standard tests in the selection of students in schools of education. She administered the American Council Psychological Examination, Co-operative General Culture Test, Meier Art Judgment Test, Seashore Tests of Musical Talents, Strong Vocational Interest Blank, Allport-Vernon Study of Values, Bell Adjustment Inventory, Bernreuter Personality Inventory, and Humm-Wadsworth Temperament Test, to 125 students of education. Ratings of success in two practice-teaching assignments were obtained for 31 of these students, and were correlated with the test scores (1945b). No significant relationships were found between the tests of intelligence, special aptitudes, achievement, interest, or values and the ratings of success in practice teaching; relationships between personality inventory scores and ratings were significant, those for the Bell keys being —.40 (total adjustment) and that for the Bernreuter Self Confidence scale being — 38 Twenty-five of these students were followed up after two years of teaching in the field, using rank in the faculty as judged by the school administrator as criterion (1946) ; the Bell and Bernreuter were again found to have some validity, as did ratings by critic teachers; grade-point ratio had none.

The numbers in Seagoe's studies, as in other studies of the same type, are small and criteria of success need to be improved, before objective selection procedures can be considered adequate in this field. But as long as teaching remains an underpaid occupation with too few applicants for available positions there is not likely to be much pressure for the development of better selection methods, at least in most training institutions.

The National Teacher Examinations (Educational Testing Service, annually since 1939) provide school systems and graduate schools of education which can afford to be selective with a standard battery of tests for the evaluation of teachers' mastery of subject matter, reasoning, and judgment. These are, obviously, only intellectual aspects of ability to teach, and do not include interest in children, emotional stability, and other factors which are generally believed to be important to teaching success. But Flanagan (1941) found that scores on this battery of tests had a correlation of .51 with ratings of 49 teachers in 22 school systems made by two supervisors and five students in each case, which indicates that the tests have value in selecting good teachers despite the fact that they do not measure everything that is to be considered. As Flanagan points out, other characteristics must be appraised by means of interviews, ratings, and recommendations in the absence of more objective methods.

REFERENCES FOR CHAPTER XV

Achilles, P. S. "The consulting services of the Psychological Corporation," *J. Consult. Psychol.*, 10 (1946), 120-126.

Adams, W. M. "Prediction of scholastic success in colleges of law: I. The experimental edition of the Iowa Legal Aptitude Test. II. An investigation," *Educ. Psychol. Measmt.*, 3, 291-305 and 4, 13-19 (1943).

Assessment Staff. *The Assessment of Men.* New York: Rinehart, 1948.

Bass, B. M. "The leaderless group discussion," *Psychol. Bull.*, 51 (1954), 465-492.

Bellows, R. M. "Status of selection and counseling techniques for dental students," *J. Consult. Psychol.*, 4 (1940), 10-14.

Benton, A. L., and Perry, J. D. "A study of the predictive value of the Stanford Scientific Aptitude Test," *J. Psychol.*, 10 (1940), 309-312.

Bills, M. A. "Relation of scores on Strong's Interest Blank to success in selling casualty insurance," *J. Appl. Psychol.*, 22 (1938), 97-104.

———— "Selection of casualty and life insurance agents," *J. Appl. Psychol.*, 25 (1941), 6-10.

Bransford, T. L., et al. "A study of the validity of written tests for administrative personnel," *Amer. Psychol.*, 7 (1946), 279 (abstr.).

Brush, E. N. "Mechanical ability as a factor in engineering aptitude," *J. Appl. Psychol.*, 25 (1941), 300-312.

Cavett, J. W., et al. "Tests of medical aptitude at Minnesota," *J. Assn. Amer. Med. Coll.*, 12 (1937), 257-268.

Chesney, A. M. "Evaluation of the Medical Aptitude Test," *J. Assn. Amer. Med. Coll.*, 2 (1936), 15-32.

Coleman, W. "An economical test battery for predicting freshman engineering course grades," *J. Appl. Psychol.*, 37 (1953), 465-467.

Crider, B. "A school of nursing selection program," *J. Appl. Psychol.*, 27 (1943), 452-457.

Douglass, H. R. "Prediction of success in the Medical School," *University of Minnesota Studies in Prediction of Scholastic Achievement*, 2 (1942), 1-16.

————, et al. "Prediction of success in the Law School," *University of Minnesota Studies in Prediction of Scholastic Achievement*, 2 (1942), 46-60.

————, and Maaske, R. S. "Prediction of success in the School of Business Administration," *University of Minnesota Studies in Prediction of Scholastic Achievement*, 2 (1942), 32-45.

————, and McCullough, C. M. "Prediction of success in the School of Dentistry," *University of Minnesota Studies in Prediction of Scholastic Achievement*, 2 (1942), 61-74.

————, and Merrill, R. G. "Prediction of success in the School of Nursing," *University of Minnesota Studies in Prediction of Scholastic Achievement*, 2 (1942), 17-31.

Du Bois, P. H. (ed.). *The Classification Program* ("AAF Aviation Psychology Report," No. 2.) Washington, D. C.: Government Printing Office, 1947.

Edgerton, H. A., and Britt, S. H. "The Science Talent Search," *Occupations*, 22 (1943), 177-180.

————, ————, and Norman, R. D. "Later achievements of male contestants in the first annual Science Talent Search," *Amer. Scientist*, 36 (1948), 403-414.

Ferson, M. L., and Stoddard, G. D. "Law Aptitude Examination: preliminary report," *Amer. Law School Rev.*, 6 (1927), 78-81.

Flanagan, J. C. "A preliminary study of the 1940 edition of the National Teachers Examination," *Sch. and Soc.*, 54 (1941), 59-64.

———— *The Aviation Psychology Program in the AAF* ("AAF Aviation Psychology Report," No. 1.) Washington, D. C.: Government Printing Office, 1947.

Flemming, E. G., and Flemming, C. W. "A qualitative approach to the problem of improving selection of salesmen by psychological tests," *J. Psychol.*, 21 (1946), 127-150.

Flory, C. D., and Janney, J. E. "Psychological services to business leaders," *J. Consult. Psychol.*, 10 (1946), 115-119.

Griffin, C. H., and Borow, H. "An engineering and physical science aptitude test," *J. Appl. Psychol.*, 28 (1944), 376-387.

Guilford, J. P. (ed.). *Printed Classification Tests.* ("AAF Aviation Psychology Report," No. 5.) Washington, D. C.: Government Printing Office, 1947.

——— "Factor analysis in a test development program," *Psychol. Rev.*, 55 (1948), 79-94.

Harris, A. J. "Relative significance of measures of mechanical aptitude, intelligence, and previous scholarship for predicting achievement in dental school," *J. Appl. Psychol.*, 21 (1937), 513-521.

Holcomb, G. W., and Laslett, H. R. "A prognostic study of engineering aptitude," *J. Appl. Psychol.*, 16 (1932), 107-115.

Jenkins, J. G. "Naval aviation psychology. II. The procurement and selection organization," *Amer. Psychologist*, 1 (1946), 45-49.

Kelly, E. L., and Fiske, D. W. "The prediction of success in the VA training program in clinical psychology," *Amer. Psychologist*, 5 (1950), 395-406.

Kelly, E. L., and Fiske, D. W. *The Prediction of Performance in Clinical Psychology.* Ann Arbor: University of Michigan Press, 1951.

Kornhauser, A. W., and Schultz, R. S. "Research on the selection of salesmen," *J. Appl. Psychol.*, 25 (1941), 1-5.

Kriedt, P. H. "Vocational interests of psychologists," *J. Appl. Psychol.*, 33 (1949), 482-488.

Kurtz, A. K. "Recent research in the selection of life insurance salesmen," *J. Appl. Psychol.*, 25 (1941), 11-17.

Laycock, S. R., and Hutcheon, N. B. "A preliminary investigation into the problem of measuring engineering aptitude," *J. Educ. Psychol.*, 30 (1939), 280-289.

Lepley, W. M. (ed.). *Psychological Research in the Theaters of War.* ("AAF Aviation Psychology Report," No. 17.) Washington, D. C.: Government Printing Office, 1947.

Mandell, M., and Adkins, D. C. "Validity of written tests for the selection of administrative personnel," *Educ. Psychol. Measmt.*, 6 (1946), 293-312.

Moon, G. R. "Study of premedical and medical scholastic records of students in the University of Illinois College of Medicine," *J. Assn. Amer. Med. Coll.*, 13 (1938), 208-212.

Moss, F. A. "Report of the Committee on Aptitude Tests for Medical Schools," *J. Assn. Amer. Med. Coll.*, 17 (1942), 312-215.

Murray, H. A., and MacKinnon, D. W. "Assessment of OSS personnel," *J. Consult. Psychol.*, 10 (1946), 76-80.

North, R. D. "Tests for the accounting profession," *Educ. Psychol. Measmt.*, 18 (1958), 691-714.

Ohmann, O. O. "A report of research in the selection of salesmen at the Tremco Manufacturing Co.," *J. Appl. Psychol.*, 25 (1941), 18-29.

Otis, J. L. "Procedures for the selection of salesmen for a detergent company," *J. Appl. Psychol.*, 25 (1941), 30-40.

Pierson, G. A., and Jex, F. B. "Using the Cooperative General Achievement Tests to predict success in engineering," *Educ. Psychol. Measmt.*, 11 (1951), 397-402.

Potts, E. M. "Testing prospective nurses," *Occupations*, 23 (1945), 328-334.

Schultz, R. S. "Standardized tests and statistical procedures in the selection of life insurance sales personnel," *J. Appl. Psychol.*, 20 (1936), 552-556.

Schwebel, M. *The Interests of Pharmacists.* New York: Columbia University Press, 1951.

Seagoe, M. V. "Permanence of interest in teaching," *J. Educ. Res.*, 38 (1945), 678-684.

——— "Prognostic tests and teaching success," *J. Educ. Res.*, 38 (1945), 685-690.

———— "Prediction of in-service success in teaching," *J. Educ. Res.,* 39 (1946), 658-663.

Smith, R. V. "Aptitudes and aptitude testing in dentistry," *J. Dent. Educ.,* 8 (1943), 55-70.

Stokes, T. M. "Selection research in a sales organization," *J. Appl. Psychol.,* 25 (1941), 41-47.

Strong, E. K., Jr. "Vocational guidance of executives," *J. Appl. Psychol.,* 11 (1927), 331-347.

———— *Vocational Interests of Men and Women.* Stanford: Stanford University Press, 1943.

———— "The interests of forest service men," *Educ. Psychol. Measmt.,* 5 (1945), 157-171.

———— "Interests of senior and junior public administrators," *J. Appl. Psychol.,* 30 (1946), 55-71.

Stuit, D. B. "Prediction of scholastic success in a college of medicine," *Educ. Psychol. Measmt.,* 1 (1941), 77-84.

Super, D. E., and Bachrach, P. B. *Scientific Careers and Vocational Development Theory.* New York: Teachers College Bureau of Publications, 1957.

Thompson, C. E. "Selecting executives by psychological tests," *Educ. Psychol. Measmt.,* 7 (1947), 773-778.

Viteles, M. S. "Getting results from a program of testing for sales ability," *Market. Ser. Amer. Mgmt. Assn.,* 1941.

————. "The aircraft pilot: 5 years of research; a summary of outcomes," *Psychol. Bull.,* 42 (1945), 489-526.

Welker, E. L., and Harrell, T. W. "Predictive value of certain 'law aptitude' tests," *Educ. Psychol. Measmt.,* 2 (1942), 201-207.

Williamson, E. G., et al. "The selection of student nurses," *J. Appl. Psychol.,* 22 (1938), 119-131.

XVI

THE NATURE OF INTERESTS

INTERESTS have been the object of much attention from vocational and counseling psychologists during the past generation. Three scholarly books (Fryer, 1931; Strong, 1943; and Darley and Hagenah, 1955), at least ten significant monographs (Garretson, 1930; Strong, 1931; Super, 1940; Darley, 1941; Carter, 1944; Barnett et al., 1952; Brogden, 1952; Guilford et al., 1954; Strong, 1955; and Layton, 1960), and a number of reviews of research published in the journals (Berdie, 1944; Super, 1945, 1947, 1954), all dealing with the nature and role of interests, are the result.

Psychologists in other specialties have paid less attention to interests, Vernon and Allport (1931) and Thorndike (1935) being among the few to study interests, and they have used somewhat different methods. Clinical psychologists have tended to devote their energies to intelligence and to personality; students of individual differences have focussed on abilities; and personologists have been challenged more by problems of the organization of personality. Developmental psychologists are perhaps an exception, as they have paid some attention to the development of play interests in a type of study illustrated by those of Lehman and Witty (1929, 1930, 1934).

It is worthy of note that, when these differing approaches to the psychology of individual differences have briefly met, the result has tended to be confusion, even after 40 years of research in this field. Thus Lehman and Witty (1932) loosed a broadside at vocational interest inventories, decrying their use on the grounds that interests are unreliable, but their evidence to that effect was based on *expressions* of interests and throws no light on *inventories* of interests. This is an important distinction which will shortly be made clear. Because of the practical importance and complexity of the great amount of material now available on the nature and development of interests, these topics are dealt with at length in this section. The role of interests in vocational adjustment will be considered later, in connection with the validity of specific instruments.

Definitions. There have been four major interpretations of the term interest, connected with as many different methods of obtaining data. In an attempt to clarify thinking in this area Super (1947a) classified them as *expressions, manifestations, tests,* and *inventories* of interests.

Expressed interest is the verbal profession of interest in an object, activity, task, or occupation, what Fryer (1931) called "specific interest." The subject states that he likes or dislikes something. There has been relatively little research with expressed interests since Fryer (1931) reviewed early work, as shown by later reviews by Carter (1944) and Berdie (1944). The expressed interests of children and adolescents are unstable and do not provide useful data for prediction. For older adolescents and adults the data are somewhat more promising, for Strong (1943, p. 657) has shown that constancy of responses to the 400 items in his inventory ranges from 53 per cent for high school juniors after six years to 83 per cent for women physicians after one day. More recently, Rothney (1958) and Schmidt and Rothney (1955) reported the results of a longitudinal study of the stability of expressed interests in adolescence. In the latter study 347 sophomores in four representative Wisconsin high schools were interviewed and counseled at the end of each school year. The vocational preferences of 35 per cent of the students were consistent over the three year period, and 67 per cent (24 per cent of the total group) were engaged in that field as students or workers six months after graduation. Only 54 per cent of the vocational preferences of the last year in high school were the same as the field actually being pursued at the time of follow-up, but this percentage was higher than that for the preceding years of high school (46 of the tenth grade and 49 per cent of the eleventh grade choices were implemented).

The importance which may be attached to expressions of specific interests clearly varies with the maturity of the individual. As Gilger (1942), Lurie (1942), Trow (1942), Hamburger (1958) and others have shown, it also depends upon the phrasing of the question, for some questions concerning vocational preferences are so put as to elicit information concerning *expectations,* some so as to ascertain *preferences,* and some to evoke *fantasies.* The degree of realism of preferences varies with the question asked.

Manifest interest is synonymous with participation in an activity or occupation. Objective manifestations of interest have been studied in order to avoid the subjectivity of expressions or the implication of a static quality in interest. Thus Kitson (1925, Ch. 8) urged that the verb "to be interested" be used, indicating that a process and activity are involved. In this approach it is assumed that the high school youth who was active in the dramatic club has artistic or literary interests, and that the accountant who devotes two evenings per week to building and operating a model railroad system is interested in mechanics or engineering. It is generally appreciated that such manifest interests are sometimes the result of interest in the concomitants or by-products of the activity rather than in the activity itself. The high school actor may have merely been seeking association with others, which he may later need less or obtain by different means. In other cases the opportunities for the manifestation of an interest may be limited by the environment or by financial considerations, so that an expressed interest has no manifest counterpart. For these reasons, manifest interest has not been used as a predictor of interest in many studies, although it has often served as a criterion, the reasoning being that anything as dynamic as interest should in most cases find an outlet.

Tested interest is here used to refer to interest as measured by objective tests, as differentiated from inventories which are based on subjective self-estimates. It is assumed that, since interest in a vocation is likely to manifest itself in action, it should also result in an accumulation of relevant information. Thus interest in science should cause a person to read about scientific developments, whether in a science course or in the daily paper, and to acquire and retain more information about science than would other people. Fryer (1931, p. 664ff.) has reviewed the attempts which were made by O'Rourke, Toops, Burtt, McHale and others during and after World War I to measure interest by means of the amount and type of information retained, and has pointed out that these were not followed up because of the cumbersomeness of memory and information tests.

With the improvement of testing and statistical techniques which subseqently took place, however, interest in the development of interest tests revived. At this time Greene published his Michigan Vocabulary Profile Test (1940), measuring interest through specialized vocabularies. The Co-operative Test Service brought out a general information test which Flanagan (1939) described as a measure of interest in several areas. Super and his students at Clark University (Super and Roper, 1941; Super and Haddad, 1943; Older, 1944) began a series of investigations designed to develop attention or recent-memory test of interest in vocational activities. During World War II the Aviation Psychology Program brought together several psychologists who had been working along these lines (R. N. Hobbs, R. R. Blake, D. E. Super, J. C. Flanagan, and F. B. Davis). Their efforts resulted in the development of a General Information Test which gave differential scores for pilots, navigators, and bombardiers and which proved to be the most valid single test in the Air Force's selection and classification battery (Flanagan, 1946; Du Bois, 1947). Since then similar tests have been used in the selection of pilots for commercial airlines, and other civilian applications are also being made. The technique will in time probably prove to be generally useful for selection and counseling.

Inventoried interest is assessed by means of lists of activities and occupations which bear a superficial resemblance to some questionnaires for the study of expressed interests, for each item in the list is responded to with an expression of preference. The essential and all-important difference is that in the case of the inventory each possible response is given an experimentally determined weight, and the weights corresponding to the answers given by the person completing the inventory are added in order to yield a score which represents, not a single subjective estimate as in the case of expressed interests, but a pattern of interests which research has shown to be rather stable. The apparently logical objection that no statistical combination of unstable elements can yield a stable total is met by Strong's study (1943, p. 871) of the effect of changes of responses to specific items on inventory scores; although changes of expressions of liking or disliking of as many as 125 of his 400 items were found, these shifts had no appreciable effect on scores for occupational interest. The reason for this is that shifts in one direction are balanced by shifts in the other direction, the underlying pattern or trend of interest being constant. Strong's work provided a foundation for a great many studies in the psychology and measurement of interest, and made possible the development of practical instruments for use in counseling and selection. He has summarized most of the significant research with his Vocational Interest Blank in two volumes (Strong, 1943, 1955) which are classics in the field of measurement. Other inventories have been developed by Kuder (see Chapter XVIII), Garretson and Symonds (1930), Lee and Thorpe (see Ch. XVIII), and others.

The term interest is also used to convey other concepts, the most relevant of which are *degree of interest* or strength of motivation and *drive* or need. The former needs no discussion, as it is a matter of degree rather than of kind: When it is said that someone is vitally interested in attaining a goal, the statement is one concerning the degree of some underlying (inventoried) interest or the strength of some drive. The concept of interest as drive does require discussion, for when it is said that an individual is interested in winning friends or in gaining prestige, the type of interest referred to is not covered by any of the concepts so far discussed. Interests or drives of this type are of a different and more fundamental order than either specific or underlying interests; they constitute a deeper layer of personality. Unlike interests, which are sometimes included under the heading personality and sometimes not, drives or needs are generally considered to be one of the central aspects of personality. They are therefore discussed, together with their vocational significance and methods of measuring them, in a later chapter.

Types of Interests. As in the case of intelligence testing, progress in the measurement of interests was first made possible by a shotgun approach which was concerned less with specific nature of that which was being measured than with the fact that is could be measured. The all-important discovery made by Strong and his students was that the interests of men in a given occupation, e.g., engineering, were different from those of men-in-general (Strong, 1943, Ch. 7). It was only after scales had been developed for the measurement of the interests of men in a number of occupations that factor analysis and item analysis revealed the nature of these interests. For this reason the logical sequence of topics which follows is not the historical order in which discoveries were made.

Interest factors were first studied by Thurstone (1931), who applied factor analysis to 18 occupational scales of the Strong Vocational Interest Blank. Strong (1943, Ch. 8, 14) later made several factor analyses, in the last of which he used data from 36 occupational scales, first without rotating the axes (like Thurstone) and then by rotating them. For clarity's sake, the results of these three analyses are presented in Table 29, together with data from four other studies, the latest of which is the most complete (Guilford et al., 1954).

Allport and Vernon developed their Study of Values as a measure of the values postulated by Spranger. Lurie (1937) also devised an instrument for appraising these values, and unlike Allport and Vernon, subjected it to factor analysis. Brogden (1952) factor analyzed the Allport-Vernon itself. These lists of factors are also presented in Table 29.

Further evidence concerning the nature of interest factors is provided by Kuder's work with his Preference Record (see Ch. XVIII). This inventory gives scores for ten types of interests, which cannot be called factors in the statistical sense of the term as they were not isolated by factor analysis methods, but which amount to about the same thing as they are based on item analysis and are therefore internally consistent and mutually independent. Kuder originally developed seven scales by this method; these are listed in Table 29. He later added three more which are listed in parentheses because, unlike the others, they had substantial correlations with other keys: e.g., mechanical interests correlated .405 with scientific; and clerical correlated .50 with computational.

The most searching study of interest factors is that by Guilford and associates (1954), who hypothesized the existence of 33 such factors and developed brief but fairly reliable inventories for each of these. The combined inventory was administered to 800 airmen and to 800 Air Force officers. When the subscores were factor analyzed, 24 factors were isolated for the airmen, and 23 for the officers, 17 of these factors being identical. Eight of these factors are clearly interest factors, but the others tap aspects

TABLE 29

THE NATURE OF INTERESTS

Interest and Value Factors Revealed by Seven Studies

Thurstone	Allport-Vernon	Lurie	Strong Unrotated	Rotated	Kuder	Brogden	Guilford
Science	Theoretical	Theoretical	Science	Science	Scientific	{ Scientific / Theoretic }	Scientific
People	Social	Social	People	People	Social-Service	Humanitarian	Social-Welfare
Language			Language	Language	Literary	Cultural	
			Things vs. People	Things vs. People	(Mechanical)		Mechanical
					(Outdoor)		Outdoor
					(Clerical)		Clerical
					Computational		
Business	{ Economic / Political }	Materialistic	Business	{ System / Contact }	Persuasive		Business
	Aesthetic				Artistic	Fine Arts	Aesthetic-Expression
					Musical	General Aesthetic	Aesthetic-Appreciation
	Religious	Religious				Liberal	
						Individualistic	Personality-Factors
						Antireligious	
						Antiaggression	

of personality which are normally classified as adjustment or temperament. Only the former are listed in Table 29, where it is clear that they are essentially the same as those identified in other studies with one important difference: What in Kuder's less rigorous work appear to be three factors of literary, artistic, and musical interest, and in Strong's less searching study of some of these fields appear to be literary and musical interests, in Guilford's work appear as two aesthetic factors of *expression* and *appreciation* regardless of the subject matter. As Strong's work with artistic and musical interests is somewhat limited, but his studies in the literary or linguistic occupations are substantial, there may be justification for retaining the concept of a linguistic factor, while accepting Guilford's finding of general aesthetic (expressive and appreciative) factors.

After a study of the factors appearing in Table 29, together with the literature upon which they are based, the writers have developed their own list of interest factors. But the naming of statistically isolated factors is a highly subjective and arbitrary process. For example, three authorities have variously named the same factor "interest in male association," "interest in order or systematic work," and "non-professional interests" (Strong, 1943, pp. 164–166). In one sense, therefore, the writers are justified in attempting a synthesis of the findings of various investigators and in applying their own names to the various categories; in another sense the whole process of naming interest factors is open to criticism as a potentially misleading one. It can be justified, perhaps on the grounds that a cautiously named concept, cautiously used, is better than no concept at all; it merely behooves the name-giver to point out the need for caution.

Table 29 brings out complete agreement on the first interest factor, the *scientific*, which may be defined as an interest in knowing the why and how of things, particularly in the realm of natural science (only the Allport-Vernon attempts to assess interest in *scientia* in the philosophical sense). There is agreement also on the second factor, interest in *social welfare* or in people for their own sake. The third factor is not provided for by Allport and Vernon or by Lurie, who were limited by Spranger's postulates; but as factor analysis, like qualitative analysis in chemistry, can isolate only the elements which were originally put into the compound, the lack of positive findings in these studies can be disregarded. The Thurstone-Strong-Kuder data can be accepted as evidence of the existence of a *literary* interest factor, consisting of interest in the use of words and in the manipulation of verbal concepts (Guilford's failure to find a literary or linguistic factor casts some doubt on this, but this may again be a function of items used). A fourth factor, again not revealed by the Spranger-inspired studies, by the Thurstone analysis (which was presumably based on too few occupations), nor by the Kuder procedure (though perhaps partly covered by his mechanical scale), but found in Strong's two analyses and in Guilford's mechanical factor, might best be called the *material* or concrete, although Strong named it "things vs. people" or, on the basis of negative loadings in the literary and linguistic occupations, "language." The writers prefer Kitson's term "material" because the occupations in which it has heavy positive loadings tend to involve working with tangibles. Carpenter, high school mathematics-science teacher, farmer, printer, production manager, engineer, chemist (these last two have heavier scientific loadings), and even policeman and accountant may be included in this category, since they are concerned, respectively, with the protection and the management of property.

The fifth factor, one concerning which there is considerable agreement, is the *systematic* or perhaps record-keeping; it emerged most clearly in Strong's more refined analysis but he refused to name it, although he states that it might be called the C.P.A. factor. Kuder's computational interest appears to be similar, and it is probably covered also by Thurstone's business, Allport and Vernon's economic, Lurie's misnamed philistine (or materialistic), and Guilford's clerical factor. The sixth, or *contact* factor, is also probably included in the too comprehensive complex of factors called business and economic in the Thurstone, Spranger and Guilford categorizations, refined by Strong's final analysis. It is the second factor which Strong thought it wise to refrain from naming until more occupations were found to have loadings of it. It seems to involve interest in meeting or dealing with people not for their own sakes but for material gain. Kuder's persuasive interest appears to be identical with it. Finally there are the aesthetic expression and appreciation factors identified as artistic by Allport and Vernon and by Thurstone (1931), as artistic and musical only by Kuder and therefore quite tentatively. The failure of Strong and Thurstone to find a musical factor proves little in view of the presence of only one musical occupation in their lists, but Guilford's recent searching study seems to justify the acceptance of two general aesthetic factors which differ in role rather than in content.

Occupational differences in patterns of interests were, it has already been pointed out, the basic discovery which made possible subsequent studies of the nature and role of vocational interests. Beginning his work in interest measurement as a member of the outstanding group of applied psychologists who were assembled at the Carnegie Institute of Technology after World War I, Strong continued to experiment with the vocational interest inventory technique after he joined the faculty at Stanford University, and there succeeded in establishing the fact that the inventoried interests of men who are engaged in different occupations differ significantly from those of men-in-general (Strong, 1943, Ch. 7).

Some occupational groups, however, were not distinguishable from men-in-general; Strong's early attempts to develop scales for executives and for teachers failed (1943, 20, 161 ff), and in his later studies (1946, 1947) of the interests of public administrators he encountered difficulties which were essentially similar. The reason for the failure to establish patterns of interest peculiar to executives and teachers, and for the lack of validity of the public administrator scale for some groups of administrators, may lie in the fact that these are not truly occupational groups. Strong's work in the development of teachers' scales has shown, for example, that interests of men social-studies teachers seem to be primarily those of social-welfare workers (r with YMCA secretary = .87), those of high school mathematics-science teachers resemble those of skilled tradesmen (r with carpenter = 68, with printer = .72), and the correlation between the interests of men in these two types of teaching occupations is practically zero (r = .13), as shown in Strong's table of intercorrelations (1943, opposite p. 716). Similarly, the executive group was made up of men who were essentially engineers, lawyers, or other specialists (Strong, 1927), and the public administrators also included many men who were professional men at heart but who had been given administrative responsibility (Strong, 1946). There do, however, appear to be differences between administrators and specialists in a given field (Strong, 1948, 1949).

The occupations which were differentiable on the basis of interest patterns of the men engaged in them could be grouped, Strong found (1943, Ch. 8), according to the degree of similarity which existed between their interests. Some of the occupational interest scales were positively intercorrelated, others negatively, in varying degrees. Strong therefore grouped the various occupational scales on the basis of these intercorrelations, establishing .60 as the minimum intercorrelation necessary for two occupations to be assigned to the same family. The resulting families may be characterized as follows:

Biological Science Occupations	e.g. Physician
Physical Science Occupations	e.g. Chemist
Technical Occupations	e.g. Printer
Social Welfare Occupations	e.g. Y Secretary
Business Detail Occupations	e.g Accountant
Business Contact Occupations	e.g. Life Insurance Salesman
Linguistic Occupations	e.g. Lawyer

The terminology is essentially Darley's (1941), but not that used by Strong, who has been extremely reluctant to name groups which seem at all heterogeneous. He characterized the second group as "mathematics and physical sciences," the fourth as "handling people for their presumed good," the fifth as "office," the sixth as "sales," and the seventh and last as "linguistic" (1943, p. 160), but felt that the presence of such vocational groups as artists and architects in the first or biological science group (r artist-physician = .79) makes it difficult to name, and that aviators, carpenters, mathematics-science teachers, and policemen make odd bedfellows in the so-called technical group, even though their intercorrelations with the printer scale are .65, .73, and .72 respectively. As Strong points out in his discussion (1943, pp. 159–160), the sub-professional technical group appeared originally as part of a general scientific group which included also the biological and physical-science occupations, but which broke up into the three scientific or near-scientific groups of the current classification when more occupational scales were devised. As additional occupational scales are developed, it is probable that the so-called technical group will further subdivide, an hypothesis for which Strong provides some important substantiating data in the analysis of the effect of the point of reference (1943, Ch. 21 and 22).

Another group which seems likely to subdivide as more keys are added is the contact or sales group. The danger involved in either of these names is brought out by the fact that public utility salesmen belong more in the business detail group (r office worker = .69) than in the contact family (r life insurance salesman = .39). Strong therefore feels that there will in time be a new sales group, consisting of house-to-house salesmen. In a study discussed in Ch. XVII Hughes and McNamara have demonstrated the need for a further breakdown. The classification of occupations on the basis of interests must therefore be considered tentative, and one must not let the very natural desire to give names to categories lead to the making of false generalizations.

The data on differences between kinds of teachers and salesmen raise a question concerning other occupations. They prompt one to ask whether a sufficiently refined analysis would reveal similar differences between mechanical, electrical, civil, and chemical engineers, for example, or between various types of secretaries in the YMCA. Using his standard techniques of comparing one occupational group with men-in-general (described in the section dealing with the inventory), Strong found no differences between the interests of the various types of engineers, the correlation between civil and electrical engineer, for example, being .86 (1943, p. 118). He obtained similar results with scales for interests of YMCA general and boys' work secretaries, only the physical directors being distinct enough (r combined Y secretary scale = .74) to warrant a separate key. These results would seem to point to the conclusion that some occupations can be broken down into specialized subgroups on the basis of interests, and that others cannot. To the first category one might add accountants, teachers, and public administrators, already discussed in another connection, and certain types of sales work; to the latter, sales managers and salesmen in certain fields such as life insurance and vacuum-cleaners. In view of the evidence accumulated by Strong it seems that, when compared with the interests of men-in-general, the interests of men in a broadly defined occupation are generally so similar as to obscure differences between specialties. A mechanical engineer, when compared to non-engineers, is more like unto than different from a civil or electrical engineer, for then the common factor, engineering, is crucial; this is true also of physicians and surgeons (Strong, 1943, p. 697).

It has been shown, however, that when a different point of reference is used, men in specialties within an occupation can be differentiated. Using engineering students as subjects, Estes and Horn (1939) compared the interests of each type of engineer, mechanical for example, with those of all other types of engineers studied. The point of reference in this study was therefore not men-in-general, but engineers-in-general. Under these conditions the differences between the interests of the various specialty groups became visible, and separate scales could be developed. Strong recognized the possibilities of this approach (1943, p. 120), but has not attempted to capitalize them except for accountants (1949) and medical specialties (Strong and Tucker, 1952). Kriedt (1949) developed specialty scales for clinical, counseling, experimental, and industrial psychologists. The method is one which might well commend itself to professional schools interested in providing better guidance services for their students or in improving their selection procedures.

The point of reference used in constructing occupational scoring keys for interest inventories has been found to have one other important effect on our knowledge of occupational differences in interests. The first men-in-general group used by Strong consisted, for reasons of convenience, of men for whom test data were on hand and who were not in the occupation under investigation (1943, p. 555). This happened to be an economically somewhat select group, for the first scales constructed were for occupations which were of either professional or managerial calibre. When Strong's Vocational Interest Blank was used with men from the lower half of the occupational hierarchy, little differentiation of interests was found: printers, carpenters, policemen, and farmers, coming from the skilled trades level, had so much in common, when compared with a professional-managerial-clerical men-in-general group, that the differences between them were not very significant (the intercorrelations approximate .70), and persons habitually employed at the semiskilled levels seemed to be undifferentiated on the basis of their interests (Berman et al., 1934).

These findings led the staff of the Minnesota Employment Stabilization

Research Institute to hypothesize concerning the differentiation of semi-skilled and unskilled workers on the basis of interests (Berman et al., 1934), and prompted Strong to pursue a line of research already suggested by his work with the women's blank (1943, p. 554). He therefore developed occupational scales based on three different points of reference. These consisted of: 1) business and professional men earning $2500 or more per annum in 1943 (rather like the original scales), 2) a proportional sample of all occupational levels averaging, like the general population, at the skilled trade level, and 3) a proportional sample of skilled, semiskilled, and unskilled workers, averaging at the semiskilled level. For convenience these three reference points, called P_1, P_2, and P_3 by Strong, may be referred to as the white-collar, general, and blue-denim groups. Three hypotheses were set up to be tested by means of these occupationally similar, but referentially different, keys. These were:

1. Certain occupations at different levels have the same types of interests (e.g., engineers at the professional and mechanics at the skilled) ;

2. The rank and file cannot be differentiated by their interests (e.g., semi-skilled workers tend to make no high scores) ;

3. Men in the lower-level occupations have their own occupationally-specialized interests (e.g., when compared to other semiskilled workers, drill-press operators have interests which are different from those of electrical-unit assembly workers).

Using scales based on the general point of reference (P_2), Strong found that the correlation between the printer and carpenter scales was .24, whereas it was .73 when the white-collar point of reference (P_1) was used; similarly, the correlation between printer and policeman was —.27 instead of .59. In other words, when an appropriate point of reference is used, differences between the interests of men in a given occupation and those of men in the reference group appear significant; when an inappropriate reference point is used, differences between the interests of men in the occupation being studied and those of "men-in-general" are obscured. This holds whether it is men in a low-level occupation being studied against a high-level men-in-general group, or men in a high-level occupation being studied with a low level men-in-general group as point of reference. Strong's third hypothesis was therefore confirmed, and it is to be expected that in due course occupational interest scales will be developed which will be useful with men of less than average socio-economic level and for counseling and selection for more occupations at the skilled and semiskilled levels, many of which should be found to have differentiating patterns of interests. Work by Clark and by Long, discussed in Ch. XVIII, has begun to implement this idea.

Lest it appear from the preceding paragraphs that all of our knowledge concerning the differentiation of occupational groups on the basis of interests is based on work with Strong's inventory, it should perhaps be mentioned that various researchers (see Ch. XVIII) have confirmed Strong's general findings for some 200 occupations with Kuder's Preference Record. The Allport-Vernon Study of Values has shown similar trends with pre-occupational groups in colleges (Duffy, 1940), but has not been much used with men and women actually engaged in occupations even in more recent years. Reference has been largely to work with Strong's Blank simply because, as a more thoroughly studied vocational interest inventory, it provides more data from which to draw conclusions.

Socio-Economic Differences. The preceding discussion of the effect of the point of reference on the identifiability of patterns of interests was virtually a treatment of research which has been carried out on socio-economic differences in occupational interests, at least in so far as methodology is concerned. There still remains the task, however, of describing the differences in interests which characterize the various occupational levels and the evident effects of status on interests. It has been shown in several studies that socio-economic status is related to the development and manifestation of interests. Using the Strong, McArthur and Stevens (1955) found that inventoried interests are better predictors of the regular adult occupation than are expressed preferences when the subjects are mobile middle-class young men, but that preferences are better predictors of adult occupation in the case of young men of upper-class status. Jordaan (1949) found that mechanically gifted boys tend to have the expected scientific and technical interests except when their fathers are executives. And Hyman (1956) found that, although Kuder-inventoried interests are not related to social status when considered alone, they are related when intelligence is taken into account; for example, social service interests tend to be high in bright boys of upper middle-class status, but low in equally bright boys of middle-class backgrounds. One would infer from these findings that certain social environments encourage the development and expression of certain kinds of interests while inhibiting the development or manifestation of others.

The basic work on the measurement of socio-economic differences in interests was done by Strong (1943, Ch. 10), in connection with his scale for measuring occupational interest level, or the socio-economic level at which an individual would be placed on the basis of similarity of interests. Men who are successfully employed in the higher level occupations tend to have more interest in literary and legal activities and in business contact work, and less social welfare and sub-professional technical interest, than men in lower level occupations. Men in legal and literary occupations, salesmen, and scientists tend to make high occupational level scores, although there is no relationship between the scientific and occupational level scales on Strong's Blank. Senior public administrators score higher on occupational level than do junior public administrators (Strong, 1946). Strong suggests that the scale measures managerial ability.

It has been suggested by Darley (1941, pp. 60 and 66) and by Darley and Hagenah (1955) that occupational interest level is indicative of aspiration level, that it "represents the degree to which the individual's total background has prepared him to seek the prestige and discharge the social responsibilities growing out of high income, professional status, and recognition or leadership in the community; at the lower end of the scale, the individual's background has prepared him for the anonymity, the mundane round of activities and the followership status of a great majority of the population." Darley suggests, also, that those who are characterized by a low level of occupational interest are likely to lack the motivation which results in staying power in college. Kendall (1947) attempted to validate this hypothesis with three groups of 100 men each at Syracuse University, selected from the entering freshman class on the basis of high, average, and low occupational level scores on Strong's Blank. These three differing occupational level groups were found to differ also in mental ability as measured by the Ohio State Psychological Examination. Those who were high on these measures made higher hour-point ratios during the first semester. When intelligence was held constant the academic achievement of the three occupational level groups was again found to differ, the differences being significant at between the one percent and the 5 percent levels. The differences are therefore not completely clear cut, but they do suggest that those with extremely low occupational interest levels are likely to find college work foreign to their taste, whereas it will be congenial to those who are characterized by high occupational interest levels.

However, the results of a number of studies, discussed by Barnett, Handelsman, Stewart, and Super (1952), by Darley and Hagenah (1955), and by Strong (1955, Ch. 12), are conflicting. Morgan (1952), unlike Kendall, found no differences in the occupational level scores of achieving and under-achieving students; Gustad (1954) found no relationship between OL scores and actual or desired socioeconomic status among college students; Terman and Oden (1948) reported that the most successful gifted men in their study made significantly higher OL scores than did the least successful when tested at age 30; and Barnett (1952) found that OL scores had a high negative correlation with satisfaction with being unemployed in a period of prosperity. As interpreted by Barnett and associates in their monograph (1952), the results of these studies suggest that only the most parsimonious interpretation of occupational interest level is justifiable:

a high OL score indicates that a person's interests are like those of people at high socio-economic levels, and are therefore most likely to find appropriate outlets in high-level occupations. But whether this means that he has the drive to seek these outlets is apparently not shown by having this type of interest.

Strong and Darley, however, reject this interpretation and continue to equate occupational interest level with drive, Strong because people tend to seek appropriate outlets for their interests (better demonstrated for *field* than for *level*), Darley because he prefers his own interpretation of the relevant studies. Thus Darley and Hagenah write (1955, p. 117): "Handelsman . . . . finds about the same relationship between OL and school grades, with intelligence held constant, as has been found by other investigators", and conclude that "there seems to be a certain disjunction between the findings of these three separate studies (Barnett, Stewart and Handelsman) and the conclusions drawn in the monograph. From our (Darley and Hagenah's) standpoint, we find the actual data quite in accord with our general interpretation of the OL scale . . ." It should be noted that the data in Handelsman's study, referred to by Darley and Hagenah, involve relationships between OL scores and grades which are not only low but *non*significant, in line with what has been found by other investigators but not with the Darley-Hagenah conclusions. It is the preponderance of such *negative* findings that requires an economical interpretation of such positive findings as do exist.

Avocational Differences. What has been found true of occupations has been found to apply also to avocations. In a study of model engineers, amateur photographers, amateur musicians, and stamp collectors, Super (1940) found that men who were active in the first three avocations had patterns of interests which differentiated them from each other, and that the first two interest patterns resembled each other ($r = .58$), whereas the first and third had nothing in common ($r = .02$). Although the number of avocations studied is small this suggests that they are differentiated and may be classified in ways similar to occupations. The interest patterns of stamp collectors were found to be similar to those of other men, suggesting that philately is an avocation which, like the vocation of executive, cuts across basic interest patterns which are much more important than the interest common to men engaging in it. It is noteworthy, also, that the three differentiable avocational interest patterns resemble those of the expected occupation, e.g., the model engineers have interests like those of professional engineers, whereas the interests of stamp collectors are difficult to classify vocationally.

Sex Differences. Popular stereotypes as to the masculinity and femininity of interests are widespread, and it is natural to ask what research in the psychology of interests found in this area. Studies made by Terman and Miles (1936), Carter and Strong (1933), Yum (1942), Strong (1943, Ch. 11), and Traxler and McCall (1941), all agree that men tend to be more interested in physical activity, mechanical and scientific matters, politics, and selling. Interest in art, music, literature, people, clerical work, teaching, and social work is more characteristic of women. It is especially worthy of note that masculinity and femininity are scaled traits rather than dichotomies: people are not masculine or feminine in their interests, but more or less masculine or feminine. It is interesting to speculate as to whether the higher incidence of cultural (artistic, literary, musical, and social) interests in women means that they are constitutionally the carriers of culture, or whether they have simply taken on that role because nature forced men, as the stouter animals, to take on the competitive, constructional, and provisioning roles. Anthropological studies suggest the latter, since there are a few societies in which men are the domestics and women the providers. But physical constitution seems to play a part, as shown by the preponderance of active-male societies. A good illustration is Miles' (1942) case study of a boy raised for 17 years as a girl: despite the seemingly overwhelming feminine influences to which he was subjected, he made definitely masculine scores on the Terman-Miles Masculinity-Femininity Test and on Strong's Vocational Interest Blank (scored for masculinity-femininity of interests).

Age Differences. Counselors and psychologists who have not carefully studied the literature on change of interest with age frequently question the wisdom of giving much weight to measures of interests because of the possibility of change of interest with age. This question overlaps to some extent with that of the permanence of interests, discussed below, but it is distinct in that it focuses on the relationship between age and change, rather than on the effects of experience.

Several important studies have been made of the differences in interests which are associated with differences in age. The first of these was by Strong (1931), incorporated and brought up to date in his later book (1943, Ch. 12–13); the second was a series of follow-up studies by Strong (1943, pp. 358–362); the third was part of the Adolescent Growth Study of the University of California, written up in a series of articles by Carter and others and summarized in his monograph (1944) and in a journal article (1940). More recent studies have been published by Tutton (1955), Rosenberg (1953), Herzberg et al. (1953, 1954), Long and Perry (1953), Trinkaus (1954), Powers (1956), Verburg (1952), and Strong (1951, 1955).

Strong's first approach consisted of comparing the interests of men at ages 15, 25, 35, and 55, both by analysis of individual items (age 15, 25, and 55) and by the construction of interest-maturity scales for each of the four age levels selected for study. These analyses revealed that age differences are less significant than occupational differences. The interests of 15-year-olds agree in large measure with those of 25-year-olds ($r = .57$), are more like those of 35-year-olds ($r = .66$), and even more like those of 55-year-olds ($r = .89$) (1943, p. 279) ; as about one-third of the change that takes place between ages 15 and 25 occurs during the first year (15.5 to 16.5), one-third during the next two years, and one-third during the next seven years (1943, p. 259) it is clear that interests are fairly well crystalized by age 18. Boys' interests tend to become less like those of physicians, dentists, and engineers as they approach age .25, and more like those of office workers, salesmen, accountants, physical directors, social science teachers, and personnel managers; those whose interest-maturity scores on Strong's Blank are high have been thought to be least likely to show changes of interest patterns, whereas the interests of those whose interest-maturity scores are low are most likely to undergo change, conclusion not supported by research (see below).

The slight changes that take place after age 25 tend to be an undoing of those that took place prior to that time, as shown by the higher correlations between the interests of 15 and 35 or 55-year-olds than those of 15 and 25-year-olds already cited. Strong has confirmed this with two different sets of data (1943, pp. 283–285). A study by Bullenberger (1940) provides a basis for the conclusion that increases in hormone activity in adolescence account for the changes that take place in boys at that stage; perhaps it is decreases in hormone activity after the mid-twenties [suggested by studies of sex habits conducted by Kinsey (1948)] which account for the reversal. This tendency toward an undoing of the 15 to 25-year-old changes should not, however, be interpreted as a reversal of all trends, for the decreased interest in physical activity and daring continues beyond age 25 and is the most striking change during that period of little change; others are a decreased interest in occupations involving writing, and a lessened liking for change or interference with established habits. Strong summarizes his work as follows: "The primary conclusion regarding interests of men between 25 and 55 years of age is that they change very little. When these slight differences over thirty years are contrasted with the differences to be found among occupational groups, or between men and women, or between unskilled and professional men, it must be realized that age, and the experience that goes with age, change an adult man's interests very little. At 25 years of age he is largely what he is going to be and even at 20 years of age he has acquired pretty much the interests he will have throughout life" (1943, p. 313).

The second series of studies conducted by Strong were follow-ups of 175 Stanford freshmen, retested nine years later, and of 168 Stanford seniors, retested ten years after graduation. The average correlation between test and retest scores was .56 for those first tested as freshmen (ages 18 and 27) and .71 for those first tested as seniors (ages 21 and 31). These findings from longitudinal studies confirm the conclusions drawn from Strong's cross-sectional analyses in revealing a fair degree of permanence of interests in 18-year-olds, and a substantial degree in 21-year-olds. The lowest retest reliabilities at these ages were in the social welfare occupations, and the highest in the scientific and literary occupations; that this is partly due to decided increases in social welfare scores and relative stability in literary scores is shown by critical ratios ranging from 2.5 to 5.1 for the test-retest means of the former, and by critical ratios of —0.6 and —.15 for those of the latter (1943, p. 363). As those for the test-retest means of the scientific occupations ranged from 0.6 to 4.2, showing a tendency for some increase in scores to take place there, it must be deduced that the changes in scientific scores are regular and do not generally affect the rank order of the persons tested, while the changes taking place in social welfare interests are irregular and do generally affect the rank order of the persons tested. In other words, those who make the lowest scientific scores as seniors tend to remain lowest, while some of those who made the lowest social-welfare scores make substantial gains in this area and others do not. Strong's early findings showed that those with the lowest interest maturity scores make the most radical gains, finding since contradicted (see below).

The Adolescent Growth Study investigations were, as the title implies, longitudinal studies of high school pupils who were tested in the tenth or eleventh grades and retested each year until graduation from college. These studies showed that the correlations between interest patterns in tenth or eleventh grade and the last year of college are about as high as those between interests in the first year of college and five years after graduation, for Taylor's study (1942) revealed a mean correlation of .52 for eleventh grades retested six years later, as compared with Strong's average correlation of .56 for college freshmen retested nine years later. Carter (1940) and Taylor and Carter (1942) have similarly demonstrated that the interest patterns of high school boys and girls (in practically the only studies of change in girls) remain fairly stable throughout the high school years. Carter concluded that "the Strong scales are almost, but not quite, as reliable and stable when used at the high school level as when used with adults," and Taylor stated that "vocational interests, as measured by the Strong inventories, appear to be almost as permanent during the high school years as during adult life". It may be well at this point, however, to remember Strong's more cautious conclusions already quoted above.

The stability of interests as measured by Strong's Blank has been thorroughly considered by Darley and Hagenah (1955, pp. 34–53) , hence only selected studies are discussed in detail here. Recent short-term studies by Stordahl (1954), Hoyt (in Layton, 1960), Hoyt, Levy, and Smith (1957), and King (1958), with college students, and long term studies by Trinkaus (1954) with college students arrived at the middle years, and by Powers (1956) and Verburg (1952) covering the span from middle adulthood to old age, are significant.

Most noteworthy is the fact that the long-term studies have shown reliabilities averaging about .70. In Trinkaus' study, 46 percent of the Yale freshmen tested and rating A on a given scale rated A or B+ 15 years later on the same scale, while 80 percent of those who made C on a given scale as freshmen made C or C+ in middle adulthood. That Powers got similar results with a group from a lower socio-economic level is also noteworthy. Strong's (1951, 1955) college students followed up 20 years later showed, like others, a high degree of permanency of interests, the retest reliabilities again being about .70.

Stordahl failed to find support for Strong's (1943) early finding that the Interest Maturity Scale predicts stability of vocational interest scores. Hoyt obtained similar results but found that 83 percent of his high-school senior to college-sophomore groups had stable interests. Hoyt and associates used an Index of Depth of Strong scores (ill-described) which had a correlation of .37 with stability of Strong scores over a four-year period. A study by King (1958), of 242 college freshmen retested after nine months, examined the relationships of age, intelligence, social status, Strong's Interest Maturity Scale, number of "reject" patterns, etc., to stability of inventory scores, finding correlations of —.17 with number of "primary" patterns and .24 with the Depth Index developed by Hoyt et al. (1957), both significant at the .01 level, other results being negative.

As Darley and Hagenah conclude from earlier studies, in the great majority of cases one can expect strong positive or negative interests to remain the same during high school and college years, and, the data just cited show, during the rest of the life span. But what causes stability or instability, and how to predict them, is still virtually unknown. Hoyt's Depth Index is the most promising approach to prediction.

A number of studies of the stability of interests measured by Kuder Preference Record, Vocational, have also been carried out. As they suggest less stability than do those with the Strong, they raise questions not so much concerning the permanence of interests as of the long-term reliability of the instrument used. They are therefore discussed in the section on the Kuder as a test (in Ch. XVIII) .

Communality of Interests. The significance of differences in the interests of occupational, socio-economic, avocational, sex, and age groups obscures an important fact brought out by Strong's research (1943, Ch. VI), namely, the fact that people's interests are far more similar than different, regardless of sex, age, or occupational status. It is not really surprising to learn that people are human, and yet the fact is easily lost sight of when they are studied as men and women, boys and men, or professional men and skilled workers. The likes of college men and women are very similar $(r = .74)$, those of 15-year-old boys and 55-year-old men are no less simliar $(r = .73)$, and those of unskilled workers and professional-managerial men resemble each other even more closely $(r = .84)$. Underneath the very real differences among various groups of people we find an even larger common core which is of great social and philosophical importance.

Effects of Experience. The question of the permanence of interests is closely tied up with that of change of interests associated with age. We have seen that age changes do take place in adolescence, but that the patterns of interests which begin to manifest themselves by age 15 tend to be those which are revealed at ages 25, 35, and 55. Most of the change which does take place with maturity is complete by age 18; the type of change which may take place at that age is systematic and predictable on the basis of interest inventory data (interest-maturity scores). It is still pertinent, however, to inquire concerning the permanence of interests when they are subjected to influences which may change them in one direction or another. Kitson (1942), for example, has described a series of projects designed by O'Rourke to modify interest in vocational activities. The evaluation in terms of changes in *expressed* interests showed that pleasant experiences do change overt attitudes toward activities. But whether or not underlying interests, or interest patterns as measured by Strong's Blank or the Kuder, are thereby modified remains to be ascertained.

The relationship of change of inventoried interests to college grades among Yale students was studied by Burnham (1942), who found no relationship; such changes in interests as did take place could not demonstrably be attributed to the kind of grade achieved in college courses. Klugman's (1944) contrary findings concerning the clerical interests of high school girls probably prove little, in view of the general tendency for girls and women to make high clerical scores. Van Dusen (1940) worked with engineering students at the University of Florida, a group whose mean scores, as Strong points out (1943, p. 278), were very low, suggesting that they may have been, not a selected group, but rather a heterogeneous collection of state university freshmen who thought they would like to study engineering. He found a slight and statistically insignificant decrease in the retest scores of students who had given up their freshman choice by their senior year, and similar increases in the engineering scores of students who remained in that field throughout college. Strong failed to find the last trend in Stanford engineering students, but confirmed the others in studying the occupational histories and test scores of his Stanford seniors who were followed up ten years later: Those who were finally employed in a field other than that preferred when they were seniors made retest scores which were 3.6 standard score points lower than their original scores in the latter field; the critical ratio approached significance (2.5). The retest scores on the finally-entered occupation were higher by a comparable amount than were the original scores for that occupation. It is significant that there were no changes in the scores of those who entered and remained in the field of their preference as seniors: Ten years of occupational experience did not increase interest in the field of employment. Strong also analyzed the employment histories and test scores of Stanford freshmen retested nine years later, and found essentially the same results.

Mather, as reported in Strong (1943, p. 379), found no increase in home economics teacher scores after practice teaching in that field (a limited sample of experience, and a group already somewhat selected by training) ; she did, however, find substantial increases (4.7 standard score points, or one-half sigma) in the appropriate interests of 45 students who were retested after their first two years of exposure to the field of home economics. These studies suggest, either that experience in a field *inappropriate* to one's interests causes one to become even less interested in that field (and, conversely, more interested in appropriate occupations), or that it helps to bring about a better understanding of one's likes and dislikes and obtain more nearly true scores on an interest inventory. In the case of *appropriate* experience, however, there seems to be no effect, perhaps because understanding is already good enough not to be affected. As the inventory is a self-portrait technique, the second explanation seems acceptable.

Not in keeping with this interpretation are Glass' results (Strong, 1943, p. 379), which showed that the interests of unselected engineering freshmen who remained in engineering college until graduation became less like those of engineers (shift from B+ average to B) while the interests of those who dropped out as freshmen were interpreted as having become somewhat more like those of engineer. In the latter instance, however, it was an insignificant raw score increase of two points, but one which happened to change letter grade from B to B+. The decline in the interest of the graduates may have been due to poor guidance and selection, such as frequently results in many able but uninterested students persisting until graduation; thus many graduate engineers never enter engineering occupations, but become salesmen, accountants, etc.

After formulating a "theory of vocational interests as dynamic phenomena" Bordin (1943) directed several studies designed to test relevant hypotheses. With Wilson (1953) he tested 256 entering freshmen, classified them according to whether or not their curricular choices were consonant with their vocational interests as measured by the Kuder, and followed them up at the end of the first year in college to retest and to ascertain their current curricular choices. Bordin and Wilson interpret this study as having provided "unequivocal support for the assumption that inventoried vocational interests are dynamic phenomena reflecting changes in the individual's perceptions of himself", and consider this study a demonstration of the modifiability of interests as a result of experience. The conclusion is based on the fact that there was a tendency for the Kuder test-retest correlations for the stable-choice group to be higher than those for the unstable-choice group (six out of nine, using a one-tail test).

The fragility of the data involved is partly recognized by Darley and Hagenah, who note in passing that using the Kuder to test hypotheses based on Strong's Blank is unfortunate, but is minimized by them and disregarded by both Bordin and Wilson. It is highly relevant that the Kuder is a less reliable instrument that the Strong: The test-retest reliabilities for high school and college students, in the study of a similar age, sex, and educational group by Herzberg and others (1954b), ranged from .59 to .75 (.58 to .86 if the working group is included). Studies of the relationships between inventoried and self-rated interest (Berdie, 1950) show, furthermore, that the Kuder is more sensitive to the conscious attitudes of the subject; apparently it reflects more conscious stereotypes and attitudes than the Strong, which appears to measure interests at a deeper, more stable, level. Curricular choice, when expressed by an entering freshman, is also likely to be a fragile type of datum: The student is often unsure of his preferences, they are of no immediate practical importance until eight months or more in the future, and he is swayed by external influences such as the attitudes of his friends. It is not surprising that two unstable preference variables, the Kuder Preference scores and the curricular "choices" of college freshmen, vary in the same way at the same time.

Also using the Kuder, Ewens (1956) and Matteson (1955a,b) studied the relationships between interests and experience, measuring the latter by self-report inventories designed to parallel the areas covered by the Kuder. They found moderate correlations between experience and interest, which might of course indicate only that the two vary concomitantly, perhaps having a common cause. Matteson's second study was longitudinal: In students retested after two years of college, the greatest gains in experience were associated with the greatest gains in interest, in fields in which the interest-experience disparity had been greatest at college entrance. Matteson has thus provided a better test than Bordin and Wilson's of the relationship between experience and interest. But it must be recognized that he used the same sensitive or perhaps even superficial measure of interest, and a self-report inventory of experience so like the inventory of preferences in content and method that the correlation may be due to contamination.

The most rigorous study of the effect of experience on inventoried interests was conducted by Stordahl (1954), who followed up students first tested with Strong's Blank as seniors in high school and retested at the University of Minnesota during their second year. Dividing the students into an urban group of 125 boys and a rural group of 85 boys, he postulated that the experiences of the urban students at the urban university were not greatly different from their urban high school experiences, whereas the rural environment of the rural school group did result in their encountering a variety of new experiences at the urban university. He then hypothesized that the urban-urban group would therefore be characterized by higher retest reliability coefficients than the rural-urban group. This hypothesis was not sustained. It thus seems from this longitudinal study, which used a criterion which is not essentially a variation of the predictor (Bordin's and Mattoson's error), that experience has no significant effect on the interests of the average college student.

This is not to deny, however, the occurrence of occasional significant changes, which appear to take place in individuals who, encountering a type of experience which is quite new to them, discover abilities and interests which they had not suspected. Roe's scientists (1951 a, b), some of whom had as young men discovered in a science course that it is possible and exciting to find things out by experiments, are a case in point. But these seem to be the exceptions, and changes of measured interests are not as common as changes of expressed preferences.

Two studies have considered the relationship between length of time in an occupation and similarity of interests to those of men successful in that field. Both of these (Ryan and Johnson, 1942; Strong, 1943, p. 487) found insignificant correlations (.00 to —.12) between the interest scores and length of experience of sales and service men in the one case, and of life insurance salesmen in the other.

It is perhaps not so difficult to synthesize these findings into a theory of the effect of adolescent and adult experiences on vocational interests as their occasional apparent discrepancies suggest. Strong (1943, p. 380) concludes that "the interests of occupational groups are present to a large degree prior to entrance into the occupation and so are presumably a factor in the selection of the occupation," rather, the implication being, than the result of experience in that occupation. This conclusion is legitimate and adequate enough as a generalization concerning the permanence of interests, but it does not go as far as the data warrant in describing the modification, as opposed to the creation or destruction, of interests by experience. Before citing the attempts of others to provide such a synthesis and interpretation, however, three more aspects of the problem of the origin and development of vocationl interests need to be dealt with. These are family resemblances, and the roles of aptitudes and of personality factors.

Family Resemblances. The inventoried vocational interests of 110 pairs of fathers and sons were correlated by Strong (1943, p. 680), the sons ranging in age from 15 to 28 with a mean of 22 years. The range of correlations for 22 vocational interest scales was from .11 to .48, the average intercorrelation being .29; the average intercorrelation for randomly assorted men and boys, from the same total group, was .03. A later study by Strong (1957) with 100 father son pairs, yielded correlations of .30 to .35. The interests of 125 pairs of fathers and sons were studied by Forster in a thesis cited by Berdie (79, p. 145); in this study the sons were all students at the University of Minnesota. The range of intercorrelations for 25 occupational interest scales was from .00 to .48, with an average of .33. Berdie (1943) found that the sons of men in the skilled trades and in business tended to have inventoried interests in those fields, although the relationship did not hold for other fields. The reason may lie in the fact that, as shown in a study by Super (1939), these two occupational fields are near the top of the blue-denim and white-collar occupational ladders, making it socially acceptable for sons of business men and skilled workers to aspire to emulate and identify with their fathers, but less easy for the sons of unskilled, semiskilled, or clerical workers, who are not at the top of either ladder, to do so. It would be difficult to explain the lack of relationship among the interests of professional men and their sons in Berdie's study in terms of this hypothesis, since they are already high on the white-collar ladder, were it not for positive results which he reports from a study by Dvorak. She found that the interests of physicians and their sons were similar. This suggests that sampling errors may have affected Berdie's results for this one occupational level, in which case the hypothesis that family resemblances are most likely to be found at the levels which are considered near the top of a social ladder would be confirmed.

Other family relationships studied are those of twins, both identical and fraternal, in a report by Carter (1932). His subjects were 120 pairs of twins, 43 of the pairs being monozygotic. For these latter the average correlation was .50, whereas that for dizygotic twins was .28. Carter, Strong, and others have argued that the closer resemblance of the interests of identical than of fraternal twins does not prove that heredity plays a part, for "the environments of identical twins are more similar than those of fraternal twins" (Carter, 1944, p. 51). This is an oft repeated statement, but one which has not, to the writers' knowledge, ever been demonstrated. It is even more logical to maintain that the environments of fraternal twins are more similar than those of fathers and sons, in view of the differences in age, generation, and daily routines in the latter case; *but we have seen that the interests of fathers and sons resemble each other just as closely as do those of fraternal twins* ($r = .29$ or .33 and .28 respectively). It seems necessary, then, tentatively to conclude that the greater similarity of the interests of identical twins, as contrasted with those of fraternal twins, is not due to the *potentially* greater similarity of their environments, but rather to the *demonstrably* greater similarity of their heredities. Perhaps it is relevant that Stewart (1959) and Henderson (1958) have shown that identification with father or mother is related to vocational interest.

This viewpoint is that espoused by Strong (1943, p. 682), who points out that if environment is so predominantly important it is odd that boys and girls learn different interests by the time they are 15 years of age and unlearn them so little thereafter (see the discussion of sex differences), and that occupation-like differences which are found in the interests of adolescents are affected so little by subsequent training and experience.

Aptitude as a Source of Interest. The necessary conclusion, as Strong (1943, p. 682) sees it, is that "interests reflect inborn abilities." There is little evidence, however, by means of which this inductive hypothesis can be verified or rejected. It has been demonstrated that there is some relationship between intelligence and inventoried interests: Strong (1943, pp. 332–333) has summarized the various studies, showing that the correlations range from about −.40 to .40 depending upon the type of interest. The positive correlations are with scientific and linguistic interests, while the negative relationships are with social welfare, business contact, and business detail interests. As scientific and linguistic occupations deal primarily with abstractions, and social welfare and business occupations at least partly with tangibles, these relationships suggest that, without the ability to understand, there can be little genuine interest.

There have been fewer studies of the relationship between special aptitudes and inventoried interests. Adkins and Kuder (1940) correlated scores on the Primary Mental Abilities Tests with those on the Kuder Preference Record, and found that only one correlation was above .30: that between number ability and computational interest in women. Although this one relationship seems logical, it did not hold for men, and other equally appropriate relationships were not found in a high enough degree to justify any positive conclusions concerning the relationship of aptitude to interest. However, Darley (1941) found somewhat clearer indications of relationships between PMA Test scores and six representative Strong scales (r's ranged from —.04 to .31), and Long (1945) found the expected relationships with the Stanford Scientific Aptitude Test. Gustad (1951), on the other hand, found no relationship between verbal or quantitative superiority on the A.C.E. and occupational interest pattern on the Strong. Other comparable data were reported in a thesis by Leffel (1939), who found positive relationships (r = .46 and .42) between the O'Rourke Mechanical Aptitude Test and engineering and chemical interests on Strong's Vocational Interest Blank, and negative relationships between O'Rourke and Strong's social science teacher and lawyer scales (—.25 and —.25) and by Holcomb and Laslett (1932), who obtained similar findings with Stenquist's mechanical (paper-and-pencil) test. As the O'Rourke is to an indeterminate degree a measure of information, and therefore of interest as well as of aptitude, it would be difficult to draw any pertinent conclusions from Leffel's findings were it not that Holcomb and Laslett and Moore (1931) cite comparable data for the MacQuarrie and the Bennett Mechanical Comprehension Test. It seems, then, that there is some relationship between aptitudes and interests, but it is not strong.

And so little research has been carried out to test Strong's hypothesis concerning the relationship of aptitudes to interests, it may be well to reproduce his reasoning on this point. "An interest is an expression of one's reaction to his environment. The reaction of liking-disliking is a resultant of satisfactory or unsatisfactory dealing with the object. Different people react differently to the same object. The different reactions, we suspect, arise because the individuals are different to start with. We suspect that people who have the kind of brain that handles mathematics easily will like such activities and vice versa. In other words, interests are related to abilities and abilities, it is easy to see, can be inherited." (Strong, 1943, pp. 682–683). Strong believes that there are two reasons for this: Interests must reflect the environment; and they are evaluated by the environment. Whereas a primitive Indian boy with fine finger dexterity might make arrowheads, the concomitant satisfaction of finger dexterity might make an urban American boy aspire to the occupation of dentist or watch repairman. Interpreting this aspiration in terms of socio-economic levels, the professional man's son might want to be a dentist, the son of a skilled tradesman might want to be a watchmaker. Establishing a causal relationship between aptitude and interest is difficult under these circumstances.

A conclusion diametrically opposed to Strong's was reached by Berdie after reviewing a number of studies of the relationship between ability and vocational interests, most of which actually dealt with choices or expressed preferences rather than with inventoried interest (Berdie, 1944, p. 142). He wrote: "The available evidence indicates, however, that a person's ability is not a very important factor in determining his interests, and although a relationship can be found between the two factors, this relationship is so small that we must look further if we are to understand the sources of vocational interests."

The discussions of the roles of aptitudes, personality, and other variables in the development of interests which were published during the nineteen-thirties and forties often showed a substantial degree of scientific and logical näiveté. The arguments ran somewhat as follows: "Since the role of aptitude (or personality, or something else) is not important, some other factor must be the major determinant of vocational interest." Another variable was then selected as likely to be most important, and positions were taken on virtually an all-or-none basis, instead of with recognition of the fact that most human events and characteristics are the products of a number of causes. If a particular writer did not actually take an extreme, unifactorial, position, his critics were likely to make him seem to have done so. The reader who is interested in the history and development of these controversies may wish to refer to the original sources; bibliographies and discussions are available in the first edition of this text and in Darley and Hagenah's recent treatise; it seems better here, with the majority of test users in mind, not to try to summarize old positions or to correct misinterpretations, but to cite typical relevant data and conclusions.

Personality and Interests. Social attitudes are the least fixed of personality traits in the sense of being most clearly and readily affected by the environment. In a preliminary study of the relationship between these and vocational interests during the Great Depression, Darley (1938) found that students with interests like those of personnel managers and YMCA secretaries had the highest morale, and those with interests like those of engineers and chemists were lowest on morale, as these are respectively measured by Strong's Blank and the Minnesota Scale for the Survey of Opinions. Such results in a preliminary study led to an analysis of data from 1000 cases tested at the University of Minnesota (Darley, 1941, pp. 63–65). This revealed that, contrary to the findings of the preliminary study, there was no relationship between morale scores and type of interests. On the other hand, differences in liberalism were found: Those with welfare interests were most liberal, those with business interests least so. Darley and Hagenah (1955) have reported confirmation of these findings with 1000 college freshmen.

If values are thought of as representing a layer of personality which is deeper than those at which vocational interests and social attitudes are found, then it is significant that there is also some relationship between these two types of interests. Sarbin and Berdie (1940) obtained Strong and Allport-Vernon scores from 52 college students, and found positive relationships between scientific interests and theoretical values, welfare interests and religious values. Duffy and Crissy (1940) obtained similar data from 108 college women, reporting intercorrelations which were in the expected directions and generally in the .30's. Burgemeister (1940) confirmed these findings with another group of 164 college women, reporting that the interests of librarians, artists, and authors, for example, tend to be associated with aesthetic values, and that those of physicians and science teachers tend to go with theoretical values. Ferguson, Humphreys, and Frances Strong (1941) have also confirmed these trends, with 93 college men.

Personality traits at a somewhat deeper level were also included in Darley's investigations (Darley, 1941, p. 63 and Darley and Hagenah, 1955, p. 118ff). These were measured by means of the Bell Adjustment Inventory and the Minnesota Scale for the Survey of Opinions in the early study, the Minnesota Personality Scale in the later research, the first yielding scores for home and emotional adjustment, the second for feelings of inferiority and family adjustment which are of interest to us here, and the third a combination of these. Darley reports that home and emotional adjustment were not related to any occupational interest patterns; inferiority feelings were somewhat less common in those with welfare interests than those with a technical or no primary interest patterns, but neither inferiority feeling nor family attitudes differentiated between other interest groups. The business contact group and the social service group tended to be better adjusted socially than literary and technical groups. Berdie (1943) used the Minnesota Personality Scale and Strong's Inventory, and found that high school seniors with interests like those of engineers had inferior social adjustment, whereas those with social welfare interests were better adjusted socially and emotionally. Similar results were reported by Tyler (1945), scientific interests being related to poor social adjustment, business contact to good, but emotional adjustment being unrelated to interests. Alteneder (1940) found no correlations which exceeded .25 between men's adjustment and interest scores for six occupations, and only four which exceeded that for seven women's occupations. These latter were .39 and .38 between social adjustment (Bell) on the one hand and teaching interest on the other. Although the results of Alteneder's women's study are intriguing, the lack of positive results for the men's occupations makes them merely suggestive.

A still deeper level of personality organization was studied by Triggs

(1947), who correlated cyclical, paranoid, schizoid, and other temperament traits as measured by the Minnesota Multiphasic Personality Inventory with vocational interests measured by the Kuder Preference Record. Significant relationships reported in that paper were, for 35 college men, those between depression and social service ($r = -.34$) and clerical (.36) interests; psychopathic deviation and mechanical interests ($-.41$); femininity and mechanical interests ($-.37$); paranoia and computational ($-.42$) and scientific ($-.38$) interests; psychasthenia and scientific ($-.33$), musical (.33), and clerical (.33) interests; and schizoid trends and musical (.39) and clerical (.32) interests. It is perhaps worth noting that these relationships are suggestive of more positive personality adjustments being found with mechanical, computational, scientific, and social service interests, and of more maladjustments being associated with musical (psychasthenic, and schizoid) and clerical (depressed, psychasthenic, and schizoid) interests. These relationships are all significant at the 5, and occasionally almost at the 1, per cent levels. When the same techniques were applied to women college students, 60 in number, no relationships were found except between lie score and musical and social service interests (the mean lie score for the whole group was normal). The apparent discrepancy between the sets of data for men and for women may be the result of the small size of the samples; the data certainly require confirmation with larger numbers, but it is also possible that certain vocational interests could have pathological significance in men and yet be quite wholesome in women. Triggs, at least, felt that the relationships which she found were significant.

As Darley has pointed out, Terman and Miles', and Strong's data on masculinity and femininity of interests indicate a relationship between temperament and vocational interests, the endocrine basis of which has been demonstrated by Sollenberger (1940). Work with an information test designed to measure temperament factors through information and interest (Guilford, 1947, Ch. 14, 25; Wickert, 1947, pp. 68–74) tends further to substantiate the hypothesis that interests are related to temperamental factors.

In a review of relevant work, Patterson (1957) concluded that neurotics and psychotics tend more frequently than normals to be interested in talent and social service occupations, for which they lack abilities and aptitudes.

Origin and Development of Interests. The first published attempt to synthesize findings such as those reviewed above into a theory of the development of vocational interests was made by Carter (1940). As he sees it, the individual derives satisfaction from identification with some group, by which means he attains status. If his abilities permit, this identification is strengthened; if insurmountable obstacles are encountered, the process of identification is interfered with, the self-concept is changed, identification with another group must take place, and with it a new pattern of interests is developed which is more compatible with the aptitudes of the person in question. Carter goes on to state that the interest patterns of adolescents tend to become increasingly practical, that in the beginning many adolescent interest patterns provide very unsatisfactory solutions of the problem adjusting their aspirations to personal abilities and social demands. He writes (1940, p. 186) : "In this process of trying to adjust to a complex culture, the individual finds experiences which offer some basis for the integration of personality. The pattern of vocational interests which gradually forms becomes closely identified with the self . . . The pattern of interests is in the nature of a set of values which can find expression in one family of occupations but not in others."

This is essentially the line of thought developed independently by Darley (1941, p. 57), who quotes Carter in a briefer discussion of the same subject, and subscribed to by Berdie (1944). The writers see three possible defects in it:

First, it stresses an environmentalistic interpretation of Strong's, Carter's, and Berdie's data on family resemblances, interpretation which, as we have seen above, seems imbalanced when viewed objectively, however laudable it may be to believe in the essential modifiability and improvability of man.

Secondly, although it takes into account the role of aptitudes, personality is postulated as the basic factor, modified by the interaction of aptitudes and environment. But this, we have seen, is on the basis of evidence which is not much more convincing than that on the role of aptitudes which caused Strong to postulate that aptitudes are the fundamental factor. Why, one may ask, seek a unifactorial explanation?

Thirdly, although Carter's description of the process of identification, trial, disruption, and reshaping of the identification is convincing and is accepted as a promising hypothesis by the writers, there is actually no evidence for it in the intensive analyses which Carter and other members of the California Adolescent Growth Study had published when he wrote, nor in the publications of other psychologists. On the contrary, we have seen that everything that had been published on the development or stability of interests from the beginnings of adolescence on suggests that the form in which interest patterns begin to crystallize is essentially the form in which they remain, except as they are modified by glandular changes associated with age or, perhaps in rare instances, by a change from an inappropriate environment to one providing experiences appropriate to the aptitudes or needs of the individual.

An environmentalistic theory which attempts to take into account the stability of inventoried interests has been advanced by Bordin (1943, pp. 59, 53) . As he put it, "One of the major facts which Strong has established concerning his blank is the continuity of interest patterns. In general he has found that these patterns become more stable as the group studied is older. Reading in between the lines of most of the discussions of the interest test phenomena, this fact is taken to mean that Strong interest patterns are fixed, once developed, and therefore any actual changes are due to unreliability or other types of error. But our theory can encompass the same phenomena without recourse to the catch-all concept of error. First of all, we assume that it would be acknowledged as a social-psychological and sociological fact that the older the individual is, the more likely it is that he will have established himself occupationally and the less likely it is that conditions will require a change in his occupation . . . *In answering a Strong Vocational Interest test an individual is expressing his acceptance of a particular view or concept of himself in terms of occupational stereotypes.*"

Bordin therefore agreed with Carter in thinking of inventoried interests as the reflection of a self-concept, which, although developed as a result of the interplay between the endowments of the individual and the environment in which he lives, is attributable largely to experience. He went on to set up a series of challenging hypotheses and corollaries.

Bordin's basic assumption, as indicated in the quotation above, is that in answering an interest inventory a person is guided by his self-concept and by occupational stereotypes. Thus the student who sees himself as a lawyer answers as he believes a lawyer would answer: The self-concept results in responses which match the stereotype. Accordingly, Bordin hypothesized that interest and preference will tend to agree when the occupation is one with a clear and well-known stereotype, will be less likely to agree when the occupation is not well-known and has an unclear stereotype. Similarly, he hypothesized that changes of occupational preference are accompanied by changes of inventoried interests, an hypothesis tested in the Bordin and Wilson (1953) study already discussed.

It seems to the writers, however, that Bordin's assumption that the individual answers the items in an interest inventory in terms of some guiding general concept of how people in the occupation to which he aspires would answer it is gratuitous. It is true that experiments have been conducted in which the subjects were told to respond as though they were members of some occupation and were able to distort the picture of themselves in the desired direction (Cross, 1950; Longstaff, 1948) . But one can theorize, equally plausibly and more parsimoniously, that *in answering the questions in an interest inventory an individual records a series of self-perceptions, which in turn are summated by the scoring scale in such a way as to reveal the similarity or dissimilarity of his self-concept to the self-concept which has been found to be characteristic of persons in the occupation being scored.*

This reformulation makes fewer assumptions than Bordin's. Some of Bordin's hypotheses are relevant, while others are not: For example, the hypothesis concerning the familiarity of the occupational stereotype and the agreement of preferences and interests becomes relevant only to the deliberate or unconscious distortion of scores; but his hypothesis concerning the effects of experience (which in our terms might modify the self-percepts) is still relevant, although, as we have pointed out, the study designed to test it was poorly designed and inconclusive. The hypothesis concerning the son's identification with his father as a determinant of similarity of father-son interests was tested in a doctoral dissertation by Henderson (1958), who, using Strong's Blanks questionnaires completed by the fathers and sons of the Career Pattern Study's ninth grade group and a similar twelfth grade sample, found a significant relationship between the son's identification with his father and the similarity of father-son interest scores: boys who see themselves as resembling their fathers tend to have interest patterns like those of their fathers, particularly in early adolescence.

In their recent monograph, Darley and Hagenah (1955, pp. 147 and 190–193) discuss Darley's original formulation of interests as derived from personality, and restate their position in the light of subsequent research and insights. Although critical in their review of inadequate previous attempts at theorizing concerning the development of interests, they allow for limitations in their own reformulation with the statement that "it is unlikely that we can produce for some time to come any complete theory regarding the origin and development of occupational interests." They recognize that, in Darley's early formulation, there was a failure "to realize that occupational adjustment is a complex and multidimensional criterion." They now assign aptitudes the role of determining the level at which an interest may develop and seek outlets, but consider values, needs, and motivations the determinants of occupational interests and choice. In the Carter (1940), Bordin (1943), and Super (1949, p. 404ff; 1951; 1953) tradition, occupational status is viewed as the social role in which the person seeks self-actualization; like Super, they allow a more important place for constitutional factors in development than did Carter and Bordin.

In thus formulating what they refer to modestly as a "better description of the process of choice" rather than a theory, Darley and Hagenah (1955, p. 193) have drawn conclusions which are very similar to those which the writers consider justified by the data. This is what Super in the first edition of this text (p. 405) referred to as a tentative "theory of interests" in his attempt to organize, in the low-order, descriptive manner which is still the only possible method, that which is known about the development of vocational interests.

It should be noted in passing that Roe (1957) has now outlined a systematic, higher-order theory of vocational interest and choice, tracing these through orientation-to-persons versus orientation-to-non-persons, through parental loving-casual-neglecting-overdemanding-overprotecting behavior, through parental acceptance-rejection attitudes, to the basic warmth or coldness of the emotional climate of the childhood family environment. The theory has commanded considerable interest because of its neatness and plausibility, and particularly because it leads to explicit hypotheses which can be tested. Several studies of this sort have been reported (Grigg, 1959; Hagen, 1960; Utton, 1960), all with results which are generally negative. These will not be discussed here, for more defini-tive work needs to be done; but the fact that they are negative suggests that the theory, in achieving rigor, puts too much emphasis on one type of determinant (personality as formed in early childhood) and neglects other possible determinants (e.g., later influences on personality, aptitude, opportunity, social evaluation of experience, etc.). Perhaps mere description is still all that is possible, as an essential prelude to higher-order theory construction.

In summary, the inventoried interests of fathers and sons resemble each other about as much as do those of fraternal twins, whereas those of identical twins are considerably more alike, suggesting, since fraternal-twin environments are more similar to each other than are father-son environments, that heredity plays a part in the development of interests. Interest patterns are related to degree of general intelligence. There is no satisfactory evidence as yet concerning special aptitudes and interests. Attitudes such as liberalism and social adjustment are related to interest patterns, even prior to occupational experience. This is true also of values, which are presumably more deep-seated aspects of personality. Personality adjustment in the sense of feelings of adequacy and security has not been shown to be related to interest patterns, but social adjustment does appear to be. There is some evidence that temperament and endocrine make-up may be related to interest patterns, at least insofar as they affect masculinity and femininity, but the experiments in question are limited in number and in scope.

Experiences such as courses in school and college, and staying in an occupation over a long period of time, appear to have no appreciable effect on inventoried interests, although the experiences of the first two years of college training in professional field have been shown, perhaps because of the importance of the first real contact with a field, to have some effect on inventoried interests. Those who leave a field of training while in college tend to undergo a decline of interest in that field after leaving, and those who change to a field tend to show some increase in related interests after they have made the change, but these changes are not on the whole very great. They are significant enough so that it is evident that some persons do show real changes of interest, perhaps those whose prior experience has been inappropriate for the development of an adequate self-concept.

A theory of interests which would take into account all of the above facts, without going beyond them, must recognize the significance of heredity, as shown in family resemblances and as implied in the data of aptitudes, personality, and endocrine factors; it must also recognize the role of experience, as shown in the data on modification of inventoried interests with change of type of experience. An adequate theory of interests must build on the findings concerning the relationship between general aptitude and interest, which imply that in some instances aptitude probably does come first, resulting in approval, satisfaction, and interest. It seems probable that ability plays a part in the development of personality traits, as shown in certain studies of the effects of social skills on adjustment (McLaughlin, 1931; Jack, 1934; Page, 1936), and therefore in the development of interests as these are affected by personality. The theory must recognize the fact that as there are relationships between interests and the deeper layers of personality such as values, temperament, personality traits, and needs as Bordin's students (Weinstein, 1953; Segal, 1954; Nachman, 1960) have demonstrated, and that these relationships are in some instances causal. In other words, an adequate theory would recognize the fact of multiple causation, the principle of interaction, and the joint contribution of nature and nurture. It would read more or less as follows:

Interests are the product of interaction between inherited neural and endocrine factors, on the one hand, and opportunity and social evaluation on the other. Some of the things a person does well as a result of aptitudes bring him the satisfaction of mastery or the approval of his companions, and result in interests. Some of the things his associates do appeal to him and, through identification, he patterns his actions and his interests after them; if he fits the pattern reasonably well he remains in it, but if not, he must seek another identification and develop another self-concept and interest pattern. His needs and his mode of adjustment may cause him to seek certain satisfactions, but the means of achieving these satisfactions vary so much from one person, with one set of aptitudes and in one set of circumstances, to another person with other abilities and in another situation, that the prediction of interest patterns from needs and from modes of adjustment is hardly possible. Because of the stability of the hereditary endowment and the relative stability of the social environment in which any given person is reared, interest patterns are generally rather stable; their stability is further increased by the multiplicity of opportunities for try-outs, identification, and social approval in the years before adolescence. By adolescence most young people in developed areas have had opportunities to explore social, linguistic, mathematical, technical and business activities to some extent; they have sought to identify with parents, other adults, and schoolmates, and have rejected some and accepted others of these identifications and the related social roles; self-concepts have begun to take a definite form. For these reasons interest patterns begin to crystallize by early adolescence, and the exploratory experiences of the adolescent years in most cases merely clarify and elaborate upon what has already begun to take shape. Some persons experience significant changes during adolescence and early adulthood, but these are most often related to normal endocrine changes, and less often to changes in self-concept resulting from having attempted to live up to a misidentification and to fit into an inappropriate pattern, or to experiences which greatly broaden previously narrow horizons. Vocational interest patterns generally have a substantial degree of permanence at this stage; for most persons, adolescent exploration is an awakening to something that is already there.

REFERENCES FOR CHAPTER XVI

Adkins, Dorothy C., and Kuder, G. F. "The relation between primary mental abilities and activity preferences," *Psychometrika*, 5 (1940), 251-262.

Alteneder, L. E. "The value of intelligence, personality, and vocational interest tests in a guidance program," *J. Educ. Psychol.*, 31 (1940), 449-459.

Barnett, G. J., Handelsman, I., Stewart, L. H., and Super, D. E. "The Occupational Level Scale as a measure of drive," *Psychol. Monog.*, 342 (1952).

Berdie, R. F. "Factors associated with vocational interests," *J. Educ. Psychol.*, 34 (1943), 257-277.

———— "Factors related to vocational interests," *Psychol. Bull.*, 41 (1944), 137-157.

———— "Scores on the Strong Vocational Interest Blank and the Kuder Preference Record in relation to self-ratings," *J. Appl. Psychol.*, 34 (1950), 42-49.

Berman, I. R., Darley, J. G., and Paterson, D. G. "Vocational interest scales," *University of Minnesota Bull. Employ. Stab. Res. Inst.*, 5 (1934).

Bordin, E. S. "A theory of vocational interests as dynamic phenomena," *Educ. Psychol. Measmt.*, 3 (1943), 49-66.

————, and Wilson, E. H. "Change of interest as a function of shift in curricular orientation," *Educ. Psychol. Measmt.*, 13 (1953), 297-307.

Brogden, H. E. "The primary values measured by the Allport-Vernon tests, 'A Study of Values'." *Psychol. Monog.*, 348 (1952).

Burgemeister, B. B. "The permanence of interests of women college students," *Arch. Psychol.*, 255 (1940).

Burnham, P. S. "Stability of interests," *School and Soc.*, 55 (1942), 332-335.

Carter, H. D. "Twin similarities in occupational interests," *J. Educ. Psychol.*, 23 (1932), 641-655.

———— "The development of vocational attitudes," *J. Consult. Psychol.*, 4 (1940), 185-191.

———— "Vocational interests and job orientation," *Appl. Psychol. Monog.*, 2 (1944).

————, and Strong, E. K., Jr. "Sex differences in the occupational interests of high school students," *Pers. J.*, 12 (1933), 166-175.

Cross, O. H. "A study of faking on the Kuder Preference Record," *Educ. Psychol. Measmt.*, 10 (1950), 271-277.

Darley, J. G. "Preliminary study of the relationships between attitudes, adjustment, and vocational interest tests," *J. Educ. Psychol.*, 29 (1938), 467-473.

———— "Relationships among the Primary Mental Abilities Tests, selected achievement measures, personality tests, and tests of vocational interests," *University of Minnesota Studies in Higher Education*, (1941) 192-200.

———— *Clinical Aspects and Interpretation of the Strong Vocational Interest Blank.* New York: Psychological Corp., 1941.

————, and Hagenah, Theda. *Vocational Interest Measurement.* Minneapolis: University of Minnesota Press, 1955.

Du Bois, P. H. (ed.). *The Classification Program.* ("AAF Aviation Psychology Report," No. 2.) Washington, D. C.: Government Printing Office, 1947.

Duffy, Elizabeth. "A critical review of investigations employing the Allport-Vernon Study of Values and other tests of evaluative attitudes," *Psychol. Bull.*, 37 (1940), 597-612.

————, and Crissy, W. J. E. "Evaluative attitudes as related to vocational interest and academic achievement," *J. Abnorm. Soc. Psychol.*, 35 (1940), 226-245.

Estes, S. G., and Horn, D. "Interest patterns as related to fields of concentration among engineering students," *J. Psychol.*, 7 (1939), 29-36.

Ewens, W. P. "Experience patterns as related to vocational experience," *Educ. Psychol. Measmt.*, (1956), 223-231.

Ferguson, L. W., Humphreys, L. G., and Strong, Frances W. "A factorial analysis of interests and values," *J. Educ. Psychol.*, 32 (1941), 197-204.

Flanagan, J. C. "Measuring interests," *Psychol. Bull.*, 36 (1939), 529-530.

———— "The experimental evaluation of a selection procedure," *Educ. Psychol. Measmt.*, (1946), 445-466.

Fryer, D. *The Measurement of Interests.* New York: Holt, 1931.

Garretson, O. K. "Relationships between expressed preferences and curricular abilities of ninth grade boys," *Teachers Coll. Contrib. to Educ.*, 396 (1930).

Gilger, G. A., Jr. "Declaration of vocational interest," *Occupations*, 20 (1942), 276-279.

Greene, E. B. "Vocabulary profiles of groups in training," *J. Educ. Res.*, 33 (1940), 569-575.

Grigg, A. "Childhood experience with parental attitudes: an empirical test of Roe's hypothesis," *J. Counsel. Psychol.*, 6 (1959), 153-156.

Guilford, J. P. (ed.). *Printed Classification Tests.* ("AAF Aviation Psychology Report," No. 5.) Washington, D. C.: Government Printing Office, 1947.

————, Christensen, P. R., Bond, N. A., Jr., and Sutton, M. A. "A factor analysis of human interests," *Psychol. Monog.*, 375 (1954).

Gustad, J. W. "Vocational interests and Q-L scores on the ACE," *J. Appl. Psychol.*, 35 (1951), 164-168.

———— "Vocational interests and socioeconomic status," *J. Appl. Psychol.*, 38 (1954), 336-338.

Hagen, D. "Careers and family atmospheres: an empirical test of Roe's theory," *J. Counsel. Psychol.*, 7 (1960), 251-256.

Hamburger, M. "Realism and Consistency in Early Adolescent Aspirations and Expectation." Unpublished Ph.D. dissertation, Teachers College, Columbia University, 1958.

Henderson, H. L. "The Relationships Between Interests of Fathers and Sons and Sons' Identification with Fathers." Unpublished Ph.D. dissertation, Teachers College, Columbia University, 1958.

Herzberg, F., and Russell, D. "The effects of experience and change of job interest on the Kuder Preference Record," *J. Appl. Psychol.*, 37 (1953), 478-481.

——, Bouton, A., and Steiner, B. J. "Studies of the stability of the Kuder Preference Record," *Educ. Psychol. Measmt.*, 14 (1954a), 90-100.

——, and Bouton, A. "A further study of the stability of the Kuder Preference Record," *Educ. Psychol. Measmt.*, 14 (1954b), 326-331.

Holcomb, G. W., and Laslett, H. R. "A prognostic study of engineering aptitude," *J. Appl. Psychol.*, 16 (1932), 107-115.

Hoyt, D. P., Smith, J. L., and Levy, S. "A further study in the prediction of interest stability," *J. Counsel. Psychol.*, 4 (1957), 228-233.

Hyman, B. "The relationship of social status and vocational interests," *J. Counsel. Psychol.*, 3 (1956), 12-16.

Jack, L. M. "An experimental study of ascendant behavior in pre-school children." *University of Iowa Studies in Child Welfare*, 3 (1934).

Jordaan, J. P. "The Relationship Between Socioeconomic Status and the Vocational Interests of Mechanically Gifted Boys." Unpublished Ph.D. dissertation, Teachers College, Columbia University, 1949.

Kendall, W. E. "The occupational level scale of the Strong Vocational Interest Blank," *J. Appl. Psychol.*, 31 (1947), 283-288.

King, L. A. "Factors associated with vocational interest profile stability," *J. Appl. Psychol.*, 42 (1958), 261-263.

Kinsey, A. C., et al. *Sexual Behavior in the Human Male*. Philadelphia: W. B. Saunders, 1948.

Kitson, H. D. *The Psychology of Vocational Adjustment*. Philadelphia: Lippincott, 1925.

—— "Creating vocational interest," *Occupations*, 20 (1942), 567-571.

Klugman, S. F. "Test scores for clerical aptitudes and interests before and after a year of schooling," *J. Genet. Psychol.*, 65 (1944), 89-96.

Kriedt, P. H. "Vocational interests of psychologists," *J. Appl. Psychol.*, 33 (1949), 482-488.

Layton, W. L. (ed.). *The Strong Vocational Interest Blank: Research and Uses*. Minneapolis: University of Minnesota Press, 1960.

Leffel, E. S. "Students' Plans, Interests, and Achievement." Unpublished Master's thesis, Clark University, 1939.

Lehman, H. C., and Witty, P. A. "Constancy of vocational interest," *Pers. J.*, (1929) 153-165.

——, and Witty, P. A. "A second study of play activities in relation to school progress," *Social Forces*, 8 (1930), 409-415.

——, and Witty, P. A. "Vocational counseling—the interest inventory," *Amer. J. Psychol.*, 44 (1932), 801-805.

——, and Witty, P. A. "Vocational guidance: some basic considerations," *J. Educ. Sociol.*, 8 (1934), 174-184.

Long, L. "Relationship between interests and abilities: a study of the Strong Vocational Interest Blank and the Zyve Scientific Aptitude Test," *J. Appl. Psychol.*, 29 (1945), 191-197.

——, and Perry, J. D. "Academic achievement in engineering related to selection procedure and interests," *J. Appl. Psychol.*, 37 (1953), 468-471.

Longstaff, H. P. "Fakability of the Strong Interest Blank and the Kuder Preference Record," *J. Appl. Psychol.*, 32 (1948), 360-369.

Lurie, W. A. "A study of Spranger's value types by the method of factor analysis," *J. Soc. Psychol.*, 8 (1937), 17-37.

———, and Weiss, A. "Analyzing vocational adjustment," *Occupations*, 21 (1942), 138-142.

Matteson, R. W. "Experience-interest relationships as measured by an activity check list," *J. Counsel. Psychol.*, 2 (1955a), 13-14.

——— "Experience-interest changes in students," *J. Counsel. Psychol.*, 2 (1955b), 113-121.

McArthur, C., and Stevens, Lucia B. "The validation of expressed interests as compared with inventoried interests: a fourteen year follow-up," *J. Appl. Psychol.*, 39 (1955), 184-189.

McLaughlin, Sister Mary Aquinas. "The genesis and constancy of ascendance and submission as personality traits," *University of Iowa Studies in Educ.*, 5 (1931).

Miles, C. C. "Psychological study of a young male pseudo-hermaphrodite." In McNemar, Q., and Merrill, Maude A.: *Studies in Personality*. New York: McGraw-Hill, 1942.

Moore, B. V. "Analysis of tests administered to men in engineering defense training courses," *J. Appl. Psychol.*, 25 (1941), 619-635.

Morgan, H. H. "A psychometric comparison of achieving and nonachieving college students of high ability," *J. Consult. Psychol.*, 16 (1952), 292-298.

Nachmann, Barbara. "Childhood experience and vocational choice in law, dentistry, and social work," *J. Counsel. Psychol.*, 7 (1960), 243-250.

Older, H. J. "An objective test of vocational interests," *J. Appl. Psychol.*, 28 (1944), 99-108.

Page, M. L. "The modification of ascendant behavior in pre-school children," *University of Iowa Studies in Child Welfare*, 3 (1936).

Patterson, C. H. "Interest tests and the emotionally disturbed client," *Educ. Psychol. Measmt.*, 17 (1957), 264-280.

Powers, Mabel K. "Permanence of measured vocational interests of adult males," *J. Appl. Psychol.*, 40 (1956), 69-72.

Roe, Anne. "A psychological study of eminent physical scientists," *Genet. Psychol. Monog.*, 43 (1951a), 121-239.

——— "A psychological study of eminent biologists," *Psychol. Monog.*, 331 (1951).

——— "Early determinants of vocational choice," *J. Counsel. Psychol.*, 4 (1957), 212-217.

Rosenberg, N. "Stability and maturation of Kuder Interest patterns during high school," *Educ. Psychol. Measmt.*, 13 (1953), 449-458.

Rothney, J. W. M. *Guidance Practices and Results*. New York: Harper, 1958.

Ryan, T. A., and Johnson, B. R. "Interest scores in the selection of salesmen and servicemen," *J. Appl. Psychol.*, 26 (1942), 543-562.

Sarbin, T. R., and Berdie, R. F. "Relation of measured interests to the Allport-Vernon Study of Values," *J. Appl. Psychol.*, 24 (1940), 287-296.

Schmidt, J. L., and Rothney, J. W. M. "Variability of vocational choices of high school students," *Pers. Guid. J.*, 34 (1955), 142-146.

Segal, S. J. "The Role of Personality Factors in Vocational Choice: a Study of Accountants and Creative Writers," Unpublished Ph.D. dissertation, University of Michigan, 1954.

Sollenberger, R. T. "Some relationships between the urinary excretion of male hormones by maturing boys and their expressed interests and attitudes," *J. Psychol.*, 9 (1940), 179-189.

Stewart, L. H. "Mother-son identification and vocational interest," *Genet. Psychol. Monog.*, 60 (1959), 31-63.

Stordahl, K. E. "Permanence of Strong Vocational Interest Blank scores," *J. Appl. Psychol.*, 38 (1954), 423-427.

Strong, E. K., Jr. "Vocational guidance of executives," *J. Appl. Psychol.*, 11 (1927), 331-347.

——— *Change of Interest With Age.* Stanford: Stanford University Press, 1931.

——— *Vocational Interests of Men and Women.* Stanford: Stanford University Press, 1943.

——— "Interests of senior and junior public administrators," *J. Appl. Psychol.*, 30 (1946), 55-71.

——— "Differences in interests among public administrators," *J. Appl. Psychol.*, 31 (1947), 18-38.

——— "Vocational interests of accountants," *J. Appl. Psychol.*, 33 (1949), 474-481.

——— "Interest scores while in college of occupations engaged in 20 years later," *Educ. Psychol. Measmt.*, 11 (1951), 335-348.

——— *Vocational Interests 18 years After College.* Minneapolis: University of Minnesota Press, 1955.

——— "Interests of fathers and sons," *J. Appl. Psychol.*, 41 (1957), 284-292.

———, and Tucker, A. C. "The use of vocational interest scales in planning a medical career," *Psychol. Monog.*, 341 (1952).

Super, D. E. "Occupational level and job satisfaction," *J. Appl. Psychol.*, 23 (1939), 547-564.

——— *Avocational Interest Patterns: A Study in the Psychology of Avocations.* Stanford: Stanford University Press, 1940.

——— "Strong's 'Vocational interests of men and women': a special review," *Psychol. Bull.*, 42 (1945), 359-370.

——— "Vocational interest and vocational choice," *Educ. Psychol. Measmt.*, 7 (1947a), 375-384.

——— "The Kuder Preference Record in vocational diagnosis," *J. Consult. Psychol.*, 11 (1947b), 184-193.

——— *Appraising Vocational Fitness by Means of Psychological Tests.* New York: Harper, 1949.

——— "Vocational adjustment: implementing a self-concept," *Occupations*, 30 (1951), 88-92.

——— "A theory of vocational development," *Amer. Psychologist*, 8 (1953), 185-190.

——— "The measurement of interests," *J. Counsel. Psychol.*, 1 (1954), 168-173.

———, and Haddad, W. C. "The effect of familiarity with an occupational field on a recognition test of vocational interest," *J. Educ. Psychol.*, 34 (1943), 103-109.

———, and Roper, Sylvia. "An objective technique for testing vocational interests," *J. Appl. Psychol.*, 25 (1941), 487-498.

Taylor, Katherine von F. "Reliability and permanence of vocational interests of adolescents," *J. Exp. Educ.*, 10 (1942), 81-87.

———, and Carter, H. D. "Retest consistency of vocational interest patterns," *J. Consult. Psychol.*, 6 (1942), 95-101.

Terman, L. M., and Miles, Catherine C. *Sex and Personality.* New York: McGraw-Hill, 1936.

———, and Oden, Melita H. *The Gifted Child Grows Up.* Stanford: Stanford University Press, 1948.

Thorndike, E. L. *Adult Interests.* New York: Macmillan, 1935.

Thurstone, L. L. "A multiple-factor study of vocational interests," *Pers. J.,* 10 (1931), 198-205.

Traxler, A. E., and McCall, W. C. "Some data on the Kuder Preference Record," *Educ. Psychol. Measmt.,* 1 (1941), 253-268.

Triggs, F. O. "A study of the relationship of measured interests to measured mechanical aptitude, personality, and vocabulary," *Amer. Psychologist,* 2 (1947), 296 (Abstr.).

Trinkaus, W. K. "The permanence of vocational interests of college freshmen," *Educ. Psychol. Measmt.,* 14 (1954), 641-646.

Trow, W. C. "Phantasy and vocational choice," *Occupations,* 20 (1941), 89-93.

Tutton, Marie E. "Stability of adolescent vocational interests," *Vocational Guid. Q.,* 3 (1955), 78-80.

Tyler, Leona E. "Relationships between Strong Vocational Interest Blank scores and other attitude and personality factors," *J. Appl. Psychol.,* 29 (1945), 58-67.

Utton, A. C. "Recalled Parent-Child Relations as Determinants of Vocational Choice." Unpublished Ph.D. dissertation, Teachers College, Columbia University, 1960.

Van Dusen, A. C. "Permanence of vocational interests," *J. Educ. Psychol.,* 31 (1940), 401-424.

Verburg, W. A. "Vocational interests of retired YMCA secretaries," *J. Appl. Psychol.,* 36 (1952), 254-256.

Vernon, P. E., and Allport, G. W. "A test for personal values," *J. Abnorm. Soc. Psychol.,* 26 (1931), 231-248.

Weinstein, M. S. "Personality and Vocational Choice." Unpublished Ph.D. dissertation, University of Michigan, 1953.

Wickert, F. (ed.). *Psychological Research on Problems of Redistribution.* ("AAF Aviation Psychology Report," No. 14.) Washington, D. C.: Government Printing Office, 1947.

Yum, K. S. "Student preferences in divisional studies and their preferential activities," *J. Psychol.,* 13 (1942), 193-200.

XVII

MEASURES OF INTERESTS

THE discussion of definitions at the beginning of the preceding chapter pointed out that the most productive work so far in the measurement of interests has been done with the *inventory* technique. For this reason, several *inventories*, but only one *test*, of interests are considered in this and the following chapters.

As interest inventories have been developed in greater numbers there is, in that respect at least, a broader field from which to choose. But it has apparently been much easier to write "like-indifferent-dislike" items than to ascertain their significance for counseling and selection. Some interest inventory authors have launched their instruments without validation data and have not followed them up sufficiently to make them useful. Others, such as Garretson (1930) and Dunlap (1935) at the junior high school level, and Cleeton (1935) at the adolescent and adult, have made careful and intensive studies prior to or immediately after publication, but have not followed through with further investigations of the nature of the traits measured by, or the validity of, their instruments. Their inventories cannot therefore be considered as more than potentially useful tools. One or two others, such as that by Lee and Thorpe (Thorpe, 1948), may in time be found useful, but data have yet to be made available to demonstrate their value. Any user of such a relatively untried inventory in counseling or selection operates on faith alone—and faith is a poor substitute for facts in psychology.

Two interest inventories and one values inventory have been studied over a period of years, and sufficient data have been accumulated to make them extremely valuable appraisal instruments. These are the *Strong Vocational Interest Blank,* the *Kuder Preference Record: Vocational,* and the *Allport-Vernon Study of Values.* The first-named inventory has been the subject of intensive study from many viewpoints over more than thirty years, its author and others having assumed responsibility for integrating and interpreting the results of relevant research (Strong, 1943, 1955; Super, 1945, 1949; Darley and Hagenah, 1955; Layton, 1960); the second

417

was experimented with for several years before publication, has since been revised, and new studies by its author and others are continually appearing in the journals or in new editions of the manual; the last-named inventory has been used since 1931, during which time numerous psychologists have reported on it, several have assumed responsibility for bringing these reports together and discussing the significance of the traits measured (Cantril and Allport, 1933; Duffy, 1940), and 1951 and 1960 revisions incorporate needed improvements. These three inventories are therefore treated at some length in this and the next chapter. Much briefer treatments of the *Cleeton Vocational Interest Inventory,* and the *Lee-Thorpe Occupational Interest Inventory* are also included, as well as the *Michigan Vocabulary Profile Test,* as these are widely used and well-publicized instruments, including some novel features.

Several studies have compared existing interest inventories in order to assess their relative value. Some of these have used occupational criteria, effectively demonstrating the superiority of the Strong over the Hepner and Brainard inventories (Berman, et al., 1934). But others have merely compared one test with another (e.g., Gordon and Herkness, 1942), thereby proving nothing unless one is willing to postulate the validity of one of the indices, the validity of which is in question.

Specific Tests

The Strong Vocational Interest Blank (Stanford University Press, 1927 and 1938; inventory and rev. Manual, Consulting Psychologists Press, 1959). The history of early interest research has been recounted by Fryer (1931, Ch. 3) and need not be repeated here, beyond stating that Strong began his work with the inventory technique as a member of the Carnegie Tech group, and took it with him to Stanford University, where Cowdery (1926) and other students worked with him in establishing it as an effective method of differentiating between occupational groups. Strong published his first edition of the blank in 1927, after several preliminary studies had shown the validity of the approach; a revision that is currently in use was brought out in 1938, based on the work of the intervening years; the many studies of the nature of the traits measured and of their validity in educational and vocational counseling and selection were brought together in monographs (Strong, 1943, 1955); new scoring keys are added from time to time as studies are completed; an 18-year follow-up study has been reported (Strong, 1955); and the journals continue to carry new studies of various aspects of the Blank's significance and use. It is without question one of the most thoroughly studied and understood psychological instruments in existence.

Applicability. Strong's Vocational Interest Blank was developed for use with and standardized upon college students and adults employed in the professions and in business. Because of this it includes some terms which are unfamiliar to high school students and to adults in lower level occupations. For example, even high school juniors and seniors filling out the blank often ask the meaning of terms such as "sociology," "physiology," and "smokers" and reveal a complete unawareness of the nature or existence of the magazine *System*. For these reasons the question of the use of Strong's Blank with persons of less than college level has frequently been raised. It can be answered from two sets of data: Strong's and Carter's studies of the interests of adolescents and adults, already discussed in some detail, and an investigation by Stefflre (1947).

The age and stability studies, both cross-sectional and longitudinal, have been seen to show that meaningful data can be obtained by means of Strong's Blank from boys and girls as young as 14 or 15, and that by the time they are 18-to-20-year-olds their Strong scores are rather well fixed. This suggests that, despite the apparent difficulty of some of the words used in the inventory, it is sufficiently well understood at those age levels to be applicable to most high school students.

The vocabularies of the Strong, Kuder, and other inventories were analyzed by Stefflre, who reported that the Strong Blank has a tenth grade vocabulary. This fits in with the data on its usefulness with 17-year-olds, and suggests that it should be used below that level only with the more able and more advanced students.

Potential users of interest inventories often ask whether a subjective technique such as this is subject to faking when used in selection programs, and even in counseling, because of the desire to make high scores in some occupations. The job applicant wants to appear in the best possible light, and even if he is above conscious distortion there are many genuine opportunities to give oneself the benefit of the doubt in answering an inventory. The student seeking guidance may be eager for self-insight and for an objective picture of himself, but in answering the questionnaire he is nonetheless guided by his self-concept, set of occupational stereotypes, and a desire to appear favorably in the eyes of the counselor. Strong (1943, p. 684), Steinmetz (1932), and Longstaff (1948) have experimented with deliberate faking, first administering the inventory in the standard way, and at a subsequent session administering it with directions to attempt to raise the score on a specific occupation or group of occupations. Very great changes resulted, the mean scores shifting to such an extent that the majority received A ratings, in contrast with B+'s (engineers as engineers) and C's (business students as engineers, education students as administrators, etc.). Other scores were affected by these distortions, as would be expected in view of the intercorrelations. In Longstaff's study, the Strong was found to be more susceptible to upward faking, the Kuder to downward faking.

Faking by job applicants, a much more important issue than directed faking by students, was also checked by Strong (1943, pp. 688–690) who administered the Blank to 118 men responding to an advertisement which he inserted in newspapers. The inventory was given as a preliminary hurdle for life insurance sales positions; some, according to Strong, took the questionnaire out of mere curiosity, but an indeterminate number of others were more serious in their purpose. The scores made by these men in their then occupations were compared with their scores as life insurance salesmen, with the finding that only groups whose averages were above a standard score of 40 on the sales key were already employed in some kind of sales work. The conclusion was that, although some individuals may have intentionally raised their scores somewhat, the majority did not achieve, or perhaps even try, any appreciable distortion. According to Strong (1943, p. 688), Bills did find that applicants under 24 years of age who scored A on both sales keys were less likely to succeed as insurance salesmen than those who scored B+, or B+ and A, on the two scales, presumably because of bluffing. Green (1951) and Heron (1956) have also demonstrated, in hiring experiments, the distorting effect of the selection situation on self-descriptive inventories. In selection, therefore, the use of other checks on interest inventories is probably desirable.

As for counselees, there is no experimental evidence that their scores are or are not affected by the desire to appear, to themselves or to the counselor, in a certain light. While Spencer (1938) has shown that some personality inventory items are answered differently when a name is signed than when answered anonymously, he also showed that answers to other items, the least personal and the most like those in interest inventories, are not changed because the respondent can be identified. Conscious distortion in counselees or students can therefore probably be dismissed as negligible.

Sinnett's (1956) study of relationships between Strong scores, Kuder scores, and expressed preferences throws further light on distortion in counselees. The temporal order of understanding occupations and the complexity of occupations (rated by psychologists) is correlated with agreement between Strong's scores and self-ratings of interests, but not with agreement between Kuder scores and self-ratings of interest. Sinnett suggests that this may be a function of the lesser transparency or distortability of Strong's Blank.

Content. The Vocational Interest Blank Form M (men) consists in its present form of 400 items grouped according to type of content. The first group is a list of many types of occupations at and above the skilled level, emphasizing the business and professional fields. This is followed by lists of school subjects, amusements (games, magazines, sports, etc.), activities (hobbies, pastimes, etc.), peculiarities of people, vocational activities, factors affecting vocational satisfaction, well-known persons exemplifying occupational stereotypes, offices in clubs, and ratings of abilities and personality characteristics (the actual grouping is not quite as in this list, which is based on content rather than on form of item). The women's form has 263 items in common with the men's and a total of 400 in the revised form.

Administration and Scoring. There is no time limit for the Vocational Interest Blank, as the task is to answer all questions; the time required ranges from a little over 30 minutes for superior, well-adjusted, adults to something more than an hour for less able or less stable individuals. It is well to allow an hour when testing groups, and to administer the blank at the end of a test session, e.g., just before a rest period, when it is part of a battery. This makes it possible to dismiss subjects as they finish, but does not put too much pressure on those who have not finished. In guidance centers the inventory is often given to older adolescents and adults to complete on their own time at home; this works well when the client has a place to work without having his responses affected by the comments of on-lookers, and when he understands the importance for himself of filling it out rapidly and without consultation.

In answering the blank, the subject marks each item according to whether he likes, dislikes, or is indifferent to it. The answer to each item is assigned a weight based on the degree to which the answers of men in a given occupation, e.g. engineering, differ from those of men-in-general. This procedure is sufficiently different from those normally used in developing scoring procedures to be worth describing, for understanding it means practically an understanding of Strong's Blank. Table 30 presents the Strong's data for one item, "Actor," showing the responses of engineers and of men-in-general.

It is made clear by the "difference" row in Table 30 that engineers are less likely to indicate a liking for the occupation "actor" than are men-in-general, slightly more likely to indicate indifference, and much more likely to show a disliking for it. By means of a formula based on the significance of the difference between two percents these data are converted into the weights shown in the bottom row. In scoring the inventory of a young man who thinks he wants to be an engineer, but who indicates that he would like being an actor, one would therefore deduct one point from his engineering score; he has shown that, in this respect at least, he is more like other men than like engineers. It is perhaps worth

noting that this is true, even though other men tend not to like being
an actor, for they indicate a liking for it more often than do engineers.

TABLE 30

DETERMINATION OF WEIGHTS IN STRONG'S BLANK: ITEM "ACTOR"

Group	% Like	% Indifferent	% Dislike
Engineers	9	31	60
Men (Gen'l)	21	32	47
Difference	—12	—1	13
Weight	—1	0	1

The score for engineer, then, is the algebraic sum of the weights corresponding to each answer marked by the client, a total of 400 weights.
A comparable addition and subtraction must be made for every occupational or other score (e.g., masculinity-femininity) desired by the counselor. To do this by hand is time-consuming, for it takes a novice about 15
minutes to score one blank for one occupation even with the stencils
provided for this purpose, and the men's inventory is scored for more
than 50, the women's for about 30, occupations and traits. With the aid
of two Veeder counters (Nos. ZD-18-T and ZD-8-T, Veeder Mfg. Co.,
Hartford, Conn.) an experienced scorer can cut the time in half, averaging about ten occupational scores per hour. As this would still mean about
four hours scoring time per men's blank when all keys are used, machine
scoring is necessary except as a device for getting to know the test.

Strong describes the methods in his manual. Briefly, they are: the IBM
method, in which a special answer sheet and electrographic pencil are
used (as with most standard tests for machine-scoring), at a cost of $1.85
to $2.00 for all scales; and the Hankes method (Testscor, 1554 Nicollet
Ave., Minneapolis 3, Minn.), requiring a Hankes answer sheet at somewhat lower cost. The names and addresses of organizations having scoring
machines and offering scoring services to others are listed in Strong's manual, which is kept up to date.

The cost of scoring Strong's Blank has been something of a deterrent
to its use in some institutions, more often in public schools than elsewhere, and other inventories with less expensive scoring have for this
reason had a wide appeal. Many a user has bought them frankly as less
expensive substitutes for Strong's Blank. Because of the pressure to cut
down costs, Strong and many others have attempted to simplify the scoring as much as possible; these attempts have been summarized in Strong's
book (1943, Ch. 24) and followed up by another study (1945). Only
Strong's conclusions can be cited here: Weighted scores differentiate better
than the unit scores proposed by Dunlap and others and should therefore
be used in counseling and selection. Weighting each item one, instead of

from —4 to 4, would, Strong has shown, lead to different counseling in from one in every twelve to one in every six cases. When the cost is approximately $1.50 per case the price of greater validity does not seem unduly high. Public schools and other institutions spend far more per pupil on things of less significance than finding out what kinds of educational and vocational activities are most likely to challenge them. As a compromise, Strong has devised six group scales, one each for the biological science, physical science, social welfare, busines detail, contact and linguistic groups. These correlate fairly well with the specific keys and can be used when only directional counseling is needed, but Cooper (1954) has shown that they are less satisfactory than the occupational scales.

Scores on Strong's Blank are recorded in many different ways by users of the inventory. One frequently sees reports in which the occupational scores are arranged in order of magnitude, all occupations in which A's are made being grouped first, the B+'s next, and so on. This is done on the assumption that the counselor and client are most interested in the A scores or, in their absence, in the B+'s. This method has two drawbacks: it focuses attention on specific occupations, and it makes it difficult to perceive patterns of scores. Each of these is worthy of brief discussion.

The Vocational Interest Blank can be scored for about 40 occupations, and the number may conceivably be increased to 45 or 50 in due course. But there are nearly 30,000 jobs in the *Dictionary of Occupational Titles* (U.S. Dept. of Labor, 1949), and, while many of these are more specific than those in Strong's Blank, and could be combined to make a smaller number, it would still be true that interest in most occupations cannot be scored on Strong's Blank. It is manifestly unwise, then, to focus solely on scores on specific occupations. The result too often is that a student says, "I rate A as a minister, but I don't have any desire to be a minister," and the insights into interests which might be gained from that score are lost in the negative reaction to a stereotype of a specific field; or, a client leaves the counselor and reports to his family, "One test showed that I should be a personnel director. I wonder what the boss will think of that?" missing the more general implications of that high score.

When occupational interest scores are grouped according to their factorial composition, however, the result is often quite different. This puts related occupations together in families; it permits the analysis of scores in terms of types of occupations rather than specific occupations, and it makes it easy to see whether or not a high score in one occupation is supported by high scores in related occupations. Thus an A as physician, for example, is a much surer basis for encouragement in choosing a premedical or biological sciences major if supported by A's or B+'s as psychologist, dentist, chemist, and engineer than if the scores of these occupations are largely B+'s and C's. The report sheet published by Strong, the Hankes Report Form, and many others are organized in such a way as to make possible this type of pattern analysis (see Fig. 7).

Pattern analysis was first described in some detail in a booklet by Darley (1941, Ch. 2), in which a distinction is made between *primary, secondary,* and *tertiary* interest patterns. The last-named category having been found inadequate, Darley and Hagenah (1955, Ch. 3) have now substituted a *reject* pattern, a family in which significantly low scores are made. They define as primary interest patterns those fields in which the letter ratings received are largely A's and B+'s, as secondary patterns those occupational families in which scores are predominantly B+ and B, and as reject those in which they tend to be below the "chance score" zone (gray, in Fig. 7). Using this classification of the letter ratings received by a counselee makes it possible to focus attention on the kinds of occupations which he is likely to find congenial. It is more helpful to know, for example, that his primary interest patterns are in the scientific and literary occupations with a secondary pattern in the social welfare field, than to know that he made A's as psychologist, physician, physicist, chemist, engineer, personnel director, public administrator, advertising man, author-journalist and president of a manufacturing concern. Darley and Hagenah tabulated the frequency of interest types or patterns for 1000 men at the University of Minnesota; it is worth noting that 19 percent of these men had no primary interest pattern, that 41 percent had only one primary pattern, and 39 percent multiple (largely double) primaries. This is discussed at great length in connection with the use of Strong's Blank. The use of interest patterns has been found more valid, with entry into an occupation as criterion, than specific occupational score by Wightwick (1945), in a study of college women. But McArthur (1955) found, in a 14-year follow-up of college men, that the occupational scales have more predictive value than does Darley's pattern analysis. The latter is useful largely for considering occupations for which no scale exists.

Norms. The question of norms is in fact a double-barreled question, for it concerns both type and number of cases. As the details of both of these are given in Strong's manual and in his book (1943, pp. 694–702) they need not be reproduced here, but one frequently encounters mis-statements made by presumably well-informed users of Strong's Blank. For example, a specialist in the selection and training of nurses once stated that the nursing scale of the women's form was of little value because it was based on about 100 nurses from one hospital in Chicago; it was actually based on approximately 400 nurses, 283 located in, but not necessarily natives of, the nurse-importing city of New York, the other 117 from up-

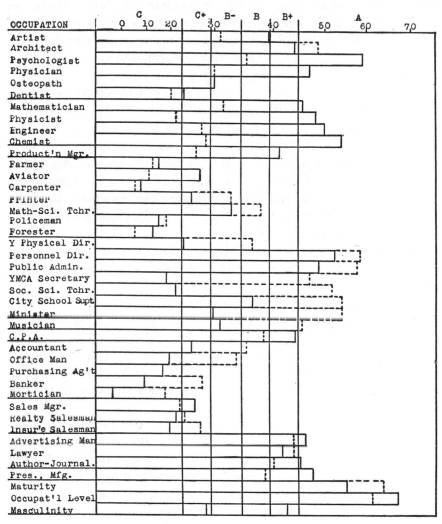

FIGURE 7

INTEREST PROFILE OF A YOUNG MAN AT AGE 23, SOCIAL STUDIES
INSTRUCTOR, AND AT AGE 37, AS PSYCHOLOGIST (STRONG'S BLANK).
(Broken lines at 23, solid lines at 37).

state New York and elsewhere. This is not a balanced sample, but neither is it as unbalanced as the above-quoted critic implied; as data on the validity of the women's form will later make clear, it is also not the reason for the lack of correlation between scores and grades in nursing schools. Some generalized statements concerning the norms of the Vocational Interest Blank follow, in order to provide the orientation to the base of this inventory which many users apparently lack.

The data concerning numbers are simple enough. Cowdery's early work (1926) showed that occupational differentiation could be achieved with groups of as few as 35 persons. For this reason, Strong's first keys were based on about 150 cases each, surely a conservative application of Cowdery's findings. Subsequent work (1943, pp. 639–650), however, led him to increase the number in order to increase the discriminating power of the test; the numbers were therefore raised first to 250 cases per occupation, and then to between 400 and 500 cases. Accordingly, the earliest scales are based on groups of from 150 to 200 cases per occupation, the newest scales on between 400 and 500 persons. Evidence reported by Strong shows that these numbers are large enough to minimize shrinkage of mean scores in cross-validation.

The question of type or quality is more complex, and can itself be broken down into several questions. Outstanding among these are: 1) the criterion of success which warrants inclusion of a given case in the criterion group; 2), the representativeness of the sample; and 3), the timelessness of the sample or the degree to which the interests of successful psychologists of 1928 can be representative of the interests of successful psychologists in 1948 or 1968.

The criterion of success varies from one occupation to another, as one might expect in view of the differences in occupations: output may measure success in electrical unit assembly work, but not in teaching. Strong's life insurance salesmen sold at least $100,000 worth of insurance annually for three years. In the cases of occupations which have some accrediting or other evaluative procedure of their own it was used: Architects were members of the state board of architecture; carpenters were union members; certified public accountants were certified in their states; chemists were non-professorial members of the American Chemical Society; and psychologists were Fellows (full members) of the American Psychological Association. When no such criterion of being established in a field was available, other evidence of status was used: The journalists were editors listed in *Editor and Publisher Yearbook;* city school superintendents were employed in cities of more than 10,000 inhabitants; personnel managers were "carefully selected by competent authorities"; and YMCA physical directors were selected by a YMCA college. All members of criterion groups had been employed in their occupation for at least three years, and none were over 60 years of age. In some cases the criterion was probably not as stringent as in others: The apparently miscellaneous collection of office workers was probably not as highly selected, in that field, as the physicians who graduated from Yale and Stanford were in theirs, especially when it is considered that the great majority of the physicians practiced in favored areas. Sometimes the criterion was established and the group selected by Strong (e.g., psychologists) and sometimes it was others who did these things (e.g., men teachers) . On the whole, however, there is little to quarrel with in the criterion.

The representativeness of the sample is more difficult to judge, and little attention has been paid to the serious questions which can be raised concerning some of the groups. The purchasing agents were located in Northern California, Los Angeles, Washington, D.C., and Cleveland; the psychologists were scattered throughout the United States and constituted 35 percent of the population from which they were drawn; the personnel managers came from New England, the Middle Atlantic States, the Great Lakes, and the Pacific Coast; and the city school superintendents were located in various parts of the States. These seem reasonably likely to prove representative. But the male social-science teachers were all from Minnesota, and may have had interests quite different from those of their confreres in Vermont and Alabama; the real estate salesmen were all from California, and may differ considerably from those of Massachusetts, though they are perhaps very much like those of Florida; and the farmers were all from the West Coast, and perhaps unlike those of Maine and Georgia. A check has been made of the possible existence of regional differences in occupational interest patterns by Braasch (1954), who found that the interests of social studies teachers in the Deep South are like those of social studies teachers in the norm (Minnesota) group, and that Southern pharmacists resemble New York State pharmacists. Strong reports an unpublished study by Pallister and Pierce (1943, pp. 674–677) which compares the interests of Scotsmen with those of Americans; the former were artists, journalists, ministers, and policemen living in or near Dundee. The interests of Scottish artists and policemen were very much like those of their American counterparts, while those of ministers (possibly) and journalists (clearly) were different. Strong concludes that the differences cannot be attributed to language usage, since at most two occupational groups differ; he believes that they are due to differences in sampling, and points out that the American journalists were a highly selected group (listed in *Who's Who*, etc.) while the Scots constituted all the literary employees of one local publishing house. There is also the possibility of national, and therefore regional, differences in the selection of persons in some occupations. Second-generation Japanese high school boys, born in America, were found to resemble white Americans in their interests in another study reported by Strong (1943, pp. 677–679), leading him, as in the case of the Scottish study, to conclude that richness of meaning has little effect upon responses to interest items, and that the omission of some terms which are not understood does not appreciably affect interest inventory scores. These findings indicate that regional differences in vocational interest patterns in the United States may not be as important as *a priori* reasoning might suggest.

The temporal validity of Strong's occupational interest scales, like their regional validity, has now been the subject of published investigations. Professional self-consciousness and the rapid development of their own profession have made psychologists conscious of the problem. It is frequently pointed out, for example, that Fellows of the American Psychological Association in 1928 were largely laboratory psychologists, more interested in problems of mental organization and functioning as shown in experimental studies of learning in humans and in animals than in problems of human adjustment, and that, in contrast, the tremendous growth of industrial, counseling, and clinical psychology in recent years now puts the heirs of these theoretical psychologists in the minority. The interests of the two generations of psychologists could be quite different, or, on the other hand, the common core of interest in the scientific study of man could be so important that, when compared with other professional men, they would seem quite similar. Kriedt (1949) has confirmed the fact that these changes in the profession are reflected in measured interests, and has revised the psychologist scale and made available a set of specialty scales. Only 56 per cent of the 1948 psychologists, as contrasted with 82 per cent of the 1927 sample, rated A or B+ on the old scoring key; the median score of the new sample was still an A. Occupational change was significant, but not radical. Caution will be needed in the use of scales for other occupations which may have changed. Berdie (in Layton, 1960) has reviewed other such studies, which tend to show little change, women social workers being one outstanding exception.

Another aspect of the norming of the inventory which needs consideration is the *form in which its scores are expressed* and the *normative group* to which it compares a person. Strong provides distributions of raw scores based on the appropriate criterion group (e.g., engineers), standard scores and letter grades for the same groups, and percentile scores for the criterion group, Stanford freshmen, and Stanford seniors. It is the norms for the criterion group which should be used. The letter ratings have the advantage over percentiles and standard scores in that they indicate clearly and readily whether or not a person's interests resemble those of men or women successful in the occupation in question, without obscuring the issue with the problem of little understood differences of degree. For although the difference between the 60th and 90th percentiles on an aptitude test has known significance, that between the same percentiles on an interest inventory such as Strong's does not; there is no reason for thinking that a *high* degree of resemblance to the interests of the *average* successful worker is superior to a moderate degree of resemblance. The man at the 60th precentile might actually differ from the average successful worker in ways which make him more like the most successful or satisfied workers than the man whose 90th percentile rank indicates closer resemblance to the average established man. In both counseling and selection, therefore, it has been thought better to use the letter ratings. Strong's long-term follow-up (1955) has, however, shown that the higher the standard score, the greater the likelihood of entering a given occupation, which suggests use of the standard scores.

The letter ratings are so established that the top 69 percent of workers in the occupation are assigned scores of A, and the bottom 2 percent are assigned scores of C. Thus anyone resembling the majority of established workers is assigned an A or at worst a B+, and all persons who rate C on an occupation are quite unlike the bulk of men in the field in question. Scaled scores may be useful in certain types of studies, as when differences between groups are being studied.

Standardization and Initial Validation. Much of what might normally be discussed under this heading has already been treated under the sections on scoring and norms, because of the unique nature of the Vocational Interest Blank as an inventory based on group differences and scored by different keys for each occupation on which it has been standardized. It is also difficult, in a sense, to distinguish between initial validation and subsequent validation, because of the basic nature of some of the later studies which Strong has made of his inventory. However, it will clarify matters briefly to outline the steps gone through in the first validation of each occupational scale of the Strong Blank.

The Blank itself, it will be remembered, was the result of several years of experimentation by Strong and his associates and students; his list of 420 items, later abbreviated to 400, consisted of those which had been found most useful in these various studies. In devising the scoring scale for each occupation the inventory was administered, often by mail, to men or women who had been in the occupation in question for at least three years and who, in most cases, were distinguished by having been nominated by well-informed persons as leaders in their fields, by being listed in the appropriate *Who's Who,* or by professional certification. The scores made by these 200 to 500 persons were distributed on the normal curve and converted into standard scores and letter grades. It should be noted that in this procedure the norm group consists of the same persons who constituted the criterion group, and that experience has repeatedly shown that when these two groups are the same, the mean scores of subsequent groups will be lower than those of the norm, even though all groups are random samples of the same population. This has been noted and pointed out by Strong (1943, pp. 649, 675), in experiments which showed that, when the criterion-norm group consists of 250 persons, the shrinkage of scores will be about 1.50 standard scores. He felt that it was wise to continue this procedure, however, in order to have the largest possible criterion groups. This was justified by the fact that the shrinkage for a criterion group of 300 was only 0.90 standard scores. As there was very little change for numbers above 300, Strong's choice of criterion groups of between 400 and 500 seems wise, but users of the blank must allow for a shrinkage of about one standard score—not enough to be important in most individual instances, but at times making the difference between a B and a B+, a B+ and an A. The experience of psychologists during World War II, when, for example, norms were regularly gathered for 400 aviation cadets per day in one center, brought home the need for cross-validation as a means of avoiding shrinkage; even supposedly similar groups of 1000 cases frequently showed significant differences. It is therefore to be regretted that Strong did not correct his norms by the amount appropriate to the number of cases used, or subsequently obtain data from new normative groups.

The procedure described above is the standard method of developing an occupational scale for Strong's Blank. Many other studies have been conducted which validate the inventory, either through cross-validation or by other means; we have, for example, seen studies of the validity of responses (faking), age changes, and the effect of experience. Other studies have considered the relationship between interest-inventory scores and grades or sales production, but as these fit more naturally into the dicussion of field validation they will be taken up after the next section.

Reliability. The odds-evens reliability coefficients of 36 of the revised men's scales are reported in the manual as averaging .88, based on the records of 285 Stanford seniors; only one coefficient was below .80, the reliability of the CPA scale being .73. Taylor (1942) found retest reliabilities averaging .87 for high school boys and .88 for girls, on the appropriate forms. The retest reliability was ascertained for college students by Burnham (1942) with eight of the original scales, the average being .87. Strong obtained retest reliabilities after five years, the first testing being when the 285 men in question were college seniors. These averaged .75, and must be thought of as not only an index of the reliability of the scales, but also as a measure of the stability of interests in early adult-hood. For tenth graders retested after two years the mean for 7 typical scales was .57 (Canning et al., 1941); for eleventh graders after three years it was .71 (Taylor, 1942). It is evident that the scales are reliable enough for confident use in individual diagnosis at least after age 17.

Validity.   The validity of Strong's Vocational Interest Blank has been investigated by relating the scores of its various scales to those of other tests, to grades in school and college, to completion of training, to earn-ings in sales work, to ratings of success in various types of work, to per-sistence in an occupation, to differences between occupational groups, and to job satisfaction. As this suggests, there has been accumulated an unusual amount of validation data, even for an instrument which has been in existence for twenty years.

To attempt to review all of these validation studies would be not only a sizable task [Strong's (1943) monograph attained 746 pages even after whole sections had been ruthlessly cut], but, because of Strong's thorough-ness, and that of Darley and Hagenah (1955) and Berdie (in Layton, 1960), an unnecessary one. There are, however, two reasons for discussing certain selected studies here at some length: 1) An understanding of these details is essential to adequate use and interpretation of Strong's Blank; and 2) they should become an integral part of the literature on vocational tests in order that the first objective may be attained. Some of the studies discussed by Strong are therefore treated here, together with others of special significance which have appeared since he compiled his review.

Tests of intelligence have been correlated with Strong's scales in eight studies summarized by Strong (1943, pp. 333–334) and in others subse-quently published. The various investigators agree that the relationships with scientific and linguistic interests are positive, the former being mod-erate or low but significant and the latter so low as to be of little meaning, as shown in Table 31.

The correlations with social welfare and business interests tend to be negative, although most of the coefficients are so low as to make them of little practical significance despite their theoretical implications. Typical data are reproduced in the lower half of Table 31. It will be noted that, although there are occasional discrepancies, there is sufficient agreement so that analyzing the nature of the groups and of the intelligence tests used in an attempt to reconcile them is unnecessary.

Special aptitudes have been correlated with scores on Strong's Blank. The relationship between the Stanford Scientific Aptitude Test and Strong's six group scales was ascertained by Long (1945) for 200 college students although, as he points out, it is not at all certain what the former test measures. He found significant positive correlations (.26 and .50) with

TABLE 31

RELATIONSHIP BETWEEN INTELLIGENCE AND INTERESTS
(Taken from Strong, 1943, Table 90)

Occupational Scale			*Correlations*			
Psychologist	.37	.43	.41	.36	.15	.38
Physician	.16	.27	.19	.04	.10	.24
Engineer	.21	.20	.14	.17	.08	.28
Chemist	.30	.34	.15	.31	.03	.35
Advertising Man	.02	.14	.12	—.11	.45	.01
Lawyer	.07	.21	.20	.13	.39	.13
YMCA Secretary	—.22	—.19	—.18	.14	—.15	—.18
Personnel Manager	—.16	—.10	—.13	.27	—.07	—.02
City School Superintendent	—.12	.03	.01	.32	.06	—.06
Office Worker	—.31	—.27	—.28	.09	—.38	—.25
Purchasing Agent	—.25	—.33	—.31	.00	—.07	—.21
Life Insurance Sales	—.35	—.34	—.31	—.19	.00	—.26
Vacuum Cleaner Sales	—.36	—.40	—.40	—.14	—.36	----

Strong's two scientific scales, and a significant negative relationship with the business-contact scale (—.37); the others were negligible, and none could be explained on the basis of intellectual differences as measured by the A.C.E. Psychological Examination. Gustad (1951) found no significant differences in the interests of two groups of college students, those whose linguistic aptitude (A.C.E. scores) exceeded their quantitative, and those whose quantitative aptitude surpassed their linguistic. Leffel (1939) correlated scores on the O'Rourke Mechanical Aptitude Test with Strong scores, showing positive relationships (.42 and .46) between the O'Rourke and the keys for chemist and engineer, and negative relationships (—.25 and —.25) with the scales for social studies teacher and lawyer. Holcomb and Laslett (1932) found comparable results for the Stenquist Mechanical Aptitude Test. This suggests that aptitude, being more fundamental than interest, may have some causal effect on the latter, but as noted previously the O'Rourke and the Stenquist are information tests the scores of which are no doubt influenced by both aptitude and interest, making it impossible to infer causal connections. The latter study also used the MacQuarrie, which correlated .22 with Strong's engineer scale. Moore's study (1941) showed correlations of .30 and .35 between the Bennett Mechanical Comprehension Test and the engineer key, and of .21 and .26 with the aviator scale, while the correlation between Bennett and Strong production manager and carpenter scales were negligible. As the MacQuarrie and Bennett tests are more strictly measures of aptitude than the O'Rourke and Stenquist, it may perhaps be inferred that aptitude plays a part in the development of interest. This seems warranted despite Klugman's (1944) contrary finding with the Minnesota Clerical Test and Strong's women's clerical keys; clerical interests appear to have too little significance in women to attach importance to findings based on them (see below).

Interest and values inventories with which the Strong Blank has been correlated include the Allport-Vernon Study of Values and the Kuder Preference Record. Data from three studies of the Allport-Vernon were discussed in the preceding chapter.

As the Strong Blank is the better understood of the two interest inventories, the discussion of its relationship with the Kuder Preference Record will be postponed until that instrument is the focus of attention.

Personality inventory scores have been related to Strong's scales with results which are somewhat contradictory. These studies are discussed in the preceding chapter and, as there is little in the way of generalizations to be drawn from them which is of value in using Strong's Blank, they are not summarized here.

Grades and scores on achievement examinations have frequently been correlated with scores on Strong's inventory in the hope that the prediction of educational success would thus be improved. The predictive value of scholastic aptitude tests being far from perfect, it was reasoned that motivation might account for part of the discrepancy, and that motivation and interest should overlap to some extent. Accordingly, a number of studies were made, many of which were not published and only a few of which are cited here. Townsend (1945) ascertained the relationships between Strong's scales and scores on objective tests of school achievement made by groups of 50 to 100 boys in private secondary schools, and reported that they were few and significant only in the case of mathematics-science teacher and chemistry ($r = .36$), accountant-chemistry (.49), CPA-chemistry (.42), and mathematician-geometry (.31). Achievement in English and history were not related to social science teacher or author-journalist interest scales. A procedure used by Segel (1934) is suggestive, for after correlating Strong's scales with Iowa High School Content Examination Scores and obtaining correlations between scientific scales and scientific subjects which ranged from .28 to .49, but which were not significantly related in other expected ways except for some negative relationships, he proceeded to use differential achievement scores. These consisted of the differences in the scores of two achievement tests, for example, the difference between literature and science, which had a correlation of .25 with life insurance sales interest. The correlations, both positive and negative, were generally higher, those for scientific interests and differential scientific achievement (e.g., science minus history and social science scores) ranged from .29 to .57. Similar relationships were found when school grades were used instead of achievement test scores in this study, although the trends were not so clear cut, presumably because of the more numerous other factors which affect grades. The reason for the relationships between differential achievement and interests being greater than the relationship between achievement and interests is that, in the former, the effects of general ability are held constant and those of differential motivation and application are emphasized. If a student consistently makes B+ in one field, and A in another, the relationships with interests will not be clear, but if his relative superiority in the second subject is brought out and correlated with interests, and the relative inferiority of his performance in the former subject is similarly treated, the role of interest is more likely to manifest itself.

Grades in college were related to scores on Strong's scales by Alteneder (1940), who worked with freshmen at New York University. The relationships were low (r's ranged from —.28 to .30), but she reported that low scholarship men tended to make higher engineering interest scores than high scholarship men, who tended to have interests more like those of teachers and CPA's, while low scholarship women had interests somewhat more like those of insurance saleswomen and stenographers than high scholarship women, whose scores as librarians, social workers, and lawyers tended to be high.

Melville and Frederiksen (1952) found significant relationships between eight interest scales and grades (r = .20 to .32), compared with twelve (r = .20 to .36) when intelligence was held constant. The scientific scales tended to have positive validities, the business detail and contact negative. Morgan (1952) confirmed the latter finding, but found that his achievers tended to have social welfare interests. Rust and Ryan (1954) found over-achievers at Yale tended to rate higher than under-achievers on scales for occupations requiring extended professional preparation, lower on others.

Typing and stenography grades of about 100 women liberal arts college students were studied with the women's stenographer scale by Barrett (1946) at Hunter College. She reported only the data from tests which showed some validity; as the Strong scale "failed to show any significant relationship to grades," data concerning it were not reported.

Engineering grades were correlated with Strong's engineering scale by Berdie (1944), Campbell (in Strong 1943, p. 521), Holcomb and Laslett (1932), and Long and Perry (1953). In the first study the honor-point ratios of 154 University of Minnesota students were the criterion; their correlation with interest scores was .13. It is worth noting that having a variety of interests, rather than only scientific, had no detrimental effect on achievement. In the second study the correlation was .32. In Campbell's study of 270 engineering students at Stanford it was .185. For this same group the correlation between social-science interests (social studies teacher) and grade-point ratios in social science was .31. Holcomb and Laslett reported a similar correlation (.32) between engineering interest and engineering grades, but Long and Perry found no significant relationships with four-year engineering grades.

Dental grades were used as a criterion for the dentist scale by Robinson and Bellows (1941), who found a significant relationship ($r=$ .13, .18, .19). Data on 141 dental students were reported by Strong (1943, p. 523), who found that those rating C on his scale made inferior grades (grade-point ratio of 2.01), while those of others were slightly higher (2.41 to 2.58). The significance of the difference is not reported.

Medical school grades were studied by Douglass (1942), Jacobson (1942), and Hewer (cited by Berdie in Layton, 1960). Douglass reported that Strong's Blank was not useful in predicting success. Jacobson, however, found that the first year grades of students who were characterized by scientific and other interests were better than those with other interest patterns, those with medical interests as their only strong scientific interest but with other types supplementing these ranked second, and those with no scientific interests ranked at the bottom. Hewer found no relationship between differential interest scores (e.g., physician vs. social-studies teacher) and differential grades (e.g., natural vs. social sciences). In connection with the top-ranking, broad-interest, students, it is interesting that Berdie (1943) found that those with many "likes" get better grades than those with few "likes."

Psychology graduate students studied by Kelly and Fiske (1951) were scored with Kriedt's Psychologist scale, yielding correlations of .46 with an examination in clinical psychology and .27 with grades.

In schools of veterinary medicine Layton (1952) found a validity of .30 for the veterinary scale and first year grades, significant at the one percent level, but Hannum and Thrall (1955) found no relationship with four-year grades.

Teachers' college students were the subjects of studies by Goodfellow (1932), Mather (in Strong, 1943, p. 526), and Seagoe (1945). Goodfellow found, as Strong did with dental students, that those who rated A on the appropriate scale made better grades than those who rated C, the differences being significant. Mather and Seagoe, however, both found no relationships between grades and interests. Berdie (in Layton, 1960) has reviewed other such studies.

These contradictory findings in different studies of the relationship between interests and achievement, reported even for the same subject-matter or professional fields, might be explained on the basis of the unreliability of the criteria in some studies, the limited range of interests in most specialized schools, and perhaps other factors which vary from one institution to another. It is interesting that in few of the published studies has the criterion been subjected to careful scrutiny, either as to distribution of grades or as to reliability, although in numerous studies (e.g., Williamson et al., 1938) it has been demonstrated that the apparent lack of validity of the predictor is attributable in the first place to lack of reliability in the criterion. The limited range of scores in professional-student groups has been commented on by Strong (1943, pp. 525-526), who contrasted the percentages of dental students receiving the various letter ratings on his scale with the percentages of college students in general: The latter received fewer A's and more C's. This phenomenon suggests the need to use an approach other than the correlational in studying the relationship between interests and educational achievement, and perhaps a criterion other than grades. Several studies have used another approach, but before describing their results attention should be focused on one study of interests and grades in which the range of the former was relatively great.

Personnel psychology students in the Army Specialized Training Program, 95 in all, were the subjects of a study by Strong (1944), after the publication of his book and the expression of opinions which might have been somewhat modified had this study been completed first. In this investigation the correlation between intelligence and grades in psychology courses was only .20, whereas that for psychologist interest was .275. Neither of these is quite significant (.31 required), but when individual course grades are considered the picture is clearer: Correlations for testing and social psychology courses were .355 and .150 for intelligence, and .32 and .34 for psychologist interests. As the tendency in other studies has been for intelligence tests to be considerably better predictors than interest inventories, possible reasons were investigated. It was found that, since the soldiers in question had all been selected partly on the basis of scholastic aptitude (minimum score of 115 on the AGCT or in the top quarter of white soldiers), the range of intelligence in the group was restricted: in fact, 90 of the 95 made scores of 120 or above. In the typical college freshman class, however, the tail of the distribution does not end so abruptly. The range of interest in psychology was considerably greater, from low C to A, with a mean of low C. Some of the men in the class reported, in conversation with Strong, that they had been assigned to personnel psychology training without being consulted. This is quite different from the typical college situation, in which the student is more generally in college for some reason of his own, and has something to say about the curriculum in which he studies. Even the required courses are then in one sense electives, something accepted because they lead to some desired goal, be it no more than playing football or being with friends.

In the typical college class a student can therefore make the grade if he has the ability, regardless of interest in the subject-matter of the course; in the ASTP many students lacked the motivation to use their ability. In such circumstances one would expect to find, as Strong did, that interest has approximately as high a correlation with achievement as does aptitude.

Completion of training is the other criterion of educational achievement used by some researchers. It avoids the fine distinctions which grades attempt to make, stressing the more carefully considered and perhaps more clear-cut distinctions between: 1) passing and failing; and 2) liking and not liking. In Goodfellow's study (1932), for example, it was noted that the education students who changed to other curricula made lower scores than did those who remained in education, and Strong (1943:524) found that only 25 percent of the dental students who rated C on his dentist scale graduated in from four to six years, whereas 91 percent of those who rated A, 93 percent of those rating B+, and 67 percent, each, of those rating B and B—, graduated. These findings fit in with Strong's explanation of the role of interest in educational achievement (1943, p. 529):

If a student has sufficient interest to elect a course, his grade will depend far more on his intelligence, industry, and previous preparation than on his interest. Interest affects the situation, however, in causing the student to elect what he is interested in and not to elect courses in which he is not interested. When a student discovers he has mistakenly elected a course in which he has little interest, he will finish it about as well as other courses but he will not elect further courses of a similar nature.

To this should be added, in view of the one study in which the range of interest was adequate: When a student is compelled to take a course or to study in a field not of his own choosing, the relationship between interests and achievement will be more nearly comparable to that of intelligence and achievement.

Vocational preference has been frequently demonstrated to have little long-term reliability or realism in adolescence (e.g., Rothney, 1958; Schmidt and Rothney, 1955), although in college students it has generally proved more stable and realistic (Strong, 1943, p. 355, 1952, 1953; McArthur and Stevens, 1955). It is often asked, however, whether the scores of interest inventories provide one with information sufficiently different from expressions of vocational preference to justify the time and expense; and, as the preferences of some groups of college students have proved rather stable, it has been suggested that in their case the inventories may be of little value (Wightwick, 1945). Counselors working with clients in schools, colleges, and guidance centers frequently comment on the large number of cases in which Strong's Blank merely confirms what one already knew from interviewing the client and, what is more, what the client already knew himself. It is therefore pertinent to inquire concerning the relationship between Strong scores and expressed preferences; some relationship would presumably be evidence of validity, while a nearly perfect relationship would suggest substituting a single question for the whole inventory.

In two investigations (Laleger, 1942; Skodak and Crissey, 1942), the conclusion was drawn that scores on Strong's Blank were less useful than expressions of preferences. In both instances the conclusion was based on low correlations between inventory scores and vocational preferences of high school girls, and on the tendency of the former to be more concentrated in a few fields than the latter. But both studies involved the Women's Blank, in which the clustering of scores has been seen to be due to the strength of one factor which is common in women and in many women's occupations.

Bedell (1941) found that only two of 17 women's scales had correlations of more than .50 with the self-estimated interests of freshmen women. Data for 1000 men at the University of Minnesota were analyzed by Darley (1941, pp. 21-25), with a resulting contingency coefficient of .43 between claimed vocational choices and inventoried interests as determined by his classification of Strong scores into primary, secondary, tertiary, and no interest patterns. An examination of the basic data is perhaps more revealing of the inadequacy of expressed preferences as indices of measured interests. Scientific choices were indicated by 374 men, of whom only 71 had primary measured interests in the scientific field, 214 had no primary interest patterns, 45 had business detail interests, and the rest were scattered among the other fields; 137 claimed linguistic choices, of whom 26 had measured primary interest patterns of that type, 65 had no primary patterns, 21 had social welfare interest patterns, and the rest were scattered; 169 claimed business detail preferences, while 60 had measured primary patterns of that type, 69 had no primary pattern, 16 had business contact patterns, and the rest were scattered throughout other categories. Allowance must be made for the fact that many had secondary patterns in the field of their claimed interests, but even then the discrepancies are substantial.

Using a more refined measure of expressed interests Berdie (1950) found a median contingency coefficient of .43 with inventoried interests; his subjects ranged in age from 14 to 37. Moffie (1942) worked with NYA boys averaging 18.7 years of age, who rated their interests in the fields assayed by Strong's Blank and were scored with Strong's group and specific scales; the correlations ranged from —.07 to .47 and from —.05 to .54, respectively. Moffie's explanation is that lack of maturity and experience on the part of adolescents invalidates their judgments of their interest in different types of work, while the pattern scores of an inventory succeed in tapping their interests more adequately. It might be suggested, also, that this lack of experience and insight is greater in some areas than in others. Some occupational fields, e.g. teaching, are more open to observation by the average youth than others, making easier the formation of preferences on the basis of interest, while others such as certified public accountant (which has the least reliable scale so far developed) are not so readily observed. Great variations in the agreement of ratings and inventory scores of individuals were found by Arsenian (1942), further substantiating the hypothesis that maturity and experience, which vary from one person to another, account for the differences in agreement between measured interests and preference or choice. Finally, data reported by Wrenn (1935a, b) show that the more intelligent college students are more likely to "choose" occupations in which they make high scores (45 percent of the superior group rate A on chosen occupation, 3 percent C), while the less able are more likely to make low scores in their preferred occupational field (22 percent rate A, 20 percent C). This suggests either that the more able students have more insight into their interests than the less able, or that their superior verbal ability enables them more adequately to integrate their rationalizations concerning interests. Whether or not we are dealing with rationalizations or insights can be ascertained from the extent of the relationship between inventory scores and objective criteria such as completion of training, grades, and stability of employment in a field.

The relative predictive value of inventoried interest and expressed preference has been studied by Wightwick (1945), by Strong (1955) and by McArthur and Stevens (1955). Wightwick found that 44 percent of 115 college women were employed in the field of the freshman choice four years after graduation, and 73 percent in the field of their senior choice, in contrast with 58 percent employed in occupations in which they had as freshmen made A or B+ ratings. This led the author to the conclusion that measured interests are not as valid predictors of vocational choice as expressed preferences, conclusion which seems rather odd as it can be based only on a comparison of *freshmen* inventory scores with *senior* preferences (58 vs. 73); a comparison of freshmen test results and freshmen preferences suggests, instead, that inventories are superior to expressed preferences (58 vs. 44). The greater validity of senior preferences is no doubt due to the nature of the criterion: field entered. It is to be expected that senior preferences would reflect an element of realism, including considerations of finances, opportunities, and family pressures which would make them perhaps less valid indices of interest than test scores, but more valid predictors of occupation entered.

Unfortunately Strong's nine-and ten-year follow-up studies (1943, pp.

393-403) and his 18-year study (1955, pp. 174-175), were not analyzed in the same manner as Wightwick's. They do show that about three-fifths of his college students were employed in the field of their freshman or senior choice five and ten years after graduation; they also show a substantial relationship between interest scores in college and field of subsequent employment, as seen in the discussion of the permanence of interests and as brought out below in the material on job satisfaction, but the data are not so organized as to show what percentage of men entered and remained in fields in which they made A, B+, or lower scores.

In his 18-year follow-up Strong gives data on the predictive value of both expressed and inventoried interests, but not in terms that make them directly comparable. About 50 percent of his subjects were employed, 18 years later, in the field of their college freshman choice or in one closely related to it, 30 percent were in somewhat related occupations, and 20 percent were in quite unrelated occupations: this may be summarized by the statement that freshman choice was highly predictive for 50 percent of the group, somewhat predictive for 80 percent. The data on inventoried interests showed that there were 78 chances in 100 that a freshman scoring A in an occupation will be found employed in it 18 years later, but only 17 chances in 100 that a freshman scoring C in an occupation will be employed in it 18 years later. These findings may be summarized as showing that high or low scores on Strong's Blank are more predictive for college freshmen in a university such as Stanford than are expressed preferences.

At Harvard University, McArthur and Stevens (1955) found that sophomore expressed and inventoried interests were about equally predictive, giving about 50 percent good predictions, 25 percent poor predictions, and 25 percent "clean misses" of occupation 14 years later. These results are about what Strong found for *expressed* interests, inferior to what he found for *inventoried* interests. In another report McArthur (1954) makes the reason for this discrepancy clear: Expressed interests are more predictive than inventoried for upper class persons (who enter occupations considered appropriate by their families regardless of underlying interests), inventoried interests are more predictive for middle class persons (whose families tend to encourage self-actualization). The different over-all predictive values at Harvard and Stanford may therefore be a reflection of the differing extents to which the two student bodies come from the sub-cultures in question.

The stability of occupational preference in relation to inventoried interests was investigated by Traphagen (1952), with the conclusion that preferences are stable when supported by appropriate inventoried interests, but likely to change when inventoried interests are not appropriate.

Unfortunately, the subjects in his study were students being counseled at the time data were collected, and whose Strong's Blank scores were obtained for use in this counseling. There is therefore every likelihood that test scores were used to evaluate choice, thus invalidating the study. It should be repeated without the contamination of counseling on the basis of the predictor variable.

The relatively low correlation between expressed preferences and inventoried interests in high school, the tendency of the less able students to prefer fields in which they lack measured interests, and the superiority of inventories to the expressed preferences of college freshmen in the dominant middle class culture, suggest that inventories can improve the quality of counseling and prediction. With college students and adults expressed and inventoried interests will often be found to agree [Berdie (1950) reports an r of about .40], but in many cases insights of this type are lacking, especially when external pressures have been at work on the client.

Vocational achievement has served as a criterion of the validity of Strong's Blank particularly in work with life insurance salesmen. It might be argued that the criterion of the validity of an interest inventory should be satisfaction, rather than achievement; certainly satisfaction should be one of the outcomes of interest. But if interest produces satisfaction it should also result in achievement, granted the necessary abilities, for the satisfied worker should throw himself more wholeheartedly into his work. This might not be true of all occupations, for theoretically there might be some fields in which the work can be done equally well regardless of interest and satisfaction in the work, provided the end-result (pay, prestige, etc.) is desired; but in other fields the congeniality of the activities engaged in might be important to success.

That insurance sales is one of these latter is indicated by a number of studies by Strong (1934), Bills (1934, 1938, 1941), Ghiselli (1942) and others, most of which are summarized in Strong's book (1943, pp. 487-500). Only illustrative data are therefore considered here.

Only one of Strong's studies used as subjects a group of applicants for employment as insurance salesmen, the other groups consisting of men already employed or, in one instance, released, by their company (Strong, 1943, pp. 487-488). In the pre-employment study, the applicants were tested in a small agency, 20 were employed, and only 16 remained more than three and one-half months. The data of the pretested group are therefore not very conclusive, although they do show a clear tendency ($r = .48$) for the higher-scoring men to sell more insurance. When data from all groups, all agencies, were combined the relationship between interest scores and sales (criterion reliability $= .81$) is as shown in Table 32, adapted from Strong (1943).

TABLE 32

PERCENTAGE OF AGENTS IN EACH LIFE INSURANCE INTEREST
RATING WHO PRODUCE $0 TO $400,000-AND-UP ANNUALLY

Annual Production	N	Percent in Each Rating Producing				
		C	B—	B	B+	A
$0 to $ 49,000	38	52	33	27	22	9
$50,000 to $ 99,000	52	24	17	45	34	16
$100,000 to $149,000	31	18	17	14	7	19
$150,000 to $199,000	37	6	17	9	13	22
$200,000 to $399,000	47	0	17	0	20	31
$400,000 up.	6	0	0	5	4	3
Total		100	101	100	100	100
Number	211	17	6	22	45	121

There is a rather clear tendency for those who made high scores to be those who sold the most insurance: 56 percent of the A men sold enough insurance to make a living by then-current standards ($150,000), as compared with only 6 percent of the C men. Although the coefficient of correlation for 181 of these cases is only .37, the relationship is statistically and psychologically significant, for it must be remembered that most of the men were tested after a long period of employment, after the low-producing and low-scoring men had been eliminated by natural selection. The greater range of scores and sales which would characterize applicants would undoubtedly yield a higher correlation coefficient. If these men had all been tested as applicants for employment, or better still as college students, and had made similar scores, findings would be quite convincing. As all but 16 of them were tested after they had been on the job some time, it is possible, however, that some of the poorer salesmen indicated liking for fewer of the sales items than did their more successful fellows, not because they actually liked sales work less, but because they were somewhat dissatisfied with the financial results of their work. Apparently Strong has not taken this possible rationalization of failure into account, for he makes no mention of the possible differences between pretested and posttested responses. But even if such forces were at work, the relationship between inventoried interests and success in selling life insurance is noteworthy.

The life insurance and real estate salesmen's scales of the Vocational Interest Blank were combined in Bills' study of 588 newly employed casualty insurance salesmen and compared with ratings of success after one year on the job. She found that 76 percent of those who made low scores were failures, while only 22 percent of the high scoring group failed. Ghiselli worked with a much smaller group of casualty insurance salesmen, 29 in all, finding significant relationships for the CPA and occupational level scales (.38 and .27). He reports that they tended to make high scores on the business contact and detail keys, but that contrary to Bills' findings the contact scales did not correlate with performance. As his cases are far fewer in number, the relation can hardly be considered disproved by this one study.

Another type of salesman, selling detergents on a wholesale basis over large territories and acting as service men on related matters (service time correlated .51 with profits), was investigated by Otis (1941). The group was necessarily small, as there were few territories and the turnover rate was low $(N = 17)$. His criterion was selling cost, with which the combined life insurance and real estate salesmen's scales correlated .50. With numbers as small as these the data are merely suggestive, but promising.

Accounting-machine salesmen, 143 in number, and 283 service men of the same types of machines, were studied by Ryan and Johnson (1942). They found that the two groups were differentiated from the general population by especially constructed standard-type scales, but that scores on these scales had no relationship to success. They then developed another set of scales based on the differentiation of successful from unsuccessful men in the occupations in question. These scales did differentiate other groups of successful and unsuccessful men in the same jobs, the critical ratio for the service men being 4.8.

The relationships between interests and achievement in several other occupations have been summarized by Strong, often from unpublished studies; it is from him (1943, pp. 501–504) that the following are taken, except when otherwise indicated.

Psychologists who were starred in *American Men of Science* averaged 48.7 on the psychologist key. Strong explains this slightly below average score on the basis of the low scores made by some applied psychologists, two of whom scored below 30 and later went into business, but this explanation seems unnecessary in view of the expected shrinkage in the means of new groups when criterion and norm groups are one and the same. It can therefore only be said that eminent psychologists taken as a group do not seem to differ from somewhat less eminent psychologists (the Fellows of the standardization group).

Teachers were rated by Ullman and by Phillips for success of performance; the ratings did not correlate with interest inventory scores.

Engineers rated as outstanding by an engineering dean were compared with full and associate members of the four engineering societies. The outstanding engineers made higher scores than the associates.

Aviators who failed in flying training were not significantly lower on the aviator scale than were those who were successful in training, perhaps because of the small size of the samples. Another set of pilot scales was constructed in a study initiated by Super in the Air Force (in Guilford,

1947, pp. 608–611) . A total of 650 aviation cadets were tested with the Vocational Interest Blank, and scales were developed on the basis of item validities, the scale based on even-numbered cases being cross-validated on odd-numbered cases, and vice versa. The correlations between these scales and success in primary flying training were insignificant (—.03 and —.10), confirming what Strong found with smaller groups.

Advertising men, 36 in all, were rated by three officials of their agency. Although the significance of the relationship was not tested, the men with higher ratings tended to have higher scores on Strong's advertising scale.

Foremen, 59 of those employed by a large chemical plant, were rated for characteristics which are not described. The correlations between ratings and Strong scores were .34 for chemist, .31 for engineer, .25 for CPA, and —.31 for life insurance salesman. These relationships are such as might be expected in a sub-professional technical job, except that with CPA. Thirty others were tested by Shultz and Barnabas (1945) , and were rated for budget-control efficiency and employee relations. The correlations between Strong's scales for production manager and occupational level, on the one hand, and combined ratings were respectively .38 and .22.

Janitor-engineers rated above average in their work $(N = 44)$ were found by Berman, Darley, and Paterson (1934) to make higher scores on the technical and scientific but not on other scales than did a group of 23 who were rated below average. In the same study 123 policemen rated by their captain were found to be differentiated on the basis of scales which measure interest in social contacts.

The gifted group studied by Terman and Oden (1948) were tested with Strong's Blank after they had reached the age of about 30; only those who indicated a desire to take it when asked did so, giving a group of 627 men. The least successful group five years later, as evaluated by judges who rated the subjects on the basis of a study of case records, included five times as many men with low interest scores in their occupations as did the most successful group. "Few men", concluded Terman and Oden, "are very successful who score low in the occupation in which they are engaged".

Psychologists in the clinical training program of the Veterans Administration were studied with a variety of instruments, including Strong's Blank, by Kelly and Fiske (1951). Scoring keys included the 1938 Psychologist scale, a custom-built scale for VA Clinical Psychologist, and Kriedt's keys for Psychologist and for Clinical Psychologist. The first-named scale had validities of .33 to .43 for ratings of academic performance and of research competence and for achievement examinations in psychology, but no predictive validity for rated success in diagnostic, therapeutic, or other aspects of practical work as shown in the internship.

The Kriedt Psychologist scale, now generally in use, had validities of from .20 to .46, for the same academic criteria but also for general clinical competence and employability. The VA Clinical scale had validities of from .20 to .24 for rated research and clinical competence, rated employability, and tested clinical knowledge, while Kriedt's Clinical scale had validities of .20 to .26 for rated specific and general clinical skills (and only for these).

In a quite different kind of work, positive results were obtained also by Knauft (1951), who developed a special scale for 38 managers of retail bakeries and cross-validated it on 32 new applicants, using as criterion the ratio of controllable costs to sales. The bake-shop manager's scale had a predictive validity, in this second study using a model longitudinal cross-validation design, of .53.

Summarizing the evidence on the relationship between inventoried interests and success in an occupation, we have seen that it is significant in the case of several quite different types of sales jobs, although in some this is so only when success-failure rather than occupational-differences keys are used. Success in psychology (judged by starring in *American Men of Science*) and in teaching were not related to the degree of similarity of interests to those of persons employed in those fields, but success in psychology (clinical training), bake shop management, advertising, technical foremanship, janitorial work, and policework were. Successful and unsuccessful aviators were not differentiated by success-failure scales.

The sales data are consistent with Super's hypothesis concerning interest and achievement, for selling life insurance requires a substantial degree of self-direction and willingness to persist in the face of a cool welcome; presumably only a person who finds a real challenge in locating prospects and in making himself pleasant and helpful to them could make enough calls to earn a living. Congeniality of the work is important, and there is a significant relationship between interest and achievement. The same is true of casualty insurance salesmen, and of wholesale salesmen in whose work service to customers is an important function. But in somewhat more routine sales work interest is related to success only when the interests of successful men in the occupation are contrasted with those of failures in the same field rather than with those of men-in-general.

The other findings are more difficult to synthesize or rationalize. The apparent contradictions may lie in the differences in the criteria of success: being starred in *American Men of Science* for one's research contributions is not comparable to being rated highly for performance as a student or an intern or for the successful management of advertising accounts. Perhaps advertising is partly a sales occupation (r life insurance salesman $=.59$), in which case the importance of interest is explainable in the same

terms. Psychological research and teaching are non-competitive, and success in both fields can be achieved in a great variety of ways; perhaps
congeniality is less crucial to them because of their varied outlets. Just
why interest should so clearly play a part in success in non-competitive
fields such as clinical psychology, foremanship, janitorial work, and police
work is difficult to see. Congeniality could be important, in that all three
groups have to put up with tht vagaries of a variety of people, but then
so do teachers. More studies, with more detailed analyses of the duties of
those involved, are needed before the significance of these findings will be
clear. In the meantime, it seems that the refinement of measures and of
criteria of success has necessitated attributing more predictive power to
interests than has been customary.

Occupational differentiation being the basis on which the Strong Vocational Interest Blank was constructed, most of what might be covered in
this section has already been dealt with in earlier sections, particularly
those concerned with the construction of the occupational interest scales.
Some occupations have been studied without scales having been developed
for them: for example, Bluett (1945) ascertained the patterns of interest
scores characterizing vocational rehabilitation officers. The applicability
of the adult scales to pre-occupational groups was verified by Goodman
(1942), who found that engineering students differed in the expected ways
from liberal arts students, and by Barrett (1945), who found that women
college students majoring in art made higher scores on the artist scale than
did other students.

The importance of adequate job description and classification in developing and using interest scales has been demonstrated by Hughes and
McNamara (1958), who showed that Strong's sales keys correlated *positively* with a custom-built scale for data-processing machine rental salesman, *negatively* with a scale for electric typewriter salesman, but did not
differentiate either specialty. The custom-built keys were valid when tried
on new groups of 220 and 358.

The study of occupational specialties, as well as of broadly defined
occupations, has been shown to be possible and worthwhile as discussed
in Chapter XVI, as further shown by Hughes and McNamara cited above,
by Kriedt's (1949) psychologist scales, and by Dunnette (1957) with engineering specialties.

The most significant problem still to be discussed is that of the differentiation of women's vocational groups on the basis of their interests.
Women's and girls' interests have been investigated with Strong's Blank
by Laleger (1942), Skodak and Crissey (1942), Crissy and Daniel (1939),
and others besides Strong himself (1943, pp. 162–168) . These studies have
shown that it is more difficult to differentiate women on the basis of their

interests than it is men. The manual for the Women's Blank shows a surprisingly large number of substantial correlations between occupations which would not, on the basis of data for the men's form, be expected. The correlation between the women's office worker and nurse scales, for example, is .55, while that between office worker and housewife is .84. It has frequently been noted that populations of high school girls and college girls tend to make far more high scores as nurse, office worker, elementary school teacher, and housewife than should be found in a random sample. Stuit (1938) found this even among teachers' college students. A suggestion as to why this may be the case emerges when it is noted that the correlations between the housewife scale, on the one hand, and those for nurse, physical education teacher, elementary school teacher, office worker, and stenographer on the other, are respectively .59, .56, .84, .77, .80.

The factor analysis by Crissy and Daniel (1939) referred to earlier carries this thought further. They found four factors in women's vocational interests, three of which were like those found by other psychologists in studying men, but one of which they called "male association." It is this factor which others have called interest in multiplicity of detail, interest in the convenience of others, interest in order, and non-professional interests. It has a very slight loading in the masculinity-femininity scale. Whatever the factor is, it seems to be present in a great many women, especially in those in the occupations named, and it is present in negative form in other women, particularly those who make high scores as authors, librarians, artists, physicians, and social workers.

It is worthy of note that the occupations in which the so-called male association factor is important in a positive way are those which may be entered after a relatively brief and easily obtainable education, whereas those in which it is of negative importance are by and large those which require a longer and less easily obtained education or which are entered only by the persistent and highly motivated. It would be helpful to have the marriage rates in each of these occupations, in order to ascertain whether or not those who are characterized by a strong "male association" factor do in fact marry in greater numbers. Observation suggests that the loss of women office workers through marriage is greater than the loss of women authors, physicians, and social workers for the same reason, but this is no doubt partly because the latter groups frequently continue their work even after marriage. If both groups of occupations marry with more or less equal frequency this factor can hardly be named "male association"; and if it really is that, why is there no evidence of a "female association" factor in men, most of whom also marry? As the factor has been isolated only in women, is positively related to stopgap and negatively related to career occupations, and is more important in the occupation of housewife than in any other (factor loading .83), it is suggested that this is in reality a home-vs.-career factor. The home or career decision is one which many women have to make, and which most decide in favor of the home. It is presumably the presence of this factor which makes it difficult to measure the vocational interests of women in Strong's technique, for it outweighs vocational interests in many instances. As will be seen in connection with the Kuder Preference Record this difficulty is not an insurmountable obstacle to the measurement of women's interests, but to overcome it it is necessary to use a different type of inventorying device.

Satisfaction in one's work has seemed to most psychologists and counselors to be the objective of counseling or employment on the basis of interest inventories. But the appraisal of vocational satisfaction is not a simple matter, for a multiplicity of factors is involved and not all of them are easily accessible. The criteria of vocational satisfaction in studies of interests have consisted of stability in the occupation (in contrast to the position), and expressions of satisfaction or dissatisfaction by the worker.

Occupational stability was the criterion favored by Strong (1934, pp. 384–388) and used in his earlier follow-up studies. It is reasoned that *interest* determines the *direction of effort, ability* the *level of achievement*. The criterion of a vocational interest inventory should therefore be the extent to which it predicts the direction of effort. College students who enter an occupation and remain in it for ten years after graduating from college are presumed to be interested in and satisfied with the direction of their efforts, even though a few are known to persist because of family or economic reasons. Those who change from one field to another are presumed to do so because they find the first field of activity unsatisfactory, and expect that the second will prove more so, despite the fact that some individuals change fields of work for economic reasons. If these assumptions can be granted, and they probably can in higher-level economic groups such as graduates of a private university, then occupational stability is a good index of vocational satisfaction and a suitable criterion of the validity of a vocational interest inventory.

The ten-year follow-up (Strong, 1943, p. 393) consisted of 287 Stanford University seniors tested in 1927 and followed up in 1928, of whom 223 were retested in 1932, and 197 again retested in 1937. The nine-year follow-up was based on 306 Stanford freshmen tested in 1930, of whom 174 were retested in 1939. The principal findings and conclusions, largely confirmed in McArthur's (1944) 14-year follow-up of 61 Harvard sophomores, are as follows:

1. Men continuing in an occupation for 5 or 10 years after college made

higher scores in it than in other occupations (mean standard score 50.2 vs. 47.7);

2. They tended to make higher scores in that occupation than did other men (data too complex to reproduce here);

3. They made higher scores in that occupation than did men who changed from that occupation to some other (standard score 48.0 vs. 44.0);

4. Men changing from one occupation to another after employment in the first field did not make higher scores on the latter occupation when in college, but their average scores were substantially lower in both the first and the second occupation than were those of men in groups 1, 2, and 3, above (standard scores 42.4 and 40.5), which suggests that those who change occupations have less clearly defined interests, or less insight into them, than do those who remain in the occupation of their first post-college choice.

In his 18-year follow up Strong (1955) abandoned occupational stability as a criterion of success against which to validate an interest inventory, at least for his subjects. They had started to work during the economic depression of the 1930's, they had experienced both the rapid advancement that came to many during the defense and war booms and the disruption that came to others with military service, and they had, with experience and expanding opportunity, changed jobs and even occupations as they advanced. Strong therefore doubts whether the stability criterion is a valid one over such a long period of time. Instead, he used occupation-engaged-in at the time of the follow-up as the criterion with which to evaluate the predictive value of interests, arguing that men engaged in an occupation at about age 40 must be at least moderately successful in it: By that time, in an expanding economy, they have had time to shift to other work if not performing to their employer's satisfaction. We have seen, in the discussion of preferences and interests, that college interest scores predict this criterion with considerable accuracy, and better than do expressed preferences.

It was noted, in the preceding chapter, that Bordin has explained the stability of inventoried interests in terms of the stability of the self-concept and of the individual's stereotype of the occupation which Bordin believes guide him in answering an inventory. It is possible thus to argue that when the self-concept and the occupational stereotype match, and when these are valid, occupational stability results: Strong's nine and ten-year studies can be thus explained. It would be interesting to have data on the adequacy of the self-concept and occupational stereotypes in a longitudinal study such as Strong's, to see if these are indeed determinants of stability, occupational interest, and choice, and on the similarity of the individual's self-concept to his concept of the occupation. Two issues are involved insofar as stereotypes are concerned: 1) does the occupational stereotype guide the individual's responses in answering an inventory? and 2) does the adequacy of the concept of the occupation correlate with stability of occupational choice? The writers, unlike Bordin, would suggest that *responses to an inventory under normal counseling conditions reflect the self-concept* but not, appreciably, the occupational stereotype (the scoring translates the self-concept into a measure of similarity to the occupational group's self-concept). That the adequacy of the concept of the occupation will be related to stability of occupational interests seems a plausible, but distinct, notion.

A study of 1400 Air Force officers by England and Paterson (1958) showed that men with appropriate measured interests wanted to remain in their specialties (accounting or personnel).

Women were followed up eight years after testing and four years after graduation from college by Wightwick (1945). Of her 115 subjects, 58 percent were employed in occupations in which they had made A or B+ ratings, while 77 percent were in fields in which they had at least tertiary patterns. The data were not analyzed for stability of employment in the same way as in Strong's study, but in 1941, 43 percent were employed in occupations in which they had made A or B+ scores in 1933.

These findings seem to be confirmed by trends brought out in a study of 76 adult men by Sarbin and Anderson (1942), in which the client's statement of vocational satisfaction or dissatisfaction was related to his primary interest pattern. They found that 82 percent of the men who expressed dissatisfaction with their current occupations did not have primary interest patterns in the fields in which they were employed, but there is no indication as to how many satisfied workers possessed primary interest patterns in the field of their endeavor. If their data are recomputed to permit another comparison, it appears that 57 percent of those who had a primary interest pattern in the field of employment were dissatisfied, as compared with 52 percent of those who lacked the appropriate primary interest pattern. This would seem a strange finding, were it not that the subjects were clients of an adult guidance center, and therefore were, as might be expected, a predominantly dissatisfied group. Although Sarbin and Anderson's (1942, p. 35) statement, "Adults who complain of occupational dissatisfaction show, in general, measured interest patterns which are not congruent with their present or model occupation," is exactly what one would expect to find, it can hardly be said that they have demonstrated the truth of the statement.

Satisfaction in a professional curriculum was correlated with inventoried interest in that field by Berdie (1944), in a study of 154 engineering sophomores who had been tested as freshmen. Satisfaction was measured by a modification of Hoppock's Job Satisfaction Blank, in which the term "curriculum" was substituted for "job" and "occupation". The correlation between scores on Strong's engineer scale and satisfaction score was .10, too low to be significant. When the data for 43 men whose blanks had been scored for all occupations were subjected to analysis of variance, it was found that those with no interest pattern in the engineering field were significantly less satisfied than those with a primary, secondary, or tertiary pattern in the physical sciences. The numbers were so small, however, as to make conclusions highly tentative.

Fortunately, Strong (1955) used a rated satisfaction criterion as well as an employment criterion in his 18-year follow up of 655 Stanford students tested as students. Each man was asked, in the follow-up as an adult, to rate his satisfaction with his *occupational career* and, if dissatisfied, to indicate the main source of dissatisfaction; to rate his desire to continue in or to leave his *occupation*, considering only the nature of the work itself; and to rate his desire to continue in or leave his present *position,* considering working conditions. Strong believes that although the distinctions were not clearly understood the five-point ratings provide an adequate general measure of work satisfaction. Recognizing the restriction of range of interest and of satisfaction scores in a group which has had opportunity to find and become established in suitable employment (e.g., 80 percent were satisfied), Strong reports tetrachoric correlations of .23 and .30 between inventoried interest in one's occupation and work satisfaction, the correlation with occupational career satisfaction being somewhat lower than that with position (that with occupation, the most relevant to interest, is not reported, perhaps because of the misunderstanding of directions).

This finding of Strong's confirms findings by Schwebel (1951), studying 450 pharmacists, and by Kates (1950a, b), studying 100 clerical workers and 25 policemen with the somewhat more refined Hoppock measure of general job satisfaction; the correlations with appropriate Strong scales were respectively .30, .21, and .35, low but significant in each study.

The evidence concerning interest and job satisfaction which consists of occupational stability data is impressive, and, combined with the less impressive data on subjective satisfaction, indicates that vocational interest is related to vocational satisfaction as one of a number of possible determinants.

The Non-occupational Scales. There has been increasing interest, during the past decade, in developing varieties of empirical scales for inventories which have large numbers of heterogeneous items; the Minnesota Multiphasic Personality Inventory and Strong's Blank have been the prime instruments for such efforts. The Masculinity-Femininity, Occupational Level, and Interest Maturity Scales of Strong's Blank have long been in use and are generally known, even though not necessarily well understood. To these Strong has added a Specialization Level Scale. Various investigators have reported attempts to develop personality scales, none of which has been published by Strong's publishers. One of the most interesting and thorough-going of these studies is that by Garman and Uhr (1958), who developed and validated an Anxiety (or, they suggest, Neuroticism) Scale for Strong's Blank, which correlated .42, corrected to .51, with a combination Taylor-Winne Anxiety Scale for the MMPI. It also yielded correlations of .42 with MMPI Psychasthenia, .43 with Cattell's 16 PF Anxious-Insecurity Scale, —.40 with Edwards' PPS Dominance Scale, .40 with the Allport-Vernon Aesthetic Values, .54 with Strong's Artist Scale, and —.39 with Strong's Sales Manager Scale. The construction and interpretation of the available non-occupational scales is conservatively dealt with by Strong in his 1959 manual.

Interest maturity cannot, as we have seen, be treated as a measure of the maturation or stability of interests. Super and Moser (in Layton, 1960) have reported that it correlates .37, significant at the .01 level, with agreement between inventoried and expressed interests, but its highest positive correlations, as shown by Strong (1943), tend to be with the social welfare occupations, its highest negative with scientific and technical occupations.

Occupational level, as brought out in the previous chapter, measures the similarity of a person's interests to those of men in higher or lower level occupations. The statement in the manual which attributes the interpretation of this scale as a measure of drive to Super is an odd error [it originated with Darley (1941) and Strong (1943)] in view of Strong's (1955, p. 132) extensive discussion of the Barnett, Handelsman, Stewart, and Super (1952) monograph, his recognition in that place of Super's rejection of the drive interpretation, and his partial agreement with Super and his students that the OL Scale indicates the socioeconomic level at which a person will find outlets for his interests. Since OL scores change with age and experience (unlike most Strong scores in adulthood), the usefulness of the scale is open to question; the occupational scales give the same information, more consistently over time.

Masculinity-femininity of interests simply means that a person's interests are more like those of men (high scores, on the Men's Blank; low, on the Women's) or more like those of women. Since men's interests tend to be scientific and technical, and women's interests linguistic, social, and artistic, high scores on the men's M-F scale simply mean what high scores on the Engineer or Aviator Scales mean. The M-F scale may be helpful when it does not agree with the occupational scales in a specific case; exploration of conflicting interests may prove meaningful.

Specialization level has not been extensively studied. As the manual points out, it was developed to differentiate specialists from generalists in medicine, and has also proved useful in distinguishing Ph.D. from subdoctoral chemists. It may measure willingness to concentrate one's activities in a narrow field, a specialty.

Use of Strong's Vocational Interest Blank in Counseling and Selection. The findings of research which have been reviewed in the preceding sections have shown that there seems to be something magnetic about interests, pulling people in their direction and holding them in place once there.

The development of interests has been seen to be well under way by adolescence, for by age 14 or 15 the interest patterns of boys and girls have begun to take forms similar to those of adults, and these patterns are generally modified by increasing maturity, by becoming more clear cut, and by a tendency, in boys at least, toward great socialization of interests. By the time boys and girls are from 18 to 20 years of age their interests are fairly well crystalized, and in most cases change very little thereafter.

The occupations for which Strong's inventory has been validated are primarily professional, managerial, and clerical, although a few skilled occupations are included among the scales. Its usefulness is therefore primarily with those persons whose intellectual and educational level is high enough to provide a sound basis for aspiration to the middle or upper half of the occupational ladder. The men's form can be scored for about 40 occupations, the women's for more than 20; while these seem like very few, compared to the large number of jobs which have been differentiated in other ways, the limitations of the instruments are not as great as this suggests. The occupations are more broadly defined than in the *Dictionary of Occupational Titles* (U.S. Dept. of Labor, 1949), for example, and what is more, the intercorrelations have shown that they fall into interest families, that these occupations can be grouped according to common underlying interests. This means that by using this inventory and scoring it for a relatively small number of occupations one can tap interest in a few core fields in which most known occupations could probably be placed. It is important to bear in mind, however, that interest is not necessarily a predictor of success, even when needed abilities are present, for interest seems to be related to success only when the congeniality of the activities in question affects application, and when the effects of application are readily determined, as in competitive work such as sales. It seems to be more important to satisfaction and stability in a field than to quantitatively judged success, and here largely with persons who have middle class attitudes and values which favor self-actualization. The women's form is not as satisfactory as the men's, because of the commonness of one interest factor in women; it is only in the cases of those with clear-cut career interests that it is likely to prove valuable.

In school and college the Vocational Interest Blank is sufficiently well understood by tenth graders to be used with them, and their maturity is great enough to give their scores meaning despite the fact that there is some subsequent modification of interests. The occupational interest scores have value for the prediction of educational achievement when screening on an ability basis has already taken place, and when there has been no screening on the basis of interest. In most situations, however, the choice of curricula or courses by students gives them enough of an elective character to nullify the relationship between interests and grades. Completion of a sequence of courses or of professional training is, however, related to interests as measured by the Strong Blank, for those whose interests are unlike those of people in the same occupational field tend to drop out more frequently than do students with appropriate interests. The inventoried interests of high school students are of more value in vocational diagnosis than are their expressed preferences; on the other hand, the preferences of college students are likely to be mature enough to warrant more serious consideration, particularly among the economically privileged, and are likely to be not much less significant in freshmen, and slightly more significant in seniors, than measured interests. The younger and less able the boy or girl, the more need there is for a good interest inventory; Strong's Blank seems to meet this need within the normal ranges of male high school juniors and seniors, college students, and adults; it does so less well for girls and women, because of the career-vs.-home factor. The older and brighter the individual, the less likelihood there is that Strong's Blank will reveal anything new to the subject, although the confirmation of interests is often very helpful and new light is sometimes thrown on confused or poorly understood situations.

The counseling use of Strong's Blank in school and college can therefore be both for choice of curriculum and for choice of occupational field. Students may be encouraged to major in fields in which they have primary interest patterns, with the knowledge that they are more likely to complete work in those fields than in those in which their interests are not so strong. Their choice of occupations for which they have appropriate measured interests may be viewed with more confidence that they will still prefer those fields after five, ten, or twenty years of employment in them. Despite the possibility of faking scores in an attempt to impress, the inventory has similar value in student selection programs.

In working with high school and college students one not infrequently encounters cases in which there is no primary interest pattern. As these are usually students or clients who have no clearly defined expressed preferences and who hope that the interest inventory will discover some hidden interest, this experience is one which is especially frustrating to novice counselors. The frequency of such cases in a college population has been investigated by Darley and Hagenah (1955), who found that slightly more than 19 percent of 1000 University of Minnesota students had no primary (A and B+) interest patterns, while 2 percent had no distinguishable interest patterns. Darley (1941) set up the hypothesis that students with high interest maturity and no primary interest pattern would make poorer grades in college than students who had primary interest patterns, but this was not verified by his evidence. As he puts it, "the case with no primary pattern will continue to be clinically difficult for the counselor . . . as usual, more and better research is necessary . . ." Strong (1943, p. 420) showed that the interests of business students are less clear cut than those of professional students; he suggests that people with widespread interests and often without primary interests should consider business, particularly if they have secondary interests in the business groups; but he, like Darley, ends by giving up: "These are the hardest of all people to counsel, because they have so little to contribute and either they have a lot of half-baked plans that change from interview to interview or they sit back and expect the counselor to prescribe the remedy" (1943, p. 441). In the writers' experience with college students it also seemed that the undifferentiated students were those who entered business, for lack of something more challenging. We are somewhat reluctant to let the matter rest there, however, in view of Strong's findings concerning the differentiation of people at lower occupational levels when a different point of reference is used. Research in the "undifferentiated" group both in college and elsewhere should presumably be pressed, using other points of reference than that of the standard scales. It seems equally possible that the person with no primary interest pattern is a person of diversified interests which are an asset in the divers activities of business management.

In guidance centers the counseling use of Strong's inventory is similar to that in schools, with the exception that there it is often given to entire classes as a part of a routine testing program, whereas in a guidance center it is part of a tailor-made battery individually administered. In mass testing which has been properly motivated the examinee's answers are likely to be frank and free, for even though motivated to co-operate he is likely to feel that he has relatively little at stake. In the individual testing program there is more likelihood of self-scrutiny and of unconscious warping of responses to make them congruent with an acceptable self-concept. In the former case scores may not be as high, but they reveal the patterning of specific interests more truly; in the latter case, they are more indicative of verbalized self-concepts. Both types of data have their value, provided the counselor knows with what it is he may be working.

A guidance center has an advantage over employment services and departments in the use of inventories such as this, in that its functions are recognized as being more advisory than administrative, the former role being one which encourages frankness on the part of examinees. Despite this fact, consultants making evaluations need to be alert for case history material which tends to support or to contradict the evidence of the inventory. It might be well if two inventories, or subtle and obvious scales for one inventory such as those for the Minnesota Multiphasic Personality Inventory, known to differ in their transparency, were used, to provide an index of tendency and of direction of distortion of interest scores. The germ of the idea is to be found in a paper by Paterson (1946).

In employment services inventories such as this are rarely used, as the type of counseling offered there has generally to do with employment rather than with choice of a field of work, and the interests of employment applicants have generally seemed assessable by less complex methods. As more attention is paid to the needs of inexperienced youth, on the one hand, and to the careful appraisal of adults applying for competitive jobs, on the other, interest inventories should probably find more use in employment services.

In business and industry the use of Strong's Blank has been confined to the selection testing of applicants for sales positions, particularly those in which the importance of the congeniality of the work, the independence of the salesmen, the intangibility of the item sold, or the competitive nature of the selling have been notable. These items include life insurance, casualty insurance, real estate, business machines, and vacuum cleaners. As work with this type of instrument began in an attempt to distinguish sales engineers from technical engineers one would expect to see more use of the instrument as a classification or placement tool. Here, more even than in guidance centers, the possibility of faking unduly high scores needs to be considered. The indications are that despite this tendency the Blank is a useful sales selection instrument; an index of distortion such as those available for certain other instruments would make it even more so.

REFERENCES FOR CHAPTER XVII

Alteneder, L. E. "The value of intelligence, personality, and vocational interest tests in a guidance program," *J. Educ. Psychol.*, 31 (1940), 449-459.

Arsenian, S. "Own estimates and objective measurement," *J. Educ. Psychol.*, 33 (1942), 291-302.

Barnett, G. J., Handelsman, I., Stewart, L. H., and Super, D. E. "The Occupational Level Scale as a measure of drive," *Psychol. Monog.*, 342 (1952).

Barrett, Dorothy W. "Aptitude and interest patterns of art majors in a liberal arts college," *J. Appl. Psychol.*, 29 (1945), 483-492.

———— "Prediction of achievement in typewriting and stenography in a liberal arts college," *J. Appl. Psychol.*, 30 (1946), 624-630.

Bedell, R. "The relationship between self-estimated and measured vocational interests," *J. Appl. Psychol.*, 25 (1941), 54-66.

Berdie, R. F. "Likes, dislikes, and vocational interests," *J. Appl. Psychol.*, 27 (1943), 180-189.

———— "Prediction of college achievement and satisfaction," *J. Appl. Psychol.*, 28 (1944), 239-245.

———— "Scores on the Strong Vocational Interest Blank and the Kuder Preference Record in relation to self-ratings," *J. Appl. Psychol.*, 34 (1950), 42-49.

Berman, I. R., Darley, J. G., and Paterson, D. G. "Vocational interest scales," *University Minnesota Bull. Employ. Stab. Res. Inst.*, 5 (1934).

Bills, M. A. "Relation of Strong's Interest Blank to success in selling casualty insurance," *J. Appl. Psychol.*, 22 (1938), 97-104.

———— "Selection of casualty and life insurance agents," *J. Appl. Psychol.*, 25 (1941), 6-10.

————, and Ward, L. W. "Testing salesmen of casualty insurance," *Pers. J.*, 15 (1936), 55-58.

Bluett, C. H. "Vocational interests of vocational rehabilitation officers," *Occupations*, 24 (1945), 25-32.

Braasch, W. F. "Regional Differences in Occupational Interests." Unpublished Ph.D. dissertation, Teachers College, Columbia University, 1954.

Brophy, A. L. "Self, role, and satisfaction," *Genet. Psychol. Monog.*, 59 (1959).

Burnham, P. S. "Stability of interests," *Sch. and Soc.*, 55 (1942), 332-335.

Canning, L., Taylor, Katherine van F., and Carter, H. D. "Permanence of vocational interests in high school boys," *J. Educ. Psychol.*, 32 (1941), 481-494.

Cantril, H., and Allport, G. W. "Recent applications of the Study of Values," *J. Soc. Psychol.*, 28 (1933), 259-273.

Cleeton, G. U. "Occupational adjustment in Allegheny County," *Bull. of the Pittsburgh Personnel Assn.* (1935).

Cooper, Alva C. "A Study of the Group Scales of the Strong Vocational Interest Blank as Predictors of Academic Achievement and of the Relationship of the Group Scales to Primary Interest Patterns." Unpublished Ph.D. dissertation, Teachers College, Columbia University, 1954.

Cowdery, K. M. "Measures of professional attitudes," *J. Pers. Res.*, 5 (1926), 131-141.

Crissy, W. J. E., and Daniel, W. J. "Vocational interest factors in women," *J. Appl. Psychol.*, 23 (1939), 488-494.

Darley, J. G. "Preliminary study of the relationships between attitudes, adjustment, and vocational interest tests," *J. Educ. Psychol.*, 29 (1938), 467-473.

———— *Clinical Aspects and Interpretation of the Strong Vocational Interest Blank*. New York: Psychological Corp., 1941.

————, and Hagenah, Theda. *Vocational Interest Measurement*. Minneapolis: University of Minnesota Press, 1955.

Douglass, H. R. "Prediction of success in the Medical School," *University of Minnesota Studies in Prediction of scholastic Achievement*, 2 (1942), 1-16.

Duffy, Elizabeth. "A critical review of investigations employing the Allport-Vernon Study of Values and other tests of evaluative attitudes," *Psychol. Bull.*, 37 (1940), 597-612.

————, and Crissy, W. J. E. "Evaluative attitudes as related to vocational interest and academic achievement," *J. Abnorm. Soc. Psychol.*, 35 (1940), 226-245.

Dunlop, J. W. "The predictive value of interest test items for achievement in various school subjects," *J. Appl. Psychol.*, 19 (1935), 53-58.

Dunnette, M. D. "Vocational interest differences among engineers employed in different functions," *J. Appl. Psychol.*, 41 (1957), 273-278.

England, G. W., and Paterson, D. G. "Relationship between measured interest patterns and satisfactory vocational adjustment for Air Force officers," *J. Appl. Psychol.*, 42 (1958), 85-88.

Fryer, D. *The Measurement of Interests.* New York: Holt, 1931.

Garman, G. D., and Uhr, L. "An anxiety scale for the Strong Vocational Interest Inventory," *J. Appl. Psychol.*, 42 (1958), 241-246.

Garretson, O. K. "Relationships between expressed preferences and curricular abilities of ninth grade boys," *Teachers Coll. Contrib. to Educ.*, 396 (1930).

Ghiselli, E. E. "Use of the Strong Vocational Interest Blank and the Pressey Senior Classification Test in the selection of casualty insurance salesmen," *J. Appl. Psychol.*, 26 (1942), 793-799.

———, and Brown, C. W. *Personnel and Industrial Psychology.* New York: McGraw-Hill, 1955.

Goodfellow, L. D. "A study of the interests and personality traits of prospective teachers," *Educ. Admin. Supervision*, 18 (1932), 649-658.

Goodman, C. H. "Comparison of the interests and personality traits of engineers and liberal arts students," *J. Appl. Psychol.*, 26 (1942), 721-737.

Gordon, H. C., and Herkness, W. W. "Do vocational interest questionnaires yield consistent results?" *Occupations*, 20 (1942), 424-429.

Green, R. F. "Does a selection situation induce testees to bias their answers on interest and temperament tests?" *Educ. Psychol. Measmt.*, 11 (1951), 503-515.

Guilford, J. P. (ed.). *Printed Classification Tests.* ("AAF Aviation Psychology Report," No. 5.) Washington, D. C.: Government Printing Office, 1947.

Gustad, J. W. "Vocational interests and Q-L scores on the ACE," *J. Appl. Psychol.*, 35 (1951), 164-168.

Hannum, T. E., and Thrall, J. B. "Use of the Strong Vocational Interest Blank for prediction in veterinary medicine," *J. Appl. Psychol.*, 39 (1955), 249-252.

Heron, A. "The effects of real-life motivation on questionnaire response," *J. Appl. Psychol.*, 40 (1956), 65-68.

Holcomb, G. W., and Laslett, H. R. "A prognostic study of engineering aptitude," *J. Appl. Psychol.*, 16 (1932), 107-115.

Hughes, J. L., and McNamara, W. J. "Limitations on the use of Strong's sales Keys for selection and counseling," *J. Appl. Psychol.*, 42 (1958), 93-96.

Jacobson, C. F. "Interest patterns and achievement in medical school," *J. Assn. Amer. Med. Coll.*, 17 (1942), 153-163.

Kates, S. L. "Rorschach responses related to vocational interests and job satisfaction," *Psychol. Monog.*, 309 (1950a).

——— "Rorschach responses, Strong Blank scores, and job satisfaction among policemen," *J. Appl. Psychol.*, 34 (1950b), 249-254.

Kelly, E. L., and Fiske, D. W. *The Prediction of Performance in Clinical Psychology.* Ann Arbor: University of Michigan Press, 1951.

Klugman, S. F. "Test scores for clerical aptitude and interests before and after a year of schooling," *J. Genet. Psychol.*, 65 (1944), 89-96.

Knauft, E. B. "Vocational interests and managerial success," *J. Appl. Psychol.*, 35 (1951), 160-163.

Kriedt, P. H. "Vocational interests of psychologists," *J. Appl. Psychol.*, 33 (1949), 482-488.

Laleger, Grace E. "Vocational interests of high school girls," *Teachers Coll. Contrib. to Educ.* 857 (1942).

Layton, W. L. "Predicting success of students in veterinary medicine," *J. Appl. Psychol.*, 36 (1952), 312-315.

———— (ed.). *The Strong Vocational Interest Blank: Research and Uses.* Minneapolis: University of Minnesota Press, 1960.

Leffel, E. S. "Students' Plans, Interests, and Achievement." Unpublished Master's thesis, Clark University, 1939.

Long, L. "Relationship between interests and abilities: a study of the Strong Vocational Interest Blank and the Zyve Scientific Aptitude Test," *J. Appl. Psychol.*, 29 (1945), 191-197.

————, and Perry, J. D. "Academic achievement in engineering related to selection procedure and interests," *J. Appl. Psychol.*, 37 (1953), 468-471.

Longstaff, H. P. "Fakability of the Strong Interest Blank and the Kuder Preference Record," *J. Appl. Psychol.*, 32 (1948), 360-369.

McArthur, C. "Long-term validity of the Strong test in two sub-cultures," *J. Appl. Psychol.*, 38 (1954), 346-353.

———— "Predictive power of pattern analysis and of job scale analysis of the Strong," *J Counsel. Psychol.*, 2 (1955), 205-206.

————, and Stevens, Lucia B. "The validation of expressed interests as compared with inventoried interests: a fourteen-year follow-up," *J. Appl. Psychol.*, 39 (1955), 184-189.

Melville, S. B., and Frederiksen, N. "Achievement of freshman engineering students and the Strong Vocational Interest Blank," *J. Appl. Psychol.*, 36 (1952), 169-173.

Moffie, D. J. "Validity of self-estimated interests," *J. Appl. Psychol.*, 26 (1942), 606-613.

Moore, B. V. "Analysis of tests administered to men in engineering defense training courses," *J. Appl. Psychol.*, 25 (1941), 619 635.

Morgan, H. H. "A psychometric comparison of achieving and nonachieving college students of high ability," *J. Consult. Psychol.*, 16 (1952), 292 298.

Otis, J. L. "Procedures for the selection of salesmen for a detergent company," *J. Appl. Psychol.*, 25 (1941), 30-40.

Paterson, D. G. "Vocational interest inventories in selection," *Occupations*, 25 (1946), 152-153.

Robinson, J. B., and Bellows, R. M. "Characteristics of successful dental students," *Assn. Coll. Registrars*, 16 (1941), 109-122.

Rothney, J. W. M. *Guidance Practices and Results.* New York: Harper, 1958.

Rust, R. M., and Ryan, F. J. "The Strong Vocational Interest Blank and college achievement," *J. Appl. Psychol.*, 38 (1954), 341-345.

Ryan, T. A., and Johnson, B. R. "Interest scores in the selection of salesmen and servicemen: occupational vs. ability-group keys," *J. Appl. Psychol.*, 26 (1942), 543-562.

Sarbin, T. R., and Anderson, H. C. "Preliminary study of the relation of measured interest patterns and occupational dissatisfactions," *Educ. Psychol. Measmt.*, 2 (1942), 23-36.

————, and Berdie, R. F. "Relation of measured interests to the Allport-Vernon Study of Values," *J. Appl. Psychol.*, 24 (1940), 287-296.

Schmidt, J. L., and Rothney, J. W. M. "Variability of vocational choices of high school students," *Pers. Guid. J.*, 34 (1955), 142-146.

Schwebel, M. *The Interests of Pharmacists.* New York: Columbia University Press, 1951.

Segel, D. "Differential prediction of scholastic success," *Sch. and Soc.*, 39 (1934), 91-96.

Seagoe, May V. "Prognostic tests and teaching success," *J. Educ. Res.*, 38 (1945), 685-690.

Shultz, I. T., and Barnabas, B. "Testing for leadership in industry," *Trans. Kans. Acad. Sci.*, 48 (1945), 160-164.

Sinnett, E. R. "Some determinants of agreement between measured and expressed interests," *Educ. Psychol. Measmt.*, 16 (1956), 110-118.

Skodak, Marie, and Crissey, O. L. "Stated vocational aims and Strong interest scores of high school senior girls," *J. Appl. Psychol.*, 26 (1942), 64-74.

Spencer, D. *The Fulcra of Conflict.* Yonkers, N. Y.: World Book, 1938.

Stefflre, B. "The reading difficulty of interest inventories," *Occupations*, 26 (1947), 95-96.

Steinmetz, H. C. "Measuring ability to fake occupational interest," *J. Appl. Psychol.*, 16 (1932), 123-130.

Strong, E. K., Jr. "Interests and sales ability," *Pers. J.*, 13 (1934), 204-216.

—— *Vocational Interests of Men and Women.* Stanford: Stanford University Press, 1943.

—— "Personnel psychologists at Stanford University," *Psychol. Bull.*, 41 (1944), 474-489.

—— "Weighted vs. unit scales," *J. Educ. Psychol.*, 36 (1945), 193-216.

—— "Amount of change in occupational choice of college freshmen," *Educ. Psychol. Measmt.*, 12 (1952), 677-691.

—— "Validity of occupational choice," *Educ. Psychol. Measmt.*, 13 (1953), 110-121.

—— *Vocational Interests 18 Years After College.* Minneapolis: University of Minnesota Press, 1955.

Stuit, D. B. "A study of the vocational interests of a group of teachers college freshmen," *J. Appl. Psychol.*, 22 (1938), 527-533.

Super, D. E. "Strong's 'Vocational interests of men and women': a special review," *Psychol. Bull.*, 42 (1945), 359-370.

—— *Appraising Vocational Fitness by Means of Psychological Tests.* New York: Harper, 1949.

Taylor, Katherine van F. "Reliability and permanence of vocational interests of adolescents," *J. Exp. Educ.*, 10 (1942), 81-87.

Terman, L. M., and Oden, Melita H. *The Gifted Child Grows Up.* Stanford: Stanford University Press, 1948.

Thorpe, L. P. "The California Interest Inventory." In Kaplan, O. J.: *Encyclopedia of Vocational Guidance.* New York: Philosophical Library, 1948.

Townsend, A. "Achievement and interest ratings for independent school boys," *Educ. Res. Bull.*, 43 (1945), 49-54.

Traphagen, A. L. "Interest patterns and retention and rejection of vocational choice," *J. Appl. Psychol.*, 36 (1952), 182-185.

United States Dept. of Labor. *Dictionary of Occupational Titles.* Washington, D. C.: Government Printing Office, 1949.

Wightwick, Marie I. "Vocational interest patterns," *Teachers Coll. Contrib. to Educ.*, 900 (1945).

Williamson, E. G., et al. "The selection of student nurses," *J. Appl. Psychol.*, 22 (1938), 119-131.

Wrenn, C. G. "Aiding the fit," *J. Higher Educ.*, 6 (1935), 357-363.

—— "Intelligence and the vocational choices of college students," *Educ. Rec.*, 16 (1935), 217-219.

XVIII

OTHER MEASURES OF INTERESTS

The Kuder Preference Record (Science Research Associates: *Vocational,*
1939, 1942, 1946, 1948, 1950, 1951, 1956; *Short Industrial Form,* 1948;
Occupational, 1956, 1957). Work with the Kuder-Vocational was initiated by its author early in the 1930's, leading to the publication of the inventory in 1939. Three forms were tried out during this experimental
period. After the 1939 edition had been in use for several years it seemed
desirable to cover mechanical and clerical activities more adequately, and
the second edition was developed and published, incorporating also a
change in the form of the items. The current form, which includes a
measure of interest in outdoor activities, was published in 1948, as was a
short form for use in business and industry. The most recent development
in the Kuder series was the introduction of the Kuder-Occupational in
1956, an inventory which closely resembles the Strong Blank in purpose
and construction. In the sections which follow, however, the discussion
focuses upon the older editions of the Kuder rather than the Occupational,
since no research on the latter (other than preliminary data in the manual) has been located and as a result its vocational usefulness is largely
unknown. The Kuder-Personal is considered at length in the chapter on
personality inventories.

Publication of the Kuder-Vocational was welcomed by many counselors
in schools, colleges, and guidance centers, because it was more economical
to score than Strong's Vocational Interest Blank, then practically the only
inventory which had been well validated, and because it also showed signs
of having been subjected to a good deal of research. Furthermore, its
format and marking device had an immediate appeal to students taking
it. Users of vocational tests therefore often included the Preference Record
in their batteries, interpreting its results in very much the same terms as
those of Strong's Blank, simply on the basis of the general similarity of the
types of items and scores, which seemed like those of Strong's group scales.
Today the Kuder is one of the most widely used vocational tests and inventories, and additional evidence concerning the nature and vocational

significance of the traits it measures is published practically every month in the professional journals.

Applicability. The Kuder Record was designed for use with high school and college students, and with adult men and women. The items were so written as to be applicable to both sexes, the vocabulary was kept as nearly as possible at the high school level, and the content seems to have been selected for its familiarity to adolescents as well as to adults. Two reports on the suitability of the inventory for high school students have been published. Christensen (1946) tried it out on 27 ninth graders and ascertained that many of the items were not understood; when the class was instructed in the meaning of the items and retested, the scores changed appreciably. The reading difficulty of the Kuder was checked by Stefflre (1947), who used the Lewerenz formula for vocabulary grade placement; he found that the vocabulary difficulty grade level was 8.4, and that it is easier than that of the Strong (10.4), the Allport-Vernon Study of Values (11.3), and the Cleeton (12.0), but somewhat more difficult than that of the Lee-Thorpe (6.8) and Brainard (6.4). These findings suggest that the Kuder can be administered to typical eighth grade boys and girls, although the less able will have difficulty with some items; its use at the ninth or tenth grade levels is likely to prove satisfactory in this respect. The "usefulness" of the Kuder in counseling at different educational levels for men and women was evaluated by clients, counselors, and judges in a study by Malcolm (1950) who found that the Kuder was *preferred* for both sexes at the high school level and, in addition, for women at the college and graduate school levels because it was believed that it generally led to a greater understanding of interests and provided a better test of expressed interests. The Strong was favored for college and graduate school men because it was considered more effective in uncovering unknown interests and seemed to lead to more constructive planning.

Because of the rather obvious vocational content of the Kuder items, many users have raised the question of whether responses to them can be either deliberately faked or unconsciously distorted. Data of investigations in actual work settings and evidence from studies in which definite interest patterns were simulated according to instructions suggest that the Kuder can be faked but not consistently on all scales and not equally well by all people. A study by Paterson (1946), who administered the Kuder and the Strong inventories to a clerical employee being considered for transfer and promotion to a desired personnel position, revealed that the employee's interests were truly clerical, that he wanted to appear in the best possible light as a potential personnel appointee, that his scores were distorted in the direction of personnel interests by this attitude, and that the Kuder was more affected by distortion than the Strong. Although based upon only one case, some of these conclusions have been subsequently supported by a more extensive study of candidates for transfer.

Green (1951) found that 70 patrolmen who had applied for reassignment differed significantly from a control group of 45 patrolmen who had not applied. The differences, which favored the applicants on the persuasive and social service scales, were attributed to their "faking good" to assure transfer. They might have been due to other differences between the two groups, however, since no data were reported which indicated that the patrolmen had similar interests before they were compared or that when compared they were equivalent on characteristics other than the desire for reassignment. However, Heron (1956) confirmed Green's findings with 400 bus company employees, half of whom were tested before, half after, hiring. Clearcut findings have been obtained in studies in which a deliberate attempt to stimulate certain interest patterns was made. Longstaff (1948), in a study of 59 adult male and female students who were instructed to fake-up or down on selected Kuder and Strong scales, found that both inventories can be faked, that some interest categories can be faked more readily than others, and that the Kuder is easier to fake-down whereas the Strong is easier to fake-up. Bordin (1947) and Berdie (1950) have reported data on the relationship of measured to professed interests in a group of college students which suggest that both the Kuder and the Strong contain scales which are transparent and fakable. And Cross (1950) and Durnall (1954) have gathered clear-cut evidence of ability to lower and to raise Kuder scores according to directions. The ability to fake, however, evidently varies not only with interest category, interest inventory, and direction of simulation, but also with intelligence and sex. Durnall found a correlation of .39 between faking ability and Otis IQ, and Longstaff reported that men were more successful than women in feigning given interest patterns on the Kuder.

Another aspect of this question of the meaning of inventory items and the orientation of respondents was investigated by Piotrowski (1946), who tested 18 superior students in a school of social work with the Kuder and the Rorschach. All subjects scored high on the social service scale, but psychiatric interviews led to the conclusion that only 11 of the inventory scores were "valid," while 7 were "invalid"; in other words, 7 of the social workers were not genuinely interested in social welfare, but made high scores because of conscious or unconscious distortion. The Rorschach responses of the two groups were then compared, with the conclusion that those who really had social service interests (as confirmed by interview data) were closer to reality, had a wider range of psychological experiences, were more realistic in their aspirations, more interested in people for their own sakes, more self-confident, and less frequently subject to despondent moods. While the results for other preoccupational or occupational groups might reveal fewer invalid scores (assuming the validity of the psychiatric interview) than a field such as social work, the evidence does indicate that distortion of scores on the Kuder can seriously affect the results.

That the Kuder can be faked, then, seems to be a valid conclusion well-documented by observation and experimentation. The problem now is to identify the faker. As an initial attempt to construct a scale which will detect simulation on an interest inventory, Kuder (1950) has formulated three hypotheses for testing: (1) subjects who fake and who are sincere can be differentiated by their responses to inventory or test items; (2) the responses of subjects who try to answer items insincerely will be distributed randomly; and, (3) the faker will mark more items which are generally approved than will the sincere examinee. Using the Kuder Preference Record-Personal with approximately two thousand subjects in eight different occupational and curricular groups, he obtained results which substantiated the hypotheses. An H or *honesty scale,* or V or *verification scale,* and a combination of both identified with fairly high probability not only subjects who tried to fake but also those who succeeded. Despite these encouraging preliminary findings, however, Kuder cautions that further work needs to be done to identify the faker, namely, the use of more refined statistical methods in the analysis of data and the development of scales for homogeneous groups and specific situations.

There is, finally, the question of changes in responses to this type of inventory with increasing age. During the past decade, as compared with previous years, there has been a surprising number of studies on the stability or development of vocational interests as measured by the Kuder. Retest reliabilities obtained by Reid (1952), Rosenberg (1953), Silvey (1951), and Stoops (1953) on groups of high school and college students for periods varying from 15 months to 3 years are comparable to coefficients reported earlier by Traxler and McCall (1941) and DiMichael and Dabelstein (1947): they cluster in the 60's and 70's, indicating that some changes occur. According to Herzberg and Bouton (1954b), the direction of these changes in the interests of high school students who continue to college is toward the social science and away from the clerical and scientific areas. These are average trends, however, and are not consistent for both sexes. In an earlier study of college students and adult workers, Herzberg, Bouton, and Steiner (1954) found that females tend to have more stable interests than males regardless of interest area, but that both men and women change more in social science and musical than in artistic and mechanical interests. What factors are related to these changes was the subject of a study by Forer (1950), who reported considerable (median $rho = .68$) interest stability in a group of 36 disabled male veterans who had experienced occupational frustration between test and retest. He concluded that neither emotional disturbance nor occupational frustration is apparently related to interest stability. But this conclusion should be accepted only tentatively until comparisons can be made between equivalent groups in which these factors are and are not present.

Change in interest as a function of shift in curricular orientation was studied by Bordin and Wilson (1953), who hypothesized a positive relationship between (a) interest stability and (b) consistency of curriculum with inventoried interests. The findings tended to support the hypothesis: test-retest reliabilities were generally higher (but significantly so in only three instances) for students whose interests were consistent with their curriculum on the second testing. To conclude, as Bordin and Wilson (1953, p. 305) did, that "The results of this study provide unequivocal support for the assumption that inventoried interests are dynamic phenomena reflecting changes in the individual's perception of himself" is, however, hardly justified by the research design and data (See Ch. XVI). Not only were variables which could have produced change in either interests or curricular plans left uncontrolled but, as Darley and Hagenah (1955, p. 154) note, the test-retest coefficients indicated ". . . considerable stability of measured interests for both subgroups, even though the hypothesis of differential stability is supported in three of the nine pairs."

These findings on the stability of Kuder interests have been interpreted in many ways. Some contend that the relatively high retest reliabilities indicate considerable interest stability. Others, like Dressel (1954), maintain that with the highest stability coefficients only about fifty per cent of the total variance in the criterion can be accounted for by variance in the predictor. For the practitioner an interpretation which is statistically sound and theoretically meaningful can be made, however, based upon a study by Mallinson and Crumrine (1952). A group of 250 high school students were tested in the ninth grade and retested in the twelfth grade. Scores on the nine Kuder scales (outdoor excluded) were ranked in descending order for the two testings, and the percentage of cases in which the three lowest and three highest areas of interest remained the same was determined. For the total sample 70 per cent of the two lowest and 64 per cent of the three lowest areas remained among the lowest three, and 74 per cent of the two highest and 67 per cent of the three highest remained in the highest three interest areas. In other words, the odds were about 2 to 1 that an individual's three highest and lowest Kuder scores would not change over a three year period. This suggests that Kuder interests are stable enough to afford a basis for prediction in counseling, yet changeable enough to allow modification when appropriate through counseling.

Content. The Preference Record consists of preference items arranged in triads. Item 13 illustrates the principle:

> Build bird houses
> Write articles about birds
> Draw sketches of birds

The examinee decides which of these three activities he likes best and marks it to show his first choice; then he decides which he likes least, and marks it to show his third choice. The activities in each item are so written as to tap three or more different types of interest, in this case *mechanical, literary,* and *artistic.* There are 168 such items (standard form), assessing interest in a total of ten different types of interests.

The relative merits of the Kuder forced-choice and the Strong L-I-D type items have not been studied directly with these inventories, and only inconclusive relevant research evidence is available. Using extent of discrimination between groups as a criterion Zuckerman (1952) and Perry (1955) have compared the two item formats. In Zuckerman's study the L-I-D test item arrangement was clearly superior in discriminating the interests of professional groups, whereas in Perry's study the forced-choice item yielded lower percentages of overlap between college student and military samples. Shortcomings in the former's experimental design (Zuckerman, 1953) may account for the discrepant findings. But as Perry notes the entire problem requires further exploration, particularly with a greater variety of occupational groups. Work with the triadic as well as the doublet type forced-choice item is also needed.

Administration and Scoring. There is no time limit, as there are no right or wrong answers; the time required by high school students is from thirty minutes to one hour, by college students approximately forty minutes. It is necessary to make sure that the directions for using the response pins are correctly followed, but, as examinees are usually intrigued by the mechanics of the inventory, motivating them to follow directions is relatively easy. Scoring may be done by hand, using appropriate answer sheets and a pin to prick answers, in which case the common procedure is to have examinees do the scoring themselves. The directions are clear, and it takes about fifteen minutes to obtain all nine scores. Profile sheets are provided on which examinees convert their scores to percentiles and plot them graphically. This method has generally been found to be a good device for getting pupils interested in their scores and to provide a springboard for discussion of vocational interests. Machine-scoring is also possible, with the use of special answer sheets. The scores obtained are for outdoor, mechanical, computational, scientific, persuasive, artistic, literary, musical, social service, and clerical interests.

Because of the relatively long administration time required for the Kuder, Canfield (1953) experimented with a half-length version which, if reliable and valid, would reduce testing time appreciably. A total of 301 completed records were scored for each interest area using first the entire booklet and then only odd and even numbered pages. Regression equations were developed on both the original and a cross-validation sample of 100 for predicting the total scores from scores on either half. The correlations, which were quite high, ranging from .90 to .97, indicated that the shortened form was essentially equivalent to the longer one. Conservative practice would suggest, however, that further validation data be accumulated before administering the Kuder half-length.

Norms. Various editions of the manual contain norms for four different base groups. The first consists of 3418 boys and 4466 girls in high school grades, published separately, in the January, 1950 revision of the Form C profile, because sex differences are significant. The second is made up of 1000 adult men telephone subscribers distributed in a stratified sample of 138 cities and towns obtained from the Postal Guide. The bulk of this group are in professional, managerial, clerical and sales occupations, according to the USES classification. The third norm group is composed also of adult men but is supposedly a sample representative of the population. The 1956 edition of the manual (p. 23) states: "After considerable thought and discussion, the norms from telephone subscribers were used on the February, 1951 revision of the adult profile sheet, on the theory that these people are probably more similar in background to adults usually counseled than a cross section of the population would be." The data for two norm groups were essentially the same, with the exception of the representative sample's higher outdoor and lower persuasive scores. Finally, there are norms for women based upon 1429 cases for scales 1 through 9, which were transmuted from the norms for Form B, but only 100 cases for the outdoor scale, which was developed in conjunction with Form C. More extensive normative data are being collected for adult women. In addition, there have been periodic reports of norms for special groups which are of some interest. Comprehensive data on sales trainees, including general biographical information such as marital status, education, previous work experience, and military service, as well as Kuder norms, have been compiled by Eimicke (1949). Hanna and Barnette (1949) have presented comparable data on 780 male veterans, as have Guba and Getzels (1956) on Air Force officers (both rated and non-rated). But while these norm groups are helpful in providing a backdrop against which to view the interests of an individual, their composition is not as vital a question as in the case of Strong's Blank, for with the Kuder one studies the relative strength of each of ten different interests *within an in-*

dividual, whereas in the Strong the comparisons are basically *between groups of individuals* classified by occupations.

Having obtained a profile of scores which shows the relative strength of the different types of interests in the person being examined, the next question which arises is that of the occupational significance of the profile. It was the absence of occupational norms which made many users of vocational tests hesitate to use Kuder's inventory, despite the care with which it was constructed and the economy with which it could be used. It was not until after World War II, for example, that some counselors were willing to use it in counseling on anything other than an experimental basis, just because it did not seem sufficient to know that a client was more interested in mechanical activities than in any other type, when what counts in vocational adjustment is how his interests compare with those of persons who have succeeded in the field. This point has effectively been made by Diamond (1948), in an important study of the occupational significance of Kuder percentile scores.

Recent editions of the manual have largely made good this deficiency by providing occupational profiles for 144 men's occupations and 68 women's, supplemented by curricular norms in a number of different fields. The numbers in any one group are sometimes quite small, e.g., 17 forest supervisors, but are often quite sizeable. Needless to say, as Strong's work suggests, caution must be used in interpreting profiles based upon only a few cases. Particularly is this true in light of the incomplete evidence in the manual concerning the type of employment, skill levels, degree of permanence, level of attainment, and regional location of the representatives of any given occupation.

The occupational norms consist of the means and standard deviations of each occupational group on each interest scale, and graphic profiles based on these same means. The profiles permit a more rapid inspection of the data than do means, and enable the counselor to compare quickly his client's profile with that of the various occupational groups. As the work of the Minnesota Employment Stabilization Research Institute (Dvorak, 1935) and the United States Employment Service (Dvorak, 1947) has demonstrated, however, this technique has serious defects. Not only is it impressionistic rather than exact, but the criterion upon which judgment is based is unsound, for the counselee is compared with the average person in the occupation rather than with the marginal worker. To put it concretely, if the counselee is significantly below the mean of the occupational group at two points of the profile, and significantly higher at two other points, does that mean that the choice of that field would be unwise? It would be more helpful to know the critical scores of each trait being measured, for then a "low" score would be known to indicate a critical lack of a trait which has been found to be related to success or satisfaction in the occupation in question. This is the procedure now used by the United States Employment Service in its General Aptitude Test Battery (Dvorak, 1947; see also Ch. XIV). Diamond's data (1948) are again highly relevant.

To provide a less impressionistic method of comparing individual profiles with those of persons established in various occupations, Kuder has developed *occupational indices* which are a statistical summation of the similarity of the examinee's interest profile to that of the occupation in question. The principle is similar to that used by Strong, although Strong applied it to a series of items whereas Kuder applied it to scores on a series of scales. Only two occupational indices have so far been published, those for accountant-auditor and for carpenter (Manual).

Despite the work which remains to be done, some progress has been made in the development of other techniques for assessing the similarity of individual and group Kuder profiles. Adapting Hathaway's coding system for the MMPI to the Kuder, Wiener (1951) has suggested a procedure for coding the occupational norms and a client's profile for ready comparison. All scales with scores above the 75th percentile are listed in descending order of size by scale number to the left of a hyphen and those below the 25th percentile are arranged in ascending order of size by scale number to the right of the hyphen. If no scores are above the 75th or below the 25th percentiles, and X is placed to the left or right of the hyphen, as the case may be. Commenting upon this system Frandsen (1952) has observed that it often results in the same codes for such diverse occupations as bank officials, carpenters, county agricultural agents, and engineers. This lack of discrimination among quite different occupational groups arises because the codes are based upon inappropriate cutting points. The 65th and 35th percentiles, instead of the 75th and 25th, are the proper cutting points for group profiles, because significant deviations are based upon the standard error of the mean rather than the standard error of measurement (as in the individual profiles). When the appropriate percentiles are used discrimination between occupations is increased considerably. In an extension and elaboration of Wiener's approach, Callis, Engram, and McGowan (1954) have discussed various uses for the coding system, but caution that since it is based upon mean profiles any comparisons of individual profiles should be qualified by consideration of the homogeneity of interest in the group. The less homogeneous the group the less typical will be the mean profile and the greater the error will be in assessing the similarity of individual cases.

A more empirical approach to the problem of profile analysis and interpretation has been taken by Holland, Krause, Nixon, and Trembath (1953) in the classification of Kuder profiles into appropriate interest groups. Samples of profiles for men and women were selected from the manual; the scales were ranked according to magnitude of scores from high to low and intercorrelated, using *rho* as an index of profile similarity. Profiles were then grouped according to patterns of intercorrelations. A "core" occupation, defined as the occupation which showed the greatest number of correlations equal to, or greater than, .70 with other occupations in the same category, was designated for each group, and the remaining occupations in the group were ranked by magnitude of their rhos with the "core" occupation. The interest groups which the analysis produced were then ordered with respect to the intercorrelations of the "core" occupations for the various groups. Seven interest groups for men emerged: I. Skilled and Technical; II. Managerial; III. Scientific; IV. Drugstore Managers and Pharmacists; V. Welfare; VI. Clerical; and VII. Expressive. As the authors of the study point out, these classifications are empirical but they have a number of limitations: (1) The representativeness of the profiles upon which the system is based is largely unknown; (2) refined statistical analysis of the data is restricted by the unorthodox use of *rho* and the ipsative nature of Kuder scores; and (3) the criterion groups for the profiles were heterogeneous, including successful and unsuccessful, satisfied and dissatisfied, experienced and inexperienced workers. A further limitation can be added: *rho* as an index of profile similarity expresses the shape but not the elevation of a profile. Whether modification of the groupings will be necessary when elevation is considered remains to be determined, but it is likely since elevation rather than shape is more important in the interpretation of interest profiles.

Standardization and Initial Validation. Many users of the Kuder Preference Record have been puzzled by the method of weighting the items in the inventory. The mental set established by Strong's work led them to believe that Kuder's interest scales were occupational in nature, that his scientific scale, for example, was the scale for a scientific family of occupations. But the early manuals and published studies showed no evidence of occupational standardization. The alternative explanation seemed to be that the keys were based on a factorial analysis of interests, such as were made with Strong's data, but again there was no evidence of such work. Lacking any such empirical basis, the scales were not infrequently suspected of being the product of nothing more than *a priori* reasoning.

Succeeding editions of the manual have attempted to make clear exactly how the scales were developed. The first step was the construction of *a priori* scoring keys, in one of which all seemingly literary items were scored, in another all scientific, and so on. The second step was to score the blanks of several hundred persons with these scales. The third step was to make an item analysis to ascertain the internal consistency of these scales. If it was found that those persons who had made high *a priori* literary scores tended to choose a given item more often than those who had made low scores, the item was retained in the literary scale; if it was not so chosen, it was discarded. After this procedure had been applied to all the *a priori* keys it was found that some of the empirically purified scales (the seven published with the first edition) were internally consistent, independent of each other, and reliable, whereas others (athletic, religious, and social-prestige interests) were not internally consistent or independent —they were, in fact, purified out of existence by the item analysis (the social-prestige scale actually split in two). The item analysis therefore gave an empirical basis for stating that some of the interest scales measure something, and that these entities are independent of each other and unchanging in their composition. The method of naming traits is then comparable to that in factor analysis and depends on inspection of the items and judgment as to their nature. The names given by Kuder seem warranted, as might be anticipated when the items are rather transparent. The two scales added with the second edition were for mechanical and clerical interests, and were based only on internal consistency; they are correlated somewhat more highly with the scientific and computational scales. The outdoor scale, developed in response to an expressed need for a measure related to agricultural and naturalistic activities, was included in the third edition.

The intercorrelations of the ten scales in Form C range from —.52 for the outdoor and persuasive scales to .54 for the computational and clerical scales, when based upon 1000 adult men in a variety of occupations. These correlations are somewhat higher than those reported previously in the manual, probably because of the greater interdependence of the new scales but possibly because of chance fluctuations in sampling.

Reliability. The reliability of the Kuder scales in its various Forms has been ascertained for several different age groups and summarized in the manuals by Kuder. For Form C the Kuder-Richardson (Case IV) reliability coefficients, which are conservative estimates, range from .84 to .90 (100 girls); from .85 to .93 (100 boys); from .87 to .90 (100 women); and, from .85 to .92 (1000 men). These are quite adequate reliabilities for cross-sectional measurements. In counseling and personnel selection, however, where the concern is primarily with longitudinal measurements or the reliability of scores over time, it is retest reliabilities that are important. It is worthy of note that these are considerably lower than the reliability coefficients cited above. In a study of 140 high school boys and 171 girls, Tutton (1955) studied changes from the end of the eighth grade to the end of the eleventh grade. She reported that 70 percent of the interests which ranked highest in eighth grade still ranked in the first three

places at the end of the eleventh, but that 30 percent of the highest interest scores had changed significantly in rank order. Rosenberg (1953) obtained somewhat similar results with 177 similar subjects, the retest reliabilities ranging from .47 to .75, and clustering around .60. Persuasive and
musical interests in boys, and persuasive, computational, social service, and
clerical interests in girls increased considerably with time; girls' mechanical and scientific interests declined. Caution is clearly called for in using
the Kuder in long-range counseling with adolescents.

At the college level the results have been reviewed by Herzberg and
others (1954) : Retest reliabilities ranged from .50 to .90 over a one-year
interval. In their own study, they ranged from .63 to .84 for a group retested from 1 to 3 years after high school. Over a four-year period in college, Long and Perry (1953) found that clerical and mechanical scores
had reliabilities of —.22 and .14, persuasive interest scores .27, and others
from .49 to .66. The accumulated evidence thus suggests that the Kuder
may give a helpful picture of aspects of a person's interests at a moment in
time, but not one which is sufficiently stable over a several year period to
be very useful in career counseling; the Strong appears to be significantly
better for that purpose.

Validity. Beginning in 1940, and in increasing numbers each year,
studies of the relationship between Kuder scores and other variables have
been appearing. Most of these pertain to the construct validity of the
Kuder but not a few concern the predictive validity of the instrument.
They are summarized and discussed in the sections which follow.

Intelligence has not frequently been correlated with Kuder scores, perhaps because other problems seemed more vital. Adkins and Kuder (1940)
reported one study of the relationship of interest scores to primary mental
abilities, an investigation which has special interest because the mental
abilities measured were specific. Their data were obtained from 512 university freshmen. The correlations between Kuder and PMA Test scores
were low, except for one of .39 between number ability and computational
interest, a readily understandable relationship. Triggs (1943) correlated
the Kuder with A.C.E. Psychological Examination scores, also finding low
correlations, except for one of .40 between literary interests and verbal
scores, and another of .40 between computational interests and quantitative scores, but these relationships held for women only. Why they were
not found in men, if not merely chance findings in women, is difficult to
explain. Perhaps social pressure makes college men develop a modicum of
computational interest regardless of special ability, whereas women do so
only if they have unusual aptitude for such work. But this would not explain the relationship between literary interests and verbal ability in
women, who are normally both more verbally and more literarily inclined

than men. More and better studies are needed to clarify these matters.

Aptitudes as measured by the Bennett Mechanical Comprehension and Minnesota Paper Form Board Tests were correlated with Kuder scores in a study of 40 aircraft factory foremen by Sartain (1946). For the mechanical scale the two correlations were .13 and .15, for the scientific scale .19 and .15, high enough to show some connection, but too low to make the relationship practically important. A novel approach to the study of the intra-individual relationship between interests and special abilities was taken by Wesley, Corey, and Stewart (1950), who computed correlations between ranked Kuder scores and similarly ordered scores on the corresponding aptitude tests, such as the Minnesota Clerical Test, for a group of 156 male college students. They obtained *rhos* which ranged from —.57 to 1.00, indicating considerable individual differences. For any one individual it was shown that predictions from the extreme ranks of ability to comparable interest ranks was much better than predictions from intervening ranks.

Interests as measured by Strong's Vocational Interest Blank have been related to Kuder scores in a number of studies, particularly in a series by Triggs (1943, 1944a, 1944b), and Wittenborn, Triggs, and Feder (1943). Peters (1942) first reported correlations ranging from .38 to .52 for 24 college women tested with the Kuder and Strong's Women's Form. The correlations between Kuder scientific and Strong physicians' interests, computational and office workers' interests, literary and authors' interests, and social service and lawyers' interests (heavily loaded with the "people" factor in women) were significant, as one would expect. So also was that between scientific and lawyers' interests, which is difficult to explain, except on the grounds of their common correlation with intelligence as shown by Strong. Cottle's (1950) extensive correlational study of all possible combinations of the 34 scales of four personality and interest inventories, including the Kuder and the Strong, in a sample of 400 male veterans, generally supports expected relationships between these two measures of interests, but the data are difficult to analyze intensively because the group scales of the Strong were used. The findings by Triggs were not subject to this limitation.

Male subjects provided the basis of Triggs' (1944a) final study, in which the trends were similar to those reported for women by Peters. For these 166 men the relationships for typical, presumably similar, scales were as given in Table 33.

These relationships tend to be what one would expect, but they are low enough so that it would not be possible to use one instrument as a substitute for the other, as many had hoped would be possible. On the other hand, the varying degrees of relationship make it possible to use either inventory with better understanding of what is being measured, or both inventories together in order to make a more penetrating analysis of a client's interests.

The existence of a higher degree of relationship between the Kuder scientific and Strong chemist scales (.73) than between the mechanical and the chemist scales (.51), when contrasted with the inverse order of relationship for the Strong engineer scale (.54 and .72), suggests that the Kuder scientific scale assesses a more theoretical, laboratory, or biological type of interest than does the mechanical, and that in testing a would-be engineer it is well to attach more weight to the mechanical scale, while for a would-be chemist the scientific scale should be stressed. It is noteworthy that Kuder has revealed an awareness of these relationships in his occupational classification in the manual, for chemist is placed in the scientific group, while the various engineers are placed in the mechanical-scientific group. It would have been even more accurate, judging by these data, to place the chemists in a scientific-mechanical group (note the order) and leave only the more purely biological occupations in the scientific group.

TABLE 33

CORRELATIONS BETWEEN KUDER AND STRONG SCALES
After Triggs (1944a)

| | | | | *Kuder* | | | | |
Strong Scale	Sci.	Mech.	Soc. Serv.	Comput.	Cler.	Pers.	Lit.
Physician	.50						
Psychologist	.36						
Engineer	.54	.72					
Chemist	.73	.51					
Carpenter	.26	.67					
Math.-Sci. Teacher	.47	.46					
YMCA Sec'y			.35				
Social Sci. Teacher			.30				
City School Supt.			.42				
Accountant				.49	.55		
Office Worker				.25	.38		
Life Insurance Sales						.58	
Lawyer							.50
Author-Journalist							.28

The almost identical correlations between the Strong mathematics-and-science teacher scale on the one hand, and the Kuder scientific and mechanical scales on the other (.47 and .46), provide an interesting contrast with both of the sets of relationships discussed in the preceding paragraph, and the closer relationship between the carpenter and mechanical scales as compared with that between the carpenter and scientific scales (.67 and .26) further strengthens the interpretation suggested.

The clerical scale correlates more closely with both the accounting and the office work scales (.55 and .38) than does the computational (.49 and .25) . This might be taken as a reflection on the computational scale, but it should be remembered that a good measure of a factor need not necessarily have the most significant relationship to any variable in which it plays a part; in other words, the computational factor may be a very real one in some occupations, which actually can be classified in an occupational field in which other factors are more important. Accountants do computational work, but they are also concerned with other aspects of office work and record-keeping, as reflected in their clerical interests.

The much higher correlation between literary and lawyer (.50) than between literary and author-journalist (.28) scales is worth noting, for it suggests that the Kuder literary scale is likely to be more valid for legal than for literary occupations. Strong's factor analysis of his scales (Strong, 1943, pp. 143 and 319) shows that his lawyer and author scales have approximately the same loading of his "things vs. people" factor (—.92 and —.98) , while the lawyer scale has a slightly heavier loading of the "system" (.26 vs. —.19) and lighter loading of the social welfare (—.22 vs. —.01) factors. It is difficult to rationalize these two sets of data. More investigation of the differences between Kuder and Strong scores is clearly needed.

Counseling experience has suggested (Super, 1947) that the apparent discrepancies between Kuder and Strong scores may have diagnostic significance. Some persons who made high persuasive scores on Kuder's inventory but low life insurance salesman scores on Strong's seemed on the basis of case history and interview material to be interested in promotional activities, but to dislike activities in which they need to push people to the point of action as in closing a sale. The diagnosis and counseling of a number of clients on the basis of this interpretation of differences between persuasive and salesman scores has seemed fruitful, in a few cases even dramatic, but too few have been handled to justify any conclusions. It is also possible, for example, that such discrepancies are the result of effects such as those described by Paterson (1946), and that the higher Kuder persuasive score is the result of self-delusion or of an attempt to impress the consultant, whereas the lower Strong salesman score reflects more accurately the true interests of the client. If this were the case the selection of salesmen could be improved by using both inventories and devising an index of distortion based on discrepancies between the two scores; the better salesmen would presumably be those whose discrepancy scores were smallest. The hypothesis would be worth testing.

Two studies now available on the relationship between Kuder scores and ratings on the Lee-Thorpe Occupational Interest Inventory are discussed below in connection with the latter instrument.

Personality traits have, we saw in connection with Strong's Blank, generally been assumed to be related to interests. This hypothesis was checked by Evans (1947) with the Minnesota Personality Scale and the Minnesota T(hinking), S(ocial), E(motional) Inventory, in relation to the Kuder Preference Record. She tested 190 women students at Indiana University and reported that social introverts tended to score low on the Kuder persuasive interest scale, as did thinking introverts, while extroverts of both types tended to make average or high persuasive scores. Thinking extroverts were low also on literary interests, although thinking introverts made average scores on the literary scale. Triggs (1947) correlated the scores of 35 male and 60 female college students on the Kuder and on the Minnesota Multiphasic Personality Inventory, finding that in men mechanical interests were significantly and *negatively* correlated with psychopathic

TABLE 34

CORRELATIONS BETWEEN SCORES ON THE PREFERENCE RECORD AND
ON THE MINNESOTA MULTIPHASIC INVENTORY FOR 35 MALE
STUDENTS FROM THE UNIVERSITY OF WASHINGTON
FROM TRIGGS (1947), UNPUBLISHED PAPER

Scales of the Preference Record	*?* 1	*L* 2	*F* 3	*Hs* 4	*D* 5	*Hy* 6	*Pd* 7	*Mf* 8	*Pa* 9	*Pt* 10	*Sc* 11
1. Mechanical	.27	.23	—.17	.29	.03	—.06	—.41*	—.37*	—.18	—.22	—.21
2. Computational	—.11	.00	—.22	—.13	—.14	—.15	—.16	—.15	—.42†	—.25	—.18
3. Scientific	—.02	.07	—.27	—.14	—.30	.15	—.18	—.29	—.38*	—.33*	—.22
4. Persuasive	.01	—.22	.13	.14	.21	—.06	.08	.11	.16	.23	.06
5. Artistic	—.01	—.14	.24	.09	.20	.12	.21	.02	.07	.19	.16
6. Literary	—.15	—.07	.14	—.25	.07	—.10	.19	.04	.05	.07	.19
7. Musical	.11	—.10	.29	—.25	.17	.22	.30	.30	.25	.33*	.39*
8. Social Service	.01	.03	—.27	.10	—.34*	.15	—.18	.17	.14	—.16	—.25
9. Clerical	—.01	.03	.19	—.15	.36*	—.24	.20	.12	.01	.33*	.32*

Scales of the Minnesota Multiphasic Inventory

Level of significance:
* 5% = .329
† 1% = .424

and feminine tendencies, computational interests with paranoid, scientific with paranoid and psychasthenic, and social service with depressed tendencies, while musical interests were significantly and *positively* related to psychasthenic and schizophrenic, clerical interests to depressed, psychasthenic, and schizophrenic tendencies. Her data are reproduced in Table 34. In women no significant relationships were found between interests and personality traits, although two relationships with validating scores were significant.

Cottle (1950, p. 27) interpreted his matrix of 561 intercorrelations among the 34 scales of the MMPI, Bell Adjustment Inventory, Kuder Preference Record, and Strong Blank to indicate, "There is a marked relationship shown in this matrix between many of the scales of the Kuder and the Strong, and between the scales of the MMPI and the Bell, which counselors would expect to be related. Between the personality and interest inventories, however, there were only low positive or negative correlations and more frequently these coefficients were zero." In a factor analysis of these data he extracted seven meaningful factors, two of which were common to the personality inventories and five to the interest inventories. He concluded: "This study indicates little overlap between the two personality and the two interest inventories." This conclusion is unacceptable, however, to Darley and Hagenah (1955) who, in endeavoring to adduce evidence in favor of the personality-interest hypothesis, maintain that Cottle's interpretation of his results is incorrect. They state, quite correctly, that for a sample of 400, correlation coefficients of .10 and .13 are significant at the .05 and .01 levels, respectively; by these criteria, 43 r's were identified as significant at the 5 per cent level or less. But it should be noted that even when the highest coefficient (.35) is considered the amount of common variance between the personality and interest inventories is practically if not theoretically negligible, being only about 10 percent of the total. Consequently (with the limitation that no tests for linearity of regression were made), Cottle's results and interpretations appear sound: interests and personality, as operationally defined, are not appreciably related. A number of other studies, however, do not consistently support this conclusion.

Klugman (1950) devised a measure of spread of interests, defined as the sum of deviations of all scores from the mean of an individual's Kuder profile, and correlated it with general adjustment status as evaluated by the Bell in a sample of 108 male veterans. He obtained a nonsignificant product-moment correlation of .01. One positive finding was that veterans with stronger scientific and weaker artistic interests tend to be better adjusted. But in general the data indicated a lack of clear-cut relationships between interests and adjustment. This was not the case in Feather's (1950) study of 503 University of Michigan students. Divided into "maladjusted" and "normal" groups according to elevation of MMPI T scores (70 or above), the subjects exhibited reliable differences on a number of Kuder scales. The most notable trends were for the "normal" subjects to score higher on the mechanical and scientific scales and the "maladjusted" students to have stronger musical, literary, and (to a lesser degree) artistic interests. The tendency for this "aesthetic" triad—musical, literary, and artistic—to accompany poorer adjustment has been corroborated in investigations by Newman (1955) and Sternberg (1956) but has been most fully explicated by Steinberg (1952), who compared Kuder profiles for neurotic veterans, non-neurotic veterans, and Kuder's Base Group. Increasing mean trends from neurotic to non-neurotic to Base Group occurred on the mechanical, computational, scientific, and social service scales; decreasing mean trends from neurotic to non-neurotic to Base Group were evident in the persuasive, literary, and musical areas. Biserial correlations between group membership (Base Group, non-neurotic, neurotic) and interest scores ranged in the .30s for the literary (positive), musical (positive), and mechanical (negative) scales. Steinberg (1952) concluded that since maladjustment is associated with low interest in the mechanical and scientific areas and high interest in the literary and musical areas on the Kuder, this inventory might be used ". . . to alert a vocational counselor to problems of general personality adjustment."

But Klugman (1957), in a second study, has questioned this assumed relationship between interests and adjustment. Selecting (from an alphabetized file) the Kuder records of the first 100 male psychotic patients in remission, he prepared a mean profile for comparison with Steinberg's "neurotics" and Kuder's "normals" (Base Group). With the exception of a significantly lower psychotic mean on the mechanical scale, the differences between the psychotics and normals were negligible. The differences between the psychotics and neurotics were essentially the same as those between neurotics and the Base Group: The neurotics scored significantly higher on the literary and musical scales and lower on the scientific and mechanical scales. Because these results indicate that the psychotic group is less, rather than more, deviant from the Base Group as compared with the neurotics, Klugman concludes that if there is a relationship between adjustment and interests, then it would have to be admitted that ". . . hospitalized psychotics in remission are in better mental health than outpatient neurotics and in just as good emotional state as normals." Since this reasoning does not seem plausible to Klugman, he prefers the alternative hypothesis that ". . . no definite relationship exists between emotional states, personality traits, or diagnoses and vocational interest patterns as presently measured." But endorsing this hypothesis, in the light of Steinberg's positive results, necessitates the assumption that differences in adjustment are quantitative only. If it is as reasonable to assume that they are qualitative as well, then it does not necessarily follow that psychotics should be more deviant from normals than neurotics on the same continuum. In other words, if the differences between neurotics and psychotics are qualitative, then neurotics and normals may differ in one psychological dimension, such as interests, whereas psychotics and normals may differ in another.

Obviously a great deal of work remains to be done before it is possible to attribute differences in the patterning of interests to variations in adjustment to self, others, and the environment. Available evidence on the relationship of interests to personality depends upon the type of tests used, the characteristics of the subjects studied, and the sophistication of the research methodology employed. Yet some reliable conclusions and observations do emerge from the results. The correlations between the Kuder and various personality inventories are generally low, and, in most instances, not any greater than those between abilities and interests. Certainly they are not high enough to warrant substituting interest for personality appraisals in individual vocational diagnosis. But some are high enough to support certain interpretations of interest-personality patterns when measures of each are used together. The most notable trends have been extrapolated by Sternberg (1956) from interest and personality characteristics which are consistently associated in either a positive or negative direction. These are the familiar interests (aesthetic and scientific-technical) which are seen as expressions of different ways of handling interpersonal relationships. Persons with aesthetic interests probably tend toward art, literature, and music, according to Sternberg, because of their ". . . need for feelings of individuality or uniqueness, which can best be satisfied in pursuits where opportunities for self-expression, active or passive, are greatest." For the person who wants to remain emotionally uninvolved with people, yet needs their applause, aesthetic activities appear to offer an opportunity to carry on interpersonal relationships at a distance while gaining the recognition of others. They may also provide greater freedom from rules, regulations, fixed procedures and set standards for the person who chafes under the proscriptions of society In contrast, the ". . . more formal, highly ordered, concrete, and easily directed or controlled" components of scientific-technical activities appear to be more congenial to the person who seeks security through conformity to regulations and gains reassurance from the low emotional demands and less-threatening nature of work in which interpersonal relationships are peripheral. These interpretations of the two interest clusters seem meaningful and should lead to a greater understanding of the part which personality plays in vocational choice. But the counselor should remember, first, that they are only tentative working hypotheses subject to test and modification and, second, that they must be related to appraisals of corresponding abilities, since an interest pattern (particularly the aesthetic) is effective as a means of personality expression only to the extent that it can be adequately implemented through successful performance.

Grades or other indices of academic achievement have been correlated with Kuder scores in at least sixteen studies. Triggs (1943) found correlations of .42 (women) and .32 (men) between scientific interests and general science achievement, .40 (men) and .33 (women) between literary interests and achievement in English literature, .34 (men) and .36 (women) between computational interests and mathematical scores. Yum (1942) found significant relationships between the literary interests and grades of men (.335) and between the computational interests and average grades of women (.295) at the University of Chicago, but the comparable relationships for the opposite sex were in each case not significant. Crosby (1943) reported significant differences between the chemistry and biology grades of high- and low-scoring scientific interest groups (critical ratios = 7.6 and 12.2), and between the accounting grades of high- and low-scoring computational interest groups (6.9). The manual cites a thesis by Mangold, in which she found significant relationships between scientific interests and scores on the co-operative Natural Science Test (.385), literary interests and Co-operative English Test scores (.31), and literary interests and literary scores on the Co-operative Contemporary Affairs Test (.59). Detchen (1946) developed a scale based on 109 of the 785 Kuder items which were found to differentiate A and B students from D and E students, and obtained a validity coefficient of .60 with a social science comprehensive examination as her criterion; her subjects were 247 students in the original group, 106 in the cross-validation group for whom the validity coefficient shrank to a still significant .55. The typewriting and stenography grades of women liberal arts students, 96 and 75 in number, were related to Kuder clerical scores by Barrett (1946), who found that the interest scores did differentiate superior (A and B) stenography students from inferior (D and F) students, the cut-off score being the 55th percentile; the scale had no validity for typing. Dentistry grades were the criterion used by Thompson (1944); he found no relationship (—.06) between mechanical interests and dental practicum, but the validity of the social service scale was .24. These seemingly odd results may perhaps be explained by the very high mean mechanical interest scores (91st percentile) and their restricted range, whereas the social service scores had a lower mean (67th percentile) and presumably a greater range. On the other hand, scientific interests correlated .28 with theory grades, as anticipated. Correlations of essentially the same order were obtained by Long and Perry (1953) with the four-year college average of 172 engineering students as the criterion: the r's ranged from —.18 (artistic) to .21 (literary). They concluded: "These correlations are, of course, lowered to some extent by the fact that the academically weaker students have dropped out of engineering, as have many of those students with little or no interest in engineering." This explanation would account for the low relationships between interests and grades in homogeneous curricular groups but not unselected ones, such as those studied by Hake and Ruedisili (1949) and Romney (1950). These investigators found uniformly low correlations between the Kuder scales and course grades in groups of 2189 and 1085 male and female college students, the highest r being .30 (literary vs. English achievement). Scientific interest and achievement in science courses, with general academic achievement controlled, were similarly unrelated in a study reported by Givens (1953).

Achievement on the USAFI Tests of General Educational Development was related to Kuder scores in a well designed study by Frandsen (1947). Achievement in the natural sciences correlated .31 with computational and .50 with scientific interests; in the social studies, —.37 with social service but .31 with literary and .34 with scientific interests, probably because of the respectively negative and positive correlations between those types of interests and academic ability. Frandsen cites a master's thesis in which Turner reported correlations of .29 and .32 between scientific interests and grade-point-ratio in several courses in the biological and physical sciences, and .49 between computational interest and grades in physical sciences. Frandsen (1953) reports a median *rho* = .27 for rankings of Kuder interests and achievement in related high school courses for 137 male and female seniors. On the basis of his and other findings Frandsen appropriately concluded, "science and mathematical interests are definitely related to general achievement in parallel areas. For other areas, significant and logically consistent interest-achievement relationships have not been so clearly indicated, though some slight relationships have been noted for literature and social studies." Exceptions, Frandsen goes on to state, appear to be due to more fundamental negative relationships between social service interests and mental ability.

Completion of Training. From this point Frandsen proceeded to check Strong's hypothesis that interest would result in remaining in rather than leaving a field of endeavor, by correlating Kuder scores with percent of total credit in scientific and social studies. The correlations are shown in Table 35.

TABLE 35

CORRELATIONS BETWEEN KUDER SCORES AND CHOICE OF COURSES

Kuder Interest Scale	Percent Total Credit in Natural Sciences	Social Studies
Scientific	.54	—.35
Social Service	—.17	.32

These data support Strong's hypothesis: Students with social service interests tend to choose more social studies courses, and students with scientific interests tend to elect more scientific courses. Further confirmation is found in a study by Bolanovich and Goodman (1944), in which the engineering grades of 66 women students of electronics in the Radio Corporation of America's war-training program correlated only .09, .18, and .10 with mechanical, computational, and scientific interests on the Kuder, but the scientific and computational interests of the cadettes who successfully completed training were significantly higher than those of women who did not complete it, while those who were released scored significantly higher than others on the persuasive scale. Similar findings were obtained by Stewart and Roberts (1955) on the relationship of persistence in teacher training to the interests of 124 female student teachers. Those who remained were clearly differentiated by multiple discriminant functions (using all Kuder scales, including outdoor) from those who left. But clear differences on individual scales occurred only in the outdoor and persuasive areas, with the drop-outs scoring lower on the former and higher on the latter. These three studies seem to provide convincing evidence that what Strong found with his inventory is also true of the educational predictive value of Kuder's inventory.

To determine the relationship between interests and job turnover Tiffin and Phelan (1953) developed a Job Tenure Key for the Kuder and computed a multiple regression equation for predicting length of job tenure from Kuder sub-scores. The tenure key was based upon standardization samples of male workers in a metal parts factory who remained on the job for 11 to 14 months (high criterion group: $N=250$) and who voluntarily quit their jobs (low criterion group: $N=200$). Item analysis revealed that the high criterion group tended to express greater preference for manual activities whereas the low criterion group professed greater liking for verbal activities. Cross-validation of the tenure key supported its ability to differentiate long- from short-tenure workers in their vocational interests. Similar results were obtained from a multiple correlation based upon a combination of scores from the Kuder outdoor, mechanical, persuasive, and clerical scales, as one variate, and length of job tenure as the other. Workers with stronger outdoor and mechanical than persuasive and clerical interests tended to remain on the job longer. This is a plausible relationship, but how general it is needs to be established by study of other work groups at the same and different skill levels.

Occupational choices, or, more accurately, expressed interests, have been related to Kuder scores by Crosby and Winsor (1941), Kopp and Tussing (1947), Rose (1948), Berdie (1950), DiMichael (1949), and Brown (1951). The first authors asked college students to estimate their interest in the seven types of activities measured by the then current form of the Preference Record, and correlated these estimates with scores on the interest inventory; the average coefficient was .54, and there was more agreement between the two indices for the more intelligent (as measured by the A.C.E.) than for the less intelligent students. Kopp and Tussing found similar results with approximately 50 high school boys and an equal number of high school girls ($r = .59$ and .50), using the nine categories of the revised Preference Record. Rose used a similar procedure with 60 veterans, finding a correlation of .61 between inventoried and expressed preferences. Those who had specific objectives showed no closer agreement than others. About two-thirds of the group preferred occupations in fields in which they made high scores. Brown, who asked clients to evaluate whether their interest profiles were too high, too low, or "just about right," found high agreement between measured and expressed interests, perhaps because the judgments were contaminated by knowledge of the results, but Berdie and DiMichael obtained results which largely agreed with earlier studies. For the counselor Berdie's (1950) conclusion is quite relevant: "As long as measured interests have a relevancy for vocational satisfaction and as long as self-estimated interests play an important role in the vocational deliberations of individuals, both types of interests must be considered."

In an interesting follow up of Berdie's study, with the same data but a different analysis apparently suggested by Bordin's (1943) theory, Sinnett (1956) attempted to identify correlates of the variation in degree of agreement between expressed and measured interests (from one occupational area to another). Three hypotheses were tested: First, that there would be a positive relationship between degree of expressed-measured interest agreement in different occupational areas and ". . . the temporal order in which the average individual in our society would acquire a realistic perception of the purposes, skills, and duties involved in these areas"; second, that there would be a positive relationship between degree of expressed-measured interest agreement and ". . . the order of the complexity or difficulty in acquiring a realistic perception of the purposes, duties, and skills of the job area"; and third, that there would be a positive relationship between temporal order of understanding and the complexity of occupations, because ". . . the simpler jobs are those likely to be understood early in life, whereas the complex ones are likely to be understood relatively later." The mean contingency coefficients between self-ratings of interest and Kuder scores for 500 male college students were ordered according to magnitude; occupational areas, e.g., technical, computational, clerical, etc., were ranked according to the dimensions of temporal order of understanding and complexity; and, *tau*'s were computed between the various sets of ranks. There was a high positive (*tau* = .87) relationship between the rankings of occupational areas according to temporal order of understanding and complexity but neither the *tau* between temporal order and contingency coefficients nor the *tau* between complexity and contingency coefficients was significant, both being equal to .16 (*P*<.30). In other words, agreement between expressed and Kuder-inventoried interests is not related to temporal order of understanding nor to complexity of occupations. The negative findings were attributed to the fact that ". . . the Kuder may be closer to the self-percept," that is, more transparent, than, for example, the Strong (with which Sinnett's hypotheses were sustained).

Manifest interests have been related to inventoried interests in a number of studies, but the results do not show any consistent trends. Ewens (1956) obtained correlations between preference and experience scores for 329 male and 350 female high school juniors and seniors: the r's ranged from .05 to .52 (boys) and from .13 to .50 (girls). Dressel and Matteson (1952), using DuMas' coefficient of profile similarity, had previously found considerable agreement between Kuder profiles administered (1) according to regular directions and (2) with instructions to answer the items on the basis of related experience. However, since the instructional variable was introduced after the standard administration and appropriate control groups were not used, interpretation of these results is difficult. Bateman's (1949) finding that high school students with no work experience had more realistic interests than those with work experience is contrary to expectation. Perhaps uncontrolled factors produced the reversal, but variables such as socioeconomic and intelligence were controlled. The work experience may have been inappropriate to the development of interests: e.g., having a paper route to earn some extra money for dates may not have much effect upon a young person's vocational interests.

In another study of manifest interests Magill (1955) investigated two questions: Does the Kuder distinguish between different activity groups? And, are there relationships between the Kuder scales and activity group counterparts, such as musical interests and participation in band? The findings for 603 male and 203 female University of Pittsburgh students distributed in all college years and 13 activity groups provided affirmative answers to both questions. There were some differences between the sexes: The women had less distinctive profiles characterizing activity group membership, and, in contrast to the men, they scored higher on the persuasive than the literary scale in the dramatics group. Herzberg and Russell (1953) compared the interests of novice and experienced workers seeking employment in another field. They found that, although the interest patterns of entry and experienced workers are quite similar, the entry group is characterized by higher scores on those scales appropriate to the occupation.

In the one study reported so far with implemented occupational choice as the criterion Levine and Wallen (1954) discovered notable relationships between adolescent vocational interests and later occupation. A sample of 215 men who had taken the Kuder when in high school were followed up by questionnaire from 7 to 9 years later. Items on the questionnaire elicited information such as amount of education, present occupation and length of time in it, job satisfaction, and the effect of counseling upon occupational choice. Respondents and non-respondents were compared on age, intelligence, and Kuder scores obtained at the original testing; with the exception of the respondents' lower musical mean score (.05 level), no statistically significant differences were found. Since the respondents were adjudged a fairly unbiased sample of the total group, their current occupations were classified according to appropriate interest areas (following the Kuder manual), and the mean Kuder scores of those in occupations belonging to an interest area were compared with all others. For six of the areas men currently engaged in a related occupation made significantly higher scores 7 to 9 years previously than did men engaged in unrelated occupations. The areas in which differences occurred at either the .05 or .01 level of significance were: mechanical, computational, scientific, persuasive, literary, and clerical. (Comparisons for the artistic and musical scales were not made because there were too few subjects employed in these areas, and the outdoor scale was not scored.) The nonsignificant difference on the remaining interest scale, social service, was attributed by the authors of the study to inadequacies in the sample rather than the scale, since the group was quite heterogeneous, with eight of the ten cases being students in liberal arts, medical or dental programs and only one in a graduate school of social work. In interpreting these findings the investigators consider the possible confounding of the effects of counseling with the relationship between interests and occupation entered and conclude that, although the relationship could be due to the influence of counseling, it is not likely because (1) Strong's data indicate a positive relationship between interests and later occupational membership without an intervening counseling experience, and (2) only 35 per cent of the respondents in the study said that counseling influenced their occupational plans. In other words, "interests will out." This is reassuring evidence of the longitudinal validity of the Kuder but presents a rather unhappy case for the effectiveness of vocational counseling!

Success in an occupation has been increasingly used as a criterion for the validity of Kuder interests. In an early study, Sartain (1946) administered a battery of tests to 40 foremen and assistant foremen in an aircraft factory who were rated by their supervisors. The ratings had an interform reliability of .79, but yielded significant correlations with none of the instruments; that for the Kuder mechanical scale was .07, social service scale —.06, and clerical scale .003. In a second study, initiated by Super and reported by Guilford (1947, pp. 613–616), the Kuder was administered to 937 AAF pilot cadets who later took primary training. The correlations with success in training were statistically significant for only one scale, and that coefficient was only —.10, between social science interests and success. The validity coefficient for the mechanical scale was only .02, and the musical and artistic scales, which on the basis of results from information tests and biographical data blanks would be expected to have negative validities, actually had low but nearly significant positive validities (.05 and .08). Guilford suggests that this is because the Kuder scales sample interest and appreciation, whereas the more valid (for predicting success) tests of information and biographical data sample experience. Thompson (1947) found superior management engineer executives more interested in mechanical and less interested in social service activities than average men in similar jobs.

In an unpublished study, reported in an abstract of a paper by Di-Michael and Dabelstein (1947), efficiency ratings of 100 vocational rehabilitation workers were correlated with Kuder scales. Of 48 relationships computed, the first two of those which follow were significant at the one percent level, the third at the 5 percent level:

r promotional work and persuasive interest score = .32,

r professional reading and scientific interest score = .26,

r employer contacts and persuasive interest score = .19.

These findings suggest that, although uncorrelated with overall success in a job, interest as measured by the Kuder may be related to success in some aspects or duties of a varied job.

The more recent, extensive occupational aptitude pattern research of Barnette (1950, 1951) includes a comparison of the Kuder profiles of 103 successful and 45 unsuccessful engineers, the criterion of success being continuation of approved training or completion of such training after veteran's vocational advisement and no expressed desire to make basic changes in goals. The profiles of the successes and failures were relatively distinct, as indicated by the coefficient of profile similarity and *rho*. The successful engineers were significantly higher on the computational, scientific, and clerical scales, but lower on the persuasive scale, and differed from the Base Group on six of the nine scales. (Which scales and in which direction were not reported).

In contrast to these positive findings are the essentially negative results obtained in three other studies using performance on the job rather than continuation in education or training as criterion. Wolff and North (1951) used the Kuder to predict the success of municipal fireman, but found no significant correlations with the criterion, ratings of ability as firemen by the captain. Whether the criterion was adequate, however, could not be determined from the reported data. Successful and unsuccessful life insurance salesmen, classified by sales production, were differentiated on only the clerical scale (successful lower) by Kahn and Hadley

(1949), but again the criterion was questionable. The criteria constructed by Comrey and High (1955) for evaluation of the performance of production department supervisors were considerably better than those generally used but were uncorrelated with Kuder scores. Why there was an expectation of intercorrelations is not clear; perhaps the supervisor's job is not highly differentiated, successful supervisors having moderately strong interest in a number of areas rather than very strong interest in a few areas.

More encouraging results have been presented by Lattin (1950), who conducted a follow-up of 595 former students in hotel administration at Cornell 14 years after their graduation. The total sample was divided into successful and unsuccessful groups, using progression or persistence in the field a a criterion. The successful graduates had higher persuasive and musical interests, whereas those who were unsuccessful had stronger mechanical and computational interests. Evidently the social demands of hotel administrative work were inconsistent with the latter's preference for thing- rather than people-oriented activities.

It seems that the extent to which Kuder interests are related to job success varies with the occupation, skill level of the job (e.g., supervisors vs. engineers), and the nature and adequacy of the criterion. Success in occupations which are characterized by a cluster of relatively homogeneous activities in one, or possibly two, interest areas can probably be predicted by interest scores much more efficiently than success in more heterogeneous occupations. Similarly, the more general the skills and knowledge required for an occupational position or job, such as foreman, the less likely it is that success can be predicted with interest scores. Continuation in a field may be more closely related to interest than is job performance. And, needless to say, the predictive power of interests is limited by the reliability, stability, freedom from bias, etc., of the success criterion.

Occupational differentiation on the basis of Kuder scores has been most extensively reported in the manual, in which Kuder reports patterns for a number of men's and women's occupational groups. Over the years profiles for more than 200 occupational groups have been accumulated on approximately 1,500 workers (Manual). Also available are data on the interest patterns of majors in various college curricula. Borg (1950) has reported Kuder profiles for art students; Borg and Healy (1952) for student nurses; and, Shaffer (1949) for business school students. And Shaffer and Kuder (1953) have provided a comparison of the interest profiles of medical, law, and business school graduates. Brief verbal summaries of the patterns revealed in Kuder's work, and that of others, are given below as tentative guides to the interpretation of the scores.

Men in social welfare occupations, e.g., vocational rehabilitation supervisors, clergymen, social workers, school administrators, and teachers of social studies in high schools, tend to make high social service and literary scores; personnel managers, however, are somewhat less distinguished by high scores in these areas, and unlike the social welfare group tend to make equally high scores on the persuasive scale.

Men in literary occupations, such as writers, English teachers, and actors, tend to make high literary and musical scores, but actors are also high in artistic interests; lawyers and judges differ even more in that they make high scores in the persuasive area as well as in the literary and musical.

Scientists such as chemists and engineers tend to make high scores on the scientific scale, electrical and especially industrial and mechanical engineers also making high scores on the mechanical scale. The computational scores of these groups are higher than average, but only in the case of the industrial engineers are they significantly high. The only significantly high score made by the 26 draftsmen was in the artistic area. Spear (1948) found similar trends in engineering freshmen, as did Baggaley (1947) with liberal arts college freshmen.

Clerical workers, including accountants, auditors, bookkeepers, and cashiers tend to make high computational and clerical scores, the higher-level groups being outstanding in computational and the lower-level groups in clerical interests.

Salesmen and sales managers make their highest scores on the persuasive scale, this being the only outstanding score of salesmen who sell to individual consumers, while those who sell to distributors or manufacturers tend also to make high clerical interest scores. Judging by pattern inspection, life insurance agents ($N = 24$) do not differ appreciably from other salesmen, a finding which is at variance with Strong's data, previously discussed.

The patterns for women are in most cases similar to those of men in the same field, and like the men's, they tend to agree with expectation. Women physicians tend to make high scores in scientific and mechanical fields, as do laboratory technicians, but neither group is high in computational interests (no similar men's groups were tested). Nurses make their high scores in scientific and social service areas and score low on the clerical scale. Women telephone operators, stenographers and typists, teachers of home economics, and teachers of social studies are relatively undifferentiated, as Strong's work would lead one to expect.

Groups of 50 male life insurance salesmen and 50 social workers were tested by Lewis (1947), who found the former significantly higher than the general population in persuasive and the latter significantly higher in social service interests. Profile analysis was not made, however. Lehman

(1944) followed up students of home economics at Ohio State University, finding from 10 to 125 in each of several subdivisions of the field. Teachers, the largest group, scored high on social service, artistic, and scientific interests; hospital dieticians were high in social service, scientific and computational areas; restaurant and tea room managers scored high on the artistic and computational scales; home service and equipment workers made high scores in social service and persuasive fields; and journalists in the literary and artistic fields. Women marines were tested by Hahn and Williams (1945), who found relationships between interest patterns and duty assignments which, like those just reviewed, were in line with expectation.

Job satisfaction has so far been used as a criterion in only a few studies. Hahn and Williams, in the study just referred to, found that satisfied clerical workers were significantly more interested in clerical activities as measured by the Kuder than were dissatisfied clerical workers, the critical ratios for three sub-groups being 2.28, 2.41, and 2.97. Clerk-typists who were dissatisfied tended to be more interested in mechanical matters; general clerks who were satisfied were also more interested in computational activities.

DiMichael and Dabelstein (1947) correlated satisfaction with various job duties, as rated by 100 vocational rehabilitation counselors, with scores on appropriate Kuder scales administered five months previously. The correlation between enjoying "contacting employers to secure jobs" with the Kuder persuasive scale was .28, and between "handling clerical details" and clerical interest scores .32. None of the expected relationships between social service aspects of the job and social service interests were significantly correlated for this group. Another group of 46 male counselors were tested *after* they had made the job satisfaction ratings, and it is interesting that here the correlation between enjoyment of the job as a whole and social service interest score was .29 as opposed to .13 for the other group. In addition, the correlation between enjoying interviewing clients and social service interest score rose from .06 to .43, and other expected relationships became closer. This might be attributed to either of two factors: The first group may have lacked insight into their interests when they filled out the Preference Record, the subsequently completed satisfaction questionnaire therefore being a more accurate picture of their interests. Or the second group, having filled out the satisfaction questionnaire first, may have answered the interest inventory more searchingly and insightfully, perhaps even distorting answers in order to make them consistent with what they had already said. As the first group had had 2.5 years experience on the job, and the second only 1 year, it does not seem likely that the first explanation is correct. The first group knew its work, but did not know it was going to rate it for job satisfaction; the second group also knew its work, though less well, and had already rated it for satisfaction. The closer agreement between the two indices in the latter group must therefore be related to having job satisfaction in mind when they took the Preference Record. It would be interesting to know to what extent the greater agreement represents, respectively, stereotyping, insight, and distortion.

In a carefully designed and executed investigation of 516 accountants Jacobs and Traxler (1954) used satisfaction with job as a criterion for comparing the interest profiles of sub-groups with each other and with Kuder's Base Group. Satisfied accountants scored significantly higher on the computational and clerical scales and lower on the outdoor and artistic scales. As compared with the norms the accountants had stronger computational, clerical, and literary interests and weaker social service interests. Using a different approach Lipsett and Wilson (1954) related self-ratings of job satisfaction to suitability of vocational interests. A subject's interests were classified as suitable if one of his two highest percentile scores corresponded to Kuder's classification of his present occupation. The sample consisted of 108 former clients of the Rochester Institute of Technology counseling center. The results indicated that of the 59 subjects who had interests suitable to their current employment 32 per cent felt that their job was the best one possible, and only 5 percent were indifferent to or disliked it, whereas of those with unsuitable interests only 8 percent reported great job satisfaction and 33 percent expressed indifference toward their jobs or only minimal satisfaction. The differences were significant at the .01 level. A relationship has thus been established between the Kuder and job satisfaction.

Use of the Kuder Preference Record in Counseling and Selection. It has been established that the traits measured by the Kuder are internally consistent and relatively independent of each other. They are not closely related to intelligence, although there appears to be a degree of relationship between some primary mental abilities and the expected interests. Similarly, special aptitudes such as mechanical comprehension seem to be somewhat related to appropriate interests. The relationships between Kuder and Strong scores are generally found according to expectation, but they are not high enough to justify using Kuder scores as though they were obtained from Strong's Blank. The reason for this is obvious enough: The Kuder scores measure relatively pure interest factors, whereas Strong scores measure the interests of people in occupations. Chemists, for example, are characterized by interests which are partly scientific and partly mechanical, while mechanical engineers have a combination of mechanical, scientific, and computational interests. Personality traits have also been found to be related, in some instances, to interests as measured by the Preference Record: The aesthetic triad of the literary, artistic, and musical scales and the scientific-technical cluster of interests seem to represent vocational expressions of different ways of handling interpersonal relationships. Kuder scores are distorted when obtained under circumstances when there is motivation to portray oneself favorably, limiting their usefulness in selection, and even in counseling clients who lack insight into fixated expressed preferences.

The development of interests as measured by Kuder's inventory is characterized by both stability and change, rather than one or the other. That the change which does occur can be predicted is likely, since there is at least some indication that factors such as curricular orientation, and possibly achievement, financial condition, etc., are systematically related to the stability of interests over a period of time. But these are only suppositions at present.

Occupational significance of scores on the Preference Record has been demonstrated largely by compilation of means and percentile ranks for people employed in various occupations. Although the numbers are sometimes small, the data indicate differences between groups such as would be hypothesized on the basis of Strong's results. The development of occupational indices, or procedures for the statistical comparison of an individual's scores with those of people in various occupations, will make the occupational interpretation of the Kuder more objective, but it will take some time to make an appreciable number of these available, especially as a different form, the Kuder-Occupational, has been developed for occupational scoring keys. In the meantime we have seen reason for thinking that Kuder's classification of occupations by interest types has some validity, although the published materials indicate that as yet much of the classification has no empirical basis. The little material available on the relationship between Kuder scores and success on the job is less encouraging than for Strong's inventory, although a few studies have shown some relationship between interest and success.

In schools and colleges the Kuder does seem to have real possibilities even for the prediction of success in courses, for scores are significantly related not only to the completion of training, as for Strong's Blank, but also to grades in some appropriate subjects, specifically the scientific, mathematical, and literary. Validity for other subjects is more doubtful, at least when the interest-range is as restricted as it generally is. The scorability of this inventory, the ease with which student participation in scoring, converting scores, and plotting profiles lends itself to interpretation of results and discussion of their implications, give the Kuder many advantages for use in school and college guidance programs. Its transparency is presumably less important in counseling than in selection programs, and the fact that scores have only moderately high correlations with expressed preferences shows that it can contribute something to the diagnosis of interests, especially for the least able students for whom the discrepancy between choices and scores is greatest.

In guidance centers, whose clients are generally somewhat more mature and more experienced than students, it is especially desirable to make a careful study of the manifest interests of clients to whom the Kuder is administered, as a precaution against overemphasis on the literary, musical, and artistic scores which seem often to be high simply on an appreciation basis. Even in schools this can be similarly checked, but there the counselor may need, and be able, to depend partly on try-out experiences. Differences between Kuder and Strong scores often suggest new interpretations worth exploring in interviews, making the use of both instruments desirable in difficult cases.

The value of the Kuder in employment centers and in business and industry is still virtually unknown, as it has been little used in such situations. Despite its "industrial" short form it was apparently not designed with such use in mind, and its transparency has militated against it. For it to be valuable in personnel selection or evaluation programs more research should be done in connection with the possibility of a distortion score and the development of occupational indices appropriate to the jobs of the specific company or institution.

The Allport-Vernon Study of Values (Houghton-Mifflin, 1931, 1951). This inventory was originally developed by G. W. Allport and P. E. Vernon in an attempt to measure the personality traits postulated by Spranger in his *Types of Men* (1921). The first edition appeared in 1931 and was revised in 1951 with Lindzey as a new coauthor; the main changes, according to the new manual, were simplification of wording and a modernization of certain items, an improvement in the diagnostic power of the items, a more economical scoring scale, fresh norms, and a redefinition of the social value. The traits measured, as just implied, are best described as values or evaluative attitudes, although some of them verge on needs (see next chapter). We have seen that they closely resemble interests but are perhaps correctly described as more basic, for they concern the valuation of all types of activities and goals, and they seem in some instances to be more closely related to needs or drives. In practice, however, values and interest inventories are often used more or less interchangeably, and their relationships warrant treating them as interest inventories. The Allport-Vernon is by no means the only values test, but it is the first of its kind, has been the most thoroughly studied, and is still the most widely used. A review of early work with this and other values tests was published by Duffy (1940).

Applicability. The Study of Values was designed for use with college students, more as an instrument for research in the theory and organization of personality than as a practical aid in counseling or selection. Its vocabulary level is therefore higher than that of most inventories; Stefflre (1947) has shown that it has a vocabulary grade placement of 11.3, and that only the Cleeton Vocational Interest Inventory, among the widely used blanks, is more difficult to comprehend. For these reasons the Allport-Vernon should be used only with superior high school juniors or seniors, college students, or superior adults. Even for these some of the items may be difficult to accept, if not to understand, because of their seemingly esoteric nature. College students usually take them in their stride, but employment applicants are often impatient with some of the mystical and aesthetic items.

Changes in scores on the old form during the four years in college have been studied by Harris (1934), Schaefer (1936), and Whitely (1938), and summarized by Duffy (1940) as showing: ". . . the lowest coefficients of correlation are found always between the first and other administrations of the test, and that the trend (perhaps not statistically significant) is toward an increase in aesthetic, social, and theoretical values, and a decrease in religious, political, and economic values." Subsequent studies by Arsenian (1943) and Burgemeister (1940) with college men and women do not alter these conclusions, which fit in with conclusions concerning the increase in social welfare interests with age in adolescence, but contradict other data on scientific interests, and have no counterpart in so far as aesthetic and other values are concerned. It may be that the increases in aesthetic and theoretical interests, and decreases in religious and other values, are the result not of maturation but rather of college experiences. It would be helpful to have retest data for these same persons five and fifteen years after graduation from college, but none are available. Neither are there studies of age changes in other more typical populations.

Content. The Allport-Vernon consists of 45 items, the first 30 of which are paired comparisons and the last 15 multiple-choice, making 120 alternatives in all. As in the Kuder Preference Record each of the choices represents one of the types of interests or values; the corrected sum of the examinee's choices of any one kind of item constitutes his score for that type of value. As in the Kuder, a higher score on one type of value automatically makes for a lower score on some other. The items are designed to tap theoretical (interest in truth and knowledge), economic (interest in the useful or material), aesthetic (interest in form and harmony), social (interest in social welfare), political (interest in prestige and power), and religious (described as interest in unity with the cosmos but actually adherence to the forms of religion) values. The use of Spranger's esoteric terminology has created many misunderstandings of the traits measured, not only among users of the test but also in some investigators who have taken the terms in their common rather than very special sense. Even Spranger's definitions are misleading, as just noted in the case of religious values, because of poor implementation of the authors' intentions. The writers have frequently noted, for example, that high school students from traditionally religious homes, in whom observation and study revealed no real depth of religious feeling or belief, make high religious scores on the Study of Values. In their cases the scale seems to measure only verbal conformity to formal religion. Similarly, the meaning of the social value has been ambiguous. Originally it was represented by love in any form—conjugal, familial, philanthropic, or religious. In the new edition it has been limited to measure only altruistic love or philanthropy, expressed as an interest in the welfare of others. Any user of the inventory should therefore study the items carefully, as well as the authors' definitions, before making interpretations.

A factor analysis of item intercorrelations, which sheds some light upon the composition of the unrevised form of the Study of Values, has been reported by Brogden (1952). Eleven first-order and three second-order factors were extracted from the intercorrelation matrix and intercorrelations of the oblique factors, but since some of these were largely uninterpretable and others accounted for only negligible portions of the total variance, only those factors which could be identified with some degree of confidence will be mentioned here. The first of these is a general *aesthetic interest* factor which corresponds closely to the aesthetic measure obtained from the regular scoring procedure. The second factor, *interest in the fine arts,* is less well established and less general because its content seems restricted to the fine arts. *A belief in "culture"* factor is described as determined by intuitive or mystical processes and is characterized by a desire to appear cultured. Opposing reactions toward conventional religious creeds or indoctrination by the Christian church as an institution are the substance of the *antireligious evaluative tendency. Antiaggression* is idenfiable but its description is limited to statements concerning individual differences in interests or evaluations pertaining to conflict or war. A factor named *humanitarian tendency* seems more related to social issues rather than personal or face-to-face social interests, although the basis for this factor is more sympathetic than rational. The *interest in science* factor is definitely related to a high evaluation of, or interest in, the physical sciences. In contrast to the humanitarian tendency found in another factor, the *tendency toward liberalism* is characterized by a liberal viewpoint on social issues which appears to be more intellectual than emotional in origin. The *theoretic interest* factor is closely related to Spranger's definition of the theoretical value and the value measured by the Allport-

Vernon. Finally, there is a *rugged individualism* factor which is heavily loaded with items reflecting individual differences in acceptance or rejection of the traditional American credo.

Administration and Scoring. The blank requires from 20 to 40 minutes to administer, depending upon the verbal ability of the examinee. There is no actual time limit, but rapid work should be encouraged. Directions are simple and clear. Scoring is by means of a self-explaining scoring and profile sheet, readily understood by college students. The scoring procedure is more time-consuming than most in current use, but this is of minor importance when the inventory is used as a part of class work and is scored by the students. The use of the profile is helpful in stimulating discussions of values and goals and in bringing about self-insight.

Norms. The college student norms provided by the manual appear to be reasonably adequate, with variations which seem explainable in terms of the clientele and emphasis of the colleges in question. But these norms are general, and serve, like Kuder's, only as a backdrop against which to study the variations of part scores within an individual. Occupational norms are also desirable, in order to throw light on the vocational significance of the scale, but are not available except for a few groups. The new manual reports means and standard deviations for only 53 engineering students, 173 business administration majors, 93 medical students, 68 graduate students in education, 24 clergymen, and 15 theological students. Other information on the nature and composition of these groups is not provided. There is enough additional research evidence on both editions, however, to lend support to the practice of interpreting Allport-Vernon scores in vocational terms.

Standardization and Initial Validation. The diagnostic efficiency of the old inventory was tested by the internal consistency method in the original study (1931), in which it was found that the scales were relatively reliable and independent, only the social values scale (since revised) being of questionable reliability (.65). Scores correlated .53 with students' self-ratings on similar traits on the average (range of r's $=$ —.06 to .69), even though the reliability of the ratings was only .59, suggesting consistency between most self-concepts and self-described behavior. The one low intercorrelation was for social values. Expected differences were found between curricular groups, science majors, for example, being high on theoretical and low on economic values, while business students tended to score high on economic values.

Data on the restandardization are sketchy, but results seem adequate. The final item analyses on the revised edition showed a positive correlation between each item and the total score for its value at the .01 level of significance. The mean split-half reliability coefficient was .82 as compared with .70 for the old form, the range being from .73 (Theoretical) to .90 (Religious). It is noteworthy that as a result of the revision the reliability of the Social scale increased from .65 to .82. Norms based upon both sexes revealed expected differences, with women being on the average more religious, social, and aesthetic than men.

Reliability. As indicated above, the split-half reliability of the new form is satisfactory, particularly when it is considered that each value is measured by only 20 questions. The test-retest reliability is even better, a fact somewhat hard to explain. For an interim of one month the co-efficients range from .77 (Social) to .92 (Economic) for a group of 34 cases. These reliabilities are considerably higher than those for the old form, but the latter were over longer periods of time.

Validity. Scores on the Allport-Vernon have been related to most of the variables which can be studied in college populations, although to relatively few which are observable only in other groups.

Intelligence test scores have been correlated with values scores, for example, by Pintner (1933) in a study of 53 graduate students of educational psychology, for whom the correlations were .24 with theoretical, .38 with social, —.28 with political, and —.41 with economic values, those with other values being practically zero. Other studies, summarized in the manual, in Cantril and Allport (1933), and in Duffy (1940) reveal similar trends except for social values, the results for which are generally not so clearly positive in studies of the old form.

Grades were used as a criterion in Pintner's study (1933), but as they were based partly on performance in test administration they are somewhat atypical: Social values correlated .46 with grades, while the other coefficients were so small as to be negligible. Cantril and Allport (1933) found theoretical values correlated with sociology grades at Dartmouth to the extent of .25. In a study of students at Sarah Lawrence College, Duffy and Crissy (1940) found a validity of .34 for a combination of values scores, using ratings of academic achievement at the end of the freshman year as their criterion. Theoretical and aesthetic values had positive weights, economic and political negative. With the Co-operative Test of General Culture as a criterion, Schaefer (1936) found relationships of .58 and —.47 between the literary achievement and aesthetic and economic values of 51 women sophomores, .47 and —.28 between fine arts and aesthetic and economic values, .37 and —.37 between history and the same values, and .31 between general science and theoretical value. These relationships seem unduly high, and may be peculiar to the local situation (Reed College); they would in any case need confirmation before being applied elsewhere. A safe generalization from the studies reviewed would seem to be that there is a slight tendency for students with theoretical values to make better grades than students in whom other values are dominant, a conclusion which is congruent with the definition of the trait, and that in some situations other values will be associated with success in appropriate fields of endeavor.

Personality, as measured by the Kuder Preference Record-Personal, has been related to the Allport-Vernon by Iscoe and Lucier (1953) who used the more recent edition of the Study of Values. They formulated specific hypotheses concerning expected relationships between the two instruments on the basis of the trait definitions given in the manuals. Positive intercorrelations were anticipated between (1) the theoretical scores on both inventories, (2) the Economic scores of the Allport-Vernon and the practical scores of the Kuder, and (3) the Allport-Vernon Political scale and the sociable and dominant scales of the Kuder. A negative relationship was predicted between the Aesthetic scores on the Study of Values and the theoretical scores on the Kuder. None of the variables were related significantly, however, in a group of 90 college males at the University of Texas. The highest positive correlation (.47) was between the two scales which were expected to be negatively related, the Allport-Vernon Aesthetic and Kuder theoretical. As the authors of the study point out, these findings highlight the dangers involved in using similarly defined trait measures as if they were interchangeable.

Success on the job has not, to the writers' knowledge, been related to scores on the Allport-Vernon Study of Values.

Occupational differences have not been studied by means of employed men or women, but numerous studies have shown that professional students are differentiated by the Study of Values in accordance with expectations. *Theoretical* values are found in students of education (Harris, 1934), engineering (Harris, 1934), medicine (Harris, 1934; Stone, 1933), natural science (Schaefer, 1936), and social studies (Schaefer, 1936). *Economic* values characterize only students of business (Stone, 1933; Tutton, 1955). *Aesthetic* values are strong in students of drama (Golden, 1946), education (Stone, 1933), literature (Schaefer, 1936; Stone, 1933), and the social studies (Schaefer, 1936). *Social* values have not so frequently been studied, as the scale was not, in the old form, reliable enough for individual appraisal; it was adequate for the study of group trends, which show that YWCA secretaries (Anderson, 1938) stand high on it, but, surprisingly, that students majoring in the social studies (Schaefer, 1936) tend to make low scores. *Political* values are significantly high in engineering students (Harris, 1934), physical education students (Shaffer, 1949), and law students (Harris, 1934; Stone, 1933). *Religious* values have been found to be high in seminarians (McCarthy, 1942) and in

YWCA secretaries (Anderson, 1938), but the high scores of high school commercial students (Triplett, 1934) and low scores of college students of business (Stone, 1933) suggest that the religious value scores do not, in some cases, represent more than the lip service of immature persons who have as yet experienced neither deep religious feeling nor intellectual doubts concerning religion. In one study of within-group differences Karn (1952) found that students in different engineering specialties could be differentiated but that the group as a whole followed the expectation of scoring significantly high on theoretical values when compared to the norms.

Satisfaction in one's work has not been related to scores on the Study of Values, as might be expected in view of its limited occupational use.

Use of the Allport-Vernon Study of Values in Counseling and Selection. The traits measured by this inventory resemble those measured by the other inventories studied in this chapter. Like the Kuder, it taps interest factors which play a part in a variety of occupational fields, usually in ways which would be anticipated in view of the nature of the items. However, the traits appear to be somewhat more fundamental and more closely related to basic needs and drives than those measured by other interest inventories. They have been found to change somewhat during the college years, social interests increasing (perhaps with physical maturation, as other studies have also reported); increases in theoretical and aesthetic values may be related to specific college influences, together with decreases in religious and economic values. Too little is known concerning age changes in values. Values are related to intelligence in the same way as interests.

Occupations for which the Study of Values has significance appear to be largely at the professional and executive levels, but that is due to the vocabulary and intended use of the instrument. Values are related in expected ways to choice of training in fields such as art, business, drama, education, engineering, law, literature, medicine, natural science, psychology, the priesthood, social studies, and social work. Only in the last-named field have experienced workers been tested, but the data for training groups are consistent enough to justify some confidence in their occupational significance. As no norms are available, the counselor must interpret on the basis of peaks and valleys in the profile, a procedure which is safer with this instrument than with most when drawing conclusions from high scores because of the method of construction, but more dangerous with low scores or valleys in the profile because interest in such a field may be very strong even though pressed down artificially by the mutually-exclusive response technique.

In schools and colleges this inventory may have some value in determining appropriate major fields, although it generally has less value for predicting grades than an intelligence test. The nature and degree of the relationships between values and grades in various types of courses are likely to vary with the institution, because of the importance of climates of opinion in attracting students and in modifying values. Differences in predominant values or climates of opinion in different colleges give the test some value in helping students choose congenial colleges. The self-scoring feature of the inventory makes its use in orientation and psychology classes easy, and it lends itself well to the starting of discussions of values, interests, and vocational objectives, such as is appropriate to orientation programs. The esoteric nature of some of the items limits its usefulness, however, to moderately well motivated persons, and the vocabulary limits it to superior high school and to college students.

In guidance centers the Study of Values can be helpful in aiding potential college students in the choice of colleges in which they will find the psychological atmosphere congenial and conducive to growth, although for this purpose comparisons between the mean scores of students in different colleges need to be made more systematically than has so far been done. A survey of the literature with this purpose in mind should yield some useful material. More important than this use, in guidance centers, is the diagnosis of interests when it is suspected that Kuder or Strong scores are distorted by a clear-cut but inappropriate self-concept. The non-vocational nature of the Allport-Vernon items presumably makes them less subject to choice on the basis of vocational stereotypes, and more on their own merits, than the more clearly occupational items in the Kuder and even the non-occupational parts of the Strong. Unfortunately this hypothesis has never been tested. Until it is, the clinical counselor in search of an understanding of a puzzling client cannot afford to neglect this test and so to miss the chance to sink a shaft into the interest field which is slightly different from those sunk by other instruments.

In employment services, business, and industry this inventory is likely to be less useful than in other types of counseling or selection situations. The vocabulary and subject-matter make it seem out-of-place to employment applicants, and the norms and validation do not lend themselves to as effective use in selection programs as do those of certain other interest inventories. An industrial and business version might presumably be constructed and be of considerable value in selection because of the differences between it and the standard vocational interest inventories. But such a project has yet to be planned and carried out.

The Cleeton Vocational Interest Inventory (McKnight and McKnight, 1937, 1943). This inventory appears to have been developed in an attempt to simplify the scoring of Strong's Vocational Interest Blank, and incorporates many items used in it and in other inventories constructed in the Carnegie tradition. It has been rather widely used in schools, colleges, and guidance centers, but has not enjoyed the popularity of either the Strong, which is more complex to score, or the Kuder, which captured a large segment of the vocational-test-using public almost on publication. This may be due partly to misgivings concerning the transparency of items grouped according to their occupational significance, and partly to such an irrational thing as dislike of the meaningless and difficult-to-remember codes used to designate the occupational families since, whether scientific or not, a convenient set of handles helps. Some evidence is now available concerning the first possibility which indicates that item transparency apparently is not a problem. The criticism has been that, because the items have been grouped in occupational families, the examinee would respond to the obvious groupings rather than to the items. Kelleher (1955) reasoned that, if this is the case, then there should be significant differences between scores of subjects on the standard form and one in which items are arranged at random. He found no significant differences between two groups tested with the different forms and concluded: "This finding would seem to suggest that S's respond to the item rather than to the scale in which it is placed."

Description. The Cleeton Inventory was designed for use in grades 9 through college and with adults, but was constructed on the latter and has a vocabulary grade placement of 12 (Stefflre, 1947), making it the most difficult of the well-known interest inventories. Both men's and women's forms consist of ten groups of items, each group representing an occupational family (e.g., OCA: clerks, stenographers, typists, and other office work occupations) and consisting of 70 items, 30 of which are occupational titles, 20 names of school subjects, magazines, prominent persons, etc., and 20 leisure-time activities, work activities, and peculiarities of people. Scoring is done by adding unitary weights for each item marked in a given group. It was standardized by administering it to some 7000 individuals engaged in a variety of occupations, principally in the Pittsburgh area. In 76 per cent of 1,741 cases the highest inventory rating agreed with the occupation engaged in, while in 95 per cent one of the three highest ranking groups included the occupation engaged in. The scores are quite reliable, ranging from about .82 to about .91 (manual).

Validity. There have been few studies of the validity of the Cleeton, further testimony of the fact that it has not challenged most vocational psychologists; most of the published studies are not concerned with the relationship between inventory scores and external criteria. It was administered to students of education by Congdon (1940) , who found significant differences between men and women who planned to teach, on the one hand, and who planned not to teach, on the other. She also found that scores in the field of claimed interest were higher than scores in fields in which no interest was claimed, but this is not surprising in an inventory as seemingly transparent as this. Even the former finding may be spuriously high because of the same sort of halo effect or stereotyping.

The correlations between Cleeton scores and Strong's scales were computed by Arsenian (1941) for 150 Springfield College freshmen who took the two inventories at intervals of one week (Strong Blank first). Scores for the Strong scales which belong to the same occupational family were combined to yield group scores comparable to Cleeton's, and the two sets were correlated. The coefficients of correlation ranged from .16 (LFJ and Lawyer-Author-Journalist) to .68 (TMD and the social welfare scales), the average being .45. This is slightly lower than the correlations between the Strong and the Kuder, which have less item-similarity than the Strong and the Cleeton. It would clearly not be wise to use the Cleeton as a substitute for the Strong Blank, although there is considerable similarity in the inventories and in the meaning of the scores.

Use of the Cleeton Vocational Interest Inventory. In view of the availability of more thoroughly studied inventories such as the Strong, the Allport Vernon, and more, recently, the Kuder, there is little justification for using an instrument concerning which there is still so much room for question and for which there is still little in the way of field validation. Although Cleeton's standardization data are rather impressive, there has not yet been enough follow-through on the inventory to make it a well-understood instrument.

The Lee-Thorpe Occupational Interest Inventory (California Test Bureau, 1943). This inventory has been available long enough for the paucity of publication concerning it in the professional journals to be disturbing. The writers have located a few studies of its validity, but practically all that is known concerning it is in the manual and "Occupational Selection Aid" supplied with it, documents which use the concepts of construct and content validity and avoid the issue of predictive validity.

Description. The items were written in simple language, with a vocabulary grade placement of only 6.8 (Stefflre, 1947); it (Advanced Form A) is therefore easily understood by junior and senior high school boys and girls. The paried comparison form is easily handled also at that level. The items are not, however, offensive to adults; they are based on the *Dictionary of Occupational Titles* (U. S. Dept. of Labor, 1949), and so have the aura of authenticity. It is scored for fields somewhat like Kuder's, by simple item-count. The inventory itself therefore looks attractive to users of vocational tests. The manual shows that it is reliable (.71 to .93). The norms are based on 1000 twelfth grade students and are said to be applicable to any high school grade and to adults—a fact which seems improbable, in view of Strong's and Carter's work and of tentative findings reported by Lindgren (1947).

Validity. The only claims for validity set forth by the manual are based on the source of items, the design of the items, the balance of activities sampled, and the presentation of items (content and to a lesser extent construct validity). All of these, it should be noted, are internal, not external, criteria, and are dependent upon the good judgment of the test authors. This judgment was checked experimentally in at least one instance, however, and was found to be sound. To determine whether the items are properly representative of the Fields of Interest measured by the inventory, Bridge and Marson (1953) had 38 judges with considerable experience in vocational counseling assign each of the 240 test items to the field in which they felt it belonged. Each item was given a dissent score which was the total number of times it was placed by the judges in a field different than that designated by the test authors. The judges agreed that 183 items, or 76 per cent of the total, were correctly assigned; of the remainder the judges agreed that 24 items were misclassified but could be used if reassigned; they could not agree upon the proper Field of Interest designation for 33 items. It is noteworthy that the largest number of misclassifications were in the Mechanical field, since these may lower the validity of this scale. Other studies of the validity of the inventory typically fail to use occupational membership or success criteria. Lindgren (1947), Roeber (1949), and Jacobs (1951) have reported substantial relationships between appropriate Lee-Thorpe and Kuder scales; Brown (1951) has obtained relationships between Occupational Interest Inventory ratings of interest and expressed interests comparable to those found in similar studies with the Strong and the Kuder.

Only MacPhail (1954) and MacPhail and Thompson (1952) have validated the inventory against college major and occupational membership with sizeable numbers of students and veterans. But these are only preliminary, even though encouraging, attempts at validation. The Lee-Thorpe is still in the embryonic stages, much as it was twenty years ago. Appropriate data on relationships to job success, job satisfaction, intelligence, grades, personality, and information concerning changes in scores over a period of time are not available.

Use of the Lee-Thorpe Occupational Interest Inventory. The nature of the inventory makes it attractive to potential users, but it is at present a purely experimental form which has yet to be validated against satisfactory occupational criteria. It may therefore be used in research by those who have the resources for conducting validation studies, or as an interview aid, but has no demonstrated value at this point as a diagnostic or prognostic instrument.

The Michigan Vocabulary Profile Test (World Book Co., 1939, 1949). Unlike the other instruments discussed in this chapter, this is a test rather than an inventory. It is virtually the one information test of interests now available, although the Army Air Forces (Guilford, 1947, Ch. 14) developed one which was quite valid for pilot and navigator selection and which should have stimulated civilian counterparts. The Michigan test was developed by E. B. Greene, as a test of specialized vocabulary which might be prognostic of interest and success in several fields of activity. It was little used before World War II, but has since been widely used in work with veterans.

Description. Two forms are available, each of which was designed for high school and college use and has eight divisions: human relations, commerce, government, physical sciences, biological sciences, mathematics, fine arts, and sports. There are 240 items divided among these eight areas, each phrased as a definition followed by four terms from which the one which corresponds to the definition must be selected. Items are arranged in ten levels of difficulty, three items per level. An attempt was made to eliminate terms which could be guessed by knowledge of roots, prefixes, etc., thus reducing the effects of reasoning and restricting the test to information. The items were selected from more than 6000 submitted by students in the various fields. Groups of items were refined by internal consistency analysis, all items being required to correlate .30 or above with the score on that part. The inter-form reliabilities range from .78 to .94, with a median of .81. Administration is untimed, most college students finishing in about one hour and high school students sometimes requiring as much as one and one-half hours. The test can be machine or hand-scored with stencils; the score is the number right for each part. A profile chart is provided on the answer sheet. Norms are expressed in percentiles, are based on 4677 students from ninth grade through college, and are available for both part and total scores; this means that each norm group contains an average of slightly less than 600 persons. Because of the limited number of items in each scale, the percentiles change rapidly: a raw score of 16 on the human relations scale places a college freshman at the 31st percentile, while one of 17 places him at the 50th. This is the unfortunate result of a steeply graded test; it would probably have been better to have separate forms for high school and college, and to have more items working at each level, in order to get a better spread of raw scores and of percentiles. As it is, too much emphasis is put upon chance factors which affect the answering of any one item. Increases in scores with grade occur, as would be expected in a vocabulary test. Finally, profiles are given for students in several professional curricula, including law, nursing, engineering, business administration, medicine, education, and social studies, the numbers for these groups ranging from 125 to 182. These do not actually constitute norms, as only the means are given, but they do aid in interpretation.

Validity. Unfortunately there have been almost no studies of the relationship between scores on the Michigan Vocabulary Profile Test and other variables, although data are needed on the relationships with intelligence, inventoried interests, grades, completion of training, occupational choice, success in various occupational fields, job satisfaction, and other external criteria. It is surprising that an instrument which has been as widely used as this during the postwar years has had so little publication. The evidence which is available is contained largely in the manual, which shows that none of the part scores correlate more than .54 with any other, the averages for each scale ranging from .15 to .34. Occupational norms as reported in the revised manual have been accumulated for twenty-four occupations in such fields as human relations, physical sciences, clerical and commercial, etc., but the number of cases in each occupation is small, the average being fifty.

Some data on the external validity of the instrument have been published, but they are either sketchy or on restricted, atypical groups of workers. Thompson (1947) found differences between more and less successful executives; Abt (1948) was able to differentiate editors rated high and low in performance by their scores in the Commerce, Government, Sports, Biological Sciences, and Human Relations divisions; and, according to Greene (1951), Swartz and Schwab (1941) obtained a validity coefficient of .87 between combined Physical Science, Biological Science, and Mathematics scores and successful performance by 37 research engineers. Greene (1951) also reports that a psychologically naive person sorted the profiles of 156 sales clerks from those of 117 general clerks with 91 per cent accuracy.

Use of the Michigan Vocabulary Profile Test. Like many other published tests this one is still in an embryonic stage because there has been little follow-through in the collection and publication of validation data and vocational norms. It has been widely used since World War II in work with veterans, because its grade norms for specialized vocabularies have made easier the evaluation of the readiness to resume a high school or college education of somewhat mature young men whose education had been interrupted. Clients whose informal education has given them much of the vocabulary of a special field can be assumed (there is no actual published evidence) to have some of the prerequisites of success in that field.

The usefulness of the Michigan Vocabulary Profile Test will probably be limited to such cases, and to the diagnosis of reasons for failure in educational programs, until more complete validation has been carried through.

Trends in the Measurement of Interests

Although it is not the purpose of this treatise to deal with topics other than standard methods of measuring aptitudes and traits which have been found to play a part in vocational development, with the objective of helping the counselor and personnel worker to make more effective use of available instruments, in closing this chapter it seems appropriate to devote a few words to trends in this dynamic branch of measurement. Occasional symposia and papers have dealt with such matters (Kuder, 1951, Super 1954); only a few points will be touched upon here.

The problem of developing measures of interests appropriate to the unskilled and semiskilled levels has been difficult to solve with conventional interest inventories, for these were developed for use with business and professional men or with college and high school students aiming at the middle and upper levels of the occupational hierarchy (Strong, 1943). As Long (1952) has pointed out, inventories such as the Kuder and Strong characteristically focus upon occupational fields, specific jobs, and recreational activities with which the lower ability job applicant (and the person of low socioeconomic status) is not familiar. Moreover, as we have seen, because they contain transparent items they are susceptible to falsification by the examinee. To overcome some of these limitations of standard interest inventories Clark (1948, 1949, 1955) and Long (1952) have developed inventories with items appropriate for lower occupational levels and standardized them on appropriate groups. Clark worked with Navy enlisted men and with trade unions, Long with applicants for industrial employment. Long devised a Job Preference Survey (JPS) based upon independent components of work interest which include samples of job activity preferences at a non-professional level. Extensive analysis of preliminary data from standardization and cross-validation of experimental forms of the Job Preference Survey yielded six bipolar dimensions of work interest which should be meaningful to the less skilled worker. These essentially independent work components, and examples of the 20 paired-statement items upon which each is based, are listed in Table 36. The reliabilities of the scales, although not uniformly high, are acceptable: Three of the scales have internal consistency reliability coefficients greater than .80; two are above .70; and one is slightly less than .70. Validity data for this promising instrument have not been published, nor have normative data been accumulated. The Job Preference Survey is in an early stage of development and should be used only for research purposes. If followed up, however, it has the earmarks of a potentially useful counseling and selection device for the measurement of low-grade work interests.

TABLE 36

WORK INTEREST COMPONENTS AND SAMPLE ITEMS FROM THE LONG (1952)
JOB PREFERENCE SURVEY

Work Interest Component	*Sample Item*
1. Routine—Varied	1. Pack glassware for shipment. Design decorative patterns for glassware.
2. Indoor—Outdoor	2. Operate a large batch mixer in a foods plant. Operate a large mixer making ready-made concrete.
3. Hazardous—Non-hazardous	3. Pour melted metals from overhead ladles into molds. Prepare molds for making heavy castings.
4. Sedentary—Bodily Active	4. Keep records of materials in stock. Deliver materials to machine operators.
5. Isolative—Gregarious	5. Look up statistical data in a reference library. Operate the loan desk of a library.
6. Precise—Approximate	6. Lay individual tiles for a shower room wall. Lay concrete blocks for a building partition.

Note—The item pairs were formed so that the alternatives were judged to be equivalent in prestige or social acceptability and performance skill level.

Clark's systematic work in the measurement of interests at the lower occupational levels has been pursued over a period of years under contract with the Office of Naval Research. A series of methodological problems has been solved, and the work should in due course bear fruit in the form of an instrument useful at the semi-skilled and skilled levels.

Because verbal interest inventories are limited by perceptual selectivity on the respondent's part in accepting and rejecting items, as well as by non-valid stereotypes surrounding words, ambiguous meanings of words, and the reading difficulty level of item content, Pierce-Jones and Carter (1954) developed a pictorial interest inventory to measure preferences in areas comparable to those on the Kuder. From a preliminary pool of 109 photographs depicting activities in the various Kuder interest areas, 50 photographs were chosen and arranged in 144 pairs for the experimental inventory, which was then administered to 52 male and 57 female college students. The pictures were projected onto a screen for approximately 8 seconds, long enough for the subjects to choose either the left-hand or right-hand photograph as the preferred activity. To reduce spurious response consistency from the use of the same picture more than once, the photographs were alternated in the left and right positions of the pair. A value of one was assigned to each preference in a particular category; an item which was classified in two categories was scored once in each interest area. In addition to the pictorial inventory the Kuder was administered for purposes of comparison.

Split-half reliabilities for the new Pierce-Jones-Carter inventory ranged from .46 to .92, with a median of .81 for men and women combined; for men alone they were generally higher, ranging from .70 to .88. Correlations among the scales for men varied from —.60 (artistic *vs.* computational) to .74 (clerical *vs.* computational); for women they ranged from —.95 (clerical *vs.* social service) to .56 (artistic *vs.* mechanical). Most of the correlation coefficients, however, were in the moderate to low ranges, indicating a fair degree of independence among the scales. The correlations between the pictorial subtests and cognate Kuder scales ranged from .27 to .75 (men and women), with a median value of .61. This novel, although not unique, approach to interest measurement thus has promise and may find useful applications after validation studies have been completed with a number of different occupational samples.

REFERENCES FOR CHAPTER XVIII

Abt, L. E. "A test battery for selecting technical magazine editors," *Pers. Psychol.*, 2 (1948), 75-93.

Adkins, Dorothy C., and Kuder, G. F. "The relation between primary mental abilities and activity preferences," *Psychometrika*, 5 (1940), 251-262.

Anderson, Rose G. "Technological aspects of counseling adult women," *J. Appl. Psychol.*, 22 (1938), 455-469.

Arsenian, S. "A further study of the Cleeton Vocational Interest Inventory," *Occupations*, 20 (1941), 94-99.

———. "Change in evaluative attitudes during four years of college," *J. Appl. Psychol.*, 27 (1943), 338-349.

Baggaley, A. R. "The relation between scores obtained by Harvard freshmen on the Kuder Preference Record and their fields of concentration," *J. Educ. Psychol.*, 38 (1947), 421-427.

Barrett, Dorothy W. "Prediction of achievement in typewriting and stenography in a liberal arts college," *J. Appl. Psychol.*, 30 (1946), 624-630.

Barnette, W. L., Jr. "Occupational aptitude pattern research," *Occupations*, 29 (1950), 5-12.

———. "An occupational aptitude pattern for engineers," *Educ. Psychol. Measmt.*, 11 (1951), 52-66.

Bateman, R. M. "The effect of work experience on high school students' vocational choice: as revealed by the Kuder Preference Record," *Occupations*, 27 (1949), 453-456.

Berdie, R. F. "Scores on the Strong Vocational Interest Blank and the Kuder Preference Record in relation to self-ratings," *J. Appl. Psychol.*, 34 (1950), 42-49.

Bolanovich, D. J., and Goodman, C. H. "A study of the Kuder Preference Record," *Educ. Psychol. Measmt.*, 4 (1944), 315-325.

Bordin, E. S. "A theory of vocational interests as dynamic phenomena," *Educ. Psychol. Measmt.*, 3 (1943), 49-66.

———. "Relative correspondence of professed interests to Kuder and Strong interest test scores," *Amer. Psychologist*, 2 (1947), 293 (abstr.).

————, and Wilson, E. H. "Change of interest as a function of shift in curricular orientation," *Educ. Psychol. Measmt.*, 13 (1953), 297-307.

Borg, W. R. "The interests of art students," *Educ. Psychol. Measmt.*, 10 (1950), 100-106.

————, and Healy, I. "Personality and vocational interests of successful and unsuccessful nursing school freshmen," *Educ. Psychol. Measmt.*, 12 (1952), 767-775.

Bridge, L., and Marson, M. "Item validity of the Lee-Thorpe Occupational Interest Inventory," *J. Appl. Psychol.*, 37 (1953), 380-383.

Brogden, H. E. "The primary values measured by the Allport-Vernon test, 'A study of values'," *Psychol. Monog.*, 348 (1952).

Brown, N. M. "Expressed and inventoried interests of veterans," *J. Appl. Psychol.*, 35 (1951), 401-402.

———— "Evaluation of Lee-Thorpe Inventory ratings by veteran patients," *Educ. Psychol. Measmt.*, 11 (1951), 248-254.

Burgemeister, B. B. "The permanence of interests of women college students," *Arch. Psychol.*, 255 (1940).

Callis, R., Engram, W. C., and McGowan, J. F. "Coding the Kuder Preference Record-Vocational," *J. Appl. Psychol.*, 38 (1954), 359-363.

Canfield, A. A. "Administering Form BB of the Kuder Preference Record, half length," *J. Appl. Psychol.*, 37 (1953), 197-200.

Cantril, H., and Allport, G. W. "Recent applications of the Study of Values," *J. Abnorm. Soc. Psychol.*, 28 (1933), 259-273.

Christensen, T. E. "Some observations with respect to the Kuder Preference Record," *J. Educ. Res.*, 40 (1946), 96-107.

Clark, K. E. "The vocational interest patterns of members of A. F. of L. trade unions," Minneapolis, Minnesota: University of Minnesota, Dept. Psychol., 1948 (Tech. Rep. No. 1).

————. "A vocational interest test at the trade level," *J. Appl. Psychol.*, 33 (1949), 291-303.

————. *The Use of Interest Measures with Naval Enlisted Personnel.* Minneapolis: Department of Psychology, University of Minnesota, 1955 (Mimeographed).

Comrey, A. L., and High, W. S. "Validity of some ability and interest scores," *J. Appl. Psychol.*, 39 (1955), 247-248.

Congdon, N. A. "A study of Cleeton's Vocational Interest Inventory," *Occupations*, 18 (1940), 347-352.

Cottle, W. C. "Relationships among selected personality and interest inventories," *Occupations*, 28 (1950), 306-310.

————. "A factorial study of the Multiphasic, Strong, Kuder, and Bell inventories using a population of adult males," *Psychometrika*, 15 (1950), 25-47.

Crosby, R. C. "Scholastic achievement and measured interests," *J. Appl. Psychol.*, 27 (1943), 101-103.

————, and Winsor, A. L. "The validity of student estimates of their interests," *J. Appl. Psychol.*, 25 (1941), 408-414.

Cross, O. H. "A study of faking on the Kuder Preference Record," *Educ. Psychol. Measmt.*, 10 (1950), 271-277.

Darley, J. G., and Hagenah, Theda. *Vocational Interest Measurement.* Minneapolis: University of Minnesota Press, 1955.

Detchen, L. "The effect of a measure of interest factors on prediction of performance in a college social sciences comprehension examination," *J. Educ. Psychol.*, 37 (1946), 45-52.

Diamond, S. "The interpretation of test profiles," *J. Appl. Psychol.*, 32 (1948), 512-520.

Di Michael, S. G. "The professed and measured interests of vocational rehabilitation counselors," *Educ. Psychol. Measmt.*, 9 (1949), 59-72.

————, and Dabelstein, D. H. "Work satisfaction and efficiency of vocational rehabilitation counselors as related to measured interests," *Amer. Psychologist*, 2 (1947), 342 (abstr.).

Dressel, P. L. "Interests—stable or unstable?" *J. Educ. Res.*, 48 (1954), 95-102.

————, and Matteson, R. W. "The relationship between experience and interest as measured by the Kuder Preference Record," *Educ. Psychol. Measmt.*, 12 (1952), 109-116.

Duffy, Elizabeth. "A critical review of investigations employing the Allport-Vernon Study of Values and other tests of evaluative attitude," *Psychol. Bull.*, 37 (1940), 597-612.

————, and Crissy, W. J. E. "Evaluative attitudes as related to vocational interest and academic achievement," *J. Abnorm. Soc. Psychol.*, 35 (1940), 226-245.

Durnall, E. J., Jr., "Falsification of interest patterns on the Kuder Preference Record," *J. Educ. Psychol.*, 45 (1954), 240-243.

Dvorak, Beatrice J. "Differential occupational ability patterns," University of Minnesota, *Bull. Empl. Stab. Res. Inst.*, 8 (1935).

————. "The USES General Aptitude Test Battery," *Occupations*, 26 (1947), 42-44.

Eimicke, V. W. "Kuder Preference Record norms for sales trainees," *Occupations*, 28 (1949), 5-10.

Evans, M. C. "Social adjustment and interest scores of introverts and extroverts," *Educ. Psychol. Measmt.*, 7 (1947), 157-167.

Ewens, W. P. "Experience patterns as related to vocational preference," *Educ. Psychol. Measmt.*, 16 (1956), 223-231.

Feather, D. B. "The relation of personality maladjustments of 503 University of Michigan students to their occupational interests," *J. Soc. Psychol.*, 32 (1950), 71-78.

Forer, B. R. "The stability of Kuder scores in a disabled population," *Educ. Psychol. Measmt.*, 15 (1955), 166-169.

Frandsen, A. N. "Interests and general educational development," *J. Appl. Psychol.*, 31 (1947), 57-66.

————. "A note on Wiener's coding of Kuder Preference Record profiles," *Educ. Psychol. Measmt.*, 12 (1952), 137-139.

————, and Sessions, A. D. "Interests and school achievement," *Educ. Psychol. Measmt.*, 13 (1953), 94-101.

Givens, P. R. "Kuder patterns of interest as related to achievement in college science courses," *J. Educ. Res.*, 46 (1953), 627-630.

Golden, A. L., "Personality traits of drama school students," *Q. J. Speech*, 26 (1940), 564-575.

Green, R. F. "Does a selection situation induce testees to bias their answers on interest and temperament tests," *Educ. Psychol. Measmt.*, 11 (1951), 503-515.

Greene, E. B. "The Michigan Vocabulary Profile Test after ten years," *Educ. Psychol. Measmt.*, 11 (1951), 208-211.

Guba, E. G., and Getzels, J. W. "Interest and value patterns of Air Force officers," *Educ. Psychol. Measmt.*, 16 (1956), 465-470.

Guilford, J. P. (ed.). *Printed Classification Tests* ("AAF Aviation Psychology Report," No. 5.) Washington, D. C.: Government Printing Office, 1947.

Hahn, M. E., and Williams, C. T. "The measured interests of Marine Corps Women Reservists," *J. Appl. Psychol.*, 29 (1945), 198-211.

Hake, Dorothy T., and Ruedisili, C. H. "Predicting subject grades of liberal arts freshmen with the Kuder Preference Record," *J. Appl. Psychol.*, 33 (1949), 553-558.

Hanna, J. V., and Barnette, W. L., Jr. "Revised norms for the Kuder Preference Record for Men," *Occupations,* 28 (1949), 168-170.

Harris, D. "Group differences in values within a university," *J. Abnorm. Soc. Psychol.,* 29 (1934), 95-102.

Heron, A. "The effects of real-life motivation on questionnaire response," *J. Appl. Psychol.,* 40 (1956), 65-68.

Herzberg, F., and Bouton, A. "A further study of the stability of the Kuder Preference Record," *Educ. Psychol. Measmt.,* 14 (1954b), 326-331.

———, Bouton, A., and Steiner, Betty J. "Studies of the stability of the Kuder Preference Record," *Educ. Psychol. Measmt.,* 14 (1954), 90-100.

———, and Russell, Diana. "The effects of experience and change of job interest on the Kuder Preference Record," *J. Appl. Psychol.,* 37 (1953), 478-481.

Holland, J. L., Krause, A. H., Nixon, M. Eloise, and Trembath, Mary F. "The classification of occupations by means of Kuder interest profiles: I. The development of interest groups," *J. Appl. Psychol.,* 37 (1953), 263-269.

Iscoe, I., and Lucier, O. "A comparison of the Revised Allport-Vernon Scale of Values (1951) and the Kuder Preference Record (Personal)," *J. Appl. Psychol.,* 37 (1953), 195-196.

Jacobs, R. "A brief study of the relationship between scores on the Lee-Thorpe Occupational Interest Inventory and scores on the Kuder Preference Record," *Educ. Rec. Bull.,* 57 (1951), 79-85.

———, and Traxler, A. E. "Use of the Kuder in counseling with regard to accounting as a career," *J. Counsel. Psychol.,* 1 (1954), 153-158.

Kahn, D. F., and Hadley, J. M. "Factors related to life insurance selling," *J. Appl. Psychol.,* 33 (1949), 132-140.

Karn, H. W. "Differences in values among engineering students," *Educ. Psychol. Measmt.,* 12 (1952), 701-706.

Kelleher, R. T. "The effect of randomizing the Cleeton Vocational Interest Inventory items," *J. Appl. Psychol.,* 39 (1955), 357.

Klugman, S. F. "Spread of vocational interests and general adjustment status," *J. Appl. Psychol.,* 34 (1950), 108-114.

——— "A study of the interest profile of a psychotic group and its bearing on interest-personality theory," *Educ. Psychol. Measmt.,* 17 (1957), 55-64.

Kopp, T., and Tussing, L. "The vocational choices of high school students as related to scores on vocational interest inventories," *Occupations,* 25 (1947), 334-339.

Kuder, G. F. "Identifying the faker," *Pers. Psychol.,* 3 (1950), 155-167.

——— "Expected developments in interest and personality inventories," *Educ. Psychol. Measmt.,* 14 (1954), 265-271.

Lattin, G. W. "Factors associated with success in hotel administration," *Occupations,* 29 (1950), 36-39.

Lehman, R. G. "Interpretation of the Kuder Preference Record for college students of home economics," *Educ. Psychol. Measmt.,* 4 (1944), 217-223.

Levine, Phyllis R., and Wallen, R. "Adolescent vocational interests and later occupation," *J. Appl. Psychol.,* 38 (1954), 428-431.

Lewis, J. A. "Kuder Preference Record and MMPI scores for two occupational groups," *J. Consult. Psychol.,* 11 (1947), 194-201.

Lindgren, H. C. "A study of certain aspects of the Lee-Thorpe Occupational Interest Inventory," *J. Educ. Psychol.,* 38 (1947), 353-362.

Lipsett, L., and Wilson, J. W. "Do 'suitable' interests and mental ability lead to job satisfaction?" *Educ. Psychol. Measmt.,* 14 (1954), 373-380.

Long, L., and Perry, J. D. "Academic achievement in engineering related to selection procedures and interests," *J. Appl. Psychol.,* 37 (1953), 468-471.

Long, W. F. "A job preference survey for industrial applicants," *J. Appl. Psychol.,* 36 (1952), 333-337.

Longstaff, H. P. "Fakability of the Strong Interest Blank and the Kuder Preference Record," *J. Appl. Psychol.*, 32 (1948), 360-369.

MacPhail, A. H. "Interest patterns for certain degree groups on the Lee-Thorpe Occupational Interest Inventory," *J. Appl. Psychol.*, 38 (1954), 164-166.

———, and Thompson, G. R. "Interest patterns for certain occupational groups: Occupational Interest Inventory (Lee-Thorpe)," *Educ. Psychol. Measmt.*, 12 (1952), 79-89.

Magill, J. W. "Interest profiles of college activity groups; Kuder Preference Record validation," *J. Appl. Psychol.*, 39 (1955), 53-56.

Malcolm, D. D. "Which interest inventory should I use?" *J. Educ. Res.*, 44 (1950), 91-98.

Mallinson, G. G., and Crumrine, W. M. "An investigation of the stability of interests of high school students," *J. Educ. Res.*, 45 (1952), 369-383.

Mangold, B. J. "An Analysis of the Kuder Preference Record." Unpublished Master's thesis, MacMurray College, Jacksonville, Ill.

McCarthy, T. J. "Personality traits of seminarians," *Stud. Psychol. Cathol. Univer. Amer.*, 4 (1942).

Newman, J. "The Kuder Preference Record and personal adjustment: a study of tuberculosis patients," *Educ. Psychol. Measmt.*, 15 (1955), 274-280.

Paterson, D. G. "Vocational interest inventories in selection," *Occupations*, 25 (1946), 152-153.

Perry, D. K. "Forced-choice vs. L-I-D response items in vocational interest measurement," *J. Appl. Psychol.*, 39 (1955), 256-262.

Peters, E. F. "Vocational interests as measured by the Strong and Kuder inventories," *Sch. and Soc.*, 55 (1942), 453-455.

Pierce-Jones, J., and Carter, H. D. "Vocational interest measurement using a photographic inventory," *Educ. Psychol. Measmt.*, 14 (1954), 671-679.

Pintner, R. "Comparison of interests, abilities, and attitudes," *J. Abnorm. Soc. Psychol.*, 27 (1933), 351-357.

Piotrowski, Z. A. "Differences between cases giving valid and invalid inventory responses," *Ann. N. Y. Acad. Sci.*, 46 (1946), 633-638.

Reid, J. W. "Stability of measured Kuder interests in young adults," *J. Educ. Res.*, 45 (1952), 307-312.

Roeber, E. C. "The relationship between parts of the Kuder Preference Record and parts of the Lee-Thorpe Occupational Interest Inventory," *J. Educ. Res.*, 42 (1949), 598-608.

Romney, H. K. "The Kuder Literary scale as related to achievement in college English," *J. Appl. Psychol.*, 34 (1950), 40-41.

Rose, W. "A comparison of relative interest in occupational groupings and activity interests as measured by the Kuder Preference Record," *Occupations*, 26 (1948), 302-307.

Rosenberg, N. "Stability and maturation of Kuder interest patterns during high school," *Educ. Psychol. Measmt.*, 13 (1953), 449-458.

Sartain, A. Q. "Relation between scores on certain standard tests and supervisory success in an aircraft factory," *J. Appl. Psychol.*, 30 (1946), 328-332.

Schaefer, B. R. "The validity and utility of the Allport-Vernon Study of Values test," *J. Abnorm. Soc. Psychol.*, 30 (1936), 419-422.

Seashore, H. G. "Validation of the study of values for two vocational groups at the college level," *Educ. Psychol. Measmt.*, 7 (1947), 757-764.

Shaffer, R. H. "The measured interests of business school seniors," *Occupations*, 27 (1949), 462-465.

———, and Kuder, G. F. "Kuder interest patterns of medical, law, and business school alumni," *J. Appl. Psychol.*, 37 (1953), 367-369.

Silvey, H. M. "Changes in test scores after two years in college," *Educ. Psychol. Measmt.*, 11 (1951), 494-502.

Sinnett, E. R. "Some determinants of agreement between measured and expressed interests," *Educ. Psychol. Measmt.*, 16 (1956), 110-118.

Spear, G. S. "The vocational interests of engineering and non-engineering students," *J. Psychol.*, 25 (1948), 357-363.

Spranger, E. *Types of Men*. New York: Stechert, 1928.

Stefflre, B. "The reading difficulty of interest inventories," *Occupations*, 26 (1947), 95-96.

Steinberg, A. "The relation of vocational preference to emotional adjustment," *Educ. Psychol. Measmt.*, 12 (1952), 96-104.

Sternberg, C. "Interests and tendencies toward maladjustment in a normal population," *Pers. Guid. J.*, 35 (1956), 94-99.

Stewart, L. H., and Roberts, J. P. "The relationship of Kuder profiles to remaining in a teachers college and to occupational choice," *Educ. Psychol. Measmt.*, 15 (1955), 416-421.

Stone, C. L. "The personality factor in vocational guidance," *J. Abnorm. Soc. Psychol.*, 28 (1933), 274-275.

Stoops, J. A. "Stability of the measured interests of high school pupils between grades nine and eleven," *Educ. Outlook*, 27 (1953), 116-118.

Strong, E. K., Jr. *Vocational Interests of Men and Women*. Stanford: Stanford University Press, 1943.

Super, D. E. "The Kuder Preference Record in vocational diagnosis," *J. Consult. Psychol.*, 11 (1947), 184-193.

—— "The measurement of interests," *J. Counsel. Psychol.*, 1 (1954), 168-173.

Swartz, B. K., and Schwab, R. E. *Experience with Employment Tests*. ("Studies in personnel policy," No. 32.) National Industrial Conference Board, 1941.

Thompson, C. E. "Personality and interest factors in dental school success," *Educ. Psychol. Measmt.*, 4 (1944), 299-306.

—— "Selecting executives by psychological tests," *Educ. Psychol. Measmt.*, 7 (1947), 773-778.

Tiffin, J., and Phelan, R. F. "Use of the Kuder Preference Record to predict turnover in an industrial plant," *Pers. Psychol.*, 6 (1953), 195-204.

Traxler, A. E., and McCall, W. C. "Some data on the Kuder Preference Record," *Educ. Psychol. Measmt.*, 1 (1941), 253-268.

Triggs, Frances O. "A study of the relation of Kuder Preference Record scores to various other measures," *Educ. Psychol. Measmt.*, 3 (1943), 341-354.

—— "A further comparison of interest measurement by the Kuder Preference Record and the Strong Vocational Interest Blank for Men," *J. Educ. Res.*, 37 (1944a), 538-544.

—— "A further comparison of interest measurement by the Kuder Preference Record and the Strong Vocational Interest Blank for Women," *J. Educ. Res.*, 38 (1944b), 193-200.

—— "A study of the relationship of measured interests to measured mechanical aptitudes, personality, and vocabulary," *Amer. Psychologist*, 2 (1947), 296 (abstract).

Triplett, R. J. "Interests of commercial students," *J. Abnorm. Soc. Psychol.*, 29 (1934), 409-414.

Tutton, Marie E. "Stability of adolescent vocational interest," *Voc. Guid. Q.*, 3 (1955), 78-80.

United States Dept. of Labor. *Dictionary of Occupational Titles*. Washington, D. C.: Government Printing Office, 1949.

Vernon, P. E., and Allport, G. W. "A test for personal values," *J. Abnorm. Soc. Psychol.*, 26 (1931), 231-248.

Wesley, S. M., Corey, D. Q., and Stewart, Barbara M. "The intra-individual relationship between interest and ability," *J. Appl. Psychol.*, 34 (1950), 193-197.

Whiteley, P. L. "The constancy of personal values," *J. Abnorm. Soc. Psychol.*, 33 (1938), 405-408.

Wiener, D. N. "Empirical occupational groupings of Kuder Preference Record profiles," *Educ. Psychol. Measmt.*, 11 (1951), 273-279.

Wittenborn, J. R., Triggs, Frances O., and Feder, D. D. "A comparison of interest measurement by the Kuder Preference Record and the Strong Vocational Interest Blanks for Men and Women," *Educ. Psychol. Measmt.*, 3 (1943), 239-257.

Wolff, W. M., and North, A. J. "Selection of municipal firemen," *J. Appl. Psychol.*, 35 (1951), 25-29.

Yum, K. S. "Student preferences in divisional studies and their preferential activities," *J. Psychol.*, 13 (1942), 193-200.

Zuckerman, J. V. "Interest item response arrangement as it affects discrimination between professional groups," *J. Appl. Psychol.*, 36 (1952), 79-85.

———— "A note on 'interest item response arrangement'." *J. Appl. Psychol.*, 37 (1953), 94-95.

XIX

PERSONALITY, ATTITUDES, AND TEMPERAMENT

Nature and Development

A DISCUSSION of the various theories of personality which abound today in the field of psychology is hardly a topic for a book on the use of tests in vocational guidance and personnel selection. An understanding of the major theoretical positions concerning the nature and development of personality is, however, essential as background for the administration and interpretation of personality inventories and techniques, particularly the projective methods for appraising personality. Treatments of the subject which were current when most of the available tests and inventories of personality were being developed will be found in psychological works by Allport (1937) and Shaffer (1936). Murphy (1947) published a comprehensive treatment of the subject, with which he also dealt earlier in his collaborative synthesis of work in experimental social psychology (Murphy, Murphy, and Newcomb (1937)). Hunt (1944) edited a generally excellent symposium of encyclopedic dimensions and scope; the chapter on inventories was, however, unfortunately weak. For more up-to-date presentations of theories of personality Shaffer and Shoben (1956) and Hall and Lindzey (1957) are recommended. It is relevant to consider the subject here from the point of view of the vocational counselor or personnel officer; that is, from the perspective of the user of personality tests for vocational purposes.

Definitions. Some psychologists like to consider the personality as a whole, to think of it as a global unit, complex in nature but unanalyzable, a viewpoint often arrived at in the Gestaltist's protest against the unduly atomistic approaches of some behaviorists. To the scientifically minded person this point of view often seems mystical, vague, and of little value in practice. Another approach defines personality with respect to the reactions an individual arouses in others. To many psychologists this social stimulus value approach seems too limited in its empiricism, since it defines personality as a function of the evaluations of persons who may not

514

react uniformly. A third definition treats personality as a pattern of traits or ways of reacting to external stimuli. Personality is then both analyzable and unitary; moreover, the operationalism of this definition appeals to the scientist. The organismic or global approach to personality has something to contribute to this last viewpoint, however, for one can think of the individual as a more or less organized and integrated unit, in addition to conceiving the process of emotional development as one in which an attempt is made to organize a variety of reaction patterns or modes of behavior into an integrated, smoothly working whole. An individual in whom a degree of integration has taken place which is appropriate to the demands made upon him by society is an emotionally adjusted person, whereas one in whom the integration has not taken place to the extent required by the demands of the environment, or one in whom the integration has partly broken down because of demands with which he was unable to cope, is an emotionally maladjusted person.

Psychologists interested in vocational guidance and personnel work seem to have found the concept of personality as a patterning of traits most helpful in their work, for discussions of emotional or personal adjustment and of personality traits abound in the literature, and attempts to measure both general adjustment and specific traits and to ascertain their significance for vocational success have been numerous. In an otherwise excellent discussion Warren (1948) states that the vocational counselor is less concerned with the degree of integration achieved by the client than with the nature and degree of his specific characteristics, since these determine his adjustments to the environment. To the writers, this seems to be too limited a view, since adjustment to oneself is to a considerable extent a matter of the degree to which the various traits of one's personality are integrated. In a well-integrated personality the various internal needs and reactions to the various external pressures are harmonious; the person is impelled, driven, or attracted in one general direction (the opposing minor needs and pressures being controlled by the more strongly integrated unit), and he is able to function effectively. In the unintegrated or disintegrated personality, in contrast, the reaction patterns are not harmonious; the individual is pulled and driven in various directions, he experiences internal conflict, and his functioning in society is impaired. The vocational counselor and psychologist, and the personnel man who wants an effective employee, are therefore very much concerned with the degree and type of integration as well as with the specific traits which are organized into the whole personality.

Role of Personality in Education and Occupation. Approaches to the study of the significance of personality and temperament traits for success and satisfaction in school and work have generally followed one of two patterns: First, there is the clinical analysis, in which case-history material is cited in order to illustrate dynamics and document hypotheses; second, there is the psychometric appraisal in which reliance has been placed necessarily upon the imperfect instruments available for the measurement of personality. In the former approach the findings prove little because of subjectivity and lack of controls, although they stimulate speculation; in the latter, they prove little because of technical defects, although they do underline the need for better instruments. The end result is that our current knowledge of the role of personality in education and in work is impressionistic, or, when quantitative, largely superficial. It has been shown by surveys of employment records, for example, that personality problems are the most common cause of discharge from employment (Brewer, 1930; Hunt, 1936). Observation leads to the suggestion that some people considering social work as a career are motivated by an unconscious desire to solve their own problems rather than to help solve those of others. But data which would enable one either to measure the extent and nature of the characteristics involved, or to predict their interference or non-interference with success in any specific type of educational or vocational endeavor are lacking.

One reason for the lack of adequate objective evidence on the vocational and educational significance of personality traits is that students of vocational and educational adjustment have generally been interested, not in vocations or in education, but in management, aptitudes, or instruction, while students of personality have generally been interested, not in vocations or education, but in psychological theory or clinical diagnosis. Some personality inventories (e.g., Bell, Bernreuter) represent an exception to this rule, but they suffer from the defects of the inventory technique, which are most serious in the field of personality. And the more penetrating instruments (e.g., Minnesota Multiphasic, Rorschach, Thematic Apperception Test) were devised for the study of personality organization or for the diagnosis of emotional disturbances. For our purposes, what is needed is a penetrating measure applicable and applied to occupational rather than to hospitalized populations.

In view of the lack of sufficient objective evidence for a practically useful discussion of personality in vocational success and satisfaction, the results of what studies have been made will be reserved for the sections dealing with specific instruments. Some comments are, however, called for in explanation of the failure to find clear-cut relationships between personality and occupations in the few studies which have been made with the better tests.

Although it has been assumed that there should be linear correlations between certain personality traits and adjustment in some occupations—for example, social dominance and selling, submissiveness and bookkeeping, introversion and research or writing—such relationships have in fact been found in very few occupations: A somewhat higher degree of dominance is more characteristic of salesmen than clerical workers (Dodge, 1935; Paterson, 1934) , but otherwise few significant differences have been reported, as will be seen later. The fact that some real differences do exist, and that some personality measures do have a degree of clinical validity, suggests that the general failure to find occupational personality patterns may be because personality is not related to occupational choice and success in the commonly expected manner. For example, even in an occupation such as bookkeeping, a dominant individual may find outlets for this trait through advancement into supervisory and managerial positions; research may accommodate extroverts as well as introverts in sociological field studies, industrial chemistry, and the supervision of projects; and the literary extrovert may find outlets in public relations work, some forms of advertising and radio, or even fiction writing, in which formulas rather than creative imagination and insight are required. A lawyer may be a bookworm or a dramatist, a scholar or a promoter; a carpenter may work in morose silence, or exchange remarks and jibes with associates and passers-by during pauses in his activity; a packer may daydream or talk about the movies and the neighbors while placing batteries in cartons. Roe's stimulating exploratory studies seemed to confirm this hypothesis for artists (Roe, 1946a) but to contradict it for paleontologists (Roe, 1946b) .

But if personality traits and temperament are not generally related to occupational choice or success, how, if at all, do they play a part in vocations? If the hypothetical examples given above are indeed valid, then personality as defined in this discussion determines the kinds of adjustment problems which the worker will encounter and the role he will play in any occupation he enters. If he is outgoing and his associates are withdrawn, he will have one kind of difficulty, but it may be solved by changing associates rather than changing occupations; if he likes sedentary mental work rather than active contact work, he may be a writer of books on his research rather than a promoter of the financing of more research or the administrator of a research project; if he is socially dominant, the assembly worker may be the social leader or the thorn in the flesh of his fellows, rather than a follower or isolate in the group. They will all be happy or unhappy in their work, depending upon the ease with which they make the modifications which it requires in their modes of behavior or alter the role requirements to suit their personalities. That such modifications are indeed made has been demonstrated not only with nursery school children by Page (1936) and Jack (1934) , but also with college students by McLaughlin (1931) . Although these studies did not demonstrate that the underlying traits were modified, they did show that the surface modes of adjustment were changed in ways which made the persons concerned function more effectively in their social groups. Since personality traits have been defined as modes of behavior, they may be said to have been modified. Adjustments to work probably are accomplished in the same manner.

If one were to ask, then, why bother to measure personality and temperament traits in personnel and vocational guidance work, there are two answers: First, a poorly integrated personality (one with general adjustment) may have trouble adjusting in any training or work situation, and should either be screened out or given professional assistance in solving his emotional problems; second, a person with traits which are likely to make for adjustment difficulties in certain types of positions (1) may be placed in a situation which is structured so that his liabilities are turned into assets or are at least minimized, or (2) he may be given psychotherapy to modify his personality in such a way as to facilitate adjustment, or (3) environmental methods may be used to help him develop new modes of behavior which are more effective. Many instances of maladjustment which appear at first to be vocational prove, after more careful examination, to be deep-rooted in the personality (Fisher and Hanna, 1931; Korner, 1946). When this is true, treatment by changing work situations or by on-the-job counseling may be necessary. The reason for making a personality diagnosis in vocational guidance and personnel work is, then, to screen problem cases and to assist in the making of more effective adjustments.

Measures of Personality

Until about 1935 only two types of instruments for measuring personality and temperament traits were widely used in the United States: rating scales and inventories. These were first put into extensive use and popularized during World War I, when Woodworth developed his Personal Data Sheet and various experimental rating scales were used by the Army; the details of these initial attempts at personality assessment have frequently been written up and will be found in a summary by Symonds (1931). By 1935 several hundred personality inventories had been developed, but very few of them had been systematically studied after their first tentative launchings, and the sophisticated segment of the test-using public had become wary of them (Super, 1942). Rating scales also had proved disappointingly unreliable and invalid, but like personality inventories they were still used in many places either because the users were not fully aware of their limitations or, more often perhaps, because there seemed to be nothing better to use.

In the thirties, however, another type of personality measure was introduced to the United States with the development of interest in the Rorschach (1932) , a series of inkblots first devised as a projective technique by a Swiss psychiatrist by that name, and with the publication by Murray (1938) of the Thematic Apperception Test, a series of semistructured pictures about which the subject makes up stories. In these, as in other projective techniques, the examinee is presented with an ill-defined situation (inkblot, clouds, collection of toys, clay, or ambiguous pictures) and permitted to make what he will of it; the tendency is to structure it according to his own needs. As a result, and without his awareness, he reveals his personality traits. The clinician must then draw upon his own skill and insight to tease out the meaning of the figures, objects, scenes, or stories constructed by the examinee. Although methods have been devised for obtaining seemingly quantitative scores from some of these tests, they are still essentially clinical techniques rather than tests. The fact that they appear to be more penetrating than personality inventories and have captured the interest of clinicians and researchers suggests that they will in time be greatly improved and transformed into more objectively scorable tests (Buhler et al., 1948; Cronbach, 1949a,b) , but for the time at least they are limited primarily to clinical use. During World War II interest was revived in other little-used projective techniques, such as the incomplete sentences test and the unstructured situation test, the former being adapted from a type of intelligence test item. Although work is being done on them (Rotter, 1950; Rohde, 1957) , they are still in the experimental stages.

In selecting specific tests for discussion in this chapter choices are limited to two types of instruments, personality inventories and projective tests, neither of which is presently very satisfactory or valuable to the vocational counselor or personnel man, and only one of which is of much value to the counseling or personnel psychologist. Rating scales are not discussed, since they are filled out by persons other than the examinee. Space is devoted to inventories and projective tests, however, for two reasons: First, increasing use is being made of both types of measures in both personnel work and vocational counseling despite widespread disillusionment with one type and skepticism regarding the other; and, second, workers in the field need to know what has been done and is being done in the field of personality measurement, so that they may handle inquiries and take advantage of progress as it is made. Personality tests and inventories are intriguing; it is well for the potential user to know the nature of their limitations in some detail.

Two personality inventories, the *Bernreuter Personality Inventory* and the *Bell Adjustment Inventory,* which were dealt with in some detail in the previous edition of this book, have been omitted from the survey that follows. Since 1949 research on these two instruments has been quite scarce and has not indicated the need for changes in the conclusions which were reached concerning their vocational validity. Moreover, inventories which incorporate technical improvements and which have gained greater acceptance among test users have been published during the past ten years, have been subjected to substantial research, and hence command our immediate attention.

Although the vast amount of research which has accumulated on the *Minnesota Multiphasic Personality Inventory* has been largely clinical rather than vocational in nature, it is dealt with in this chapter, partly because it does have potential value for the assessment of both personality integration and traits as these relate to vocational choice and adjustment, and partly because it represents probably the most sophisticated approach to the assessment of personality and adjustment now available. Other personality inventories discussed more briefly are the novel *Edwards Personal Preference Schedule,* which features a forced-choice item format designed to control the social desirability of items, and the *Kuder Preference Record —Personal,* which yields scores in five different areas of personal and social activities supposedly related to occupational endeavors. Many other inventories might be commented on but the discussion of the above-named instruments should help the reader to examine the tests critically and to select those which are most appropriate for a given psychometric problem. If space had permitted, the *California Psychological Inventory* (Gough, 1956) and the *Guilford-Zimmerman Temperament Survey* (1949) would also have been discussed.

Two graphic projective techniques, the *Rorschach Inkblots* and the *Murray Thematic Apperception Test,* are treated in some detail, although only from the vocational counseling and personnel selection point of view, both because of the widespread interest in them and because they are now being used in occupational research. Finally, work with the *Incomplete Sentences Test* (Rotter, 1950) is briefly discussed for the same reasons.

The Minnesota Multiphasic Personality Inventory (University of Minnesota Press, 1943; Psychological Corporation, 1945). This personality inventory was developed by Hathaway and McKinley (1940) at the University of Minnesota as a clinical instrument for use in psychiatric diagnosis. They did not intend it to be a test for use in educational and vocational counseling or in personnel selection. Their purpose was to develop one personality inventory which would measure those aspects of personality which bear on psychiatric diagnosis. They wished to make more objective the judgments that are reached in a clinical situation by providing more systematic coverage of behavior and attitude items than is generally possible in an interview. But there has long been, in many counseling centers and consulting services, an interest in applying this instrument to vocational guidance and selection, which apparently arose from the belief that since it is a better clinical inventory than most others on the market, it should also be a better vocational test. This is a nonsequitur, but it has led to relevant research and has opened up possibilities which make desirable some consideration of the test in this chapter. No attempt will be made to go into its clinical validity in any detail.

Applicability. The Multiphasic was designed for use in mental hygiene and psychiatric clinics with older adolescents and adults who had at least some formal educational background. It has been administered to junior high school boys and girls, but according to Hathaway (1948) it has not been validated at that age, for which many items might conceivably have quite different significance. The authors report that several of the traits which are measured change within relatively short periods of time, as would be expected of such cyclical tendencies as depression and hypomania. Some of the other traits might be expected to be less subject to the effects of experience and of mood, as in the case of masculinity and psychopathic deviation.

Content. The MMPI consists of 550 self-descriptive items such as are found in the Bernreuter and in other personality inventories on which it was based. They are classified under 26 categories, ranging from general health and the gastrointestinal system through habits, family, occupation, sex, phobias, and morale to items designed to show whether the examinee is trying to describe himself in improbably good terms. Some items such as the first two listed below are quite innocuous, while others, like the last four, are more likely to seem somewhat offensive, at least to the relatively normal examinee:

> I like to read newspaper editorials.
> I hate to have to rush when working.
> Someone has it in for me.
> Peculiar odors come to me at times.
> At times I feel like smashing things.
> There is something wrong with my mind.

It should be noted that, although at least one of the traits measured by the MMPI may be thought of as one aspect of temperament (masculinity-femininity), two others seem to be mood-manifestations of another aspect of temperament (hypomania and depression), and still another may be the pathological extreme of a personality trait (schizophrenia), the remainder are traits made up of modes of behavior which are not usually considered components of the normal personality but rather clinical syndromes or even disease entities. On logical grounds one might therefore question the soundness of applying such measures to normally adjusted persons and drawing conclusions concerning vocational behavior, but to do so is consistent at least with Rosanoff's (1938) theory of temperament and with recent research on college populations (Drake, 1954; Drake and Oetting, 1959).

Administration and Scoring. There is no time limit for the inventory, but testing normally takes from 60 to 90 minutes, depending upon the education and adjustment level of the examinee. Instructions for administration can be found in the manual for the two forms of the test, one consisting of a set of cards administered individually and to be sorted into three stacks (True, False, Cannot Say) and the other a booklet with an IBM answer sheet.

The card test is recorded on special forms, and both are scored by means of stencils, or the booklet can be machine scored. A simplified, shorter method of scoring the individual form, based upon a notched-card and needle-sorting procedure of the Key-sort type, has been proposed by Krise (1947), who has also noted a common error in scoring the card form. He points out that failure to record "Cannot Say" items often results in spuriously high or deviant profiles (Krise, 1949). A number of scores can be derived from the MMPI, including measures on specially developed scales (Welsh and Dahlstrom, 1956), but the test is usually scored only for the following reaction patterns: hypochondriasis (Hs or 1), depression (D or 2), hysteria (Hy or 3), psychopathic deviate (Pd or 4), masculinity-femininity (Mf or 5), paranoia (Pa or 6), psychasthenia (Pt or 7), schizophrenia (Sc or 8), hypomania (Ma or 9), and social introversion (Si or 0). Although these scales were formerly referred to by their respective abbreviations (e.g., Si), current practice encourages the use of numbers (e.g., 0) to foster greater objectivity in interpretation and to facilitate the coding of profiles. In addition to the clinical scales four validity scores (question, lie, validity, and a suppressor variable), valuable in assessing the test-taking attitudes of the examinee, are obtained and included in the profile code when they indicate possible response distortions. The "suppressor variable" (K) (Meehl and Hathaway, 1946), in particular, has been useful not only in the identification of "faked" profiles but in the evaluation of an individual's defensiveness or his self-criticalness in completing the inventory (Welsh and Dahlstrom, 1956).

Caution should be exercised, however, in the interpretation of K-corrected profiles. Tyler and Michaelis (1953) found that, for a group of 56 female student teachers, the K-correction did not make the T-scores more discriminative. This conclusion agrees with the observation of Welsh and Dahlstrom (1956, p. 59) that the routine use of the K-correction in scoring the MMPI is not always warranted. They write: "Evidence is adduced, it is true, to indicate the amount of improvement over the 'uncorrected' values in discriminating criterion groups. But it must be noted that the suggested weights of K to be applied are optimal for the population used by the (test) authors. They themselves point out that the *same* weights would not very likely be found to operate in other populations." Suggestions as to what weights should be used were not made. Until data on other groups are available, probably the best procedure is to correct with K in scoring the MMPI and interpret the profile as if it had not been corrected. Whatever errors are then made should be in the direction of conservative estimations.

Because there are two forms of the MMPI, individual and group, the question of their comparability is often raised, not only because one might be more appropriate for certain groups of examinees than the other, but because the validation data for one might not be applicable to the other. For older persons, disturbed or hospital patients, and those of low education and mental ability, the test authors strongly recommend the individual form of the test. For individuals more in the normal range of background, behavior, and development they suggest the group form, since for these persons results from the two forms are practically identical. Wiener's (1947) study of 200 veterans in a guidance center, for example, yielded no differences in group trends on the two forms. Similarly, with college students, Gilliland and Colgin (1951), Cottle (1950a), and McQuary and Truax (1952) found that there were no systematic differences in scores on the two forms. In the latter two studies, however, a tendency for a majority of students to score higher on the booklet form was noted. Cottle suggested that, in making an individual diagnosis, a counselor should adjust the interpretation to account for this trend. The subjectivity of this procedure, however, might introduce more error into interpretations than would basing them upon the obtained scores.

The effect of random answers to items on the MMPI was assessed in an exceptionally well-designed and conceived study by Cottle and Powell (1951). MMPI profiles, based upon answers to the booklet form which were determined by throwing dice and reference to a table of random numbers, were essentially the same but had more scores falling above a T-score of 70 than the profiles of 400 veterans previously studied by Cottle (1950b). When all items were answered in the True response position a "psychotic" profile (high Pa, Pt, and Sc) resulted, whereas all False answers produced a "neurotic" profile (high Hs, D, and Hy). Another finding was that scale intercorrelations for the veteran group and a group of 179 males tested at the University of Kansas were considerably higher than those for the randomly answered booklets. These results suggested a number of conclusions. First, because chance or True-False MMPI's are deviate, it follows that a "normal" profile is more systematic, more non-chance, and hence may reflect the more effective operation of censoring or integrating tendencies in the personality. Second, since the intercorrelations of chance-scored scales are much lower than those based upon subjects, the intercorrelations cannot be attributed solely to item overlap; they evidently result also from communalities in personality structure as measured by the MMPI. And, third, due to the format of the inventory, a True response set yields a "psychotic" profile and a False response tendency produces a "neurotic" profile. The latter finding is consistent with the observation that neurotics often are negativistic in their general outlook on life and agrees with Berdie's (1943) finding that a "dislike" response set on the Strong Blank produces a primary interest pattern in the verbal-linguistic area which, in turn, is related to poorer adjustment.

Norms. The standardization group consisted of about 700 men and women who were typical of the general Minnesota population in age and education, but who were not under medical care at the time of testing. The norms were based on hospitalized patients (averaging about 50 in each diagnostic category) for all scales except Si, which was developed first on University of Wisconsin women (Drake, 1946) and then further validated on a male college sample (Drake and Thiede, 1948). The development of norms for psychiatric classification is difficult because of the impurity of cases in actual practice and the consequent difficulty of classification in any one category. Clinical users of a test such as this should therefore examine published data on the norm groups more carefully than is appropriate here.

There is increasing evidence that the original norms are not appropriate for use with college students. Collegiate norms are necessary not only because both college males and females differ in their scores as compared with the original norm group but because the male and female groups of students differ considerably. A codebook of normative data for college students has been made available by Drake and Oetting (1959). From a comparison of the results from a number of studies and from an analysis of possible regional differences in MMPI patterns Goodstein (1954, p. 578) concluded: "While there is a characteristic profile for the college male that differs little from college to college, it is markedly different from the characteristic profile of the noncollege male and from the characteristic profile for the college female." College males generally have peaks on Ma, Mf, Sc, Pt, Pd, and Hy, which suggests that they tend toward greater femininity in their interests, are more active, and worry more than men-in-general. Their relatively greater disregard of social dictates and norms may reflect the typical adolescent personality in our culture; at least this interpretation would agree with Hathaway and Monachesi's (1950) finding that the "normal" adolescent's MMPI is quite similar to that of the adult psychopathic deviate. The differences between the average college male and female are less in the shape of the MMPI profile than in the elevation of the overall pattern. The peaks and valleys in the mean patterns for the two groups are essentially the same, the difference being that the women's profile is generally lower. The exceptions occur on the Pa scale, on which the male and female scores practically coincide, and on the Mf scale, where the college females are less masculine than the males are feminine in their interests as compared with the general population. As noted above Goodstein found no regional differences, in either average trends or variability, for college males.

No occupational norms have been published, but some data on small, selected groups of workers have accumulated and are discussed below.

Standardization and Initial Validation. Hathaway and McKinley (1940) relied partly on the Humm-Wadsworth Temperament Scale, partly on the Bernreuter and the Bell, as sources of items for their inventory, which is essentially a pool or reservoir of items. In addition, they made up other items of their own on the basis of psychiatric manuals and clinical experience. Items were assigned to scales on the basis of the extent to which they differentiated 221 classified psychiatric patients from 724 normal persons, who had accompanied friends or relatives to the University of Minnesota Hospital, 265 college-entrance applicants at the University, and other similar persons presumed to be normal. The first clinical group consisted of 50 carefully screened hypochondriacs (McKinley and Hathaway, 1940) , a cross-validation group of 25 hypochondriacs, and control groups of 699 normals, 50 normals with physical disease, and 45 miscellaneous psychiatric cases. The hypochondriacs were significantly (C.R. = 10.9) distinguished from the normals; the other non-normal groups were also, but the overlapping in their cases was much greater (C.R. = 4.0 and 2.5) . The other clinical groups were equally small; the depressed also numbered 50 (Hathaway and McKinley, 1942) . But the tendency to distinguish appropriate groups from others was in each case cross-validated and stood the test. The various scales of the Multiphasic may therefore be said to have been empirically developed and validated against appropriate external criteria.

Reliability. As the test authors point out, there are a number of difficulties in securing adequate indices of the reliability of the MMPI: Some of the traits vary from time to time within a given person; the scales are composed of heterogeneous items which may have different reliabilities; and coefficients of consistency and stability change with the homogeneity of the groups tested and the extent to which they are normal, and hence less fluctuating in their behavior. Despite these difficulties, however, reported test-retest reliabilities have been generally favorable (Cottle, 1953), ranging from approximately .71 to .83. There are some exceptions which fall as low as .56 for Pa and .57 for Hy, but most of the coefficients are about as high as those of most personality inventories.

An empirical check on the authors' hypotheses concerning variations in scores due to intra-individual changes over a period of time was made by Layton (1954), who analyzed the MMPI scores of 15 subjects administered the booklet form once a week for 18 successive weeks. The group profile remained essentially unchanged from one week to the next, but individuals shifted considerably from occasion to occasion. The shifts were in profile elevation, however, not in the configuration or shape of the MMPI pattern. Since it is the latter which is used primarily in analysis and diagnosis, the stability of the total profile therefore seems sufficient for use with individuals. It would nevertheless be desirable to obtain independent ratings of intra-individual changes on MMPI traits and relate these to changes in actual scores. Although such ratings are themselves not very reliable, if made each time by the same person they would presumably have a sufficiently high degree of reliability as indices of increase or decrease in the type of behavior under study. A more objective basis would thus be provided for identifying the variations attributable to the individual and to the unreliability of the test.

Validity. The *clinical* validity of the MMPI has been the subject of numerous studies, but because of its extensive nature and tangential relevance for the vocational use of the inventory, it will not be reviewed and summarized here, a task which has been aptly performed by Cottle (1953). The competent counselor and personnel worker will familiarize himself with this fund of information. To use the MMPI properly and effectively with individuals within the normal range of behavior or to identify those aspects of behavior which are predominantly abnormal in nature, as in vocational rehabilitation counseling, a knowledge of deviant patterns and trends is not only desirable but essential. For a general introduction to the clinical significance of the MMPI, its nature and use, Welsh and Dahlstrom's (1956) compilation of sixty-six articles, including previously unpublished material on the development of the inventory, is a valuable source. Case history summaries, categorized by profile code high and low points, for 968 cases have been compiled in Hathaway and Meehl's (1951) *Atlas for the Clinical Use of the MMPI,* a handbook to which continual reference should be made. And Drake and Oetting (1959) have made available a compilation of many carefully made observations of college students characteristics related to MMPI profiles.

The vocational validity of the MMPI is far less well-established than the clinical validity of the instrument, partly because fewer studies of the relationship of MMPI scores to occupational choice, success, and satisfaction have been conducted, but mostly because the studies which have been made have dealt with single scores rather than patterns of scores. They have investigated the relationship of profile elevation, or the *absolute* magnitude of scores, to vocational criteria but have largely neglected the relationship of profile shape, or the *relative* magnitude of scores with respect to each other, to these same criteria. In general clinical work, however, as Hathaway and Meehl note (in Welsh and Dahlstrom, 1956, p. 137), "the shape of the total profile is of greater significance than the elevation of single scores. To get the most out of this instrument, the clinician must treat the data in a configural rather than an *atomistic* fashion." The failure to find relationships between the MMPI and vocational behavior in some of the studies discussed below can probably be attributed to lack of emphasis upon the configural approach. A notable exception to this is a study by Drake and Oetting (1957) on the prediction of academic achievement.

Achievement criteria of various types are of particular interest to vocational guidance and personnel workers, who need to know not only the effectiveness of the test in screening maladjusted persons who may need special attention, but also the significance, if any, of the various personality trends which are related to educational-vocational success. Because they provide this kind of empirical data on the predictive validity of MMPI patterns for a criterion of college grade point average, as well as a model for configural research, the investigations by Drake and Oetting (1957, 1959) are unique.

In a previous study Drake (1954) had found that clients at a university counseling center, who were described as "lacking academic motivation" by their counselors, typically had MMPI profiles with the pattern 89-0 (Ma-Sc paired high with Si low) more frequently than a large group of unselected students. Also, scale 5 (Mf) occurred less frequently in the client group than would be expected from its incidence in the general student body. From these findings two hypotheses were formulated for testing: First, it was predicted that students with the 89-0 pattern (5 not coded) would obtain lower grade point averages their first semester in college than the total freshman group; and second, it was predicted that students with the 89-0 pattern, but with 5 coded high, would not have academic averages less than the total group of freshmen. Both hypotheses were supported by the results: The "lacking academic motivation" group (89-0 pattern), which had more masculine (5 not coded) and hence more deviant interests in terms of the predominantly feminine (people, language, and ideas) college culture, received lower grades than the total freshman group; in contrast, the "intense academic motivation" group with more feminine interests (5 coded high) actually excelled the larger group of freshmen in grade point average, probably because their personality tendencies were such that they compensated for the low academic motivation level. These considerations suggest that, although MMPI patterns have some predictive validity for achievement criteria, they are nevertheless difficult to identify. As Drake and Oetting (1957, p. 246) point out: "In order to predict behavior for a group, the group must be selected on the basis of as many underlying traits as possible. In this study three scales were used to select the group and it was still necessary to include a fourth scale as a suppressor in order to predict the criterion."

Other studies on the prediction of educational achievement or success with the MMPI have yielded at best only moderately positive results; in general, they have produced negative findings. Frick (1955) included the MMPI in a multiple regression equation with the A.C.E. and was thereby able to improve the prediction of academic achievement over that yielded by aptitude data alone. The overall multiple correlation, for the group of 267 University of California freshmen women in the study, when both intellectual and non-intellectual variables were included as predictors, was .64 as compared to the zero-order correlation of .48 between the A.C.E. and the criterion (grade point average for the freshman year). With very small samples ($N = 11$) of upper and lower quarter junior year medical students at the University of Minnesota, who were matched on the A.C.E. for scholastic aptitude, Schofield (1953) found that the poorer students tended to peak on the Hy, Pd, and Sc scales of the MMPI, but that an elevation on any one scale was not predictive of inferior academic performance. Hovey (1954) concluded that the relationship between supervisors' ratings of the ward-practice of student nurses and their scores on the Hs, D, Pd, and Pt scales might be curvilinear, with the least successful trainees obtaining MMPI scores in the range 55-59, but he did not offer an explanation for the finding. Other attempts to predict achievement with the MMPI have been less productive, as in studies by Glaser (1951) of medical students, Weisgerber (1951) of student nurses, and Michaelis and Tyler (1951) of student teachers, none of which yielded sufficiently high correlations with various criteria of educational success to be useful in prediction. Similarly, although they identified certain MMPI signs which were predictive of success in practice teaching, Gough and Pemberton (1952) were unable consistently to differentiate more from less successful student teachers by their scores on single scales. A comparison by Morgan (1952) of achievers and nonachievers, who were equated for scholastic aptitude, indicated no differences on the MMPI clinical scales; achievers scored higher, however, on specially devised scales which purportedly measure such traits as optimism, dependability, and self-confidence, thus suggesting that variations on these more normal personality dimensions rather than deviations in syndromes of abnormal behavior may be related to achievement.

New scales, developed primarily to tap this normal range of behavior as it might be revealed by responses to the MMPI, have met with varied degrees of success as valid measures of nonintellective achievement factors, work attitudes, and predictors of job success and failure. Altus (1948) developed a twenty-five item achievement scale which on cross-validation correlated .40 with grades in an elementary psychology course and .39 with honor point ratio. Students who attained higher grades were characterized by their MMPI responses as more socially introverted and masculine (contrary to Drake and Oetting's findings), but evidently they were also more intelligent since the achievement scale correlated .21 with verbal aptitude. Even less promising results were obtained with an achievement scale developed by Clark (1953), who found not only that certain items which were common with Altus' scale were scored in the opposite direction but that an initial correlation of .282 with honor point ratio shrank to .064 on cross-validation. Using over- and under-achieving groups, as defined by the difference between A.C.E. scores and college grades, McQuary and Truax (1955) made an item analysis of the MMPI. Twenty-four items, including only 3 from Altus' scale, were selected for an experimental achievement key which was then cross-validated on another group. Cut-off scores identified 54.5 percent of the underachievers and 52.8 percent of the overachievers in this group when the entire distribution was used. When intelligence was partially controlled, however, by ignoring the extremes of the distribution, the percentages increased to 77.2 for underachievers and 90.9 for overachievers, presumably because those of very low or very high ability have less opportunity to under- or over-achieve. Achievement scales for the MMPI which are effective predictors of academic performance can thus be developed, but evidently only on local groups since the item content and validity varies from one setting to another.

To determine whether MMPI items could be used to measure work attitudes prognostic of desirable job performance and adjustment Tydlaska and Mengel (1953) had seven judges select 58 items which would indicate unfavorable dispositions toward work. These were then reduced in number to the 37 items which were most differentiating between a group of 50 civilian employees who had completed two or more years of "satisfactory work" (based upon merit ratings), and a group of 60 "poor work attitude" airmen, which included 43 AWOL cases, 7 disciplinary problems, 8 malingerers, and 2 miscellaneous offenders. A critical score of 13, based upon unit weights for the total set of items, correctly identified approximately 88 per cent of the employees and 85 per cent of the airmen. The scale was then cross-validated by Tesseneer and Tydlaska (1956) on groups of "poor work attitude" and "good work attitude" students ($N=26$ for each group), which were matched on mean I.Q., mean age, and proportion of freshmen and sophomores. These two groups had been constituted by asking faculty members to classify students they knew very well on the work attitude criterion. The work attitude (Wa) scale differentiated the two groups in the expected direction at a high level of significance. Further validation is obviously necessary, however, before the scale will be ready for other than experimental use. Not only were the standardization and initial validation groups small, but they were probably quite heterogeneous in personality characteristics other than work attitudes, which could have contributed to the differences between them. Until relationships with known variables are determined, it cannot be said what the scale is measuring.

Two other new scales for the MMPI have been reported, both of which pertain to the prediction of job performance. Gowan and Gowan (1955) made an extensive analysis of all MMPI items which distinguished between two groups of prospective and experienced teachers ($N = 200$ for each group), one of which had been judged more "able" than the other. This empirical approach produced a teacher prognosis scale which not only was highly reliable (.90) but which was relatively valid. It correlated .54 (uncorrected) and .75 (corrected) with instructors' ratings of probable teaching effectiveness for an independent group of 200 teaching candidates, and .72 (uncorrected) and .83 (corrected) with similar ratings for an additional student group. Relationships with other tests indicated moderate concurrent validity. Using a different approach, Wiener (1948) devised subtle and obvious keys for 5 MMPI scales (D, Hy, Pd, and Ma) which he related to the success and failure of counseled veterans in school and on-the-job training. Only the obvious key, composed of items which are relatively easy to detect as indicative of emotional disturbance, was associated with the criterion; veterans who scored high on it tended to fail their training programs. Because the successful and unsuccessful veterans were not matched on intelligence, however, the latter's failure to complete training might be as much related to this factor as to personality difficulties or deviations, especially since Wiener (178) reported that less intelligent persons score higher on the obvious key.

Prevocational or educational differences were studied in two investigations by Lough (1946, 1947). In the first she found that 185 unmarried women undergraduate students of education were a relatively stable group with a very slight tendency for elevation on Ma and that there were no significant differences between those preparing to be elementary or music teachers. In the second paper she reported findings for 300 unmarried women undergraduates, including the original group and 115 liberal arts college students. A slight tendency toward a peak on Ma was found in the new group as in the original, but, if Hathaway and Monachesi's (1950) data are generalizable, this trend is characteristic of adolescents, who typically obtain a double-spike pattern with high points on Pd and Ma. There were no differences between curricular groups, to which nurses and the various liberal arts majors were added. She concluded: "It is not a useful instrument for differentiating between those who are more suited for one occupation than another. The primary value of the MMPI seems to be to give some insight into the emotional life of the individual and to detect those who may be in need of psychological or psychiatric counseling." It should be noted that her first conclusion is based not on success but simply on choice (a somewhat questionable criterion, since some who choose fail and some who might succeed do not choose), and that her second conclusion is based on the evidence of other studies.

Sternberg (1955) studied prevocational personality differences with a somewhat novel approach which was designed to identify interest, value, and personality factors characteristic of students enrolled in various college academic curricula. Kuder Vocational, Allport-Vernon, and MMPI scores for groups of 30 males majoring in biochemistry (premedical), chemistry, economics, English, history, mathematics, music, political science, and psychology were intercorrelated and factor analyzed, with subsequent comparisons of the factor scores for the nine subject areas both separately and in combinations. Seven factors were extracted, but only five differentiated the fields of study. Of these, three had loadings on MMPI scales: Mf correlated .52 with the positive pole of a factor identified as *Aesthetic Communications* (English and music) vs. *Practical Science* (biochemistry and psychology); D, Pd, Mf, Pa, Pt, and Sc had negative correlations with another bipolar factor termed the *Go-getter* (economics and psychology) vs. *Passive Aesthete* (English and music); and, Pd, Sc, and Ma were positively loaded on a third bipolar factor named the *Driven Extrovert* (economics and political science) vs. *The Pure Scientist* (chemistry and mathematics). Although the factor designations are somewhat unusual and even picturesque, the loadings of the MMPI scales are explicit and reasonable. College males with more feminine interests or, probably more accurately, interests in people, language, and ideas, usually prefer literary and musical activities in which aesthetic values are readily expressed. Similarly, individuals with these interests, in conjunction with tendencies toward maladjustment as indicated by a generally elevated MMPI profile, typically have artistic preferences and aesthetic values, particularly the latter as an expression of interest in form and harmony. And extroversion, high activity level, and superficiality in interpersonal relationships (as indicated by higher Sc scores) characterize persons with material values and persuasive interests, which often lead to preparation for business, law, and related occupations.

Two other studies of differences between college major groups, neither of which used the configural approach, present conflicting results. Striking similarities, with only a few significant differences, were obtained by Clark (1953) in an extensive analysis of 707 male and 763 female college students distributed in a variety of educational curricula. In contrast, Norman and Redlo (1952), presumably because they used seniors and graduate students who were more homogeneous in personality characteristics within a major group, found a number of significant differences, most of which would be expected from the nature of the course of study. Psychology and sociology majors had high points on Pd and Ma; mathematics, chemistry, and physics students scored high on D but low on Pd, Ma, and Sc; engineers were not high on any scale, being low on Pd, Ma, Hy, and Mf; anthropology students were characterized by high Mf; business administration majors had a high point on Ma with low points on D and Mf; and, art and music students had peaks on Mf, Hy, Sc, Pd, Ma, and Pa, and generally had the most elevated or maladjusted profile. Because the number in each of these classifications is small (highest $N = 29$ engineers), the results must be interpreted as tentative only; they do not constitute norms for college major groups but do suggest some trends, if they are further validated, in the relationship between personality and preoccupational choice.

Students in more specialized training programs than college curricula were the subjects of three further studies on the relationship of the MMPI to vocational choice. The first was an investigation conducted by Wiener and Simon (1950) of 36 veterans who planned to become embalmers. They were compared on mean scores for the various scales with an unmatched "control" group of veterans who did not have the same vocational goal. The embalmer trainees were significantly higher on only the Hs and Ma scales, whereas the controls obtained higher scores on D, Mf, and Pa. The authors concluded that the findings do not support the generally held hypothesis that persons interested in dead bodies tend toward shallow emotionality, femininity, and compulsiveness, but do suggest the reasonable conclusion that individuals who want to become embalmers have an overconcern with personal health (elevated Hs) which, through projection, may be the basis of their interest in preparing the dead for burial. As interesting as this interpretation is, however, it needs to be further documented.

The second investigation involved a comparison of women students in occupational therapy and nursing programs. Schmidt (1951) was able to differentiate the two groups, with the nurses scoring higher on Hs, Pd, Pt, and Ma, when the raw scores were not K corrected; with the correction, however, the only difference was on the K scale, the score being higher for the occupational therapists. Whether the differences on the uncorrected scores were due more to inequalities between the groups in socioeconomic status than in personality characteristics was not determined, but this seems plausible because K is related to status, the occupational therapy group had higher K scores, and no differences were found when K was added and the groups were, in effect, equated on this variable. In the third study Mahler (1955) compared student nurses with members of a women's physical education class at Drake University and found that the former scored higher only on the Hs scale.

Change in occupational choice was the criterion used by LaBue (1955) to determine whether there is a relationship between personality traits and persistence of interest in teaching. Groups of males and females, who applied for admission to a teacher preparation program at Syracuse University, were defined as persistent if they completed the course of study and subsequently accepted a teaching position. They were designated as nonpersistent if after applying for admission (at which time the MMPI was administered) they did not matriculate. The mean scores for both sexes in the persistent and nonpersistent groups were less than 70 on all MMPI scales, but those who did not follow their initial interest in teaching had a greater percentage of scores above 70. Significant differences occurred, however, on only the Pd scale for men and the Pd and Ma scales for women: Men who persisted with teaching as a career tended to have attitudes toward social standards and authority more like the typical individual; women teachers, in addition to this tendency, were more like the average female in general activity level. These personality characteristics seem to agree fairly well with the commonly held stereotype of teaching as an occupation and are consistent, for the women at least, with Black's (1953) description of high and low scoring college females on the Ma scale.

Occupational differences have not been extensively studied and the data which have accumulated are based upon groups of small numbers. The interpretation of MMPI patterns as characteristic of certain occupations should therefore be tempered with the realization that norms on occupational groups of sufficient size are not available and present findings can be considered at best as only tentative. Daniels and Hunter (1949) presented mean scores on the Mf, Pd, Sc, and Ma scales for 26 occupations, a majority of which contained from about 5 to 13 members with only one having as many as 33. These scores were interpreted as "work needs" which the "personality demands" of the occupation could satisfy, but from the report it was not clear whether this was supposition or fact since there was no indication whether the veterans who were studied had only expressed a desire to enter the occupations or were actually engaged in them. Moreover, not only is the interpretation of MMPI scores as "work needs" rather unique but since it is not documented it seems to add only surplus meaning when empirical evidence is needed.

Women clerical workers, department store saleswomen, and women optical workers were tested by Verniaud (1946), the samples numbering 40, 27 and 30 respectively. The workers came from several different offices and stores, and from several departments of one factory. The profiles of the two white-collar occupational groups differed very little from the norms, except for a somewhat low point on Hs for the clerical workers and a high point on Mf for the salesclerks, but the optical workers were decidedly elevated on Ma and Pt with slightly less accentuated peaks on Pa and Pd.

In view of what is known of the interest patterns of women clerical workers, it is not surprising to find them a normal group, resembling women in general. The masculinity of department-store salesclerks is understandable, although they deal largely with feminine items, because their work is a relatively impersonal type of sales, being considerably more thing- than person-oriented. This interpretation, however, would bear further investigation.

The findings concerning the factory women raise several questions, for they may be peculiar to the local situation (one company in one town), to the occupation (blocking, roughing, emery grinding, polishing, finishing jobs), to the socio-occupational level, or to the population (e.g., a minority group). There is no description of the status of the women but the factory workers were all employed on war jobs (Navy contracts), whereas the others were engaged in more normal, peacetime operations rather than in war industries. This suggests that they may have been a quite atypical group of women workers: drifters, thrill seekers, and others who might flock to a boom industry on a temporary basis. Verniaud does not go into this possibility, but does state that "In terms of the expected meanings of the characteristics (MMPI scales), we would expect these workers as a group to be restless, 'full of plans', alternating between enthusiasm and over-productivity in energy output and moods of depression, more inclined toward anxieties and compulsive behavior than the average individual, disinclined or unable to concentrate for long periods on one task, somewhat oversensitive or suspicious of the good-will of others, somewhat more inclined than the average woman to disregard social mores." Only three sample case studies are presented in this report of her master's thesis, but Verniaud states that the test profiles are borne out by case-study material which she collected in the thesis. Before any vocational guidance or selection applications are made of such findings, it would be imperative to ascertain whether the factory workers whom she studied are in fact typical of women factory workers in general, this type of occupation only, only this plant at this time, or merely of women war-plant workers.

Life insurance salesmen and women social workers, 50 subjects in each group, were studied with the MMPI by Lewis (1947), each group being compared with the norm group of the same sex. The insurance salesmen were significantly higher on D, Hy, Pd, Mf, Pa, and Ma, but the highest mean T-score was only 58.1 on the last-named scale. The social workers were significantly higher on D and Hy, but significantly lower on Mf, Hs, Pt, and Sc, their psychological sophistication being perhaps a contributing factor to their low scores. For this reason pre-training tests, evaluated after employment in the field, would have provided more convincing evidence of occupational differentiation in this type of work. Lewis also found that those whose interests, as measured by the Kuder Preference Record—Vocational, were least appropriate for their work, tended in each occupation to be the least well adjusted, but the differences were not clearly significant in most comparisons.

Fifty professional actors and fifty non-actors were compared by Chyatte (1949), the two groups being matched within 3 years on age and 5 Otis I.Q. points. Significant differences indicated that the actors scored higher on Pd, Mf, and Ma, and lower on Hy. This is a quite likely personality pattern for actors, at least as they are generally stereotyped, since it reveals tendencies to "act out" anxiety and hostility; to have more feminine interests, i.e., be interested more in the cultural aspects of life, such as language and ideas; and, to be somewhat egocentric, independent, and strongly motivated. Adjectival descriptions (found by Hathaway and Gough and reported by Black, 1953), which are characteristic of persons (such as actors) with high points on Pd and Ma include, among others, "sociable," "frank," "individualistic," "irresponsible," "adventurous," and "undependable." These traits may be ameliorated to some extent by the greater femininity of actors but would probably still be predominant, particularly since they would be supported by the low scores on Hy.

Job satisfaction has not been studied by means of this inventory, although the findings just reviewed have implications for that topic if confirmed by other studies.

Use of the Minnesota Multiphasic Personality Inventory in Counseling and Selection. The future promise of the Minnesota Multiphasic in educational and vocational diagnosis would seem to lie in the validation of specific personality patterns rather than the differentiation of preoccupational and occupational groups by scores on single scales. Clinical work with the inventory has indicated that it is primarily the configuration of scores which is significant in making accurate and valid predictions about behavior, yet such a total profile analysis approach has not been used to determine its value in the vocational setting. As we have seen, the test has little validity for differential vocational counseling or classification at present: Occupational differences are either nonexistent or, when present, questionable because of too few cases and too great variation within groups; new scales to measure achievement and work attitudes have not been successfully or meaningfully cross-validated; and there is little or no evidence on the relationship of the MMPI to job success and satisfaction. Consequently, all that could be written at this stage of its development would concern its clinical significance rather than its vocational implications. Such material has a very important place in a manual of clinical psychometrics, but not in a book designed for the evaluation of tests for the prediction of vocational success and satisfaction. Not, that is, until more is known about the vocational significance of clinical data.

In schools and colleges the Minnesota Multiphasic Personality Inventory may be useful as a device for screening students in need of further study and perhaps of counseling in relation to personality adjustment; more often, it is helpful as a diagnostic device following such screening by other less elaborate inventories or after referral by other staff members, to provide the counselor with some orientation to the nature and extent of the maladjustment. It is not recommended as an aid to vocational counseling except when the counselor is a counseling or clinical psychologist and the client is a maladjusted person in need of help with an immediate problem of vocational choice or adjustment.

In guidance and employment centers the Multiphasic has more of a place because the larger number of persons with personality problems who come to such centers makes careful screening imperative. This inventory may therefore be helpful in a secondary test battery when a shorter routinely administered personality inventory, the psychometrist's or preliminary interviewer's observations, or the referring source suggests the presence of psychopathology. Positive findings would then be an indication of need for therapy beyond the scope of the typical vocational or placement counselor, through referral to a clinical or counseling psychologist or a psychiatrist, or for co-operative work with a psychotherapist, the vocational counselor helping the client to make a vocational adjustment which contributes to his general adjustment by making one aspect of his life that much more successful and satisfying. Differential occupational prediction on the basis of Multiphasic scores, such as is suggested and practiced by some counselors, is still premature except in a highly tentative way and on the basis of confirmation by case-history material. In evaluating persons being considered for referral for employment or referred for evaluation by employers the inventory may have some value as a screening or selective-placement device, but in view of what is known about the distortion and faking of scores on other inventories, the results in such cases should be very critically viewed.

In business and industry this inventory may be helpful as a means of screening out maladjusted employment applicants, as those who make high scores are extremely likely to have personality problems; but low scores may include persons who are successful at disguising their true characteristics. It may also be of use in personnel evaluation, either for the selective placement of handicapped persons or for the improvement of supervisory and executive functioning. In this type of work the interpretation should be done only by a qualified clinical or counseling psychologist, as the results might otherwise be bad both for the individual and for the company, and referral facilities should be available if psychotherapy is indicated. The inventory may prove to have value in the selection of salesmen and other contact personnel, and perhaps with other types of employees, but local validation and normative studies must be carried out before such use is possible.

The Edwards Personal Preference Schedule (The Psychological Corporation, 1954, 1959). A relative newcomer in a long line of paper-and-pencil personality inventories, the Edwards PPS was devised, according to its manual, "primarily as an instrument for research and counseling purposes, to provide quick and convenient measures of a number of relatively independent *normal* personality variables." The measures of the normal personality are based upon fifteen needs defined by Murray (1938) and include the following:

1. *Achievement* (ach): To do one's best, to be successful, to accomplish tasks requiring skill and effort, to be a recognized authority, to accomplish something of great significance, to do a difficult job well, to solve difficult problems and puzzles, to be able to do things better than others, to write a great novel or play.

2. *Deference* (def): To get suggestions from others, to find out what others think, to follow instructions and do what is expected, to praise others, to tell others that they have done a good job, to accept the leadership of others, to read about great men, to conform to custom and avoid the unconventional, to let others make decisions.

3. *Order* (ord): To have written work neat and organized, to make plans before starting on a difficult task, to have things organized, to keep things neat and orderly, to make advance plans when taking a trip, to organize details of work, to keep letters and files according to some system, to have

meals organized and a definite time for eating, to have things arranged so that they run smoothly without change.

4. *Exhibition* (exh): To say witty and clever things, to tell amusing jokes and stories, to talk about personal adventures and experiences, to have others notice and comment upon one's appearance, to say things just to see what effect it will have on others, to talk about personal achievements, to be the center of attention, to use words that others do not know the meaning of, to ask questions others cannot answer.

5. *Autonomy* (aut): To be able to come and go as desired, to say what one thinks about things, to be independent of others in making decisions, to feel free to do what one wants, to do things that are unconventional, to avoid situations where one is expected to conform, to do things without regard to what others may think, to criticize those in positions of authority, to avoid responsibilities and obligations.

6. *Affiliation* (aff) : To be loyal to friends, to participate in friendly groups, to do things for friends, to form new friendships, to make as many friends as possible, to share things with friends, to do things with friends rather than alone, to form strong attachments, to write letters to friends.

7. *Intraception* (int) : To analyze one's motives and feelings, to observe others, to understand how others feel about problems, to put one's self in another's place, to judge people by why they do things rather than by what they do, to analyze the behavior of others, to analyze the motives of others, to predict how others will act.

8. *Succorance* (suc) : To have others provide help when in trouble, to seek encouragement from others, to have others be kindly, to have others be sympathetic and understanding about personal problems, to receive a great deal of affection from others, to have others do favors cheerfully, to be helped by others when depressed, to have others feel sorry when one is sick, to have a fuss made over one when hurt.

9. *Dominance* (dom) : To argue for one's point of view, to be a leader in groups to which one belongs, to be regarded by others as a leader, to be elected or appointed chairman of committees, to make group decisions, to settle arguments and disputes between others, to persuade and influence others to do what one wants, to supervise and direct the actions of others, to tell others how to do their jobs.

10. *Abasement* (aba) : To feel guilty when one does something wrong, to accept blame when things do not go right, to feel that personal pain and misery suffered does more good than harm, to feel the need for punishment for wrong doing, to feel better when giving in and avoiding a fight than when having one's own way, to feel the need for confession of errors, to feel depressed by inability to handle situations, to feel timid in the presence of superiors, to feel inferior to others in most respects.

11. *Nurturance* (nur) : To help friends when they are in trouble, to assist others less fortunate, to treat others with kindness and sympathy, to forgive others, to do small favors for others, to be generous with others, to sympathize with others who are hurt or sick, to show a great deal of affection toward others, to have others confide in one about personal problems.

12. *Change* (chg) : To do new and different things, to travel, to meet new people, to experience novelty and change in daily routine, to experiment and try new and different things, to eat in new and different places, to try new and different jobs, to move about the country and live in different places, to participate in new fads and fashions.

13. *Endurance* (end): To keep at a job until it is finished, to complete any job undertaken, to work hard at a task, to keep at a puzzle or problem

until it is solved, to work at a single job before taking on others, to stay
up late working in order to get a job done, to put in long hours of work
without distraction, to stick at a problem even though it may seem as if no
progress is being made, to avoid being interrupted while at work.

14. *Heterosexuality* (het): To go out with members of the opposite sex, to engage in social activities with the opposite sex, to be in love with someone
of the opposite sex, to kiss those of the opposite sex, to be regarded as
physically attractive by those of the opposite sex, to participate in discussions about sex, to read books and plays involving sex, to listen to or to
tell jokes involving sex, to become sexually excited.

15. *Aggression* (agg) : To attack contrary points of view, to tell others what
one thinks about them, to criticize others publicly, to make fun of others,
to tell others off when disagreeing with them, to get revenge for insults, to
become angry, to blame others when things go wrong, to read newspaper
accounts of violence.

These highly operational definitions of the "manifest" needs, which are
merely rewordings of the items, reflect Edward's approach to the development of this new instrument, particularly in designing items which minimize the operation of the social desirability factor in the responses of
examinees to the inventory. It is somewhat unfortunate therefore that,
although the item content was largely derived from Murray's need constructs, the variables were termed "manifest needs." This designation has
introduced more confusion than clarity into the interpretation of scores
to clients, particularly by less experienced counselors, not only because
clients often have difficulty in understanding what is meant by "needs"
but because the items themselves, at least superficially, elicit a person's
preferences rather than needs or states of deprivation. When scores on the
fifteen variables are interpreted to clients as "needs" their misunderstanding seems to focus upon whether this means that they are wanting in
certain areas of adjustment to others and the environment, or that they
have some needs which are stronger than others but which they are
satisfying. Since neither the manual nor the accumulated research data
on the EPPS provides answers to these questions, it is probably best to
interpret scores as indicating the relative strength of personal preferences
for a variety of different activities and interpersonal relationships. Until
more extensive evidence on the inventory's validity is available, this procedure should yield interpretations which are as parsimonious and objective as can be made at present, and hence less subject to error, since they
are based upon the face or content validity of the items rather than the
surplus meanings often associated with the concept of needs.

Applicability. The emphasis in constructing the EPPS was upon the
measurement of those aspects of the personality in which relatively normal
people would differ: variations in personal preferences within the normal
range of behavior rather than deviations from some norm in the direction

of maladjustment. In this respect, then, the EPPS is like the Kuder Personal and unlike the Minnesota Multiphasic. And, because of its focus upon the various behavioral expressions of the normal instead of abnormal personality, appropriate settings for its use are the vocational advisory service, secondary school guidance office, university counseling service, and personnel office. It is not designed, as is the Minnesota Multiphasic, primarily for use in mental hygiene and psychiatric clinics or mental hospitals. As would be expected, the item content is generally less offensive to the normal person than that of the Minnesota Multiphasic and is therefore probably more desirable for use with students and job applicants, particularly those at the high school and college levels, since innocuous items are more likely to promote more sincere test-taking attitudes, prompt fewer extraneous remarks in group testing situations, and produce more accurate self-reports in response to items which are assumed to have *a priori* validity. Although no studies of the reading difficulty of the EPPS have been reported, it has been used with high school seniors, who evidently did not have trouble in understanding the items, and could probably be used with high school juniors and sophomores. Below these levels not only the difficulty of the item content but also the nature of the items might restrict the applicability of the inventory, for activity and experience preferences are asked for which the younger person has not had the opportunity to develop. There would not seem to be an upper limit of applicability for the EPPS, however, the variables being quite relevant to the feelings and attitudes of the middle-aged and mature adult.

Content.   There are 225 items in the EPPS, each of which has two self-descriptive statements arranged in a forced-choice format, such as in the following example:

   A. I like to talk about myself to others.

   B. I like to work toward some goal that I have set for myself.

All of the statements are in the first person singular, and most of them use either *like* or *feel* as an active, transitive verb. Each of the statements is supposedly matched with the other on the extent to which they are socially desirable, and each of the statements for the fifteen personality variables is paired twice with statements for the other variables. The examinee is instructed to indicate which of the two statements is more characteristic of what he likes or how he feels. It is to be noted that a factor analysis of EPPS items by Levonian, Comrey, Levy, and Proctor (1959) yielded item groups which differed from Edwards', and that inter-item correlations in Edwards' scales were low, e.g., only about 35 percent of the need-Achievement items had r's of .10 or above, significant at the .01 level.

Administration and scoring.   The items of the EPPS are printed in a reusable booklet with covering instructions, which can be administered either individually or to large groups. Responses are recorded by the examinee on a separate answer sheet. For the average college student testing time is approximately 40 minutes, but is probably somewhat longer at lower educational levels. There is no time limit, but the Manual stresses that the examinee should be encouraged to work rapidly, indicating his initial reactions as much as possible.

Although outlined in detail with each step fully explained, the scoring process is nevertheless complicated and errors can easily be made. Until machine-scoring is available, extreme caution must therefore be exercised. At present all scoring is by hand with the aid of an especially designed template which is used for obtaining one of two special scores in addition to those for the fifteen personality variables. The first of these special scores is a measure of consistency in response to fifteen items which are repeated twice throughout the inventory, e.g., item 1 is the same as item 151, item 25 is the same as 175, etc. If the respondent answers the duplicated items in the same way each time he encounters them, then he receives a higher consistency score. Based upon the probability of making identical choices more frequently than would be expected on the basis of chance, a cut-off score of 11 was selected for the consistency variable: If a subject obtains this score or higher, his responses would be due to chance only 6 times out of 100; if his score is less than 9, there is reason to doubt the validity of his scores on the personality variables. The second additional score, which is derived from the answer sheet, is a measure of profile stability. It indicates the degree of correlation between partial scores for each of the fifteen variables measured by the schedule. The manual gives the distribution of profile stability coefficients for a random sample of 299 cases, the average r being .74, but does not further clarify the meaning and possible use of this special score.

Norms. The original normative sample consisted of 749 college women and 760 college men, enrolled in various liberal arts curricula in a number of different colleges and universities. Separate norms are reported for males and females, since the former had significantly higher means on Achievement, Autonomy, Dominance, Heterosexuality, and Aggression and the latter scored higher on Deference, Affiliation, Intraception, Succorance, Abasement, Nurturance, and Change. All subjects were high school graduates with some college training (amount not reported in the manual), but they differed in age. Most of the sample were in the age range 15 to 29; a significant few, however, were older, falling in the range 30 to 59. Whether these variations in age are important enough to warrant age norms is yet to be determined; differences might be expected, however, on some of the variables, such as Heterosexuality, Change, and possibly Aggression. At the lower end of the age distribution, Klett (1957a) found that separate norms were necessary for high school students.

The manual (p. 6) states that "No attempt will be made to define precisely just what constitutes a high or low score on any of the personality variables. It is felt that this is something that each user of the EPPS can determine best for the particular group under observation and in terms of his own objectives." Certain guides are provided, however, as approximate criteria for the evaluation of scores. The possible raw score range for an individual on any one personality variable is from 0 to 28. Because the items are of the forced-choice variety, some indication of the relative strength of response tendencies *within the individual* can be obtained from the various raw score totals. For the comparison of an individual's scores with those of others, standard scores and percentiles are available in the manual as well as on the profile sheet. In addition, there are descriptive labels for T-score and percentile ranges, such as Very High for T-scores of 70 and above or percentiles of 97 and above.

No occupational norms have been published as yet. Consequently, the suggestion in the manual (p. 10), "The EPPS can add a good deal to the vocational and educational counseling of college students," must be based upon unpublished data or merely upon subjective evaluation. In either case, it would seem that for general use the EPPS has potential, not demonstrated, value as a device for vocational appraisal or personnel classification.

Standardization and Initial Validation. Two studies of the relationship between EPPS variables and ratings of one kind or another are summarized in the manual but without references or presentation of relevant statistical data. To evaluate these investigations adequately is thus extremely difficult, but since Edwards is quite critical of them any error in reporting them here will probably be on the conservative side. One study involved the agreement between subjects' self-rankings on the EPPS variables, as based upon definitions which were provided for them, and their actual scores as measured by the test. Some sets of rankings and scores agreed perfectly, whereas others were quite divergent, perhaps due to variations in the ways in which the definitions were interpreted by the subjects or to the effects of the social desirability variable which was controlled in the scores but not in the rankings. The second study compared EPPS scores with the subjects' Q sorts of EPPS items printed on individual cards. Again, the degree of agreement between the scores and sorts varied considerably from one subject to another. Since each item in the Q sort had a social desirability scale value, it was possible to determine the influence of this variable upon the extent of agreement between the self-ratings and objective scores. There was a definite effect: For subjects who regarded the more socially desirable statements as most characteristic of themselves the correlations between scores and sorts were quite low. Commenting upon these findings, Edwards (Manual:13) reached a conclusion to which we can readily subscribe: "It is believed that studies such as the ones described above between self-ratings and scores on an inventory can do little more than establish agreement, or lack of it, between the ratings of a particular subject and his scores on the inventory. The interpretation to be placed upon this agreement, or lack of it, is another matter and one involving many difficult and complex problems. It is not clear, however, how even perfect agreement between self-ratings and inventory scores could be interpreted as bearing upon the nature of the variables being measured by the inventory."

A second approach used by Edwards in the initial validation of the EPPS was based upon the construct validity of the instrument. This approach involved the correlation of scores on the EPPS variables with scores on variables measured by other personality inventories. It was reasoned: "If the direction of such relationships can be predicted in advance of their actual establishment, this may give the investigator additional confidence in his understanding of the nature of the variables supposedly being measured by the inventory," (Manual:13). This procedure, it will be noted, requires that predictions be made *before* correlations between variables are obtained; note further that in conducting the following study Edwards did not fulfill this requirement, except perhaps in the most general way. In merely correlating scores on the EPPS and other inventories he was proceeding upon the hypothesis that there might be a relationship between them, but the direction of the relationship on particular scales was not specified. He found a few marginally significant (5 percent level) r's, which did not fall into any meaningful pattern, for the EPPS, the Guilford-Martin Personnel Inventory, and the Taylor Manifest Anxiety Scale. There was one moderately high correlation of —.51 between Aggression and Agreeableness (Guilford-Martin), but most of the other coefficients were in the twenties and low thirties, with the exception of a —.39 between Succorance and Objectivity (Guilford-Martin). From these findings Edwards concluded that the correlations were in the expected direction, although some of them could be accounted for by common variance on the social desirability factor. Even though the results are in accordance with "expectation," they cannot be accepted as legitimate data in support of the construct validity of the EPPS because the "expectations" were based upon a *posteriori* reasoning rather than a *priori* predictions. That is, they cannot be accepted, as Cronbach and Meehl (1955) point out, until they have been cross-validated upon a new sample.

For the same reasons as those just mentioned the intercorrelations of the EPPS scales do not directly support the validity of the instrument but they do reveal the nature of its internal structure. For the 749 women and 760 men in the normative sample the intercorrelations of the personality variables were generally quite low. The highest correlation was .46 between Affiliation and Nurturance, the next largest being —.36 between Autonomy and Nurturance. Some of the remaining 103 r's were in the low thirties, but most of them were in the teens and low twenties. The various scales are thus relatively independent and hence are fairly efficient measures of different constructs.

Reliability. Two types of reliability are reported in the manual. Split-half reliabilities or coefficients of internal consistency for the fifteen personality variables, based upon the scores of the 1509 subjects in the normative group, and corrected by the Spearman-Brown formula, ranged from .60 (Deference) to .87 (Heterosexuality), with the majority clustering in the mid-seventies. Although somewhat lower than would be desired and would be found for ability or aptitude tests, these coefficients are approximately comparable to those for other paper-and-pencil personality inventories. In fact, they tend to be generally higher than those for the more widely used Minnesota Multiphasic. The test-retest reliability, or stability, coefficients for the EPPS were even more acceptable than the internal consistency estimations. For a group of 89 students at the University of Washington, who were re-examined after a one-week interval, the reliabilities ranged from .74 (Achievement and Exhibition) to .88 (Abasement), with most of the coefficients falling in the eighties. On the basis of both kinds of reliability the three most consistent and stable scales were Heterosexuality, Endurance, and Abasement, whereas the least reliable were Deference, Exhibition, and Affiliation.

Validity. The unique feature of the EPPS is its forced-choice item format which was designed to control or, more accurately, eliminate the influence of the social desirability factor in the responses of examinees. This factor has been defined by Edwards (1957) in two interrelated ways: first, as the social desirability scale values of personality statements; and, second, as the tendency of respondents to endorse as characteristic of themselves those statements with socially desirable scale values and to reject those with socially undesirable scale values. The first aspect of the definition is quite straightforward and operational in nature. The social desirability scale values of the personality statements are obtained by "performing certain operations upon a set of observations made under specified conditions. The observations are the judgments of social desirability made by the subjects in the judging group. The operations are those of a particular psychological scaling method. The specified conditions are the instructions given to the members of the judging group," (Edwards, 1957, p. 7). The scaling techniques which Edwards used include paired comparisons, the method of successive intervals, and the method of equal-appearing intervals. Various groups have been used for judging purposes.

Because the groups which can be used for judging purposes may vary in nature, i.e., be representative of different populations, the second aspect of the definition of social desirability is not only more complex than the first but is closely related to it. For the tendency of persons to attribute the more socially desirable characteristics to themselves may stem from more than one source. A person may endorse a personality statement as self-descriptive not because it is actually characteristic of him but because it is a socially desirable characteristic ("faking good"). But he may also endorse it because in the group of which he is a member (men, teen-agers, hospitalized patients) this trait is fairly common or dominant. To determine which of these response sets accounts for his answers to the personality items it is necessary to hold one of the sets constant. Because the effects of group membership can be controlled whereas faking can only be assessed, an effort has been made to establish the generality of the social desirability stereotype, i.e., to demonstrate that it varies little from group to group. Since if most groups entertain the same conception of social desirability, then the group of which a person is a member will not *differentially* affect his responses to the personality inventory.

That the social desirability factor is relatively stable has been indicated in a number of studies. Men ($N = 86$) and women ($N = 66$) scaled the 140 statements from the EPPS for social desirability by the method of successive intervals, and their judgments were quite similar. Of the total, 95 statements had the same scale value, regardless of whether determined by males or females. Only 2 of the 140 statements were as dissimilar in their scale values as one interval. The concept of social desirability apparently transcends subcultural as well as sexual differences. Fujita (1956) obtained a product-moment correlation of .95 between items scaled by a group of 50 Japanese-American college students and the original scale values based upon the judgments of the American norm group. Similarly, statements from the EPPS which were translated into Norwegian by Lovaas (cited by Edwards, 1957) and judged for social desirability by 50 male and 36 female students at two *gymnasiums* in Oslo were correlated .78 with the criterion set. And, Klett (1957a) found that there were no differences in the scale values of items judged by high school students from different socio-economic levels. Moreover, there were no differences in the judgments of high school and college students.

In another study, Klett (1957b) compared the judged social desirability of EPPS statements made by psychotic and non-psychotic hospitalized patients with those made by the high school and college groups. Again, there were no significant differences for the total set of items, but there was a tendency for the hospitalized group (both psychotics and non-psychotics) to rate Deference, Order, and Aggression statements as more socially desirable and Affiliation and Intraception items as less socially desirable. Finally, Edwards (1957) has reported that the social desirability factor varies only slightly with age, three different age groups agreeing to a high degree in their scale values for the items. Thus, regardless of sex, cultural, social and economic, adjustment, and age differences, individuals tend to describe themselves in essentially the same socially desirable rather than undesirable terms. The importance of this rather general tendency lies in its relationship to the probability of endorsing self-descriptive personality statements.

The relationship between probability of endorsement, i.e., the proportion of examinees who indicate that a given statement is characteristic of them, and the social desirability scale value of a personality item is extremely high. For the original set of 140 items Edwards (1957) found that in a group of college students the correlation between the two variables was .87. Using similar methodology this finding was replicated on other samples with slightly different sets of personality statements by Edwards (1957), Kenny (1956), and Hanley (1956). A somewhat different approach to the study of the relationship between probability of endorsement and social desirability was taken by Navran and Stauffacher (1954), who asked a group of 25 student nurses to take the EPPS and then three months later to rank a stack of cards with the names and definitions of the fifteen personality variables printed on them. Two rankings were obtained: first, from least to most characteristic of themselves; and, second, from least to most socially desirable. The rank-order correlation coefficient for raw scores on the EPPS and the first ranking was —.03; for raw scores and the second ranking it was —.01; and, for the two rankings it was .90. From these findings Edwards (1957, p. 86) drew the justifiable conclusion: "Under any circumstances, if a statement has a high social desirability scale value and if a subject endorses it in self-description, our interpretation of his response is complicated. We have no way of knowing, for example, whether the statement is, in fact, descriptive of the subject or whether he simply says that it is because he regards it as a socially desirable characteristic. Similarly, if a subject fails to endorse a statement with a low social desirability scale value, he may do so because the statement is not, in fact, descriptive of him, or because he does not choose to acknowledge what he may regard as a socially undesirable characterization." To control this confounding of the social desirability factor with the probability of endorsement in the EPPS the self-descriptive personality statements which are presented to the examinee in pairs were matched, as far as possible, on their social desirability scale values.

Results on the effectiveness with which the items have been matched are not uniform. Some indicate that the matching is fairly successful, whereas others suggest that social desirability is still operative to a significant degree. The intraclass correlation (a measure of within-group homogeneity) for the various item sets, as determined by Edwards (1957), was .85. A coefficient this high supports the similarity of the item pairs in social desirability as does the finding, also by Edwards, that there is a low relationship between the differences in the scale values of the two statements in a pair and the probability that the first statement will be endorsed.

Less favorable results, however, were obtained by Corah, Feldman, Cohen, Gruen, Meadow, and Ringwell (1958). When a group of 50 men and 31 women were asked which statement in 30 item pairs "would make another person look better to other people if it were said of him," their judgments revealed that each statement does not have an equal chance of being endorsed. Those items containing statements about Achievement and Order were more frequently selected as being more socially desirable, whereas those concerning Heterosexuality were identified as less socially desirable. An additional finding was a product-moment correlation of .88 between the percentage of another group (other than the judging group) which answered the first alternative in each pair and the rated social desirability of the item statements. In other words, 77 per cent of the total variance in responding to EPPS item pairs could be accounted for by the social desirability of the statements. The investigators (Corah et al., 1958, p. 72) concluded: "It appears likely that Edwards, in using the method of successive intervals to scale his items, achieved only a first approximation of equal pairings and that additional judgments of the item pairs themselves are necessary along with revisions in pairings before the variable of social desirability can be eliminated from the EPPS."

This conclusion is perhaps open to criticism, however, because the social desirability factor was not operationally defined in the same way as Edwards defined it: Different instructions were given to the judges for determining the social desirability of an item. This variation in procedure might account for the divergent results. But this is unlikely since Klett (1957a), using exactly the same procedure as Edwards, found that the matching of items by scale values in his high school group was not as good as in the college sample. Moreover, his hospitalized group differed from the norm group in their ratings of the social desirability of subsets of items for certain personality variables. To what extent these inequalities between items in social desirability significantly affect responses to the items clearly requires further research before any definitive statement can be made. Perhaps the most that can be said at present is that the matching of items in the EPPS has reduced but not eliminated the effects of social desirability upon test-taking attitudes.

This conclusion applies equally well to the operation of the social desirability factor at the variable level. Correlations of measures of social desirability with scale scores are much lower for the EPPS than for other personality inventories, but they are not negligible. Correlations between a specially constructed measure of social desirability and the three scales of the Guilford-Martin Personnel Inventory were .63 (Cooperativeness), .53 (Agreeableness), and .71 (Objectivity). A coefficient of similar magnitude for social desirability and the Taylor Manifest Anxiety Scale, on which low scores indicate less anxiety, was —.60 (Manual). The only significant correlations of the social desirability scale with the EPPS were —.32 (Succorance) and .32 (Endurance). Comparable results have been reported by Silverman (1957), who correlated the K scale of the MMPI and difference scores between the Taylor Manifest Anxiety Scale and the Heineman Forced Choice Manifest Anxiety Scale with the EPPS variables. Only three coefficients were significant, the highest being —.35 between K and Aggression.

An experimental rather than correlational analysis of the effects of social desirability, as well as personal desirability, upon EPPS variables was made by Borislow (1958), who assessed the relationship between fakability and indices of profile similarity and stability. Some subjects were instructed to respond as they believed a "perfect individual characterized by those traits that society considers highly desirable" (social desirability) would respond; others were told to answer items according to how they would "like to be" rather than how they actually are (personal desirability); and, still others were given the standard instructions for taking the test (control group). The findings indicated that the inventory can be faked under structured personal and social desirability instructions; that the consistency score and coefficient of profile stability are not adequate devices for detecting faking; and that there is a real difference between social and personal desirability response sets as determinants of responses to the EPPS. Thus Navran and Stauffacher's (1954) conclusion that "the EPPS not only has eliminated the influence of social desirability at the item level, but has also considerably reduced its operation at the variable level" must be qualified at least to agree with the less than perfect matching of item statements on social desirability scale values and the possible influence of a personal as well as social desirability factor upon total scores.

The extent to which the social desirability factor is operative as a determinant of responses to the EPPS has direct implications, of course, for the validity of the instrument. If the factor is eliminated or minimized, then considerably greater confidence can be placed in studies which demonstrate the relationship of the EPPS to other variables. At least those relationships cannot be attributed in large part to the tendency of examinees to appear in as favorable a way as possible. This advantage of the EPPS has not accrued as yet, however, for the vocational validity of the instrument. No studies of the occupational predictive value of the inventory have been noted in the literature, but one study of its construct validity, two investigations of its relationships with other tests, and one study of its relationship to achievement, ability, and college major have been located which have some implications for the use of the EPPS in vocational guidance and selection work.

A well-conceived but inadequately executed piece of research by Bernardin and Jessor (1957) was designed to determine whether two of the scales have *construct validity* for the measurement of dependency, which was defined as (1) reliance on others for approval or importance of approval from others, (2) reliance on others for help or assistance, and (3) conformity to opinions and demands of others. Since the EPPS does not contain a direct measure of dependency a combination of scores on two scales, Deference and Autonomy, was used to define an Independent and a Dependent group of subjects: The former had high scores on Autonomy and low scores on Deference, whereas the latter had low scores on Autonomy and high scores on Deference. These two groups were then used to test three hypotheses.

The first hypothesis was that Dependent subjects "under conditions of negative verbal reinforcement (critical comments) would perform less efficiently on a finger-maze learning task than either independents under the same conditions or a control group of dependents and independents receiving no negative verbal reinforcement." In other words, Dependent-Experimentals (DE) would be less efficient than Independent-Experimentals (IE), Dependent-Controls (DC), and Independent-Controls (IC). This prediction was based on the assumption that Dependent subjects, who supposedly rely more upon others for approval, the first aspect of the dependency construct, would be frustrated to a greater extent by criticism or disapproval. And, because frustration is related to quality of performance, they would do less well on the experimental task. To test this hypothesis the various experimental and control groups were compared on three measures of quality of performance in learning a finger-maze. The experimental groups differed as expected, the results being interpreted as in support of the hypothesis. This conclusion, however, does not seem justified.

The hypothesis required that the DE and IE groups be compared under the same experimental condition. That is, the amount of frustration must be invariant for the two groups. If the amount of this condition varies between the groups, then it is confounded with the effects of Dependence-Independence upon the criterion variables. That it did vary between the two groups is apparent from the data which were reported. What Marx (1951) has termed an Experimental-Control definition of frustration was operationally established in the DE group by a significant performance difference between it and the DC group, but such a difference was not demonstrated in the IE group; comparable differences between it and the IC group were not obtained on any of the quality-of-performance criteria. In fact, even if a difference between IE and IC had been established, the amount of frustration for DE and IE might have been different. There is no way of knowing because they were compared with different control groups. This failure to define frustration adequately destroyed the equivalence of the DE and IE groups on this variable. As a result, it is not known whether to attribute the performance differences between them to differences in degree of Dependency or amount of frustration since these two variables were confounded.

The second hypothesis which was tested by Bernardin and Jessor was: "Dependent persons confronted with a difficult problem-solving task will request help significantly more often than independent persons, when both groups are informed that assistance may be gotten upon request." In this phase of the experiment the Independents and Dependents were given a difficult Chinese puzzle to solve and instructed that they could ask for assistance from the experimenter if they wished. The number of times that the two groups asked for help or corroboration of what they were doing was tabulated, and they were then compared on the frequencies. The results indicated that the Dependents sought assistance significantly more than the Independents. Thus the hypothesis was supported, and the validity of the scales for measuring the second aspect of the Dependency construct, reliance on others for help or assistance, was demonstrated. There were no apparent flaws in the experimental procedure which would lead to a qualification of this conclusion.

To test the third hypothesis that "In a situation requiring perceptual judgments to be made before a group, dependent S's will conform more to the judgments of the group than will independent S's," the subjects were asked to make sixteen judgments of line lengths in a group which was making incorrect judgments. There were no significant differences between Independents and Dependents in the extent to which they conformed to the judgments of the group: Members of both experimental groups adhered closely to the consensus of the group although the latter's judgments were purposefully incorrect. Commenting upon this part of the study the investigators say (Bernardin and Jessor, 1957, p. 67) : "Unfortunately the situation was so constructed that conformity to the group (which gave 13 out of 16 objectively incorrect judgments) was attainable only at the expense of disagreeing with a fairly objective reality situation. A less structured situation where the correct response is less apparent to the S might be successful in differentiating dependents from independents." They suggest the use of ambiguous colors which must be named instead of judgments of line lengths. Moreover, they point out that the use of group members of higher status than the subjects might elicit a greater degree of differential conformity behavior from independents and dependents.

These difficulties in carrying out a unique and otherwise ingenious and potentially productive approach to the construct validation of EPPS scales, as well as those of other personality and interest inventories, necessarily limit the inferences which can be drawn from the results. Nevertheless, there was one definite finding: A relationship evidently exists between independence-dependence, as defined by combinations of high and low scores on the Autonomy and Deference scales of the EPPS, and asking for help in solving a problem. Individuals with low scores on Autonomy but high scores on Deference rely more upon others for assistance in problem-solving activities than individuals with high scores on Autonomy and low scores on Deference. This relationship was expected from the definition of the Deference and Autonomy scales.

Correlations of the EPPS with other tests have been studied by Graine (1957), Bendig (1957), and Allen (1957). These studies investigated the congruent validity of certain EPPS scales by relating them to already existing, and presumably valid, measures of the same traits. In the first study Graine's purpose was to determine whether there is a relationship between the Group Conformity Rating of the Rosenzweig Picture Frustration Study and the EPPS Autonomy scale. He found that in a group of 83 college students (40 male and 43 female) correlations between the two instruments for the total group, males, and females were .24, .12, and .26, respectively. He concluded that these relationships, which are contrary to expectation, being positive instead of negative, might be due to the atypicality of the groups' responses to the Picture Frustration Study, since the norm group for these conformity measures responded differently for two of the categories. Another possibility is that the criterion in this instance, the Rosenzweig Picture Frustration Study, has questionable validity (and perhaps reliability) for the measurement of conforming or autonomous behavior. The article does not consider evidence on these characteristics of the criterion variable, a task which would seem incumbent upon the investigator, particularly in a study of the congruent validity of a test.

Bendig's (1957) study of the relationship of the Taylor Manifest

Anxiety Scale and McClelland n-Achievement Scale to the EPPS Achievement scale suffers from a similar deficiency, although an inadequacy of one of the congruent measures was noted. In this investigation 244 college students (136 men and 108 women) were administered the various scales in a group situation, correlations then being determined for males and females combined since preliminary analysis of the data revealed no sex differences. The findings were uniformly negative: Taylor Manifest Anxiety Scale *vs.* EPPS Achievement $= -.05$; McClelland n-Achievement Scale *vs.* EPPS Achievement $= .11$; and, Taylor Manifest Anxiety Scale *vs.* McClelland n-Achievement Scale $= .06$. The author concluded: "The results indicate that the three scales are measuring quite independent traits. The small correlation between the two measures of 'need Achievement' suggests either that each scale measures a different type of 'need Achievement,' or that the low stability of McClelland's scale results in considerable attenuation of the relationship." Another explanation of the low correlations might be based upon the possible homogeneity of the group of college students with respect to "need Achievement." A restricted range on this variable would, of course, tend to depress the relationships between various measures of it. Assuming that there were sufficient individual differences in the need to achieve, however, for the relationships to emerge if real, it is worth noting that evidently the social desirability factor was not operating to any great extent in this study and therefore was not responsible for the nonsignificant correlations. For 106 college students, presumably like those used by Bendig, Edwards (1957) found that his specially constructed social desirability scale correlated only .09 with the Achievement scale but was significantly related to the Taylor Manifest Anxiety Scale $(-.60)$. Since the latter scale was unrelated to either the McClelland or the Edwards Achievement measures, the tendency of examinees to present themselves in a socially favorable manner did not influence their responses to these instruments. Moreover, it can be concluded that the McClelland n-Achievement Scale is apparently as free of the effects of the social desirability factor as the EPPS Achievement scale. At least this conclusion seems valid if the Taylor scale and social desirability were related as highly in Bendig's as in Edwards' sample. In any case, it must be recognized that there is little, if any, evidence for the congruent validity of the EPPS. Allen (1957) reported negligible correlations between EPPS and MMPI scales.

Achievement, ability, and *college major* were related to scores on the EPPS variables by Gebhart and Hoyt (1958) in a study of various groups of college students which numbered from 40 to 120. The experimental design was factorial, in which the relationships of the three variables to EPPS scores were considered simultaneously. Two college majors (Engineering and Arts and Sciences), three ability levels (high, average, and low), and two achievement levels (under and over) were defined for investigation. Using analysis of variance, results were obtained which indicated that overachievers score higher on Achievement, Order, Intraception, and the Consistency Score, whereas underachievers score higher on Nurturance, Affiliation, and Change; that high ability students have higher scores on Achievement, Exhibition, Autonomy, Dominance, and Consistency Score, whereas low ability students have higher scores on Deference, Order, Abasement, and Nurturance; and, that engineering majors score higher on Endurance, whereas Arts and Science majors score higher on Dominance. In addition to these main relationships, it was found that certain interactions existed: Overachievers with low ability score higher on Heterosexuality than underachievers with low ability, and underachievers with high ability score higher than overachievers with high ability on the Consistency Score. From these findings the investigators reached the following conclusion: "On the basis of the present study, three different patterns of overachievement can be hypothesized: (a) overachievement associated with a drive to compete (Achievement); (b) over-achievement associated with a drive to organize or plan (Order); and (c) over-achievement associated with intellectual curiosity (Intraception). Similarly, two patterns of underachievement may be hypothesized: (a) that associated with a need for variety (Change), wherein academic studies may appear boring and routine; and (b) that associated with social motives (Affiliation, Nurturance), wherein friendship may be placed above scholarship. The fact that the scales involved do not intercorrelate significantly supports the notion that several relatively distinct patterns, rather than a single pattern, are involved" (1957, pp. 127-128).

To these general observations can be added a fuller personality description, suggested by the definitions of EPPS variables. The overachiever with a drive to compete strives to do his best in tasks which require skill and effort, attempts to accomplish something of great significance and do difficult jobs well, and desires to excel others in what he does; the overachiever whose predominate attitude is to organize or plan his activities quite extensively appears as more highly controlled, with his energy channelled into systematized ways of doing things; and the overachiever with intellectual curiosity seems more sensitive, being attuned more to the feeling of others, and more introspective as he analyzes his own as well as others' feelings and motives. In contrast, the underachiever whose behavior is characterized by change wants to do new and different things, to travel, to meet new people, to experience novelty in daily routine, and to try new and different jobs; and the underachiever who tends to place friendship above scholarship prefers to help friends when they are in trouble, to have others confide in him about personal problems, to assist others who are less fortunate, to participate in friendly groups, and to do things with friends rather than alone.

The need patterns of 366 Chicago area teachers were analyzed with tthe EPPS by Jackson and Guba (1957), who reported that veteran teachers were more docile than novices.

Use of the Edwards Personnel Preference Schedule in Counseling and Selection.   In a few years there will probably be enough accumulated evidence concerning the personality variables measured by the EPPS to justify a discussion of its significance paralleling that for other, more fully validated inventories, but all that can be written at this stage of its development is based upon the few research investigations which have been reviewed, none of which directly pertains to the vocational significance and implications of the test.

As we have seen, most of the research activity thus far with the EPPS has focused upon the study of the effects of the social desirability factor as a response determinant, primarily because this is the first inventory which has been specifically desgined to control the operation of this variable. That it has been controlled to a considerable extent, on both the item and variable levels, but has not been eliminated completely, is well documented by the evidence. The approach might profitably be used in the construction of other kinds of inventories. The problem of faking interest blanks and records has never been solved with the conventional inventory but might be more amenable to solution if items were matched for social desirability, or, perhaps more accurately, occupational desirability. Or, for the personl selection situation, special keys might be developed to detect the use of occupational stereotypes as response sets in simulating an interest pattern on the Kuder, for example, which would be consistent with the job the applicant was seeking.

In schools and colleges the EPPS may be useful not only as a general aid for facilitating discussion of a client's preferences, as suggested in the manual, but it may be helpful in determining the extent to which a client is actively involved in the process of occupational choice. It seems reasonable to conclude from the findings of Ginzberg et al. (1951) and particularly of Super and Overstreet (1960) that some persons who are confronted with the problem of occupational choice approach it more or less actively. Some individuals need only minimal stimulation to take positive steps toward a solution of the choice problem on their own behalf; they become actively engaged in the search for an appropriate occupational outlet for their capacities without leaning heavily upon the counselor for motivation and assistance. These are the persons, for example, who can be referred to the occupational information library with the expectation that

they will use it to advantage. In contrast, other individuals are quite
passive in their approach to selecting a satisfactory occupation; they respond to external pressures, particularly the wishes of parents, and characteristically react to major forces in the environment rather than attempting to control them. They have difficulty in using the resources at their
disposal, whether in the community or in the counseling situation. Because the counselor would plan the counseling process differently for individuals who are more or less active and independent in their decision-
making, he would find information about these response tendencies very
useful. The patterns of high and low scores on the EPPS Autonomy and
Deference scales, discussed above, which indicate degree of reliance upon
others in the solution of problems, should provide some basis for the identification of clients who might be more active or passive in the search for
a suitable occupation.

The use of the EPPS in diagnosing patterns of overachievement and
underachievement seems justified, at least tentatively. It would be desirable to have cross-validation data on the patterns which have been reported before too much confidence is put in them. But since they seem to
jibe with experience quite well, they can probably be used to advantage
without gross error. College majors which may be appropriate or inappropriate for those who have certain patterns of scores cannot as yet be listed.
Similarly, there is no knowledge of which patterns are related to either
occupational field or level, although Roe's (1956, 1957) theory of the relationship of needs to occupational membership has obvious implications
for research along these lines, as does the work of Bordin and his students
(Nachman, 1960).

In guidance and employment centers and in business and industry the
EPPS would seem to have tested value only for the purposes already mentioned, but since these are not directly related to the placement and selection processes the inventory's significance at present is primarily as a
promising instrument for research. Certainly the potentiality of the EPPS
as a test which reduces the possibility of faking will not go unrecognized
for long in the employment situation.

The Kuder Preference Record—Personal, Form A (Science Research
Associates, 1948).   This inventory is included in this chapter, not because
there is considerable evidence of its validity in vocational counseling or
personnel work, nor because it is especially widely used and needs to be
understood, but simply because it has apparent promise as a unique measure of personal characteristics (in addition to interests and other personality traits), which may be significant in occupational choice and adjustment. The scales of the Kuder—Personal were developed along lines quite
similar to those used in the construction of the Kuder—Vocational. Sam-

ples of 2,500 adults and 2,000 students, who participated in the original studies, were administered an experimental form containing approximately 900 items distributed in three activity areas. Intercorrelations of scales in this initial form revealed seven which were relatively independent from each other and from the Kuder—Vocational scales, and which had reliabilities ranging from .68 to .83. Correlations of items with each of the scales then provided a basis for a revised form, which was subsequently administered to a new group of about 1,100 men and women. Of the seven experimental scales two were not sufficiently independent and reliable and were consequently discarded, leaving the five scales which constitute the present form.

Description. These five scales measure preference for five different kinds of situations or activities. Originally termed Sociable, Practical, Theoretical, Agreeable, and Dominant activities they have been renamed (1953 manual) preference for being active in groups, preference for familiar and stable situations, preference for working with ideas, preference for avoiding conflict, and preference for directing others. A high score in the first of these areas, preference for being active in groups, supposedly indicates that a person enjoys working with people, meeting new people, taking the lead or being the center of attention in a group, but not necessarily dominating or controlling the activities of others. Industrial engineers, sales and distribution managers, retail store managers, and public school superintendents, among others, would *presumably* obtain high scores on this scale, whereas physicians and farmers would score low, but the hypotheses need to be validated. Preference for familiar and stable situations, rather than new experiences and the possibility of improbable events is expected to be most characteristic of such occupational groups as toolmakers and clergymen and least typical of business executives, insurance salesmen, and reporters. Similar relationships are hypothesized for other traits and other professions, but, again, validity data must be examined before such interpretations can be justified.

Terms designed to measure preference for these various activities and situations are arranged in the familiar triadic format, the examinee being instructed to decide which of the three activities he likes the most and which he likes the least. A typical item is:

> P. Exercise in a gymnasium
> Q. Go fishing
> R. Play baseball

Because the choice is forced and because each alternative is keyed for a different preference scale, the scores on the Kuder—Personal, as on the Kuder—Vocational, are ipsative. That is, they are interrelated so that they indicate the relative strength or magnitude of personal preferences *within* the individual. An expressed preference for an activity keyed, for example, to the working-with-ideas scale necessarily increases the score in this area while it decreases the score in the being-active-in groups area. Statistical treatment of scores from the Kuder—Personal must consequently allow for their ipsative nature, since, as Guilford (1952) has pointed out, certain statistical procedures, such as product-moment correlational techniques, are not appropriate for certain problems. Interpretations of Kuder scores in counseling must also be adjusted to account for their forced interrelationships.

The inventory is self-administering, testing time usually ranging from 40 minutes to one hour. It is available with a machine-scoring answer sheet as well as the hand-scoring form with the step-down booklet, answer pad, and pin. It is designed for use with upper level high school students and adults. Several sets of norms are available; boys (3,650), girls (3,924), men (1,000), and women (532). Mean scores and corresponding percentile ranks of men and women who liked their work are given in the 1953 edition of the manual, but most of the occupational groups contain so few cases they should be used only tentatively. A verification scale, for the identification of persons who answer carelessly or without understanding, is based upon items which almost everyone marks. Because a positive correlation was discovered between age and scores on the preference for familiar and stable situations and avoiding conflict scales, a relationship which would be expected from Strong's (1943, Ch. 17) research on change of interests with age, appropriate corrections are made on the profile sheet for adults. The scales are quite reliable, most of the coefficients ranging between .80 and .89 for the various norm groups, with only one as low as .76.

Validity. To the extent that the statistical independence of the several scales is an indication of validity the Kuder—Personal compares favorably with other preference inventories, as well as with most multifactor aptitude tests. The highest intercorrelation (1953 manual) is between scales A (preference for being active in groups) and E (preference for directing or influencing others), but this apparently varies with the group upon which it is based, being .384 for 1,000 men in the norm group, .353 for 500 college women, and .272 for 250 college men. The other correlation coefficients (some negative, some positive), cluster in the mid-twenties, with a few in the .00 to .10 range. Scores in the five activity areas are evidently contributing unique information and fostering efficient measurement, which was, of course, the intent in developing them by item and intercorrelational analysis.

Ratings of dominance constituted the criterion used in a study by Birge (1950) of fraternity and sorority members, who had also taken the Kuder—

Personal. A "high dominant" group $(N = 47)$ and a "low dominant" group $(N = 45)$ were compared on their mean scores for the five scales. Differences significant between the .04 and .02 levels indicated that the more dominant person prefers to take the lead and be in the center of activities involving people, likes activities involving the use of authority and power, and enjoys activities ordinarily chosen by people trying to make a good impression. Unfortunately, the high and low dominant groups were not matched on factors which might have influenced their scores (such as age and intelligence) and the reliability of the behavior ratings was not reported, but these shortcomings are not severe enough to render the findings, which are in the expected direction, completely invalid.

Occupation entered in relation to personal preferences was studied by Mosier and Kuder (1949) in the only other published report on the validity of the inventory. A total of 577 cases, representing twenty different occupations distributed at the professional and managerial, clerical and sales, skilled and semi-skilled levels, were surveyed for differences in Kuder —Personal scores. Each occupational group was compared with a norm group of 450 unselected cases, and the three skill levels were compared with each other. On scale A (preference for being active in groups) five occupations scored higher than the average: personnel and counseling workers, sales managers, insurance salesmen, foremen, and salesmen who sell other than to the consumer. Those occupations scoring lower than the average in this area were office managers, accounting clerks and tellers, consumer salesmen, carpenters, and telephone linemen, all of which are generally more solitary in nature or do not require active participation in groups. On scale B only chemical engineers showed an above average preference for familiar and stable situations; as might be expected, sales managers and non-consumer salesmen were below average in their liking for activities in this area. With respect to differences between skill levels, the clerical and sales workers scored lower on this scale than the skilled and semi-skilled workers, thus reflecting the latter's greater desire for stability and probable security. Significantly high scores on scale C, preference for working with ideas, were obtained by business managers, account clerks and tellers, and personnel and counseling workers; only carpenters, who are definitely thing-oriented according to Strong's (1943, Ch. 17) research, scored lower than the average on this scale. Occupational level differences were found between the professional and clerical classifications, on the one hand, and the trade categories on the other, with the former scoring higher. Insurance salesmen, teachers, office managers, and mechanical engineers, as well as the professional and clerical occupations in general, expressed more preference for avoiding conflict (scale D).

Preference for directing the activities of others (scale E) was endorsed more than the average by business managers, personnel and counseling workers, sales managers, and the broader levels of professional and clerical occupations, but was indicated less than the average by factory workers and workers at the skilled and semi-skilled levels. Occupations which did not differ from the base group on any of the scales included accountant, plant manager, retail manager, general office clerk, and electrician. There were no differences between the professional and clerical levels on any of the five scales.

The job satisfaction and *personal preferences* of men and women in eight different occupational classifications are included in the manual (1953 edition). Satisfied and dissatisfied-workers in each occupation were compared for significant differences in mean scores on the various scales. In general, the results were those that would be expected from the nature of the occupation and the preference activities, but there were some exceptions. Lawyers and judges (men), who differed in expressed degree of job satisfaction, were not differentiated by their Kuder—Personal preferences; similarly, there was no relationship between job satisfaction and activity preference in the group of insurance salesmen (men). Satisfied accountants and auditors, however, expressed greater liking for familiar situations and avoiding conflict. Public school superintendents, who reported that they were satisfied with their jobs, scored higher in the areas of preference for being active in groups and directing others. Dissatisfied retail managers preferred fewer activities which involved being active, and dissatisfied mechanics and repairmen scored lower on preference for familiar and stable situations than their satisfied co-workers. For the two women's occupations, grammar school teacher and housewife, there were no differences between satisfied and dissatisfied teachers but there was a relationship of satisfaction to preference for familiar situations and avoiding conflict among housewives. No other validation studies have been located.

Use of the Kuder Preference Record—Personal in Counseling and Selection. As there is only minimal evidence upon which to base suggestions for the use of this inventory in educational and industrial personnel work the discussion which follows is necessarily limited. The empirical data which have accumulated on the Kuder—Personal indicate that it is sufficiently reliable (although some of the coefficients might be higher) for use with individuals and is fairly economical due to the low interrelationships among the scales. Adequate validity data are still wanting, but the findings which are available seem positive and encouraging. Some of the scales have demonstrated construct validity; others are related to expressions of vocational satisfaction; and, most were effective in the one study of the differentiating of occupational groups in ways which are psychologically meaningful. How homogeneous these occupations are, however, in the activity preferences which distinguish them, is not known (standard deviations are not given in the manual), nor has the relationship between preferences and occupational performance or success been determined.

A further problem, particularly for the employment situation, is the identification of those who distort their responses to the inventory. Kuder has reported progress in the development of an honesty scale for detecting falsified records but it is still in an experimental stage. These gaps in knowledge should be recognized, and the inventory should be utilized only within its present limitations, but its potential value should not be overlooked. In particular, the Kuder—Personal seems peculiarly adapted to the measurement of those aspects of the normal personality which may contribute to differential vocational success and satisfaction. Unlike other personality inventories, which are either too broadly conceived to differentiate among occupations or too narrowly restricted to measure other than deviant behavior, the Kuder taps personal reactions to the types of activities which, because of their intimate relation to those found in work, can constitute sources of satisfaction and accomplishment, or stress, strain, and frustration. Further research may reveal that it can be used to establish empirically the hitherto elusive relationship between personality and occupations.

The Rorschach Inkblot Test (Grune and Stratton; first published in Switzerland in 1921). This series of inkblots was developed by a Swiss psychiatrist, Hermann Rorschach, as a measure of the underlying structure of the personality, was experimented with by him and his students for a number of years before it was introduced into the United States during the 1930's, and has grown rapidly in popularity as a clinical instrument since that time. The result has been a vast amount of publication concerning it, most of which has consisted of discussions of its use in personality study and clinical diagnosis rather than of conclusions based upon reliable research knowledge. Although some proponents of the technique have advocated its use in vocational guidance and selection (e.g., Piotrowski, 1943a, b), little satisfactory evidence has been adduced to justify or contradict some of the sweeping claims made for it.

The fundamental differences between this and other types of tests, the varied aspects of the personality which it is purported to measure, the internally consistent logic upon which it is based, and the dramatic use to which it has sometimes been put, have given the Rorschach a wide appeal. At the same time, the enthusiasm of its proponents and the extent to which it has been based on clinical intuition and subjectivly rather than quantitatively analyzed experience have antagonized many more scientifically minded psychologists. However, the proper approach is an open-minded study of the instrument in which one can assess its demonstrated value and establish hypotheses concerning its potential usefulness, which can be tested experimentally. It is in that spirit that the writers have attempted to deal with it in the following pages, for though they have used the inkblots, both in research and in clinical and counseling practice, and believe they may yet prove to be of value, they are not "Rorschachers."

To attempt to treat the clinical validity of this complex and subjectively scored test is too sizable a task for a book such as this. To explain the technique alone requires a whole volume, or volumes, as has been shown by Rorschach (1932) and later by Beck (1937, 1944, 1945), Klopfer and Kelly (1942 and 1946), Klopfer et al. (1954, 1957), and Sarason (1954); a volume on its validity is also needed, but—significantly—has yet to be produced, although the recent Klopfer and Sarason books deal with the issue. The pattern followed in discussing personality inventories will therefore be departed from, and this section will attempt only to describe the test in sufficient detail to provide an orientation to the procedure and to the nature of the test, and to discuss the studies which have been made of its significance for educational—vocational counseling and selection. Its clinical validity will not be treated, a decision which seems justified by the fact that the inkblots are in any case a diagnostic rather than a screening device.

Description. The Rorschach Inkblot Test was designed originally for use in the diagnosis of psychiatric disorders in adults. It has since been used, however, with normal adults, adolescents, and children, and has been found applicable to any person of school age provided the interpretation is made in terms of the age group to which the examinee belongs. The test consists of ten white cards, on each of which is reproduced one large inkblot. Some of the inkblots are monotones (gray), while others include color. The test is administered individually in clinical and sometimes in personnel practice. The examinee tells what he thinks each inkblot might be and the examiner records the responses on a blank which includes outlines of the inkblots. This is followed by an inquiry in which further details concerning responses are elicited, and by a testing of the limits, in which the psychologist ascertains whether or not the examinee is capable of giving certain types of responses which he has not previously given. When used for screening (as it occasionally is), for personnel selection, or for research the test is often administered as a group test, the inkblots being projected onto a screen and the examinees recording their responses on diagrammed blanks; this is followed by a modified inquiry, in which the examinees locate their responses for the examiner but there is no testing of the limits. A multiple-choice form of the group test has also been developed (Harrower and Steiner, 1945), which, as will be seen below, is of doubtful value.

Scoring the Rorschach is a time-consuming task, which often takes two or three hours, when a detailed clinical picture of the person being studied is desired. When Munroe's (1941) inspection technique is used merely in order to derive an index of total adjustment the time may be reduced to 15 minutes per examinee. In either case the person doing the scoring must have had intensive training in the use of the test, combined with a good background in clinical psychology, for despite the lengthy and helpful discussions of scoring now available the procedures are quite subjective. Some users of the test are, in fact, convinced that to objectify the procedure would be to destroy its clinical value (Klopfer and Kelley, 1942, pp. 20–21).

The norming of the Rorschach has also been a sore point with many psychologists. In general, Rorschachers have felt that clinical experience and insight are sufficient to justify the interpretations commonly made, and Rorschach's original insights are often appealed to as evidence of the significance of a response. Others have been concerned with the accumulation of norms for the various types of responses, for various normal and clinical groups, in order that the clinical significance of a response might be objectively demonstrated and verified by reference to quantitative data. For example, Beck's (1937) first monograph on the inkblots was quite normative in its approach, but his later books (1944, 1945) have been more subjective and more dependent on clinical intuition. It is this very lack of objective norms for many aspects of the test which makes clinical training and experience necessary for the users of the Rorschach; it also makes essential a scientific attitude and a tendency to seek objective evidence to justify clinical intuitions. The problem is not as simple a one as to collect or not to collect norms, however, as the scoring and interpreting often require the relating of one variable to others in ways which do not lend themselves well to quantitative treatment as we now understand it.

Since responses and scoring have so far been discussed in abstract terms, it may be well to make the subject tangible by describing some types of responses and their scoring. One inkblot, for example, may look to the examinee like a leopard skin, and the inquiry may indicate that this is because of the shape and because of differences in the furry texture. In scoring this response three items are of interest: the examinee responded to the *whole* picture rather than to details, seeing the inkblot as a unit rather than as a number of disparate units; he responded thus partly because of the *form*, and partly because of the *texture* which he used as color.

These three items are added to similar items obtained in response to other pictures, giving scores, respectively, for the W, F, and Fc responses. Interpretation of the test then proceeds on the basis of each of these scores, seen in the light of other related scores. W is thought of as revealing a tendency to respond to wholes, to organize and synthesize; a high score is taken as revealing superior intelligence, unless it is so high or so superficial as to take on another meaning. F is thought of as a sign of emotional control, although if it is high and certain other indices are low it may mean rigidity. Fc, or the use of texture, is interpreted as a sort of shock absorber, an indication of controlled sensitivity to the environment. A variety of other modes of response to the inkblots, and the content of the responses, are also analyzed, various ratios are computed, and a profile is plotted in order to facilitate study of the pattern of responses. A verbal summary or personality sketch is then prepared on the basis of this analysis. Most of the justification for these interpretations, it should be emphasized again, lies in the intuition of clinicians who have used the test and studied the responses of persons whom they had come to know well by other clinical methods. Only a few attempts have been made to validate them by objective methods, generally with disappointing results.

Validity.   It should be clear from what has preceded that the validity of the Rorschach in personality diagnosis has been demonstrated largely by the extent to which clinicians have thought it agreed with psychiatric diagnoses. Studies with the Rorschach on its clinical value have been reviewed by Hertz (1941), and subsequent reviews have been published by White (in Hunt, 1944) and Sarason (1954). In addition, however, some attention has recently been given to the vocational significance of the Rorschach. Studies of the vocational validity of the technique have been reviewed through 1956 by Steiner (1949), Williams and Kellman (in Klopfer et al. 1956), and Patterson (1957). The evaluations of these reviewers have varied from optimistic enthusiasm for the Rorschach in the vocational setting to hypercritical rejection of it. The favorable comments have generally acknowledged the lack of empirical support for the vocational use of the Rorschach but have rationalized the negative research evidence by pointing to deficiencies in it or inadequacies in the experiments which have produced it; the unfavorable opinions have often been based upon exacting criteria of research excellence.

Grades in college were used as a criterion against which to validate the total adjustment score of the Group Rorschach in a study by Munroe (1945). Her subjects were students at Sarah Lawrence College, where grades were not those usually given for specific course work, but faculty ratings of academic standing, a more general evaluation of the student's status. The correlation was .49, as contrasted with one of .39 for the

A.C.E. Psychological Examination. This promising finding has not, however, been replicated at other colleges in which more traditional marking methods are used. Cronbach (1950) obtained correlations of only .17 and .25 between grade-point average and number of checks on the Inspection List and overall adjustment rating, respectively, but obtained a correlation of .45 between the criterion and the A.C.E. Similarly, Cooper (1955) found nonsignificant relationships between average grade for three semesters and Munroe scores, and Rust and Ryan (1953), using Davidson's 15 signs of adjustment rather than the Inspection Technique, were unable to differentiate groups of overachievers, normal achievers, and underachievers. There were, however, some nonlinear relationships between certain Rorschach variables and achievement which, even though tentative because not cross-validated, formed a meaningful picture of the overachiever as follows: He is "overconventional and a conformist (high P); he is practical-minded, tending to 'see what's there' and exhibiting 'stereotypy in thinking' (high A percent); he shows little 'introversion or self-preoccupation' (low M) and is probably emotionally immature (FM greater than M)." This line of investigation, based upon the analysis of Rorschach configurations in well-defined groups at different levels of achievement, would appear as the most productive approach and should be pursued further, since, as Cronbach (1950, p. 81) points out, the need is for inquiry into "what elements or patterns in the Rorschach are associated with particular behaviors and criteria, rather than attempting blind prediction of marks or over-all ratings."

In two studies of the relationship of the Multiple-Choice Rorschach to achievement, one of which attempted to establish sign patterns for achievers and nonachievers, Osborne and Sanders (1949) were moderately successful in identifying predictors of academic performance. They first evaluated different systems of weighting the multiple-choice responses, two of which were proposed by Harrower-Erikson, and found that weights based upon the magnitude and reliability of biserial correlations between average fall quarter grades and Rorschach responses were the most efficient. Correlations between the criterion and weighted responses were .47 (first quarter) and .43 (second quarter); for the criterion and the A.C.E. they were only slightly higher, being .56 and .50 for the successive quarters; and, the multiple correlation between grades and the best combination of Rorschach responses and A.C.E. scores was .62. It is evident that the factors assessed by the Rorschach in this instance contributed to a better prediction of achievement than that based solely upon a measure of scholastic aptitude. In the second study (Osborne et al., 1950) they compared groups of probationary and nonprobationary students and found that the latter, with only one exception, chose what Harrower-Erikson has designated as "good" responses on the Multiple-Choice Rorschach. In addition an item analysis yielded signs predictive of probationary status which were highly efficient: The results indicated only 13 per cent false positives and 32 per cent false negatives. These findings have not been cross-validated, however, and it is noteworthy that in the comparison of the probation and nonprobation groups intelligence was not controlled. Consequently, differences between the groups on this factor may have contributed to their differences in Rorschach responses, particularly those which are supposedly related to intelligence, such as M and the ratios in which it appears.

Other attempts to differentiate between academically successful and unsuccessful groups or upper and lower scholastic aptitude groups have produced either negative findings or findings which have quite restricted validity. McCandless (1949) compared high and low academic performance groups of merchant marine officer candidates ($N = 13$), who were matched on such variables as age and sex but not intelligence, and found that the only difference between the groups was that the more successful students gave a slightly greater number (8.1 to 6.6) of popular responses. This finding is consistent with Rust and Ryan's characterization of the overachiever as "overconventional or a conformist (high P)" but should be accepted only tentatively due to the small number of cases and lack of controls. Similarly, Thompson's (1948, 1951) results from two studies must await replication before their stability and reliability is demonstrated, but they are nevertheless suggestive. She was able to develop, through a process of extensive item analysis, achievement scales based upon responses to the Group Rorschach which correlated highly with semester grades but only minimally with concurrent measures of verbal aptitude. These correlations with final grades in a psychology course (reliability of criterion $= .96$) were .38 in one study and .32 in the other; with intelligence test scores they were .04 in the first study and $-.07$ in the second. Unfortunately, the second study, which was termed a "follow-up" study, was not a cross-validation of the scale which was originally constructed; a new scale based upon different responses by different groups of subjects was developed. Consequently, both scales need further research before they can be used.

Occupational differences as shown by the Rorschach have been studied by Prados (1944), Kaback (1946), Reiger (1949), and Roe (summarized in Roe, 1956). Prados accomplished an intensive analysis of a very few Rorschach protocols of creative artists and painters, whom, he concluded, can be characterized by certain unique aspects of their handling of the Rorschach cards. He summarized these common personality features as: "A superior mentality which emphasizes the abstract form of thinking, the logical and constructive activities, with an obvious disregard for the routine problems of every-day life and a certain fear of mediocrity. These intellectual potentialities are efficiently used, since they are accompanied by a strong drive for achievement and a richness of the inner interests and stimuli (for) spontaneous creative thought." These traits were suggested by the subjects' high normal number of responses, their overemphasis upon W and underemphasis upon D, their high number of M which was greater than FM, and their dilated *Erlebnistyp* (large number of both M and C). Whether responses of these kinds and quantities are typical only of artists and painters and therefore would differentiate them from other occupational groups and from the general population was not determined by Prados. Until appropriate comparisons with other groups are made, then, these data support only the inference that a particular configuration of responses to the Rorschach may occur more frequently than others within a group of artists; they do not support the conclusion that artists are different than members of other occupations merely because they respond as they do.

Kaback used the Group Rorschach results of 300 pharmacists and accountants, dividing them into professional and preprofessional (student) groups. She found point-biserial coefficients of correlation (to be distinguished from biserial coefficients) of .54 and .65 between 24 Rorschach components and professional or pre-professional group membership. Kaback points out, however, that the overlapping of groups is so great as to make the application of her findings to individuals highly questionable. The picture is further confused by the finding of equally great differences between the employed and student groups (point-biserials of .625 and .62) , the thumbnail sketch of the employed pharmacists having practically no resemblance to that of the student pharmacists, although those of the two accounting groups are more similar. The sketches of the two professional groups are summarized here as illustrations of Rorschach results.

Pharmacists: intelligent adults whose impulse control functions well in general with one limitation—their conscious suppression of impulses (F per cent = 47) plays a relatively greater role, and inner stability a relatively smaller role (M = 2.09) . Fairly marked amount of anxiety (presence of K and k responses) which is counterbalanced by sensitivity to inner and outer conditions (FK + Fc:FK + K = 2.28:1.19) . Intellectual flexibility marked (W,D,d,S present) . Spread of interests somewhat limited (H + A:5 other content categories) . However, in terms of general adjustment, the group falls within the normal range.

Accountants: superior adults. Well-balanced impulse control; function smoothly in conscious impulse control (F per cent = 44), rational behavior in emotional situations (FC:CF + C = 92.59) , inner stability (number of M present) . This group has a tendency to attend more to stimulations from within than to external stimulations (M:sum C = 3.1) , and use them productively (W:M = 12:3). Conscious control refined by use of shock-absorbing functions

(FK $+$ F $+$ FCR $=$ 56) by being sensitive to inner and outer conditions. Small amount of anxiety (some K and k) and a slight tendency to overcautiousness in emotional contact with outside world (FC $+$ CF $+$ C:Fc $+$ c $+$ C' $=$ 1.5:3). Good mental elasticity (W,D,d,Dd,S present) with widespread interests (H $+$ A:8 other content categories). In general, a well-adjusted group.

Reiger's subjects were distributed in a number of occupational groups as follows: Sales, 55; Engineers, 53; Supervisors, 36; Administrators, 64; Clerical, 66; Personnel workers, 24; Merchandizing trainees, 32; and, miscellaneous, 22. She compared these various occupational groups on five Rorschach scoring categories (W,D,Dd,M, and C), using the critical ratio technique in some instances and the *chi*-square test in others. The data of these statistical analyses are not reported directly but only summarized. They were largely negative: Most of the differences appeared to be related to variations in total number of responses (R), i.e., if R was higher in one group than in another, the two groups would tend to differ in the proportion of responses in the location and determinant scoring categories. Aside from these differences the various occupations appeared to be quite similar in their reactions to the Rorschach materials. Only two groups tended to be differentiated from the others; these were the administrators and the supervisors. The former were characterized chiefly by their facility in producing and handling ideas (high R, low A per cent), whereas the latter typically had low R, high A per cent, high F+ per cent, and low M and C. Reiger concluded that no single personality type could be associated with any of the occupational groups, and that it cannot be assumed that any particular type of personality occurs more frequently in one occupation than in another.

Artists were the subjects of Roe's (1946) first study. Her results showed that the group was extremely heterogeneous on the Rorschach: general adjustment scores ranged from 3 to 18 with a mean of 10.3, approximately that which Munroe (1945) found predictive of maladjustment in college but higher than the mean of 7.7 which Roe (1946b) found in paleontologists. The latter group, as compared with the artists, differed also in number of sex responses and animal anatomy responses, as might be expected in a group of men whose work involves spending hour after hour with bones. Moreover, color shock, or inability to handle color, which is considered indicative of inability to handle social relationships effectively, was also common in this group of men whose work permits them to live in relative isolation and carry few social obligations. In fact, this finding was fairly general among what might be termed natural scientists. Both biologists (Roe, 1949, 1951b) and physical scientists (Roe, 1950a, 1951a, 1951c, 1951d) were less than optimally adjusted in a social sense, tending to dissociate themselves from interpersonal relationships in general. In other respects, however, these two groups differed in significant ways, at least as far as their Rorschach performances are concerned. The most notable difference was the biologists' greater concern with form and accuracy of form, and the physicists' attention to three-dimensional space and inanimate movement. The biologists also seemed to handle their anxiety more effectively by structuring it through greater use of intellectualized controls (high number of F present). These similarities and differences seemed to obtain whether more or less eminent biologists and physicists were compared; that is, the differences between the two groups were more outstanding than the differences within the groups with respect to success in the occupation.

The final group studied by Roe (1952, 1953) was composed of psychologists and anthropologists. These social scientists differed considerably from the biologists and physical scientists not only as to their early developmental histories, on which Roe collected considerable information, but in their responses to the Rorschach. They gave many more responses, the mean numbers being 66 for psychologists and 69 for anthropologists, and evinced relatively less concern with the formal qualities of the blots, as compared with biologists, and with inanimate movement, as contrasted with the physical scientists. Rather, they tended to concentrate upon enriching the stimulus materials by attributing to them the kinesthetic qualities of human and animal movement, particularly the former, which Roe interpreted as evidence of considerable empathic capacity. This tendency is evidently accompanied by a need to hold and feel nurturant attitudes, as well as "uncritical attitudes, and a sort of haphazard use of rational controls—that is, (they are) rational when they wish to be but generally feel no compulsion to make a point of being so," (Roe, 1953). Concerning all of the scientists she studied, including both the eminent and the less eminent, Roe (1953) concluded: "(the) similarities are greater than the differences. This is to be expected from the fact that there is considerable heterogeneity within the separate groups, and from the fact that these men are all functioning adequately."

Success on the job has been studied with the Rorschach in various ways, using different groups, and with sometimes conflicting results. One of the first attempts to predict job success by means of Rorschach assessments was made by a research team headed by Piotrowski and others (1944). These investigators were able to identify four Rorschach signs which differentiated more from less outstanding mechanical workers, in a group which numbered 450 male New York City high school graduates, ranging in age from 16 to 23. With a performance criterion based upon foremen's evaluations, counselor's interview ratings, and shop records Rorschach protocols were analyzed for responses which seemed to characterize those workers who scored high and low on the composite standard. The signs which appeared to be most discriminative were the following: m, scored in the conventional manner and credited if it occurred at least once in the protocol; Frsx, a contraction of "four-six" and pertains to quality of performance on Cards IV and VI; hEvd, "high evidence" of superior performance or the production of three or more distinct ideas (which are not incongruous) on the first seven cards; and no WF, no whole responses when form is the main determinant on plates VIII, IX, and X. These signs, which seem to have considerable face validity, particularly m which Roe found to be prominent also in the records of physical scientists, were not cross-validated. Moreover, although the investigators concluded: "it appears improbable that the signs test specific mechanical aptitudes," their relationship to mechanical aptitude was not determined. Consequently, it is wholly possible that, if they are related to degree of mechanical aptitude, the differences between the more and less efficient mechanical workers might be explained by the former's superior mechanical ability rather than by personality variables, since mechanical aptitude is known to be related to success in this type of work.

Fortunately, there is evidence on both of these possible criticisms in a well designed and executed but rather poorly reported study (no tabled statistical data were published for evaluation) conducted by Anderson (1949). She found that, although the results were not as dramatic as those of Piotrowski, his four signs correctly identified 64 per cent of the high efficiency machinists in a group of 34 men who had been rated on four job efficiency criteria: quality of performance, quantity of performance, rate of learning, and job knowledge. Moreover, in a further analysis of the data, she found that Piotrowski's hypothesis concerning what the signs measure—mechanical aptitude or non-specific personality traits—was substantiated by the validity of predictions for machinists whose efficiency ratings were inconsistent with their measured mechanical aptitudes. She writes: "In four of these eight machinists with conflicting efficiency ratings and test scores (e.g., low aptitude, high efficiency), the direction of the Rorschach predictions would agree with that of the test results. The Rorschach results might suggest compensating factors for the low test scores in one; and possible handicapping factors against the effective use of abilities in the other three men."

That personality may operate in this manner, as a compensating or handicapping factor in the attainment of job success, was further indicated by interview data on the workers who had conflicting ratings and aptitude test scores. For example, one high efficiency-low aptitude worker was rated by both his supervisors as high in cooperative attitude, quality of work, and job knowledge but lower in quantity of work, and rate of learning. Apparently this man's persistence compensated for his slowness and contributed to a high rating despite lack of high aptitude. Similarly, but conversely, high aptitude-low efficiency workers were identified as less cooperative as rated in interviews, and more neurotic and less socially dominant on the Bernreuter Personality Inventory. From the findings of these two studies, which seem to be the best to date on the relation of the Rorschach to vocational behavior, a significant implication becomes apparent: Although occupations are not highly differentiated with respect to personality, it is quite possible that personality can act as a suppressor variable in the prediction of vocational success and vocational satisfaction. That is, given a particular pattern of aptitudes and interests, a worker may be more or less successful and satisfied in his job depending upon the extent to which his personality affects the fulfillment of his vocational capabilities.

The Multiple-Choice Rorschach was used to predict a criterion of accident-proneness in a study of bus and street car operators by Miller (1955), who analyzed both specific factors and patterns of responses in the test protocols. In the factor approach 136 quantitatively scored items were tested for significance in discriminating subjects who had no accidents or had three or more accidents for the previous year. The subjects varied in years of experience from approximately 1 year 6 months to 5 years (one subject had been on the job for a period of about 6 years). From this part of the analysis, 50 items were selected and weighted, following a method similar to that used by Strong, and then were cross-validated on an independently selected sample which met the same criterion for accident-proneness. The results were not only negative, but they were opposite to expectation, the high accident-prone subjects in the cross-validation group being more like the low accident-prone subjects in the standardization group. Negative results were also obtained in the attempt to discriminate high and low accident-prone subjects by patterns of responses to descriptive statements on accident-proneness which were keyed to Rorschach terminology. Only two configurations discriminated in the standardization group, and these did not stand up upon cross-validation. Miller points out that the lack of validity of the Rorschach in this instance may be due to the fact that it measures characteristics which are too deeply imbedded in the personality to have a relationship to accident-proneness; he suggests that more superficial personality traits, probably such as those inventoried by a paper-and-pencil test, might discriminate the highs and lows. Another explanation may lie in the inadequacy of the criterion: Three accidents does not seem enough to establish "accident-proneness", nor does one year's driving history seem sufficient. Furthermore, no attempt was made to control age which might have a suppressor effect upon differences between the highs and lows. That is, if age is negatively related to accident proneness but positively associated with personality functioning then the relationship between accident-proneness and personality might be cancelled out.

Cox (1948) had sales managers rank their salesmen in dress and millinery departments along a continuum of sales success and then compared the top 25 per cent with the bottom 25 per cent. The comparisons were made on responses to the Multiple-Choice Rorschach, the analysis following a modification of Fisher's "discrimination of groups by means of multiple measurements" (the procedure was not further explained). The items which discriminated between the upper and lower groups of salesmen were weighted, the Rorschachs were rescored using these weights, and the number of positive and negative scores in the successful and unsuccessful groups was determined. As might be expected, because the scores were derived from items which discriminated, the successful salesmen had mostly positive scores and the unsuccessful salesmen had mostly negative scores. This finding should be cautiously interpreted, not only because it has not been cross-validated on an independent sample, but because cross-validation is practically impossible: The criteria for ranking subjects according to their success in sales work were not specified; the method of analysis was not clearly identified; and the characteristics of the sample were not reported, e.g., age, educational background, etc. Moreover, since the investigator assisted the sales managers in making adjustments in their rankings, only he could actually repeat the experiment. This study, like many with the Rorschach, contributes little to reliable knowledge about the technique because the procedures which were followed were not explicitly defined and were thus more private than public and scientific.

Essentially the same criticism can be made of a study by Symonds and Dudek (1956), who obtained a relatively high rank-order correlation of .60 between rankings of the effectiveness of 19 teachers, as evaluated from interviews, observation of classroom performance, the Thematic Apperception Test (discussed below), and information made available by the teachers' supervisors and principals, and rankings of Rorschach protocols according to their indications of differential teacher effectiveness. It should be noted that the criterion includes a projective test (the TAT), as well as the predictor. Consequently, the results are quite restricted; in fact, they apply only to these investigators with these data on this one occasion. No conclusions concerning the use of the Rorschach in predicting teacher effectiveness can be made or are justified. One implication of the study is noteworthy, however, and that is the importance of knowledge of the criterion (job and its demands) as well as the predictor (Rorschach) in making predictions from one to the other. As Symonds and Dudek point out: "A person who both knows the Rorschach and also the qualities that make for successful teaching should undoubtedly be able to predict teaching success corresponding to a correlation of well over .60."

That knowledge of both the occupational and personality variables in studies with not only the Rorschach but other instruments, in particular the MMPI, is often lacking is reflected in the gross, unrefined hypothesis which is frequently tested, namely, that members of this occupational group differ from members of that occupational group in their personalities or that successful members of an occupation differ from unsuccessful members. Very seldom are the specific differences, the reasons *why* certain findings are expected, specified in more than a general way. Perhaps this is the most telling criticism of Roe's (1953) work: Vague statements, such as "these differences in personality structure (between physicists and biologists) can be definitely related to the content of the vocations," are made about how personality and vocation *must* be related but *why* they are related is never made explicit. Bordin and his students (Nachman, 1960) have succeeded in avoiding this error.

Teacher effectiveness was also the criterion used in an analysis of signs of maladjustment on the Multiple-Choice Rorschach by Cooper and Lewis (1951), who selected high and low groups of teachers (30 in each) from 72 in service and 153 student teachers rated by 4730 pupils on a check list for evaluating teacher-student relationships. They found that neurotic signs correlated .52 (tetachoric coefficient) with unfavorable pupil ratings and that the less-liked teachers tended to be more emotionally constricted (sum of achromatic responses in excess of sum of color responses). The percentage of poorly adjusted teachers in the two groups was essentially the same: 42 per cent of the less-liked and 47 per cent of the liked teachers had Munroe Inspection scores greater than 10, which is considered the maximum number for optimum adjustment. As the authors of this study point out, however, although the results are suggestive, they pertain to groups and not to individuals, and because of the considerable overlap between the groups, no predictions concerning the probable effectiveness of teaching candidates are warranted.

A large-scale study of clinical psychologists reported by Kelly and Fiske (1951), using a variety of educational and clinical performance criteria, yielded largely negative results despite various treatments of the Rorschach data. Only one phi coefficient was significant (.39) for professional promise.

Dulsky and Krout (1950) studied the relationship of the individually administered Rorschach to promotion potential in a small group of 14 supervisors, who were rated by three executives on a continuum which included consideration of such qualities as adaptability to change, rapidity of learning new duties, capacity for learning a new job, and getting along with new associates. The subjects averaged 42 years of age, had 14 years of service, and had been in their present positions for 5 years; on the Wonderlic Personnel Test they placed as a group at the 50th percentile (variability was not reported). The four highest and lowest of the group were selected for intensive analysis of their Rorschach protocols, which revealed that the lowest had greater A per cent, rejected more cards, and had more F— and C responses. Those rated highest had higher Fc per cent. From these rather sketchy findings, which do not seem to fall into any meaningful pattern, it was concluded that "the Rorschach test is of great value in personnel evaluation. However, its interpretation must be in terms of every day concepts and meaningful work-situations, rather than in terms of the more formal academic constructs of personality structure which are frequently used in dealing with Rorschach data." With the last comment there would seem to be little argument; as noted above the relationship between personality and occupation needs to be translated into work-behavioral terms. Whether the Rorschach has "great value" for personnel selection, evaluation, and guidance is another question.

Although research activity with the Rorschach in vocational counseling and personnel selection has increased during recent years, the only conclusion which can be drawn from these various studies is that if the Rorschach has validity for the selection of personnel for various types of work (or, by implication, the counseling of people concerning the appropriateness of vocational choices), there is as yet no evidence to indicate just what single or combined Rorschach traits might confirm one choice or contra-indicate another, the only possible exception to this generalization being the four signs identified by Piotrowski and partially cross-validated by Anderson as predictive of success in mechanical work.

Job satisfaction as related to Rorschach performance was the problem of two studies by Kates (1950a,b). In the first of these he found no relationship between job satisfaction, as measured by a modified version of Hoppock's form, and either total adjustment as indicated by the Munroe Inspection Technique or specific Rorschach scoring categories in a sample of 100 routine clerks. In the second study, however, the relationships among these variables were significant. The subjects in this instance were 25 New York City policemen who had an average age of 32.8 years and mean educational level of 12.2 years. The more satisfied the policemen were with their jobs, the more they tended to manifest signs of maladjustment, the correlation between job satisfaction and Munroe scores being .47. Kates concluded that "the individual's maladjustment might contribute to his job satisfaction rather than to his job dissatisfaction." This inference accords with Roe's observation on the adjustment of the scientists which she studied, particularly the biologists and physical scientists: By clinical and social standards they would be considered as rather poorly adjusted, yet vocationally they seemed quite satisfactorily adjusted, at least if their eminence and the personal satisfaction they derived from their work are any criteria. Their work, which in many cases filled most of their waking hours, was their major source of satisfaction precisely because it supported, and most likely kept intact, those aspects of their personalities which, according to the Rorschach, appeared as maladjusted.

The extent to which this relationship between job satisfaction and personality adjustment exists in other occupational groups remains to be determined by further research. The expectation would be that it would vary in magnitude and direction, depending upon the extent to which the nature of the work involves more or less adequate personal and social adjustment. For example, because counseling demands not only a high degree of self-awareness but considerable facility in engaging in interpersonal relationships, successful and satisfying performance in this occupation, as contrasted, for example, with biological research, probably bears a high, positive relationship to good personal and social adjustment. At any rate this would seem to be an hypothesis well worth testing.

Use of the Rorschach Inkblot Test in Counseling and Selection. No attempt has been made to assess, in this section, the validity of the Rorschach as an instrument for the clinical study of personality, although it is obvious that such validity would be helpful in counseling and evaluation because of the insights it would give into the types of adjustment problems an individual might encounter and the amount of difficulty he might have in handling them. The making of such an assessment would require more space than is warranted here. Attention has been limited, therefore, to the relationship between Rorschach scores and pre-vocational or academic achievement, occupational differences, job success, and job satisfaction.

Suggested uses of the Rorschach technique in vocational counseling and personnel selection can be evaluated against the background of what is known about these relationships. In two papers Piotrowski (1943a,b) has proposed a number of uses for the Rorschach in vocational work, some of which are fairly general in nature but others of which are specific. The latter pertain to the identification of empirically based signs predictive of occupational success and failure, which were found to have validity for the selection of efficient machinists. In addition, Piotrowski has introduced eight formulae, based upon Rorschach scoring combinations, which he believes to be helpful in educational and vocational guidance but which, unlike the signs for mechanical work, have not as yet been validated. Levine (1954) has reported a number of general uses of the

Rorschach, as well as other projective techniques, which purportedly commend its application in vocational cases, but the studies so far completed would suggest that its validity for use with individuals is extremely restricted. Much more must be learned about the vocational significance of the Rorschach before it can be used with sufficient confidence for such purposes as Levine proposes, an example of which is the "Determination of what type of work environment would be compatible with the individual's personality so that destructive work environments could be avoided."

Because the data on the vocational validity of the Rorschach have a number of limitations, some of which are due to methodological errors and some of which are attributable to failure to perform cross-validations, the technique can be considered only an instrument which may be worth using in validation studies, as one which research may yet prove valuable in vocational counseling and selection, but about which too little is now known to justify its use in practical counseling or personnel work.

The Murray Thematic Apperception Test (Harvard University Press, 1935, 1943; Grune and Stratton, 1949). This projective technique is, even more than the Rorschach, a clinical device rather than an objective test, and its occupational significance is unknown. It is briefly described here for two reasons: It has so challenged the interest of test users that questions concerning it are common; and it has promise as a research technique for the study not only of personality adjustment but, more specifically, of the determinants of vocational choice and satisfaction. Unlike the Rorschach, it is not a measure of the structure or organization of personality, but rather a technique designed to bring out the content of the personality, the needs, strivings, and environmental pressures which are felt by the person being studied. This fact might lead one to question its potential value as a device for use in directional vocational counseling or selection, were it not that the needs or strivings which it reveals may well be the determinants of vocational choice and vocational interest.

Description. The TAT, as this test is generally called, was designed for use with older adolescents and adults, but pictures have since been added which make it administrable to older children and younger adolescents; the examiner merely selects the appropriate pictures. As most of the studies made with it have been made with the older group, however, more is known about its scoring and interpretation at that level. The test consists of a series of 20 pictures for a given age and sex group. The pictures are semistructured, that is, their content is more like a specific object or scene than is the content of an inkblot or a cloud picture, but expressions are sufficiently ambiguous and action poorly enough defined so that it is possible for the subject to project himself into the situation and shape it somewhat according to his own needs and fears. Thus one scene depicts a human figure seated or kneeling next to a seat, a small object on the floor or ground before him, head bent and face hidden. To one person this figure represents a boy who has just broken his mother's favorite vase; to another, a girl who has just shot her lover and, dropping the pistol in front of her, is overwhelmed by her deed; to someone else it is a young man, fondly gazing at a flower given him that night by his sweetheart. Each person sees what he needs or wants to see in such a picture.

The test is administered individually, sometimes the examiner, and sometimes the examinee, writing down the examinee's story of how the scene came about, what is going on at the moment, what the characters feel, and what the end result will be. Scoring methods vary with the objectives of the examiner, and might better be called interpretive methods, for they are neither objectively based nor objectively expressed. Instead, the examiner analyzes the content in order to determine the underlying themes (hence the name of the test), to ascertain whether or not the plots are happy, logical, probable; and to find out with what kinds of heroes the subject identifies himself and the forces to which he feels subjected. The manual presents a somewhat more quantitative but time-consuming method for obtaining a weighted count of the needs (e.g., abasement, aggression, dominance) and "press" or forces (e.g., affiliation, aggression, loss) affecting the hero or examinee, a scheme useful when research is being conducted in group differences or in relationships between test and criteria. The norms in this scoring system consist of the responses of normal college students; in certain other methods there are none, and the data are used simply as clinical or case-history material to be interpreted in the light of other personal data to make a dynamic and meaningful picture of an individual. It is obvious that, like the Rorschach, this test can be used only by well-trained and experienced clinical and counseling psychologists. Bellak (1954) and Tomkins (1948) have published scoring aids and manuals, each differing from the others in important aspects.

Validity. The most intensive clinical validation of the technique is reported by Murray (1938) in a study of Harvard undergraduates, which showed a high degree of consistency between TAT and other clinical evaluations made independently. Harrison (1940) found that conclusions based on it agreed well with case-history material and psychiatric diagnoses in a mental hospital. As the question of clinical validity is not one of primary concern in this context, however, these and subsequent related investigations will not be detailed; it is important only that there are some indications of validity in what is still a clinical device likely to develop into a test.

Occupational differences in TAT patterns have been touched upon by

Roe (1956) in her various studies of eminent scientists and her earlier investigation of artists. She found the test difficult to administer to her 20 artists, as they were so critical of the artistic quality of the pictures that they found it difficult to focus on the telling of a story. Interpretation of results was made correspondingly difficult. With the scientists a tally sheet was used to summarize their responses to the TAT, but Roe did not push the analysis of these data as well as she did for that from Rorschach protocols.

Use of the Thematic Apperception Test in Counseling and Selection. This brief account of the TAT has attempted to make clear its embryonic status and at the same time to suggest its promise as a device for measuring, more subtly than any personality inventory, the needs which drive people and the forces which they feel pressing upon them. Although virtually no use has been made of the instrument for vocational counsel ing or selection, and none should be made at present, the technique is one which should be developed to a point which will make it useful in studying the needs and drives which are related to vocational choice and success and for ascertaining the relationship between these and satisfaction in various types of work. It would be helpful, for example, to know that the need for affection is more often satisfied in social work or in teaching than in medicine or law, and to have an objective method of measuring that need. Such developments in the TAT are remote, but they are mentioned in the hope that research will be prosecuted which will bring them about.

The Rotter Incomplete Sentences Test (Psychological Corp., 1950). In this approach, made available in test form by Rotter (1950), by Rohde (1957), by Forer (1957) and by Dole (1958), the examinee is presented with a series of incomplete sentences such as "I wish . . .", "Most girls . . .", "My father . . .", and "The work I do . . .". The specific stimulus phrases vary with the purpose of the test, with the attitudes, needs, or aspects of adjustment which it is desired to assess. Such tests were apparently first experimented with by Payne (1928) and by Tendler (1930), then by Lorge and Thorndike (1941), Sanford (1953), and, with more follow-through, by Rohde (1946, 1957), and Dole (1958). The technique originates in the intriguing word-association method developed by Jung, experimented with rather fruitlessly at first by many investigators (Symonds, 1931), and more recently reviewed by White (in Hunt, 1944) and revived by Payne, Rotter, and Rohde in its present more objective form. The special advantage of this open-end or sentence completion technique is the freedom which it leaves the examinee to reveal his feelings by the way in which he structures the semi-structured situation (incomplete sentence). This complicates scoring, but procedures have been developed for the categorization of responses in such a way as to make possible the rapid classification and scoring of the completed sentences.

Rotter's approach has been to develop, standardize, and validate a total adjustment score, whereas Rohde's has been to devise more complex methods of scoring various needs and traits, as in other projective devices. Little research has been done with this need approach to incomplete sentences tests, but it is significant that Mehenti (1954) found no relationships between presumably identical need scores on an incomplete sentences test and on selected cards of the TAT, except in the case of need-Aggression.

There is more evidence, and more promising evidence, concerning Rotter's approach. Rotter and Rafferty (1950) summarize two studies of the validity of the instrument in the identification of disturbed persons in college and in a convalescent hospital, which showed some validity for the college and adult version of the test. Rotter, Rafferty, and Lotsof (1954) have reported similar data for the high school form, which differentiated at the .001 level between normal and clinic-referred high school boys and girls: With psychologists' interview ratings of total adjustment, the correlations were .20 and .37 for boys and girls respectively, while for sociometric status the correlations were .20 and .32 (data are reported so that positive correlations indicate agreement of adjustment data). The discrepancies in the data for boys and girls are noteworthy, and may stem from the greater conformity of feminine behavior, and hence more favorable evaluation of well-adjusted girls than of well-adjusted boys.

More college student data are reported by Churchill and Crandall (1955) at Antioch College. Test-retest reliability for one year was about .52, and for three years about .40; an adult (mother) group yielded a 20-month retest reliability of .70, reflecting either more constant testing conditions or more stable life conditions in the case of the mothers than of the college students. The IST scores correlated .49 with psychologists' ratings of the mothers' adjustment. Students entering psychological counseling while in college were differentiated from those who did not seek counseling, but not as markedly as in the original Rotter-Rafferty-Schachtitz (1949) study, which yielded biserial r's of .50 for women and .62 for men. The biserial r's obtained by Churchill and Crandall were still moderately high, however, being .42 for women and .37 for men. Norms at Antioch College were comparable to those reported in the manual for the Ohio State University.

Tindall (1955) has reported correlations with a variety of other measures of adjustment, as have Super and Overstreet (1960). In Tindall's study of 66 14-year-old orphan boys, the correlations with Munroe-Rorschach, Guess Who, and Heston Personal Adjustment scores were negligible; with the California Personality Test social and self adjustment scores they were .32 and .32, with psychologists' ratings the correlation was .36, all three being significant at the .01 level. In the Super and Over-street study of 105 ninth grade boys the correlations of Rotter total adjustment scores with TAT total adjustment scores (using a scoring method comparable to Rotter's) and sociometric peer acceptance scores were negligible (or marginal and in the direction opposite to that predicted), and only the correlation with parental occupational level (out of 21 status, adjustment, and achievement variables) was significant at the .01 level, r being .26. Tindall does not indicate whether he used the unpublished high school or the published college scoring manual for the Rotter; Super and Overstreet used the appropriate high school scoring manual, made available by Rotter.

The data so far available thus make the Rotter Incomplete Sentences Test appear a promising clinical screening device for use with college students, and even more promising with adults; with high school students its use is much more open to question, although further studies should be made before final judgments are reached. In any case, without encouraging educational and vocational validity data, the utility of the instrument in vocational counseling or in personnel selection is not demonstrated. The technique is still merely a research and perhaps a clinical instrument.

Trends in the Measurement of Personality.

Perhaps the major trend in the development of instruments for the measurement of personality during the years prior to the first edition of this text was in technique and toward various projective devices, illustrated by the rapid growth in popularity of the two best-known but complexly scored projective tests. More recently there has been a contrary trend of considerable importance, an interest in the refinement of inventory techniques, illustrated by the publication of instruments such as the Minnesota Multiphasic and Edwards Personal Preference Schedule and the other self-report methods (Bass and Berg, 1959) which in current forms have seemed more likely to be valid.

Both trends can be traced to the low validity which characterized early personality inventories. In the first it caused a search for a more subtle and penetrating type of test which would probe underneath the sophistications and rationalizations of the subject in order to get at the structure and content of his personality; in the second it resulted in a greater emphasis on purity of factors in some inventories and on empirical weighting in others. The improved personality inventories and biographical data blanks seem to the writers to be better stopgaps while the subtler projective techniques are being objectified and validated.

REFERENCES FOR CHAPTER XIX

Allen, R. M. "Relationship between Edwards Personal Preference Schedule variables and the Minnesota Multiphasic Personality Inventory scales," *J. Appl. Psychol.*, 41 (1957), 307-311.

Allport, G. W. *Personality: A Psychological Interpretation.* New York: Holt, 1937.

Altus, W. D. "A college achiever and non-achiever scale for the Minnesota Multiphasic Personality Inventory," *J. Appl. Psychol.*, 32 (1948), 385-397.

Anderson, Rose G. "Rorschach test results and efficiency ratings of machinists," *Pers. Psychol.*, 2 (1949), 513-524.

Bass, B. M., and Berg, L. A. (ed.). *Objective Approaches to Personality Assessment.* Princeton, N. J.: Van Nostrand, 1959.

Beck, S. J. "Introduction to the Rorschach method," *Amer. Orthopsychiat. Assn., Monog.* 1 (1937).

———. *Rorschach's Test: I. Basic Processes.* New York: Grune and Stratton, 1944.

———. *Rorschach's Test: II. A Variety of Personality Pictures.* New York: Grune and Stratton, 1945.

Bellak, L. *The TAT and CAT in Clinical Use.* New York: Grune and Stratton, 1954.

Bendig, A. W. "Manifest anxiety and projective and objective measures of need achievement," *J. Consult. Psychol.*, 21 (1957), 354.

Berdie, R. F. "Likes, dislikes, and vocational interests," *J. Appl. Psychol.*, 27 (1943), 180-189.

Bernardin, A. C., and Jessor, R. "A construct validation of the Edwards Personal Preference Schedule with respect to dependency," *J. Consult. Psychol.*, 21 (1957), 63-67.

Birge, W. R. "Preferences and behavior ratings of dominance," *Educ. Psychol., Measmt.*, 10 (1950), 392-394.

Black, J. D. "The Interpretation of MMPI Profiles of College Women," Unpublished Ph.D. dissertation, University of Minnesota, 1953.

Borislow, B. "The Edwards Personal Preference Schedule (EPPS) and fakability," *J. Appl. Psychol.*, 42 (1958), 22-27.

Brewer, J. M. "Religion and vocational success," *Relig. Educ.*, 25 (1930), 1-3.

Buhler, Charlotte, Buhler, K., and Lefever, D. W. *Development of the Basic Rorschach Score with Manual of Directions.* Los Angeles: Rorschach Standardization Studies, 1, 1948 (mimeographed).

Churchill, Ruth, and Crandall, V. "The reliability and validity of the Rotter Incomplete Sentences Test," *J. Consult. Psychol.*, 19 (1955), 345-350.

Chyatte, C. "Personality traits of professional actors," *Occupations,* 27 (1949), 245-250.

Clark, J. H. "Grade achievement of female college students in relation to non-intellective factors: MMPI items," *J. Soc. Psychol.*, 37 (1953), 275-281.

——— "The interpretation of the MMPI profiles of college students: a comparison by college major subject," *J. Clin. Psychol.*, 9 (1953), 382-384.

Cooper, J. G. "The inspection Rorschach in the prediction of college success," *J. Educ. Res.*, 49 (1955), 275-282.

———, and Lewis, R. B. "Quantitative Rorschach factors in the evaluation of teacher effectiveness," *J. Educ. Res.*, 44 (1951), 703-707.

Corah, N. L., Feldman, M. J., Cohen, I. S., Gruen, W., Meadow, A., and Ringwall, E. A. "Social desirability as a variable in the Edwards Personal Preference Schedule," *J. Consult. Psychol.*, 22 (1958), 70-72.

Cottle, W. C. "Card versus booklet forms of the MMPI," *J. Appl. Psychol.*, 34 (1950a), 255-259.

—— "Relationships among selected personality and interest inventories, *Occupations*, 28 (1950b), 306-310.

——, and Powell, J. O. "The effect of random answers to the MMPI," *Educ. Psychol. Measmt.*, 11 (1951), 224-227.

—— *The MMPI: a Review*. Lawrence, Kansas: University of Kansas Press, 1953.

Cox, K. J. "Can the Rorschach pick sales clerks?" *Pers. Psychol.*, 1 (1948), 357-363.

Cronbach, L. J. "Statistical methods applied to Rorschach scores: a review," *Psychol. Bull.*, 9 (1949a), 149-171.

—— "Pattern tabulation: a statistical method for analysis of limited patterns of scoring with particular reference to the Rorschach test," *Educ. Psychol. Measmt.*, 9 (1949b), 149-171.

—— "Studies of the Group Rorschach in relation to success in the College of the University of Chicago," *J. Educ. Psychol.*, 41 (1950), 65-82.

—— , and Meehl, P. E. "Construct validity in psychological tests," *Psychol. Bull.*, 52 (1955), 281-302.

Daniels, E. E., and Hunter, W. A. "MMPI personality patterns for various occupations," *J. Appl. Psychol.*, 33 (1949), 559-565.

Dodge, A. F. "Occupational ability patterns," *Teachers Coll. Contrib. to Educ.* 658 (1935).

Dole, A. A. "The Vocational Sentence Completion Blank in counseling," *J. Counsel. Psychol.*, 5 (1958), 200-205.

Drake, L. E. "A social I. E. scale for the MMPI," *J. Appl. Psychol.*, 30 (1946), 51-54.

—— "MMPI profiles and interview behavior," *J. Counsel. Psychol.*, 1 (1954), 92-95.

——, and Oetting, G. "An MMPI pattern and a suppressor variable predictive of academic achievement," *J. Counsel. Psychol.*, 4 (1957), 245-247.

——, and Oetting, E. R. *An MMPI Codebook for Counselors*. Minneapolis: University of Minnesota Press, 1959.

——, and Thiede, W. B. "Further validation of the social I. E. scale for the MMPI," *J. Educ. Res.*, 41 (1948), 551-556.

Dulsky, S. G., and Krout, M. H. "Predicting promotional potential on the basis of psychological tests," *Pers. Psychol.*, 3 (1950), 345-351.

Edwards, A. L. *The Social Desirability Variable in Personality Assessment*. New York: Dryden, 1957.

Fisher, V. E., and Hanna, J. V. *The Dissatisfied Worker*. New York: Macmillan, 1931.

Forer, B. R. *The Forer Vocational Survey*. Los Angeles: Western Psychological Services, 1957.

Frick, J. W. "Improving the prediction of academic achievement by use of the MMPI," *J. Appl. Psychol.*, 39 (1955), 49-52.

Friesen, E. P. "The incomplete sentences technique as a measure of employee attitudes," *Pers. Psychol.*, 5 (1952), 329-345.

Fujita, B. "An Investigation of the Applicability of the EPPS to a Cultural Subgroup." Unpublished Master's thesis. University of Washington, 1956.

Gebhart, G. G., and Hoyt, D. P. "Personality needs of under- and overachieving freshmen," *J. Appl. Psychol.*, 42 (1958), 125-128.

Gilliland, A. R., and Colgin, R. "Norms, reliability, and forms of the MMPI," *J. Consult. Psychol.*, 15 (1951), 435-438.

Ginzberg, E., Ginsburg, S. W., Axelrod, S., and Herma, J. L. *Occupational Choice*. New York: Columbia University Press, 1951.

Glaser, R. "Predicting achievement in medical school," *J. Appl. Psychol.,* 35 (1951), 272-274.

Goodstein, L. D. "Regional differences in MMPI responses among male college students," *J. Consult. Psychol.,* 18 (1954), 437-441.

Gough, H. G. *The California Psychological Inventory.* Palo Alto: Consulting Psychologists Press, 1956.

———, and Pemberton, W. H. "Personality characteristics related to success in practice teaching," *J. Appl. Psychol.,* 36 (1952), 307-309.

Gowan, J. C., and Gowan, May S. "A teacher prognosis scale for the MMPI," *J. Educ. Res.,* 49 (1955), 1-12.

Graine, G. N. "Measures of conformity as found in the Rosenzweig P-F Study and the Edwards Personal Preference Schedule," *J. Consult. Psychol.,* 21 (1957), 300.

Guilford, J. P. "When not to factor analyze," *Psychol. Bull.,* 49 (1952), 26-37.

———, and Zimmerman, W. S. *The Guilford-Zimmerman Temperament Survey.* Beverly Hills: Sheridan Supply Co., 1949.

Hall, C. S., and Lindzey, G. *Theories of Personality.* New York: Wiley, 1957.

Hanley, C. "Social desirability and responses to items from three MMPI scales: D, Sc, and K," *J. Appl. Psychol.,* 40 (1956), 324-328.

Harrison, R. "Studies in the use and validity of the TAT with mentally disordered patients. II, III," *Char. and Pers.,* 9 (1940), 122-138.

Harrower, Molly R., and Steiner, Matilda E. *Large-Scale Rorschach Techniques.* Springfield, Ill.: C. C. Thomas, 1945.

Hathaway, S. R. "The Minnesota Multiphasic Personality Inventory," In Kaplan O. J. *Encyclopedia of Vocational Guidance.* New York: Philosophical Library, 1948.

———, and McKinley, J. C. "A multiphasic personality schedule: I. Construction of the schedule," *J. Psychol.,* 10 (1940), 249-254.

———, and McKinley, J. C. "A multiphasic personality inventory: III. The measurement of symptomatic depression," *J. Psychol.,* 14 (1942), 73-84.

———, and Meehl, P. E. *An Atlas for the Clinical Use of the MMPI.* Minneapolis: University of Minnesota Press, 1951.

———, and Monachesi, E. D. (eds.). *Analyzing and Predicting Juvenile Delinquency with the MMPI.* Minneapolis: University of Minnesota Press, 1950.

Hertz, Marguerite R. "The validity of the Rorschach method," *Amer. J. Orthopsychi.,* 11 (1941), 512-519.

Hovey, H. B. "MMPI aberration potentials in a nonclinical group," *J. Soc. Psychol.,* 40 (1954), 299-307.

Hunt, H. C. "Why people lose their jobs or aren't promoted," *Pers. J.,* 14 (1936), 227.

Hunt, J. McV. (ed.). *Personality and the Behavior Disorders.* New York: Ronald Press, 1944.

Jack, L. M. "An experimental study of ascendant behavior in pre-school children," *University of Iowa Studies in Child Welfare,* 3 (1934).

Jackson, P. O., and Guba, E. G. "The need structure of in-service teachers—an occupational analysis," *Sch. Rev.,* 65 (1957), 176-192.

Kaback, Goldie R. "Vocational personalities," *Teachers Coll. Contrib. to Educ.,* 924 (1946).

Kates, S. L. "Rorschach responses related to vocational interests and job satisfaction," *Psychol. Monog.,* 309 (1950a).

——— "Rorschach responses, Strong Blank scales, and job satisfaction among policemen," *J. Appl. Psychol.,* 34 (1950b), 249-254.

Kelly, E. L., and Fiske, D. W. *The Prediction of Performance in Clinical Psychology.* Ann Arbor: University of Michigan Press, 1951.

Kenny, D. T. "The influence of social desirability on discrepancy measures between real and ideal self," *J. Consult. Psychol.,* 20 (1956) , 315-318.

Klett, C. J. "Performance of high school students on the Edwards Personal Preference Schedule," *J. Consult. Psychol.,* 21 (1957a) , 68-72.

—— "The social desirability stereotype in a hospital population," *J. Consult. Psychol.,* 21 (1957b) , 419-421.

Klopfer, B., Ainsworth, Mary D., Klopfer, W. G., and Holt, R. R. *Developments in the Rorschach Technique* (Vol. I. Technique and Theory; Vol. II. Fields of Application.) New York: World Book Co., 1954, 1957.

——, et al. "Shall the Rorschach method be standardized?" *Amer. J. Orthopsychi.,* 9 (1939) , 514-529.

——, and Kelly, D. M. *The Rorschach Technique.* New York: World Book Co., 1942.

Korner, Anneliese F. "Origin of impractical or unrealistic vocational goals," *J. Consult. Psychol.,* 10 (1946) , 328-334.

Krise, E. M. "A short method of scoring the MMPI," *J. Clin. Psychol.,* 3 (1947) , 386-392.

—— "A common error in scoring the MMPI," *J. Clin. Psychol.,* 5 (1949) , 180-181.

LaBue, A. C. "Personality traits and persistence of interest in teaching as a vocational choice," *J. Appl. Psychol.,* 39 (1955) , 362-365.

Layton, W. L. "The variability of individuals' scores upon successive testings on the Minnesota Multiphasic Personality Inventory," *Educ. Psychol. Measmt.,* 14 (1954) , 634-640.

Levine, Phyllis R. "Projective tests in a vocational guidance setting," *J. Counsel. Psychol.,* 1 (1954) , 209-214.

Levonian, E., Comrey, A., Levy, W., and Proctor, D. "A statistical evaluation of the Edwards Personal Preference Schedule," *J. Appl. Psychol.,* 43 (1959) , 355-359.

Lewis, J. A. "Kuder Preference Record and MMPI scores for two occupational groups," *J. Consult. Psychol.,* 11 (1947) , 194-201.

Lorge, I., and Thorndike, E. L. "The value of response in a completions test as indicators of personal traits," *J. Appl. Psychol.,* 25 (1941) , 191-199; 200-201.

Lough, O. M. "Teachers college students and the Minnesota Multiphasic Personality Inventory," *J. Appl. Psychol.,* 30 (1946) , 241-247.

—— "Woman students in liberal arts, nursing, and teacher training curricula and the Minnesota Multiphasic Personality Inventory," *J. Appl. Psychol.,* 31 (1947) , 437-445.

Mahler, I. "Use of the MMPI with student nurses," *J. Appl. Psychol.,* 39 (1955) , 190-193.

Marx, M. H. *Psychological Theory: Contemporary Readings.* New York: Macmillan, 1951.

McCandless, B. R. "The Rorschach as a predictor of academic success," *J. Appl. Psychol.,* 33 (1949) , 43-50.

McKinley, J. C., and Hathaway, S. R. "A multiphasic personality schedule: II. a differential study of hypochondriasis," *J. Psychiat.,* 10 (1940) , 255-268.

McLaughlin, Sister Mary Aquinas. "The genesis and constancy of ascendance and submission as personality traits," *University of Iowa Studies in Educ.,* 5 (1931) .

McQuary, J. P., and Truax, W. E., Jr. "A comparison of the group and individual forms of the Minnesota Multiphasic Personality Inventory," *J. Educ. Res.,* 45 (1952) , 609-614.

——, and Truax, W. E., Jr. "An under-achievement scale," *J. Educ. Res.,* 48 (1955), 393-399.

Meehl, P. E., and Hathaway, S. R. "The k factor as a suppressor variable in the MMPI," *J. Appl. Psychol.*, 30 (1946), 525-564.

Mehenti, Perin M. "Agreement Between Vocational Preference and Inventoried Interest in Relation to Some Presumed Indices of Vocational Maturity." Unpublished Ph.D. dissertation, Teachers College, Columbia University, 1954.

Michaelis, J. U., and Tyler, F. T. "MMPI and student teaching," *J. Appl. Psychol.*, 35 (1951), 122-124.

Miller, Carmen. "A comparison of high-accident and low-accident bus and street car operators," *J. Proj. Tech.*, 19 (1955), 146-151.

Morgan, H. "A psychometric comparison of achieving and nonachieving college students of high ability," *J. Consult. Psychol.*, 16 (1952), 293-298.

Mosier, Mary F., and Kuder, G. F. "Personal preference differences among occupational groups," *J. Appl. Psychol.*, 33 (1949), 231-239.

Monroe, Ruth L. "Inspection technique," *Rorschach Res. Exch.*, 5 (1941), 166-190.

——— "Prediction of the adjustment and academic performance of college students by a modification of the Rorschach method," *Appl. Psychol. Monog.*, 7 (1945).

Murphy, G. *Personality*. New York: Harper, 1947.

———, Murphy, Lois B., and Newcomb, T. M. *Experimental Social Psychology*. New York: Harper, 1937.

Murray, H. A. *Explorations in Personality*. New York: Oxford University Press, 1938.

Nachmann, Barbara. "Childhood experience and vocational choice in law, dentistry, and social work," *J. Counsel. Psychol.*, 7 (1960), 243-250.

Navran, L., and Stauffacher, J. C. "Social desirability as a factor in Edward's Personality Preference Schedule performance," *J. Consult. Psychol.*, 18 (1954), 442.

Norman, R. D., and Redlo, M. "MMPI personality patterns for various college major groups," *J. Appl. Psychol.*, 36 (1952), 404-409.

Osborne, R. T., and Sanders, Wilma B. "Multiple-choice Rorschach responses of college achievers and non-achievers," *Educ. Psychol. Measmt.*, 9 (1949), 685-691.

———, Sanders, Wilma B., and Greene, J. E. "The prediction of academic success by means of 'weighted' Harrower-Rorschach responses," *J. Clin. Psychol.*, 6 (1950), 253-258.

Page, M. L. "The modification of ascendant behavior in pre-school children," *University of Iowa Studies in Child Welfare*, 3 (1936).

Paterson, D. G. (ed.). "Research studies in individual diagnosis," *Bull. Empl. Stab. Res. Inst., University of Minnesota*, 4 (1934).

Patterson, C. H. "The use of projective tests in vocational counseling," *Educ. Psychol. Measmt.*, 17 (1957), 533-555.

Payne, A. F. *Sentence Completions*. New York: New York Guidance Clinic, 1928.

Piotrowski, Z. A. "Use of the Rorschach in vocational selection," *J. Consult. Psychol.*, 7 (1943a), 97-102.

——— "Tentative Rorschach formulae for educational and vocational guidance in adolescence," *Rorschach Res. Exch.*, 7 (1943b), 16-27.

———, Candee, B., Balinsky, Holtzberg, S., and Von Arnold, B. "Rorschach signs in the selection of outstanding young male mechanical workers," *J. Psychol.*, 18 (1944), 131-150.

Prados, M. "Rorschach studies on artists-painters: I. Quantitative results," *J. Proj. Tech.*, 8 (1944), 178-183.

Reiger, Audrey F. "The Rorschach test in industrial selection," *J. Appl. Psychol.*, 33 (1949), 569-571.

Roe, Anne. "The personality of artists," *Educ. Psychol. Measmt.,* 6 (1946a), 401-408.

——— "A Rorschach study of a group of scientists and technicians," *J. Consult. Psychol.,* 10 (1946b), 317-327.

——— "Analysis of group Rorschachs of biologists," *Rorschach Res. Exch.,* 13 (1949), 25-43.

——— "Analysis of group Rorschachs of physical scientists," *J. Proj. Tech.,* 14 (1950), 385-398.

——— "A psychological study of eminent physical scientists," *Genet. Psychol. Monog.,* 43 (1951a), 121-239.

——— "A psychological study of eminent biologists," *Psychol. Monog.,* 331 (1951b).

——— "A study of imagery in research scientists," *J. Pers.,* 19 (1951c), 459-470.

——— "Psychological tests of research scientists," *J. Consult. Psychol.,* 15 (1951d), 492-495.

——— "Analysis of group Rorschachs of psychologists and anthropologists," *J. Proj. Tech.,* 16 (1952), 212-224.

——— "A psychological study of eminent psychologists and anthropologists and a comparison with biological and physical scientists," *Psychol. Monog.,* 352 (1953).

——— *The Psychology of Occupations.* New York: Wiley, 1956.

——— "Early determinants of vocational choice," *J. Counsel. Psychol.,* 4 (1957), 212-217.

Rohde, Amanda R. "Explorations in personality by the sentence completion method," *J. Appl. Psychol.,* 30 (1946), 169-181.

——— *The Sentence Completion Method.* New York: Ronald, 1957.

Rorschach, H. *Psychodiagnostik.* Bern: Hans Huber, 1932.

Rosanoff, J. *Manual of Psychiatry and Mental Hygiene.* New York: Wiley, 1938.

Rotter, J. B., Rafferty, Janet E., and Lotsof, Antoinette B. "The validity of the Rotter Incomplete Sentences Blank: High School Form," *J. Consult. Psychol.,* 18 (1954), 105-111.

———, Rafferty, Janet E., and Schachtitz, Eva. "Validation of the Rotter Incomplete Sentences Blank for college screening," *J. Consult. Psychol.,* 13 (1949), 348-356.

———, and Rafferty, Janet E. *Manual for the Rotter Incomplete Sentences Blank.* New York: The Psychological Corp., 1950.

———, and Willerman, B. "The incomplete sentences test," *J. Consult. Psychol.,* 11 (1947), 43-46.

Rust, R. M., and Ryan, F. J. "The relationship of some Rorschach variables to academic behavior," *J. Pers.,* 21 (1953), 441-456.

Sanford, R. N., et al. *Physique, Personality, and Scholarship.* Washington, D. C.: Soc. Res. Child Devel., 1943.

Sarason, S. B. *The Clinical Interaction, with Special Reference to the Rorschach.* New York: Harper, 1954.

Schmidt, H. O. "Comparison of women students in occupational therapy and in nursing," *J. Psychol.,* 31 (1951), 161-174.

Schofield, W. "A study of medical students with the MMPI: III. Personality and academic success," *J. Appl. Psychol.,* 37 (1953), 47-52.

Shaffer, L. F. *Psychology of Adjustment.* Boston: Houghton-Mifflin, 1936.

———, and Shoben, E. J., Jr. *The Psychology of Adjustment.* (2nd ed.). Boston: Houghton-Mifflin, 1956.

Silverman, R. E. "The Edwards Personal Preference Schedule and social desirability," *J. Consult. Psychol.,* 21 (1957), 402-404.

Steiner, Matilda E. *The Psychologist in Industry.* Springfield, Ill.: C. C. Thomas, 1949.

Stemberg, C. "Personality trait patterns of college students majoring in different fields." *Psychol. Monog.,* 403 (1955).

Super, D. E. "The Bernreuter Personality Inventory: a review of research," *Psychol. Bull.,* 39 (1942), 94-125.

———— *Appraising Vocational Fitness.* New York: Harper, 1949.

————, and Overstreet, Phoebe L. *The Vocational Maturity of Ninth Grade Boys.* New York: Teachers College Bureau of Publications, 1960.

Symonds, P. M. *Diagnosing Personality and Conduct.* New York: Appleton-Century, 1931.

————, and Dudek, Stephanie. "Use of the Rorschach in the diagnosis of teacher effectiveness," *J. Proj. Tech.,* 20 (1956), 227-234.

Tendler, A. D. "A preliminary report on a test for emotional insight," *J. Appl. Psychol.,* 14 (1930), 123-136.

Tesseneer, R., and Tydlaska, Mary. "A cross-validation of a work attitude scale from the MMPI," *J. Educ. Psychol.,* 47 (1956), 1-7.

Thompson, Grace M. "College grades and the Group Rorschach," *J. Appl. Psychol.,* 32 (1948), 398-407.

———— "College grades and the Group Rorschach: a follow-up study," *J. Genet. Psychol.,* 78 (1951), 39-46.

Tindall, R. H. "Relationships among indices of adjustment status," *Educ. Psychol. Measmt.,* 15 (1955), 152-162.

Tomkins, S. S. *The Thematic Apperception Test.* New York: Grune and Stratton, 1948.

Tydlaska, Mary, and Mengel, R. "A scale for measuring work attitude for the MMPI," *J. Appl. Psychol.,* 37 (1953), 474-477.

Tyler, F. T., and Michaelis, J. U. "K-scores applied to MMPI scales for college women," *Educ. Psychol. Measmt.,* 13 (1953), 459-466.

Verniaud, W. M. "Occupational differences in the Minnesota Multiphasic Personality Inventory," *J. Appl. Psychol.,* 30 (1946), 604-613.

Warren, N. D. "Personality measurement." In Kaplan, O. J. *Encyclopedia of Vocational Guidance.* New York: Philosophical Library, 1948.

Weisgerber, C. A. "The predictive value of the Minnesota Multiphasic Personality Inventory with student nurses," *J. Soc. Psychol.,* 33 (1951), 3-11.

Welsh, G. S., and Dahlstrom, W. G. *Basic Readings on the MMPI in Psychology and Medicine.* Minneapolis: University of Minnesota Press, 1956.

Wiener, D. N. "Individual and group forms of the Minnesota Multiphasic Personality Inventory," *J. Consult. Psychol.,* 11 (1947), 104-106.

———— "Subtle and obvious keys for the MMPI," *J. Consult. Psychol.,* 12 (1948), 164-170.

————, and Simon, W. "Personality characteristics of embalmer trainees," *J. Appl. Psychol.,* 34 (1950), 391-393.

XX

APPRAISING INDIVIDUAL VOCATIONAL PROMISE

Preliminary Considerations

Focus on the Individual. IN THE early chapters our attention was focused on the logic and steps of test construction and validation, on the nature and occupational significance of a variety of aptitudes and traits, and on instruments for their measurement. This focus was chosen because in actual work with tests one begins perforce with a test result, and proceeds to study the significance of that score for the occupational plans of the person being counseled. But in appraising individual vocational promise, whether in a counseling or in a personal capacity, there are other steps which precede and follow the selection and interpretation of tests. When the focus is on the individual rather than on a test the perspective changes and other considerations come to the fore. For these reasons it is the purpose of this chapter to consider the use of tests in appraising individuals.

What is said here does not bear on the work of the psychologist or personnel man who is using tests mechanically in large-scale selection programs; in such work the procedures are those of test development, described in another chapter; test interpretation is then simply the statement of chances of success as expressed in a numerical score. In such operations there is neither a problem of selecting appropriate tests nor one of synthesizing the results and evaluating their significance for a given individual, for test selection has been taken care of in the test development program, and synthesizing results and teasing out meaning has been taken care of by the validation and scoring processes.

But the material of this chapter is of importance to the worker who must operate without extensive previously validated test batteries. It is important to most persons working in small organizations, with small departments, to executives even in large organizations, and to private consultants. Many of the applicants appraised in these situations are considered for positions which have not been thoroughly studied with tests, and which sometimes cannot be so studied in time to help with the solution of immediate problems. In such instances the user of tests must operate more as a counselor or clinician, bringing together bits of information about tests and about jobs in order to make the best possible appraisal.

The material in this chapter is even more important to the vocational counselor whose function it is to help his clients to obtain the most accurate possible picture of their abilities and interests in relation to occupational opportunities. In such work the counselor usually has to help the client do what he should have been doing for some years: review his school, leisure-time, and work experiences in order to understand what they reveal concerning his vocational abilities. Vocational appraisal in counseling, of course, often requires the analysis of a much greater number of abilities, and the consideration of the requirements of a much greater variety of occupations, than does appraisal in selection work. Needed occupational norms are often not available, and those that might be used are often for populations of such specialized characteristics as to make generalization to other seemingly related occupations questionable.

The use of tests by a vocational counselor is therefore of necessity generally not a predictive process but rather a clinical procedure. A variety of data have to be studied in relation to each other, and hypotheses are established for the consideration of the client. It should be noted that the term hypotheses is used, rather than conclusions, as their bases are not definitive enough to warrant the term conclusion. The client decides which hypothesis seems most likely to him, aided by the mature experience and accepting attitude of the counselor, and proceeds to test it by embarking upon an appropriate plan. This plan is subject to review and revision on the basis of subsequent experience, either with the continuing aid of the counselor or by the client alone.

Selecting Appropriate Tests. When utilizing psychological tests for the appraisal of vocational promise, the first problem with which one is confronted is that of selecting tests suitable to the person and purpose at hand. This is no mean problem. At least four considerations must be kept in mind in making the selection.

The person to be tested must be understood. The psychometrist or counselor selecting the tests must know certain obviously important facts such as age, amount of previous education and approximate intellectual level. All of these affect, for example, the choice of the Kuder or the Strong interest inventories; age and intelligence, the choice of the Bennett or Owens-Bennett mechanical aptitude tests. The cultural background of the client is equally important, as has been well demonstrated by the investigations of social psychologists interested in race differences and by the experience of vocational counselors working with refugee groups. Even when there are no language differences, differences in experiences peculiar to a sub-culture can affect the appropriateness of a test. It has been found, for example, that in a picture-completion test standardized on American children and depicting, among other things, a boy about to kick something which he has just dropped from his extended hands, Scottish children often make the mistake of giving the boy a pumpkin to kick instead of the oval football. The reason is clear: Their football game is soccer, in which a round ball is used, and they are familiar neither with oval balls (despite English Rugby-football) nor with pumpkins. Some tests, designed by and standardized upon residents of the Northeastern and Middle Western states, are not fully applicable to those who reside in other parts of the country.

The purpose of testing must also be clear to the selector of tests. Is the objective a survey of the abilities and interests of the client, in order to ascertain which areas might profitably be explored either by tests or by life experiences? If so, a combination of tests which tap a number of fundamental abilities and interests is desirable, even though occupational norms may be defective, for the important thing is to locate strengths for further study. Or is the aim to make an intensive analysis of some one or two areas, in order better to understand and evaluate the possibilities of assets already known to exist? In this case, a number of tests measuring varied aspects or manifestations of the same aptitudes may be desirable, to make possible a detailed study of an area. For example, a number of tests of manual dexterity may be used to determine just what type of hand-and-finger operations the client performs with the most skill, or several interest inventories may be administered so that discrepancies between patterns on tests constructed in different ways and using different types of items may suggest special outlets to be avoided or sought.

Whether the testing is to aid in guiding development over an extended period or to help in making an immediate decision is another aspect of the purpose of testing. A young man who has left school with no intention of continuing his education but who wants to get started in a field in which he may be able to learn and progress on the job is in quite a different position from another who expects to go to college and wants help in deciding what to major in and at what field to aim. Directional guidance is sufficient for the latter case, and this calls for a variety of tests and inventories in order to check the level at which he may work and to point out occupations which he may do well to explore in courses, extra-curriculum, and summer jobs. But, reluctant though one may be to work in such a way, the case of the young man deciding on an entry occupation requires careful study of qualifications for immediate employment. The study must cover previous experience, and that is often very helpful; but in other instances test results are the most tangible and clear-cut guide available. The battery of tests must therefore be one which throws direct light on qualifications for entering at once into any one of several occupations under consideration. To fail to get all possible meaning from tests in such a case is to leave the making of the decision largely to chance.

The vocational aspirations of the client are a third factor determining the selection of tests. The psychometrist or counselor must know not only the background of the client and the nature of the service being rendered, but also the ambitions or goals which the client has in mind. He must know what educational and occupational level he hopes to attain, as some aptitudes are more important at some levels than at others (e.g., clerical perception); he must also consider what type of occupation the client hopes to enter, as that will help him decide how fully to test in special areas such as the technical and linguistic.

Test data constitute the last type of information necessary in the selection of tests for use in counseling. Knowing the client's status and goals, one must choose tests which have appropriate contents and norms, which are known to measure traits relevant to the choices in question, which measure these reliably, and which can be administered and scored in the time available. There should be no need to elaborate on these points in such a treatise as this.

Three Methods of Vocational Appraisal

Historically and currently, there are three methods of appraising the vocational promise of an individual with the aid of tests: One is clinical and two are psychometric. Their fundamental differences lie in the way in which tests are used. In the *clinical* method the results of each test are viewed singly and in relation to other tests and to personal and social data. All of these are weighted mentally, and a subjective judgment is made on the basis of this weighting. In the *psychometric profile* method test scores and other quantifiable data are compared with occupational norms, as when an individual's test profile is plotted and visually matched with those of various occupational groups to ascertain which he resembles most clearly. In the *psychometric index* method quantification is carried one step further to permit the expression of the individual's summarized test scores in one total score or index. This shows how he compares with members of the occupation in question. For example, in the Aviation Psychology Program of the Army Air Forces the scores of each cadet were statistically weighted and combined to yield three scores or stanines which expressed his standing as a prospective pilot (the pilot stanine), navigator (the navigator stanine), and bombardier (the bombardier stanine). These procedures are discussed at some length in the following sections.

The Clinical Evaluation of Test Data. The clinical method of evaluating test scores was the first to be used in vocational counseling, because occupational data were not available to make possible the psychometric methods. Until recently it has not often been described in the literature, perhaps because its very subjectivity makes it difficult to describe; in a good discussion of test interpretation Harmon (1947) emphasized the profile method but included the clinical, and Meehl (1954), McArthur (1954), Koester (1954), and Super (1957) have explored it further. Its advocates are many, and there are many who claim that it is not only the first method to have been used but also the ultimate method, to which all will turn when the defects and limitations of the psychometric methods are more clearly understood. This argument is met with the reply that, as psychometric methods improve, more factors will be more adequately taken into consideration and judgments made subjectively by the counselor will be made objectively by psychometrics. The reasoning underlying this statement is that anything that exists can be measured, and that any relationships which exist can be quantitatively expressed: If the clinician can do it, science can do it more accurately. The writers are inclined to agree with this latter position, but to recognize also that science must make a good deal of progress before all significant factors and relationships can be quantitatively measured and expressed. For this reason the clinical method of test interpretation is of great practical importance and should be adequately described.

The objective of the clinical method is to describe the individual in dynamic terms, in the expectation that a good picture of the person will make possible inferences concerning occupational success and satisfaction. The underlying hypothesis is that genuine understanding of a person, combined with insight into a situation, permits one to foresee the interaction of forces and predict the outcome. More humbly and accurately put, they permit one to set up hypotheses concerning the probable outcomes. Even when stated in these terms, it is clear that the clinical method takes on no mean job and makes claims as great as those of the psychometric, perhaps even greater, for the best psychometric predictions are made with full consciousness of the limited basis upon which they are founded, whereas the clinical method attempts to take into account all that is relevant. It puts great weight on the training, insight, and objectivity of the counselor.

In the experience of the writers, as counselors, supervisors of counselors, and counselor-trainers, there have seemed to be three principal techniques

of utilizing the clinical method. These are the case conference, discussion
with the client, and the preparation of psychometric reports. Separate
chapters are devoted to the last two topics, so they will be only briefly
mentioned here.

In the case conference the test scores are presented so that all in attendance may see them, generally on a blackboard. Sometimes they are simply
listed, and sometimes they are plotted in graphic or profile form. The
counselor orally summarizes the background information, giving the staff
an outline of the socio-economic status, education, previous experience,
interests, aspirations, and presented problem of the client. The counselor
or psychometrist then reviews the test scores, commenting on any observations made during testing that may add to the data. The case is then
thrown open for factual questions, after which members of the case conference raise questions of interpretation, propose interpretations of their
own, and make suggestions for further investigation or counseling. At the
close of the conference the counselor or chairman summarizes the discussion, perhaps attempting to present an integrated picture of the case as
seen by the conference. The focus may be on appraisal, but in practice it
generally includes also the nature of the counseling and the resources
which may be utilized in implementing the counseling.

Case conferences such as these are unfortunately rarely held in service
agencies other than hospitals and special institutions, largely because of
the amount of time they require. They are common in training situations,
whether academic or institutional, and some service agencies make a practice of holding them occasionally as an in-service training or supervisory
device. They have a number of advantages as a clinical appraisal technique: 1) They utilize the insights and resources of more than one counselor; 2) they are a safeguard against blindspots and biases; 3) they force
the crystallization of ideas which might otherwise not be made clear and
concrete.

Discussion with the client resembles the case conference as a technique,
but with the important difference that at least one of the discussants is
untrained in the use of tests and is emotionally involved in the proceedings. Despite these facts such discussion does a great deal to clarify the
counselor's thinking about the significance of the test scores, partly because of the freshness of another person's point of view, and partly because
the opportunity to think out loud brings ideas to the surface. Furthermore, the client's reactions to the data and to the counselor's tentative
interpretations (often put in the form of a question beginning with
"Could that mean . . . ?") provide a healthy corrective for the counselor's
own possible biases. This procedure is discussed at length in the next
chapter, from a somewhat different viewpoint.

The preparation of test reports is perhaps the commonest and best technique for the application of the clinical method of test interpretation. In writing up the results of testing the counselor not only expresses the test scores in verbal form, but discusses the significance of background data, observed behavior, and client attitudes and statements for the interpretation of test scores, relates test scores to each other and to these non-test data, and draws conclusions concerning the true characteristics of the individual being studied. These are then related to each other in a final summary or thumbnail sketch of the client as seen through the interpreted test data. This process, like the others described, forces the counselor to crystallize his ideas and to justify his interpretations, at least in his own eyes and in the eyes of any potential reader. It thus ensures more thorough exploration of the data than would a mere mental interpretation of test scores, and provides something of a safeguard against the indulgence of bias and the riding of hobbies. This technique also is treated at greater length and for a different purpose in a later chapter.

The picture of a person obtained by the above methods is probably as adequate as any. The interpretation of test data and case-history material, if the data themselves are skillfully obtained, is in fact the only method available for the psychological description of an individual. But from the point of view of vocational counseling, the defects of the clinical method are two: 1) The evaluations or judgments made are subjective, so that even a group of experienced counselors may be wrong, and 2) the best techniques for describing the psychological characteristics of an individual may be lacking in data concerning their occupational significance.

In the occupational applications the judgment of the counselor again becomes of fundamental importance. One might cite the O'Connor Tweezer Dexterity Test as an example, interpreted for years as a measure of significance for success in dental school, but shown by the majority of studies to have doubtful validity for that purpose. Several wartime aviation psychologists were certain that they could make better predictions of success in flying training by clinical interpretations of test data than were provided by the objectively obtained stanines, but, either because of the inadequacy of some of the tests used or because of their lack of knowledge of flying, or both, their predictions had no validity (Guilford, 1947, p. 669). As it is known that many instruments are good measures of psychological characteristics of one kind or another, and relatively few have been validated for many occupations, it is probably in the making of occupational and related behavioral applications that the clinical method makes the gravest errors. It is one which should be used only by counselors who have acquired both an intimate knowledge of tests and an even greater fund of information concerning occupational activities and requirements.

Methods of drawing on a general fund of occupational information for the clinical interpretation of vocational tests, and of adding to that fund when it is not sufficiently great or detailed, deserve some mention; they are even less frequently treated in the literature than are methods of analyzing test results in order to prepare a psychological sketch of an individual. They amount to the making of a job analysis by the psychometrist or counselor. If he has a good fund of vocational information the job analysis is of the armchair variety: The counselor mentally reviews the functions, duties, and tasks of workers in the occupation, and makes deductions concerning the aptitudes and traits which seem to be required; he checks these deductions against what he knows of the published material on test validities and against the expressed opinions of others who are familiar with the work in question. The list of characteristics thus drawn up in his mind, and perhaps put on paper, serves as a guide in considering the client's qualifications for work of the type in question.

If the counselor lacks sufficiently detailed information concerning the occupation in question, the job analysis must be made from a vantage point other than the armchair. The first step may be familiarization with printed material in the form of occupationial and industrial descriptions such as are listed in Shartle (1959), in Baer and Roeber (1951), in Hoppock (1959), and in Forrester (1959). But such data are often too general to provide the insights needed into the aptitudes and traits which make for success on the job. The counselor then needs to go to the job itself, observing workers in action, familiarizing himself with the knowledge, tools, processes, and problems of the occupation. This takes time, but it is the accumulation of information acquired in such first-hand contacts with vocations and workers which distinguishes the vocational counselor and the counseling psychologist from the clinical psychologist. The last-named knows diagnostic and counseling techniques, and has insight into the dynamics of human adjustment, but unless he has had a great deal of contact with workers and has studied their work he is not qualified to do vocational appraisal and counseling. The techniques used in these field studies and observations are of course the standard techniques of job analysis as used in the preliminary work of test development. Shartle (1959) has described them in his text on the collection and organization of occupational information.

The Psychometric Profile Method. The first attempts to objectify the clinical method of test interpretation consisted of administering batteries of tests to persons in a variety of occupations in order to ascertain the nature of the patterning of test scores. This was the method developed by the Minnesota Employment Stabilization Research Institute (Paterson and Darley, 1936), which used a standard battery of intelligence, clerical, mechanical, spatial, and manual dexterity tests, administering this battery to groups of clerical workers, department store clerks, policemen, janitors, accountants, casual laborers, and others. The mean scores made by each group on each test were ascertained, and a profile plotted for each group, as shown in Figure 8. This made it possible to give the same battery of tests to a client, and to compare the patterning of his scores with that of accountants if he aspired to be an accountant, or to the patterning of the aptitudes of policemen if that was an occupation to be considered.

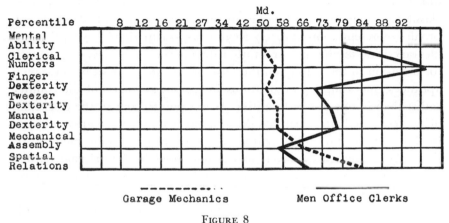

FIGURE 8

OCCUPATIONAL ABILITY PATTERNS
After Andrew and Paterson (1934).

The technique had a number of serious limitations, of which its originators were well aware. One was the limited number of occupations for which patterns could be obtained; this was in part remedied by the generalizations of experts in the *Minnesota Occupational Rating Scales* (Paterson et al., 1941, 1953). Another was the difficulty of deciding when an individual's profile differed significantly from that of an occupational group, discussed in connection with the USES General Aptitude Test Battery; this was then remedied only by the judgment of the counselor, making the method partly clinical in nature. A third was the limited number of characteristics appraised by the test battery and included in the profile; this also had to be remedied by the counselor's clinical skill and occupational knowledge. As in the case of the clinical method, too often counselors have knowledge of tests or knowledge of occupations without having both. Finally, the populations used to establish occupational ability profiles in the Minnesota project were selected as representing the local population, leaving the question of their applicability in other localities unanswered.

The Occupational Analysis Division of the United States Employment Service carried work with this technique further, partly for selection and partly for guidance purposes. In the former program batteries of the most valid tests were used in varying combinations to establish profiles for each job studied; in the latter, a standard battery was administered to persons employed in various families of occupations and patterns of aptitudes were ascertained. This work has been described in Chapter 14, its outcome being the USES General Aptitude Test Battery. The difficulties discovered in the MESRI work were minimized in the USES project by classifying occupations in families in such a manner as to make some 200 profiles represent approximately 2000 major occupations, basing the profiles on critical minimum scores rather than mean scores, selecting the tests for inclusion in the battery on the basis of a factor analysis of vocational aptitudes, and sampling occupations in various key parts of the country rather than in one or two localities. As was pointed out in the discussion of the tests, the battery still has defects, but it represents a great advance in the occupational ability pattern or psychometric profile method. Its usefulness is limited, however, to the tests used in the original battery (not available except through state employment services) and to the occupations already studied. It makes one further contribution, in that a counselor who knows the patterns established by the General Aptitude Test Battery, and who has a real understanding of vocational processes and requirements, can use this fund of information to provide an objective foundation for the exercise of clinical insight when working with tests and occupations for which occupational ability pattern data are lacking.

The Differential Aptitude Tests of the Psychological Corporation, also described in Chapter XIV, are another attempt to improve and extend the occupational ability pattern or psychometric profile method, although to date it has been applied largely to school populations. *The American Institute for Research* is conducting large scale research in its Talent Project which should facilitate developing occupational ability profiles. Existing multifactor batteries which may in due course yield such data have been described elsewhere and evaluated by Super (American Personnel and Guidance Assn., 1957).

The usefulness of this method of appraising vocational promise depends, as might be expected in the case of an empirical method, upon the accumulation of objective evidence. It has been seen that only a bare minimum of such data are now on hand, enough to reveal the promise and the defects of the technique, to provide a concrete basis for the making of some decisions, and to make somewhat less intuitive some of the clinical judgments which have to be made when objective data are lacking.

The Psychometric Index Method. The combining of test scores in order to provide a single score or index of vocational promise has long been practiced, both in the arbitrary weighting of scores on the basis of *a priori* judgments of their relative importance in a job, and in the statistical weighting of test scores on the basis of their respective correlations with the criterion. This has been a selection technique, however, rather than a method of appraising an individual for counseling, largely because data were lacking for the statistical weighting of tests for counseling and because counselors were properly reluctant to give the appearance of objectivity to their judgments by arbitrarily weighting the scores and combining them. Perhaps two exceptions to these statements may now be made.

In the Kuder Preference Record a series of scores (those for the ten types of interests) can be weighted on the basis of their relationship to membership in an occupation, and combined to show how closely an individual's interests resemble those of members of that occupation. This is a limited application of the technique, both because the scores involved represent only interests, and because such occupational indices, as Kuder calls them, have so far been developed for very few occupations.

The stanines of the Air Force's Aviation Psychology Program (Du Bois, 1947) may be a second exception. Although these were developed for selection purposes rather than for counseling, the fact that they are available for three different flying jobs and are all obtained from the same basic test battery means that they could also be used in counseling concerning the choice of any one of those three specialties. This too is a limited application of the technique, but it illustrates its possibilities.

The fundamental argument for the use of the psychometric index is that it does away with the subjectivity of the profile; instead of leaving to the counselor the making of an over-all judgment of the similarity of the client's psychological characteristics to those of members of the occupation in question, this "judgment" is made by an empirically based statistical process which is more precise than the subjective judgment of the counselor. Each aptitude and trait is weighted on the basis of its occupational significance, and the similarity of the individual to others who have succeeded in that occupation is expressed by the final score or index. In the Air Force, for example, a cadet with a pilot stanine of 9 is known to have aptitudes, interests, and temperament very much like those of other cadets, 84 percent of whom succeeded in learning how to fly, while another cadet with a stanine of 1 is clearly shown to have characteristics like those of cadets, 81 percent of whom failed to learn to fly in the alloted time (Du Bois, 1947, p. 145).

This procedure, as well as that of the psychometric profile method, has sometimes been criticized as too mechanical, as failing to take into account the multiplicity of personal and social factors which affect success and satisfaction. Probably no one would contend that it does take all of these into account: Its proponents would argue only that what it does consider is taken into account in the most accurate manner possible. The adequacy of that kind of appraisal is a matter, not for discussion (except for the establishment of hypotheses), but for experimentation. Meehl (1954) has reviewed relevant research in a much cited monograph. Several studies are considered here, because of the importance of the issue. All of these are experiments in a selection rather than a counseling situation; unfortunately the lack of psychometric indices for use in counseling has precluded the possibility of making such experiments in counseling programs.

In the *Clinical Techniques Project* of the Army Air Forces, aviation psychologists experimented with a number of clinical evaluation tests for the selection and classification of pilots (Guilford, 1947, Ch. 24, p. 616). These tests included ratings of prospects of success based on observations made while the cadet responded to a confusing sequence and combination of signals in a miniature cockpit, while he worked with three others to assemble the parts of three sets of Wiggly Blocks, and while he sat in a waiting room surrounded by odds and ends of wrecked airplanes, bombs, and similar objects; they also included the Group Rorschach, which was scored in the usual manner and also evaluated impressionistically to yield a rating of promise as a flier. None of the techniques had any substantial validity, and those which showed some slight promise in the first validation were proved invalid in the cross-validation. At the same time, the objectively derived stanines had their usual substantial correlations with success in pilot training. It should be pointed out that this was a very limited evaluation of the clinical method, for each clinical evaluation was based on only one source of data, however global in approach the test was. Although it had been planned to make evaluations on the basis of a clinical synthesis of all data for each cadet, this part of the plan broke down because of the sheer bulk of the data to be handled and the impossibility of assigning the required number of psychologists to the project over such a long period of time.

The Surgeon's Classification Board provided an opportunity for a more comprehensive clinical evaluation of cadets being considered for flying training during several months in which it was experimented with during World War II (described in a military report by W. M. Lepley and H. D.

Hadley). The board consisted of a flight surgeon and an aviation psychologist, who interviewed each cadet with stanines below the required levels for all three air crew assignments (at that time 3 for pilot and bombardier, 5 for navigator). The interviews lasted approximately eight minutes each, ranging in length from five to twenty minutes. A total of 1524 cadets were interviewed during the six months of the board's existence at this one classification center, and 285 were sent to pilot training because the board's review of the test scores and interview data led it to believe that the cadet would make a good pilot. Follow-up data were obtained for 259 of these cadets, who were test-matched with 146 cadets sent to training at a somewhat earlier date when standards were lower and without having been passed on by a board. Various analyses were made by class and time of training; in the most legitimate comparison, 68.9 percent of the cases passed by the board failed in training, whereas 73 percent of those with similar stanines who went automatically to training failed. The critical ratio was 0.50, showing that cadets who were clinically evaluated by a board of experts were no more likely to succeed than others who had the same stanine or psychometric index but were not clinically evaluated. Despite certain defects in the design of this real-life experiment (e.g., elimination rates were not quite the same when the two groups were in training, being slightly lower for and therefore favoring the board cases), Lepley and Hadley seem to have definitely put the burden of proof upon those who claim that the clinical method is superior to a comprehensive battery of objectively validated and summated tests. At present, one can only conclude, with Meehl (1954) that the costly clinical methods have been proved no more effective than the less time-consuming objective methods.

A Balanced Approach in Counseling.

The preceding sections have brought out the facts that use of the clinical method is often necessitated by the lack of data basic to the use of psychometric methods, and that the fully developed psychometric index method is not easily improved by adding clinical evaluation to it. It has also been made clear that both methods depend for their success on the use of a variety of relevant and well-understood tests. In view of the scarcity of psychometric occupational indices, the clinical method, made as objective as possible by occupational norms, must generally suffice as the technique of individual appraisal for vocational counseling.

Since the publication of Meehl's review of research on *Clinical Versus Statistical Prediction* (1954) considerable interest has been shown in how the clinician and counselor function in making the predictions which are a part of appraisal. We have already referred to this process as one in which the counselor studies a variety of data in relation to each other and sets up hypotheses for the consideration of the client; it is this concept which has been the theme of recent writing on this subject.[1]

The description of the clinical or appraisal process as the setting up of hypotheses for subsequent experimentation or "testing" was probably first undertaken by Allport (1937), who referred to it as the "integrational hypothesis." Williamson, (1950), Meehl (1954), and the Pepinskys (1954), among others, have discussed the appraisal function as one in which the counselor or clinician formulates and tests hypotheses. The psychologist reviews a number of diverse facts, relates these facts to each other, judges how to interpret and combine them, and with them constructs a picture of his client. Meehl refers to this as a "conception of a person," McArthur calls it a "clinical construct," while the Pepinskys call it a "hypothetical person," a term which well conveys the notion of a picture, the validity of which is to be tested by trying it. As Murray (1938) put it, "By the observation of many parts one finally arrives at a synthetic conception of the whole, and then, having grasped the latter one can re-interpret and understand the former." The whole itself serves as the basis for prediction.

Actuarial prediction enters into the counselor's or personnel man's thinking as he takes into account data such as the fact that most men with abilities like those of the person with whom he is working fail in a particular type of occupation, but many psychologists have concluded that it is the "hypothetical person," the picture of a client developed by studying and synthesizing available data in ways not now possible by statistical methods, that gives the best prediction. Thus McArthur's (1954) analysis of how clinicians work led him to conclude that "It was from that clinical construct and not from any single datum that good predictions were made . . . The good predictions came from the construct as a whole."

In developing this clinical construct McArthur's best clinicians were guided, not by preconceived psychological theories nor by experience with other cases, but rather by a theoretical framework derived from study of the case in question. They developed, that is, a theory for each client as they worked with him. The data for each person were paramount. Those who applied existing theories in a doctrinaire fashion turned out to be the poorest appraisers.

A more systematic study by Koester (1954) had counselors do their appraisal work out loud so that it might be electronically recorded. The process of appraisal appeared to be an orderly one, beginning with ex-

---

[1] The material which follows is based largely on Super's paper on "The preliminary appraisal in vocational counseling," *Personnel and Guidance Journal*, 1957, 36, 154-161.

amination of data, interpretation of these facts, formulation of hypotheses on the basis of combinations of facts, and evaluation of the hypotheses in the re-examination of the data. The procedure was eclectic, inductive as in the work of McArthur's clinicians, with the focus on making a theory to fit the data rather than on making the data fit a theory. The best counselors made an effort to ascertain whether their data might cause them to refute a hypothesis already developed. Understanding came as data began to fall into combinations and hypotheses emerged.

In a study of clinical prediction of success and failure in flying, Holtzman and Sells (1954) reported that their clinicians tended to agree remarkably well with each other but to be consistently wrong, leading Shoben (1956) to conclude that this suggests that the psychological theories which currently guide the organization of data by clinicians are less useful than theories which are derived from data concerning the individual being appraised. As McArthur pointed out, theory may help to explain a specific fact; it may give clues which help to place the fact in the picture of a person which is emerging from studying him.

Meehl raised the question of when creating hypotheses is likely to help prediction, and suggested that for " 'open-ended' prediction problems the intermediate construct-building steps will show up to greater advantage than they have in the prediction problems hitherto studied." When regression equations can be developed for a particular situation, as for example in the selection of students and interns in clinical psychology, statistical methods are best (Kelly and Fiske, 1951), but when one is counseling concerning a career, in which any number of occupations are open to the counselee (Meehl's "open-ended" situation) and specific validity data and regression weights are not available, clinical appraisal and prediction by means of a hypothetical person is the only possibility.

Since, however, it is easy to fall into the error of predicting on the basis of inappropriate preconceived theories and stereotypes, it is relevant to consider how one can construct hypotheses without falling into the classical clinical error. Several writers on the subject have attempted to provide the answer, which consists of remembering that one is dealing with hypotheses, of testing these hypotheses against the original data, against new data, against the insights of professional colleagues, and against the client's own perceptions and in actual experience, and finally of constructing new hypotheses as the results of experience require.

It is important to point out (Super, 1957) that vocational counseling is not always open-ended. The counselor is often presented with selection-like situations in which he must appraise fitness for a particular occupation, for clients ask whether they should study accounting, take a job as a salesman, or seek an apprenticeship in printing. The judgments to be made are the same as in selection work, and they are not open-ended. The psychologist often must make predictions which are not truly open-ended but which lack regression data. How well, then, does appraisal work?

The Office of Strategic Services used assessment or appraisal methods during World War II to predict success in the unstudied occupation of secret agent; psychologists in the Veterans Administration psychology selection project used them to predict success in an occupation they knew well, clinical psychology; Holtzman and Sells used them for the job of pilot; and the Menninger Clinic staff attempted to forecast success in psychiatric training by clinical methods. It is by now an old story that the appraisals generally had little value. Thus, although the clinical appraisal of a person is the only kind one can make when regression data are lacking, it is still true that it is in the making of occupational predictions that the hypothetical picture of a person is most likely to lead one astray. Lacking information as to the occupational predictive value of one's data about a person, it is difficult to forecast his vocational behavior; lacking appropriate knowledge of the occupational context in which he may work, the likelihood of making an informed guess is still further reduced. As Cronbach put it in the *Annual Review of Psychology* for 1956, "Assessment encounters trouble because it involves hazardous inferences . . . The clinical judge adds valid variance. But he makes overbold predictions, underweights relevant scores in favor of his clinical data, employs stereotypes instead of admitting his ignorance of what makes a good pilot or psychiatrist, and commits himself to a single 'most likely' personality structure instead of reporting the tentative alternative." One ounce of statistics (e.g., one Strong's Blank scale) appears to be worth a pound of clinical judgment (e.g., the counselor's hypothetical person).

Granted the defects of the appraisal method, it is still the only method available in most counseling and in much selection work. The question of immediate importance to the test user is, then, how to improve it. The following suggestions emerge from the discussions:

1. The situation in which vocational behavior is to be predicted should be analyzed as thoroughly and as objectively as possible;

2. The appraisal data which should be relied on most heavily are those having well-established significance for future behavior (validity);

3. Inferences about the personality of the client should be made from relevant data, hypotheses concerning his other characteristics and behavior should be derived from these inferences, and these hypotheses should be tested for congruity with all of the data;

4. The hypothetical picture of the client should be related to the hypothetical picture of the situation in which his behavior is to be

predicted, and hypotheses ("predictions") as to the behavior which may be anticipated by that type of person in that type of situation are set up;

5. The hypothetical client thus pictured, the vocational situation described, and the behavior predictions thus made, should be tested against the perceptions of other observers, including the client himself;

6. The predictions should be expressed as probabilities, that is, as hypotheses the validity of which may be tested by experience, and the probabilities of alternative outcomes should be considered.

In closing this discussion, a word of caution needs to be put on record concerning the mechanical use of test results. The presumed superiority of completely validated and objectively summated test data over clinical interpretations does not mean that test results should be used mechanically, if "mechanically" is taken to mean applied indiscriminately and regardless of the background of the person taking the tests, his health and morale at the time of testing, and the conditions of testing. Clinical interpretation in this sense is always necessary, and in counseling it should be easier than in a large-scale selection program. One illustration will perhaps suffice to make the point. It will be remembered from the discussion of test administration that Meltzer (1944) reported a correlation between manual dexterity and output in an industrial job which changed from —.27 to .30 with a change in supervision. The attitudes of the persons taking the tests and producing the output are important. When such factors are involved the clinical insight of the test user is crucial. He cannot know whether or not such factors are present unless he has insight and is alert to use it.

REFERENCES FOR CHAPTER XX

Allport, G. W. *Personality*. New York: Holt, 1937.

American Personnel and Guidance Association Staff. *The Use of Multifactor Tests in Guidance*. Washington, D. C.: American Personnel and Guidance Association, 1957.

Andrew, P. M., and Paterson, D. G. "Measured characteristics of clerical workers," *University of Minnesota, Bull. Empl. Stab. Res. Inst.*, (1934).

Baer, M. F., and Roeber, E. C. *Occupational Information*. Chicago: Science Research Associates, 1951.

DuBois, P. H. (ed.). *The Classification Program*. ("AAF Aviation Psychology Report," No. 2.) Washington, D. C.: Government Printing Office, 1947.

Forrester, G. *Occupational Literature*. New York: H. W. Wilson Co., 1958.

Guilford, J. P. (ed.). *Printed Classification Tests*. ("AAF Aviation Psychology Report," No. 5.) Washington, D. C.: Government Printing Office, 1947.

Harmon, L. R. "Test patterns in the vocational clinic," *Educ. Psychol. Measmt.*, 7 (1947), 207-220.

Holtzman, W. H., and Sells, S. B. "Prediction of flying success by clinical analysis of test protocols," *J. Abnorm. Soc. Psychol.*, 49 (1954), 485-490.

Hoppock, R. *Occupational Information*. New York: McGraw-Hill, 1957.

Kelly, E. L., and Fiske, D. W. *Prediction of Performance in Clinical Psychology*. Ann Arbor: University of Michigan Press, 1951.

Koester, G. A. "A study of the diagnostic process," *Educ. Psychol. Measmt.*, 14 (1954), 373-386.

McArthur, C. "Analyzing the clinical process," *J. Counsel. Psychol.*, 1 (1954), 203-208.

Meehl, P. E. *Clinical vs. Statistical Prediction*. Minneapolis: University of Minnesota Press, 1954.

Meltzer, H. "The approach of the clinical psychologist to management relationships," *J. Consult. Psychol.*, 8 (1944), 165-174.

Murray, H. H. *Explorations in Personality*. New York: Oxford University Press, 1938.

Paterson, D. G., and Darley, J. G. *Men, Women, and Jobs*. Minneapolis: University of Minnesota Press, 1936.

————, et al. *The Minnesota Occupational Rating Scales*. Chicago: Science Research Associates, 1941; and Minneapolis: University of Minnesota Press, 1953 (2nd. ed.).

Pepinsky, H. B., and Pepinsky, Pauline N. *Counseling Theory and Practice*. New York: Ronald Press, 1954.

Shartle, C. L. *Occupational Information*. New York: Prentice-Hall, 1959.

Shoben, E. J., Jr. "Counseling," *Annual Rev. Psychol.*, 7 (1956), 147-172.

Super, D. E. "The preliminary appraisal in vocational counseling," *Pers. Guid. J.*, 36 (1957), 154-161.

Williamson, E. G. *Counseling Adolescents*. New York: McGraw-Hill, 1950.

XXI

USING TEST RESULTS IN COUNSELING

THE interpretation of the results of psychological tests, whether by the counselor for his own appraisal purposes as discussed in the preceding chapter, or for the counseling of clients as considered in this chapter, has been strangely neglected by most authors of books or articles on the use use of tests in guidance. In the texts of the mid-thirties there was some mention of problems of technique, but it was only with the focusing of attention on interview techniques which resulted from the work of the non-directive school that it began to be written about in detail. In view of the relative recency of some of these developments and the controversy which still surrounds them, it seems wise to describe the techniques of transmitting test results to clients as they have been reported in the literature before attempting to suggest a method which combines the strengths of several.

In a treatise such as this it is difficult to observe the distinction between test interpretation and counseling; indeed, it could be maintained that there is none, for test interpretation is one technique of counseling. But it is only one technique, and a very limited one, despite the fact that for some time psychologists more skilled in psychometrics than in counseling acted as though it were the principal method of counseling. As a technique, it can legitimately be singled out for discussion by itself; it must be remembered, however, that it can be fully understood only within the framework of counseling in general. Chapter I was devoted to a discussion of counseling; in this chapter, the focus is therefore as narrowly as possible on test interpretation. With this caution in mind, we may proceed to survey methods of test interpretation.

Directive Test Interpretation. One of the first specific discussions of interpreting test results to clients appeared in 1937 in Williamson and Darley's (1937) *Student Personnel Work.* After describing the types of material included in the synthesis of test and other personal data, they wrote: "It is the job of the counselor to integrate this material, to interpret the present abilities and achievements of the case in terms of his background, and to draw conclusions from these interpretations. The final act of counseling the case is not performed by instructing the student to train for this or that particular profession, but by presenting to the student his possibilities in certain lines of endeavor; alternative goals, with the evidence for and against a choice, help to clarify the student's thinking and provide needed data for a tentative decision. He is urged to try, at least, that course which seems to suit his abilities and interests most favorably; the tentative nature of the try-out and the necessity for further interviews, before a final decision, are emphasized" (p. 166). Again: "The *recommendations upon which prognoses are based must be in terms of alternatives so that the student may make his own choice.* It is at this point in the case work that the counselor translates his two basic principles, about prediction for success in training and prediction based upon the characteristics of goal groups or occupational groups, into terms that the student can understand in relation to his own problems" (italics in the original) (p. 175).[1] Williamson and Darley gave no more space to test interpretation in this book, but this brief discussion makes it clear that they viewed the process as one of explaining logically and in everyday language the significance of tests and their vocational implications to the client.

These points were elaborated upon somewhat in later books by the same authors. In *How to Counsel Students* Williamson (1939) wrote: "The counselor must begin his advising at the point of the student's understanding, i.e., he must begin marshaling, orally, the evidence for and against the student's claimed educational or vocational choice and social or emotional habits, practices, and attitudes. The counselor uses the student's own point of view, attitudes, and goals as a point of reference or departure. He then lists those phases of the diagnosis which are favorable to that point of reference and those which are unfavorable. Then he balances them, or sums up the evidence for and against, and explains why he advises the student to shift goals, to change social habits, or to retain the present ones. The counselor always tells what a relevant set of facts means, i.e., their implications for the student's adjustment, in other words he always explains why he advises the student to do this or that; and he does the explaining as he orally summarizes the evidence. If in this way the student's confidence in the counselor's integrity, friendliness, and competence has been secured, the student should be ready to discuss the evidence and to work out cooperatively a plan of action."[2] Although there is little mention of tests in the preceding material, it is clear that in a University Testing Bureau such as Williamson then directed much of the evidence presented to the student would be in the form of test data. After

---

[1] By permission from *Student Personnel Work*, by Williamson, E. G., and Darley, J. G. Copyrighted 1937, McGraw-Hill Book Co.

[2] By permission from *How to Counsel Students*, by Williamson, E. G. Copyrighted 1939, McGraw-Hill Book Co.

a survey of other methods of counseling, and with only a passing reference to passive or indirect methods (as the non-directive were then called), Williamson took up the *explanatory method* in more detail: "In using this method the counselor gives more time to explaining the significance of diagnostic data and to pointing out possible situations in which the student's potentialities will prove useful. *This is by all odds the most complete and satisfactory method of counseling* [italics original], but it may require many interviews. With regard to vocational problems the counselor explains the implications of the diagnosis (of test and personal data) and the probable outcome of each choice considered by the student. He phrases his explanation in this manner:

"'As far as I can tell from this evidence of aptitude, your chances of getting into medical school are poor; but your possibilities in business seem to be much more promising. These are the reasons for my conclusions: You have done consistently failing work in zoology and chemistry. You do not have the pattern of interests characteristic of successful doctors which probably indicates that you would not find the practice of medicine congenial. On the other hand you do have an excellent grasp of mathematics, good general ability, and the interests of an accountant. These facts seem to me to argue for your selection of accountancy as an occupation. Suppose you think about these facts and my suggestion, talk with ..., see ..., and return next Tuesday at 10 o'clock to tell me what conclusion you have reached. I shall not attempt to influence you because I want you to choose an occupation congenial to you. But I do urge that you weigh the evidence pro and con for your choice and for the one I suggest'" (pp. 139–140).

In *Testing and Counseling in the High School Guidance Program* Darley (1943, Ch. 7) wrote in the same vein. The counseling interview, he stated, may be thought of as an unrehearsed play in which the counselor "carries" the action; a special learning situation for the student; a cathartic experience for a student suffering from great emotional pressure; or a sales situation. In all but the cathartic type of interview Darley conceived of the counselor as taking the lead, for in the play he must "organize the conversation" and "summarize the action"; in the learning situation he "explains the assembled test material and non-test data to the student, and then follows this by a discussion of the material"; and in the sales situation he "attempts to sell the student certain ideas about himself, certain plans of action, or certain desirable changes in attitudes. Persuasion and logic will facilitate and hasten the sale of such ideas by a counselor." Darley continued: "Many books on guidance insist that the counselor must not *tell* the student what to do. While such a generalization seems unsound, since it emasculates most of the purpose of data collecting and since it would be of no assistance to a student who needs help in making a decision, it is still true that the student who chooses one from among several suggested plans of action will feel a more active participation in planning with the counselor."[3]

Experience and the contributions of others have led both Williamson (1950) and Darley to modify their viewpoints since the above texts were written, for much progress has since been made in the clarification of counseling methods, but these writings have influenced and are influencing many users of tests and many counselors. For this reason it is necessary to present them in some detail. Perhaps the best way to see the limitations of this method is to present the antithetical point of view, and then to attempt a synthesis.

Nondirective Test Interpretation. Most active and severest critics of the directive approach of Williamson, Darley, and many other vocational psychologists and counselors have been the nondirective counselors, led by Rogers (1946). His most detailed discussion of the use of tests in nondirective counseling first points out that tests do not stand up well as a "client-centered" counseling technique, because in suggesting tests the counselor implies that he knows what to do about the client's problem, in administering them routinely or early in a contact he proclaims that he can find out all about the client and tell him what to do, and in interpreting them he poses as an expert who knows all the answers and will impart them to the client. "By every criterion, then, psychometric tests which are initiated by the counselor are a hindrance to a counseling process whose purpose is *to release growth forces.* They tend to increase defensiveness on the part of the client, to lessen acceptance of self, to decrease his sense of responsibility, to create an attitude of dependence upon the expert" (italics are ours) (p. 141). As one might expect from the italicized clause, however, Rogers went on to point out that there are stages in counseling at which clients are emotionally ready to study their abilities and interests and to compare them with those of others as a part of the formulation of objectives and the making of plans. Rogers believes that this does not occur frequently in practice, and that it is not the factual test results which are important, but rather the attitudes of the client toward them. He therefore sees little place for tests in practice while admitting that there is one in theory.

Rogers' views may have been conditioned unduly by selective experience. His theories were formulated while working in a child guidance clinic. After that his work in a university counseling center undoubtedly brought him cases in which emotional problems were much more com-

---

[3] By permission from *Testing and Counseling in the High School Guidance Program,* by Darley, J. G. Copyrighted 1943, Science Research Associates.

mon and more serious than they are in cases going to the vocational counseling center of the same university. It is a commonplace that people are referred to and gravitate toward persons who are interested in their types of problems: psychoanalysts encounter sex problems, ministers religious problems, attitude (nondirective) counselors attitudinal problems. It is significant that those of Rogers' students who have worked in centers which specialized more in vocational and educational counseling have found their viewpoints modified by that experience. It is from them that some very helpful formulations of the role of tests in counseling and of the methods of interpreting test results to clients have come. Contributions from the Bixlers, Combs, and Covner are cited below.

The use of nondirective *techniques* in vocational counseling was considered by Covner (1947) in a review of his experience in a vocational counseling center. Concerning tests he wrote: "A second major locus of fruitful application of the nondirective approach was the area of *preparation for testing and interpretation of test results*. . . . Test interpretation called for all the skill the counselor could muster. . . . As an introduction to interpretation it was frequently found helpful to sound out a client on his reactions to the tests. His mode of response served as a guide and warning to the counselor as to what sort of session test interpretation would be. For example, when a client who did very poorly on certain tests reported that he 'knocked them for a loop,' the counselor took notice to proceed with caution. The same approach on a number of occasions showed that clients were able to do a remarkably accurate job of interpreting their relative strengths and weaknesses, and to reveal considerable understanding of themselves." Covner goes on to point out that rejection of the counselor's interpretations often seemed to be the result of failure to give the client sufficient time to react, and that exploration of client reactions was facilitated by reflecting feelings, as in the statement, "The results are rather disappointing to you." To the experienced vocational counselor who had not been unduly influenced by highly directive writings, these insights into test interpretation did not seem very surprising; such nondirective *techniques* had been the stock-in-trade of good vocational counselors since the origin of modern vocational guidance, but because of greater interest in occupational information and in the counselor's use of tests, they simply had not been written up.

Types of problems best handled by directive and by nondirective techniques have been analyzed by Combs (1947) who worked in a university counseling center in which educational and vocational problems outnumbered emotional adjustment cases by three to one (Hahn and Kendall, 1947). One type of case best handled nondirectively was that in which the level of aspiration is definitely higher than demonstrated ability or in which there is a wide discrepancy between expressed and measured interests. Combs points out that such discrepancies are warning signals, and that the emotion likely to be aroused by being brought face to face with them is best handled nondirectively. He does not elaborate on method in this connection, but it consists primarily of accepting the client's feelings and of reflecting them in such a way as to make it possible for him to discharge the emotion, to accept himself, and then to discuss the situation and its implications objectively. This subject has been most adequately covered by the Bixlers, whose contribution is discussed below.

Bixler (1945, 1946) served as a counselor in the Student Counseling Bureau (formerly the University Testing Service) of the University of Minnesota, in which the test-oriented philosophy of Williamson and Darley tended to prevail; he therefore made a point of studying the use of non-directive techniques in vocational test interpretation which, strangely enough in a nondirective counselor, he seems to consider synonymous with vocational counseling. Bixler begins by pointing out that there are two aspects to the problems of test interpretation: 1) presenting test results to the client in such a way that they are understood, and 2) dealing with the client in such a way as to facilitate his use of the information. It seems to the writers that Williamson and Darley focused on the former and did it rather well, except that, as implied in Covner's report, they may not have allowed the client to react to the presented facts enough to guarantee an understanding of them. They appear to have failed to deal with the client in such a way as to ensure his being able to use the facts, depending entirely on his being sufficiently well adjusted emotionally to assimilate a mass of personal and therefore emotionally toned information. As Rogers pointed out, this is sometimes the case, perhaps more often than Rogers recognized, but it is certainly not always so. As the Bixlers (1946) put it: "The grading of examinations at the end of the quarter verifies the ineffectiveness of books and lectures in giving information to students. Vocational test interpretation is much more personalized and there is greater opportunity and reason for the student to distort or disregard information given to him." How many innocent counselors have not been shocked when clients or former clients reported that "You told me my tests showed that I would make a good personnel manager . . ." merely on the basis of one Strong's Blank score? The rules evolved by the Bixlers for interpreting vocational tests to clients are given below.

1. *Give the client simple statistical predictions based upon test data.* Examples: "Eighty out of 100 students with scores like yours on this test succeed in agriculture." "You have more of this type of aptitude than 65 out of 100 successful accountants." This can of course be elaborated upon.

2. *Allow the client to evaluate the prediction as it applies to himself.* After merely stating the facts the counselor pauses, perhaps longer than he feels he should, in order to let the client react to the facts.

3. *Remain neutral towards test data and the client's reactions.* The counselor expresses no opinions, gives no advice, but in a warm and respectful manner listens to what the client has to say. This is called acceptance; it is not the same as agreement.

4. *Facilitate the client's self-evaluation and subsequent decisions.* The counselor recognizes and reflects the feelings and attitudes of the client. Example: "You expected this, but it's hard to take." This makes it easier for the client to explore his feelings further, to release any related tensions, and to view the data and their implications more objectively.

5. *Avoid persuasive methods.* The counselor need provide no artificial motivation; the test data and the exploration and release of related feelings should do that. If they do not, neither will the exhortations or cajolements of the counselor.

Some sample excerpts from cases are given by the Bixlers (1946, pp. 151-152); one of these is reproduced and commented on below, in order further to illustrate the technique.

C1. There are studies which demonstrate that students' ranks in high school, along with the way in which they compare with other entering students in mathematics, are the best indication of how well they will succeed in engineering. Sixty out of one hundred students with scores like yours succeed in engineering. About eighty out of one hundred succeed in the social sciences (names several). The difference is due to the fact that study shows the college aptitude test to be important in social sciences, along with high-school work, instead of mathematics.

S1. But I want to go into engineering. I think I'd be happier there. Isn't that important?

C2. You are disappointed with the way the test came out, but you wonder if your liking engineering better isn't pretty important?

S2. Yes, but the tests say I would do better in sociology or something like that. (Disgusted.)

C3. That disappoints you, because it's the sort of thing you don't like.

S3. Yes, I took an interest test, didn't I? (C nods.) What about it?

C4. You wonder if it doesn't agree with the way you feel. The test shows that most people with your interests enjoy engineering and are not likely to enjoy social sciences—

S4. (Interrupts.) But the chances are against me in engineering, aren't they?

C5. It seems pretty hopeless to be interested in engineering under these conditions, and yet you're not quite sure.

S5. No, that's right. I wonder if I might not do better in the thing I like— Maybe my chances are best in engineering anyway. I've been told how tough college is, and I've been afraid of it. The tests are encouraging. There isn't much difference after all—being scared makes me overdo the difference. (He decided to go into engineering and seemed at ease with his decision.)

Several good features of this interview illustrate points made by the authors, and are worth pointing out, together with some defects in the use of the technique. The first statement of the counselor (C1) is a factual statement of an actuarial sort, without explicit personal applications of evaluations. In these respects it is good. It fails, however, to achieve simplicity and clarity. What kind of score or scores are referred to in the "sixty out of one hundred" sentence: high school rank, mathematics grades, or mathematics achievement test scores? If the last is meant, is that the score which predicts success in eighty out of one hundred students in the social sciences? The last sentence in the paragraph suggests that a scholastic aptitude test is the predictor for social sciences, a mathematics test that for engineering. This may have been made clear in unreported passages preceding this one, but as it stands the paragraph has to be carefully analyzed in order to be understood. It need be no longer to be clear by itself.

The client's first response (S1) illustrates the value of the method in obtaining free expressions of the client's feelings on the matter, and the counselor replies (C2) by recognizing and reflecting the feeling. This causes the client to bring up the counter argument himself (S2), putting him rather than the counselor in the position of the weigher of evidence; the client is taking responsibility for working out a solution. The counselor helps him continue the thought process by again reflecting feeling (C3).

The client pursues the matter further and it occurs to him that another test he took might throw some light on the matter (S3). This natural introduction of test results and discussion of them as one more bit of evidence is one of the very real strengths of this technique. It should be noted that the client is putting the test data to use with the help of the counselor, rather than the counselor telling him what their implications are. A follow-up of such cases might be expected to show much less distortion of test data and of counseling by the client, for the client has done his own thinking and reached his own conclusions in the presence and with the help of the counselor, rather than after he left the counselor's office. However, studies by Dressel and Matteson (1950), Lane (1952) and Lyle Rogers (1954), suggest that this may not be so, for counselor attitudes seem to be more important than mere techniques resulting in differences in client participation.

The counselor then reports the relevant test results (C4), reflecting feeling in the process in order to help the client clarify his thinking. The client continues to keep control of the diagnostic process, interrupting (S4) to make a tentative interpretation for the counselor to check. The counselor reflects feeling (C5), rather than repeating statistics. The result is a summary weighing of evidence by the client, in which he reaches a conclusion based on an understanding and acceptance of his own limitations and an awareness of the assets which he may draw on to help carry out his plans.

A Synthesis of Suggestions for Interpreting Test Results to Clients. The preceding sections have made it clear that the nondirectivists and others influenced by them who have worked in vocational counseling have made a significant contribution to the literature on test interpretation. Their insistence on analyzing counseling experiences and techniques has led them to formulate principles and to describe the use of methods of test interpretation which have long been in use by many counselors. In verbalizing what is done they have crystallized thinking on the subject and thereby helped to improve practice. As the nondirectivists approach the problem from the point of view of a systematic school of thought they have made some unique contributions in pointing out the implications of various interpretive techniques for counseling; they also run the risk, as shown in Rogers' paper on the subject, of failing to see other implications and other possibilities because of theoretically produced blindspots. There are values also in some of the more directive procedures, and occasions when they are more effective. For these reasons the writers prefer a more eclectic approach. If the suggestions outlined in the paragraphs which follow appear more nondirective than directive, that is because the writers' philosophy and approach, like those of Dewey, Kilpatrick, Kitson, Brewer, Taft, Allen, Roethlisberger, Cantor, and Rogers, are client-centered and nondirective, even though not those of a "school" of counseling. The writers' philosophy is also pragmatic, in that they are willing to use whatever works, and do not feel compelled to use only the techniques which are compatible with a system, valuable though systems are as means of making one conscious of the implications of the procedures used.

Structuring the Counseling Relationship. It may seem odd to begin a discussion of methods of test interpretation with a consideration of the structuring of the counseling relationship, but experience has repeatedly shown that the client's attitude toward test results is an important factor in his first contacts with the counselor, and that what happens in these first contacts makes it easy or difficult for the counselor to use the test results constructively in counseling. As Bordin and Bixler (1946), Bordin (1955), Covner (1947), and others have put it, most new clients feel that their problems will be solved by the counselor and that tests will play a major part in the process, and many are confused as to what vocational counseling is like. One prerequisite to good test interpretation, then, is the establishing of an appropriate mental set in the client; this is generally referred to as structuring the relationship. The techniques are partly verbal, partly nonverbal.

Verbal structuring may be done by asking the client what kind of help he wants the counselor to give him, and if (as often happens) the reply is, "Give me some tests to tell me what I will succeed in," by replying, "You feel that tests will solve your problem for you." Most clients react negatively to this type of bald but accepting statement by another of what they have actually been thinking; it brings to the surface the realization that they must assume more of the responsibility for their actions, and that tests are not likely to provide any such clear-cut answers. For the client to formulate and express these ideas himself is much more effective than for the counselor to do so for him: The former constitutes the achievement of insight, while the latter may be no more than indoctrination. Verbal structuring is also accomplished by an explanation of the counseling procedure, to make it clear that it consists of two persons, one of whom is trained in counseling and in occupational information, discussing the other person's aspirations, status, abilities, interests, and plans, surveying relevant facts, and considering their implications. It brings out the fact that testing is one way of getting some types of data, that there are other types of data and other ways of obtaining them, and that discussion is the crucial process.

Nonverbal structuring is based on the old adage that actions speak louder than words. If the counselor creates a permissive situation, acts as though he were interested in the client, and "accepts" the client's expressions of feeling, the client will generally sense that discussion is the essence of the vocational counseling, and that his own participation is the essence of the discussion; he will usually welcome the opportunity to make a genuine exploration of his vocational aspirations and status and will assume responsibility for working actively with the counselor in this enterprise. Once this type of relationship is established, the counselor need have no fear that the use of tests will unintentionally result in the imposition of a vocational prescription on the client.

Test Administration and Interpretation.　In the chapter on test administration attention was devoted exclusively to the problems and techniques of administering tests to individuals and to groups. But what has been said about interpreting test results to clients has made it clear that it has broader implications, for the way in which testing is done has an important effect on the client's expectations of tests. As Rogers (1946) pointed out, the routine administration of tests or the giving of tests early in the counseling process, i.e., in an unstructured relationship, implies both that the counselor knows what to do about the problem and that he can find out what he and the client need to know by means of tests. Such test administration is, in fact, a nonverbal or behavioral structuring of the situation. The antidote is not necessarily, as Rogers implies, to refrain from testing early in the relationship; it may consist of so structuring the relationship by discussion and behavior as to make it possible to test without creating this undesirable mental set. As clients often come with it already partly established, to do so requires special attention to the problem and a degree of skill, but it can be done. The essential factor is that testing be done by mutual agreement for jointly established purposes. Ways of accomplishing this are considered in the paragraphs which follow.

Routine test administration is often administratively desirable. In schools and colleges it is most economical to give tests to entering classes, in order to have the data for sectioning, screening, appraisal, and counseling purposes when and as needed. In guidance centers it simplifies scheduling, cuts down expenses, and is a safeguard against failure to obtain and consider basic objective data such as intelligence and interest test results. The question then is, can these values be preserved, without creating the mental set criticized by the nondirectivists and most other counselors? The writers are not familiar with any systematic experimentation with this problem, but experience and observation suggest that it may be done by two methods, one applicable to academic testing programs and one to guidance centers.

In *school or college testing* programs a large number of the students taking tests do so as a routine matter, because they are asked to do so rather than because they want to take them. Others are more immediately interested because they have problems of curricular or vocational choice to the solution of which they believe tests will contribute. Both of these groups can be helped by a brief explanation of the fact that the testing program is part of the institution's method of obtaining information which may be useful in problems of choice and adjustment, and that the test-obtained data are just one part of the information secured over the years, and added to the student's record. It is stressed that the other data, such as the previous school record, grades, extracurricular activities, part-time and summer work experience, and the student's own feelings on these matters of vocational choice and educational adjustment, are of central importance, test data being just one kind of helpful information. The procedure is like a routine medical examination: It may not turn up anything of special significance, but on the other hand some items may help to give a better understanding of a situation. This type of explanation will not uproot any strongly imbedded ideas that tests give all the answers, but it will help prevent their taking root and may help pave the way for more individualized structuring when a student comes for counseling.

In *guidance centers* to which individuals come for help with problems of vocational and educational adjustment test administration is always preceded by some sort of intake or registration interview. This can be and too often is handled as nothing more than a registration procedure, in which the basic data concerning the client are obtained, the presented problem is ascertained, the type of test battery to be given is determined, and an appointment is made for testing. But it can also be made an occasion in which the client finds an opportunity to discuss his problem in a permissive atmosphere and to develop an often-needed orientation both to his situation and to the kind of help which can be given by a guidance center. If the intake or preliminary interviewer (whether or not he is the final counselor) is nondirective at first and permits the client freely to explore his problem he will generally get better insight into its nature and into the kind of testing and counseling which is needed than if he proceeds at once systematically to take a history; he will establish a relationship in which the client is an active participant; and with this as a foundation he can help the client to understand that the information asked for in taking the history and the data sought in administering tests are simply part of the background material which the counselor uses in getting an orientation to him as a person. It can also be stated that some of the background data, such as the type of education received, grades earned, jobs held, and scores made on tests, may at various points in the counseling be facts to which the client and counselor will want to refer and which they may want to discuss. Testing may then occupy the same position in the counseling sequence as it now does in most guidance centers, and it may stand out as such administratively, but the client no longer views it as *the* procedure which gives the counselor and himself the answers they seek; instead, he sees it as simply one more data-collecting device, and he begins to understand that data collecting is only one small part of the counseling procedure. It then devolves upon the counselor to establish a permissive relationship with the client, carrying on that begun in the early part of the intake interview.

This is done by keeping the focus on and the responsibility in the client. The counselor may begin the first interview, for example, with a statement that "Mr. Doe, the first interviewer, has told me something about you, and of course I have looked over the records, but I think it would be most helpful if you would tell me, in your own words, just what you have been thinking about and with what you think we might help you." The new relationship thus begins as one in which the client is active rather than passive, in which the counselor can accept and reflect feelings, and in which the client uses the superior knowledge and insights of the counselor to develop his own understandings.

After routine testing and the re-establishment of a permissive relationship, *test interpretation* may be done at various points during the interviews. When the client wants to evaluate himself in comparison with other students or occupational groups, and asks how he stood on some test, the counselor reports the results in actuarial, nonevaluative terms in the manner previously described, permits the client to react to the facts, reflects his feelings, and facilitates further self-evaluation as the client continues to explore the significance of the facts for himself. This reporting of test results is often scattered throughout a series of interviews, the data being introduced only as they are relevant and requested by the client. More often in practice, but perhaps less desirably, the reporting of test results is done in one session, in which the counselor gives the client a profile of his test results to help him visualize them while he explains their actuarial significance. The results should be expressed in percentiles (without I. Q.'s!) so that relative standing will be easily understood by the client, and the nature of each group with which a comparison is made must be explained as briefly recorded on the test profile. Having the data in front of him permits the client to take in both his standing on each test and the nature of the comparison. This process is unfamiliar to the client and therefore requires much more of a mental adjustment than the counselor, used to test reports, generally realizes. It makes it possible for the counselor either to complete his explanation of the whole battery, allowing the client to come back to and discuss each score, or to stop after each test score has been briefly explained and allow for as thorough an exploration of that datum as the client wants to undertake. The writers are not ready to recommend one procedure rather than the other, but suspect that whichever method the client wants to use is best. If so, the effective counselor will pause long enough and be permissive enough after each brief explanation for the client to be able to take the initiative any time he is ready to use it. It is, after all, the client who must use the test results, and as their use is an emotionally loaded process it is well to let it be nondirective.

Client-determined test administration is perhaps the best term for what Rogerians would call client-centered testing, for the type of routine testing which has already been described is also client-centered in that tests are selected on the basis of relevance to the client and results are used as he needs them to clarify his thinking. This procedure has been described by Bordin and Bixler (1946) in a way which evokes considerable criticism from some counselors, as they proposed that the client choose his tests himself with little or no help from the counselor. It is not necessary, however, to go to this extreme in order for test selection and administration to be client-determined. If counseling has been begun nondirectively and the relationship is one in which the client works on problems of his own choice at his own speed, he may, to quote Rogers (1946), "reach a point where, facing his situation squarely and realistically, he wishes to compare his aptitudes or abilities with those of others for a specific purpose. Having formulated some clear goals, he may wish to appraise his own abilities in music, or his aptitude for a medical course, or his general intellectual level." When such desires are expressed the counselor may give the test or tests himself, giving the client the resulting information in the way already described. Better still in some cases, the counselor lets the client obtain the information himself by working up the percentiles and test profile together, thus continuing the mutual processes and joint activity of the counseling relationship, the client reacting to test data as they are obtained and the counselor explaining actuarial aspects and reflecting the client's feelings.

Combs (1947) believes that the difficulties in the way of the counselor who attempts to provide information and clarify attitudes are so great as to make reliance on a third person as test administrator and interpreter desirable, with the client then returning to the original counselor for nondirective clarification of feelings and reaching of conclusions. As he points out, it takes a good deal of skill to shift from one relationship ("directive" supplier of facts) to the other (nondirective acceptor and reflector of feeling), but then so does any aspect of counseling, and the writers believe that it is a technique which can be learned and used like any other. Whether or not it is learned and used depends upon the counselor's theoretical orientation, personal preferences, and work situation. In Combs' case all three were in favor of not having one counselor shift back and forth from more to less directive techniques; in most cases the requirements of the work situation and the desirability of continuity of relationships and work lead the writers to believe that skill in the use of both techniques and in shifting from one to the other is desirable.

The Counselor's Moral Responsibilities: Breaking Bad News and Sharing Good. As a user of psychological tests and as an appraiser of vocational aptitudes and interests the counselor has available information which may be of crucial importance to the client and of value to society. But neither the individual nor society may be aware of the availability and significance of that information; the client may never ask for it, and the counselor may never seek to obtain or to share it, if strictly nondirective procedures are used. One might ask whether it is ethical for a counselor to let a high school student work through his attitudes toward going to college and to make college plans without checking up on his mental equipment for going to college. Does a counselor who knows that a young man who is planning to enter a skilled trade actually has abilities and interests which might make him a scientist of considerable stature owe it to his client to make him aware of that fact? And does he owe it to society? It is not only attitudes which make for success and satisfaction:

abilities, opportunities, and awareness also play a part. The counselor has an obligation beyond that of assisting the client to assume responsibility for his own action, although that seems to be the sole objective of counseling set up by the nondirective school. He also has responsibilities for the detection and optimum use of talent, and for helping some clients to achieve insights into themselves and into society which they might not develop in sufficient time if left to direct the entire course of counseling themselves.

The counselor or test interpreter therefore needs to make sure that certain facts basic to the solution of the problems being worked on by the client are secured and considered. Intelligence tests may not be asked for in considering the choice of college or of occupational level; in such a case the counselor must either be sure from other evidence that the client has the ability to implement his plan or help the client see the need for the obtaining and considering of such evidence. Interest inventories may not be requested or interest scores discussed in considering the choice of a field of work; but if the counselor does not see good evidence in the cumulative record or case material that the field being considered is compatible with the client's interests, he owes it to the client and to society to lead the client to want to obtain such evidence. Psychotherapy cures some seemingly physical illnesses and solves some seemingly vocational problems, but it leaves other body ailments and other vocational adjustment problems untouched: Not to make a diagnosis when diagnosis may be important is as potentially serious an omission in a counselor as in a physician. The counselor or psychologist need be no more apologetic about being directive in such instances than is the physician. The crucial question has to do with how the counselor brings such evidence to the attention of the client. This is primarily a problem of counseling rather than of test interpretation, but as the solution is sometimes sought in test interpretation it should be briefly considered here.

To put it in negative terms, a client should not be confronted with an unsuspected low intelligence test score, low musical aptitude scores, or an unfavorable personality inventory score. The counselor must instead lead the interview into channels which help the client to explore these characteristics. This may be done by getting him to talk about his school grades, his success as a member of a glee club or band, or his relations with fellow-students or fellow-workers. Discussion of any of these matters in a permissive atmosphere usually leads the client to examine his aspirations and his disappointments, his strengths and weaknesses (Margolis, 1945; Rheingold, 1945). Reflection of the related feelings encourages the pursuit of these topics. During the course of such discussions it is generally easy enough for the counselor to introduce relevant objective data with which the client should be familiar; in fact, the client will often ask for them before the counselor has to take the initiative, in a way which shows that he has some insight into their probable nature. From then on the process is strictly one of counseling, and beyond the scope of this book.

REFERENCES FOR CHAPTER XXI

Bixler, R. H., and Bixler, Virginia H. "Clinical counseling in vocational guidance," *J. Clin. Psychol.,* 1 (1945), 186-192.

———, and Bixler, Virginia H. "Test interpretation in vocational counseling," *Educ. Psychol. Measmt.,* 6 (1946), 145-156.

Bordin, E. S. "The implications of client expectations for the counseling process," *J. Counsel Psychol.,* 2 (1955), 17-21.

———, and Bixler, R. H. "Test selection: a process of counseling," *Educ. Psychol. Measmt.,* 6 (1946), 361-374.

Combs, A. W. "Non-directive techniques in vocational counseling," *Occupations,* 25 (1947), 262-267.

Covner, B. J. "Nondirective interviewing techniques in vocational counseling," *J. Consult. Psychol.,* 11 (1947), 70-73.

Darley, J. G. *Testing and Counseling in the High-School Guidance Program.* Chicago: Science Research Associates, 1943.

Dressel, P. L., and Matteson, R. W. "The effect of client participation in test interpretations," *Educ. Psychol. Measmt.,* 10 (1950), 693-706.

Hahn, M. E., and Kendall, W. E. "Some comments in defense of non-nondirective counseling," *J. Consult. Psychol.,* 11 (1947), 74-81.

Lane, D. "A Comparison of Two Techniques of Interpreting Test Results to Clients in Vocational Counseling." Unpublished Ph.D. dissertation, Teachers College, Columbia University, 1952.

Margolis, B. D. "The problem of 'facade' in the counseling of low scholarship students," *J. Consult. Psychol.,* 9 (1945), 138-141.

Meltzer, H. "Approach of the clinical psychologist to management relationships," *J. Consult. Psychol.,* 8 (1944), 165-174.

Rheingold, H. L. "Interpreting mental defect to parents," *J. Consult. Psychol.,* 9 (1945), 142-148.

Rogers, C. R. "Psychometric tests and client-centered counseling," *Educ. Psychol. Measmt.,* 6 (1946), 139-144.

Rogers, L. B. "A comparison of two kinds of test interpretation interview," *J. Counsel. Psychol.,* 1 (1954), 224-231.

Williamson, E. G. *How to Counsel Students.* New York: McGraw-Hill, 1939.

——— *Counseling Adolescents.* New York: McGraw-Hill, 1950.

———, and Darley, J. G. *Student Personnel Work.* New York: McGraw-Hill, 1937.

XXII

PREPARING REPORTS OF TEST RESULTS

WRITTEN reports of the results of psychological tests are generally prepared for one or more of the following reasons: 1) to provide a permanent record of the interpretations made by the person who counseled the client; 2) to provide an interpretation of the results for the use of other professional workers; 3) to insure that the user of the test results makes a thorough analysis of his data rather than relying on clichés or stereotypes; and 4) to provide clients or their parents with a record of the interpretations for future reference. The first three reasons pertain to the same type of write-up, which may be referred to as the *report to professional workers;* the last may be called the *report to clients.* Each of these is taken up in turn in this chapter, from the point of view of purpose, form, and content.

Reports to Professional Workers. Depending upon the situation in which he is working, the psychologist who administers tests and reports on test results does so in one of three ways. He may simply submit a graphic *profile of test scores* to a counselor or personnel worker in the same organization, accompanied by notes on observations. He may make *limited interpretations,* primarily from the test results, when testing for a colleague to use in working with the client, this user being a counselor, psychiatrist, social or personnel worker. Or he may draw on all the case material in making a *full interpretation,* avoiding dependence on the ability of the user to synthesize the test findings with case history material.

Profiles of Test Results. The most effective way of presenting test results in some guidance centers and business organizations has been found to be the test profile or psychograph. This is true when testing is done by psychometrists who have no more skill in interpreting test results than the counselors or executives who use them, and when the latter have been so well trained in test interpretation that it is uneconomical for the psychologist to write out detailed interpretations which the counselor or personnel worker can make himself. In the latter situation the psychologist and the user of the test results generally find that a brief discussion is all the profile ever needs by way of supplementation, or that a few notes at the bottom of the sheet on the client's behavior during testing take care of the subjective factors which the counselor should consider.

The objective of the test profile is, then, to set forth the test results in the simplest and clearest form, so that a trained and experienced user of test results, who can confer with the examiner in case he has questions, can quickly grasp their significance. It is also sometimes a useful device for study with a client, serving as a basis for discussion in which the client develops insights by analyzing both the data and his reactions to them. He is aided by the counselor's interpretations of the actuarial significance of the tests and reflections of feeling.

The principles which govern the development of test profiles and the graphic representation of standing on tests can be outlined as follows: 1) tests should be grouped according to type of aptitude or trait measured; 2) when standard batteries are used the test names should be printed on the profile sheet to the left of the grid, but when the tests used vary greatly with the client blank spaces should be left in which test names may be entered; 3) space should be provided after the name of each test for entering data concerning the norm group; 4) another space should be allowed for recording the test score or percentile; 5) the grid or graph on which the test results are plotted may be based on either percentiles or standard scores, or may show both, but the users should be conscious of the advantages and disadvantages of both types of scores; 6) some test data are not appropriately represented on the grid together with aptitude and achievement tests and need a special type of presentation on the test profile; 7) space should be provided for supplementary personal data to aid in interpretation; 8) it may be desirable to record observations made during the test sessions to aid in understanding some of the objective scores. Each of these principles is taken up in more detail below.

1. The grouping of tests according to type of aptitude or trait measured is primarily to facilitate the comparison of test scores which should be approximately the same. Although the Minnesota Spatial Relations Test and the Minnesota Paper Form Board measure the same basic aptitude, the latter test is more affected by general intelligence than the former; for this reason a client's status will not be identical on the two tests, but a study of the differences often helps give a better understanding of the person tested. This type of analysis is aided by juxtaposition of the scores. In the case of interest inventory scores, which do not lend themselves well to plotting on the grid, parallel listing of the comparable scores of the commonly used inventories is helpful in making comparisons. Two profile forms reproduced in this chapter (Figures 9 and 10) illustrate this principle. The juxtaposition of a heterogeneous battery of tests on one profile, as in the Vocational Advisory Service form (Fig. 9), can be

misleading in that the norm groups appear identical but are actually different; the DAT (Fig. 10) avoids this error, as all of the tests use the same norms.

2. The names printed alongside the grid save time and improve the appearance and readability of the profile if the clients worked with are sufficiently homogeneous in status and objectives for a standard list of tests to be appropriate, selections being normally made from within this list. This is true in selection programs in which standard batteries are used, and in specialized guidance centers. The Vocational Advisory Service profile (Fig. 9) attempts to effect something of a compromise by listing traits measured rather than the test doing the measuring. This has the advantage of focusing on psychological characteristics, but makes it necessary to write in the name of the test except when users of the report know that a certain test is routinely used for each trait, as in the case of the spatial and dexterity tests. Figure 11 shows a form on which no test names are specified, because of the variety of tests used by the agency; it provides space in which to make note of the names. Such flexibility of forms is essential in such an organization.

3. Spaces for the entering of data concerning the norm group are essential because most tests have several sets of norms from which the examiner selects the most appropriate Without these notations the counselor cannot know the significance of the client's standing, as in the case of the Minnesota Clerical Test, on which standings when compared to accountants are radically different from standings when compared to the general population or even to general clerical workers. These notations can be brief, for the counselor should know the tests well enough to remember the details if practice calls for no written interpretation by the examiner.

4. Space for recording the standard score or percentile obtained when the examinee is compared with the norm group is necessary, both as an aid to plotting the graph and as an aid to using it, for minor errors in plotting and reading graphs are common. The numerical entry permits accuracy, just as the graphic entry facilitates grasp of relationships.

5. Grids based on percentiles have the advantage of using the familiar and readily understood form of expressing standing on a test in relation to other persons, whereas standard scores are much less commonly known. But the percentile system has the disadvantage of distorting scores at the extremes, thereby minimizing the important differences in aptitude, while standard scores accurately express these same differences. For example, I. Q.'s of 135 and 190 are both expressed as the 99th percentile, despite the fact that the latter is much further from the mean than the former, making two persons with those scores seem equally intelligent instead of quite

VOCATIONAL ADVISORY SERVICE
CONSULTATION SERVICE

PSYCHOLOGICAL PROFILE

Client _____   Counselor_____

Sex: M_____ F_____ Chron. Age _____   Date_____

1 POOR	8 BELOW AV.	31 AVERAGE	71 ABOVE AV.	94 EXCEPT. 99	TEST	SCORE	ERRORS
					ACADEMIC		
					Vocabulary		
					Verbal Reasoning		
					Vbl.Speed & Alert		
					Wech.-Bel.-Verbal		
					CLERICAL		
					Number Checking		
					Name Checking		
					Simple Posting		
					Complex Classif.		
					Filing		
					Arithmetic		
					Spelling		
					MANUAL		
					Finger Dexterity		
					Tweezer Dexterity		
					Placing		
					Turning		
					SPATIAL		
					Wech.-Bel.-Non V.		
					Two Dim. Simple		
					Two Dim. Complex		
					Three Dimensional		

Comments:

Entered by_____   Checked by _____

JCS 10 (3-18-46)

FIGURE 9

INDIVIDUAL
REPORT
FORM

DIFFERENTIAL APTITUDE TESTS

G. K. Bennett, H. G. Seashore, and A. G. Wesman

THE PSYCHOLOGICAL CORPORATION

New York 18, N. Y.

NAME

SEX   AGE   GRADE

      YRS.   MOS.

PLACE OF TESTING   FORM   NORMS USED   DATE OF TESTING

Raw Score

Percentile

Standard Score	Percentile	Verbal	Numerical	Abstract	Space	Mechanical	Clerical	Spelling	Sentences	Percentile
70 –	99									99
65 –	95									95
60 –	90									90
	80									80
55 –	75									75
	70									70
	60									60
50 –	50									50
	40									40
45 –	30									30
	25									25
	20									20
40 –	10									10
35 –	5									5
30 –	1									0

FIGURE 10

Test Record and Profile Chart

Name ____________________ C-number ____________________

Test No.	Test Name and Form (or Sub-test)	Norm Group	Raw Score	T-Score or Standard Score	Percentile Rank	Standard Score Scale: 2.0 2.5 3.0 3.5 4.0 4.5 5.0 5.5 6.0 6.5 7.0 7.5 8.0 Percentile Rank Scale: 0 1 2 5 10 20 30 40 50 60 70 80 90 95 98 99 100
1						
2						
3						
4						
5						
6						
7						
8						
9						
10						
11						
12						
13						
14						
15						
16						
17						
18						
19						
20						
21						
22						
23						
24						
						σ Score Scale: -3.0 -2.5 -2.0 -1.5 -1.0 -.5 0 .5 1.0 1.5 2.0 2.5 3.0

16—43079-1

FIGURE 11

Test No.	Date of Test	Examiner	Examiner's Title	Institution	Examiner's Observations and Comments (Refer by number to any particular test; include any necessary additional explanations of special items such as norm groups)
1					
2					
3					
4					
5					
6					
7					
8					
9					
10					
11					
12					
13					
14					
15					
16					
17					
18					
19					
20					
21					
22					
23					
24					

different from each other. As standard scores are based on distances from the mean, this less-known system reveals instead of hiding this difference. However, as it is probably easier to explain this fact to test users than to get them to adopt standard scores, it is probably good practice to use the percentile system and keep its defects in mind. When space permits it is therefore wise to provide also for the recording of I. Q.'s and standard scores beside the grid.

6. Test data which do not lend themselves to presentation on the grid include the results of some interest inventories and some personality measures. Scores on Strong's Vocational Interest Blank, being measures of similarity of interests to those of men in various occupations, may not have the same meaning at the higher extremes as do aptitude tests. Strong therefore rightly recommended use of letter ratings, and these do not lend themselves to plotting on the more refined continuum of percentiles. Figure 7 (p. 425) illustrates the profile form used by Strong, combining letter grades and standard scores. Another effective way of organizing such data is to group, in parallel columns, the types of interests measured by the Strong, Kuder and Allport-Vernon inventories. It then becomes possible quickly to scan the entries in order to see in which occupational families high ratings tend to predominate. This has the advantage, also, of emphasizing the difference between aptitude and interests, frequently forgotten by clients and by relatively untrained counselors.

7. Space for supplementary personal data is something of a safeguard against interpreting test results in a vacuum. Most forms call for age and sex at the top of the first page, where they are seen before any test scores. Some provide space for the most important educational, avocational, occupational, and aspirational facts concerning the client. These make it possible for the user of test results to check quickly the client's measured interests against his expressed interests and ambitions, and to ascertain whether or not his aptitudes are reflected in experiences appropriate to them. The data may be too sketchy for complete diagnostic work, but help in case of quick reviews.

8. The recording of the observed behavior of the client often cannot and need not be a detailed and tedious task, and therefore generally does not require much space. It is important that some evaluative comments can be made on the test profile, however, in special cases. Figures 9 and 11 reproduce forms in which space is provided for such notations. These are especially desirable in the case of apparatus tests which permit the subjective analysis of the client's approach to problems.

Limited Interpretation. This is the type of report of test results which should be prepared and used routinely in guidance centers in which psychometric work is done by psychologists, and in which counseling is carried on by vocational counselors who have more knowledge of occupational requirements and of counseling techniques but less of testing. It puts the burden of test interpretation where it should be, but leaves the integration of the interpreted test data with the case history material to the skilled counselor who sees the individual and his situation both objectively on paper and dynamically in interviews. It is not a worthwhile type of report in situations in which the counselor knows more about tests than the psychometrist, for then the counselor can see more meaning in the test profile than the psychometrist can put into the write-up. Neither is it valuable in situations in which the psychologists knows case study procedures well and the counselor, psychiatrist, social or personnel worker has not had extensive, specific experience in using test results. Nor is it likely to prove useful as a report from one agency to another, except when the other agency is an equally well-staffed counseling service. In such instances full interpretation on the basis of all available supporting evidence is essential, as borne out by the experience of more than one guidance center which has attempted to render testing services to social agencies. Without full interpretation the test results generally impress the users as being of little or no practical use.

The objective, then, of the limited interpretation of test results is to put into the hands of the counselor a concise, verbal, occupationally-rather than test-oriented statement of the significance of the test scores. The counselor then relates them to other data already in his possession or obtained as he works with the client.

The principles which apply to the limited interpretation of test results may be stated as: 1) the interpretation of each test score first in the light of the appropriate norm group or groups; 2) the relation of that score and percentile to observed behavior in the test situation; 3) the relation of each such interpreted test score to any others which may have bearing on its further interpretation; 4) the modification of this interpretation in the light of any personal data affecting the suitability of the test content or of the norms; 5) the expression of these interpretations in so far as possible first in psychological and then illustratively in broad occupational terms; and 6) the summarizing of the interpretations to yield a picture of a person and of his occupational potentialities.

1. The interpretation of each test score first in the light of the appropriate norm group or groups requires only the verbal statement of what appears in the profile of test results. For example: "On the (1959 edition of the College Aptitude Test, Verbal) he stood at the 97th percentile when compared to freshmen in more than 300 colleges."

2. The relation of this interpretation to observed behavior in the test situation provides an opportunity to mention anything unusual which might have affected the client's performance, such as resistance to taking the tests, undue tension, or concentration and a systematic approach to the task at hand; e.g., "He seemed impatient with the discipline inherent in the test situation and wanted to skip the instructions given before each practice test, but controlled these reactions and worked steadily on the subtests proper."

3. The relation of each test score to others which may have a bearing on its interpretation requires the mental review by the examiner of other data, and the mention in the report of any implications noted. These may consist of such things as the seemingly discrepant scores on two tests of the same aptitude or trait, and the congruence of or lack of agreement between two tests of different types of traits such as aptitude and interest important in the same occupation. An example might be: "The evidence of aptitude for professional or executive endeavor provided by this intelligence test is not supported by the scores of the interest inventories administered."

4. The modification of interpretations such as those given above in the light of personal status affecting the suitability of test content or norms requires a reference to personal history data such as age, sex, education, and cultural background, and consideration of their resemblance to those of the standardization groups. To illustrate: "As the client is now 23 years old, it is probable that his standing when compared to freshmen on the A.C.E. Psychological Examination is somewhat biased in his favor, for it has been demonstrated that scores on this test increase with age during the age range from 18 to 22. Even if his standing on this test is really somewhat lower than it seems, however, the indications are that he is well above the average college freshman in scholastic aptitude. This is borne out by his score on the Wechsler-Bellevue, for which the comparison is with adults in general and shows him to be in the very superior category."

5. The expression of test scores first in psychological and then in educational or vocational terms ensures both the scientific accuracy of the description of the examinee and its meaningfulness to the non-psychologists who often use the results. It provides an educational or occupational sketch of the individual which is more dynamic than a profile of test results. The test summaries and case summaries which follow in this and in the next chapter will serve to illustrate this principle better, but a brief illustration follows. The interpretations which have so far been given might be followed up with "The conclusion may be drawn that this client has the scholastic aptitude successfully to complete the work of a selec-

tive four-year liberal arts college, although his interest inventory scores, which remain to be reviewed in detail, suggest that such work may not be exactly to his taste. Men with general ability comparable to his tend to gravitate toward professional or managerial work, whether or not they go to college."

6. The summary picture of the person tested, pointing up his educational and vocational potentialities and liabilities, brings together the gist of what has been brought out in connection with the results of specific tests. It attempts to integrate these findings into a dynamic picture of psychological characteristics, from which occupational inferences may be drawn by those who know occupations, and of occupational possibilities indicated by the known validities of the tests used. The summary of the test report from which the preceding excerpts have been taken attempted to implement this principle in the following way:

"In summary, the client appears to be a young man of very superior mental ability, capable of graduating from a good university and rising to positions of considerable responsibility. His speed in the perception of clerical detail, particularly numerical symbols, is comparable to that of successful accountants. His superior ability to judge shapes and sizes and mentally to manipulate them is indicative of promise in technical and artistic occupations. In ability to perceive and analyze the effects of physical forces and the operation of mechanical principles he does not compare well with engineers or skilled artisans, although he compares favorably with the general population. His interests are not highly developed in any area, although they resemble somewhat those of men who are engaged in business occupations involving contact with other persons and the management of enterprises. Experience has shown that many young men with abilities and interests such as this client's enter business and find their way into executive positions."

Common errors in the preparation of reports of test results generally consist of violations of the above principles. Psychometrists tend to write in terms of test scores of percentiles rather than in terms of aptitudes and traits; psychologists without extensive contact with business and industry sometimes find it difficult to translate psychological characteristics into occupational behavior; and those who are not well grounded in both psychology and in occupations tend to overwork the brief and somewhat stereotyped interpretive phrases of the test manuals. The result is test-centered, and the real significance and value of testing is lost. Perhaps an illustration of poor reporting, accompanied by an improved version of the same report, will help to illustrate some of these points. To facilitate comparison they are reproduced in paired, original and revised, lines when changes seem desirable.

In summary, the client's very{high scores on the Paper Form Board, the
{superior ability to visualize space relations,
performance subtests of the Wechsler-Bellevue Scale, and the Meier Art
to think in non-verbal abstractions, and to judge the quality of form and
Judgment Test,} } work or in
composition,} indicate a great deal of potential ability in art } and in re-
work involving spatial as well as aesthetic judgment} } Such as layout or pro-
lated types of work,}
duction work in an advertising agency. The low score on the mechanical
comprehension test suggests artistic rather than technical outlets for her
spatial ability.} {clerical scores and the
ability to work in spatial arrangements.} The average{ speed of perception of
48th percentile "effectiveness of expression and accuracy} of written expres-
clerical symbols and average clarity}

sion" suggest that she will not be handicapped in these activities} should they
} but that she
be involved in her work.} Her
would do well not to specialize in business detail or linguistic work.}
intelligence, which is} better than that of 97 percent of the general popula-
} very superior, suggests ability to rise high in any work.
tion, should ensure ability to succeed in any area using her other aptitudes.
utilizing her other aptitudes and providing outlets for her interests.

Briefly stated, the changes in the above summary were intended to produce a description of the client's abilities, interests, and occupational promise, rather than a summary of her test scores. Perhaps this type of report can best be made clear, after the outlining of principles which has just preceded, by reproducing *in toto* a report written for use by a trained counselor working in the same agency and for possible sending to a similar college counseling bureau. Such a report follows, with data slightly changed and identity disguised.

Report of Test Results: John F. Atkinson
(Limited Interpretation)

John Atkinson, a high school graduate, 19 years of age, was given two tests of scholastic aptitude. On the Otis-Self-Administering Test of Mental Ability he was at the 50th percentile when compared to college students, which would suggest that his chances of competing with college students and completing college work in an average college are reasonably good. On the 1944 Edition of the American Council of Education Psychological Examination he was at the 27th percentile when compared to college freshmen. His linguistic score was at the 33rd percentile and his quantitative score at the 26th percentile.

As the A.C.E. test is a somewhat longer and more appropriate instrument, this suggests that John, while able to compete with college students, is likely to find himself in the lower third of the student body and will therefore find it necessary to apply himself more effectively than the average college student in order to achieve satisfactory results.

Several tests of special aptitudes which are important in engineering and scientific occupations were administered. On the Engineering and Physical Science Aptitude Tests his mathematical score was at the 4th percentile, his physical science comprehension score at the 12th percentile, and his mechanical comprehension score at the 39th; on the other hand his arithmetic score was at the 56th percentile, his formulation score at the 70th percentile, and verbal comprehension score at the 74th, compared to men students in non-collegiate technical courses. These scores suggest that the client has more aptitude for work of a verbal nature than for mechanical or mathematical work. The relatively low standing in these latter areas is confirmed by the Minnesota Spatial Relations Test on which he scored at the 30th percentile when compared to engineering freshmen. On the O'Connor Wiggly Block his letter rating was C, which points up even more the lack of special aptitude in spatial visualization.

One test of clerical aptitude was administered: The Psychological Corporation General Clerical Test. The total score on this test was at the 29th percentile when compared to clerical workers, the lowest part score being that for clerical speed and accuracy at the 19th percentile and the highest part being verbal facility at the 49th percentile. These results fit in with the data indicating greater verbal facility than numerical or spatial, but do not indicate special qualifications for clerical work. At the same time the scores are high enough to indicate reasonable chance of success in such employment if other things are favorable.

Three measures of interest were obtained. On Strong's Vocational Interest Blank John revealed a pattern of interests most similar to those of engineers, chemists, and other men engaged successfully in physical science occupations. His interests are also similar to those of teachers of high school science, and to those of production managers and others engaged in semi-technical industrial work; they also resemble those of musicians. According to Strong's Blank his interests do not greatly resemble those of men in artistic work, biological science, social welfare, business contact, or literary and legal occupations. There is some sign of interest in business detail occupations, including office worker and purchasing agent.

The results of the Kuder Preference Record—Vocational, did not agree very well with the results of the Strong Blank, although scores on the two tests tend to confirm each other in most cases. According to the Kuder, John's interests are strongest in artistic, musical, social welfare, and mechanical activities. The moderately high interest in music and in technical work indicates some agreement with Strong's Blank, but there is a real discrepancy between the two tests on artistic and social welfare interests.

The Allport-Vernon Study of Values throws some light on this matter by showing a fairly high social welfare score and an average theoretical or scientific score, but confuses the issue by revealing a strong interest in material welfare, such as normally characterizes men in business contact occupations. What seems fairly clear from these interest test results is that John does have interests comparable to those of men who are successful in managerial work in industry; the picture is not clear cut with reference to other interests.

In summary, it would seem that John Atkinson is a young man of fair college aptitude, greater linguistic than scientific aptitude, and interests which most clearly resemble those of men engaged in managerial and supervisory positions in industry. His prospects for success in a four-year engineering or liberal arts college do not seem especially good, although such students do graduate from the less competitive colleges. On the other hand it seems likely that he would succeed in an industrial engineering course or in a business course aiming at administrative work, taken in an institution in which the competition is not too great.

Full Interpretation. As previously stated, this type of report of test results is most likely to prove valuable when reports are prepared by well-trained and experienced vocational psychologists, particularly if they are to be used by counselors, psychiatrists, and social or personnel workers who have not been trained in the use of test results. In such instances the psychologist shares the others workers' ability to make a case study, and has, in addition, the knowledge of tests, and of their occupational significance, not possessed by his colleagues. The effective use of talents then calls for full interpretation by the psychologist, although their application in counseling or in selection and promotion may be made by other specialists, depending upon the nature of the situation and of the case. The counselor may need the data in connection with educational and vocational planning, the psychiatrist in connection with therapy which calls for the most effective use of his patient's abilities and interests, the social worker as an indication of the types of vocational rehabilitation which may be effective, and the personnel worker as an aid to making decisions concerning employment and advancement. And the counseling psychologist will also find that the preparation of such a report is one of the most effective methods of forcing himself fully to explore the significance of test results and personal history data.

The objective of full interpretation is to tease the maximum of meaning from the test results by synthesizing them with other case-history material, at the same time using one type of data as a check on the other in preparing an accurate and vivid description of the person being studied.

The principles guiding the preparation of full interpretations of test results are the same as the six governing limited interpretations, with the addition of one more which follows after the fourth in the list given above. This principle specifies the necessity of *viewing the test data in the light of related case history material which it may confirm, contradict, or illuminate, or by which it may be confirmed, contradicted, or illuminated.*

Viewing test results in the light of other case material requires that the interpreter be trained and experienced in case-history taking and in the occupational and clinical significance of personal, socio-economic, educational, and avocational data. The process involves the examination of intelligence test results in the light of educational attainment; the comparison of measured interests with interests as manifested in school subjects, leisure-time activities, and previous occupational experience; and the evaluation of special aptitude test scores in the light of accomplishments in related activities. To illustrate: "The Co-operative General Mathematics Test for High School Classes was also administered. The client had three and one-half years of high school mathematics, followed by college training in accounting, a master's degree in business education, and three years as a junior accountant, in all of which he worked with figures. When compared with the four-year norm group he is at the 4th percentile, while with the three-year group he is at the 32nd. This low score is congruent with his low quantitative score on the scholastic aptitude test, his own statement that he feels weak in mathematics, and the fact that he failed the teaching examination in mathematics. The picture is clearly one of weakness in the mathematical area, although whether or not this weakness is the result of lack of aptitude, emotional maladjustment, or a combination of the two is not brought out by these data."

A somewhat more complete report of test results is reproduced below.

Report of Test Results: James L. Frank

James is an eighteen year old high-school senior, who came for help in the choice of a career. Specifically, he wanted to know whether or not he should go into engineering. His father owns a manufacturing plant; he is interested in having the boy go to college and feels that he may be better qualified for administrative than technical work. His father thinks that industrial management would probably be a good field. The boy worked in his father's plant during one summer but got a different job last summer, working as a bell hop in a resort. He preferred to go out on his own rather than into a job already made for him. He, too, feels that he is really more interested in administrative than in technical work.

James was given the American Council on Education Psychological Examination, two different forms a week apart. On the first, he scored at the 74th percentile compared to entering College Freshman; and on the second, at the 76th percentile. On both tests, his linguistic score was distinctly higher than his quantitative, which suggests that his and his father's hunch that James is not as strong in the technical field as in others has a foundation in fact.

James also took the Engineering and Physical Science Aptitude Test. His scores, when compared to recent high school graduates applying for non-collegiate technical training, were in the bottom decile for arithmetic reasoning, in the fourth decile for mathematics and formulation, almost at the 75th percentile in physical science comprehension, and in the top decile for verbal comprehension and mechanical comprehension. These results suggest that, while James is weak in mathematical ability, he does have a rather high degree not only of verbal but also of mechanical aptitude.

The Minnesota Spatial Relations Test was given, the letter grade being B—. As the norm group is the general population, it seems legitimate to conclude that James does have a relatively low degree of ability to visualize spatial relations.

The Purdue Pegboard was administered, James being near the 99th percentile on all part scores and total scores when compared with college men.

The Strong Vocational Interest Blank shows no primary interest patterns and no A ratings. The greatest concentrations of interests are in the physical sciences, technical and social welfare fields. James rates a B— as engineer and chemist, C as mathematician, B+ as mathematics-science teacher, B as production manager; B as personnel manager, B— as Y.M.C.A. physical director and social science teacher, C+ as Y.M.C.A. secretary, C as school superintendent. In the other fields, James's scores are scattered B—'s and C's. His interests are like those of many young men who go into business in that they are relatively undifferentiated. But he is somewhat stronger in the practical side of technical work and in the fields of human relations and personal contact.

The Bernreuter Personality Inventory indicates that James is an emotionally stable, somewhat dependent, extroverted, rather dominant, self-confident and quite sociable young man.

The rest of the results appear to agree quite well with the interview material. James's extra-curricular and leisure-time activities are primarily social, and indicate not only interest but considerable skill in dealing with people. His grades in mathematics are poor but are acceptable in other subjects. His general ability is better than that of the average college freshman, but he lacks some of the special aptitudes required for success in a technical curriculum. He has certain other aptitudes which would be assets to him, particularly his mechanical comprehension and his verbal ability. James would probably do well in a position such as his father's, in which facility in understanding mechanical processes is necessary, and in which finding some engineering activities congenial would help. His personality characteristics would also be an asset in the supervision and contact side of industrial management.

In choosing a college, James would probably do well to select one in which he can follow a business administration or industrial engineering major. It would be helpful if summer employment could be obtained in an industry (other than his father's) rather than in a field unrelated to his educational and vocational objectives. This would permit him to try himself out and get the experience of making his own way. It would make it emotionally easier for him to return to work in his father's plant within a relatively brief time after the completion of his education if that seemed desirable.

Reports to Clients.   The problem of preparing reports of test results for clients who have been counseled is a vexatious one. Ideally, the counseling of which testing and test interpretation are a part should have been so conducted that the client (and his parents, if they are involved) has integrated the test results into his own thinking. He then has insights into their significance which match his understanding of his school record and his vocational experiences and views them in very much the same light. Just as he does not think it necessary to have a written record of all of his jobs and of his performance on them, so he should not need to want a written report of the results of his tests. When he does, it generally means that they are thought of as a crutch of some sort.

In a world in which there are crippled people crutches are sometimes desirable. They are to be frowned upon only when they contribute to keeping a person partially crippled longer than he need be. The fact that clients often want written reports indicates a need for a crutch in some cases. When such requests are at all frequent the counselor should examine his practices, in order to find out why his clients seem to feel the need of something tangible to lean on.

This view, it should be noted, is not universally shared by psychologists who have used test results in counseling. Yoder and Paterson (1948) report a study by Stone at the Minnesota Employment Stabilization Research Institute, in which half of the adult clients who were tested were sent written reports of their test results, with occupational interpretations and employment and training suggestions, and half were personally interviewed for test interpretation and vocational counseling. The recipients of these letters, although uncounseled in the usual sense, were so appreciative that "the staff believes they represent a real contribution to vocational counseling procedures," their explanation being that the letter provides more time for learning, less opportunity for forgetting, than the interview. But it could also be contended that these data are actually irrelevant to the issue, for these were not clients who came for counseling, they were unemployed persons selected on a random basis for a study of the unemployed. It therefore seems likely that they appreciated help in any form. There is no comparison of the relative satisfaction of the two groups, nor of the outcomes in finding employment and making good on the job. Their appreciation may in fact have been appreciation of a crutch.

In the writers' experience clients have wanted copies of test reports 1) when testing has been overemphasized, 2) when the discussion of test results was not successfully integrated with counseling, 3) when the client's own insecurity led him to believe that he could use a report of test results to sell himself to a potential employer more successfully than he could on the basis of his experience, education, and conduct in the employment interview, and 4) when parents and others want tangible evidence of the results of counseling. Before discussing the form and content of such written reports to clients as are prepared, it may therefore be wise to deal briefly with methods of handling these problems.

Methods of Handling Client Requests for Test Reports. Methods of avoiding overemphasis on testing and of successfully integrating test results with counseling have been discussed in some detail in Chapter XXI, and need not be gone into here. But when a client requests a written report of test results which have already been discussed such preventive techniques are no longer usable. In the experience of the writers and the counselors whose work they have supervised it has generally been effective to ask the client how he expects to use the report. When emotionally insecure clients reply that they will show it to prospective employers as evidence of their qualifications for a job, the counselor asks the client to put himself in the place of the employer. He is to consider how he would react to an applicant who applied for a position and produced a sheet of test results to prove his qualifications. This generally brings about a realization of the artificiality of the technique and of the fact that most employers still judge in terms of other types of evidence. If this realization does not come at once it can be helped by asking how often employers have asked the client if he had any test results to show his qualifications, or had requested that he obtain such. The client then generally recognizes that if employers were inclined to depend upon or to be much impressed by the results of tests given in reports to clients they would ask for them more often.

The client may state that he would like to have the test report for incidental use when talking with employers, that they are tending to become test conscious and might be impressed by the fact that the client had taken the trouble to study himself so thoroughly before applying for a job. The counselor can use this as an opening for discussing job-hunting techniques, introducing the client to books such as Magoun's (1959). This helps the client to see that he can best demonstrate the care with which he has gone about seeking employment by an intelligent understanding of the company for which he wants to work and of the ways in which he can serve it, and that merely having a report of tests (of someone else's insights rather than of his own) is likely to be of little value. The counselor's suggestion that any employer interested in obtaining a report of the client's test results might write for such a report with the client's permission generally appeals at this point as a more effective way of putting the test results to work than taking a report with him.

In certain other cases it may be desirable to send copies of test reports to parents, school principals, or potential employers who may not be well qualified to interpret test results and whose discretion in their use cannot be taken for granted. It should be recognized that the sending of reports to parents is at best a compromise with an undesirable situation, and that if reports from the counselor to parents are necessary they should really be made as a part of counseling. School and industrial users of test results are in a different category, but even in their case it would be preferable from both client's and school's or industry's point of view if the psychologist were to make his report to the principal or employer on the basis not only of familiarity with the client but also with the school or work situation, helping the recipient of the report to integrate client-data with situational-data. Because written reports are often the best possible compromise in such situations, methods of interpreting the results in writing are discussed in the next paragraphs.

The objectives of the report to parents or other laymen are the increasing of their understanding of the abilities, interests and personality of the client. As the recipients of these reports are not thoroughly trained in psychology, testing, or counseling the report aims to describe these not in psychological terms but in terms of their educational and vocational implications.

The principles governing the writing of reports to laymen may therefore be formulated as follows: 1) test names, test scores, and most psychological trait and aptitude terminology should be avoided in favor of descriptions of probable educational and vocational performance; 2) these descriptions should be phrased in broad terms and illustrated with typical concrete examples; and, 3) a brief summary giving a dynamic picture of the individual should bring together the interpretations of the more specific aspects of probable behavior. Each of these principles is taken up briefly below.

1. The substitution of descriptions of probable behavior in educational and vocational situations for psychological terminology requires the making of statements concerning probable success in college, technical institutes, and appropriate types of occupations rather than the description of mental status; it involves comparisons of the interests of the client with those men in occupations which he is or perhaps should be considering, rather than in terms of letter ratings or percentiles. It should be noted, however, that percentiles may be given to high school students without evidence of bad effects (Rothney, 1952). These varied actuarial comparisons are both more meaningful and less traumatic than descriptions of ability levels or personality traits would be. It was written of one high school sophomore with an intelligence quotient of 90 and no A's or B's on Strong's Vocational Interest Blank: "His chances of doing good work in a college preparatory course are slight, but it is probable that he could complete the graduation requirements of the general, commercial, or trade curriculum. His general ability is equal to that of many men who have succeeded in skilled trades, such as machinist, printer, or plumber, but he might have difficulty competing in the more demanding aspects of technical work such as mathematics and blue-print reading; he could probably compete successfully with routine clerical workers such as stock clerks and general clerks, but would not be likely to rise to a position of responsibility in office work; as a machine operator or assembly worker in a factory he would be competing with men of his own ability level, and could, other things being equal, rise to a position of leadership as a foreman or supervisor. His interests do not resemble those of men engaged in engineering, business, or skilled occupations, suggesting that he may find most satisfaction in work which does not require a great deal of specialized information; instead, he may find his satisfactions more in his contacts with other people or in outside activities. Many men with interests and abilities like his are more interested in a job with regular hours, steady pay, opportunities to make friends with other people, and time off in which to indulge in special interests such as sports, association with men friends, and reading newspapers and magazines, than in the exact nature of the work they do."

2. The couching of such statements in terms sufficiently broad to avoid the appearance of prescription but concrete enough to be meaningful, and the use of specific examples which are illustrative rather than limiting, is perhaps the most difficult part of writing reports of this type. They require

considerable knowledge of occupations and of the world of work on the part of the person writing the report. Considerable help can be obtained from the literature, e.g., through the use of occupational norms such as those published for intelligence tests after both World Wars (see Chapter 6) and for various types of tests by projects such as the Minnesota Employment Stabilization Research Institute and the GATB (Chapter XIV), reviewed in Roe (1956), and through familiarity with studies of workers such as those discussed in Super (1957). The illustration in the preceding paragraph should serve for this principle also.

3. The summary statement at the close of the report serves to pull together the gist of what has been said before and to avoid the overemphasis of isolated statements which might happen to impress the reader. Of the boy partly described earlier in this discussion it might be said, for example, "In summary, John is a boy who should be able to complete a high school education in the general, commercial, or trade curriculum if he so desires. His abilities and interests suggest that he is most likely to find success and satisfaction in the middle range of occupations, and, in that group, most probably in the less competitive general office or factory jobs. It seems probable that he will derive more satisfaction from employment which permits him to have interesting friendships and recreational outlets than from some one type of work requiring special preparation over a long period of time. John's aim might well be the ability to shift readily from one type of factory operation to another, skill in getting along with people, and knowledge of a variety of industrial processes which make a valued employee in his own company and a very employable applicant in the eyes of other concerns."

REFERENCES FOR CHAPTER XXII

Magoun, F. A. *Successfully Finding Yourself and Your Job.* New York: Harper, 1959.
Roe, Anne. *The Psychology of Occupations.* New York: Wiley, 1956.
Roethlisberger, T. J., and Dickson, W. J. *Management and the Worker.* Cambridge: Harvard University Press, 1939.
Rothney, J. W. M. "Interpreting test scores to counselees," *Pers. Guid. J.,* 30 (1952), 320-322.
Super, D. E. *The Psychology of Careers.* New York: Harper, 1957.
Yoder, D., and Paterson, D. G. *Local Labor Market Research.* Minneapolis: University of Minnesota Press, 1948.

A

ILLUSTRATIVE CASES: APPRAISAL AND COUNSELING

THERE are so many different types of tests, so many tests of each type, and so many studies of the validity of some of these tests, that it is difficult in books on testing to find adequate space for discussion of the ultimate purpose of testing: achieving insight (by the client) and an understanding of a person (by the counselor). An effort has been made to deal systematically with this topic in Ch. XX, and to treat problems of reporting test results to clients in Ch. XXI; it still remains, however, to describe the appraisal and counseling of a number of individuals, and to report their subsequent vocational adjustments, in order to show how the test data were used and how well the deductions from them foreshadowed subsequent developments.

Opportunity should also be provided for the student of testing to put to work the insights which he has developed from the contents of this book and from his own experience, by presenting the test data and essential case material in such a manner as to permit him to make his own appraisals before reading those made by the counselors who actually handled the cases. The reader may also want to attempt to predict the subsequent educational and occupational histories of the boys and girls, men and women, described by the case summaries. It should prove instructive to see how well the reader's and the counselor's insights corresponded with what actually took place. From such comparisons one gains new insights into the meanings of test scores, the interplay between various types of personal characteristics, and the interaction of personal characteristics and social environment.

The cases described in this and the following appendix were tested and counseled by Super, his associates, and his students in a number of different places at various times during the past 25 years. These places were the Cleveland Guidance Service of the National Youth Administration in

Ohio, the Guidance Service operated by Clark University in co-operation with a number of high schools in central Massachusetts, the Psychological Services Branch of the AAF Regional and Convalescent Hospital in Miami Beach and Coral Gables, Florida, and the Guidance Laboratory of Teachers College, Columbia University. For ethical reasons, even the place of work with any individual case and the identity of the counselor (sometimes Super but sometimes an associate or student), as well as all more personal identifying data such as names and institutions, are disguised.

The method of presentation requires a word of explanation in order that the reader may obtain the maximum desired benefit from the material. The case histories are divided into three sections: 1) case summaries and test profiles, 2) counselors' interpretations and the immediate outcomes of counseling, and 3) follow-up reports. Within each of these three sections the cases are presented in the same order, beginning with boys and girls first counseled as high school students and closing with experienced men and women who came for counseling because they were considering changing occupations. Thus Tom Stiles' background data and test profile are presented first, followed by those for Marjorie Miller, etc. Then the sequence begins again, this time for giving the counselors' interpretations and the plans, if any, made by the client. (It may be of interest that this material was written up for publication *before* the follow-up data were obtained, to avoid contamination by hindsight.) The sequence then begins over again for the last time, to show the current status of each of the cases in turn and to consider the validity of the counselors' appraisals. It is suggested that readers interested in obtaining the maximum possible value make their own appraisal (and prognosis, if so inclined) after reading the background material and studying the test profile of each case, add anything they wish to this after reading the account of the counselors' work, and then compare their notes with the follow-up data as these are read for the first time.

Background Data and Test Profiles

The Case of Thomas Stiles: When is an Engineer an Engineer?. Tom was 17 years old, in good health, of average height and weight, a high school senior when he came to the counselor. He was enrolled in the academic course, in which he liked the work in mathematics and science better than anything else, and cared least for English and history. His leisure-time activities consisted largely of spectator sports; he liked also to read popular scientific and adventure story magazines. As a younger boy he had done odd jobs at home, and since then had had part-time and summer jobs working as a helper on a truck, operating machines in a shoe factory, helping in a garage, and working in a machine shop. Some of these jobs had been for no pay, others, the more recent, had been paid work.

The student's father was an operative in a shoe factory; the mother kept house, and several siblings, all younger than Tom, were still in school.

Tom stated that he was interested in machines, having lived among various types of machinery all his life; his junior high school ambition

FIGURE 12

GRADES: THOMAS STILES

Subjects	9th Grade	Marks 10th Grade	11th Grade	12th Grade (1st sem.)
English	C	D	E	III-G IV-C
Latin I		C		
Civics	B			
World History	B			
Prob. of Democracy			C	
U.S. History				C
Algebra I		B		
Plane Geometry		B		
Review Math.			C	
Math. (Gen.)	B			
Solid Geometry				C
Physics		D		
General Chem.				C
Phys. Education		D		

had been to be a diesel engineer or marine engineer, an ambition which had broadened to include work with almost any type of engine: steam, diesel, or airplane, especially the last-named type, as "it is the coming field." He thought he would like engineering training, but was not certain of his choice. Asked what he would like to be ten years hence he replied: "Foreman or superintendent in an airplane factory."

The cumulative record in the school office showed that Tom's high school work was mediocre. As shown in the accompanying chart, he had failed junior English, did poorly in physics, had made only C's in mathematics after the tenth grade, and was doing no better in chemistry. His I. Q. on the Henmon-Nelson Test of Mental Ability, administered at the beginning of his junior year and recorded on the school record, was 106. The profile of test results obtained by the counselor during the first semester of Tom's senior year in high school is shown in Figure 13.

Tom's questions were: "Should I go into engineering? I am interested in engines. Should I continue my education in order to prepare for such work? What about engineering college?"

FIGURE 13

TEST PROFILE: THOMAS STILES

		Norms	%ile
Scholastic Aptitude	A.C.E. Psych. Exam.	Coll. Fresh.	14
	Otis S.A. I. Q. 101	Students	19
Reading	Nelson Denny: Vocab.	Fresh.	1
	Paragraph	"	30
Achievement	Coop. Social Studies	"	11
	Coop. Mathematics	"	74
	Coop. Natural Sciences	"	5
Clerical Aptitude	Minn. Clerical: Numbers	Gen'l. Clerks	6
	Names	"	6
Mechanical Ability	O'Rourke Mechanical Aptitude	Men in Gen'l.	67
Spatial Relations	Minn. Paper Form Board, Rev.	Coll. Fresh.	65
Personality	Calif. Pers.: Self	"	35
	Social	"	40
	Total	"	40

VOCATIONAL INTERESTS

1. Biological Sciences	B+	4. Social Sciences	C
2. Physical Sciences	A	5. Business Detail	B—
3. Technical		6. Business Contact	B
Carpentor	A	7. Literary	B
Policeman	A		
Farmer	B+		

Exercise 1.

a) Prepare a written analysis of the test results of this case as though for transmittal to the grade adviser. Use the sample on page 635 as a model. Do this before reading further, and save your report to compare with the appraisal actually made by the counselor.

b) Outline the plans which you think are most suitable for this client, including your approach to counseling the client, in the light of your psychometric report. Save these for comparison with the counselor's conclusions and with the results of counseling.

Marjorie Miller: A Case of College and Choice of a Scientific Field.
Marjorie was 16 years old when counseling began. She was then an academic high school senior, in excellent health, of average height and weight, very good looking, friendly, and mature in manner. She reported that she liked chemistry, languages, and history best, and had no special dislikes in school. Her leisure-time activities consisted of photography, dramatic club, work on the school paper, scouts (Mariner, in charge of younger troop), participant sports, dancing, and painting; in this last connection, she had entered some of her work in local exhibits. Her reading consisted largely of school-required books. Her part-time and summer work experience consisted of selling Christmas cards and working in a gift shop.

This pupil's father was employed as an executive by an insurance company; the mother was a housewife; there were no brothers or sisters.

Marjorie's plans were to go to a liberal arts college, but in doing so she

FIGURE 14

GRADES: MARJORIE MILLER

Subjects	9th Grade	10th Grade	11th Grade	12th Grade to date
		Marks		
English	91	88	90	92
French			93	90
Latin	94	94	94	
History	Ancient 94			U.S. 90
Mathematics	Algebra 88	Geometry 87	Rev. Geom. 91 Rev. Math. 85	Sr. Alg. 85
Biology		94		
Chemistry			90	
Art	91	91		
Typewriting			80	
Physical Education	88	91	95	

wanted to "specialize in some definite subject so as to be ready to work" after graduation. She was considering two nearby colleges of good but not outstanding reputation, neither of which was actually a liberal arts college but both of which had good professional and business curricula. Her occupational preferences were chemical research ("I think I would like the work"), dietetics ("I like the subject") or the teaching of chemistry in high school or nursing school ("If I had to teach, I would want it to be chemistry"), but she was undecided as to her actual choice. She had previously thought of art, surgery, medical laboratory work, and tea room management, in that order, beginning in the last years of grade school. Ten years hence she wished to be "connected in some way with science or medicine."

The high school record showed that Marjorie had done uniformly superior work. Her grades were close to or above 90 in all subjects except for 85 in Review Mathematics and Senior Algebra and 80 in Typewriting. The only patterning revealed is perhaps slightly less strength in mathematics than in the more verbal subjects. She said "I would rather spend time on chemistry than on any other subject. I am interested in math but find it rather hard. I have never taken social studies (this despite a current course in history) but I'm sure I'd like them." The principal described Marjorie as "a brilliant girl with unusual ambition, with many interests, particularly in science." Marjorie's test profile, obtained during the first semester of twelfth grade, is reproduced in Figure 15.

The statement of the problem as seen by Marjorie was to choose be-

FIGURE 15

TEST PROFILE: MARJORIE MILLER

			Norms	%ile
Scholastic Aptitude	A.C.E. Psych. Exam.		Coll. Fresh.	72
	Otis S.A.	I. Q. 124	Students	87
Reading	Nelson Denny: Vocab.		Fresh.	80
		Paragraph	"	96
Achievement	Coop. Social Studies		"	59
	Coop. Mathematics		"	90
	Coop. Natural Sciences		"	70
Aptitudes	Minn. Clerical: Numbers		Clerical Workers, F.	57
		Names	"	34
	Minn. Paper Form Bd. Rev.		Coll. Fresh.	70
Personality	Calif · Self-Adjustment		"	80
		Social-Adjustment	"	40

VOCATIONAL INTERESTS

	Strong	Allport-Vernon %ile		Strong	Allport-Vernon %ile
Biological Sciences		90	Domestic Housewife	A	
Physician	B+				
Dentist	B				
Nurse	A		Business Contact		
Artist	B−	7	Life Insurance		
Math-Sci. Teacher	B−		Saleswoman	C	67
Social Sciences		35	Literary		
Y. W. Sec'y.	B		Author-Journalist	C+	
Social Wkr.	B+				
Social Sci. Teacher	C		English Teacher	C	
			Lawyer	C	
Business Detail			Librarian	C	
Office Clerk	C+		Femininity	72nd %ile	
Stenographer	C+		Political (Prestige)		47
			Religious		92

tween dietetics and chemical research, to decide what kind of training to
get and where, and to find out more about the kinds of jobs that might be
available to her after completing college.

Exercise 2.
   a) Prepare a written analysis of the test results of this case, as though for transmittal to the grade adviser. Use the sample on page 635 as a model. Do this
before reading further, and save your report to compare with the appraisal actually made by the counselor.
   b) Outline the plans which you think are most suitable for this client, including your approach to counseling the client, in the light of your psychometric
report. Save these for comparison with the counselor's conclusions and with the
results of counseling.

Paul Manuelli: A Problem of Choosing a College Major.   Paul was a 17-year-old high school senior taking college preparatory work and enjoying mathematics and science most while caring least for "history, etc." He was a very tall, well-built individual with excellent health, a pleasant appearance, and agreeable manner. His leisure-time activities consisted largely of participant sports (in which he excelled), parties, and dancing. Part-time and vacation work occupied a good deal of his time, and consisted of cooking, soda jerking, and mowing lawns; while in junior high school he had worked as a caddy, and had raised vegetables and sold them.

FIGURE 16

GRADES: PAUL MANUELLI

Subjects	9th Grade	Marks 10th Grade	11th Grade	12th Grade
Drawing	90			
Ancient History	90			
U.S. History & Gov't.				90
English	90	90	90	90
Public Expression			95	95
Latin	90	90		
French		85	95	
Algebra	90		90	
Geometry		90		(Solid) 85
College Chemistry			85	
College Physics				85
Physical Education	85			

The Manuelli family included the father, employed as an operative in a local factory; the mother, a housewife; an older brother who worked in a factory like the father; an older sister then in training as a nurse; and two younger sisters.

Paul was not sure about continuing his education beyond high school but hoped to be able to go to engineering school. He had saved his summer earnings, but needed more money to help finance his education. He was considering engineering and law as occupations, the former because he liked the related school subjects, the latter because he enjoyed debating and public speaking. He was thinking of West Point as a means of combining his engineering interest with the possibility of war, which was then going on in Europe.

Paul's school record showed a high level of achievement, his grades all being 85 or better and the bulk of them 90. His achievement in verbal subjects was slightly higher than grades in quantitative subjects, but the difference was not great enough to be conclusive. He had been given the **Otis Quick-Scoring Test of Mental Ability, Gamma Form**, at the beginning of the eleventh grade, and had been given an I. Q. of 113; it was noted

FIGURE 17

TEST PROFILE: PAUL MANUELLI

		Norms	%ile
Scholastic Aptitude	A.C.E. Psych. Exam.	Coll. Fresh.	87
	Otis S.A. I. Q. 123	Student	84
Reading	Nelson Denny: Vocab.	Fresh.	97
	Paragraph	"	96
Achievement	Coop. Social Studies	"	73
	Coop. Mathematics	"	94
	Coop. Natural Sciences	"	24
Clerical Aptitude	Minn. Clerical: Numbers	Gen'l Clerks	26
	Names	"	53
Mechanical Ability	O'Rourke Mechanical Aptitude	Men in Gen'l	53
Spatial Relations	Minn. Paper Form Board, Rev.	Coll. Fresh.	3
Personality	Calif.: Self-Adjustment	"	95
	Social "	"	90
	Total	"	95

VOCATIONAL INTERESTS

Biological Sciences	B	Social Sciences	B−
Physical Sciences	A	Business Detail	C+
Technical		Business Contact	B+
Carpenter	C+	Literary	B
Policeman	B+		
Farmer	B		

on the cumulative record, however, that he had ranked ninth in a class of 185 pupils, suggesting that there might have been something wrong with the testing. The raw score was 52; a recheck of the I. Q. shows that this is the equivalent of an I. Q. of 113. Other notations showed that he was very well thought of by the school staff, both as a student and as an athlete.

The problem as Paul saw it was to find a way to finance a higher education, and to decide in which field to major. Although attracted to both engineering and to law, he really had no definite idea as to what he wanted to do. As engineering specialization begins early, he felt the need to choose or reject it during the last year in high school.

Exercise 3.

a) Prepare a written analysis of the test results of this case as though for transmittal to his grade adviser. Use the sample on page 635 as a model. Do this before reading further, and save your report to compare with the appraisal actually made by the counselor.

b) Outline the plans which you think are most suitable for this client, including your approach to counseling the client, in the light of your psychometric report. Save these for comparison with the counselor's conclusions and with the results of counseling.

James L. Johnson: A Moderately Successful Man in Search of New Worlds. James Johnson was a 36-year-old married man, tall, well built, and athletic in appearance, with a dignity beyond his years. He had been employed on government projects as a civilian during the war, having been physically disqualified from military service. With the closing down of war plants he was soon to be released from this work, and wanted to start making definite plans for the transition back to peacetime employment.

Mr. Johnson had graduated from an outstanding technical institute with a degree in business administration, at about the time when college graduates were finding that the depression had made radical changes in the employment situation as they had understood it when they chose their major fields. He had originally planned to become an engineer, but had swerved from this objective because of the pessimism of an older friend. His first job after graduation was in a factory, where he was employed with the understanding that he would be trained for an executive position. He was soon made foreman in charge of a department, but after some time the training program was dropped because of the depression and the prospects of advancement grew slight. Although he enjoyed the production work, the hours were long and the temperature unhealthy in his department, so he left after a year to take a job with a retail clothing company. This also was for executive training, but as he could not accept this company's questionable policies he resigned after several months. His next position was with a distributor, a family-owned concern in which he was given the responsibility for setting up a new department the operation of which, once it was established, was such a routine matter, with so few outside contacts, that it bored him and left him tired at the end of each day despite its easiness. There being little prospect of promotion to jobs normally held by the family and its connections, Mr. Johnson left to become placement director of a small but well-established college. This involved a slight increase in pay, and he enjoyed the variety of contacts, the pleasant working conditions, and the educated people he generally dealt with. When the war came he took a leave of absence in order to accept employment on a government project. Here too he had executive responsibility, varied duties, and better pay.

Mr. Johnson's vocational aspirations, as he saw them, were for work as varied and with as congenial a clientele as those he had known as a college staff member and government official, with a staff to handle detail so that he could concentrate on policy, development, and other broader matters, and pay equal to or better than his wartime salary. He could have returned to his college position, but discussion of this matter with the college

FIGURE 18

TEST PROFILE: JAMES L. JOHNSON

California Test of Mental Maturity, Adv. Battery

Total I. Q.	124
Language I. Q.	123
Non-Language	118

Wechsler-Bellevue Vocabulary Test

Full Scale I. Q. equivalent 120

Minnesota Spatial Relations Test   Engineering Freshmen   94th %ile

Bennett Mechanical Comprehension

AA   "   Job Applicants   15th "

Interests	Strong Grade	Kuder %ile		Interests	Strong Grade	Kuder %ile
Biological Science				*Literary-Legal*		30
Physician	C			Lawyer	C	
Dentist	C			Advertiser	C	
Psychologist	C			Author-Journalist	C	
Physical Science		10		*Business Contact*		95
Engineer	C			Sales Manager	B	
Mathematician	C			Life Insurance		
Chemist	C			Salesman	B—	
				Real Estate		
Technical		96		Salesman	B—	
Math.-Sci. Teacher	B					
Production Mgr.	A			*Business Detail*		
				Accountant	B+	7
Artistic		54		Purchasing Agent	A	
Artist	C			Office Worker	A	7
Architect	C					
				Miscellaneous		
Social Service		72		Musician	C	76
Minister	B—			CPA	C	
Social Sci. Teacher	C					
City School Supt.	B—					
Y Physical Director	B					
Y Secretary	B+					
Personnel Manager	B+					

president had made it clear that there would be no possibility of increasing the staff of the placement office and little in the way of salary increases for him despite the institution's eagerness to have him return. The client therefore felt that he should systematically canvass other possibilities, to re-establish himself in the best possible way in returning to normal employment.

The problem with which this client wanted help was the appraisal of abilities and interests, and the analysis and evaluation of ways in which they might best be put to use to help him find work of an executive type, with congenial (educated) associates and contacts, and at a good salary (defined in 1946 as $5000 or more per year). He realized that it might be difficult to find unless he made good use of contacts, but he thought that a position as an administrative assistant might give him needed experience in some one line or industry and put him in a position to advance to executive responsibility. He was considering, in addition, selling tangibles such as cars or oil, especially if he could get an agency. He was not interested in insurance and other intangibles.

Exercise 4.

a) Prepare a written analysis of the test results of this case as though for transmittal to his adviser. Use the sample on page 635 as a model. Do this before reading further, and save your report to compare with the appraisal actually made by the counselor.

b) Outline the plans which you think are most suitable for this client, including your approach to counseling the client, in the light of your psychometric report. Save these for comparison with the counselor's conclusions and with the results of counseling.

Counselors' Appraisals and the Immediate Results of Counseling

In this section the interpretations of test and other data made by the counselors who worked with these persons will be presented, followed in each case with a statement of the immediate outcomes of counseling, that is, of the plans decided upon by the client or of the apparent status of his thinking when he left the counselor. Readers who wish to derive maximum value from this chapter should, before reading this section, have made notes on their own appraisals and prognoses as arrived at while reading the preceding section. In some cases, in which the amount of specific detail in the case record permits and the techniques of counseling are interesting, material is included to illustrate points made in Chapter XX.

Thomas Stiles: Appraisal and Counseling (case material on p. 645 ff.)

The Counselor's Appraisal. Tom's intellectual level, as shown by his Otis I. Q. of 101 and confirmed by an A.C.E. score which put him at the 14th percentile point of a typical college freshman class, was about average when compared to that of the general population. Occupational intelligence norms from both World Wars indicate that this is the ability level typical of skilled tradesmen and of the most routine clerical workers, observation confirmed by various studies made with the Otis test in industry. His mastery of school skills and subjects as shown by his scores on the achievement tests was about that to be expected from one of his mental ability level, and decidedly below that of the college freshmen with whom he was compared, except for a superior score on the mathematics achievement test—his favorite subject. This suggested that he might have abilities useful in technical occupations at the skilled level which seemed appropriate to his mental ability. His school marks, however, were not so encouraging, being only B's in mathematics prior to his junior year, and C's since then. The explanation may have lain in his being in the more abstract college preparatory course.

On the special aptitude tests Tom appeared to lack speed in recognizing numerical and verbal symbols such as is required of even routine clerical workers. Combined with his marginal intellectual ability for office work, this strengthened the basis for questioning the choice of a clerical occupation. On the other hand, Tom's scores on the tests of spatial visualization and mechanical aptitude seemed to confirm the implications of the mathematics achievement test. His inventoried interests, too, were in the physical science and subprofessional technical fields; the latter field seemed more in keeping with his intellectual level and with his poor achievement scores and fair grades in the natural sciences.

Tom's family background, leisure activities, and expressed vocational ambitions were all congruent with the implications of the test results. His father was a semiskilled worker, indicating that work at the skilled level might well be accepted by the family as a step upward. There were no older siblings who might have established a higher record for him to compete with. His leisure activities were nonintellectual, but they did show interest and achievement in mechanical and manual activities, as well as familiarity with work at those levels. He stated that he wanted to work with engines. It was true that, under the influence of a college preparatory course in the academic high school of a substantial middle-class community, he raised the question of going to college to study engineering, but in most contexts his discussions of work with engines were pitched at the skilled level.

The counselor who worked with Tom therefore felt that Tom would be wise to aim at a skilled trade, either by means of a technical school of less than college level, through apprenticeship, or through obtaining employment as a helper in an automotive maintenance shop and taking night school courses.

The Counseling of Tom Stiles. The counselor began by asking the pupil to bring him up to date on his thinking about his postschool plans. Tom did this, indicating no real change in his ideas and mentioning college only incidentally to rule it out as an impractical objective. The counselor then reviewed the evidence of the tests and school grades, discussing the intelligence test data in terms of general population percentiles and college freshmen, but focusing mostly on their occupational equivalents. Family socio-economic status and the low intellectual level of the boy's leisure interests were of course not mentioned; the acceptability of skilled work to Tom and his family was considered something for him to mention, if at all, and as an attitude for the counselor to accept, reflect, and clarify. Tom did not mention it, seeming to consider it quite acceptable. His leisure activities were mentioned by the counselor as fitting in with the aptitude and interest data; this interpretation was accepted by the client with the statement that "Yes, I always have thought I was best at mechanical things, and I like them best, too."

Ways of utilizing Tom's skilled technical potentialities were taken up next. No decisions were reached in this interview, but two nearby technical schools were discussed, and the counselor made sure that Tom had access to their catalogues, one of which was examined in order to review admission requirements, courses, and expenses, and to be sure that the student was oriented to such matters. The apprentice training program of a nearby factory, in which aircraft engines were being produced and increasing numbers of young men were being trained, was considered. Tom knew about it, and discussion helped him to plan how and when to apply if he decided on it; he saw the possible advantages of having such a specialty if he were drafted. Less formal ways of getting experience with automotive engines were looked into, and night schools offering appropriate courses were mentioned. Tom was not sure what he would do, when he left the office, but he felt that he knew a number of suitable alternatives and that he could choose between them in good time.

Exercise 5.

a) Compare your interpretation of the test results with that of the counselor, and note the ways in which they differ. Study these differences in order to locate possible inadequacies in your conception of the significance of the tests or scores in question, or ways in which your insights may be more adequate than those of the counselor.

b) Compare your tentative plans with those considered suitable by the counselor. Compare your proposed approach with that used by the counselor. What shortcomings are suggested, in your work or in that of the counselor? Evaluate these in the light of the client's reactions and the immediate outcomes of the counseling as it was done.

Marjorie Miller: Appraisal and Counseling (case material on p. 647 ff.)

The Counselor's Appraisal. Marjorie's scholastic aptitude tests indicated that she would probably stand in the top quarter of a typical college freshman class, although they did not justify the principal's characterization of her as "brilliant." Her vocabulary and reading scores suggested that this characterization might be based in part upon unusual ability to put her aptitudes to work, for her reading speed was decidedly superior to her scholastic aptitude and even to her vocabulary level. Marjorie was not outstanding on the social studies achievement test, in which subject she had had little preparation, and only moderately superior in the natural sciences which appealed to her, but this latter may have been due to not having included physics in her program. Her mathematics achievement was very superior. In general, these data were in keeping with the school grades, which we have seen to have been superior; but the trends were reversed, for her mathematics grades were slightly inferior to those in verbal subjects.

Marjorie's perceptual speed, when working with clerical symbols, was in the average range for clerical workers, her standing on the numbers test being high average and on the names test low average. Her score on the test of ability to visualize spatial relations was only moderately high for college freshmen, and would therefore not be outstanding when compared to scientific workers. It seemed high enough, however, to warrant no special consideration if other things were favorable.

The personality inventory scores revealed nothing of significance. Her interests, as measured by Strong's Blank and the Allport-Vernon Study of Values, seemed to be concentrated in the scientific field, with some signs of interest in the social and religious fields. They were quite feminine, and although she did not have much in common with office workers who tend as a group to make high housewife scores, her interests did resemble those of housewives. It seemed worth noting that her highest scientific interest score was as nurse, which hardly belongs in that group and which is heavily saturated with the interest factor which is most important in housewives. She had stated that she thought she might eventually marry, but this thought seemed to play no part in her vocational planning.

Marjorie's school and leisure-time interests did not do much to weight the balance in the direction of either scientific or social interests. Her favorite school subjects included chemistry, languages, and history. Her activities encompassed not only photography, but also the school paper, scout leadership, drama, and painting.

Marjorie's expressed ambitions were in the direction of natural sciences, in keeping with her measured interests, tested achievement, and some aspects of her school and recreational record. The counselor was inclined to give more weight to these factors than to the secondary interest pattern in social welfare work, the social welfare and literary activities, and the achievement in verbal subjects in school. He concluded that Marjorie would be wise to go to a liberal arts college where she would still have opportunity to explore both the social welfare and the scientific fields in courses and in activities. He thought that it would be well for her to select a college which had strong offerings in the natural sciences so that if she did choose this field she would be able to prepare for it as well as her abilities and drive warranted. It was the counselor's opinion that Marjorie would probably become a medical laboratory technician, dietician, or high school teacher of science.

The Counseling of Marjorie Miller. Like that of Tom Stiles, the counseling of Marjorie Miller was done in a situation in which one or at most two interviews were customary, case material being worked up ahead of time and discussed in a factual manner with the student. During and especially after the review of the data by the counselor, in terms of their actuarial significance for educational and vocational choices, the pupil had opportunity to react to them and to discuss them. The counselor then attempted to help the client understand his reactions, see the implications of the data, and consider possible lines of action. He drew on whatever informational resources were needed and available in order to help with the pupil's orientation. In Marjorie's case the review of the data seemed to bring out little that she did not already realize, although the objective and actuarial form in which they were presented impressed her, as might a view of oneself in a mirror for the first time in one's life. The possibility of keeping her program broad for the first two years of college and still finishing with a vocationally usable major had not been known to her; when this was mentioned, she suggested that she might then do well to continue to explore both the scientific and the social fields before making a decision.

Marjorie then raised the question of which college, as those she had been thinking of, rather vaguely, did not offer genuine liberal arts programs but instead specialized from the freshman year. The counselor mentioned several colleges of the type which he thought might be appropriate to her, and asked Marjorie if she had ever thought of any of them. Finances appeared to be a problem. The counselor had made note of some scholarships for which students might possibly apply, one of them being a very desirable scholarship offered by a first-rate college and limited to girls from her part of the state. Marjorie wondered whether she could qualify for such a prize. The counselor, knowing the standing of some girls who had previously been awarded it, said he thought she might and encouraged her to apply. She decided to do so, although she could not afford to go to that college without generous financial aid. There was some discussion, also, of ways in which campus activities, courses, and summer vacations could be utilized by Marjorie to get a better idea of the direction in which she wanted to turn when she came to the fork in the road.

Exercise 6.

a) Compare your interpretation of the test results with that of the counselor, and note the ways in which they differ. Study these differences in order to locate possible inadequacies in your conception of the significance of the tests or scores in question, or ways in which your insights may be more adequate than those of the counselor.

b) Compare your tentative plans with those considered suitable by the counselor. Compare your proposed approach with that used by the counselor. What shortcomings are suggested, in your work or in that of the counselor? Evaluate these in the light of the client's reactions and the immediate outcomes of the counseling as it was done.

Paul Manuelli: Appraisal and Counseling (case material on p. 649 ff.).

The Counselor's Appraisal. Paul's scholastic aptitude tests confirmed the opinion that the earlier I. Q. did not truly represent his mental level. Compared to college freshmen he seemed very superior, ranking in the top 15 percent. His vocabulary and reading speed were even higher. The achievement tests showed that he was unusually well prepared in mathematics, superior in social studies, but not well prepared in the natural sciences. This seemed surprising, as he had received an 85 in chemistry the preceding year, and an 85 in the first semester of physics at the time of testing; as his grades in the linguistic subjects were generally slightly superior to those in the quantitative, this may actually reflect true differences in his special abilities.

In ability to distinguish numerical symbols with speed and accuracy Paul ranked low when compared to clerical workers, but his facility with verbal symbols was average for such workers. His understanding of the nature and uses of mechanical, woodworking, and related tools and processes was average when compared with that of skilled workers, but his ability to visualize and mentally manipulate objects in space was quite inferior when compared with that of college freshmen. Despite the high achievement in mathematics, this poor showing in spatial visualization and relatively low standing in natural sciences, combined with high verbal ability and superior social studies achievement, appeared to lend some support to this student's second expressed interest: law. His very superior measured adjustment agreed with the opinions of the school staff.

Paul's inventoried interests were most like those of physical scientists, including engineers, and also resembled those of men in business contact work such as life insurance sales. He showed some interest also in the biological science and literary-legal occupations, but not as much as might have been expected of a boy who enjoyed public speaking and debating, had little in the way of technical hobbies, and was considering law as seriously as engineering.

The counselor was inclined to give more weight to the factors pointing in the direction of engineering than to those contradicting it. Mathematical ability and interest supported the choice, while poor achievement in science and poor spatial visualization opposed it. It seemed possible that the spatial relations score was for some reason not representative, and the poor science preparation might have been more a matter of teachers than of pupil. It hardly seemed justifiable to question seriously the choice if Paul made it after a review of the data.

The Counseling of Paul Manuelli. In view of the above, the counselor let Paul talk some about his vocational objectives. These seemed more than ever to involve engineering training, but Paul wanted to know how he compared with engineering freshmen. His profile was therefore reviewed. Paul reacted particularly to the relatively high mathematics standing, to the low Paper Form Board score, and to the greater degree of interest in physical science than in legal occupations. He was not inclined to be discouraged by the low spatial score, and might perhaps have given it no more thought, but the counselor suggested that it might be taken as a warning signal, and that if mechanical drawing or other such activities ever gave him trouble he might want to look into it further; it was mentioned also that his standing might be checked by a retest. College choices were then discussed, the client raising the question after indicating that he thought he would go ahead with engineering. Paul felt that his financial status might make choice of a co-operative training program wiser than a four-year engineering school. The nearby engineering schools operating on the co-operative system were therefore considered with the aid of catalogues, and one was most thoroughly discussed as being accessible, inexpensive, and of good standing.

Exercise 7.

a) Compare your interpretation of the test results with that of the counselor, and note the ways in which they differ. Study these differences in order to locate possible inadequacies in your conception of the significance of the tests or scores in question, or ways in which your insights may be more adequate than those of the counselor.

b) Compare your tentative plans with those considered suitable by the counselor. Compare your proposed approach with that used by the counselor. What shortcomings are suggested, in your work or in that of the counselor? Evaluate these in the light of the client's reactions and the immediate outcomes of the counseling as it was done.

James L. Johnson: Appraisal and Counseling (case material on p. 651 ff.)

The Counselor's Appraisal. Mr. Johnson was given two tests of mental ability, the Vocabulary Test of the Wechsler-Bellevue and the California Test of Mental Maturity. On the former his intelligence quotient was 120; on the latter his total I. Q. was 122, with language and nonlanguage I. Q.'s of 123 and 118 respectively. The evidence therefore agreed in showing him to be a man of superior mental ability, quite capable of performing successfully in professional or executive work.

In ability to visualize the relations of objects of different shapes and sizes Mr. Johnson exceeded even the majority of engineering students, standing at the 94th percentile on the Minnesota Spatial Relations Test. In ability to understand the operation of mechanical contrivances and to apply mechanical principles to practical situations he did not, however, compare well with graduate engineers, his score being at the 15th percentile for this group. Although scores on this test are somewhat affected by experience its effect is not very great, and in any case the client had had experience which had given him opportunity to increase his familiarity with mechanical matters and to apply his spatial visualization ability to mechanical problems.

Interests were measured by the Strong and Kuder inventories. They agreed in revealing a high degree of interest in subprofessional technical occupations such as production manager, occupations which provide outlets for mechanical interests but do not require a high level of mechanical ability or of interest in scientific matters. The Strong Blank showed some resemblance between Mr. Johnson's interests and those of successful salesmen and sales managers, but not as much interest in sales work as was suggested by the very high persuasive score on the Kuder Record. This seemed to be related to the client's statement that he was interested in promotional activities, but did not like actual selling. Strong's Blank showed considerable similarity of interest with those of men employed in business detail work, including accountants and purchasing agents, but the Kuder yielded very low scores on the clerical and computational scales. Apparently the client had interests like those of office workers but, as he himself stated, did not enjoy clerical routine once it was established. Both inventories revealed some interest in social welfare work, but this seemed secondary to business and production interests.

An attempt at personality appraisal was made by means of the Bernreuter Personality Inventory. This depicted the client as quite unstable emotionally, dependent, introverted, moderately dominant in face-to-face situations, quite self-conscious, and somewhat solitary. These results seemed to agree with interview material which suggested an underlying neurotic tendency in Mr. Johnson. This material consisted of his description of himself as a worrier, and of a possible interpretation of his vocational dissatisfactions as due to personality maladjustment rather than to vocational misplacement. These maladaptive tendencies seemed, however, to be well under control, as evidenced by Mr. Johnson's success in each of his jobs, his employers' desires to have him stay with them, and the fact that each change of employment so far had been for a definitely superior position. Although it seemed to the counselor that the client might be paying too high a price emotionally for his success, the fact that he did not take advantage of the rather permissive counseling relationship to work on personality problems led the counselor not to press him to open up that area.

In summary, it seemed that Mr. Johnson was a man of superior general mental ability capable of achieving, as he actually had, at the professional and executive level. His low mechanical comprehension and scientific interests indicated that he had perhaps done well to avoid engineering

occupations, although he did have the spatial aptitude and lower technical interests which might make industrial work appeal to him. This
probably explained the satisfaction which he found in the factory job
which he held after graduation, despite the poor working conditions and
lack of advancement which caused him to leave it. The combination of
business, technical, and welfare interests shown by the inventories, combined with his own stated preferences, indicated that he should find satisfaction in office work of a supervisory nature, in which he did no detail
work but was responsible primarily for planning and for outside contacts.
It was felt that he might have difficulty adjusting to the emotional demands of some jobs, but his success in his previous positions and in moving to progressively better jobs led to the conclusion that under favorable
conditions he would be able to make the necessary adjustments. Psycho-
therapeutic help might enable him to get more satisfaction from his work
and from other aspects of life by relieving him of the load of anxiety
which it was suspected that he carried, but it might be more appropriate
for him to seek such help after he had made the change back to a peacetime job than during the transition period.

The Counseling of James L. Johnson.　In this case the counseling procedure consisted of the initial interview for the collection of case material
and the determination of the problem to be worked on, followed by the
administration of the tests the results of which have just been summarized.
Then followed an interview for the discussion of the implications of the
test results and of the meaning of the client's experiences to date. These
were followed by three more widely spaced interviews, in which job-
seeking plans were thought through, related activities were reported and
evaluated, and the suitability of openings discovered was discussed.

In the first interview following testing, Mr. Johnson's test data were
interpreted as favoring employment in fields such as production management, personnel work, buying, and general administrative work such as
he was contemplating. It was suggested that sales work did not seem indicated, and that his former engineering interest might have proved to be an
unwise choice had it been followed through. After this rather directive
interpretation by the counselor the discussion shifted to a review of the
client's experiences in the light of the test results, and of the test results in
the light of the client's experience. In this process the counselor was
relatively nondirective, reflecting the feelings and attitudes expressed by
the client, and occasionally asking a question designed to assist the client
in his thinking. When, for example, contemplation of his low clerical
score on the Kuder and the moderately high clerical score on the Strong
caused the client to remark: "So I don't like clerical work but I do have
interests somewhat like those of office workers," the counselor asked,

"What meaning does that have for you?" This led the client to state that he supposed he would find working with that kind of people congenial, but that he would want to have duties other than responsibility for clerical detail. The question, "What kinds of jobs might offer you that combination?" led to an exploration of supervisory and public contact jobs in business. Further discussion led the client to conclude that, everything considered, the position of administrative assistant would probably offer him the best chance to do congenial work and to learn enough about some type of enterprise to enable him to assume executive responsibilities. Other supervisory and contact jobs did not seem equally open because of lack of specific experience other than clerical and educational.

In the next interview the means through which the client might locate suitable openings were explored. He revealed a good orientation to job-seeking methods, so the discussion was primarily an opportunity for him to use the counselor as a sounding board for his own analysis of each lead, of the best way in which to use it, and of the suitability of the kinds of jobs which it might yield.

Subsequent interviews were devoted to discussing the openings which the client located during his job hunting. One of these was in personnel work with an oil company; others were: accountant with supervision of an accounting department for an important foundation, industrial relations work with a rubber manufacturer, industrial engineering in an electrical equipment factory, and administrative assistant to the head of a large business enterprise. The two personnel positions had considerable appeal, but both involved certain limiting conditions which made the client hesitate, one geographic and the other the narrowness of the job because of the specialization in the office. The accounting job was with an organization which would have provided very pleasant working conditions and good pay, but the client knew that he would have to relearn a great deal about that type of work and that the work itself would not appeal to him. The industrial engineering job would have involved beginning rather low in the scale and working up, and at his age and with his experience the client did not feel he should make such adjustments. The position of administrative assistant had the most appeal, for it not only paid well, but was described as one which had, for some previous incumbents, led to higher-level executive positions in this and in other companies. Mr. Johnson was quite enthusiastic about this possibility, and the counselor felt that it was compatible with his interests and abilities. The client stated that if the offer materialized he would accept it.

Exercise 8.

a) Compare your interpretation of the test results with that of the counselor, and note the ways in which they differ. Study these differences in order to locate possible inadequacies in your conception of the significance of the tests or scores in question, or ways in which your insights may be more adequate than those of the counselor.

b) Compare your tentative plans with those considered suitable by the counselor. Compare your proposed approach with that used by the counselor. What shortcomings are suggested, in your work or in that of the counselor? Evaluate these in the light of the client's reactions and the immediate outcomes of the counseling as it was done.

B

ILLUSTRATIVE CASES: FOLLOW-UP AND
EVALUATION

*The Validity of Vocational Appraisals in the Light of
Subsequent Work Histories*

EACH of the cases discussed in the preceding appendix was followed up
some time after counseling in order to find out in what type of work he
was engaged, how well he liked it, what aspects of it he disliked, and how
well the ultimate outcomes of counseling agreed with the appraisals made
by the counselors. The time that elapsed between the closing of the case
and the follow-up varied greatly. In one case it was only three months, in
some it was six years and even longer. The cases were selected partly because enough time had elapsed since counseling to make follow-up
meaningful.

In one case the follow-up was through personal contacts which, by a
happy combination of circumstances, were renewed from time to time
over a period of several years. In certain others it was made through correspondence supplemented by the personal contacts of others living in
the same communities. And in still others the follow-up consisted solely
of a brief exchange of letters. Such methods leave a good deal to be desired, as they are not likely to yield emotionally toned material and provide insufficent opportunity for the exploration of important issues. Their
results are, however, given for the insights which they do occasionally give
into the adequacy of the understandings derived from the tests and related
appraisal procedures. Inadequate though they may be, the obtaining of
even these follow-up data represents an advance over much that is done
in the way of evaluation.

The follow-up data for each of our cases are presented in the paragraphs
which follow, accompanied by comments on the adequacy of the testing
and of the appraisal in the light of these data.

The Early Career of Thomas Stiles (see also p. 645 and p. 652)

Subsequent History. Tom was followed up by means of a personal letter some eight years after he was tested and counseled. His letter was brief and factual, giving an outline of his experiences during the intervening years but not going into detail concerning his attitudes toward these experiences. After graduation from high school he took a summer job, comparable to those he had held in previous years. He was then admitted to apprenticeship training in a large metal-products manufacturing concern, remaining for six months before illness caused him to resign and return home. Several months later he accepted employment as a tool grinder with a company within commuting distance of his home, where he worked for a period of two years. He was successful at this work, but felt the need for more training of the type that had been interrupted by his illness. He therefore gave up this job and entered one of the subprofessional technical schools which he had discussed with the counselor three and one-half years previously, taking a two-year course in steam and diesel engineering. He graduated after the normal two years, having enjoyed the training and worked during the one summer in another metal-products factory. After completing his training he was placed, by the school placement service, in a job with a manufacturer of railway locomotives. Nine months had elapsed on this job at the time of writing, and Tom felt that he had successfully begun a career of the type which appealed to him most, with a concern which would offer him security and advancement.

Validity of the Appraisal. The plans carried out by Tom seem to have corresponded rather closely with the appraisal of the counselor insofar as type of activity is concerned, although there was some floundering at the start and the ultimate achievement level was the highest of those which had been deemed likely. It will be remembered that the counselor had thought of apprenticeship or on-the-job training as equally appropriate in Tom's case as formal training in a technical institute. Although the interruption in the apprentice training which he began after completing high school seems to have been due to factors not related to his interests or abilities, the fact remains that it was interrupted, that a period of work followed which served to finance schooling and to confirm his desire for it, and that in the end he graduated from a technical institute and obtained employment at the skilled level. The only way in which Tom's history differed from that discussed in the counseling process was in the selection of steam and diesel rather than gasoline engines, but this difference is, from the standpoint of aptitudes and basic interests, quite insignificant.

One might conclude from this one case that test results and the counselor's diagnoses tend to correspond rather closely, were it not for the fact that while a case may illustrate it cannot prove. The case of Marjorie Miller, which follows, serves to bring out the complexity of people and of occupations, and to underline the fact that vocational adjustment is often a process of unfolding rather than of predicting.

Exercise 9.

Compare your interpretation of the test data and the plans which you considered suitable with the report of the subsequent history of this client. In what ways were your ideas on the case borne out by experience? In what ways do you seem to have been wrong? What do you think may have been the causes of your mistakes or of the mistakes which the tests led you to make? How do discrepancies between your test interpretations and the outcomes of the case add to your understanding of the validity data reported in investigations using the tests?

The Early Career of Marjorie Miller (see also p. 647 and p. 654)

Subsequent History.   Marjorie carried out the decision reached with the aid of the counselor and applied for the special scholarship at the high-ranking college. Drawing on the diagnostic data made available by the counselor, the principal gave her an extremely favorable and yet objective recommendation. She was awarded the scholarship, which provided all she needed to supplement her family's financial backing, for her four years in college. At the end of her freshman year the counselor had a letter from Marjorie, expressing her appreciation of the educational experience which he had helped her to obtain, and describing some of her reactions to her first year. Apparently her horizons had been so broadened by the experience that she felt considerable gratitude to the counselor for having made her aware of the advantages of the type of college she was attending and for having found a way to make it financially possible. The next contact came at the end of Marjorie's college career, when the counselor received an announcement of the graduation ceremonies in which Marjorie was to participate. The third follow-up was made through one of the college personnel officers, a year after Marjorie had graduated and six years after the counseling took place.

Marjorie's freshman program in college included chemistry, economics, English, and German. Her grades for the year were C, C, B and B, respectively. Her college personnel record showed that her goal, at the beginning of this year, was "nutritionist, chemist, or social worker." Late in her freshman year she discussed her choice of major field with a counselor, who was impressed by her intelligence, viewpoint, and enthusiasm. She talked also with the heads of the science departments in which she was most interested.

During her first summer vacation Marjorie worked as a sales clerk in a department store, and acted as head of the department in which she worked. Her employer reported that "Marjorie has better than average intelligence, good initiative, and excellent character. While at work in my store she handled selling duties very well although she had had no previous training in this field. She is ambitious and would succeed in any work which she undertook."

In her second year in college Marjorie apparently shifted from her former scientific inclinations and majored in child study. She took four courses in this subject, continued economics and German, and added physiology and psychology. Her marks for the year were all B+ or B. She continued along these lines during her third and fourth years, concentrating more and more on psychology and child study. Her marks improved steadily, and she graduated 85th in a class of about 250 students.

Marjorie's extracurricular activities consisted of working on the college newspaper, as a reporter during her first year and as assistant managing editor of a new and rival publication during her sophomore year. She was an officer, and ultimately president, of a campus religious organization. She served as co-editor of her class yearbook in her senior year.

In her last summer vacation Marjorie took a position as a playground instructor in one of the large cities, receiving ratings of "excellent" in industry, ability, attitude, and attendance. She also did field work with children in a local settlement house as part of her academic work during the year. Her supervisor's report read: "She showed a fine understanding of the needs of individual children, was responsible for completing tasks assigned to her, and showed initiative in many situations where students frequently wait for direction. She has a friendly personality and adjusts easily to new situations." Another supervisor spoke of her "good sense of orientation, quick grasp of problems. What is more, she showed good intellectual and emotional insight into the life of children."

When Marjorie registered with the placement office during her senior year she stated that she wanted to teach in a public or private nursery school. In a later contact she expressed the same interest, but hesitated about applying for specific openings because she was thinking of marrying soon and really wanted a job more than a career. A little later she expressed an interest in an opening as a field secretary for one of the scouting organizations, had an interview with a representative of the national office, and was employed in a branch near her home town.

A final follow-up revealed that Marjorie was doing well in her work, found it very satisfying, and had been promoted to a more responsible position in the same organization. Although she still had marriage in mind, it had receded into the background at least temporarily, and she looked forward to continuing in the same work for the foreseeable future.

Validity of the Appraisal. Marjorie's grades in college were in line with the counselor's expectations, when he disagreed with the high-school principal's characterization of the girl as brilliant. She did prove to be, as he anticipated, a good student in her chosen field, graduating at the bottom of the upper third of her class. It is interesting to note, however, that her work in science and freshman (but not sophomore) economics was only at the C level. Her achievement in the more verbal subjects was better than that in the more quantitative, as suggested by the analysis of her school grades. This trend was not, however, clearly foreshadowed by the test scores.

Of major interest is the predictive value of the interest inventories. These, it will be remembered, showed dominant interest in the scientific fields, with some signs of interest in social welfare and religion. Her school and leisure-time activities did not do much to decide the issue one way or the other, as they included scientific and social interests. The subsequent history showed that, contrary to the counselor's expectation, the secondary social welfare interest pattern became dominant as time went by. It has been seen that Marjorie carried out the program of exploration in both scientific and social areas which the counselor had recommended for her freshman year, and that, whether because of interest, aptitude, or some combination of the two, she then focused entirely on the social welfare field.

The counselor's private opinion, then, which he did not let influence his counseling, was mistaken. He had thought that exploration would confirm Marjorie in her adolescent choice of a scientific occupation, whereas in fact she decided to prepare for and actually entered a social welfare occupation. Stated as flatly as this, the outcome might lead one to conclude that the test results had actually been misleading in this case. But reconsideration of the data will reveal that the basis of Marjorie's subsequent actions can be seen in the high-school counseling record. Subordinate though the trends seemed to the counselor at the time, there were indications of social welfare interests. Isolated from the rest of the pattern these indices are rather impressive:

> Unusual reading speed.
> Verbal grades superior to quantitative.
> Secondary social welfare interest pattern.
> Feminine (i.e. social and literary) interests.
> Active on school paper.
> Dramatic club member.
> Scout leader.

The foundations for the choice of a social welfare or literary occupation were clearly there. It was only the more dominant interest in science supported by superior achievement in the sciences and equally important scientific avocations which led the counselor to believe that success and satisfaction were most likely to lie in the applied sciences.

Perhaps the principal conclusion to be drawn from this case, however, is that even in the case of some well-motivated, clear-thinking, able high-school seniors interests and abilities are still in the process of developing or, at least, of coming to the surface of consciousness. When more than one pattern of abilities and interests is noted, it is therefore wise for the student to plan a program of study, work, and leisure which provides for further exploration of the two or three dominant patterns. The diagnostic process may serve to reveal areas in which exploration can best be concentrated, and counseling may have as its function the planning of appropriate types of exploratory activities. Actual decision making may not come for some time, and then it will turn out to be a step-by-step process rather than an event.

Exercise 10.

Compare your interpretation of the test data and the plans which you considered suitable with the report of the subsequent history of this client. In what ways were your ideas on the case borne out by experience? In what ways do you seem to have been wrong? What do you think may have been the causes of your mistakes or of the mistakes which the tests led you to make? How do discrepancies between your test interpretations and the outcomes of the case add to your understanding of the validity data reported in investigations using the test?

The Early Career of Paul Manuelli (see also p. 649 and p. 657)

Subsequent History. Paul, like Ralph, was heard from by mail six years after he graduated from high school. He wrote as follows:

I graduated from high school with honors, a medal for excellence in United States History, and a scholarship at Carnegie Tech.

I spent my freshman year at Tech, studying mechanical engineering. I was permitted to omit Freshman English, taking Literature in its place. I played on the Varsity Football squad. I made a C+ average, which was all right as my scholarship was based more on athletics than on academic achievement.

After we got into the war I joined the Navy V-12 program and was transferred to Stevens Institute, where I graduated with a B.S. in Mechanical Engineering in 1945, and grades averaging from 75 to 80. I made the Dean's List once, in my junior year, played on the football team, belonged to the senior honorary society, was class orator, was listed in the American student "Who's Who," was company commander, was on various student committees, and took part in theatrical productions rather regularly.

Transferred to Columbia Midshipmen's School, I was commissioned an Ensign in the Naval Reserve, graduating 259th in a class of more than 1000 men. I served as company commander here also.

I was assigned to duty on a cruiser, as a junior officer in firerooms, machine shop, and main engines. Studying under the chief engineer, after seven months aboard I qualified as engineering watch officer and stood watches, in complete charge of the engineering facilities.

My discharge came late in 1946, after which I joined the Atlas Corporation as a student engineer. I completed a year's study in which I spent several months in each of their main divisions, learning all the operations from design to sales and service. After completing this course, I requested assignment to production engineering; I could have asked for development engineering, but I felt that I would be better qualified for development work if I became thoroughly familiar with the problems of improving existing designs, making them easier to manufacture, etc., before trying development work. I would like ultimately to be a senior engineer with a department of my own, but of course that is a long-term objective. Before that happened, I think I might be tempted to shift to factory administration, as I enjoy working with people and handling long-range problems.

I enjoyed my schooling, and even though I never made top grades I never had any worries about passing. I got as much out of college as most students, and never disliked any courses; I suppose I cared less for drafting, as drawing prints is an anti-climax after actually solving a problem. The Navy was all right too. My work with Atlas has gone smoothly, and I have never felt unprepared or unable to handle the work that has come my way.

I have had two substantial raises since coming to Atlas, and consider my rate of progress satisfactory. I have been given a fair amount of responsibility, having been sent to deal with other companies with power to purchase, alter designs, and in other ways represent Atlas.

Validity of the Appraisal. The subsequent history of Paul Manuelli confirms, in its general outlines, the appraisal made by the counselor and is in line with the plans discussed in counseling. Although the war changed the details of Paul's education, he developed in ways which had been anticipated in counseling. Some of the minor, specific, ways in which his history did differ from the forecast and planning are of interest, and are taken up below.

One of the counselor's misgivings, it was pointed out, concerned Paul's low spatial visualization score. This had been discussed with Paul as an indication that he might do well to check his performance in drafting and related types of activities, and that trouble there might lead him to shift to a field requiring less spatial ability. The subsequent history shows no actual difficulty with spatial visualization, but the fact that his grades were not as good as the other indices would have led one to expect may be due to weakness in this special area. It is perhaps significant, too, that drafting was the one subject that Paul liked least. Although the stated reason was the lack of intellectual challenge, it is quite possible that the underlying reason was difficulty in transferring spatial concepts to paper. There are many men as bright as Paul, with interests just as intellectual, who enjoy seeing an idea take shape on the drafting board.

If it is indeed true that Paul is somewhat handicapped by low ability to visualize space relations, his future development will be worth noting, for both production and development engineering, in the mechanical field, should require considerable ability of this type. One might hazard the guess that Paul may well eventually "be tempted to shift to factory administration" not only because of his interest in people and planning, but also because of frustration in the more technical aspects of development work.

The leadership qualities seen in Paul's high school extracurricular record and reflected in his rather high business contact interests on Strong's Blank continued to manifest themselves during his college, Navy, and business career. These also suggest that, once he is firmly established as an engineer in his company, he may want to change to administrative rather than technical work. On the whole, Paul's leadership record is superior to his academic record.

Although it is not concerned with testing, one final point is of interest. The counselor was apparently unduly pessimistic about the ability of this student to finance his way through college, pessimism which seems to have been quite unwarranted in view of the award of the four-year athletic scholarship. In this respect at least, the student may have shown more *savoir faire* than the counselor.

Further follow-up would be highly desirable in this case, not in order to provide more guidance (Paul seems to be handling his career very well), but in order to see which predominates in the end, his technical interests and abilities or his social interests and abilities. In the meantime, it may be concluded that development has been very much like that anticipated in the counseling process.

Exercise 11.

Compare your interpretation of the test data and the plans which you considered suitable with the report of the subsequent history of this client. In what ways were your ideas on the case borne out by experience? In what ways do you seem to have been wrong? What do you think may have been the causes of your mistakes or of the mistakes which the tests led you to make? How do discrepancies between your test interpretations and the outcomes of the case add to your understanding of the validity data reported in investigations using the test?

The Early Career of James L. Johnson (see also p. 651 and p. 658)

Subsequent History. The hoped-for opportunity to accept employment as administrative assistant to the head of a large business enterprise materialized, and Mr. Johnson wrote the counselor a week or so after the final interview that he had accepted the offer. He was very pleased with the nature of the work, with the associates with whom it threw him, and the excellent salary which he was paid. He expressed his appreciation of the counselor's services in helping him to clarify his objectives and to carry out his job-hunting campaign.

A follow-up letter was sent to this client two and one-half years after he took the job as administrative assistant, expressing an interest in knowing how he liked the work, the nature of his subsequent experiences, and what he thought of his present situation. An immediate reply was received, a brief but friendly letter in which Mr. Johnson summarized the experience of the intervening two years. He was still working in the same position, and had had a substantial raise at the end of his first year. He felt that the prospects with his present company were excellent, and he had developed contacts through his work which might well lead to other opportunities should he be interested. The work had proved to be very much to his taste: Detail was taken care of by a competent office force and his own duties involved development work and contacts with a variety of executives both in the company and in other concerns. There was no indication, in the letter, of anxiety or difficulty in interpersonal relations such as it was thought might develop at the time of counseling. While failure of such signs to appear in a letter proves little, it did seem significant that a formerly dissatisfied man wrote a letter in which satisfaction was the only manifest attitude.

Validity of the Appraisal. In this case, unlike Marjorie Miller's, the only follow-up data are general. They give blanket confirmation of the appraisal made at the time of counseling, insofar as type of activity in which success and satisfaction might be found were concerned. The client's work was of a type which counselor and client had agreed should prove satisfactory, and it had proved satisfactory over a significantly long period of trial.

The counselor's belief that emotional maladjustment might create difficulties for Mr. Johnson did not seem to be substantiated. As was pointed out, however, the failure to find confirmation of this belief in a letter hardly constitutes proof. The fact that the letter expresses satisfaction with the job and with its prospects may nevertheless be taken as some evidence of the fact that, as in the past, Mr. Johnson was handling whatever emotional problems he might have with considerable success, winning the confidence of his employers and carrying out his work effectively.

Exercise 12.

Compare your interpretation of the test data and the plans which you considered suitable with the report of the subsequent history of this client. In what ways were your ideas on the case borne out by experience? In what ways do you seem to have been wrong? What do you think may have been the causes of your mistakes or of the mistakes which the tests led you to make? How do discrepancies between your test interpretations and the outcomes of the case add to your understanding of the validity data reported in investigations using the test?

Conclusions

The cases summarized and discussed have served to illustrate the nature and use of data from a variety of tests, together with the need for personal data as a background against which to interpret test results. They illustrate the way in which tests sometimes serve to predict with considerable accuracy the type of field in which success will be found (Stiles), sometimes foreshadow in a general way developments which they cannot forecast (Miller, Manuelli, Johnson). In still other cases they leave one with a baffled feeling of not having gotten to the heart of the matter. In some cases tests yield important insights which could not well be obtained by other means, in others they merely seem to confirm what other data reveal (Stiles, Manuelli), and in still others they contribute to an understanding of the client but do not point the way to immediate solutions (Miller, Johnson).

Problems of test interpretation for vocational counseling at several different levels have been illustrated. Three cases were high school students, one of them considering a skilled trade, two of them college majors. And one was a man in his mid-thirties, seeking to re-establish himself on a higher plane than that at which he had worked before.

Many more cases would be necessary in order to illustrate all the points which a user of tests should be familiar with in practice. But the problems presented, and the opportunity provided for the student to work out his own answers to them before reading what actually transpired, should provide sufficient exercise with "paper cases." It now becomes incumbent upon the student-counselor to test some live clients, analyze the test results and relevant personal data, prepare psychometric reports in which he draws on all of the knowledge of the educational and occupational significance of tests which the study of this book and of the original studies on which it is based should have given him, and obtain the criticism of a qualified supervisor. As he works with students or clients, and makes his own formal or informal follow-up studies, he will gain that richer understanding of tests, of occupations, and of vocational and counseling psychology which is the earmark of the well-rounded counselor or personnel worker.

C

TEST PUBLISHERS AND SCORING SERVICES

Acorn Publishing Co.
  Rockville Center, L. I.
  New York
Bureau of Publications
  Teachers College, Columbia
  University
  New York 27
  New York
C. H. Stoelting and Company
  424 North Homan Avenue
  Chicago 24
  Illinois
California Test Bureau
  5916 Hollywood Boulevard
  Los Angeles 28
  California
Consulting Psychologists Press
  270 Town and Country Village
  Palo Alto
  California
Division of Applied Psychology
  Purdue University
  Lafayette
  Indiana
Educational Records Bureau
  21 Audubon Avenue
  New York 32
  New York
Educational Test Bureau
  720 Washington Avenue, S.E.
  Minneapolis
  Minnesota
Educational Testing Service
  20 Nassau St.
  Princeton
  New Jersey

Grune and Stratton
  381 Fourth Avenue
  New York 16
  New York
Harvard University Press
  Cambridge 38
  Massachusetts
Harcourt, Brace and World, Inc.
  Tarrytown-on-Hudson, N. Y.
Houghton Mifflin Company
  2 Park Street
  Boston 7
  Massachusetts
Institute for Personality and Ability
  Testing
  1602 Coronado Drive
  Champaigne
  Illinois
McKnight and McKnight
  Bloomington
  Illinois
Marietta Apparatus Company
  Marietta
  Ohio
Psychological Corporation
  304 East 45th Street
  New York 17
  New York
Psychological Institute
  P.O. Box 118
  Lake Alfred
  Florida
Psychometric Affiliates
  Box 1625
  Chicago 90
  Illinois

Public School Publishing Co.
  345 Calhoun Street
  Cincinnati 19
  Ohio
Science Research Associates
  57 West Grand Avenue
  Chicago 10
  Illinois
Sheridan Supply Company
  P.O. Box 837
  Beverly Hills
  California

Stanford University Press
  Stanford
  California
Testscor
  2309 Snelling Avenue
  Minneapolis 4
  Minnesota
Western Psychological Services
  10655 Santa Monica Boulevard
  Los Angeles 25
  California

AUTHOR INDEX

References to bibliographies have been set in italics in the Author Index.

OCCUPATIONAL INDEX

Vocational rehabilitation workers, 489; supervisors, 446, 487

Watchmen, 239

Welders, 197

YMCA secretaries, 385, 386, 403, 498
YWCA secretaries, 497, 498

SUBJECT INDEX

TEST INDEX